AS

FACT AND FICTION: REPRESENTATIONS OF THE ASTURIAN REVOLUTION (1934–1938)

by

SARAH SANCHEZ

MANEY PUBLISHING
for the
MODERN HUMANITIES RESEARCH ASSOCIATION
2003

Maney Publishing
for the
Modern Humanities Research Association

ISBN 1 904350 13 5

Copies may be ordered from Publications Sales, Maney Publishing, Hudson Road, Leeds LS9 7DL, UK; e-mail mhra@maney.co.uk. Further information about the activities of the MHRA and individual membership can be obtained from the Honorary Secretary, Dr David Gillespie, Department of European Studies and Modern Languages, University of Bath, Bath BA2 7AY, UK, or from the website at www.mhra.org.uk.

Produced in England by
MANEY PUBLISHING
HUDSON ROAD LEEDS LS9 7DL UK

CONTENTS

Acknowledgements vii

Introduction 1

1 The Asturian Revolution of 1934 17

2 Literary Development: From Avant-Garde Prose Narrative to the Politically Committed Novel 44

3 Political Discourse, Confession, and Journalistic Response 79

4 Non-Fictional Accounts of the Revolution 120

5 On the Border Between Fiction and Non-Fiction (I) 175

6 On the Border Between Fiction and Non-Fiction (II) 202

7 The Non-Fictional Novel (I) 240

8 The Non-Fictional Novel (II) 287

Conclusion 336

Bibliography 346

Index 356

Illustrations

Map 1 The Key Sites of the Asturian Revolution 32

ACKNOWLEDGEMENTS

I am grateful for the opportunity to thank some of the people whose help and advice have been instrumental in the writing of this thesis.

Most importantly, I would like to express my sincere thanks to Professor Nigel Dennis, my PhD supervisor, for his patience and encouragement, and without whose intellectual guidance this thesis would not have been written. Moreover, it was Professor Dennis's undergraduate course on literature and politics in Spain in the 1930s which first drew me into this field. I would like to extend my thanks to the rest of the members of the Department of Spanish at the University of St Andrews for their assistance and support over many years. I also owe a warm thank-you to Alan Hoyle whose encouragement prompted me to search for a publisher.

I am particularly indebted to the staff at the Biblioteca Pública Ramón Pérez de Ayala, Oviedo; the Centro de Estudios Asturianos, Oviedo; the municipal libraries of La Felguera and Mieres; the Servicio de Archivo of the Ayuntamiento de Langreo; the Biblioteca Nacional, Madrid; the British Library, London; the University of St Andrews library; and Senate House library, University of London. I would like to mention in particular Dr Antonio Insuela and Dra. Isabel Carrera, at the University of Oviedo for helping me out, especially in the early stages of my thesis, as well as D. José María Laso Prieto, at the Fundación Isidoro Acevedo, Oviedo, and the late Padre Patac, at the Biblioteca Pública Jovellanos, Gijón. It is difficult to imagine how I would have been able to track down the primary sources on which this study is based without the help of these individuals and institutions.

The research for this thesis would not have been possible without a bursary from the School of Modern Languages, University of St Andrews, and generous funding from the Carnegie Trust for the Universities of Scotland.

Finally, I would also like to thank my family and friends for bearing with me throughout, particularly Elena and Salvador for their 'pollo con arroz' and 'sidra' when dinner was the last thing on my mind. Above all I owe the most to my husband Juan Fondón for all he has done for me and for his constant support, and to my mother, for providing endless expert advice, and, as always, for being there when she was most needed.

INTRODUCTION

Despite the historical, political, and social importance of the Asturian Revolution, generally thought to mark the rehearsal for the Spanish Civil War, the literature which was written about it has received scant attention. Some of the writing has been briefly looked at in studies dealing with the literature of the second Republic,[1] but for the first time this thesis provides an exhaustive critical assessment of a range of textual responses not properly examined before.

Following the Revolution many versions of it were written, from the religious and the military, to the official government reports and right-wing critical accounts, while all the major left-wing factions — anarchists, communists, and socialists — provided their interpretation. In 1938 Alfonso Camín Meana gave an indication of the immense written reaction to the uprising in the last paragraph of his work:

> Sobre la tragedia del 34 en Asturias — carne nobilísima para los cuervos y para los oportunistas de la pluma — se han hecho, a raíz de los sucesos, informaciones truculentas, folletos falsos y amañados por el Gobierno, almanaques de escándalo "negros" y "rojos" — en los cuales lo que menos importaba era el fondo humano de la tragedia — y hasta libros dramáticos de mera literatura, fuertes y apasionados, que entran de lleno en el campo de la novela. [. . .] Por eso mismo, por no entrar en fila con aquellos folletos de ocasión y catecismos de escándalo de los "plumíferos" ladrantes del 34, no se publica este libro hasta principios del 38.[2]

Although I have divided the authors into two ideological groups — those on the left and the right of the political spectrum — there was little political consensus amongst those belonging to either, as both sides were split into extreme and moderate factions. Thus, although two authors may be pro- or counter-revolutionary, their interpretations of the Revolution may differ. It is the incommensurable conflict between the left and the right, and all the factions within these positions, that makes these texts particularly interesting and valuable, as they manifest how the political positions are often so extreme that it is difficult to envisage any sort of compromise.

The texts most readily available today were written by those who opposed the revolutionary action. Many of these are accessible in most of the main libraries. It is thought that many of the other works were either lost or destroyed during the dictatorship that followed the Civil War, or taken abroad, unpublished, when their authors were forced to leave the country. Taibo suggests that the disappearance of those texts has been influential in giving a right-wing bias to the events which took place in October:

> La versión de los triunfadores suele jugarle la mala pasada a la Historia de perdurar sobre la visión de los vencidos. Perdurar incluso a pesar de los historiadores que acogidos al bando de los derrotados, son incapaces de romper con las fuentes de información tradicionales, y profundizar en la maraña que oculta los hechos.[3]

The majority of left-wing texts which have been recovered and published in recent years, mainly by political organizations such as the Fundaciones Pablo Iglesias, José Barreiro and Anselmo Lorenzo, have specific political value.

The texts which I have chosen to deal with have been arranged typologically or generically. They have been selected, irrespective of considerations of literary quality, on the basis of three criteria: (1) prose narrative, as opposed to poetry or drama, of which there are a number of examples published during these years; (2) texts published between 1934 and 1938; and (3) texts which deal principally with the Revolution in Asturias (only one of the locations where it broke out). Maryse Bertrand de Muñoz highlights the importance of the documentary value of the Civil War novels, a claim which I extend to the works studied here: 'Al juzgar su valor, los resultados son muy diferentes según el punto de vista que se adopta, el documental o el literario'.[4] There is plenty of writing post 1938, but to make the discussion coherent and focused I have chosen to limit the study to the contemporary representations, in other words, to those written at the time or in the immediate aftermath of the Revolution. The temporal distance is a key factor in the writing of these texts; it would be methodologically wrong to compare those from 1938 to those from 1950.

No doubt there are many more works of narrative, in addition to those dealt with below, which could have been included in the present study but which I have been unable to find despite extensive research in numerous libraries and other cultural institutions and establishments. These include the municipal libraries of La Felguera, Mieres, and Gijón; the regional library in Oviedo; the Biblioteca Nacional in Madrid; the British Library in London; the Centro de Estudios Asturianos in Oviedo; and the Fundación Isidoro Acevedo in the Communist Party headquarters in Oviedo. In a last attempt to find the missing works I have searched through the on-line catalogues of various other libraries in the major Spanish cities, such as the Bibliotecas de Catalunya in Barcelona, Andalucía in Granada, and Valencia, and other countries, such as the Bibliotèque National de Paris, and the Biblioteca Nacional de México.

This research, however, has proved to be fruitless. All in all, many of the works consulted are unknown for most, not easily accessible, and can only be found in a few libraries, which is why I have gone to such lengths to provide a summary of each in the relevant chapter.

In essence, the purpose of this thesis is to reveal specific manifestations of the literary response to the Revolution and to bring to light these virtually unknown texts. The literature of this period is worth looking at for several reasons. Firstly, it confirms that the Revolution was fundamental in determining the politicization of literature. More generally, focusing on this specific set of texts will help situate this literature in the context of the development of the generic status of prose narrative at the end of the Republic, thus throwing light on wider literary issues. This corpus as a whole is worth examining for other less literary reasons. For example, certain historical and political details regarding the controversial Revolution emerge, details which have often been ignored. In addition, it conveys the extreme political divisions in society, the rivalry between the communists and the fascists, and how difficult it was to remain on the margins. Of course, some of the issues which are raised here continue to be relevant during the Civil War.

Even after excluding all the works which do not conform to the specific requirements outlined, the body of texts remaining is substantial. One of their main characteristics is their blend of factual and fictional discourse. Thus, I have arranged them generically, in a sequence of chapters which range from the most objective representations (political essays and journalistic accounts) to the fictional recreation (non-fictional novels and short stories) in which the historical element is central but subordinate to certain literary concerns. One of my aims is to outline the proportion of fact to fiction in these texts, suggesting in the process how an event of this magnitude impacts on people's conception of the function, form and subject matter of narrative fiction. While making no pretence to offer a full critique of the relationship between history and literature, this study will necessarily delineate and discuss the structure and role of these two narrative forms, and the characteristics which distinguish one from the other. Because this issue will be central to the thesis I will draw on the work of critics who refer to the conflict between history and literature as part of their examination of the historical novel (Georg Lukàcs, Herbert Butterfield and, previous to these, Alessandro Manzoni [1785–1873]) or do so in their analyses of the North American non-fictional novel of the1960s. Having offered these critical perspectives, I will briefly define the most problematic terms as I have used them, thus avoiding the vagueness which currently surrounds many commonly used expressions such as 'fact' and 'fiction', 'history' and 'literature'. This will stop any confusion in later chapters and prevent having to clarify what is meant by certain terms every time they are used. The most appropriate point at which to begin is with a range of critical views about the historical novel.

History and Literature

As the historical novel emerged, critics such as Manzoni divulged their opinions about the new genre. Some of the key critical texts were produced during the first half of the twentieth century, such as those of Lukàcs who does not reject the historical novel outright but sees clear problems with it, and Butterfield who is greatly in favour of it. The latter claimed that a story could be told in a number of ways, depending on the point of view and the perspective taken by the author. Manzoni, however, believed that the historical novel was deficient both as historiography and as poetry as it tried to mix two distinct types of truth, the verisimilar and the factual. Lukàcs, the most influential of the theorists, views the historical novel as an effect of socio-political events and thus maintains that its development is directly related to the historical events of the time; as these became more complex, so did literature. Thus, according to Lukàcs, the historical novel was a product of the age of nationalism, industrialization, and revolution. The French Revolution and the Napoleonic Wars made history a popular experience for the first time as the French Republic needed to create mass armies: 'If a mass army is to be created, then the content and purpose of the war must be made clear to the masses by means of propaganda.'[5] According to Lukàcs, this propaganda, in order to be more effective, could not be restricted to the isolated war; it had to reveal the social context, the historical presuppositions and circumstances of the struggle, so that the war could be connected with the entire life of the people and with the possibilities of the nation's development. For Lukàcs the historical novel had a function: to describe the present by referring to the past. In other words, the author demonstrated how the situation in the reader's present had been determined by past events. Essentially, Lukàcs believed that it mattered little whether individual details and facts were historically correct or not as detail was 'only a means of achieving historical faithfulness, for making concretely clear the historical necessity of a concrete situation' (p. 36).

Manzoni, writing prior to Lukàcs, argued in *On the Historical Novel* (1962) against the possibility of the historical novel or any work which combined reality and invention, whatever form it took.[6] He based his essay on two diametrically opposed complaints. The first of these, directed at the historical novel, centred on the argument that fact was not clearly distinguished from invention in the narrative, resulting in an unfaithful representation of history, and the consequent deception of the reader by the author. The second of the criticisms was that in the historical novel the author plainly differentiates factual truth from invention, thus creating uncertainty in the mind of the reader. Manzoni admits that both sets of critics are right, not because the historical novelists are at fault, but because the genre itself is an impossibility:

> Both those who want historical reality always to be represented as such and those who want a narrative to produce in its reader a unified belief [are right]. But both are wrong in wanting both effects from the historical novel, when the first effect is incompatible with its form, which is narrative, and the second is incompatible with its materials, which are heterogeneous. Both critics demand things that are reasonable, even indispensable; but they demand them where they can not be had. (p. 72)

Herbert Butterfield was of the opinion that history should deal more with the personal, intimate details of an era and take on board direct human experience, thereby rejecting the usual emphasis on political and military events. In order to do this, rather than suggest the invention of episodes, Butterfield proposed turning the historical information into a historical novel: 'In order to catch these things ['the human touches'] in the life of the past, and to make a bygone age live again, history must not merely be eked out by fiction, it must not merely be extended by invented episodes; it must be turned into a novel.'[7] Butterfield asserted this view at a time in which the form and role of history were being reconsidered. The problematic relationship between fiction and history had not always existed. Prior to the French Revolution, historiography had been conventionally regarded as a literary art; while the study of history was scientific, writing it down on paper was a literary exercise. The final product was thus to be assessed as much on literary as on scientific principles. However, from the nineteenth century on the writer of history avoided drawing on the imagination, stuck to the facts, and described chronologically, impartially, and faithfully what had happened. According to Hayden White:

> Historians continued to believe that different interpretations of the same set of events were functions of ideological distortions or of inadequate factual data. They continued to believe that if one only eschewed ideology and remained true to the facts, history would produce knowledge as certain as anything offered by the physical sciences and as objective as a mathematical exercise.[8]

Facts were considered to be all-important and history was regarded as a scientific study. History, in this new guise became the dominant humanistic form, running parallel with the physical and biological sciences. Butterfield wished to escape from this view of history.

Although the concept of the historical novel surfaced around the time of the publication of Sir Walter Scott's *Waverley* in 1814, Scott is not the only figure to have been linked to its emergence. Other authors include Balzac, Tolstoy, Hegel, Goethe, and Virginia Woolf. Harry Shaw claims that 'In a sense, historical fiction is as old as literature itself.'[9] Lukàcs and Manzoni refer to tragedy, epic, and historical drama and such figures as Shakespeare, while Barbara Foley refers back to ancient, medieval, and Renaissance texts, which she calls 'pseudofactual narratives', and maintains that their writers showed no confusion about the difference between history and fiction.[10] For his part, Avrom Fleishman argues that historical fiction emerged from epic tradition and national chronicle in the Romantic Movement and was finally established as a genre in the Victorian period.[11] Shaw indicates that the critical fortunes of historical fiction have tended to reflect the genre's close ties with the nineteenth century, pointing out that Scott, Dickens, Thackeray, Eliot, and Hardy all produced at least one historical novel. However, in the twentieth century the classical form of the historical novel has become less prevalent. Instead, authors such as John Dos Passos, Norman Mailer, Truman Capote, and Thomas Wolfe, writing about issues and events relevant to their time, have chosen to use documentary evidence and journalistic reports in their novels. The historical novel is one in which 'the action takes place during a specific historical period *well before* the time of writing' (my emphasis).[12] In other words, the term is not suitable for those works which have become historically significant but which, at the time of composition, dealt with contemporary issues, as is the case with the works examined here. Kathleen Tillotson solves this problem by defining a separate type of historical novel — 'the novel of the recent past'.[13]

Central to the principles behind the historical novel, the novel of the recent past, and the non-fictional novel is the relationship between fact and fiction. In his study on the American non-fiction novel of the 1960s John Hollowell, referring to Robert Scholes, uses a diagram to explain roughly the continuum from Empirical to Fictional narrative:

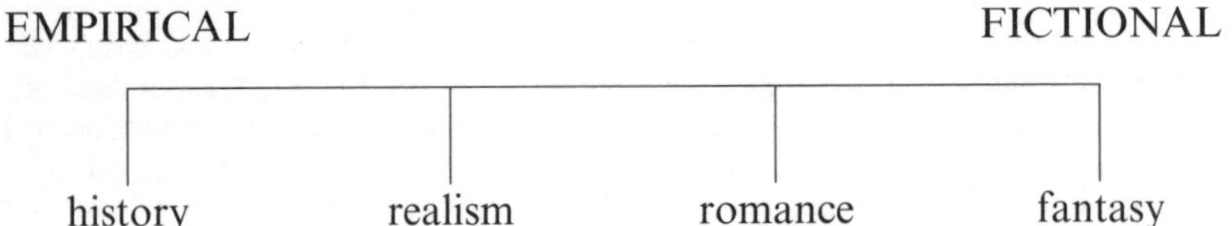

Moving from left to right along the continuum, the direct representation of experience would be history or a purely empirical narrative. The opposite extreme at the right would be fantasy or a purely imaginary world. Between the extremes lie realism and romance. Realism, according to Hollowell, strives to present the world 'as it is' and is closely allied to history; romance presents the world 'as it might be' or 'as it should be'.[14] Most narratives, however, are combinations of the various elements. As will be argued later, the very vivid events which took place during the Revolution meant that, for the works examined in Chapters 7 and 8, the authors did not need to fabricate plots and invent characters; instead they chose to confront the reality of the Revolution. Similarly, in Chapter 3 the texts are not totally empirical in nature as the authors draw on fictional techniques to depict the events more effectively.

Critics do not agree on the extent to which fact and fiction differ, and whether they can be distinguished in a text. In her study of documentary fiction Barbara Foley examines the shifting borderline between fiction and its counterparts in historical, journalistic, biographical, and autobiographical writing. She takes the documentary novel as a starting point, claiming that the historical novel, like fictional autobiography, the pseudofactual novel and the metahistorical novel are subgenres of this more general genre. Although these subgenres have been influential in literary history as far back as the sixteenth century, Foley insists that factual and fictive discourse have changed through the ages, and lists three current arguments that view the relationship between fictional and non-fictional discourse differently. The first of these is based on Robert Scholes and Robert Kellogg's proposal, labelled the 'spectrum argument'. They affirm that

> the novel has historically synthesized two narrative impulses, [. . .] one directed toward the 'empirical,' or historical, and the other directed toward the 'fictional,' or imaginary. Empirical and fictional are blended tendencies, rather than distinctive kinds; history and fantasy stand as the poles of a narrative spectrum, with different narrative forms such as autobiography, realism, and romance occupying positions at various points along the scale.[15]

Contrary to this idea of fiction and non-fiction as concepts that cannot be clearly defined, Barbara Herrnstein-Smith believes that the distinction between fact and fiction is absolute.[16] The third theory, devised by the poststructuralists, argues that all discourses, either factual or fictive, are influenced by the language and ideology of the author and are therefore fictive 'in effect if not in intent'.[17] Foley, not satisfied with any of these proposals, gives her own. Any given element in narrative 'must be scanned and interpreted as either factual or fictive in order to be read and understood' (p. 40), an opinion already asserted by Wayne Booth and shared by Celia Fernández Prieto.[18]

In her theoretical study of the principles of the historical novel Fernández Prieto argues that what is to be considered history and what is fiction depends on the readership:

> Se trata de modalidades de comunicación que se definen y se reconocen por su función socio-cultural, y que se construyen mediante un doble código: el código lingüístico común y otro *código específico fijado por la propia comunidad* que crea, define, interpreta y usa esta clase de discursos. La función socio-cultural así como la *codificación de sus propiedades discursivas* varían según se transforman los contextos históricos y los presupuestos culturales, científicos, estéticos e ideológicos de esa comunidad. Por tanto, el atributo de 'histórico' o 'literario' aplicado a un texto es una *sanción pragmática*, relativa al contexto cultural en que se realiza. De ahí que las *calificaciones de los discursos* se transformen y lo que en un tiempo se acepta como histórico, en otro se catalogue como literario. (p. 38, my emphasis)

In other words, the definitions of reality and fiction, truth and verisimilitude, according to Fernández Prieto, depend on the cultural and ideological beliefs of a given society so that 'el concepto de realidad es interdependiente del sistema de creencias vigente *en un determinado momento histórico*' (p. 40, my emphasis). She adds: 'De esta forma, la realidad no es un concepto estético sino dinámico, en permanente revisión' (p. 40).

Lars Sauerberg writes that historians working on empirical lines claim that the truth of their work lies in 'the possibility of checking it against the sources employed'.[19] However, the idea that historical narrative is definitive and objective is contradicted by the fact that on many occasions there are different accounts of the same historical event or period. It is often contended that the procedures that go into the making of a fiction are similar to those of history as the author has to equally go through a selection and editing process: 'Every supposed historical description, falling short of a complete re-creation of the original, involves a selection of what is important and what is not, involves, in other words, interpretation.'[20] William Walsh enumerates a set of factors which contribute to the disagreement among historians: (1) personal likes and dislikes for individuals, or classes of person; (2) prejudices and assumptions associated with the historian's membership of a certain group, such as nation, race, social, class, or religion; (3) conflicting theories of historical interpretation; (4) different moral beliefs and conceptions of the nature of man.[21] Similarly, Laurence Lerner reveals why he believes that a historian's objectivity is impossible: 'History cannot give us direct access to objective facts, since the ideology and the verbal strategies of the historian will determine what he chooses to notice and how he describes it, to say nothing of the connections between events that he then establishes.'[22] Linked to the growing acceptance of this idea, increasing numbers of critics have defended the concept of narrative history. For his part, R. G. Collingwood, who, with his *The Idea of History* (1946) provided the first sustained challenge to established opinion in historiography, emphasized that the historian and the novelist construct a picture which is partly a narrative of events, and partly a description of situations and analysis of characters. White claims that for historians as well as novelists there is no certain scientific or objective proof of the superiority of one response over another: 'The crisis of modern historiography lies in the fact that it finds itself squeezed into an uneasy middle position between science and literature.'[23] In *Metahistory* (1974) he concludes that historians 'should raise their linguistic consciousness, explore other literary modes for their narratives [. . .] and reanchor history in the literary imagination'.[24]

Since the possibility of the narrativization of history is defended by many, is the novel versatile enough to allow for its 'historization'? Mariano Baquero Goyanes indicates that the novel has 'una flexibilidad incomparable para adaptarse a los temas, estilos y gustos de cada época'.[25] Similarly, Chris Baldick states that the novel as a literary genre is 'exceptional' in that it

> disregards the constraints that govern other literary forms, and acknowledges no obligatory structure, style, or subject-matter. [. . .] The novel has frequently incorporated the structures and languages of non-fictional prose forms (history, autobiography, journalism, travel writing), even to the point where the non-fictional element outweighs the fictional.[26]

As two final examples of the view on the flexible nature of the novel, Darío Villanueva writes: 'La novela es el reino de la libertad, libertad de contenido y libertad de forma, y por naturaleza resulta ser proteica y abierta. La única regla que cumple universalmente es la de transgredirlas todas',[27] and Mikhail Bakhtin describes it as 'plasticity itself'.[28]

What is clear is that novel and historiography share many features. Ribbans argues that all writing, whether historiography or creative literature, involve selection, organization, and interpretation. However, he also insists that 'fiction allows a much wider scope for variation of the narrative mood or voice, for intertextuality, for the utilization of symbolic or mythological material, for metonymic or metaphorical patterns, for ironic presentation, for self-reflexive analysis, and so forth' (p. 21). Sauerberg highlights other similarities, less often considered:

> Historical accounts are seldom marked by strict adherence to the calendar. There are flash-backs and anticipations, there are alternations between emphasis on *temps* and *durée* as in literature. The aims may differ, but the technique and the effect on the reader, provided there is functional overlapping, remain identical. And a purely chronological progression would contradict the historian's declared aim of accounting for historical events. (p. 61)

John Mander explains that history enters into the making of most novels, but the strength of the documentary component depends on the author's intentions:

> While imaginative fiction can absorb large doses of history without coming to harm [. . .] this implies that there is a distinction between fiction and history. This

distinction is to be found in Aristotle's dictum that 'poetry' (i.e. epic or dramatic fiction) is 'nearer to philosophy than to history'.

Aristotle's distinction does not mean that history is truer than poetry, in the sense that fact is truer than fiction, it means that the truth of history and the truth of poetry are of a different nature. The truth of history is literal, factual truth: when did such and such an event happen, and in what particular circumstances? The truth of philosophy, on the other hand, is conceptual, abstract, and general: what general truth about the world is to be derived from this particular event? Historical truth is particular; philosophical truth is general.[29]

Finally, Fleishman also believes that the historian and the novelist share common strategies. He claims that the historian, as well as the historical novelist, uses his imagination in order to fill in all those gaps which are as yet unknown about a certain individual or event. He, like Mander, concludes that it is not in kind but in degree that the use of the imagination differs in the work of historical and fiction writers.

Generic Categories

If Todorov's assertion that literary genres are 'nothing but [. . .] choices among discursive possibilities, choices that a given society has made conventional'[30] is taken into account, genres applicable to one period may not be appropriate for others. The way today's reader perceives the work will not necessarily coincide with the contemporary reader's impression. Although today's reader may question the accuracy of the text when the aims of the narrative appear to be other than to inform about the facts, and when any data presented ostensibly as facts is not verifiable, for the reader in 1935 these requirements may not have been very significant. A reader may have been searching for something else besides factual information, such as assurance that the ideological position adopted with regards to the events was the correct one.

Generic classification, however, is important for the reader as well as for the author. It influences the work's semantic and syntactic properties; affects what the author will write about; assists the author in the composition of his work; and is important in the reader's understanding of the work. Alistair Fowler rejects the view that all genres are obsolete and that the concept of genre is outdated.[31] Instead he believes that generic types are in constant flux, or 'in a continual state of transmutation', and that while old genres survive, new ones emerge which mix existing types.[32] In other words, more rigid genres disappear giving way to new variations of subgenre. In the same way, Todorov argues that a new genre 'is always the transformation of one or several old genres: by inversion, by displacement, by combination. [. . .] It is a system in continual transformation'.[33] As Elisabeth Wesseling explains:

> For the reader, genres constitute sets of expectations which steer the reading process. Generic repertoires may be regarded as bodies of shared knowledge which have been inferred from perceived regularities in individual literary texts. As sets of norms of which both readers and writers are aware, genres fulfil an important role in the process of literary communication.[34]

According to the reader–writer pact implicitly established, before reading or writing a piece of narrative prose both parties must know what form, or what genre, it is going to take in order to facilitate the task of interpretation and understanding.

In order to classify these works generically, a number of factors have been taken into account. Although Sauerberg relies on style, intention, context, and function to determine the genre of any given work,[35] for those examined here only the first element applies. All of the authors, writing at the same time (within four years of the Revolution), aimed to produce an informative, verifiable, and credible account of the events. Where they differ is in the way they choose to render this factual content. Thus, here the balance between the documentary and historical content, and the use of techniques usually associated with creative writing has been the key determinant. Often the aims of the author are revealed in the prologue or introduction of the work and, according to Fowler, serve as a generic marker and may have a strategic role in guiding the reader.[36] The division of these works into categories is only intended to serve as a guide to reading them rather than as a conclusive statement about their form as the boundaries overlap and allow intricate mixture.

Further Definitions

In European languages the word *literature* in its current sense is quite recent, dating back to the nineteenth century. According to Raymond Williams:

> There has been a steady distinction and separation of other kinds of writing — philosophy, essays, history, and so on — which may or may not posses literary merit or be of literary interest (meaning that 'in addition to' their intrinsic interest as philosophy or history or whatever they are 'well-written') but which are not now normally described a literature, which may be understood as well-written books but which is even more clearly understood as well-written books of an *imaginative* or *creative* kind. [37]

Given that the importance of fictionality as a determinant of literariness has diminished, we should be careful to keep separate the two notions of 'literature' and 'fiction'. Here I refer to *literature* in the broadest sense of the word, referring to written material in general. *Fiction* refers to 'writing that relates imagined characters and occurrences rather than recounting real ones'.[38] I will constantly be arguing that *fact* is not definitive. Hollowell writes: '"Facts" never speak for themselves [. . .] since the writer's selection and arrangement inevitably impose a design — a fiction — not apparent in life itself' (p. 73), and quotes Tony Tanner who claims: '"Facts are silent as Conrad said, and any singing they do depends on their orchestration by a human arranger"'. Tanner's statement underscores the necessity of the human arranger's hand in any account, fictional or non-fictional. Whenever I refer to *fact* it is on the understanding that this will be borne in mind. *Documentary* 'is the presentation or representation of actual fact in a way that makes it credible and vivid to people at the time. Since all emphasis is on the fact, its validity must be as unquestionable as possible. [. . .] The heart of documentary is not form or style or medium, but always content',[39] while *history* is thought to be a social scientific subject in which assertions are made methodically on the basis of proof. In the definitions of *history* what stands out is the concept of scientific organization — methodology, record-taking, and knowledge.[40] The general term *narrative* refers to 'a telling of some true or fictitious event or connected sequence of events' and is thus an appropriate term for all the works considered here.[41] When using the expression that a certain work is *dramatized*, this is a shorthand way to describe that the narrative includes dialogue and theatrical content and belongs to a different category that involves a range of literary and rhetorical devices beyond the straightforward documentary account. Finally, I refer to Stott for a definition of *propaganda*: 'Almost all social utterances involve propaganda because almost all seek to influence opinion. [. . .] We understand that propaganda has a "double face". There is black propaganda, put forward by a covert source, using vilification and lies to spread dissention among the group it addresses. There is white propaganda, put forward from an overt source, using actual fact to educate its audience. And there are all shades of grey in between' (p. 23).

The present study is divided into eight chapters. The first two deal with the historical and literary context of the Revolution. In the remaining six chapters I concentrate on specific texts. Briefly summarizing the chapters, in Chapter 1 I will give a historical summary from the establishment of the Republic in 1931 to the aftermath of the Revolution. Most of the information for this chapter will come from P. I. Taibo, *Asturias 1934* (1984), an exhaustive study of the origins, the course and the after-effects of the Revolution, and of many of those who took part. Taibo bases the information he provides on contemporary documents and personal accounts, as well as on written testimonies and interviews which were held after the events. Having a solid grasp on the Revolution enables us to judge the accuracy of the texts examined further on. I should mention at this stage that the revolutionary action differed in degree throughout Spain, ranging from the general strike which lasted a few days, to the revolutionary insurrection in some parts of Asturias. The importance which it had in Asturias explains why many more works refer to this region than to any other.

In Chapter 2 I provide the literary context to the creation of these works. It has long been known that the Asturian Revolution had an important impact on Spanish cultural life. The literature of the Revolution is an important indicator of the process of change from the avant-garde to the social political literature of the 1930s. The mission of the writers as the period 1928–36 progressed was to make their message transparently clear, something which had been traditionally regarded as a defect. Writers felt that they had to abandon literary subtlety in favour of the message. The Revolution had been specially traumatic, and those who chose to write about the events wanted to assign a social and political function to their text. In this chapter I will give a résumé of the development from the avant-garde to the 'literatura de avanzada' and the committed social literature of the 1930s, mentioning at every step the salient features of each and those individuals who were influential. Finally for this chapter, I will examine how the October Revolution affected the intellectuals in general, before going on to examine specific works in the next chapters.

In Chapter 3 I bring together three groups of works, written from both a revolutionary and counter-revolutionary perspective: those which offer a purely political interpretation of the events, those providing evidence in the form of confessions, and finally compilations of articles published after the events by journalists. At the end of the chapter I will briefly analyse four texts which were written as a response to the repression. Despite the diverse nature of these categories, the works which they encompass present a common factor, that is, they deal with the October Revolution only as part of a more general analysis of the years of the Second Republic. The specific details of the Revolution are not at issue here; instead the more wide-ranging implications of its causes and defeat are examined within the context of the important historical period that Spain has just undergone.

In Chapter 4 the works dealt with are specifically about the Revolution, although the emphasis is still on the 'factual'. I will divide the texts into four separate categories: Government and Counter-Revolutionary, Military, Religious, and Pro-Revolutionary responses. The one feature that these texts have in common is that they relate the course of the Revolution with an aim to provide a reliable and, in most cases, conclusive version of the events. Many of them contain dialogue and re-enacted episodes which serve primarily to subjectify the experiences of the narrators or their protagonists. These elements, which are more commonly associated with fictional writing, are incorporated into the non-fictional and journalistic forms of reportage and chronicle.

In Chapters 5 and 6 I examine texts belonging to an uncertain range of narrative types which are not easily identified as fiction or non-fiction. While they do deal with factual events, the way in which they are presented resembles fictional prose narrative. Although only four texts are examined the vast number of significant issues which they raise has prompted me to divide this chapter into two, each of these dealing with two texts belonging to different generic categories: dramatized vignettes and *relato* in the first person in Chapter 5, and novelized biography and collage in Chapter 6. I will explain why I have classified these texts in this way, and what the factual and fictional features of each work are. It will transpire that re-enacted and dramatized episodes are merged with factual reports and documented accounts, where real experiences are related employing literary devices more commonly associated with fictional or novelistic writing.

I will conclude my review in Chapters 7 and 8. Just as with the previous set of works, the four included here will be dealt with in two chapters. From Chapter 3 on, each chapter has dealt with texts in which the fictional or novelistic element has been increasingly pronounced and in which the documentary aspect, although equally important, makes a less obvious appearance. In the same way, in these two chapters, although the works are fictional in their creativity and structure, they are clearly not so in content. On the whole we are dealing with literature which is simultaneous to the events and which refers to the immediate reality of the author. Because of the nearness of the Revolution to its rendering we cannot refer to the works in these two chapters as historical novels. Instead I call these pseudohistorical accounts non-fictional novels. After revealing the origins and salient features of this genre I will examine the four works in detail. Given that they too are prose narrative, I will consider five short stories. These have the added value that they were composed by significant writers of the time (as opposed to many of the longer texts examined whose authors are largely unknown). Finally, in a concluding chapter I bring together my findings and argue that the overwhelming quality and urgency of the historical event justifies these writers' abandonment of the traditional novel form.

1. For example, Fulgencio Castañar, *El compromiso en la novela de la II República* (Madrid: Siglo XXI, 1992), and J. Bécarud and E. López Campillo, *Los intelectuales españoles durante la II República* (Madrid: Siglo XXI, 1978), briefly mention the effect which the

Asturian Revolution had on literature at the time. Manuel Aznar Soler's article, 'La revolución asturiana de octubre de 1934 y la literatura española', *Los Cuadernos del Norte*, 26 (1984), 86–104, deals specifically with the Revolution. However, the restriction on the length inevitably limits the depth of his analysis.

2. *El valle negro: Asturias 1934* (Mexico: Norte, 1938), p. 507.
3. *Asturias 1934*, 2 vols (Gijón: Jucar, 1984), I, 225–26.
4. *La guerra civil española en la novela: bibliografía comentada*, 2 vols (Madrid: Ediciones José Porrúa Turanzas, 1982), p. 20.
5. *The Historical Novel* (London: Merlin Press, 1962), p. 23.
6. *On the Historical Novel*, trans. and intro. by Sandra Bermann (Lincoln: University of Nebraska Press, 1984). Bermann maintains that this work is probably Manzoni's most neglected work.
7. *The Historical Novel: An Essay* (Cambridge: Cambridge University Press, 1924), p. 21.
8. 'The Fictions of Factual Representation', in *The Literature of Fact: Selected Papers from the English Institute*, ed. by Angus Fletcher (New York: Columbia University Press, 1976), pp. 21–44 (p. 27).
9. 'The Historical Novel,' in *Encyclopaedia of Literature and Criticism*, ed. by Martin Coyle, et al. (London: Routledge, 1991), pp. 531–43 (p. 531).
10. *Telling the Truth: The Theory and Practice of Documentary Fiction* (Ithaca: Cornell University Press, 1986).
11. *The English Historical Novel: Walter Scott to Virginia Woolf* (Baltimore: Johns Hopkins University Press, 1971).
12. Chris Baldick, *The Concise Oxford Dictionary of Literary Terms* (Oxford: Oxford University Press, 1990), pp. 99–100.
13. Avrom Fleishman refers to Kathleen Tillotson, *Novels of the Eighteen-Forties London* (1961) in *The English Historical Novel*, p. 3.
14. John Hollowell refers to Robert Scholes, *Elements of Fiction* (1981) in *Fact and Fiction: The New Journalism and the Nonfiction Novel* (Chapel Hill: University of North Carolina Press, 1977), p. 20.
15. Foley, p. 29.
16. Barbara Herrnstein-Smith, 'On the Margins of Discourse', in *Critical Inquiry*, 1 (June 1975), 769–98 (p. 774).
17. Foley, p. 33.
18. In his important study on rhetoric Wayne Booth raises a number of issues about the 'reader-writer pact'. He suggests that a reader and a writer, before reading or writing a piece of narrative prose, must know what form, or what genre, it is going to take in order to facilitate the task of interpretation and understanding. In Wayne C. Booth, *The Rhetoric of Fiction*, 2nd edn (London: Penguin, 1991). For her part, Celia Fernández Prieto writes: 'Toda obra literaria debe haber sido estructurada de acuerdo con unos códigos que, al menos en parte, sean compartidos con los destinatarios. La función de esos códigos es señalar al texto como texto literario y facilitar que el receptor lo identifique y active su competencia cognoscitiva sobre el dominio semiótico de la literatura, su conocimiento de otros textos literarios, de ciertas convenciones de época, de escuela, de movimiento, y especialmente de la *poética* [author's own emphasis] particular del género. Así pues, el contexto del texto literario no es sólo lo que está en el texto, sino también y muy especialmente, la tradición textual en que ese texto se inserta, el género al que pertenece. La literatura crea su propio espacio semiótico y da lugar a tradiciones de textos, a redes textuales que llegan a generarse unas a otras.' In Celia Fernández Prieto, *Historia y novela: poética de la novela histórica* (Pamplona: EUNSA, 1998), pp. 28–29.
19. *Fact into Fiction: Documentary Realism in the Contemporary Novel* (London: Macmillan, 1991), p. 42.
20. Ilse Bulhof refers to Hayden White, *Metahistory: The Historical Imagination in Nineteenth-century Europe* (1974) in 'Imagination and Interpretation in History', in *Literature and History*, ed. by Leonard Schulze and Walter Wetzels (Lanham: University Press of America, 1983), pp. 3–25 (p. 13). In 'The Fictions of Factual Representation', White expands his argument: 'The facts do not speak for themselves, but [. . .] the historian speaks for them, speaks on their behalf, and fashions the fragments of the past into a whole whose integrity is — in its *re*presentation — a purely discursive one. [. . .]

The historian must utilize precisely the same tropological strategies, the same modalities of representing relationships in words, that the poet or novelist uses' (p. 28).

21. *An Introduction to Philosophy of History* (Bristol: Thoemmes Press, 1992), p. 100.
22. *The Frontiers of Literature* (Oxford: Basil Blackwell, 1988), p. 334.
23. Geoffrey Ribbans refers to Hayden White, *Tropics of Discourse: Essays in Cultural Criticism* (1978) in *History and Fiction in Galdós's Narratives* (Oxford: Clarendon Press, 1993), p. 8.
24. Bulhof, p. 4.
25. 'Sobre la novela y sus límites', *Arbor*, 8 (1949), 271–83 (p. 282).
26. *The Concise Oxford Dictionary of Literary Terms*, pp. 151–52.
27. *El comentario de textos narrativos: la novela* (Gijón: Ediciones Júcar, 1995), pp. 9–10.
28. *The Dialogic Imagination: Four Essays*, ed. by Michael Holquist, trans. by Caryl Emerson and Michael Holquist (Austin: University of Texas Press, 1996), p. 39.
29. *The Writer and Commitment*, 8th edn (London: Sacker and Warburg, 1961), pp. 103–04.
30. *Genres in Discourse*, trans. by Catherine Porter (Cambridge: Cambridge University Press, 1990), p. 10.
31. Alistair Fowler, 'The Life and Death of Literary Forms', in *New Directions in Literary History*, ed. by Ralph Cohen (London: Routledge and Keegan Paul, 1974), pp. 77–94.
32. Alistair Fowler, *Kinds of Literature: An Introduction to the Theory of Genres and Modes* (Oxford: Clarendon Press, 1982), p. 24.
33. 'The Origin of Genres', *New Literary History*, 8 (Autumn 1976), 159–70 (p. 161).
34. Elisabeth Wesseling, *Writing History as a Prophet: Postmodernist Innovations of the Historical Novel* (Amsterdam and Philadelphia: John Benjamins, 1991), p. 18.
35. Sauerberg, p. 47.
36. *Kinds of Literature*, p. 88.
37. *Keywords: A Vocabulary of Culture and Society* (London: Croom Helm, 1976), p. 152. The emphasis is the author's own.
38. Ross Murfin and Supryia Ray, *The Bedford Glossary of Critical and Literary Terms* (Boston, MA: Bedford Books, 1998), p. 128.
39. William Stott, *Documentary Expression and Thirties America* (London: Oxford University Press, 1973), p. 14.
40. *Oxford English Dictionary*, CD-ROM, 2nd edn.
41. Baldick, p. 145

CHAPTER 1

THE ASTURIAN REVOLUTION OF 1934

In October 1934 Asturias was the site of a major armed insurrection, led by the recently formed multiparty alliance, the Alianza Obrera, which, during the two weeks of its existence, abolished the political authority of the state and instituted new economic and social structures. As the first major outbreak of class war in Spain it clearly foreshadowed the Civil War. This armed conflict was not a spontaneous occurrence. The socio-political situation in Spain and more widely in Europe during the early 1930s had become increasingly turbulent. The longed-for Republic proved to be a disappointment to the high expectations of all those who had anxiously awaited its creation as many of the policies which had originally been promised failed to be implemented. This historical analysis starts in 1931, the year in which the Republic was proclaimed, going further back in time only when looking at the factors which led to the end of the dictatorial regime. This year marks the beginning of a new era with the end of Primo de Rivera's dictatorship (1930) and the exile of King Alfonso XIII.

From the Elections of 1931 to the October Revolution of 1934

In September 1923 General Primo de Rivera had staged a coup d'état, in response to the conduct of the war in Morocco, taking power, closing the Cortes and banning political parties. From that moment until the elections of April 1931, Spain was ruled by a military dictatorship, although Primo de Rivera himself fell from power in February 1930. According to Shlomo Ben-Ami, who examines in detail the political, social, and economic factors which led to the initial support for a republican regime, the demographic evolution which Spain went through at the beginning of the 1900s, and the desertion of the countryside and increasing urbanization caused by industrialization, were influential factors in bringing about the Republic: 'The growth of wealth, technological potentialities and urbanization, as well as the steady process of de-archaisation of the social structure, were simply becoming incompatible with autocracy', in other words, with both a monarchy and a dictatorship.[1] Although violent social protest was suppressed, its causes remained and were likely to erupt under a democratic regime.

In order to measure the degree of working-class militancy in Asturias, Adrian Shubert examines industrial development in the region from as far back as the First World War. Due to the unavailability of British coal during and immediately after the Great War, Spain had had to rely on its own domestic production of coal. As a result profits rose to unprecedented levels and miners' unions were able to agree on high wage settlements and a shorter working day; pit owners preferred to agree on high wages rather than disrupt the production of coal which would be the result of strike action. However, because the industry's prosperity was based on artificial premises, this upsurge did not last long. British coal (which was cheaper) once again began to enter Spain. Prices fell drastically and most of the mines which had been opened during the boom were shut. In the mines which remained open the managers strove to improve their competitiveness by reducing wages and increasing working hours, as well as by mechanizing production thereby reducing the manpower needed. To add to the problems facing the Spanish coal industry, the onset of the world depression severely affected the iron and steel industries, having grave repercussions on the amount of coal consumed. In addition, more countries were joining the coal market, and energy-saving technologies were being developed.

Primo de Rivera had resolved the dilemma confronting the coal industry by searching for projects at home which would sustain the demand for steel, iron and other manufactured materials, and consequently for coal. His economic policy was dominated by the expansion of Spain's infrastructure: he built roads, railway tracks and bridges. In this way the demand for steel and other products was maintained and unemployment was prevented from rising. Nevertheless, Primo de Rivera was simply delaying the inevitable and ignoring the acute problems facing Spanish industry. With the Republican government the country's expenditure was channelled into a new set of priorities, namely educational and labour reforms. Largo Caballero (as Minister of Labour) strove to introduce measures which would improve workers' wages and working hours. However, he had chosen a critical moment in the country's industry to do this. Although up to 1931 various strikes had been called by, amongst others, the largest of the miners' unions, the socialist SMA (Sindicato Minero de Asturias, founded in November 1910), the lack of positive results led to a fall in membership. The union recovered most of its support between 1931 and 1933, however, due largely to the role played by its leaders in the establishment of the Republic. Nevertheless, despite the worsening situation for the miners, throughout this period the union's policy was to avoid strikes and rely on the government and on Largo Caballero to satisfy its demands. The moderation of the socialists was in direct contrast to the behaviour of the communist and anarcho-syndicalist rivals in the SU (Sindicato Unico [Minero]), for whom there was no difference between the Republic and the monarchy. The struggle between the SMA and the SU escalated into an all-out war during the general strike called by the latter in June 1931, during which a shoot-out ensued between the groups from the two unions. This general strike was the high point of SU activity during the first two years of the Republic, and other strikes received much less support.

Another sector of society which was very much in favour of a Republic and which was without a doubt influential in bringing it about was the liberal intelligentsia. These included the greatest names of Spanish thought and letters. Indeed, once the Republic had been established many of them were to form part of the government or to be appointed ambassadors.

The municipal elections held in April 1931 turned out to be a vote of no-confidence on the monarchy and its regime.[2] These election results were to be merely a foretaste of the disastrous results for the monarchical right wing in the general elections held in June of that same year. The overwhelming majority of Spanish voters opted for a Republican government and, for the working class in particular, the new government carried with it the promise of major change.[3] The politicians who took office in April 1931 represented a broad and diverse alliance of assorted republicans and socialists. On the right stood the conservative, Catholic republicans to whom the regime's first Prime Minister, Niceto Alcalá Zamora, and Minister of the Interior, Miguel Maura, belonged. These were recent converts from monarchism anxious for a moderate Republic and eager to create a mass conservative party capable of 'republicanizing' Catholic opinion. Those nearer the centre of the political spectrum were represented by the largest and longest-established republican party, the Radical Party of Alejandro Lerroux. The Radicals' only real objective was the establishment of the Republic; only a minority pursued any reforming campaign beyond the traditional anticlericalism. During 1931 the Radical Party opened its arms to former monarchists and by the end of the year it had emerged as the main force of conservative republicanism. Left-wing republicanism was represented by various parties, notably Acción Republicana, led by Manuel Azaña. Its members were characterized by a desire to modernize Spain by, for example, reducing the role of the Church in society and developing lay education. Finally the Socialist Party, the PSOE (Partido Socialista Obrero Español), with its powerful and fast-growing union, the UGT (Unión General de Trabajadores), provided the new regime with genuine reforming objectives. This wide-ranging republican alliance made possible a landslide republican victory as it drew votes from the working, the middle and even the upper classes. The same heterogeneity which ensured the Republic's electoral success would nevertheless result in disaster once the new government was faced with the need to reconcile opposing interests.

The new Republic was faced with difficulties right from the beginning:

> With the Republic came the sudden arrival of mass politics, involving an adjustment difficult in itself and aggravated by . . . further considerations. The first was the sheer pressure for rapid and sweeping institutional and social reforms [. . .]. The second was the continued power of conservative interests, given that no social revolution occurred to precede or accompany the change from monarchy to republic.[4]

The establishment of the new government had involved merely the assumption of political office by members of a mainly professional and intellectual middle class. Although they had initially supported reform, Blinkhorn suggests that it was for fear of an outright revolution; they would only back republican measures on the condition that there be no drastic social reforms which would jeopardize their privileged position. In addition, as already indicated, the Republic was born into an economic climate very different from that of the 1920s: the world depression was undoubtedly going to make any reforms more difficult to finance and implement, and consequently the social atmosphere even more tense than it might otherwise have been. However, certain critics, such as Ben-Ami, maintain that the reason for the failure of the Republic were the actual policies which the new government hoped to implement and the reaction towards them. As early as October 1931 the anticlericalism of the left caused a rift in the republican ranks. Due to the controversial religious policies which appeared in article number 26 of the new Constitution, the Catholics Alcalá Zamora and Maura resigned from government.

In the field of labour and social reform, between 1931 and 1933 the Minister of Labour, Largo Caballero, attempted to shift the balance of economic power from the employers and landowners towards the working class and the peasantry. This partly succeeded, although the economic crisis provided the landowners and factory owners with an excuse to delay the adoption of the new measures. Thus, much of the agrarian and industrial reforms (to which there had been great opposition) proved to be unpractical and failed to be implemented. Strike action continued, making Asturias, along with Barcelona, the most strike-ridden province in the country from 1931 to 1933. Pamela Beth Radcliff distinguishes these strikes from those which took place after 1933.[5] Whilst the strikes during the first two years of the Republic were 'rooted in conventional workplace conflicts and involved moderate demands' (p. 284), after the elections of

1933 they were increasingly provoked by contentious political issues. Shubert also affirms that in the first two years of the Republic there was only one strike which could be regarded as political, whereas in the first nine months of 1934, of thirty-two strikes mentioned in the press, there were eight which were political and of these three were general strikes.[6]

By 1933 the hard core of the original republican-socialist alliance that had held office since December 1931 was crumbling. On the one hand, the republican policies had ensured a rightward drift of the Radical Party which had consequently left the governing coalition in December 1931 and joined the opposition. On the other hand, Largo Caballero and his supporters sought power for the PSOE alone in the belief that if they governed single-handedly they would be able to combat growing fascism more effectively. The result was the rupture of the PSOE's alliance with the left-republicans in the summer of 1933, a move which according to Blinkhorn was 'decidedly counter-productive [. . .] in view of the renewed vigour of the Spanish right' (p. 6).

The general elections of 1933, prompted by Azaña's fall from office in September, were won by the right-wing coalition, the CEDA (Confederación Española de Derechas Autónomas, founded in March 1933 and led by José María Gil Robles) and the Partido Radical of Alejandro Lerroux, while the PSOE representation was cut dramatically and left-republicanism nearly disappeared as a significant popular parliamentary force:

> Los resultados eran previsibles: decepción de los campesinos ante la ausencia de una reforma agraria, ausencia del voto obrero no partidario que culpaba a los socialistas de complicidad con la represión republicana y vuelco de la clase media a la busca de la «paz social» ofrecida por centristas y derechistas.[7]

The new government strove to overturn the anticlerical, labour, agricultural, and education legislation passed during the first two years of the Republic. Additionally they hoped to split and eradicate the left wing through the use of repressive measures. According to Paco Ignacio Taibo, the CEDA privately aimed to go a step further: they would initially support the Partido Radical in government, introduce a number of CEDA members into some key ministries, with a view to take power and ultimately end with democracy.[8] Nevertheless, to the electorate the CEDA presented itself as 'an anti-revolutionary movement of social defence rather than a political party',[9] accounting partly for its electoral success. In addition the middle-class support which the CEDA gathered helped to secure its victory:

> Nos hallamos ante un partido político de masas, que hábilmente se ha desligado del cadáver político de la monarquía, que ha prescindido de los nexos con los pequeños funcionarios trapicheros, con los burócratas menores ligados a los caciques pueblerinos, sobre los que melquiadistas y radicales levantan su poder. Está

> vinculado al latifundismo agrario, pero básicamente a aquél que incursiona en el comercio y la industria rural. [. . .]
>
> Es el partido que más sólidamente atado al capitalismo español se encuentra. Es el partido del poder económico, de los industriales, los banqueros, los empleados de confianza. Es el partido que se expresa a través de los abogados de las grandes compañías. [10]

The CEDA was also the most powerful political grouping committed to the defence of the Church, an important consideration if we take into account the problems which the former Republican government had encountered with its anticlerical measures.

From the point of view of the left, José Peirats suggests that the electoral boycott called by the CNT (Confederación Nacional del Trabajo, the anarcho-syndicalist trade union) during the elections had grave repercussions on left-wing support. The campaign in favour of abstentionism was intense and it was kept up throughout the election period.[11] There were also internal problems in the socialist ranks. The supporters were divided into three factions, represented by Julián Besteiro, Indalecio Prieto, and Francisco Largo Caballero. During the Republic trade union affiliation had increased massively and the PSOE was living through one of its strongest moments. Nevertheless, the socialist members of the Republican government had at times followed a repressive and non-revolutionary line due to their links with the bourgeois elements in the government, for which they came in for severe criticism from much of the working class. Subsequently, for the 1933 elections the PSOE chose not to coalesce with any other party, facing the other left-wing groups and the coalition of the CEDA alone. Although the united right had slightly fewer votes than the disunited left, the former had nearly twice as many seats due to the electoral law which encouraged alliances, giving eighty per cent of seats to the party or groups of parties with the largest vote over forty per cent.[12]

With the disastrous election results the PSOE had the choice of continuing with the drive for a change in government through the democratic parliamentary process, as advocated by Besteiro, or adopting a revolutionary stance. Whilst they had formed part of the Republican government the PSOE could hardly have opted for an insurrectionary approach. Nevertheless, now in opposition they could at least contemplate the possibility, more so as the right wing in power became increasingly reactionary towards the working class. Largo Caballero called for a Revolution; Indalecio Prieto, who had originally opted for a parliamentary approach, decided at a later stage to espouse the revolutionary cause with the underlying intention of keeping it under control; Julián Besteiro, the most conservative of the socialist figureheads, criticized the left-wing socialist position, but with no effect.

As the Republican government became more repressive and the masses more radical, power in the PSOE moved from Besteiro to Largo Caballero. On 28 January 1934 Besteiro, Saborit and Trifón Gómez resigned the leadership of the UGT following the leftist victory in the elections to the Agrupación Socialista in Madrid. They were substituted by Anastasio de Gracia, Díaz Alor, and Largo Caballero. The leadership of the FNTT (Federación Nacional de Trabajadores de la Tierra — the land workers' section of the UGT) was also taken over by the leftists, as was that of the Juventudes Socialistas, in April 1934, whose new executive included Carlos Zancajo (president), Santiago Carrillo (secretary), and José Laín Entralgo. The three major socialist organizations were therefore now led by supporters of Largo Caballero. Caballero declared that the socialists would defend themselves (violently, if need be) if the right wing became belligerent or aggressive. With the support of the Juventudes Socialistas he began to form a revolutionary plan. Indeed, throughout 1934 the Juventudes organized a paramilitary force, initially under the responsibility of Laín Entralgo and then under the Italian anti-fascist Fernando de Rosa, in preparation for any revolutionary action. The following extract from the newspaper *Adelante*, quoted by Marta Bizcarrondo, is demonstrative of Largo Caballero's attitude towards the imminent Revolution:

> Ya no es cuestión ahora de partidos intermedios, situados entre la clase trabajadora y la gran burguesía, sino de una manera tajante: a un lado la burguesía reaccionaria, al otro lado, nosotros, el movimiento obrero. Esta matización, que se va acentuando cada día más, formula, como consecuencia inmediata, o bien el poder pasa a manos de las derechas o a las nuestras. Y como las derechas para sostenerse necesitan su dictadura, la clase trabajadora, una vez logrado el poder, ha de implantar también su dictadura, la dictadura del proletariado. La hora de los choques decisivos se va acercando. El movimiento obrero ha de prepararse para la revolución.[13]

In Asturias some leadership changes were made: Juan Antonio Suárez and Teodomiro Menéndez (moderate socialists) were displaced by militant socialists such as Graciano Antuña who became president of the Federación Socialista Asturiana. However, for the most part this move to the left was hardly felt.

The victory of the right in November marked the beginning of a new period, especially as the Lerroux and Samper governments adopted a series of contentious measures and set out on a deliberate policy of repression against the labour movement. In the first place, in March the government announced an anti-strike bill and the police were increasingly used to break up strikes and demonstrations. Members of left-wing unions were discriminated against and wages decreased dramatically. In addition a black list with the names of union members was being compiled by the CEDA in all the cities and villages. Secondly, those generals responsible for the attempted coup d'état in 1932, headed by General Sanjurjo, were released from jail and given back their military posts. Thirdly, the lands which had been taken away from the landowners by the state without any form of indemnity payment were handed back. Finally, the clergy were once again to be financially supported by the state.

The socialist newspaper *Avance* was specially targeted by the repression, and its director, Javier Bueno, was jailed three times in 1934.[14] It played a key role in the fight against the government by informing and criticizing the country's move to the right: 'No fue *Avance* en 1934 un periódico que propusiera caminos tácticos o dirigiera la lucha. Más que eso, operó como un ejemplo para sus lectores.'[15] The government took strict measures against the journal with a view to remove it from circulation. As a response the journal called on its readership for support and increased the severity of its articles. On 30 August the newspaper openly proposed to its readership: 'No hay más que un camino, sin altos ni pausa: la revolución.'[16] When Bueno, as director, was jailed the journal organized mass visits to the prison where he was held and published articles written by the detainee himself criticizing the harsh conditions inside the Cárcel Modelo in Madrid. The journal's average print-run was twenty-five thousand issues, and fifty thousand issues were printed of a special edition on the first of May.

The October Revolution could well be regarded as an assault on a legitimately elected government, just as the July military rebellion which led to the Civil War has been perceived. Nevertheless, as Fernando Claudín suggests, the right-wing election victory was regarded as a serious threat to the recently established Republic, especially in view of the spread of fascism across Europe, not only in Germany, Italy, and Austria, but also in France and Great Britain:

> La derrota electoral de noviembre de 1933 no fue vista por la izquierda obrera y republicana [. . .] como una alternancia política normal dentro del juego democrático. La vio como el primer paso hacia la «pérdida de la República» y hacia la instauración del fascismo, recientemente triunfante en Alemania, ya consolidado y cada vez más arrogante en Italia, avanzando en Austria [. . .] y crecientemente activo en otros centros europeos. En consecuencia, el radicalismo latente de un sector considerable del socialismo español, reavivado ya bajo el bienio republicano-socialista debido a la decepción causada por la timidez de las reformas [. . .] se convirtió de la noche a la mañana en voluntad revolucionaria. La seducción que desde tiempo atrás ejercía la Revolución bolchevique se transformó en modelo operativo para recuperar la República y convertirla en marco adecuado de la revolución social. La izquierda socialista puso rumbo a la dictadura del proletariado [. . .] mediante la conquista del poder por vía insurreccional. [17]

Claudín does, nevertheless, suggest that there were some other aims behind the insurrection: Prieto hoped to restore the Republic to its original condition; the then fairly insignificant Communist Party wanted to participate in order to eventually take control of the insurrectionary campaign and guide any future revolutionary government; and the anarcho-syndicalists who joined in the action only in Asturias hoped to exercise their libertarian communist ideas.

The growing critical atmosphere prevailed during the month of September. The year 1934 had been marked by an employers' and landowners' counter-attack upon union rights, wage gains, and rent controls, and by a series of mainly unsuccessful left-wing responses, such as the winter Revolution of the Aragonese CNT, the Zaragoza general strike, and the peasants' strike of June. Many on the left, and not only the socialists, felt that they had to do something in order to stop the crumbling of the Republic. By the summer of 1934 the radicalization of the socialist leadership was complete, and as early as November 1933 the executive of the PSOE had discussed an armed insurrection against the government. Even Martínez Barrio, the president of the liberal Unión Republicana, closed the party's annual conference with a speech affirming that the regime governing Spain resembled that of a monarchy or a dictatorship. According to Shubert: 'In this last month before the revolution the Asturian miners were openly contesting the legitimacy of the Republic and Socialist leaders found themselves caught in a dilemma' (p. 125). They had to keep up the pressure and respond to government provocation, while at the same time hold back the angry and impatient crowds until orders from Madrid gave the insurrection the go-ahead. The growing socio-political trouble suddenly worsened as a young communist, Joaquín Grado, was killed by a group of fascists in Madrid on 29 August. In addition, on 9 September a meeting of the young right-wing CEDA was held at Covadonga, the birthplace of the Reconquest, in Asturias itself, during which Gil Robles gave a blatantly provocative speech in which he warned: 'No consentiremos ni un momento más que continúe este estado de cosas.'[18] Finally, the situation in the autonomous regions added to the trouble. The transfer of power in Catalonia from the central to the autonomous government was vetoed, and in the Basque Country the hopes for a new autonomous statute were dashed.

The left hoped that the president of the government, Niceto Alcalá Zamora, would resolve the critical political situation facing Spain by calling for elections. On 26 September the CEDA provoked a crisis by announcing that they could no longer support a minority government insisting that they should be included in the governing administration.[19] Thus, Samper resigned as head of the government on 1 October. The moderate republicans advised Alcalá Zamora not to yield to the CEDA's demands, while the socialists on the right suggested to him that he dissolve

Parliament and call for elections. It was a difficult decision for Alcalá Zamora as the CEDA, although the largest elected party, did not hold a majority in parliament and, what is more important, was opposed in principle to the Republic. Alcalá Zamora instead of deciding for himself asked Lerroux to form a new government with CEDA participation hoping that this would be limited to the holding of one ministerial post. Nevertheless, Gil Robles, not content with this, was adamant that his party should hold three posts. On 4 October the new government was announced. The three CEDA ministers included in the new government were a deliberately provocative choice: José Oriol Anguera de Sojo (Minister of Labour) had been responsible for the confiscation of a hundred issues of *El Socialista*; Rafael Aizpún (Minister of Justice) was a Carlist and openly anti-republican; and Manuel Giménez Fernández (Minister of Agriculture) represented the particularly aggressive landowners of Badajoz. Supporters of the Republic were outraged when the names of the three new anti-republican and pro-fascist CEDA ministers were announced. It proved to be the final spark, and on 4 October the socialist Revolutionary Committee in Madrid gave the insurrection the green light. When the signal was given late that night, Asturias erupted with the full force of the miners' ire and frustration.

The Preparations for the Revolution

The leaders of the working class realized that they needed to form a single force against the repression suffered by all the workers, whether they be from the countryside or from the city. The coalition of all these revolutionary groups, however, was not as easy to achieve as it may at first appear. These groups, the socialists, the communists, and the anarchists, had each followed their own political agenda, on many occasions to the detriment of the other groups. According to Joaquín Maurín:

> Durante los años de auge del movimiento obrero, en la post-guerra, los anarquistas y sindicalistas de Gijón y La Felguera hicieron una guerra a muerte a los socialistas de Oviedo y de la zona minera. Gijón contra Oviedo. La Felguera contra Sama. El eterno y trágico drama de nuestro movimiento obrero. Cuando la marea sindicalista comenzó a descender, entonces la escisión se produjo dentro de las filas socialistas. No era suficiente, al parecer, la pugna entre anarcosindicalistas y marxistas que aún debía producirse un nuevo fraccionamiento. Los que antes resistieron al ataque anarcosindicalista, luego se buscaron para entredevorarse. A un lado, el Partido Socialista; al otro, el Partido Comunista. De una parte, el Sindicato Minero; de la otra, el Sindicato Unico. Aquí, Llaneza, González Peña, Belarmino Tomás, Amador Fernández; allá, Benjamín Escobar, Loredo Aparicio, Jesús Rodríguez, Marcelino Magdalena. La guerra civil entre comunistas y socialistas fue implacable desde 1922 hasta 1934.[20]

Therefore the formation of a coalition in which the left as a whole were to co-operate and fight together was not going to be straightforward. Nevertheless, the same groups realized that if a revolutionary attempt was to succeed they had to work together. This unifying force, which was to be known as the Alianza Obrera, did not crystallize in most of Spain for a number of reasons: the rural areas of mid and southern Spain could not respond fully as the agricultural strikes had left the peasants hungry and weak; the CNT refused to join the Alianza; the communists disagreed with the socialists about the form the coalition should take; and the Alianza was largely dominated by socialists to the displeasure of the other proletariat groups. Indeed Asturias, and to a lesser degree Catalonia, were the only places in Spain where the Alianza Obrera became a reality.

The talks which had begun in Catalonia on 22 November 1933, led to the signing of a pact by the Federación Catalana of the PSOE, the UGT, the Unión Sindicalista of Cataluña, the BOC (Bloc Obrer i Camperol), the group Izquierda Comunista, the Unió de Rabassaires, the Partido Sindicalista, the Sindicatos de Oposición, the Federación Sindicalista y Libertaria, and the Federación de Sindicatos not included in the CNT, giving birth to the Alianza Obrera. In Asturias, it was the PSOE which was to take the initiative in creating this unifying force. The first important group to co-operate with the socialists in Asturias were the anarcho-syndicalists, a move which was taken by the CNT (only in Asturias) as a result of the foresightedness of its regional committee, and in particular, José María Martínez, one of the confederation's leaders. He realized that a revolutionary situation was developing and that it could only be taken advantage of in co-operation with the UGT, which was the most important labour organization in Asturias at the time.[21] On 9 March 1934 the CNT regional Committee agreed to make contact with the UGT in order to begin negotiations. The first meeting in which negotiations began was held four days later and was dominated by great suspicion on both sides. The conditions of the pact were drawn up on 28 March 1934 and signed on 31 March after some minor alterations. The terms were as follows:

1. Las organizaciones firmantes de este pacto trabajarán de común acuerdo hasta conseguir el triunfo de la revolución social en España. Estableciendo un régimen de igualdad económica, política y social, fundado sobre principios socialistas federalistas.
2. Para la consecución de este fin, se constituirá en Oviedo un Comité Ejecutivo en representación de todas las organizaciones adheridas a este Pacto, el cual actuará de acuerdo con otro nacional y del mismo carácter para los efectos de la acción general de toda España.
3. Como consecuencia lógica de las condiciones primera y segunda de este Pacto queda entendido que la constitución del Comité Nacional es premisa indispensable, en caso de que los acontecimientos se desenvuelvan normalmente, para

emprender toda acción relacionada con el objetivo de este Pacto, por cuanto el mismo trata y pretende la realización de un hecho nacional. El Comité Nacional que ha de constituirse será el único que autorizadamente podrá ordenar, al que queda en Oviedo, los movimientos a emprender en relación con el general en toda España.

4. Se constituirá en toda Asturias un Comité en cada localidad, cuya composición deberá estar integrada por delegaciones de cada una de las organizaciones firmantes de este Pacto, y aquellas otras que adhiriéndose sean admitidas por el Comité Ejecutivo.
5. A partir de la fecha en que este Pacto sea firmado cesarán todas las campañas de propaganda que pudieran entorpecer o agriar relaciones entre las partes aliadas, sin que esto signifique dejación de la labor serena y razonada de las diversas doctrinas preconizadas por los sectores que integran la Alianza Obrera Revolucionaria, conservando, a tal fin, su independencia colectiva.
6. El Comité Ejecutivo elaborará un plan de acción que mediante el esfuerzo revolucionario del proletariado asegure el triunfo de la revolución en sus diversos aspectos, y consolidándola según las normas del convenio previamente establecido.
7. Serán cláusulas adicionales al presente Pacto, todos lo acuerdos del Comité Ejecutivo, cuyo cumplimiento es obligatorio para todas las organizaciones representadas, siendo estos acuerdos de obligada vigencia, tanto en el período preparatorio de la revolución como después del triunfo de ésta. Sobreentendiéndose que las resoluciones del referido Comité Ejecutivo se inspirarán en el contenido de este Pacto.
8. El compromiso contraído por las organizaciones que subscriben terminará en el momento en que haya sido implantado el régimen señalado en el apartado primero, con sus órganos propios elegidos, voluntariamente, por la clase trabajadora y por el procedimiento que haya preceptuado la obra dominante de este Pacto.
9. Considerado que este Pacto constituye un acuerdo de organizaciones de la clase trabajadora, para coordinar la acción contra el régimen burgués y abatirlo, aquellas organizaciones que tuvieran relaciones orgánicas con partidos burgueses las romperán automáticamente para consagrarse, exclusivamente, a la consecución de los fines que determina el presente Pacto.[22]

On 1 April 1934 this pact appeared in *Avance* along with an adjoining invitation for other revolutionary groups to join. As a result the BOC and the group Izquierda Comunista applied for entry into the Alianza. They were admitted with the proviso that they accepted firstly the terms of the Alianza as they had been drawn up, without making any alterations, and secondly their absence from the Executive Committee.

The Communist Party was the last to join the alliance. Right from the start it had been against the Alianza, advocating instead a Popular Front. Nevertheless, the increasing political tension and the seemingly effective workings of the Alianza Obrera forced the communists to rectify their original stance, applying for membership on 27 September. Marta Bizcarrondo quotes Vicente Arroyo who gives reasons for the Communist Party's integration into the Alianza:

Es evidente que las "Alianzas Obreras" no eran — ni son todavía — el frente único, no pueden ser la expresión de la unidad de acción de la clase obrera y de los campesinos trabajadores, faltando en ellas sectores tan importantes como la C.N.T. [which had not joined the Alianza Obrera except in Asturias and Cataluña], la C.G.T.U., el Partido Comunista, las organizaciones campesinas y los obreros inorganizados. La misma constitución de las "Alianzas Obreras" — exclusivamente por arriba — y sus objetivos inmediatos: "hacer inmediatamente la revolución rechazando toda acción por las reivindicaciones inmediatas de los obreros", no podían merecer ninguna garantía para el P.C., que quiere realmente organizar la revolución. Por eso el Partido Comunista rechazó, en principio, en esa fecha, la aceptación de las "Alianzas Obreras" propuesta por el P.S.

Pero la situación continúa agravándose en España; las masas obreras se muestran cada vez más decididas y partidarias del frente único y cada vez desean más la unificación de las fuerzas revolucionarias [. . .]. El ingreso del P.C. en las "Alianzas Obreras" no es la completa unidad de acción [. . .]. Pero con el ingreso de nuestro Partido, que no disfraza su pensamiento ni sus propósitos de trabajar dentro de las "Alianzas" para atraer a ellas a todas las fuerzas obreras, las "Alianzas Obreras" tomarán un nuevo carácter. Nuestro Partido dentro de ellas trabajará por transformarlas de conglomerados de direcciones de partidos en organismos vivos de frente único. . .[23]

Dolores Ibárruri comments, in retrospect, on the reasons for the change in the position of the PCE: 'La situación política había empeorado considerablemente y no era posible aguardar más sin correr el riesgo de que un golpe reaccionario sorprendiera a la clase obrera dividida.'[24] Thus, on 2 October the Alianza Obrera, comprised of the three major left-wing forces, finally became a reality in Asturias, at the last moment and almost on the eve of the insurrection.

In most of Spain the principle of the Alianza lacked support, chiefly because the stance and the motives of the Socialist Party were regarded with suspicion by the other political groups. Nevertheless, during the ten days of revolutionary action in Asturias there was an extraordinary level of co-operation between the socialists on the left and right, the communists, the anarcho-syndicalists, and the Trotskyists. This co-operation, which in the short term overcame the rival doctrinaire positions between the leftist groups, gave the Asturian Revolution a legendary reputation. Indeed many argue that without the combined action of the Alianza Obrera the Asturian Revolution would never have broken out.

Although the Alianza Obrera provided the moral and ideological ground for the Revolution at rather a late stage, the more practical preparations had begun by the end of 1933, when the political situation in Spain seemed to become increasingly reactionary. The workers in Asturias had slowly but systematically been preparing for a possible future insurrection by smuggling fire arms, cartridges and bullets from several factories, and sticks of dynamite from the mines. Ingenious methods were thought up to smuggle and hide arms, as Taibo reveals: 'En los días previos al movimiento, se hizo un boquete desde el economato a un almacén de la Fabrica [de la Vega]. Las armas se sacaron ocultas en pequeños carros de patatas'; 'Un par de compañeros vestidos de ropavejeros y con sacos de esparto ocultaban las piezas [of the rifles] y las transportaban al edificio de *Avance*, donde se ocultaban entre las grandes bobinas de papel'; 'Los fusiles se sacaban por un desagüe en el probadero de ametralladoras. . . Afuera se escondían en varas de yerba. . .'; 'grandes tambores de lámina metálica enterrados con las armas cubiertas con plástico y grasa'; 'Compramos un candado y los guardamos en el sótano del kiosko de La Felguera, abajo de donde tocaba la banda de música.'[25] Some arms were bought with money from the 'fondo revolucionario' which had been set up. Other weaponry reached Asturias as contraband from Belgium and France.

Another substantial source of weapons was the cache of arms transported to Asturias by the ex-fishing boat, the *Turquesa*, which reached the Ría de Pravia on 10 September. The story behind these arms was cloaked in mystery: what the origins of the arms were, who had financed their purchase and for what reason, who had been responsible for transporting them to Asturias, and where they were hidden were some of the questions which the authorities asked themselves. According to Taibo the weapons were originally destined for a revolutionary attempt in Portugal, but the instigators there failed to come up with the money to pay for them.[26] Indalecio Prieto organized the secret purchase of these arms for the Socialist Party. These were transported from Cadiz to Asturias, where a large team organized by the Asturian Socialist Party and the Sindicato Minero were due to pick them up. Taibo claims that many individuals were involved in the *Turquesa* operation: 'Se realizó con un equipo que incluía un barco con una tripulación de 12 hombres, doscientos militantes en operaciones de transporte y cobertura, seis camiones, siete automóviles y cinco motoras con su tripulación.'[27] However, the sudden appearance of the Civil Guard and the police, alerted by the amount of movement on the coastline and the beach, meant that only one trip to the *Turquesa* could be made by the dinghies transferring the weapons from the boat to the shore. Any further trips were seriously impeded by the strict vigilance. The *Turquesa*, with many crates full of weapons still aboard, remained in the same place for several days until the crew, short of provisions and without radio contact, and under the impression that something serious with regards to the secret operation had occurred, sailed on to Bilbao and then to Bordeaux where they were eventually arrested by the French authorities. Thus, many of the arms did not reach the hands of the revolutionaries and many of those involved were jailed and interrogated by the authorities in an attempt to find out details about the operation. Little information was divulged and to add to the confusion *Avance* published a number of articles making false claims which puzzled further those investigating. Hence the mysterious nature of the affair.

By 5 October the socialists, especially, had secured a considerable supply of arms and dynamite. However, it was a relatively modest stock if we take into consideration that with it they hoped to defeat the army and the police. Although the right-wing press claimed that the initial success of the revolutionaries had been due to a well-equipped revolutionary force, as opposed to central and local government disorganization, the reality was that there were few arms for the number of revolutionaries volunteering to fight: 'Exceptuando Madrid y Asturias, en ningún otro lugar de España hay fusiles suficientes para poder plantearse combates contra el ejército en condiciones de triunfo. Se depende por tanto del triunfo del golpe de mano, de la victoria sorpresiva en el asalto a los cuarteles.'[28] Few of the crates shipped by the *Turquesa* actually reached the shores of Asturias safely, and when these were opened, mainly ammunition was found. Most of the rifles and machine guns had been left on board. Therefore, what had at one point seemed a substantial haul was finally not to be so. By the time the Revolution broke out there were fourteen storage points in Asturias, two belonging to the CNT, two to the Communist Party and ten to the Sindicato Minero and the Juventudes Socialistas. Altogether the revolutionaries had at their disposal 1300 rifles, four machine guns, and thousands of dynamite sticks. We can add to this the few thousand guns which the militants possessed. Finally, a clandestine paramilitary force, based on the 'escuadras' of the Juventudes Socialistas, the CNT and the Juventudes Libertarias, had been organized:

> Entrenados por ex sargentos, con la cobertura de grupos de excursionismo, clubes culturales; participando en falsas meriendas campestres o romerías, uniformados con sus camisas rojas y armados con pistolas, los grupos de la JS actuaron en Asturias durante todo 1934 preparándose para el enfrentamiento decisivo.
>
> La CNT aportó a este primer ejército insurreccional varios grupos organizados [. . .], en total cerca de un millar de combatientes. El Partido Comunista desdobló algunos de sus comités de radio y les dio estructura insurreccional.[29]

The Revolution: From 5 to 18 October

By October the Alianza Obrera in Asturias had at their disposal three thousand organized and armed men divided into squads, ready to take part in the fighting. All that was needed was a stimulus strong enough to bring the workers out on to the street, and that stimulus came on 4 October with the political events already examined.

The fighting was almost limited to the central core of Asturias. The Revolution spread from Mieres, Campomanes and Langreo to Oviedo,

FIGURE 1 The key sites of the Asturian Revolution

where the battle was most bloody (see Fig. 1). The insurrection started on 5 October, in Sama and in Mieres, as the miners attacked the Civil Guard posts with dynamite. The revolutionary leaders, aware of the lack of arms, regarded the attack on these posts as the main priority for the arming of the insurrection. This assault was a success but it had taken thirty-six hours, longer than had been anticipated, and thirty-eight Guards had been killed. Thus it was not until the next day, the sixth, that the miners, divided into three columns, entered Oviedo. The delay and poor co-ordination among the columns had removed the element of surprise, crucial if the insurrection was to succeed, and had allowed the forces inside the city to prepare for their defence. The fight in Oviedo was always going to be different from that in the mining towns given that the capital city possessed a considerable professional middle class, a university, numerous government offices and a garrison of around a thousand soldiers. The revolutionary troops from the surrounding mining valleys spent all of the first day on the outskirts of the capital waiting for the Revolutionary Committee based inside the city to give the order to attack. The order was not given until the day after and even then relatively few workers inside the city rose in revolt. When the siege finally began some 1400 soldiers and 300 Civil Guards were defending the city from about 1200 workers. Despite the imbalance between the two sides, some important battles were won by the revolutionaries. On 6 October a small group staged a surprise attack on the cannon factory at Trubia during which the workers inside were able to disarm the soldiers on guard. The revolutionaries managed to capture twenty-seven cannons from this one factory. The next day the explosives factory at La Manjoya was taken. And finally, a day later, on the eighth, they assaulted the small arms factory of La Vega in Oviedo, taking hold of thirty thousand rifles and a number of machine guns.[30] By the ninth the defenders had been reduced to a few isolated pockets: the barracks, the jail, the government building, and the cathedral.

At this point revolutionary victory seemed to be a real possibility. Most of the villages and towns in the heart of Asturias had been taken by the revolutionaries except for the two major cities, Gijón and Avilés. Here, the first days were dominated by the constant search for arms by Committee members. Trips to Oviedo and La Felguera in quest of arms proved to be unfruitful, and the arms which were hidden in a nearby village called Llanera, destined for Avilés and Gijón, were inaccessible as the Civil Guard and the police had guarded the village from 5 October onwards after having successfully launched a surprise attack. Gijón's position was further weakened when, on the eighth, the war ship *Libertad* bombed the areas where the revolutionaries had put up their barricades.

Meanwhile, three government columns were approaching Asturias from the east, the west and the south. On the southern front, General Bosch and his column, advancing on to Mieres along the main road from León, were encircled at Vega del Rey by between two and three thousand miners. They had made skilful use of the mountainous terrain to trap the professional soldiers who had seriously underestimated the efficiency and enthusiasm of their revolutionary opponents. Bosch's troops were trapped for six days before the arrival of enforcements enabled them to break out and retreat. On the fifteenth, almost totally out of ammunition, the miners on this front began to withdraw but the efforts of a small guerrilla force and the concern of the new commander, General Balmes, not to fall into another trap meant that the troops advanced very cautiously and never reached Mieres. As far as the eastern front is concerned, on the seventh a considerable troop of Moorish and Foreign Legion soldiers, shipped urgently from Morocco and led by Colonel Yagüe, reached Gijón where they landed and joined the column which approached the city from the east. On the tenth they took Gijón. On the twelfth the main column pushing forward from the west, under the command of General López Ochoa, joined the Moors and the Foreign Legion, which had recently conquered Gijón, in the outskirts of Oviedo. Three days of tough fighting in the streets of Oviedo continued, but it was clear by the seventeenth that the insurrectionary movement had been defeated, and Belarmino Tomás, one of the revolutionary leaders, and General López Ochoa settled on the terms for surrender which was to take place the next day. Despite their eventual defeat the military achievement of the revolutionaries was considerable for they had faced a well-armed, professional force of around twenty-six thousand men: General López Ochoa advancing on Oviedo from Galicia, Colonel Yagüe's African troops joining the attack after landing at Gijón, and General Solchaga's force marching on the Nalón valley from the east, as well as the Bosch-Balmes column trapped on the southern front.

From 9 October onwards the Revolutionary Committee based in Oviedo had changed hands three times. The first Committee, which was socialist-dominated, had considered abandoning the movement as early as the ninth, when it was clear that Asturias had risen alone. On the eleventh, with López Ochoa's troops entering the capital, the Committee fled.[31] The unannounced flight of the leaders of the Revolution caused a brief panic and indignation amongst the fighters, and in some places the men abandoned their arms on the streets and fled to the mountains. Nevertheless, the next day a second Committee composed of five communists, an anarcho-syndicalist, and two members of the Juventudes Socialistas was elected at a meeting in the town hall square in Oviedo. This Committee, which launched a counter-attack on the troops entering the city, lasted only a day. On the twelfth some of the socialist members of the first Committee returned and a third, and final, Committee was formed. This one was made up of six socialists, including Belarmino Tomás as the president, and three communists. Representatives from the CNT attended but refused to serve as members. The next day the Committee moved to Sama although the communist delegates stayed in Oviedo to mount a last defence. The Socialists' main concern was to find a way to wind up the struggle, but they had trouble convincing the local Committees and the strong-willed miners that the fight should be given up. On the seventeenth Belarmino Tomás, as president of the Committee, negotiated the revolutionary surrender with General López Ochoa. All arms were to be handed in in return for the General's promise that the Moorish troops would not be allowed into the mining villages, a promise which was not kept. The next day the Committee issued a final communiqué ordering everyone back to work. The Asturian Revolution was over.

The events of October, although targeted at the whole of Spain, only reached revolutionary proportions in Asturias.[32] The incidents which took place in Barcelona, where on 6 October Luis Companys, President of the Catalan government, proclaimed the 'Republic of Catalonia within the Federal Republic of Spain' and invited a democratic 'government in exile' to establish itself in Barcelona,[33] should also be regarded as significant. From the moment that it transpired that the insurrection had been unsuccessful in Barcelona and Madrid it was clear that the miners in Asturias would not be able to defeat the sustained attack mounted by the government forces. Nevertheless, the revolutionaries in Asturias fought right up to the last minute, hoping that when the rest of the country saw and heard of their success they too would join the fight. In addition, in an attempt to keep up morale and enthusiasm, they were supplied with false information by their own side in the form of leaflets and newspaper articles which claimed that the Revolution was succeeding throughout Spain. As late as the thirteenth, reports were spread claiming that the Revolution in the whole of Spain would successfully end in a matter of hours.[34]

Without the support from the rest of Spain the Revolution was almost certain to fail. Right from the start, and more so as Asturias was left alone, the government enjoyed far superior military force and arsenal, in terms of quality and quantity, and it had at its disposal professional military support. The rebels could not endure the fight as the battle in Asturias dragged on. Although the insurrection, in theory, had been planned, in practice it soon became apparent that the rebel groups lacked professional military tactical expertise. The ammunition and armaments taken from the various factories were carelessly used and wasted and by the end of the fighting all the rebels had at their disposal to fight with was dynamite. As far as war strategy is concerned, the revolutionaries had overestimated the importance of Oviedo, neglecting the other major city in the province, Gijón, with its large and combative working class composed of metal workers, fishermen, and dockers.[35] Oviedo was politically symbolic but Gijón and its port were strategically more significant. Finally, the revolutionary leadership was not absolutely united and differences had begun to emerge between the different ideological groupings. In his extensive study Taibo argues against the extended view that the leaders were unconditionally united in the fight and suggests instead that when the revolutionary forces did effectively fight together it was due to the initiative of the men, who felt they were fighting alongside their brothers for a common cause.

Despite its outcome, many of the revolutionaries did not consider themselves to have been defeated. One of the most important facets of the Revolution had been the new social and economic organization which various towns had managed to put in force, essentially imitating that of the Russian soviets. Each town was controlled by a local Revolutionary Committee, made up of representatives from the working-class organizations influential in that locality, which was responsible to the larger provincial Revolutionary Committee. Thus, the ideological composition of the local Committees differed from town to town. For example, the Sama Committee included the PSOE, CNT, and the communists while in Turón there were only socialists and communists represented. In Mieres, Manuel Grossi appointed the local Committee composed of two socialists, two anarchists, two communists, and himself as representative of the Alianza Obrera and the Bloque Obrero y Campesino. In La Felguera the anarchists of the FAI (Federación Anarquista Ibérica) governed alone. As indicated by Shubert, these local Committees took control of many aspects of social organization. As well as military affairs they were active in food supply and rationing, health, labour, communications, and propaganda, public order and justice. Money was abolished and replaced by vouchers issued to each family and valid for an amount of food determined after a detailed census. Radcliff writes that fifty-six bakers from the Sindicato de Alimentación rotated to keep a steady production of bread to dispense free to the citizens (p. 298). In Sama the supply committee dealt with local farmers to secure quantities of milk, eggs, and meat. According to Taibo: 'El abastecimiento de leche se realizó de una manera perfecta. Primero se atendían las necesidades de los enfermos, de los niños y de los ancianos. Después, las del resto del vecindario.'[36] In Oviedo, Sama and Mieres hospitals were organized where the wounded of both sides were treated. Nuns and doctors staffed these hospitals although the latter often had to be forcibly recruited. Collective kitchens were set up on the fronts. Works committees coordinated the conservation of mines and the operation of essential public services such as water and electricity. Explosives were produced in Mieres and armoured vehicles in Turón. In La Felguera the FAI kept the Duro-Felguera foundry going, turning out armoured cars in three eight-hour shifts per day. Trains were used to move troops and supplies. Telephone connections were extended to allow more effective communications and there was even a radio transmitter in Turón which broadcast to France and Belgium although most of the transmissions were blocked. Public order was maintained by the 'Guardia Roja', armed police forces composed of workers not involved in the fighting. In the capital, where the workers controlled the bourgeois residential and business districts, special efforts were made to prevent looting. Jails were improvised where necessary and the prisoners were generally treated well.[37] According to Maurín, even drinking alcohol was prohibited — 'la Revolución es sobria, espartana'[38] — and Jackson claims that 'for the best of the militant elements, the revolutionary regime was to be a demonstration of proletarian morality'.[39]

There were heavy casualties: around three thousand dead and seven thousand injured, most of them workers. A substantial number of Civil Guards were killed at the start of the action whilst defending their posts.[40] In Oviedo the city centre had been completely destroyed by the heavy artillery of the army and the dynamite of the miners: the University and its precious library had been razed to the ground and the cathedral tower had been damaged. In addition the Cámara Santa of the cathedral, along with the priceless treasures from the tenth and eleventh centuries which it harboured, were blown up.

Due to the extent of the destruction, both in terms of buildings and lives, the insurrection had a deep impact on the rest of Spain. The right-wing newspapers immediately started a campaign against the revolutionaries, whereby they blamed them for all the destruction and accused them of committing all sorts of barbarities. These stories included that of the nuns of the convent of the Colegio de las Adoratrices who were supposedly raped; the children of the Civil Guard from Trubia who had had their eyes gouged out; the burning alive of children, priests, and monks; and the killing of the priest of Sama whose body was later hung on a butcher's shop window with a placard advertising pig meat for sale. Although very detailed investigations were carried out by parliamentary members no indications were found that any of these claims were true.[41] This is not to say, however, that the revolutionaries were free from committing unjustified and irrational acts of violence. According to Jackson, in the two weeks following 5 October a total of around forty people were murdered by the revolutionaries. Personal vengeance and class hatred motivated the murder of a small number of engineers and businessmen, including Rafael del Riego, the well-respected owner of the minefields in Turón. The principal victims, however, were the priests and other religious figures. Taibo admits that most of the thirty-three priests shot were unjustifiably killed. For example, several convents were searched for arms and any priests trying to escape were shot at. In Turón half a dozen monks were arrested on the morning of the fifth, and on the eighth a group of revolutionaries, excluding those guarding them, marched the prisoners off to the village cemetery where they were shot. Taibo also insists, however, that many more religious figures were prevented from being shot by the angry masses as a result of the action of the Revolutionary Committees. The right-wing press took full advantage of the negative episodes in order to present the revolutionaries as evil and mad. These newspaper reports had the desired effect and Spanish public opinion immediately after the insurrection was definitely against the miners, calling for revenge and severe reprisals.

Repression

It could be argued that many of the atrocities committed by the revolutionaries, which were few in comparison to those committed by the forces of order in the months following the revolutionary surrender, were the result of the desperation which they felt as they saw the Revolution slipping away from their hands. Much of the government fighting had been carried out by the Moors and the Foreign Legion, sent from Morocco by Franco,[42] and in the last days of the fighting the revolutionaries had witnessed the brutal actions of the Moorish troops against both revolutionaries and innocent people. The use of the Moorish soldiers in Asturias was considered by some as outrageous and, for historical reasons, ironic. Asturias had been the only place in Spain which, historically, the Moors had not managed to conquer. In addition they were known for their savagery, which they openly exercised in this region. While General López Ochoa did what he could to prevent murder and rape, Colonel Yagüe of the Foreign Legion did not inhibit his troops in any way and preferred to use terror as a weapon. With the Moors free to do as they wished the citizens of Asturias were subjected to ransack and murder as the soldiers entered the mining valleys and the outskirts of Oviedo. This was despite López Ochoa's assurances to Belarmino Tomás that the Moorish troops would not be in the vanguard of the military advance. The districts of La Tenderina, El Naranco, San Lázaro, Villafría, and Los Arenales, amongst others situated on the outskirts of Oviedo, witnessed major acts of violence where sixty-one individuals were proved to have been murdered.[43]

The violence was not limited to lay individuals, however. In Oviedo, on 27 October, the liberal journalist, Luis de Sirval, was shot by a member of the Legion, Dimitri Ivan Ivanov, shortly after he had been arrested. The legionnaire had felt threatened by the journalist's articles which accused him of numerous acts of violence against the inhabitants of Villafría and San Pedro de los Arcos. Sirval had been arrested by a group of soldiers who took him to the barracks of Santa Clara. The next day while he was in his cell Ivanov, along with another two legionnaires, entered the cell, dragged Sirval out to the courtyard, and shot him eight times. The murder of Sirval was no more brutal than any of the other murders committed by the forces of repression, but he was well-known and highly respected throughout Spain. His death is particularly significant as it was followed by an outcry on the part of intellectual circles in Spain, especially as the government and the military authorities showed signs of indifference towards it. Ivanov's trial was finally held from the fifth to the seventh of August 1935. He was subsequently sentenced to six months in prison. However, after spending a few months in a hospital in Oviedo he was set free and rejoined the Legion. Sirval's death became the subject of a number of reports and the events surrounding his death are related, more or less accurately, in many of the texts dealing with the Revolution.

The violence, as exercised by the Legion, became more acute after the surrender of the miners. López Ochoa, who had shown some humanitarian traits, was removed from his influential post. Order was now in the hands of the Civil Guard and the Foreign Legion, and with Parliament suspended the extent of the repressive measures could not be debated. The death penalty was once again instituted, and press censorship became the order of the day. Thousands of miners were taken prisoner,[44] as well as those revolutionary leaders who had not managed to escape abroad. In Oviedo, on 1 February 1935 two men were executed having been sentenced by a military court: Sergeant Vázquez, who had deserted to the revolutionary militia, and a miner, Argüelles, who had supposedly commanded the squad responsible for the death of eight Civil Guards. Many of the employers who had suffered strikes and demonstrations prior to the insurrection chose this critical moment in the workers' movement to purge their workforce of not only known troublemakers but also defenceless union members who had been involved in the insurrection to a greater or lesser degree. Many of these men were not employed again until 1936. The Civil Guards were interested in particular in finding the arms which had been supposedly hidden by the revolutionaries when defeat was looking increasingly likely, and they were urged on by a desire to take revenge on those who had been responsible for the death of their colleagues. Commandant Doval, who arrived in Asturias on 23 October, was put in charge of finding the revolutionary arms stored away in hide-outs. He used many means of torture to force the miners to give him the information which he desired, as demonstrated by the numerous reports written about the severe repression in Asturias, such as those by Fernando del los Ríos,[45] Álvarez del Vayo, Clara Campoamor, Marco Miranda, and Félix Gordón Ordás.[46] These investigators established that many of the claims propagated, in particular by the right-wing press, concerning the barbarities committed by the revolutionaries, were false. They also gave evidence of the widespread arrest and torture of many revolutionaries crammed into improvised prisons throughout Asturias. Nevertheless, these reports were not released to the public until January 1936 once the censorship had been lifted.

Initially the government refused to investigate the claims of mass imprisonment and torture. However, as public opinion slowly turned against those in power the Prime Minister, Lerroux, had to reconsider the extreme measures which were being taken in Asturias. Doval was made to resign and leave the country and further executions were halted. The trials of the socialist deputies, Ramón González Peña and Teodomiro Menéndez (who had not been involved in the Revolution), were held in mid-February. They, along with other revolutionary leaders, were sentenced to death. In the interval between the Menéndez and González Peña trials, the French Socialist Party collected thousands of signatures in support of amnesty petitions. In addition a group of Spanish intellectuals wrote to Alcalá Zamora, protesting about the tortures in the prison at Oviedo revealed in a document signed by some 564 prisoners in late January. Among those that signed the letter were Unamuno, Valle-Inclán, and

Bergamín. Although Gil Robles put pressure on the government to accept the death penalties, the latter decided to commute these. This caused a governmental crisis as the CEDA refused to collaborate any longer with the government which consequently resigned. With the CEDA-Radical Party coalition broken elections were called for 16 February 1936. The Popular Front, a left-wing coalition gradually forged during 1935, were the victors on this occasion, and a left-Republican government, led by Azaña, resumed office.[47]

1. 'The Republican "take-over": prelude to inevitable catastrophe?', in *Revolution and War in Spain 1931–1939*, ed. by Paul Preston (London: Methuen, 1984; repr. London: Routledge, 1993), pp. 14–34 (p. 16).
2. In the regional capitals 1037 councillors elected were republican, while 522 were monarchists, sixty-four were constitutionalists and seventy-seven were unidentified. Ben-Ami, p. 32, footnote 61.
3. The right-wing anti-republican parties captured sixty seats, and the Socialist Party 116 seats. The rest of the seats were divided as follows: Radical Socialists, sixty; Azaña's republican Action Party, thirty; Lerroux's Radicals, ninety; Catalán Esquerra, forty-three; Alcalá Zamora's Progressive Party, twenty-two; Casares Quiroga's Galician Nationalists, sixteen.
4. Martin Blinkhorn, 'Introduction: Problems of Spanish Democracy, 1931–9', in *Spain in Conflict 1931–1939: Democracy and Its Enemies* (London: Sage, 1986), pp. 1–13 (p. 2).
5. *From Mobilization to Civil War: The Politics of Polarization in the Spanish City of Gijón, 1900–1937* (Cambridge: Cambridge University Press, 1996).
6. 'The Epic Failure: The Asturian Revolution of October 1934', in *Revolution and War in Spain 1931–1939*, pp. 113–36 (p. 124).
7. Paco Ignacio Taibo, *Asturias 1934*, 2 vols (Gijón: Jucar, 1984), I, 10. The Socialist Party dropped from 116 seats to 58, while the openly right-wing parties captured 207 seats, and Alejandro Lerroux's party 104 seats.
8. Ibid. In a speech given just before the 1933 elections Gil Robles declares: 'Debemos marchar hacia un nuevo Estado. Qué importa si ello significa derramamiento de sangre? Necesitamos una solución integral, que es lo que estamos buscando. Si queremos realizar este ideal, no debemos detenernos ni estancarnos en formas arcaicas. La democracia es para nosotros no un fin, sino un medio para llegar a la conquista de este nuevo Estado. Cuando llegue el momento las Cortes se someterán o las haremos desaparecer.' Quoted by Gerald Brenan, *El laberinto español: antecedentes sociales y políticos de la guerra civil* (Barcelona: Plaza y Janes, 1996), pp. 333–34, footnote 1.
9. Frances Lannon, 'The Church's Crusade against the Republic', in *Revolution and War in Spain 1931–1939*, pp. 35–58 (p. 38).
10. Taibo, *Asturias 1934*, I, 5.
11. The campaign in favour of abstentionism culminated in a massive meeting held in Barcelona's bull ring at which CNT speakers emphasized that if defeat for the left brought with it victory for the right, they would unleash the social revolution. According to José Peirats, this pledge prompted the revolutionary uprising of 1933 which was most severe in Navarre, Aragon, and La Rioja. José Peirats, *The CNT in the Spanish Revolution*, trans. by Paul Sharkey (Hastings: The Meltzer Press, 1996).
12. Paul Preston, 'Spain's October Revolution and the Rightist Grasp for Power', *Journal of Contemporary History*, 10 (1975), 555–78 (p. 557).
13. J.M., 'Hablando con Largo Caballero', *Adelante*, 28 February 1934, quoted in Marta Bizcarrondo, *Octubre del 34: reflexiones sobre una revolución* (Madrid: Ayuso, 1977), p. 27.
14. According to Taibo, who dedicates the whole of Chapter 3 of the first volume of *Asturias 1934* to the newspaper: '*Avance* fue creado por iniciativa del Sindicato Obrero Minero Asturiano. Llaneza impulsó la idea y Amador Fernández había sido su más enérgico promotor' (p. 34). The first issue came out on 15 November 1931 and originally 'era

concebido como un periódico republicano bajo control socialista, que influyera en un amplio núcleo de lectores de clase media y llegara hasta la clase obrera socialista' (p. 34). In the first two years of its existence the directorship of the newspaper changed hands three times, and by 1933, with Javier Bueno as director, *Avance* held an openly militant socialist stance and had become the most widely read newspaper by the working class in Asturias. More information about Javier Bueno's role in the preparations for the October Revolution can be found in Mirta Nuñez Díaz-Balart, 'Javier Bueno, un periodista comprometido con la revolución', in *Periodismo y periodistas en la Guerra Civil*, ed. by Jesús Manuel Martínez (Madrid: Fundación Banco Exterior, 1987), pp. 69–89.

15. Paco Ignacio Taibo, 'Las diferencias asturianas', in Gabriel Jackson, et al., *Octubre 1934* (Madrid: Siglo XXI, 1985), pp. 231–41 (p. 239).
16. Taibo, *Asturias 1934*, I, 97.
17. 'Algunas reflexiones sobre Octubre 1934', in Gabriel Jackson, et al., *Octubre 1934*, pp. 41–46 (p. 43).
18. A meeting was held in El Escorial on 21 April 1933 and at the same time a strike was called in protest at the right-wing gathering. Similarly, a strike was held on 8 and 9 September against the CEDA rally to be held in Covadonga on 9 September 1934. Taibo transcribes some of Gil Robles's hostile speech: 'Nosotros levantaremos la bandera de España: que salgan a nuestro encuentro. Para ensayos, ya basta. La experiencia está íntegramente hecha. Ya hemos concluido nuestra difícil tarea. No hemos puesto obstáculos: los hemos removido. No hemos derribado Gobiernos: los hemos salvado en circunstancias difíciles. No hemos sido elemento de perturbación, sino un elemento constructivo de la política española. Cuando ni aún con esa ayuda y con esa buena voluntad ha sido posible que las cosas marchen por el camino que debían, nuestro camino está despejado. Ni un momento más. Personalmente no queremos nada; pero si no se encuentran con fuerzas para hacerlo, que se aparten, porque los arrollaremos. No consentiremos ni un momento más que continúe este estado de cosas.' Taibo, I, 112.
19. The government was in power due to the support it had from the 115 CEDA deputies, seventy-nine Radical deputies, thirty-six *agrarios*, nine Liberal Democrats from Melquiadez Álvarez's party, eight Independent deputies, and the tacit support of twenty-four deputies belonging to the Catalan Lliga.
20. *Revolución y contrarrevolución en España* (Paris: Ruedo Ibérico, 1966), p. 148.
21. Out of the seventy-five thousand trade union members in Asturias, fifty-eight per cent belonged to the UGT, thirty-five per cent to the CNT, five per cent to the CGTU (Confederación General del Trabajo Unitaria — founded by the PC), and two per cent to the Catholic trade union. Figures taken from Taibo, *Asturias 1934*, I, 60.
22. Manuel Grossi Mier, *La insurrección de Asturias* (Gijón: Jucar, 1978), pp. 12–13.
23. Vicente Arroyo, 'Hacia la unidad de acción revolucionaria del proletariado: Importantísima decisión del C.C. del Partido Comunista de España', *La Correspondencia Internacional*, 49 (1934), 938, quoted in Marta Bizcarrondo, p. 43.
24. Dolores Ibárruri, *El único camino* (Mexico: Ediciones Era, 1963), p. 177.
25. Taibo refers to first hand accounts and interviews held with those who were involved. In Taibo, *Asturias 1934*, I, 52–53.
26. Taibo clears up much of this mystery in Chapter 6 of the first volume of *Asturias 1934* which he devotes entirely to the *Turquesa* and the arms it delivered.
27. 'Las diferencias asturianas', p. 237.
28. Taibo, *Asturias 1934*, I, 109.
29. Taibo, 'Las diferencias asturianas', p. 238.
30. Unfortunately most of the ammunition which had been produced in the factory was taken to the army barracks (the Cuartel de Pelayo) as a precautionary measure before the revolutionary movement broke out. For this reason the revolutionaries remained in desperate need of ammunition throughout the Revolution. They tried to overcome this problem by manufacturing bullets manually, but they were unable to keep up with the demand, and the shortage of ammunition became increasingly acute as the fighting dragged on.
31. Taibo refers to the whereabouts of the members of the first Committee: 'Martínez Dutor se queda allí [en Grullos] para no obstaculizar la fuga de sus compañeros. Ibáñez y Coca marchan juntos por los montes para recorrer un largo camino que los llevará a Rusia. Llaneza, Belarmino García y Arturo Vázquez se echan al monte. Simón Díaz Sarro

emprende una ruta que lo llevará tras mil penurias a la frontera con Portugal. González Peña y Cornelio Fernández buscan refugio en Las Regueras. Graciano Antuña se ha quedado en Oviedo.' In *Asturias 1934*, II, 44. Few of these leaders expected the fighting to continue for another seven days.

32. According to Taibo: 'Durante 1935 y en 1936 después de que se levantó la censura, abundaron explicaciones sobre el fracaso de la revolución de Octubre en otros puntos de España. Explicaciones relativas: insuficiencia en el armamento, debilidad de los dirigentes regionales, inhibición del anarcosindicalismo en algunas zonas, ausencia de organización paramilitar, derrota previa del movimiento a causa de la huelga campesina de junio-julio, etc.' In 'Las diferencias asturianas', p. 232.
33. Gabriel Jackson, *The Spanish Republic and the Civil War 1931–1939* (New Jersey: Princeton University Press, 1965), p. 148.
34. According to Taibo: 'Así, la revolución asturiana fabricó un fantasma a escala nacional, que innecesariamente engañaba a los combatientes distorsionando su perspectiva de la situación general en la que se encontraban.' Taibo, *Asturias 1934*, II, 84.
35. In her book, Radcliff examines the revolutionary situation in Gijón, and affirms that 'the rebellion in Gijón was a sideshow [. . .]. And yet, on another level, Gijón's rebellion disclosed more about the complex forces of polarization that were pulling the country apart than did the dramatic pitched battles in the rest of the province. Thus, while the latter revealed how well the labor movement could mount a militia force, the revolution in Gijón bared the reality of a mobilized and divided population.' In Radcliff, p. 295. The Revolution in Gijón ended on the tenth, although the strike carried on until the sixteenth.
36. Taibo, *Asturias 1934*, II, 24.
37. Most of the details of the role of the Revolutionary Committees have been taken from Shubert, pp. 130–31.
38. Maurín, p. 157.
39. Jackson, p. 155.
40. On their appointment the Civil Guard had to take an oath whereby they promised to stand by their mother country until death. For this reason, although in the revolutionary assault on government posts the Civil Guard were urged to surrender with the promise that no reprisals would be taken, they refused and perished. According to Taibo, seventy-three Civil Guards were killed and sixty-five were injured. In *Asturias 1934*, II, 243.
41. Even contemporary right-wing chronicles, such as Rafael Salazar Alonso, *Bajo el signo de la revolución* (Madrid: Imp. Sáez Hermanos, 1935), criticize these exaggerated claims under the pretext that any other true assertion would lose credibility in the eyes of the readers.
42. The idea to use Moorish troops had been General F. Franco's. Franco, who had been up to this point Commander of the military forces in the Balearics, was appointed by the Minister for War, Diego Hidalgo, as his personal advisor. Many of the other generals were considered by the Minister as too liberal, including López Ochoa who was an enlightened officer and a Freemason. Ochoa was nevertheless Lerroux's favourite to take charge of the military procedures in Asturias. As a result Franco was rejected and prevented from taking a more active part in the events. He nevertheless remained Diego Hidalgo's assessor, warning him that there was a strong possibility that the Spanish conscripts which made up much of the regular army would refuse to fire on the revolutionaries. The use of the Foreign Legion and the Moorish troops was regarded as an effective way to solve this problem.
43. Taibo affirms that there were more reports of murders which could not be proven 'por el miedo de los parientes a denunciar los hechos, o el traslado de las familias'. Taibo, *Asturias 1934*, II, 64.
44. The exact number of prisoners was never clear, since the authorities did not want to publicize the extent of their repression. Nevertheless, Taibo estimates that between fifteen and eighteen thousand people were processed throughout the whole province of Asturias, most of them beaten and tortured. Between three and four thousand were sentenced to one year or more in prison. Ibid., II, 159.
45. De Los Ríos 'lost' his copy of the report which subsequently reached the hands of French journalists who published it. However the Spanish government ignored this as well as all the other reports.

46. After discovering the extent of Doval's activities, Gordón Ordás, a deputy of the Radical Party, wrote a denunciatory letter in December 1935 to the Prime Minister Lerroux.
47. As 1935 progressed the republican and socialist left gradually re-emerged from near-clandestinity to form, along with the increasingly important Communist Party and other elements on the left, the Popular Front. According to Garnier: 'Es fácil constatar que, a diferencia de la Alianza Obrera, el Frente Popular es un frente "multiclasista". En cuanto al programa, no contiene estrictamente ninguna de las reivindicaciones obreras revolucionarias: nada de nacionalización de la tierra y de los bancos, nada de control obrero . . . Un solo punto es importante y bastará para la movilización popular: la amnistía de los encarcelados, la supresión de las medidas tomadas contra los trabajadores por motivos políticos.' Georges Garnier, foreword to Manuel Grossi Mier, *La insurrección de Asturias*, p. xiv. The results of the elections were: 263 deputies from the leftist block, 129 deputies from the right, and 52 deputies from the centre.

CHAPTER 2

LITERARY DEVELOPMENT: FROM AVANT-GARDE PROSE NARRATIVE TO THE SOCIO-POLITICALLY COMMITTED NOVEL OF THE 1930S

In this chapter I will discuss why the literary responses to the Asturian uprising influenced literature (more specifically, prose narrative) during the Second Republic.

Literature in Spain is marked during the period 1925 to 1936 by the transition from a relatively new type of playful, refined, elitist, and lyrical literature to a literature which gave priority to wider communication and engagement with social and political realities. Although the avant-garde movement was influential in all artistic and literary fields, here I am concentrating solely on its repercussions on prose narrative, especially the novel, a genre in which 'el vanguardismo adquiere unas dimensiones muy particulares'.[1] The date for this transition in prose writing is difficult to determine, but Fulgencio Castañar, in his study on the novel of the pre-war period, argues that its development between 1925 and 1936 can be divided into two stages. The first stage, from 1925 to 1931, is characterized by the convergence of two literary approaches, avant-garde literature and 'literatura de avanzada', a style of literature which José Díaz Fernández advocated in *El nuevo romanticismo* and in the prologue to the second edition of his novel, *El blocao* (1928). The second stage spans the years 1931 to 1936 and is marked by the further development of socially and politically committed literature as the sense of fatigue at the irresponsibility and self-satisfied elitism of the avant-garde, and a general reaction to events at home and abroad led to more intellectual involvement in social and political issues. The reaction to the repression of the Asturian Revolution of 1934 incited many intellectuals who had not already done so, to express their view on the recent events. Thus, the move towards a more decisive socio-politically committed literature took a definitive turn. The year 1936, with the outbreak of the Civil War, marks another clear juncture in the evolution of literature, but I will not deal with this stage as it extends beyond the period under review.

THE AVANT-GARDE

New literary and artistic ideas were imported into Spain shortly after the First World War. In addition, young Spanish writers who travelled abroad and came into contact with other European writers were exposed to diverse literary styles, all of which have since been encompassed under the term avant-garde literature.[2] The main driving force behind this new literary tendency was a desire to break with tradition and create an artistic style which had not been seen until then and would reflect more accurately the changes in society. It has been argued that compared to the critical attention which the poets of the avant-garde have received, the prose writers have been unfairly neglected. In an article on avant-garde prose literature, Buckley points to this paradox:

> La generación 1927 no se compone solamente de una serie de poetas superdotados (los Lorca, Guillén, Alberti, Salinas). Estas figuras fueron las más brillantes, pero, a mi juicio, no las más significativas. Para comprender el momento estético e ideológico 1927, es imprescindible leer a los prosistas (o mejor, cuentistas) de aquella generación: Benjamín Jarnés, Antonio Espina, el mejicano Torres Bodet, César Arconada, Francisco Ayala y el que fue precursor de todos ellos, Ramón Gómez de la Serna.[3]

Similarly, Francisco Blasco affirms that there was a 'nutrido grupo' of prose writers who reacted to the same 'estímulos estéticos' in a similar way as the poets.[4] According to him: 'La prosa de estos años se nos ofrece como un rico y diversificado conjunto [. . .] que va de la novela al poema en prosa; del aforismo al ensayo; del rigor crítico al experimentalismo vanguardista' (p. 528). Amongst the avant-garde prose writers which Blasco names are Benjamín Jarnés, Antonio Espina, Fernando Vela, Pedro Salinas, José M. de Cossío, and José Bergamín. He also indicates that some of the poets, such as Jorge Guillén, Luis Cernuda, Gerardo Diego, and Dámaso Alonso actually started off writing both prose and verse.

Prose writing, initially in the form of short stories or 'prosas', only really began to be affected by the avant-garde after 'ultraísmo', a major poetic literary movement from 1918 to 1923 which placed Spain in the European literary scene, permeated through into narrative writing. According to Ramón Buckley and John Crispin 'ultraísmo' was a combination of 'dadaísmo, futurismo y cubismo literario o creacionismo' and it was 'el punto de partida para la generación vanguardista del período 1925–1935'.[5] The first manifesto promulgating 'ultraísmo' and insisting on the need for a magazine devoted to this literary trend had been drawn up in 1918 by a group of writers led by Rafael Cansinos-Assens. Three years later, on 27 January 1921, the first issue of the magazine *Ultra* came out; the last issue, number 24, was published on 15 March 1922. Benjamín Jarnés, Mauricio Bacarisse and Valentín Andrés Álvarez published their first pieces of prose fiction in *Plural* (1925), another important and short-lived magazine considered by Guillermo de Torre, one of its contributors, as the last bastion of 'ultraísmo'.[6] Prose writers contributed to many of the same magazines as their counterparts engaged in verse, for example *Alfar* (1920–30), *Indice* (1921–22), *Verso y Prosa* (1927–28), *Mediodía* (1926–29), *Residencia* (1926–34), *Revista de Occidente* (1923–36), directed by Ortega y Gasset, and *La Gaceta Literaria* (1927–32), founded by Ernesto Giménez Caballero.

According to Fuentes, the development and diffusion of the new novel must be seen in the context of the growth of capitalism in the 1920s as the favorable economic conditions led to the foundation of new publishing houses and collections devoted to the promotion of avant-garde literature.[7] La Revista de Occidente, Cuadernos Literarios, La Gaceta Literaria, and la Compañía Ibérico-Americana de Publicaciones (C.I.A.P.) were some of those which published avant-garde novels. In his critical study of avant-garde fiction, Pérez Firmat summarizes the integral history of the avant-garde novel in the following way: 'The lifespan of vanguard fiction is [. . .] bracketed by the two editions of Jarnés' novel [*El profesor inútil*]: 1926 and 1934. Before 1926 there was no general awareness of the genre, nor was there a corpus of works that could have engendered it; by 1934 — after the publication of perhaps three dozen works — the interest in this sort of fiction has all but dissipated.'[8] Although Pérez Firmat surprisingly excludes Gómez de la Serna's works from his analysis, he accurately calculates when the bulk of avant-garde fiction was written. According to him this period began in the summer of 1926 with the publication of *Víspera del gozo* by Pedro Salinas, the inaugural work of the series 'Nova Novorum' (belonging to the *Revista de Occidente*), which was for the most part favourably received by many of the important critics of the day, including Eugenio d'Ors, Azorín and Fernando Vela. Blasco stresses the importance of this collection: 'Allí se fraguó un tipo de novela alegórica o simbólica, que ensaya la incorporación a la narración del estilo metafórico [. . .] propio de la poesía, del fragmentarismo en boga en las artes plásticas y de la dinámica visión aprendida en el cine [. . .]; una novela que rompe con la disposición lineal del tiempo, encaminando el relato hacia la ucronía o la retrospección' (p. 529). A few months after the publication of *Víspera del gozo*, *El profesor inútil*, by Benjamín Jarnés, appeared. Like *Víspera del gozo* it was a brief volume containing several distinct narrative texts. The third book to be published by 'Nova Novorum' was *Pájaro pinto* (1927), by Antonio Espina, also a collection of prose pieces of varying lengths. This third novel was thought to be more successful than the other two as it dealt to a greater extent with human issues. Thus, the series 'Nova Novorum' provided the initial stimulus of the new fictional form, later joined by 'Colección Valores Actuales' of Ediciones Ulises which published between 1930 and 1931 such important works as *Cazador del alba*, by Francisco Ayala, *Estación, ida y vuelta*, by Rosa Chacel, and *Tres mujeres más Equis*, by Ximénez de Sandoval.

Many new Spanish novelists had by now discarded the nineteenth-century realist novel, opting instead for a new type of fiction labelled by Ramón Feria as the 'poematic novel' or 'essayistic novel': novels with insignificant themes, brief plots and sketchy characterization, written in complicated and intricate language, aimed at a reduced cultured readership.[9] Novels which Max Aub, with hindsight, would describe as 'cagarrita literaria':

> Una obra cortísima parida con dificultad, exquisita en el escoger de sus adornos, difícil de comprender a primera vista, disfraz de ideas ingeniosas y sin trascendencia y considerada como meta última de los esfuerzos de su joven autor. [10]

Blasco, who takes a more positive attitude towards the avant-garde novel points out that there were two types of novel: the 'novela lírico-intelectual', and the 'novela humorística': 'En ambas direcciones, preside una actitud ambivalente, que acepta esperanzada todo lo que de novedad técnica, cosmopolitismo y deportismo, traen consigo los tiempos modernos; y, a la vez, ironiza desconfiada sobre los peligros de la deshumanización y frivolidad que acompaña a las novedades incorporadas' (p. 529).[11] Fuentes, who also refers to the objectives of the new authors, writes: 'Rechazan las formas novelescas tradicionales y aspiran a crear una nueva novela, basada en los descubrimientos científicos, tecnológicos y artísticos de la nueva época'; 'Descartan los módulos novelescos y el lenguaje realista-naturalista, que identifican con la represiva sociedad burguesa'; 'En sus relatos, continuamente zahieren y ridiculizan, por contrarias a la vida, las virtudes sobre las que se asienta la sociedad burguesa'.[12] Finally, according to Buckley and Crispin, with their 'arte de creación' the writers 'quieren desprenderse del falso sentimentalismo patético (tan evidente en las novelas "eróticas" y "rosas" en boga), librarse de las exigencias de la anécdota y apartarse de un realismo demasiado prosaico' (p. 12).

Carlos Blanco Aguinaga agrees that the most influential figure in the avant-garde movement was Ramón Gómez de la Serna: 'Padre y mentor en gran medida de las diversas corrientes vanguardistas.'[13] For his part Hoyle stresses Gómez de la Serna's literary importance: 'No es que Ramón alcanzara un gran éxito de ventas, pero sí un éxito de crítica y un renombre de personalidad literaria, lo suficiente para demostrar que había logrado el propósito vanguardista de llevar el arte a la vida y transformar la vida con el arte.'[14] As far back as 1909 Gómez de la Serna published in his magazine *Prometeo* (1908–12) Filippo Tommaso Marinetti's first Futurist manifesto.[15] A year later the same magazine published 'Proclama futurista a los españoles', signed by Tristán (Gómez de la Serna's pseudonym) with a new Futurist manifesto by Marinetti. He also held 'tertulias' in the café *Pombo* in Madrid where ideas on the various avant-garde styles were exchanged and their merits debated by the many famous intellectuals who attended. However, it was his prose fiction which exerted the strongest influence on the new and aspiring young novelists. Gómez de la Serna's 'greguerías', which according to Hoyle 'throw a new and unexpected light on usually quite mundane or trivial things',[16] and are described by Ricardo Senabre as 'un tipo de construcción que traduce una específica actitud del autor ante el lenguaje',[17] were essential in the development of avant-garde prose writing. Some critics, such as Mainer, go as far as to suggest that Gómez de la Serná's novels — such as *El Gran Hotel* (1922), *El Incongruente* (1922), *El novelista* (1923), *La quinta de Palmyra* (1923), and *Cinelandia* (1924) — were just as important as José Ortega y Gasset's observations on art and literature expounded in *Ideas sobre la novela* (1925) and *La deshumanización del arte* (1925), examined below.[18] Gómez de la Serna's influence is important if we agree with Hoyle's assertion that far from meaningless, the author understood his writing to be '[una] lucha contra la hostilidad de lo establecido', and 'su evasión, mediante el humor representaba [. . .] un fuerte compromiso, militante a su manera, con las realidades de su tiempo'.[19] He also affirms that 'Ramón se proponía fusionar un arte hermético de minoría con el arte popular de masas'.[20] These two assertions would contradict the wide-spread belief that the avant-garde was meaningless, 'intranscendente', and aimed only at a minority readership.

While the practical principles for many of these authors were provided by Gómez de la Serna's work, the theoretical guidelines were laid down by José Ortega y Gasset in the two essays *Ideas sobre la novela* and *La deshumanización del arte*, composed of a series of articles previously written for *El Sol* (1922–23). Both of these essays were composed by the author as a response to the increasing popularity of avant-garde art and literature. Ortega was acting as an observer of this trend and in his essays he indicates what he believed the characteristics manifest in the Spanish novel at the time were. By examining these two essays a general idea of the nature of avant-garde writing will emerge. In *La deshumanización*, Ortega endorsed the idea that art appeared to be an expression of pure and above all metaphoric language aimed at an elite erudite readership:

Aunque sea imposible un arte puro, no hay duda alguna de que cabe una tendencia a la purificación del arte. Esta tendencia llevará a una eliminación progresiva de los elementos humanos, demasiado humanos, que dominaban en la producción romántica y naturalista. Y en este proceso se llegará a un punto en que el contenido humano de la obra sea tan escaso que casi no se le vea. Entonces tendremos un objeto que sólo puede ser percibido por quien posea ese don peculiar de la sensibilidad artística. Sería un arte para artistas, y no para la masa de los hombres; será un arte de casta, y no demótico.[21]

Ortega, whose commentaries on avant-garde literature had a decisive influence on writers at the time, lists seven characteristics of the 'nuevo arte' as he sees them:

Tiende: 1.°, a la deshumanización del arte; 2.°, a evitar las formas vivas; 3.°, a hacer que la obra de arte no sea, sino obra de arte; 4.°, a considerar el arte como juego, y nada más; 5.°, a una esencial ironía; 6.°, a eludir toda falsedad, y, por tanto, a una escrupulosa realización. En fin, 7.°, el arte, según los artistas jóvenes, es una cosa sin transcendencia alguna. (pp. 20–21)

He concludes that the reality of lived experience and aesthetic expression are incompatible in art. He demonstrates this with an anecdote of a deathbed scene witnessed by the wife of the dying man, a doctor, a journalist, and a painter. According to Ortega only the latter of the witnesses can produce a work of art from the experience as only he is detached.

In *Ideas*, perhaps the more relevant of the two essays for this study, Ortega suggests that 'el género novela, si no está irremediablemente agotado, se halla, de cierto, en su período último y padece una tal penuria de temas posibles, que el escritor necesita compensarla con la exquisita calidad de los demás ingredientes necesarios para integrar un cuerpo de novela'.[22] Ortega criticizes Balzac and praises Stendhal for his art of narration. The former describes his characters while the latter presents them as they are: 'Si en una novela leo: "Pedro era atrabiliario", es como si el autor me invitase a que yo realice en mi fantasía la atrabilis de Pedro, partiendo de su definición. Es decir, que me obliga a ser yo el novelista. Pienso que lo eficaz es, precisamente, lo contrario: que él me dé los hechos visibles para que yo me esfuerce, complacido, en descubrir y definir a Pedro como ser atrabiliario' (p. 22). Ortega does not believe that the most important aspect of the novel is the plot ('un arte de aventuras') but rather the characters ('un arte de figuras'). According to him in the work of art the structure is more important than the contents: 'La obra de arte vive más de su forma que de su material y debe la gracia esencial que de ella emana a su estructura, a su organismo. Esto es lo propiamente artístico de la obra, y a ella debe atender la crítica artística y literaria' (p. 31). The primary objective of the avant-garde novelist is to transform reality, and this he realizes through the use of literary devices such as metaphors, comparisons, hyperbole, personification, mythical and biblical references, and cinematographic techniques.

Ortega points out that although the plot of the novel is not its most important aspect, it is an indispensable element. He describes the plot as the 'armazón' of the novel. The most important task of the novelist 'ha de consistir en aislar al lector de su horizonte real y aprisionarlo en un pequeño horizonte hermético e imaginario que es el ámbito interior de la novela' (p. 44). The author must be able to keep the reader in total isolation, removed from the real world and from the problems faced by that world, if the novel is to have its full effect. That is why, according to Ortega, any novel which has a meaningful theme, whether political, symbolic, satirical, or ideological, is from the start ineffective. The reader cannot leave the real world and enter the imaginary world if he is reading about the problems which may be affecting him and his society. Rather, 'El novelista ha de intentar [. . .] anestesiarnos para la realidad, dejando al lector recluso en la hipnosis de una existencia virtual' (p. 46). That is why, for Ortega, the historical novel is difficult to conceive: 'Como cada horizonte exige una acomodación distinta de nuestro aparato visual, tenemos que cambiar constantemente de actitud; no se deja al lector soñar tranquilo la novela, ni pensar rigurosamente la historia. [. . .] El intento de hacer compenetrarse ambos mundos produce sólo la mutua negación de uno y otro' (p. 47). As far as the contents are concerned Ortega argues that they are 'psicología imaginaria', and therefore the concept of 'realismo' is superfluous. Summing up, the novel should be insignificant. The novel must be a novel, and only a novel, not a sociological study or a political pamphlet.

Generally speaking, critical perspectives on the avant-garde affirm that this movement was crucial in Spain's artistic development. Derek Harris, for example, who searches for an all-embracing definition of the avant-garde not only in literature, but also in painting, music and other artistic fields, claims that the avant-garde in all of these areas has one thing in common: 'They deliberately rupture centuries of hallowed conventions so basic that most people had ceased to be aware of them as conventions.' According to him, the avant-garde signalled a fundamental change: 'It is a revolution in the relationship of art to the physical world and to human experience.' Art becomes 'autonomous, sufficient unto itself and essentially meaningless because it is no longer required to make a commentary on the world or on human behaviour'. Finally he adds: 'The avant-garde rejects transcendence and replaces serious, moral intent with play. Art becomes a game.'[23] Gareth Thomas stresses the meaninglessness of the themes: 'Art survives only in a climate in which it is not intended to mean anything, and the most radical instrument of dehumanisation is the metaphor',[24] and Castañar, referring more specifically to prose narrative, maintains that the writer's goal was 'hacer arte y sólo arte para aquellas minorías egregias que son capaces de captar y emocionarse con la belleza desnuda creada, a ritmo lento, por el narrador'.[25] Because of this lack of 'transcendencia' critics have associated this literary movement with a conservative and reactionary political attitude. On the other hand, Buckley and Crispin, taking a similar stance to that of Hoyle indicated above, do not accept that avant-garde writing was 'aséptica' or 'consciente o inconscientemente reaccionaria' (p. 13). They maintain that although in general avant-garde writers resisted taking up a politically committed posture, they did have a social objective in the sense of wanting to change man and see him 'transformado por la revolución tecnológica y liberado [. . .] de los viejos esquemas morales, económicos y sociales' (p. 14).

'Literatura de Avanzada'

In the second half of the 1920s, while avant-garde prose writing was going through its most productive period, a small group of writers realized that although they had been part of the avant-garde art, the relationship between society and literature had to be reconsidered. For some the avant-garde had meant an exciting new approach, but others saw it merely as a way of evading the problems of the present and accused it of 'elitismo, separación entre arte y vida, aislamiento del artista, belleza inútil, juegos intranscendentes, cobardía ante los problemas de la época'.[26] Between the advocates of the avant-garde and those staunchly opposed to it there was a group that, while adopting a more socially committed stance, did not entirely abandon the aesthetic principles of the avant-garde: 'En vez de oponerse a la literatura deshumanizada a favor de una literatura social de compromiso, buscan más bien reconciliar las dos tendencias al incorporar rasgos de la nueva estética a una temática actual que responda más adecuadamente a las preocupaciones de la juventud en un momento de crisis.'[27] Laurent Boetsch provides a further definition of 'literatura de avanzada': 'Aquella que ocupa un momento breve de transición entre una literatura de vanguardia "deshumanizada", característica de los años 20, y otra social de claro punto de vista partidista que predomina durante los años 30.'[28] The pressures which arose between different sectors in society due to the diverse ideological stands and, more importantly, to the impact of the economic situation, compelled the writers to take part in the socio-political struggle, for which avant-garde writing hardly seemed appropriate. Therefore, the years 1927 to 1930 were a transitional stage, both in poetry and prose writing, where writing increasingly removed itself from the avant-garde line.

Influenced by pacifist literature from Europe and the revolutionary novel from the Soviet Union, many new publishing houses and magazines appeared, showing a new political awareness, although not necessarily at the service of a particular ideological stance. According to Castañar one of the most influential factors in the defence and promotion of this 'literatura de avanzada' were the literary initiatives taken by the magazine *Post-Guerra* (1927–28). As increasing numbers of writers joined in the criticism of the avant-garde so the magazines began to change: 'Ya no serán portavoces de malabarismos mentales ejercitados por grupos pequeños para otros grupos pequeños, o refugios de intercambio para un estrecho círculo, sino vehículos de enfoque social y transformación política.'[29] The magazine *Post-Guerra*, which adopted a revolutionary leftist stance and was founded and directed by J. A. Balbontín and R. Giménez Siles 'representó un ensayo, único en las letras españolas de su época, por superar el divorcio entre vanguardia artística y política, tan acusado en los años de la dictadura de Primo de Rivera'.[30] The objectives set out in the first number clearly demonstrate this emphasis on the proposed fusion of art and politics:

> 1.°) Aproximar a los trabajadores manuales y a los intelectuales; 2.°) luchar contra la propaganda reaccionaria y arcaica de la ideología y de la cultura burguesa; 3.°) abrir paso y ayudar a la eclosión de un arte colectivo. [31]

In its articles the contributors proposed how literature should develop. These proposals 'fueron el soporte en el que algunos novelistas se apoyaron para presentar las imágenes de una nueva sociedad con el lenguaje que se consideraba más nuevo'.[32] In 1928 *Post-Guerra* became further involved in the progress of 'literatura de avanzada' when its publishing house, Historia Nueva, launched the collection 'La novela social', directed by César Falcón. The directors of *Post-Guerra* had decided to suspend the magazine and instead concentrate on book publishing with a view to avoiding Primo de Rivera's censorship which was nonetheless tolerant with books exceeding two hundred pages, in other words, books which he believed would be too expensive to be accessible to the working class. Only six titles were published in this collection — *El pueblo sin Dios* (1928) and *Plantel de inválidos* (2nd edn) (1928) by César Falcón, *El blocao* (1928) by José Díaz Fernández, *El suicidio del príncipe Ariel* (1929) by J. A. Balbontín, *El botín* (1929) by J. Zugazagoitia, and *Justo el «Evangelio»* (1929) by J. Arderíus — and although they varied greatly in quality they were an attempt to 'enfrentarse a la concepción de la literatura como juego'.[33] Santonja goes as far as to affirm that the collection as a whole 'fue la avanzadilla de la todavía incipiente promoción de la novela social-realista española'.[34]

With the fall of Primo de Rivera in January 1930 and the subsequent increase in political agitation, the publishers of 'La novela social' once again decided to pursue a different course of action and launched the weekly magazine *Nosotros* (May 1930–August 1931), directed by César Falcón. This magazine joined *Nueva España*, whose editorial board included such prominent literary figures as Antonio Espina, José Díaz Fernández and Joaquín Arderíus and which was launched a few months earlier in January, in criticising the political situation. The difference between these and *Post-Guerra* was significant, as Santonja points out:

> Media un abismo desde el reducido puñado de ejemplares de la animosa revista *Post-Guerra*, de periodicidad mensual y casi simbólica incidencia, hasta semanarios tan relativamente estables y bien asentados como *Nueva España* y *Nosotros* o diarios de la asombrosa capacidad de resistencia que acreditaría *La Tierra*. (p. 61)

Towards the end of 1930 Berenguer's censorship toughened, particularly after Fermín Galán and García Hernández's revolt in the name of republicanism which took place on 12 December 1930. Many magazines and newspapers faced financial ruin as steep fines were imposed, whole issues were withdrawn from circulation and prevented from being sold, and journalists were imprisoned and bail had to be paid.

Around the time the collection 'La novela social' was launched (1928–29) other young intellectuals were creating and, in many cases, personally financing further publishing houses with the same consideration in mind — to avoid Primo de Rivera's censorship. The most important of these include Ediciones Oriente (1928–32), Editorial Cenit (1928–36), Editorial Jasón (1929–31), Editorial Ulises (1929–31), and Editorial Zeus (1930–33). One enterprise of the new publishing houses was the translation of European socio-political works, primarily from Germany, France, and Russia, as well as some from the United States. Although the First World War had been influential in the development of the avant-garde novel, for one group of European youngsters the disastrous effects prompted the feeling that far from adopting a playful and insignificant theme the novel should deal with the horrors of the war. The harrowing experiences of the French and German soldiers were the subject of many pacifist novels, such as *Los que teníamos doce años* (1929) and *Paz* (1930) by Ernst Glaeser, *El sargento Grischa* (1929) by Arnold Zweig, *Guerra* (1929) by Ludwig Renn, and *Cuatro de infantería* (1929) by Ernst Johannsen. The most popular translated novel was *Sin novedad en el frente* by Erich Remarque, translated by Benjamín Jarnés and Eduardo Faertsch and published in Spain in 1929 by Editorial España.[35] After having been involved in the war this German writer found it inconceivable to view literature merely as a search for pure art and ideal beauty. He, as well as other European novelists, felt that literature should have a social function; they hoped to demonstrate the errors which had provoked such a war, avoiding in this way another similar war.

The Russian works translated dealt for the most part with a different subject — the Russian Revolution and the class struggle. According to Gil Casado up to 222 translated Russian works appeared in Spain between the years 1920 and 1936, featuring authors such as Fyodor Gladkov, Ilya Ehrenburg, Leon Trotsky, Maxim Gorky, Boris Pilnyak, and Konstantin Fedin.[36] In addition, reviews and information about these works could be found in literary magazines such as *Post-Guerra*, *La Pluma*, and *Revista de Occidente*. In the later years of *La Gaceta Literaria* there was a regular section entitled 'Postales rusas' by Tatiana Enco de Valero and, alongside, reviews by important writers such as Francisco Ayala, Ramón Gómez de la Serna, Benjamín Jarnés, and Giménez Caballero. Excerpts of some of the translated works were also published in literary magazines making this kind of literature accessible to a wider readership. The influx of whole translated novels provided them with plenty of examples to emulate. The following are the traits which, according to Castañar, Spanish literature adopted from literature from abroad:

> El predominio del contenido sobre la forma, el interés por acercarse a unos asuntos candentes interpretando la realidad desde una perspectiva pro proletaria, la inserción del intelectual en los movimientos obreros y su planteamiento sobre el papel de intelectual en la sociedad; además puede anotarse también un entusiasmo ferviente por la moderna epopeya — la marcha del pueblo hacia una nueva sociedad — , la admiración por los nuevos mitos — el interés por las máquinas ya impulsado por el futurismo — y una expresión con fuerte apoyatura lírica con el fin de mover al lector a cambiar la sociedad. (p. 39)

This alternative approach to literary creation is evidently directly opposed to the principles behind 'deshumanización' and the avant-garde.

Although Spain had not taken part in the First World War, the country had been involved in a series of intermittent wars in North Africa from 1904 to 1927. The opposition to the wars in Morocco was a source of pacifist literature as Spanish writers, returning from the battlefield, denounced the impact which such a conflict was having on society and in particular on the working class. Except for the books published by Giménez Caballero, *Notas marruecas de un soldado* (1923),[37] and Víctor Ruíz Albéniz, *¡Kelb Rumi!* (1922), the North African issue was not taken up until the end of the twenties and early thirties. *El blocao* (1928) by José Díaz Fernández, *Imán* (1930) by Ramón J. Sender, and *La barbarie organizada* (1931) by Fermín Galán tell of the frustration felt by the soldiers sent to desolate areas to fight a cruel and horrific war which they personally do not agree with.[38] *El blocao*, a brief novel made up of seven separate stories, similar in its composition to the avant-garde 'relatos' published around the same time by authors such as Salinas and Espina,[39] relates the isolation felt by the soldiers in Morocco who are there simply to satisfy the colonial whims of the government and the generals. Both the physical and the psychological strains of the fighting are made visible in the progressive dehumanization of the characters. In the case of *Imán*, the main character, Viance, represents the majority of the soldiers in Morocco. By the time the protagonist is able to return to normal civilian life, his personality has been utterly destroyed by the experiences suffered; the only thing he feels is hatred. In *La barbarie organizada* Fermín Galán takes a similar approach to Sender. The protagonist here has also been deeply affected by the military discipline and the terrifying experiences of the war. If we look briefly at the other end of the political spectrum, one right-wing novelist, Manuel Perera, also wrote a novel which dealt with the war in Morocco, *Tragedia proletaria* (1930). Unlike the others, this work is not critical in any way of Spanish presence in Morocco and, on the contrary, spreads the Christian notion that man must accept the destiny which God has chosen for him.

As far as the structure of these novels is concerned, Ignacio Soldevila Durante explains that the later novels dealing with Morocco were symptomatic of a period in which 'reportaje' and fiction were combined. Their similarity to the traditional novel 'hizo evolucionar a ésta hacia una temática de inmediateces, frente a la tradición de evocaciones y hacia una presentación "amontonada" sin estructura aparente, sin ordenación cronológica, sin eje de concatenaciones, en una palabra, muy de entonces: de instantáneas'.[40] As I will later show in Chapter 8 of this thesis, this technique was partially employed by Díaz Fernández in *Octubre rojo en Asturias* (1935). Leaving to one side the contents and the structure of these novels, the style of *El blocao* and *Imán* is clearly influenced by the avant-garde. Both Díaz Fernández and Sender produced creative, imaginative and artistic works. In the introduction to the 1997 edition of *Imán*, Marcelino Peñuelas writes about the novel:

> Se trata de notas y observaciones ordenadas en una estructura firme y cuidada [the author appears to be at variance with Soldevila's generalised assertion], escritas en terso y viguroso estilo que implica un dominio consumado de procedimientos y técnicas narrativas, con una mezcla equilibrada de fidelidad a los hechos y de creación imaginativa. Y en el fondo de todo ello se pueden vislumbrar definidas intenciones estéticas. . . (p. 10)

Víctor Fuentes describes Díaz Fernández's novels in general as 'novelas-puente entre la novela vanguardista, poemática y subjetivista y la social, objetiva y colectivista'.[41]

As a response to Ortega y Gasset's *La deshumanización del arte*, José Díaz Fernández wrote *El nuevo romanticismo*, a collection of essays which provided the theoretical foundations for the 'novelistas sociales', and called for the rehumanization of art: 'Esta vuelta a lo humano es la distinción fundamental de la literatura de avanzada.'[42] The most important essay of the volume for our purposes, which gives its title to the whole collection, is 'El nuevo romanticismo', according to López de Abiada, 'una llamada explícita a la politización del escritor español, frecuentemente refugiado en el estetismo estéril y alejado de los problemas de la vida real'.[43] According to Boetsch, this work is 'consciente de las aportaciones del vanguardismo pero insistente en la idea de su inadecuación, dadas las nuevas realidades sociales del país'.[44] Although José Díaz Fernández praises the achievements of the avant-garde, he criticizes the limits it imposes thematically. He believes the creativity and originality of the avant-garde should be applied to themes anchored in reality, dealing with contemporary social problems: 'La auténtica vanguardia será aquella que dé una obra construida con todos los elementos modernos — síntesis, metáfora, antirretoricismo — y organice en producción artística el drama contemporáneo de la conciencia universal' (p. 80). He maintains that literature should be about human feelings and thoughts. Díaz Fernández's 'arte de avanzada' is one in which

> Las conquistas del lenguaje artístico del arte nuevo se funden con la sensibilidad y el espíritu de la nueva democracia, la de la masa proletaria. Su ideal es la creación que, además de obra de arte, belleza, sea elemento de una nueva cultura, de un nuevo humanismo de aliento proletario.[45]

For Díaz Fernández art provided a fundamental means of spreading valuable social and political messages to the masses. For this reason he criticizes those who refuse to join a movement which he believes positively influenced civilization: 'No saben hacer un alto en las tareas del arte para acudir solícitos a la conciencia nacional y cuidar que la vida pública sea la vida civilizada y fecunda que deben tratar de construir todos los hombres inteligentes' (p. 64). Buckley and Crispin comment on the importance of Díaz Fernández's essay:

> El ensayo de Díaz Fernández constituye un hito importante en nuestra historia estética, ya que señala el momento en que los vanguardistas abandonan sus posiciones teóricas y entran en el terreno del compromiso político, bien por medio del ensayo, bien por medio de la novela social. (p. 20)

Díaz Fernández had already indicated his views on 'literatura de avanzada'. As early as 1927, in an article for *Post-Guerra*, he had proposed an 'arte novísimo con intención social'.[46] A year later in the prologue to the second edition of his novel *El blocao* Díaz Fernández continued to affirm his stance:

Trato de sorprender el variado movimiento del alma humana, trazar su escenario actual con el expresivo rigor de la metáfora; pero sin hacer a ésta aspiración total del arte de escribir, como sucede en algunas tendencias literarias modernas. Ciertos escritores jóvenes, en su afán de cultivar la imagen por la imagen, han creado una retórica peor mil veces que la académica, porque ésta tuvo eficacia alguna vez y aquélla no la ha tenido nunca. Cultiven ellos sus pulidos jardines metafóricos, que yo me lanzo al intrincado bosque humano, donde acechan las más dramáticas peripecias.[47]

He adds,

Mi libro llega a las letras castellanas cuando la juventud que escribe no siente otra preocupación fundamental que la de la forma. *El blocao* tiene que parecer un libro huraño, anarquizante y rebelde, porque bordea un tema político y afirma una preocupación humana. Me siento tan unido a los destinos de mi país, me afectan de tal modo los conflictos de mi tiempo, que será difícil que en mi labor literaria pueda dejar de oírse nunca su latido. (p. 32)

Sender (with *Imán* and *Siete domingos rojos*), Arderíus (with *El comedor de la Pensión Venecia* and *Campesinos*), Arconada (with *La turbina*), as well as Díaz Fernández (with *El blocao* and *La Venus mecánica*), are the most important examples of the first authors who adapted the style of the avant-garde to the issues which the 'novela comprometida' would deal with.

Thus 1930, the year in which *El nuevo romanticismo* is published, marks an important turning point for the avant-garde. The best indicator of what this moment meant for prose writers is demonstrated in a survey carried out for *La Gaceta Literaria*, from 1 June 1930 to 15 November 1930, in which a number of prominent literary and intellectual figures provide written responses to a questionnaire drawn up by Miguel Pérez Ferrero about their view on the avant-garde and its impact.[48] Ernestina de Champourcin believes that the avant-garde continues to exist and will continue to exist. Ramón Gómez de la Serna also firmly supports the avant-garde movement and criticizes all those who do not any longer suggesting that this is simply because it has gone out of fashion. On the other hand, Ramiro Ledesma Ramos and Mauricio Bacarisse criticize it, the first because he believes that literature should be linked to politics, and the second for its restrictive nature. Ernesto Giménez Caballero, Esteban Salazar y Chapela, and Guillermo de Torre believe that the avant-garde did once exist but that it does not any more. César Arconada also takes this position and asserts that 'el vanguardismo literario existió en un tiempo en que era preciso imponer una nueva sensibilidad de acuerdo con las exigencias de una época nueva'.[49] He goes on to list the results which the avant-garde movement has had on art:

> La quiebra de lo exquisito. Es decir, las últimas delincuencias del impresionismo: la pintura quebrada de reflejos de sol. La música acuática y vaporosa. La poesía simbolista. La arquitectura barroca de confituras de yeso. Todo esto murió bajo la acometida poco piadosa de la vanguardia. Tal vez no hizo más. Pero ya era bastante. Ensanchó los caminos, abrió los campos, limpió las ruinas. En resumen: preparó la construcción de lo que ha venido después.[50]

This response succinctly shows what the avant-garde meant for many. It was merely a step along a long road from the realist literature of the end of the previous century to the socially committed literature which would emerge in the 1930s. However, while nineteenth-century realism merely demonstrated the existence of social problems, the 'new realism' of the 1930s examined and debated the causes of social problems with a view to proposing radical reforms to solve them. For the novelist Ramón Sender 'new realism' was not about capturing individual drama or about lingering on social relations, but about the relationship between man and society. More generally for the left-wing writers 'new realism' implied concentrating on the future, and not on the past. When writing his 'Autobiografía' in the magazine *Nueva Cultura*, in 1936, Arconada states: 'Llegó un momento en nuestro país en que el proceso revolucionario rompió el idilio de los poetas con las musarañas. Fui uno de los primeros que se angustiaron ante el dilema, ante el destino de nuestro tiempo y de nosotros mismos.'[51] In his defence of 'literatura de avanzada' Díaz Fernández highlights the difference between those who have chosen to make progress and those who still favour the dehumanized approach:

> La literatura de vanguardia, el culto de la forma, la deshumanización del arte, ha sido cultivada aquí por el señoritismo más infecundo. Contra esos escritores está la generación de 1930, partidaria de una literatura combativa, de acento social, que Espina, Arderíus y yo hemos defendido en *Nueva España*.[52]

For Díaz Fernández the break with the avant-garde is decisive enough to warrant the designation of a new literary grouping: 'La generación de 1930'. Present-day critics have referred to this group in various other ways: 'La otra generación del 27' by Fuentes and Boetsch, 'Los novelistas de la pre-guerra' by Eugenio García de Nora, 'Los novelistas del nuevo romanticismo' by Pablo Gil Casado, and 'La generación de la segunda república' by Esteban.[53]

On the right of the political spectrum J. M. Carretero ('El Caballero Audaz') and Ernesto Giménez Caballero were the main figures who defended the politicization of literature from a different ideological standpoint, as the latter pointed out in 1934:

Ya no se busca la 'pureza', tal como predicaba *Revista de Occidente*, y en su lugar se persigue lo 'humano'. Nuestra literatura se empieza a interesar por la política y por realidades acuciantes. Un nuevo impulso creador ha nacido; pero es un período aún virgen, sin nombres ni obras, ni siquiera manifiestos. Pero lo cierto es que la sensibilidad de nuestros jóvenes está cambiando de rumbo.[54]

For those on the right, taking up a more committed stance was to serve to warn the readers of the dangers of a possible Marxist Revolution, and to spread the fascist patriotic and expansionist doctrines. As early as 1929 Giménez Caballero wrote his 'Carta a un compañero de la joven España' (*La Gaceta Literaria*, 52 [February 1929]) considered to be the first Spanish fascist manifesto.[55] In an interview held for the magazine *Hoja Literaria* on June–July 1933, in which prominent literary figures were asked about their literary generation, the response of this same author is indicative of the thoughts and worries of the literary youth in general, from both the left and the right, when he predicts that certain issues will stand out in the literature of the thirties, namely social and religious matters, and that politics will also play a key role in literature.

'La República de los Intelectuales'

The increasing social commitment of the writers coincided with the growing role of the intellectuals[56] in politics which came about with the establishment of the Republic in 1931, a Republic referred to by some, such as Bécarud and López Campillo, as 'la República de los intelectuales':

De una posición de vanguardia en la coyuntura del año 1930, los intelectuales han pasado a ser gente que sigue, acompaña y orquesta en el momento de iniciarse la guerra civil. En los años 1930–1931 eran líderes, iniciadores entusiastas que daban el tono [. . .]. La España de 1931 presenta el caso relativamente excepcional de un régimen anunciado, preparado, elaborado por los intelectuales. (p. 135)

The fall of the dictatorial regime of Primo de Rivera, which had ruled Spain from 1923 to 1930, had been to a certain extent the result of the efforts of the intellectuals. In 1925 a letter signed by 175 intellectuals including writers, professors, lawyers, journalists, doctors, and engineers was sent to Primo de Rivera rejecting his dictatorship. Intellectuals had begun to form political groupings, most of them of republican tendency. The most important of these was 'Acción Republicana', a group which in 1925 tried to form an anti-monarchical coalition (with the 'Partido Federal', the 'Partido Republicano Catalán', and the 'Partido Radical'), led by the University professors José Giral and Enrique Martí Java. This coalition called 'Alianza Republicana' was finally formed in 1926 and its manifesto was signed by such significant figures as Azaña, Luis Bello, Vicente Blasco Ibáñez, Marañón, Juan Negrín, Antonio Machado,

Eduardo Ortega y Gasset, Pérez de Ayala, and Unamuno. Bécarud and López Campillo explain why the intellectuals became so politically influential:

Las ansias de cambio social del proletariado del campo y de la ciudad llegan a ser tan fuertes, el malestar de las clases medias tan evidente, que, dado la ausencia de otras soluciones (fascismo o comunismo), este grupo de intelectuales ideológicamente heterogéneo resultará ser, por su *disconformidad*, el núcleo en el que cristalizarán las esperanzas revolucionarias de buena parte de los estamentos españoles. (p. 8, author's emphasis)

One institution which exerted great influence in the establishment of the Republic was the Ateneo in Madrid, which, due to its criticism of government policy, was continually closed and reopened, depending on the Minister of the Interior in office.

In April 1929 a number of leaflets circulated around Madrid in which José Ortega y Gasset, favouring a more politically committed stance, wrote:

Creemos que se impone con urgencia la necesidad de que los intelectuales españoles, muy particularmente los jóvenes, definan sus diferentes actitudes políticas y salgan de ese apoliticismo — no pocas veces reprobable — que les ha llevado a desentenderse de los más hondos problemas de la vida española.[57]

This declaration was signed by a number of prominent intellectuals including Antonio Espina, Benjamín Jarnés, Francisco Ayala, Federico García Lorca, and José Díaz Fernández. On 10 February 1931 a manifesto was launched in *El Sol* by the recently formed 'Agrupación al Servicio de la República', presided by Antonio Machado, and signed by Ortega, Gregorio Marañón and Ramón Pérez de Ayala. From February to April the 'Agrupación' addressed mass meetings and wrote stirring articles. When the Republic was proclaimed many of those in the 'Agrupación' were elected to the Spanish Cortes and although they were not registered as a political party they acted as a minority group under the leadership of Ortega. The political situation was changing, however, and public opinion seemed to be satisfied only by extreme political positions. As a result, once the statute of Catalan autonomy and the agrarian reform had been approved by the Republican government the 'Agrupación', on 29 October 1932, dissolved itself.

Once in government some of the intellectuals were satisfied with having established the longed-for Republic; both Primo de Rivera and King Alfonso XIII had left Spain. Nevertheless, for other more politically-minded intellectuals this was just the first step to a more egalitarian Spain — a socialist, communist, or anarchist Spain — and for others the chance to impose a fascist dictatorship similar to that of Italy. The development of Spanish literature cannot be fully explained without taking into account the wider European political context. The 1930s were crucial years in the consolidation of German and Italian fascism. On the one hand, liberal and left-wing intellectuals, alarmed by the rapid spread of fascism, denounced this movement in their written work. On the other hand, those right-wing intellectuals who supported Hitler and Mussolini saw it as a perfect opportunity to present the option to the Spanish people. Thus, in the fascist writings of the 1930s there was an attempt to attract eminent literary figures to their ranks, with a view to legitimize right-wing ideology and give it greater respectability. Bécarud and López Campillo stress that Spanish fascism did not emerge as a conscious political movement against the Republic. From 1928 to 1930 fascism was already a concept talked about. Unlike Hitler and Mussolini, the two Spanish figures who contributed most to the emergence of the fascist movement in Spain were intellectuals — Ernesto Giménez Caballero and Ramiro Ledesma Ramos:

> En todo momento las revistas culturales y los literatos han tenido mucho que ver con la difusión del fascismo en España pues han sido los literatos quienes han creado una mitología fascista para que las ideas pudiesen llegar al gran público.[58]

It was in *La Gaceta Literaria*, founded by Giménez Caballero, the author of the most coherent Spanish fascist theory of art and literature, *Arte y Estado* (1935), that the first fascist ideas were expressed. In an interview with Ramiro de Maeztu entitled 'Conversación con una camisa negra', which was published on 15 February 1927, the readers were urged to take sides, to either wear the 'camisa negra' or the 'camisa roja'.[59]

The Republic met increasing difficulties, including an economic recession which was affecting the whole of Europe, unemployment, a fall in wages, and strikes, as well as opposition from the land-owning and business sectors.[60] The bourgeois capitalist system had been put in doubt and the intellectuals offered the public other alternatives. On the one hand, the Revolution in Russia was admired and hopes were placed on its communist principles. On the other, Italy and Germany offered another approach to combat the European economic crisis, based on an authoritarian system, in other words fascism. A glance at the political situation in Spain during the early and the mid 1930s reveals that, generally speaking, Spanish public opinion was divided into two diametrically opposed positions. As a result art could no longer take a neutral stand and the artist had to side either with the left or the right. This stance was reflected in the literature of the time, which became increasingly politicized, right up to 1936 and the outbreak of the Civil War. Castañar observes that whether writing from the left or from the right: 'En todos está muy presente el valor que como arma de combate confieren a la novela' (p. 106).

Up to 1931 the intellectuals, united, had criticized the government from the outside. Once they were part of the government they diversified into parties with more defined ideological viewpoints. As the political commitment of the intellectuals increased divisions began to emerge between those who considered that political affairs lay out of their domain and those who felt that they had an important part to play in the social and political development of the country, as Bécarud and López Campillo indicate:

> Los 'puros', los que quisieran permanecer con la función crítica y creativa exclusivamente, lamentan esta evolución, considerándola como una traición a la cultura y una concesión a la facilidad y al arribismo político. Los militantes y organizativos expresan una hiperagresividad contra los 'puros', echándoles la culpa de la lentitud de los progresos de la organización o de sus fracasos coyunturales. (p. 137)

By 1933, after two years of Republican government, the intellectuals faced another crisis as the disillusion with the failure of the republican-socialist coalition set in.

Socially and Politically Committed Literature

As already indicated, literary developments were influenced greatly by social and political events at a national as well as a European level. As political attitudes became more extreme, so the novel, and literature in general, became more politicized. The Republic brought about a series of valuable reforms as demonstrated in Chapter 1. Nevertheless, for many the reforms, especially those regarding the Church, did not go far enough, and for others they were too radical. Even the Ateneo in Madrid (of which Manuel Azaña continued to be president despite also heading the government), having fully supported the Republican government on its formation, now criticized it and its president for being guided by bourgeois values. The criticisms directed at the Republic increased as the peasant revolts of Castilblanco (December 1931), Arnedo (January 1932) and Casas Viejas (January 1933) were ruthlessly suppressed.

One area in which the Republic was considered by the public to have been successful was in the reform of education. The reorganization of public education was one of the first steps taken by the Azaña government — the opening of more schools, the end of compulsory religious education, greater investment in libraries,[61] and an increase in the number of teachers. Amongst the reforms was the creation in May 1931, under the directorship of Manuel Cossío, of the 'Misiones Pedagógicas', groups of students who visited rural areas, gave talks, handed out medicines, set up small libraries, exhibited a small museum with copies of some of the pictures to be found in the Museo del Prado and, from 1933 onwards, performed theatrical works organized and directed by Alejandro Casona.[62] The 'Misiones' went to villages, many of them poverty-stricken, where the peasants had never come into contact with cultural activities.[63] According to Bécarud and López Campillo this organization was 'el símbolo del nuevo giro de la política educativa' (p. 39). Another similar initiative was taken by Federico García Lorca when, with the help of Eduardo Ugarte, he set up La Barraca in December of that same year. A mobile theatre company, whose members were also mainly students, and which was subsidized by the government, La Barraca began to tour round the country in July 1932 and performed until 1937 (in Valencia). García Lorca and La Barraca concentrated on putting on plays, mostly by classical playwrights such as Lope de Vega, Cervantes, and Calderón de la Barca. These two cultural projects clearly demonstrate that the socio-political commitment of the novelists, poets, and dramatists was not limited to their written work, but that they also physically reached out to the masses and undertook the mission of spreading examples of Spanish cultural heritage to all strata of society, even to the most disadvantaged. There were other cultural initiatives, the majority of which were of left-wing tendency. These included the foundation of cinema clubs, exhibitions, and theatre groups, of which the Teatro Experimental del Español (1933) and the Teatro Escuela de Arte (1933) are two examples.[64]

The electoral victory of the right in 1933 signalled an important change in the Republic's direction. The right-wing coalition government in power, led by Alejandro Lerroux, set about undoing the developments which Azaña's government had set in motion. The crisis of confidence of the left-wing and liberal intellectuals which greeted Lerroux's victory was considerable. The Radical-Socialist government was considered by both left and right to have been a failure. While many young intellectuals severely criticized the first two years of the Republican government for betraying the socialist values which had been conferred on it, the upper echelons of society were attracted by Italy and Germany's authoritative form of government, and were delighted by the right's electoral victory. In addition, both sides looked to define further their ideological stand. While the left seemed to be splitting up into splinter groups — socialists, anarchists, and communists — the extreme right was also having its internal ideological battle between Giménez Caballero and Ledesma Ramos, who disagreed on the value of intellectual participation in the fascist movement. Those who opted for neither of the extreme ends of the political spectrum found themselves astray in the midst of indecisiveness, uncertain about where their political sympathies should lie:

Entre los intelectuales que no se declaran partidarios ni del comunismo, ni del socialismo, ni del movimiento libertario reina una gran confusión. Los 'prefascistas' o 'parafascistas' siguen manifestando cierta nostalgia liberal y algunos católicos de izquierdas demuestran veleidades autoritarias; unos y otros sienten una gran desconfianza por un capitalismo en crisis y por una democracia parlamentaria que, a todas luces y por todas partes, revela su importancia y su caducidad.[65]

It was this political uncertainty which accounts for the existence of numerous magazines to which contributors with different, sometimes opposing, points of view supplied articles and other written works. The most significant of these publications was *Cruz y Raya*, founded in 1933 by José Bergamín. As founder and director, Bergamín had meant his magazine to be a view on society from the stance of progressive Catholicism, expressed in the opening editorial of the first issue:

Esta revista de colaboración abierta, libre, independiente, se propone actuar todos los valores del espíritu sin mediatización que los desvirtúe. Precisamente la razón más pura de ser de esta revista, la que la inspira y nos impulsa, quizá consista en esto: en nuestra viva voluntad de católicos para esclarecer bien las cosas; para darles a cada una el lugar que le corresponda en la vida como en el pensamiento.[66]

According to Rafael Osuna, *Cruz y Raya* reflects better than any other magazine the internal conflict which afflicted the intellectuals during these years. For example, in October 1933 Alfredo Mendizábal condemned 'nacionalismo estrecho y agresivo', and yet an article written by Rafael Sánchez Mazas, in August of that same year, praised exactly these same values.[67] Nevertheless, in October 1934, following the Asturian Revolution, *Cruz y Raya* was to undergo a critical ideological change, which I will examine further on in the last section of this chapter. Those on the right who condemned the revolutionary action in Asturias slowly abandoned the magazine; for them Bergamín's critical stance towards the government and his sympathy for the miners proved to be unacceptable.

The political plurality demonstrated by *Cruz y Raya* was not the rule, however. Indeed, the radicalization of the political positions can best be seen in the publications of the time. The critical nature of the situation encouraged the intellectuals to concentrate their attention on defending and furthering their particular socio-political convictions.[68] The years 1933 and 1934 witnessed the publication of various worthy novels, such as *Los pobres contra los ricos* (1933) and *Reparto de tierras* (1934) by César M. Arconada, *Un hombre de treinta años* (1933) by Manuel Benavides, *Uno* (1934) by Andrés Carranque de Ríos, and *Viaje a la aldea del crimen* (1934) and *La noche de las cien cabezas* (1934) by Ramón J. Sender, and the foundation of a substantial number of magazines including *Azul*

(1934–35), *Ciudad* (1934–35), *El Gallo Crisis* (1934–35), *Horizontes* (1934–35), *La Lucha* (1934), *Leviatán* (1934–36), *Los Cuatro Vientos* (1933), and *Octubre* (1933–34). The year 1935 also saw the creation of new and important magazines, such as *Caballo Verde para la Poesía* (1935–36), *El Tiempo Presente* (1935), *Línea* (1935–36), *Nueva Cultura* (1935–37), *Pueblo* (1935–36), *Sur* (1935–36), and *Tensor* (1935), to which Spanish as well as international artists from all fields contributed. In this way, photographic montages, drawings, paintings, and sketches were found next to poems, short stories, extracts from novels, chronicles, and political essays. Other magazines served primarily as mouthpieces for the political parties, as is the case with *Octubre* and *Leviatán*. Before examining further these two important magazines I should point out that Esteban's statistical evidence indicates that the number of novels published during these years fell.[69] In the first place the bankruptcy of the C.I.A.P., set up in 1927 to secure the economic survival of writers by energetically promoting and marketing new books, meant that some of the publishing houses dependent on the larger benefactor, ceased publishing.[70] Secondly, the radicalization of politics drove many writers to contribute to magazines.

Many of the magazines were directed at specific political groups. Socialist magazines included *Leviatán*, *Renovación, El Socialista* and *Claridad*; those supporting an anarchist point of view included *Tierra y Libertad*, *Tiempos Nuevos*, *Solidaridad Obrera*, and *Revista Blanca*; and *Octubre*, *Letra*, *Nuestro Cinema*, *Pueblo*, and *Mundo Obrero* advocated communism. Magazines championing the fascist cause were not as copious — *Acción Española*, which included contributors from all right-wing sectors, including monarchists, international fascists, religious figures, and even Sanjurjo, responsible for the attempted coup d'état in 1932, and *La Conquista de Estado*, Ramiro Ledesma Ramos' anti-intellectual, nationalist, anti-liberal magazine, were the main advocates of fascism. Other extreme right-wing magazines were *Azor*, *Jons*, *F.E.*, *Arriba*, and *Haz*. What stands out is that between 1933 and 1935 those publications dedicated solely to purely literary matters were few and far between, and by 1935 it is difficult to find any magazine which is not to some extent influenced by a particular political movement.

In the summer of 1933 the PSOE and UGT began a radicalization campaign which was to escalate following the socialist defeat in the elections of November of that same year. The more radical members of the Party endorsed a revolutionary socialist stance to which the working class could relate and which would once again encourage revolutionary action. *Leviatán* made the dissemination of political ideas a prime objective. From its pages, its director and one of the most important proponents of revolutionary socialism, Luis Araquistain, wrote against the moderation of Besteiro and Saborit. Schwartz claims that *Leviatán* 'deliberately eschewed literary matters to concentrate on politics, socialism, anarchism, labor unions, the economic situation of the world, life in Russia, the perils of European fascism, and agrarian reform'.[71] It nevertheless did not totally abandon literary issues and 'included matters of literary concern to reveal a continuing interrelationship of political commitment and literary endeavour in the twentieth century'.[72] Many of the contributors to *Leviatán* were young intellectuals. The valuable role of the youth of the day had already been predicted by José Díaz Fernández in *El nuevo romanticismo*:

> En el fondo de las provincias, perdida y anhelante en ciudades y pueblos oscuros, está una juventud que es espíritu vivo de la España que todos queremos. Juventud enemiga de la pobreza, ansiosa de cultura, adversaria de la injusticia, pero mal avenida también con los antiguos sistemas de educación o de política [. . .] A esa juventud no se le puede engañar.[73]

Society had changed and the younger generation wanted to participate in the socio-political development of Spain.

Octubre, founded in June 1933 by Rafael Alberti and María Teresa León, was also geared towards a younger age-group and was created as an alternative to the increasingly popular fascist movement and its Catholic and imperialist literature:

> La razón de su publicación estribaba según Alberti, en 'el peligro que ofrecía la reciente aparición de una literatura de exaltación histórica y social que está sobre todo en curso de ganar a la juventud universitaria. . .'.[74]

The magazine's main objective was to give a vision of the ideal society embodied in the Soviet Union and its social and political organisation. Thus, numbers four and five, whose publication coincided with the sixteenth anniversary of the Russian Revolution, were dedicated to the Soviet Union. Nevertheless, rather than follow the official line of the Communist Party, *Octubre's* independent and more radical position served as a forum for the expression of revolutionary ideals. Contributors to *Octubre* included renowned national and international figures, such as Antonio Machado, Emilio Prados, and Luis Cernuda, as well as André Gide, Louis Aragon, Henri Barbusse, Alejo Carpentier, Ilya Ehrenburg, and Máximo Gorki. *Octubre*, founded two months after the conservative *Cruz y Raya*, was among the first magazines to openly support revolutionary action. One reason for *Octubre*'s appeal was its aspiration to popularize culture by including pieces written by ordinary working people as well as by renowned figures. Thus Lechner writes:

Una de las facetas más importantes de la revista dentro del dominio de la poesía, nos parece el hecho de que colaboraran fraternalmente en las mismas páginas los poetas más importantes y ya consagrados, y hombres totalmente desconocidos y pertenecientes a capas que antes no solían asomarse ni se atrevían a enviar sus escritos a las revistas literarias.[75]

In this way, 'La revista se esforzó por desmitificar la figura del intelectual y trató de crear un clima de sincera comprensión entre éstos y los lectores'.[76] Both *Leviatán* and *Octubre* illustrate a growing tendency in the nature of the publications at this time: 'La transformación política y la cultural se veían como indisolubles, [. . .] política y literatura entrecruzaban sus confines: ésta, al usar la política como temario; aquélla, al usar la literatura como vehículo.'[77] While literary magazines commented on and debated current affairs, political magazines and newspapers drew in famous literary figures to their pages.

The socio-political engagement evident in the magazines also extends to the novel. Left-wing writers called for an end to bourgeois dominance and defended the revolutionary path and class struggle which would give power to the proletariat. The story-line of the novels, which encompassed these general ideals, assumed a distinctive nature as the novelist applied his particular point of view and his own personal style to the narrative. In this way, *Los pobres contra los ricos* and *Reparto de tierras* by Arconada take a communist line; *Un hombre de treinta años* by Benavides takes a socialist line; and *Uno* by Carranque de Ríos takes an anarchist line. The masses became the centre of these works — not only were they the subjects under study, but they were also, ideally at least, the recipients of the finished work. The themes of the fascist writers tended to revolve around the threat of an imminent proletarian revolution; they rejected egalitarian ideas arguing that they went against human nature; and they depicted the proletariat as greedy and avaricious, merely interested in improving their own personal situation. These writers suggest that the only way to progress and win back the glory which Spain had in the past is to trust Catholicism and the monarchy.

Each writer, whether left or right-wing, opted for a literary formula which would allow him to carry out his socio-political objectives in the most effective and compelling way. The majority of novelists used dialectical realism,[78] although allegory, satire, irony, and humour were also techniques used in committed prose writing. Castañar clearly explains what the most significant characteristic of these works is:

Es innegable que esta narrativa, al brotar de la vida de su tiempo, tiene el mérito de ser la exposición de una sociedad tremendamente conflictiva. Sus autores logran tender un puente que une la literatura y la vida del público y evitan así la disociación que existía entre el artista y sus contemporáneos. (p. 435)

This same virtue, however, meant that at times the creative piece bordered on the propagandistic, and on many occasions lessened the artistic value of the work. The novelists were too concerned with ethical and moral values to be worried about aesthetic considerations, and the urgency of the increasingly critical situation required rapid publication and distribution. Indeed many of the works have been regarded by today's critics of little literary value. For the novelists, such as Samblancat, Arderíus, Sender, Arconada, Carranque de Ríos, Mas, Ciges Aparicio, and Díaz Fernández, the pressures of the socio-political situation brought out certain qualities and a unique sensitivity in their work. As Castañar explains, their commitment did not necessarily hamper the value of their work: 'Su realismo dialéctico tiene la peculiaridad de estar impregnado de un subjetivismo lírico, con tintes neorrománticos, que sirve para embargar de emoción a quienes sintonicen con las ideas del escritor y también es una puerta abierta para engalanar las obras con abundantes recursos literarios' (p. 435).

European artists generally believed that in order to combat fascism more effectively and limit the cultural threat it posed they had to unite. This led to the creation of several intellectual movements which had in common 'un fuerte sentimiento antifascista, como elemento unitario esencial'.[79] One of the first international organizations to be set up, in April 1932, was the Unión de Escritores Soviéticos. In August 1934 they held an important conference in Moscow where socialist realism was promulgated. Rafael Alberti and María Teresa León were to take part in this conference, along with Arconada and Sender. In an interview held shortly after, Alberti comments on the participation of the Spanish delegation:

> Ante el Congreso dimos un informe sobre la situación de escritores españoles. Formamos parte de una brigada de choque de escritores, en la que los había de todas nacionalidades [. . .]. Y en el transcurso del viaje estalló la Revolución Española, la de Asturias. Las noticias las leímos en los periódicos rusos de provincia [. . .]. Había un gran entusiasmo por la Revolución Española.[80]

The Soviet Union was to provide much stimulus to the various artistic movements in Spain, as well as more generally in Europe. Apart from the already mentioned translations, Spanish artists increasingly took up Lenin's view that art should be 'un instrumento del Estado para realizar la dictadura obrera y la revolución mundial'.[81] From the moment that Fernando de los Ríos and Anguiana were despatched to Moscow in 1921 by the Spanish Socialist Party to investigate its affiliation to the Third International, there were many visits to Russia by Spanish politicians and intellectuals. Spanish communists like La Pasionaria were frequent visitors to Moscow, and Ramón Sender himself spent several months there in late

1933 and early 1934, an experience recounted in *Madrid-Moscú* (1934). Max Aub had also been a visitor in 1933. Amongst those who wrote books about their visits to Russia were politicians, syndicalists, liberals, such as Isidoro Acevedo, Álvarez del Vayo, Angel Pestaña, Diego Hidalgo, César Vallejo (who, although Peruvian, published his book in Spain), Zugazagoitia, and Rodolfo Llopis.[82]

One month prior to the creation of the Unión de Escritores Soviéticos, in March 1932, the Association des Ecrivains et Artistes Révolutionnaires (A.E.A.R.) was formed in Paris. Branches of this same organization, known in Spain as the Unión de Escritores y Artistas Revolucionarios, were set up in Madrid and Valencia. Members included Arderíus, Acevedo, Arconada, Alberti, Emilio Prados, and Rosario del Olmo. In June 1935 the A.E.A.R. held an important international conference in Paris at the Palais de la Mutualité: the I Congreso Internacional de Escritores para la Defensa de la Cultura. Gide, in one of the most important speeches of the Congress, clearly states what the role of literature was to be for the writers present:

> La literatura no es — o no es solamente, al menos — un espejo. Hasta ahora, la literatura actual de la URSS se ha contentado, poco más o menos, con desempeñar ese papel y nos ha dado así muchas obras notables. No debe reducirse a eso. Se trata también, o se trata quizás sobre todo, de ayudar a este hombre nuevo que amamos y que deseamos, a que se desprenda de las trabas, de las luchas, de las falsas apariencias; se trata de ayudarle a formarse y a perfilarse él mismo [. . .]. La literatura no se contenta con imitar: informa, propone, crea.[83]

He adds: 'El estado de la cultura depende íntimamente del estado de la sociedad, y es el amor a la cultura el que nos hace decir: mientras nuestra sociedad sea lo que es aún, nuestro primer afán estribará en modificarla' (p. 31). The issue of the role of the intellectual in society and the necessary search for unified artistic expression was highlighted by most of the speakers at the conference, as Aznar Soler points out in his detailed study of the Congress:

> La mayoría de discursos pronunciados en el I Congreso coinciden en un mínimo común denominador: denuncia de la crisis política, económica y cultural de la sociedad capitalista; condena inequívoca del fascismo que, ya en 1935, había demostrado su radical antihumanismo, su barbarie y su voluntad destructora de la cultura; defensa de una amplia unidad antifascista, que iría a concretarse en la formación de los Frentes Populares; defensa del compromiso del escritor y de una literatura revolucionaria vinculada al nuevo público de obreros y campesinos; defensa del humanismo socialista como talante intelectual de un hombre nuevo en una sociedad sin clases y de una nueva cultura jamás entendida de nuevo como monopolio de una clase social; respeto a las culturas y literaturas de las minorías nacionales, siguiendo el ejemplo de la Unión Soviética; esperanza en la victoria del socialismo y en que, con la derrota del fascismo, fuesen posibles la dignidad humana

y la libertad de los pueblos; defensa de los valores de la nueva cultura socialista, fundamentados en la fraternidad humana, el internacionalismo y la solidaridad.[84]

This first Congress has been considered to be very important as it was the first international manifestation against fascism in which intellectuals from all around the world took part. Spanish participation, however, was hardly noticeable: on the one hand many of those invited did not go, and on the other some were not invited who should have been. All in all, the Spanish delegation was composed of Julio Álvarez del Vayo (a politician and essayist belonging to the left wing of the PSOE), Andrés Carranque de Ríos (a young novelist), and Arturo Serrano Plaja (a young poet). Valle-Inclán would have gone had he not been ill, and so would have Alberti had he not been in the USSR attending the Congreso de Escritores Soviéticos. Nevertheless, a second conference was held by the A.E.A.R. in Spain in 1937, in Barcelona, Valencia, and Madrid, with the Civil War as a backdrop. Along with the first, these conferences were 'una muestra más [. . .] del predominante sentimiento de intervencionismo público, político-social, y de solidaridad entre intelectuales de distintas nacionalidades'.[85]

The Impact of the Asturian Revolution

For those who promulgated or warned of revolutionary action in their work, the attempted, and failed, Revolution in Asturias (and Cataluña) was to be a landmark in their ideological development and consequently in their literary socio-political commitment. Víctor Fuentes goes as far as to affirm categorically that 'octubre del 34 marca la fecha en que se efectúa el desplazamiento masivo de nuestros intelectuales hacia la causa popular'.[86] Most intellectuals, both from the left and the right, were deeply affected by the events. The most violent reaction came from the left as the extent of the disaster and the brutal repression exercised by the forces of order came to light. Both revolutionary supporters, such as Alberti, Arconada, and Sender, and sympathizers, such as Machado and Bergamín, took steps to denounce the government's reactionary and intransigent stance. On the other hand, the right wing, with the press on their side, wrote about the reported atrocities committed by the revolutionaries and highlighted the deaths of soldiers and policemen, religious figures, as well as innocent victims such as women and children, in order to reinforce the idea that the revolutionaries were beast-like.

According to Manuel Aznar Soler it was the death of Luis de Sirval which aroused most indignation amongst the intellectuals. They objected to the government's handling of the Revolution and the fact that a professional and serious journalist, whose only offence was to inform fully and impartially of the situation, had been a victim of a calculated killing.

In December 1934 the Radical-Socialist deputy Félix Gordón Ordás gave a speech in the Cortes about the Sirval case which was subsequently published in a pamphlet and which urged the intellectuals to pressurize the government into clearing up the allegations of violence made against the military acting on their behalf.[87] On 8 December 1934 the Madrid newspaper *El Liberal* published an article written by the board of directors of the Ateneo and directed at Alcalá Zamora, the President of the Republic, requesting that 'se depure lo que ha acontecido y está aconteciendo en España, en aldeas y ciudades, en cárceles y comisarías' for the sake of 'España, que jamás, para honor suyo, podrá avenirse a perder un patrimonio de libertades que, por significar respeto, son las bases morales esenciales de la moderna cultura civil'.[88] The long awaited trial of Sirval's killer, Dimitri Ivanov, took place in August 1935. The six months and one day sentence Ivanoff was given provoked outrage and that same month a letter signed by significant intellectuals including Unamuno, Azorín, Julián Besteiro, Juan Ramón Jiménez, and Bergamín demanding a retrial was published in *El Sol*.[89] Valle-Inclán also spoke against the repression in a banquet which he attended, as did Julio Álvarez del Vayo and Alberti who referred to the Asturian events in their speeches given at the I Congreso Internacional de Escritores and the I Congreso de Escritores Soviéticos respectively. When the death sentences of the leaders of the Revolution were passed intellectual reaction against the government increased. Aznar Soler indicates that eighty-six Professors from the University of Santiago de Compostela, and another forty Professors from the University of Zaragoza sent public letters to the President of the Republic demanding that the death sentences be overturned.[90] The excessive repression remained an issue right up to the elections of February 1936, and in the electoral proposals of the Frente Popular the left-wing coalition pressed for the release of all political prisoners and for a total amnesty. This determined largely the outcome of the elections.

Direct public criticism of the government after October 1934 was almost impossible, particularly in the press. Strict censorship had been imposed and was not totally lifted until after the elections which brought the Frente Popular to power in February 1936. Many left-wing intellectuals were thus forced into silence while government supporters were free to publish articles in right-wing newspapers and magazines, regardless of the accuracy of the information and so long as it did not jeopardize the government position. In addition, important and outspoken intellectuals such as Manuel Azaña, Javier Bueno (director of *Avance*), Zugazagoitia, and Manuel Benavides, had been imprisoned, and others had to live a clandestine existence. The criticism which was directed from abroad was for this reason all the more important. The French Socialist Party collected thousands of signatures in a petition calling for an amnesty, and the French Socialist deputy Vicent Auriol visited Lerroux on behalf of the League of the Rights of Man. Neither of these initiatives was covered in the Spanish press. Anti-governmental reports of the events, many of which were written while the authors served prison sentences, did not appear in Spain until late 1935, as the publication dates of the texts which I will examine in subsequent chapters indicate. Eventually, taking advantage of the crisis facing the right-wing government in January 1936, the working-class and liberal press was able to launch a fierce attack against the government's policy of repression in Asturias. This wave, started off by *El Socialista, La Libertad*, and *El Liberal* could not be impeded by the censors, and the entire left-wing press set out to inform about the events of October.

The revulsion with which the intellectuals regarded the governmental repression can be seen in the poetry written on the revolutionary events. These poems were in most cases included in collections dealing with a wide range of subjects. The introductory pages of some of these collections reveal how the intellectuals viewed the role of literature and the writer following October. Although poetry falls outside this study, the importance of these introductory comments makes them worth examining. *El poeta en la calle* (1931–35) by Rafael Alberti was published in 1935 and includes several poems dealing with aspects of the Asturian Revolution such as 'El alerta del minero', 'Libertaria Lafuente', and 'El Gil Gil'. In the prologue to the first edition Alberti, who had defended politically committed poetry as early as 1929, highlights the importance of writing for the masses. What he affirms is fundamental in understanding the change which took place in literature following the events of 1934:

> De mi contacto con las masas populares de España surgió en mí la necesidad de una poesía como la que se intenta — muy lejos aún de conseguirse — en este libro. Sin ignorar que todos aquellos poemas que lo integran no reúnen las condiciones necesarias para su repercusión y eficacia en la sala del mitin, en la calle de la ciudad, en el campo o en la plaza del pueblo, quiero dejarlos y justificar aquí su presencia por la sola razón de haber nacido siempre de una exigencia revolucionaria. ¡Cuántas veces a la salida del mitin, en el sindicato, en la humilde biblioteca de la barriada o en cualquier lugar de trabajo, después del recital o la conferencia, se me acercaron algunos camaradas para «encargarme» un poema que reflejara tal o cual situación política, este o aquel suceso! Y es que cuando el poeta, al fin, toma la decisión de bajar a la calle, contrae el compromiso, que ya solo podrá romper traicionando, de recoger y concretar todos los ecos, desde los más confusos a los más claros, para lanzarlos luego a voces allí donde se le reclame. De acuerdo o no de acuerdo con esta posición que es un camino, yo sé que esta salida al aire libre, este dejar de devorarnos oscuramente nuestras propias uñas, puede traernos, compañeros poetas — hoy ya lo estamos viendo — , la nueva clara voz que tan furiosamente pide España, liquidados ya estos últimos años de magnifica poesía.[91]

Rafael Alberti published another book of poems dedicated to the Asturian Revolution called *El burro explosivo*, which included the poems 'El burro explosivo' and 'Al nuncio de SS en España'.[92] In Manuel Altolaguirre's introduction to Emilio Prados' *Llanto en la sangre* the impact which the Revolution had on the writers is once again expressed: 'Fue necesario que llegara el año de la sangrienta represión de Asturias para que todos, todos los poetas, sintiéramos como un imperioso deber adaptar nuestra obra, nuestras vida [*sic*], al movimiento liberador de España.'[93] Finally, the Argentinean poet Raúl González Tuñón, previously an avant-garde poet, also included a valuable prologue in his collection of poems dedicated to the Revolution in which he writes:

Me parece que ahora hay que hacer poesía revolucionaria. Esto no quiere decir que los demás poetas, si son poetas, dejen de serlo al no sentir la necesidad de expresarse revolucionariamente, en el sentido de la propaganda. Lo que exigimos de ellos es una actitud antifascista concreta, porque el fascismo es el enemigo de la cultura y del arte, tanto como de la dignidad humana. Me parece también que hay que aclarar cuando se habla del llamado arte-purismo. Hay dos grupos en esta tendencia: por un lado están los "puros", los deshumanizados, los nuevos retóricos, cuya obra, abundante en amorcillos, metáfora por la metáfora, discos conocidos, cursilería al revés, tragedias personales sin hondo valor humano, no interesa, no es arte; es subarte, apenas, y por otro lado aquellos que barajan en sus poemas elementos calientes, que hacen, no una obra revolucionaria, pero una obra viva, llena de tierra y llanto, cubierta de raíces y de sangre. La posición de éstos últimos será discutible desde el punto de vista nuestro, pero es humana y seria. Por otra parte los escritores que no sientan el tema revolucionario serán arrastrados a él tarde o temprano por imperativo de su conciencia misma de artistas.[94]

Other poets to deal with the Revolution include Pascual Pla y Beltrán, Arturo Serrano Plaja, Juan Gil-Albert and, for the right wing, Casimiro Cienfuegos.[95]

To conclude, an analysis of the change which took place in the magazine *Cruz y Raya*, which was founded in 1933, prior to the Asturian Revolution, and which continued on after it up to 1936, will demonstrate how intellectual opinion towards the role of literature developed further. Following October Bergamín approached sympathetically the theme of the Revolution from a Christian point of view. For example, following André Gide's speech at the Congreso Internacional de Escritores in an article entitled 'Hablar en Cristiano' Bergamín wonders if communism and Christianity have the same aims and hopes:

Que el hombre, cuando es hombre, siempre es nuevo, y que el hombre sea siempre nuevo es una de las primeras verdades del Cristianismo. Del Cristianismo no histórico, ni evolutivo o progresivo: del Cristianismo revolucionario permanente. El Cristianismo nos dice del hombre que se puede novar o renovar siempre, *haciéndose de nuevas*. Pues esto, y acaso no otra cosa, quiere decir evangelizarse. También en el bajo fondo invisible de estas actitudes religiosamente comunistas ¿late un mismo afán de comuniones evangélicas?[96]

More directly relevant to the violent events, in the article 'El Estado fantasma y ¿en qué país vivimos?' Bergamín reveals the personal testimony of one of the contributors to *Cruz y Raya*, Alfredo Mendizábal, professor at the University of Oviedo, who was taken prisoner by the miners during the rebellion.[97] This testimony appeared in *La Vie Intellectuelle*, a magazine of the French Dominican order, and praised the humanity of the miners. Bécarud affirms in his study of *Cruz y Raya* that: 'Citándole como ejemplo, Bergamín se congratulaba de que un católico español hiciese oír la voz del verdadero espíritu cristiano en medio del concierto de odio y de injurias que se había desencadenado en todo el país' (p. 23). Following the Revolution this magazine ventured into the political field in a more aggressive way than it had done before, and 'su acento se volvió más apasionado, y también más angustiado'.[98] This was inevitably going to be the case in most other magazines and in literature generally speaking.

1. José M. del Pino, *Montajes y fragmentos: una aproximación a la narrativa española de vanguardia* (Amsterdam: Rodopi, 1995), p. 25.
2. The so-called avant-garde movement actually embraced numerous styles, including 'modernismo', 'creacionismo', 'ultraísmo', 'surrealismo', the 'greguerías' of Gómez de la Serna, 'dadaísmo', and 'futurismo'. Some of these were limited to poetry and others to prose writing. According to Jaime Brihuega, Gómez de la Serna's, *Ismos* (Madrid: Biblioteca Nueva, 1931) actually identified twenty-five 'ismos', or styles. In Jaime Brihuega, *Manifiestos, proclamas, panfletos y textos doctrinales: las vanguardias artísticas en España, 1910–1931* (Madrid: Cátedra, 1979), p. 23.
3. Ramón Buckley, 'Francisco Ayala y el arte de vanguardia: Hacia una nueva valoración de la generación de 1927', *Insula*, January 1970, pp. 1, 10 (p. 1).
4. Francisco Javier Blasco, 'Prosa y teatro del 27', in *Historia y crítica de la literatura española*, ed. by Francisco Rico, 9 vols (Barcelona: Editorial Crítica, 1979–), VII: *Época contemporánea: 1914–1939*, ed. by Víctor García de la Concha (1984), pp. 528–51.
5. Ramón Buckley and John Crispin, *Los vanguardistas españoles 1925–1935* (Madrid: Alianza Editorial, 1973), pp. 9–10.
6. Referred to by Buckley and Crispin, p. 10.
7. Víctor Fuentes, 'La narrativa española de vanguardia', in Víctor García de la Concha, pp. 561–64.
8. Gustavo Pérez Firmat, *Idle Fictions: The Hispanic Vanguard Novel, 1926–1934* (Durham: Duke University Press, 1993), p. 29.
9. The terms used by Ramón Feria are quoted by Firmat, p. 25.
10. Max Aub, *Discurso de la novela española contemporánea* (Mexico: El Colegio de México, Centro de Estudios Sociales, 1945), p. 95.
11. Blasco defines the two types: The 'lírico intelectual' novelist, Jarnés, 'evita las asociaciones de la lógica superficial [. . .] colocando al yo narrativo — que pasa a desempeñar la misma función que el yo lírico en la poesía — como eje aglutinador de las secuencias novelísticas' (p. 529), and Espina 'reacciona con indignación ante el medio que le rodea; pero cada uno viste su exasperación con el traje de su tiempo, y a Espina le correspondió una indumentaria cosmopolita y grotesca' (p. 531). On the other hand, 'El humor es — como la ironía o la metáfora transmutadora en la novela lírico-intelectual — una forma de distanciamiento satírico, respecto a la realidad del momento' (p. 533). In this second category the most important figure in the 1920s was Jardiel Poncela.
12. Fuentes, 'La narrativa española de vanguardia', pp. 561, 563, and 563 respectively.

13. Carlos Blanco Aguinaga, Julio Rodríguez Puértolas, and Iris Zavala, *Historia social de la literatura española (en lengua castellana)*, 3 vols (Madrid: Castalia, 1978–79), II (1979), 281.
14. *El humor ramoniano de vanguardia*, Manchester Spanish and Portuguese Working Papers, II (Manchester: University of Manchester, 1996), p. 30.
15. Filippo Tommaso Marinetti (1876–1944) was the founder of Futurism, an artistic, social, and political movement. As the first European movement of the avant-garde, Futurist poetry frequently presented an incoherent and anarchic blend of words stripped of their meaning and used for their sound alone. The first Futurist manifesto appeared in the Parisian *Le Figaro* on 22 February 1909. Marinetti's article, 'Fundación y manifiesto del futurismo', translated by Gómez de la Serna, was published in the sixth issue of *Prometeo*, in 1909. Félix Rebollo Sánchez, *Periodismo y movimientos literarios contemporáneos españoles (1900–1939)* (Madrid: Huerga y Fierro, 1998), pp. 155–56.
16. 'Ramón Gómez de la Serna and the Avant-Garde', in *Changing Times in Hispanic Culture*, ed. by Derek Harris (Aberdeen: University of Aberdeen, 1996), pp. 7–18 (p. 8).
17. Senabre's description continues: 'La lengua se le presenta a Ramón como una avalancha de vocablos y expresiones cuyo sentido se le impone. Pero el escritor puede salvarse de esta esclavitud ejercitando un acto de íntima libertad al rebelarse contra los significados y enfrentarse con el lenguaje. [...] Sólo el recurso a la pureza inicial vigorizará las palabras hasta hacerlas aptas para nuevos modos de expresión.' Ricardo Senabre, 'Técnica de la greguería', in García de la Concha, pp. 221–26 (p. 222).
18. José Carlos Mainer, *La Edad de Plata (1902–1939): ensayo de interpretación de un proceso cultural*, 4th edn (Madrid: Cátedra, 1987), p. 238.
19. *El humor ramoniano*, pp. 19 and 6 respectively.
20. Ibid., p. 21. Hoyle refers to *El Incongruente* (1922) which merged 'la escritura poética con el cine cómico'.
21. *La deshumanización del arte*, 10th edn (Madrid: Alianza, 1996), p. 19. All further references are cited parenthetically in the text.
22. *Ideas sobre el teatro y la novela* (Madrid: Alianza, 1995), p. 19. All further references are cited parenthetically in the text.
23. Derek Harris, 'Squared Horizons: The Hybridisation of the Avant-garde in Spain', in *The Spanish Avant-garde*, ed. by Derek Harris (Manchester: Manchester University Press, 1995), pp. 1–14 (p. 3).
24. *The Novel of the Spanish Civil War (1936–1975)* (Cambridge: Cambridge University Press, 1990), p. 20.
25. Fulgencio Castañar, *El compromiso en la novela de la II República* (Madrid: Siglo XXI, 1992), p. 16.
26. Ibid.
27. Laurent Boetsch, 'Una aventura de la otra generación de 1927: Díaz Fernández, Arconada y la literatura de avanzada', *Bazar*, 4 (1997), 144–49 (p. 146).
28. Ibid., p. 149.
29. Rafael Osuna, *Las revistas españolas entre dos dictaduras: 1931–1939* (Valencia: Pre-Textos, 1986), p. 55.
30. Víctor Fuentes, '"Post-Guerra" (1927–1928): una revista de vanguardia política y literaria', *Insula*, 360 (November 1976), 4. Further details on *Post-Guerra* can be found in Gonzalo Santonja, *Del lápiz rojo al lápiz libre: la censura de prensa y el mundo del libro* (Barcelona: Anthropos, 1986), pp. 99–143.
31. Quoted from the first issue brought out on 25 June 1927 by Castañar, p. 42.
32. Ibid., p. 46.
33. Ibid., p. 49.
34. Gonzalo Santonja, *Del lápiz rojo al lápiz libre*, p. 227.
35. Nine editions of the novel were published in one year and in total 106,000 copies were sold in Spain.
36. Pablo Gil Casado, *La novela social española (1920–1971)*, 2nd edn (Barcelona: Seix Barral, 1973), p. 133. Víctor Fuentes, 'Los nuevos intelectuales en España: 1923–1931', *Triunfo*, 28 August 1976, pp. 38–42, provides information on the books (mainly theoretical) published between 1923 and 1927 by Juan Andrade and other members of the PCE aimed at spreading Marxist ideology.

37. According to Douglas Foard, *Notas marruecas de un soldado* is 'a bitter indictment of Spain's political and military leadership, an angry protest against the nations of western Europe (whom he accused of profiting from Spain's misfortunes), and an uninterrupted song of praise for the vitality and patriotism of the army's enlisted men'. Douglas Foard, 'The Forgotten Falangist: Ernesto Giménez Caballero', *Journal of Contemporary History*, 10 (1975), 3–18 (p. 7). The first edition of *Notas* was sold out within two weeks.
38. José Díaz Fernández, *El blocao* (Madrid: Historia Nueva, 1928); Ramón J. Sender, *Imán* (Madrid: Cenit, 1930); Fermín Galán, *La barbarie organizada* (Madrid: Castro, 1931). *Imán* was a best-seller in Spain as well as abroad, where it sold 20,000 copies in Germany, 15,000 copies in Great Britain, 8000 in Holland, and 55,000 copies in the Soviet Union. Other books which deal with the war in Morocco are *El suicidio del príncipe Ariel* (1929) by J. A. Balbontín, and *Los caimanes* (1931) by Ciges Aparicio.
39. Víctor Fuentes, 'De la literatura de vanguardia a la de avanzada: en torno a José Díaz Fernández', *Papeles de Son Armadans*, 54 (1969), 243–60.
40. Ignacio Soldevila Durante, *La novela desde 1936* (Madrid: Alhambra, 1980), p. 63.
41. Víctor Fuentes, 'La novela social española en los años 1928–1931', *Insula*, January 1970, pp. 1, 12, 13 (p. 12).
42. José Díaz Fernández, *El nuevo romanticismo o polémica de arte, política y literatura* (Madrid: Zeus, 1930), p. 47. This text is a collection of theoretical essays in which Díaz Fernández notes down his opinions about the development of literature. All further page references in the text refer to this edition.
43. José Manuel López de Abiada, introduction to José Díaz Fernández, *Octubre rojo en Asturias* (Gijón: Silverio Cañada, 1984), p. xl. The other essays in *El nuevo romanticismo* are: 'La juventud y la política', 'Vida nueva y arte futuro', 'Objetivos de una generación', and 'Proyección social del arte nuevo'. Juan Ignacio Ferreras calls Díaz Fernández's collection 'la biblia de la tendencia' in *La novela en el siglo XX (hasta 1939)* (Madrid: Taurus, 1988), p. 124.
44. Laurent Boetsch, *José Díaz Fernández y la otra Generación del 27* (Madrid: Editorial Pliegos, 1985), pp. 48–49.
45. Víctor Fuentes, *La marcha al pueblo en las letras españolas (1917–1936)* (Madrid: Ediciones de la Torre, 1980), p. 55.
46. José Díaz Fernández, 'Acerca del arte nuevo', *Post-Guerra*, 4 (1927), 6–7. Quoted in Mainer, p. 92.
47. Prologue to José Díaz Fernández, *El blocao*, 2nd edn (Madrid: Editorial Historia Nueva, 1928). Quotation taken from José Díaz Fernández, *El blocao* (Madrid: Viamonte, 1998), p. 30. Subsequent page references are to the 1998 edition.
48. Questions included: '¿Existe o ha existido la vanguardia? ¿Cómo la ha entendido usted? ¿A su juicio, qué postulados literarios presenta o presentó en su día? ¿Cómo la juzgó y la juzga ahora desde su punto de vista político?' In Brihuega, p. 20, footnote 18.
49. Buckley and Crispin, p. 397.
50. Arconada's response is quoted by Buckley and Crispin, pp. 397–98.
51. César Arconada, 'Autobiografía', *Nueva Cultura*, 11 (1936), quoted in Boetsch, 'Una aventura de la otra generación de 1927', p. 148.
52. José Díaz Fernández, 'Los novelistas y la vida nueva: encuesta', *La Libertad*, 6 June 1931. Referred to by Juan Cano Ballesta, *La poesía española entre pureza y revolución (1920–1936)* (Madrid: Siglo XXI, 1996), p. 31.
53. Fuentes, *La marcha al pueblo*; Boetsch, 'Una aventura de la otra generación de 1927'; Eugenio García de Nora, *La novela española contemporánea* (Madrid: Gredos, 1973); Gil Casado, *La novela social española*; and José Esteban, 'Editoriales y libros de la España de los años treinta', *Cuadernos para el Diálogo*, 32, suppl. (1972), 58–62.
54. Quoted by Buckley and Crispin, p. 54.
55. According to Trapiello: 'Giménez Caballero no era en 1927 el fascista que fue luego, aunque muchas de sus simpatías estuviesen decantadas por personajes y regímenes, como el italiano, de corte autoritario. Fue sólo a raíz de uno de sus viajes kilométricos por Italia, Holanda, Bélgica y Alemania, en 1928, cuando daría forma a un pensamiento embrionariamente ducista.' Andrés Trapiello, *Las armas y las letras: literatura y guerra civil (1936–1939)* (Barcelona: Editorial Planeta, 1994), p. 29.
56. By intellectual I mean: 'Aquel que generaliza saber en forma más o menos literaria para un público más amplio que el de su círculo profesional', a definition taken by Bécarud

and López Campillo from Juan Marsal, *Los intelectuales políticos* (Madrid: Editorial Nueva Vision, 1971). According to Bécarud and López Campillo this definition 'comporta [. . .] unos criterios fundamentales, como el de audiencia y de influencia'. Jean Bécarud and Evelyn López Campillo, *Los intelectuales españoles durante la II República* (Madrid: Siglo XXI, 1978), p. 2.

57. Castañar, p. 27.
58. Ibid., p. 94.
59. Quoted by Bécarud and López Campillo, p. 28.
60. All the problems which confronted the Republic from 1931 to 1933 are explained in Shlomo Ben-Ami, 'The Republican "Take-over": Prelude to Inevitable Catastrophy?', in *Revolution and War in Spain 1931–1939*, ed. by Paul Preston (London: Routledge, 1993), pp. 14–34.
61. According to Esteban, 'El presupuesto de la monarquía para la compra de libros fue en 1930 de poco más de 40.000 pesetas; el del año 1933 fue de 1.690.000 pesetas. [. . .] Desde 1932, mil seiscientas bibliotecas públicas fueron fundadas por el Estado' (p. 61).
62. According to John Crispin the most important mission of the Misiones Pedagógicas was 'su campaña para crear en los pueblos afición a la lectura'. John Crispin, 'Antonio Sánchez Barbudo, misionero pedagógico', in *Homenaje a Antonio Sánchez Barbudo: ensayos de literatura española moderna*, ed. by Benito Brancaforte, Edward Mulvihill, Roberto G. Sánchez (Madison: University of Wisconsin, 1981), pp. 9–22 (p. 13). For Mainer the importance of the 'Misiones' lies elsewhere: 'La movilización de algunos centenares de muchachos refleja el momento culminante del populismo intelectual español, a la vez que Antonio Machado — a través de su heterónimo Juan de Mairena — soñaba con una "Escuela Superior de Sabiduría Popular", y cuando Luis Buñuel rodaba en Las Hurdes su documental *Tierra sin pan*, cuando Bergamín escribía en *Cruz y raya* sobre "La decadencia del analfabetismo", cuando lo popular [. . .] se convirtió para jóvenes y no tan jóvenes en un modo de adhesión emocional al pueblo y, por supuesto, en una implícita rectificación de los axiomas orteguianos' (p. 289).
63. Details on the role of the Misiones Pedagógicas in Asturias can be found in Leonardo Borque López, 'Las Misiones Pedagógicas en Asturias', *Los Cuadernos del Norte*, 11 (1982), 83–87. Borque López quotes the opening words of the decree responsable for the setting up of the Misiones and published on 30 May 1931: 'Según el preámbulo de aquel Decreto se trataba de "llevar a las gentes, con preferencia a las que habitaban en localidades rurales, el aliento de progreso y los medios de participar en él, en sus estímulos morales y en los ejemplos del avance universal, de modo que los pueblos todos de España, aún los apartados, participen en las ventajas y goces reservados hoy a los centros urbanos"' (p. 83).
64. Bécarud and Campillo add to these the Escuela de Estudios Arabes (1932), the Consejo Nacional de Cultura (1932), and the Universidad Internacional de Verano de Santander (1932).
65. Bécarud and López Campillo, p. 87.
66. Jean Bécarud, *Cruz y Raya (1933–1936)* (Madrid: Taurus, 1969), p. 8.
67. Bécarud and López Campillo, pp. 87–88.
68. The earliest example, recorded by Esteban and Santonja in *Los novelistas sociales españoles (1928–1936)*, of a novelist openly tackling socio-political issues in his work is Manuel Ciges Aparicio (1873–1936) who, in *Los vencidos* (1908) and *Los vencedores* (1910), incites the reader–worker to change his living and working conditions through revolutionary action. Prior to 1930, however, these novelists were few and far between and, for the most part, from the left of the political spectrum.
69. 'Editoriales y libros', p. 61.
70. The C.I.A.P.'s ambitious programme met increasing economic difficulties as the company's financier Bauer & Co. suspended its monetary contributions.
71. Kessel Schwartz, *Studies on Twentieth-Century Spanish and Spanish American Literature* (Lanham: University Press of America, 1983), p. 13.
72. Ibid., p. 13.
73. Taken from an excerpt of *El nuevo romanticismo* included in the anthology by José Esteban and Gonzalo Santonja, *Los novelistas sociales españoles (1928–1936): antología* (Barcelona: Anthropos, 1988), pp. 25–27 (p. 26).
74. Rebollo Sánchez, p. 228.

75. J. Lechner, *El compromiso en la poesía española del siglo XX* (Leiden: Universitaires Pers Leiden, 1968), p. 97.
76. Esteban and Santonja, p. 321.
77. Osuna, p. 74.
78. 'Realismo dialéctico' is a term borrowed from Castañar. He defines it the following way: 'Se creará en la ficción literaria una realidad aparente, sometida a todas las normas y leyes del mundo físico, mas, en vez de ser un espejo de la sociedad, se articularán las anécdotas subordinadas a la concepción ideológica que al escritor le interesa imbuir en las personas que lean sus obras' (p. 100).
79. *Hora de España: antología*, ed. by Francisco Caudet (Madrid: Ediciones Turner, 1975), p. 19.
80. From an interview between Rafael Heliodoro Valle and Rafael Alberti and María Teresa León, published in *Revista de Revistas*, 19 May 1935. Quoted by Robert Marrast, *Rafael Alberti en Mexico (1935)* (Santander: La Isla de los Ratones, 1984), p. 33.
81. César Vallejo, *El arte y la revolución* (Lima: Mosca Azul Editores, 1973), p. 59. Vallejo agrees with Lenin: 'La literatura proletaria debe ser una literatura de clase y una literatura de partido. Ella debe inspirarse en la idea socialista y en la simpatía por los trabajadores, que encarnan y luchan por la realización de aquella idea' (p. 61).
82. Castañar, p. 35.
83. André Gide, *Defensa de la cultura*, trans. by Julio Gómez de la Serna (Madrid: S. Aguirre, 1936), p. 24.
84. Manuel Aznar Soler, *I Congreso Internacional de Escritores para la Defensa de la Cultura (Paris, 1935)*, 2 vols (Valencia: Generalitat Valenciana, Consellería de Cultura, Educació i Ciència, 1987), I, 55–56.
85. Caudet, p. 20.
86. *La marcha al pueblo*, p. 108.
87. Gordón Ordás clarifies what he hoped to achieve with his report: 'Visité completamente solo las zonas más sospechosas [of the Asturian repression]. En ellas adquirí con toda certidumbre tal cantidad de noticias terribles que se me llenó el alma de espanto. Y como el Gobierno seguía negando o callando, sin tener en cuenta que con su actitud comprometía gravísimamente el prestigio moral y el sentido humano de la República, me creí en la obligación inexcusable de hablar en el Parlamento para exponer los hechos y pedir justicia.' Félix Gordón Ordás, *Mi política en España*, 2 vols (Mexico: [n. pub.], 1962), II, 253.
88. Quoted by Manuel Aznar Soler, 'La revolución asturiana de octubre de 1934 y la literatura española', *Los Cuadernos del Norte*, 26 (1984), 86–104 (p. 88).
89. *El Sol*, 11 August 1935, p. 1. Referred to by Aznar Soler, 'La revolución asturiana', p. 89.
90. 'La revolución asturiana', p. 103, footnote 11.
91. The prologue to *Poeta en la calle* (1935) is included in the edition, Rafael Alberti, *Poeta en la calle: obra civil* (Madrid: Aguilar, 1978).
92. Rafael Alberti, *El burro explosivo* (Madrid: Ediciones del 5° Regimiento, 1936).
93. Manuel Altolaguirre's prologue to Emilio Prados, *Llanto en la sangre* (Madrid, Valencia: Ediciones Españolas, 1937), p. 6. Quoted in Aznar Soler, 'La revolución asturiana', p. 88.
94. Raúl González Tuñón, *La rosa blindada: homenaje a la insurrección de Asturias y otros poemas revolucionarios* (Buenos Aires: Imp. Federación Gráfica Bonaerense, 1936), p. 14.
95. Pascual Pla y Beltrán, *Voz de la tierra: poema en rebelión* (Valencia: Ediciones de la Unión de Escritores y Artistas Proletarios de Valencia, 1935); Arturo Serrano Plaja, *Destierro infinito* (Madrid: Ediciones Héroe, 1936); Juan Gil-Albert, unpublished poem provided by Aznar Soler, 'La revolución asturiana', p. 102; and Casimiro Cienfuegos, *Elegía de Asturias y otros poemas del dolor trágico de España* ([n.p.]: Editorial Ibérica, 1935).
96. José Bergamín, 'Hablar en Cristiano', *Cruz y Raya*, 28 (1935), 73–83 (p. 81).
97. José Bergamín, 'El Estado fantasma y ¿en qué país vivimos?', *Cruz y Raya*, 25 (1934), 127–33.
98. Bécarud, *Cruz y Raya*, p. 50.

CHAPTER 3

POLITICAL DISCOURSE, CONFESSION, AND JOURNALISTIC RESPONSE

In this first chapter dealing with the narrative texts written immediately after the October Revolution, three groups of works have been brought together: those which provide a purely political interpretation of the events, those providing evidence in the form of confessions, and finally compilations of articles published after the events by journalists. Despite the diverse nature of these categories, the works which they encompass present a common factor, that is, they deal with the October Revolution only as part of a more general analysis of the years of the second Republic. The specific details of the Revolution are not at issue here; instead the more wide-ranging implications of its causes and defeat are looked at within the context of the important historical period that Spain has just gone through. The value of these texts, written from both a revolutionary and counter-revolutionary point of view, lies not only in the fact that they demonstrate varying interpretations of, and responses to, the events but also in that, despite their diametrically opposed ideological stance, the narrative approach of the authors is similar. Both of these factors stand out in all the texts examined, from the 'factual' narratives considered in this chapter to the more descriptive reports and increasingly literary accounts that will be examined later. This is why, despite their lack of literary value, they are vital to the overall analysis.

In addition, the October Revolution cannot be dealt with comprehensively without touching on the subsequent repression, not only for its ethical considerations but also for the political consequences that it brought about, namely the fall of the right-wing government and the victory of the Popular Front in the elections held in February 1936. Hence, at the end of this chapter I briefly analyse four texts which were written as a response to the repression. Although these texts are also 'factual' and present many similar characteristics, they are dealt with separately since they concentrate on the repression rather than on general political issues.

The texts looked at in the first part of the chapter, in ideological order from left to right, are Joaquín Maurín, *Hacia la segunda revolución* (1935), a political essay by a revolutionary supporter of the Alianza Obrera; and a compilation of socialist documents put together by a section of the Socialist Party, *Documentos Socialistas* (1935). Moving along the more moderate left-wing position we find Consuelo Bergés' political commentary sympathetic with the socialist position, *Explicación de octubre* (1935), and Manuel Azaña, *Mi rebelión en Barcelona* (1935), an explanation of the ex-President's involvement in the events. Crossing the dividing line between the left and the right we find the right-wing commentary that Antonio Oliveros makes of the Republic, *Asturias en el resurgimiento español* (1935), the collection of articles published by Francisco de Cossío, *Hacia una nueva España* (1936), and José Simeón Valdivielso, *Farsa y tragedia de España en el 1934* (1935), and the résumé which Diego Hidalgo provides about his actions as War Minister during the Revolution, *¿Por qué fui lanzado del Ministerio de la Guerra?* (1934). Finally, situated at the extreme right-wing end of the political spectrum are the political discourses of El Caballero Audaz, *Traidores a la Patria* (1935), and the fascist Mauricio Karl, *Asesinos de España* (1935), supporting Mussolini's fascism and Hitler's Nazism.[1] These 'factual' texts are examined together in an attempt to demonstrate that, despite being generically and stylistically diverse, at the time of composition their authors have certain priorities in mind, issues and characteristics which are relevant to even the most literary of the texts, as the following chapters will demonstrate.[2]

Taking first of all those works which are essentially political discourses we find that Maurín's main aim is to demonstrate that Spanish politics has arrived at a crucial juncture in which political events will determine which ideological side will govern Spain, and implies that the 1934 Revolution is at the centre of this important moment; Bergés concentrates on why and how the years of Republican government led ultimately to the October Revolution and, without looking at the course of the Revolution, lists six reasons explaining why it failed; Oliveros, whose text, like Bergés', is a commentary on the history and politics of Asturias, especially from 1898 to 1934, provides us with an introduction which is particularly interesting for the comments he makes on the nature and importance of historical writing and the difficulty of the historian's task;[3] and El Caballero Audaz and Karl criticize the government for its soft stance against the revolutionaries and the socialists in particular.[4]

Secondly, the 'confessional' works also provide first-hand documentary evidence. The collection of socialist documents — including letters, speeches, and reports — published in 1935 aims to guide the Socialist Party in its post-revolutionary development, and calls for all socialists to unite. It is specifically directed at the left wing of the Party which calls for further insurrections and reminds them of the repercussions and effects of the last attempt. Particularly interesting and relevant is the section 'Palabras pronunciadas por Ramón González Peña, en la ciudad de Oviedo, el día 15 de febrero de 1935, ante el Consejo de guerra que le condenó a la última pena' in which the 'generalísimo' comments on why he joined the Revolution and answers the allegations made against him. Azaña's text deals with the Revolution in Barcelona, as the author responds to the accusations that he was in that city in order to plot the Revolution, an accusation from which he was absolved after nearly a year in the courts.[5] Despite the fact that it only mentions Asturias in passing it provides the point of view of an ex-President, opposing any form of violence, accused of contributing to the Revolution. In addition, the prologue and other assertions that he makes throughout the book demonstrate how many intellectuals, reacting to the government backlash against the left-wing forces, united to condemn all repressive action. Hidalgo, in similar vein to Azaña, is concerned with providing information which will prove that all the allegations hurled at him criticizing the way he ran the Ministry of War, particularly in the run-up to October 1934, are unfounded. This text is interesting as Hidalgo, a member of the right-wing Radical Party, conveys the political disarray that faced Spain after the Revolution and before the 1936 general election. He concentrates on the criticisms directed at him from politicians, such as Calvo Sotelo, which were to lead to his dismissal from the government.

Finally, the third category of texts represents the journalistic response to the Revolution, be it only from a right-wing point of view.[6] Cossío gathers in his volume, published shortly after Franco's coup in July 1936, numerous articles written from 1934 to 1936 in order to provide a full report of the October Revolution and elucidate why Franco's action is so necessary. Similarly, Valdivielso compiles the reports that he published in his section of the Madrid newspaper, *El Siglo Futuro*, called 'Mirilla', as the October events unfolded. Most of these articles are political tracts examining the advent and the resulting failure of the Republic crowned by the Revolution, and aim to demonstrate the journalist's belief that democracy has failed.

On considering the principles that guide the authors in their writing, one essential factor emerges in all of the works examined here, that is, the hope that their work, despite being personal and therefore subjective in nature, should be regarded as an accurate interpretation of the events, or at least an important aid to future historical research. To this end, many of the authors state their own particular view of how the study of history must be approached and the importance which the October Revolution, as a single, unique event, and their interpretation of it, have within the context of the whole of Spanish history. Oliveros, who distinguishes 'historia' from 'Historia', the former being the anecdotal past and the latter the study and interpretation of it, is the most explicit about the role of the historian and the implications for history on current affairs, issues which he deals with in his prologue, 'Historia y mito'.[7] As part of his analysis Oliveros considers the important and difficult task of separating history/truth from myth/falsehood. Although most authors examined mention the importance of truth, achieved primarily through objectivity, few link it to its implications on history and tackle the issue in depth. While Oliveros regards history (a difficult term to define) as an ongoing process which links the past to the present, he highlights that without a guarantee of the truthfulness of the historical account, its objective nature and therefore its value is doubtful:

La Historia es, en efecto, continuidad, aunque no continuación, semejanza y no identidad, el enlace causal del instante vivido con el actuante.

[. . .] La sucesión de los hechos, sus causas, accidentes y consecuencias, corresponde, en el relato objetivo, a la verdad, sin cuya certidumbre aquélla carece de valor probatorio. (p. 5)

Taking the Reconquest of Spain, which started in the eighth century in Asturias, as an example, Oliveros aims to demonstrate that, contrary to popular belief, history ('Historia') is not definitive and its accuracy cannot be taken for granted. One of the main reasons for this is that history is narrated by men, inevitably influenced by and exposed to contemporary internal and external factors and pressures:

El historiador, como hombre, al fin es prisionero de sus pasiones. Refiere los sucesos regularmente, no como han debido ser o han sido, sino como los ve su temperamento, o como importa a ciertas circunstancias nacionales, religiosas o políticas que sean registrados. (p. 6)

Consequently, history should be taken to be a mixture of myth and reality; the distinction between them is the reader's responsibility. Oliveros elucidates his arguments with the example of the myth surrounding the Reconquest, which, according to him, did not happen in the way it is popularly believed to have. In order to appreciate the important part that Asturias has played in Spain's political destiny from the legendary battle against the Moors up to the current time, the truth regarding the events and those involved — which according to Oliveros are far from being attributable to a miracle and a Christian hero — must be realized. Only then will the Asturian people become aware of the important part played by their ancestors, and only then will the importance of the Reconquest in the shaping of Asturias and Spain be perceived. Whilst he begins his text with a brief summary of his version of the Reconquest, dealt with in the second part of the prologue, the ensuing narrative considers recent political history from 1898 to 1934, as experienced by him, and ends with the Revolution of October 1934, discussed in the epilogue. At the end of the prologue and before he begins narrating the political events which he has witnessed Oliveros advises the reader that his version of the events are 'historia vivida' (p. 15). Whilst future generations will have to take into account the issues that Oliveros has carefully expounded in their study of the development of Spanish political history, his account will undoubtedly aid in preventing the mythical recreation of this period of Asturias' past. Thus, Oliveros, whose initial concerns surround the problems of interpreting, or reinterpreting, historical events which have taken place in the distant past, 'una lejanía casi insondable' (p. 6), presents us with a critical analysis of contemporary events.

Oliveros is not the only writer concerned with leaving future generations his version of the events. The equally successful journalist Francisco de Cossío, who chose to publish a compilation of his articles as opposed to a thorough and carefully structured study, is also aware of the future value of his book.[8] Having evaluated the pros and cons of each of these two narrative styles, Cossío opts for the spirit and tone conveyed in journalistic writing, which according to him is also of historical value:

> Falta en el comentario periodístico serenidad de juicio y perspectiva, mas, en cambio, en él se recoge la vibración del momento, es decir, el espíritu de los contemporáneos, y esto muy raramente lo alcanza el historiador. (p. 9)

Similarly, Valdivielso favours a journalistic representation of the events and, despite the seemingly disorganized structure which results, he chooses to present the articles in chronological as opposed to thematic order: 'Porque en esta variedad y desorden con que los temas surgen y se desplazan me parece a mí que se refleja mejor lo ocurrido' (post-scriptum). This quotation from Valdivielso reflects the greatest dilemma facing the writers when composing their work. On the one hand, they wish to present a historical account of the events, in other words, an objective and empirical study based solely on evidence and other corroborative material. On the other hand, they want to reflect as closely as possible the tense and violent climate that prevailed in the run up to, during and immediately after the Revolution.

Following the impact of new historicism, many of today's historians would dispute the 'objective' prerequisite of and 'scientific' approach to the study of history.[9] As Oliveros demonstrates, however, these authors, writing over fifty years earlier, still assumed that their approach to the facts should be, and could be, neutral and impersonal. Thus they consider it necessary to declare to the readers (whether to warn or to attract them) that, given the extreme and sensitive nature of the events, their particular account will be based on personal experience and will be influenced by their political stance.[10] In addition, the pressing need to publish the works as close to the events as possible shaped in many cases the tone in which they were written. This is particularly true in the case of the journalists whose articles, although subsequently collected and published in book form, were originally written and published from day to day in tandem with the events. Thus Valdivielso affirms that the articles he compiled were written:

> Entre el acoso de la actualidad palpitante, en medio del fragor y la turbulencia del combate cotidiano y con la urgencia y el apremio de toda labor periodística realizada atropelladamente bajo la coacción de las horas de cierre y los requerimientos con calidad de imperativo categórico con que el regente del taller reclama su 'ración' de original. (post-scriptum)

Aware of the influence of the urgency factor, Bergés concludes that it is too early to make a proper analysis of the events. When she reveals the aims of her book, she writes:

> Toda esta trayectoria lógica [referring to her narrative] formará el hilo de una serie de crónicas que pretenden ser la historia comprimida de tres años y medio de República española. Vista, naturalmente, como la vida en la novela, a través de un temperamento. (p. 34)

Bergés' concerns are symptomatic of the ongoing debate about the extent to which political and social issues and circumstances should influence art, in all its forms, and vice-versa, a topic which, as already illustrated in Chapter 2, had been particularly contentious from 1928 to 1934. Bergés' thoughts on this controversy make her opening pages particularly relevant to a discussion of the political engagement of writers. She alludes to the difficult situation facing artists during conflictive periods[11] and scornfully comments on the allegations made by those reluctant to commit their art to a political or social cause on the grounds that 'la política mata y excluye a la literatura artística':

> Para ellos, abandonar la torre de marfil donde tiene su morada aséptica y eterna la minoría exquisita, cuesta la privación de la gracia literaria, amiga de la soledad y de la excepción, pudorosa como una colegiala. (p. 14)

Despite Ortega y Gasset's assertions, which she quotes, Bergés insists that the intellectuals' commitment is inevitable: 'Los escritores sucumben casi todos al mandato atrayente de un momento en el que la vida vibra y fermenta demasiado para que pueda permanecer incontaminada, transparente y fría ninguna clase de pureza' (p. 15), and closes her introductory pages with an 'acendrada invitación' to other writers to be committed.[12]

Karl declares at the start of his narrative that his version of the October episode is going to be purposefully subjective as his aim is to produce an interpretation of the events as opposed to an impersonal descriptive account:

> Una versión inédita, una interpretación subjetiva y un poco de pasión en los puntos de la pluma, y no ese cambalache de retazos que constituye una estafa consumada en las pacientes barbas del buen lector español. (p. 11)

Karl regards this as a positive and original attribute as most of the texts, according to him, do not attempt to analyse the events or explain the motives and instead concentrate only on their description. Likewise, El Caballero Audaz feels that, as a journalist, his duty is to 'ser fiscales y enjuiciadores de la tragedia; de sus causas y de sus responsabilidades' (p. 141). Cossío and Maurín also prefer to be openly political, although, rather than driven by a desire to blame the other party, they are motivated by an effort to encourage their own side. Cossío, who affirms that he felt 'en mi mano la pluma como un arma' (p. 11) insists that the articles that constitute his compilation were written with a clear propagandistic aim in mind:

> Yo procuré servirla [Spain] haciendo las cosas de mi oficio, lanzando palabras como proyectiles. España necesitaba también palabras encendidas, y yo abrí de par en par mi balcón, y, asomándome a él, comencé a gritar. (p. 11)

Similarly, Maurín, just like A.G. in *Documentos Socialistas*,[13] hopes that his text will be influential in restoring confidence amongst the left-wing forces:

> Las páginas que siguen, escritas al resplandor del incendio de octubre, intentan ser una contribución al esfuerzo heroico que hace nuestro movimiento obrero para marchar, audazmente, hacia un mundo mejor, hacia una estructuración social más racional, más justa, más humana que la presente. (p. 46)

Karl, El Caballero Audaz, Cossío and, on the left, Maurín, take advantage of the conflictive and sensitive political situation facing Spain and the impact of the Revolution, still fresh in people's minds. They are concerned with providing an immediate response to the most serious political episode of the second Republic as part of a more general assessment of contemporary Spanish politics, and not an account of the events for the use of any future historical study. This explains the deliberate political stand that they choose to take.

Whether the authors' ideological viewpoint is openly declared or not, however, there is no doubt that in all of these texts there exists a political bias, for example in the mere selection of the evidence or information presented:

> [The historian] selects [. . .] what he thinks important, and omits the rest; he interpolates in them things which they do not explicitly say; and he criticises them by rejecting or amending what he regards as due to misinformation or mendacity.[14]

Collingwood's affirmation, taken out of a book on the philosophy of history and the limits of historical knowledge, highlights a problem that must be raised when considering the factuality and objectivity of any testimonial text which assures that the use of first-hand evidence corroborates the truthfulness and accuracy of its claims. In his study on New Journalism, John Hellman is equally confident that 'because it is a product of the human mind and language, journalism can never passively mirror the whole of reality, but must instead actively select, transform and interpret it'.[15]

In essence, any selection of documents involves a degree of manipulation. While the authors dealt with up to now aim to provide an interpretation of the events, Hidalgo, who relates his experience as Minister of War, refrains from doing so on the grounds that a proper historical analysis of the difficulties that faced the Republic prior to the Revolution should be left, for the sake of truth ('la Verdad'), to more capable hands.[16] Instead he compiles a report with the criticisms that he was subjected to while he held his ministerial post and which resulted in his eventual dismissal, together with his responses to the allegations made against him. Hidalgo's aim, just like Azaña's, who is concerned with clearing his name and 'restaurar la verdad' (p. 22), is to provide all the information which he claims the public are certain to lack. He hopes that by reading about the events, written first-hand by the protagonist, the reader will be able to make a true judgement of the ex-Minister's conduct: 'Quisiera yo, brevemente y con claridad meridiana, dar la mayor publicidad a estos acontecimientos para que la opinión, al conocerlos, forme juicio claro sobre los mismos' (p. 14). However, even though Hidalgo claims that his is not an interpretative undertaking, the information that he provides for any future historical study is selected and therefore subjective. Similarly, Valdivielso claims that his compilation is not a critical account of the events:

> No aspiran a constituir una obra de análisis, ni de crítica sistemática y organizada, ni siquiera un relato completo y detallado. Son simplemente una "mirilla" personal abierta sobre el apasionante panorama de unos momentos decisivos para España. (post-scriptum)

And yet on reading through his text there is very little in the contents and style that differentiates it from Cossío's compilation. All of the writers examined in this chapter, despite their introductory or prefatory statements and the varying forms that their narratives take, aspire to the same end — to convince the reader that their opinion, interpretation or account of the events is the correct one.

The authors employ a series of strategies to convey an impression of accuracy and truth. One of these is to include verifiable evidence, in the form of newspaper reports and articles,[17] Parliamentary speeches,[18] government addresses regarding the Revolution,[19] political conversations and speeches pronounced at meetings and similar gatherings,[20] trial proceedings,[21] numerical data,[22] witness reports,[23] letters,[24] photographs,[25] and revolutionary documentary evidence such as leaflets and edicts.[26] Because many of the authors in this chapter openly admit their personal views, each one has to ensure that his or her version is perceived to be the real one. By basing the narrative on factual evidence, the information presented does not appear to be manipulated, in this case, in favour of a particular political line. It is interesting to note that in the more 'fictionalized' works of subsequent chapters the same verifying strategies are used.

There are other more subtle and interesting strategies used by the authors in their quest for the reader's full confidence. For example, in order to confirm the reliability of his text, Azaña begins with a statement signed by fifty intellectuals and middle-class professionals (including writers, journalists, composers, architects, and doctors) claiming that the court action taken against him is unwarranted and intolerable:

> No se ejercita en su contra una oposición, sino una persecución. No se le critica, sino que se le denosta, se le calumnia y se le amenaza. No se aspira a vencerle, sino a aniquilarle. Para vejarle se han agotado todos los dicterios. Se le presenta como un enemigo de su patria, como el causante de todas sus desdichas, como un ser monstruoso e indigno de vivir. (p. 5)[27]

By including this statement Azaña demonstrates that even if he did not enjoy their political support, he certainly had the moral support of many respectable members of society throughout Spain. Supposedly, these influential figures would not have lent their name to such a book or statement if they were not sure of Azaña's integrity and innocence. In addition, Azaña employs another common technique to corroborate the claims he has made and in this way ensure that his version is deemed to be the most truthful, against all the other 'false' suppositions about his whereabouts and deeds. He stresses that he only includes that which he has personally witnessed or which he has been told about by reliable witnesses: 'Incluyo estrictamente mis andanzas personales o las ajenas cuando me constan por referencias indisputables u observación directa' (p. 103), a technique most commonly used in the chronicles and personal testimonies examined in later chapters. It is worth noting that Karl does not only employ witness reports; he also claims to be able to provide witnesses who will back up his allegations, 'testigos (que requeriremos si por acaso fuera necesario ante la autoridad judicial)' (p. 142). Paradoxically, the fact that most of the texts rely to such a great extent on first-hand witness reports and yet contradict each other nullifies much of their credibility. Thus, the 'facts' expressed in each and every case must be taken cautiously.

The reader's faith in Azaña, who has actually taken part in the events, as a reliable source of information is sought by El Caballero Audaz and Karl with their investigative journalist technique. Although they have not directly witnessed the events they deal with, their account will in this way appear to be researched and, consequently, accurate. In Part II of *Traidores a la Patria*, the relevant section of El Caballero Audaz's text, the author relates his trip to Asturias, prompted by the desire to find out the real events that took place during October and to discover if the allegations made by the revolutionaries about the government forces are true. Given that the text will adopt a clear political stance, as indicated by the author from the start, the discovery which El Caballero Audaz purports to undertake is in essence already decided upon.[28] Initially, El Caballero Audaz structures his account around the steps taken by General Bosch and his troops as they entered Asturias charged with the mission to crush the Revolution. Thus, the author meets the principal focal points of the Revolution in chronological and geographical order. As indicated in Chapter 1, the narrative takes the form of investigative journalism as the author describes his journey to León and then across the mountains to Asturias, interviewing witnesses as he passes through the villages.[29] Accordingly, Chapters 2, 3, and 4 take the same format — the author describes how his surroundings have been visibly affected by the fighting as he drives through the region, transcribes or describes conversations between him and the witnesses (Edmundo Estevez [Chapter 2], a young telephone operator [Chapter 3], and a rebel [Chapter 4]), and concludes with a few paragraphs in which the author outlines his political position. From Chapter 5 onwards, however, the author changes his approach and the remaining five chapters take the form of political tracts where the author expresses his opinion on the political situation without introducing any other material, as he has done in the other chapters, which may divert the reader's attention. It appears as if the author has changed his priority in the course of the writing and is increasingly concerned with stating his own political point of view and less with setting out the grounds on which he has based his opinion.

Unlike El Caballero Audaz, Karl, who is more concerned with examining the main figures of the Revolution and delving into official documentary evidence, maintains his investigative format throughout.[30] Despite Karl's consistency, his narrative is clearly a propagandistic exercise in which the investigative value is cancelled out, just as in the case of El Caballero Audaz, by the palpable presence of the author's prejudiced and preconceived ideas; rather than basing his conclusion on the research carried out, the investigation simply manoeuvres around a foregone conclusion. It could be argued that this is the case in all of these texts; all the authors prior to composing their work have a clear idea of the message they want to convey. However, added to the usual misinformation, whether deliberate or not, and the manipulation of the facts, Karl's abusive language and lack of subtlety, also applicable to El Caballero Audaz, as well as the emergence of certain inconsistencies, accentuate the unreliability of the narrative, especially for those of us examining this issue with the benefit of hindsight. The most significant of these concerns the claims made by Karl about when, with regard to the Revolution, he is composing his text and, consequently, how much of his judgement about the events can be attributed to his forecasting ability and how much is based on what he has witnessed. Fifty pages into the 'Libro Segundo', the section dealing with the Revolution in which Karl examines the suspicious action of the Spanish government and its influential supporters, the writer refers for the first time to the outbreak of the Revolution: 'Cuando estábamos escribiendo este capítulo, empezaron a sonar en la calle las primeras descargas de la Revolución' (p. 180). Accordingly, all the criticisms and allegation that he makes prior to this should be attributed to his perceptiveness.[31] The fact that the predictions made in the first fifty pages are realized implies that the rest of the narrative, especially the forecasts about what may happen in the future (after the Revolution) or what may have been the result of a revolutionary victory, should also be regarded as being credible and reliable. However, there are numerous references to the Revolution in the fifty pages in question that contradict the writer's alleged wisdom and perspicacity.[32] There may be two explanations for this inconsistency. In the first place, it may be the case that Karl decided to change the order of the chapters prior to the work's publication and failed to spot the inconsistency. Alternatively, the author's assurances may have been a badly executed manipulative strategy geared towards making his predictions seem the result of his sharpness and understanding of the situation and not merely an interpretation of what he has witnessed, as stated above. Regardless of the origins of the inconsistency, the fact that it exists undermines precisely that credibility which the author pursues.

The techniques which guarantee the verifiability of the text are important if the reader is to believe the assertions which the author makes, vital given that the aim of the latter is to convince the reader to adopt a particular political stance in view of the events which he has described and interpreted. The historical and political priority in these texts means that, contrary to what we might expect, the details and the intricacies of the Revolution are not dealt with. Rather than recount its course the authors' concerns lie in the reasons for its failure, those responsible for letting such a situation emerge, and other similar politically wide-reaching issues. Thus, the factual narratives on which I am concentrating in this chapter are, for the most part, included in texts dealing with the more general issue of Spanish politics during the 1930s, which as already pointed out became increasingly polarized. The need to choose between the left and the right, or 'Moscú o Berlín',[33] is evident, as well as the idea that only extreme positions exist.[34] Accordingly, Maurín clearly indicates in his prologue that the two alternatives are: 'Socialismo libertador o putrefacción fascista' (p. 45). In the prologue written to the second edition of this same text, published in 1966, Maurín comments that the main point he was trying to make in 1935, and which, in retrospect, proved to be right was this: 'Si la España de los tiempos de la República no llevaba a cabo la revolución democrático-socialista, inevitablemente triunfaría la contrarrevolución fascista, que se eternizaría' (p. 2).

A quick glance at all the texts in this chapter reveals that one recurrent theme is the authors' judgement of what the Republic has achieved (or not) up to the point at which the government has switched from having a socialist majority (after the 1931 elections) to a right-wing majority in 1933, allegedly bordering on the fascist and prompting as a result the 1934 uprising. Clearly, each of these authors had his or her idea of what the Republic signified and what political measures should have been taken after the elections of 1933. For Oliveros the outbreak of the October Revolution is the culmination of the socio-political problems which he examines. He is more concerned with criticizing the socialist leaders for having driven the miners to slaughter while acting in the knowledge that they would be protected, than with describing the battles and revealing names and dates. Oliveros believes that the socialists used the threat of fascism, insignificant in his opinion, as a pretext for taking over the government following their electoral defeat in 1933.[35] He argues that the socialist Revolution had been a move against the Republic as voted for in 1931:

> Si la revolución hubiese triunfado, ¿subsistiría la República votada por España el 12 de abril de 1931? No, porque España no votó ese día una República federal ni socialista, sino una República de convivencia nacional. (p. 376)

This does not mean that Oliveros' opinion of the Republic is a favourable one. According to him the root of the Republic's problematic existence can be traced to the failure to adhere to the initial proposals behind it:

> Después de instaurada la República, en vez de conservadora, como se había ofrecido al país, se la hizo derivar en un izquierdismo que pretendía ser semi-soviético y semi-burgués, y que no era otra cosa que una confusión, desconcertante, sembradora de zozobras. (p. 380)

Karl, Valdivielso and El Caballero Audaz are much more critical of the Republic. While Karl describes the democratic process which elected the Republic as 'la pistola puesta en manos del pueblo niño, para que se salte la tapa de los sesos' (p. 302), Valdivielso refers to the Republic as 'el fracaso de un sistema' (p. 5) and 'una de las mayores desventuras sufridas por mi patria' (p. 7), and El Caballero Audaz goes as far as to call for a plebiscite to decide whether Spain should remain a Republic or go back to being a monarchy (194–95). For his part, Cossío uses the chaotic experience of the first years of Republican rule, the ensuing October Revolution in which he claims ex-members of the government were involved,[36] and the electoral programme of the Frente Popular with their 'glorificación de la revolución de octubre' (p. 325), to explain why Franco's rebellion in July 1936 was so necessary.

Whilst the Revolution is strongly condemned by the right-wing writers, they do not all directly criticize the working class for their involvement. Oliveros, for example, who takes a centre-right political stand, expresses admiration for the workers: 'Su natural es bondadoso, de abnegación, de adaptación a la disciplina' (p. 398). He also claims to understand the difficult situation in which they live, admitting that many of the social problems in Asturias are directly attributable to the greed and ignorance of the 'patronos' during the previous decade:

> En gran parte la culpa de que las luchas sociales tuviesen en Asturias por esos tiempos un cierto carácter cruento debióse a la incomprensión de un patronado ayuno de toda preparación intelectual moderna y con un lastre de ideas regresivas en el cerebro que le impedía asomarse a la realidad del mundo nuevo en marcha. (p. 65)

On the other hand, he does refer scathingly to the socialist leaders for not knowing how to make the most of the favourable historical and political climate offered by the new Republic. For most, the leaders of the Socialist Party, with their relentless spread of propaganda, are entirely responsible for the radicalization of the working class and for launching them into 'la locura de una insurrección fratricida'.[37] The leaders are further censured for running away and hiding while the workers bear the brunt of the consequences of the revolutionary defeat. For Cossío, who differentiates between the leaders, 'socialistas de café' (p. 47) who follow 'socialismo de club' (p. 46), and the workers, 'comunistas de la mina' (p. 47), the latter are exploited by the socialist bourgeoisie who merely desire to be back in power. For much of the right wing the issue is not the protection of the values of one social class or another but rather the defence of the 'Patria' from the 'grosera nostalgia de Poder' of the socialists.[38] In the extreme right-wing texts the only sector of society fully pledged to the 'Patria' is the army. Consequently, it is the only group that is acclaimed. For example, Valdivielso is even critical of the wealthy members of society who have not donated money to the restoration of the forces of law and order despite being the 'principales beneficiarios del sacrificio de la fuerza pública' (p. 200). As Mirta Nuñez Díaz-Balart suggests, the monopolization of the term 'Patria' by the right and the meaning which it had adopted explain some of the left-wing feelings against the notion of patriotism: 'La derecha [. . .] había monopolizado el término "patria", llamando a su defensa por encima de los intereses de clase'.[39]

What is particularly interesting about these texts is the fact that they demonstrate the political divisions that existed at this time not only between those on the left and those on the right, but also between those at the extreme and moderate ends of each political side. While right-wing criticisms against the left-wing Republican government, which ruled from 1931 to 1933, are to be expected, more remarkable is the fact that the right-wing government in power from 1933 and during the Revolution also becomes a target of its own side. Thus, Lerroux, Samper and Gil Robles come under attack from the extreme right wing for their feebleness in dealing with the Revolution,[40] and Karl ascribes the ineffectiveness of the government to the fact that it is dominated by Jews and Masons. This writer, who uses grandiloquent and exultant expressions to extol fascism and would surely dispute the insignificant status which it is given by Oliveros, is very critical of the bourgeoisie for ignoring working-class misery, the intellectuals for supporting the Republic merely for their own benefit, and the workers' leaders for leading the ordinary working man astray.[41] What concerns Karl, Valdivielso, and El Caballero Audaz most, and is certainly a widespread concern amongst the right wing in general, is the fact that those most responsible for the Revolution have been pardoned and released from prison, a situation described by Valdivielso in a figurative way:

> Después de la lucha agotadora que el país acaba de sostener, y de la que ha salido vencedor, pero exhausto, desangrándose por las innumerables heridas que le hicieron, en lugar de someterle a la intervención quirúrgica de urgencia que está pidiendo a gritos le hacemos una aplicación de emoliente parlamentario a ver si se nos queda pronto en las manos y acaba de sufrir de una vez para siempre. (p. 195)

For Karl the risk of Revolution in Spain will always be present while the country's enemies continue to be protected by the State.[42] He argues that stricter measures should be taken, not surprising in a man who is especially supportive of Mussolini's fascism and even more so of Hitler's conduct in Germany. Hidalgo, criticized precisely by these writers, is himself critical of the government in power after the Revolution for holding him, as Minister of War, responsible for the government's lack of preparations in preventing and combating the Revolution. In order to highlight his support for the army and his patriotism, which is put in doubt by sectors of the right wing, he constantly praises the army as an institution that is devoted to Spain and pays tribute to many of the commanding officers who were involved in crushing the Revolution (and which he appointed) including Doval, Yagüe, and Franco.[43]

Turning our attention to the other end of the political spectrum, although the extreme positions of the right-wing texts are not as clearly manifested in the few left-wing texts examined in this chapter, it is generally agreed that there were also deep-rooted divisions between the socialists, the communists, the anarchists, and other left-wing groups, as well as within the PSOE itself: the '"centrismo" de Prieto frente a socialismo revolucionario defendido por Largo Caballero y las Juventudes socialistas'.[44] In the introduction to *Documentos Socialistas*, A.G. explains the motivation behind this work, alluding to the increasing split in the Socialist ranks and calling for unity in order to be able to effectively hold out against fascism:

> Que su lectura y la reflexión sobre ella sirva para que nadie se sienta socialista de "Claridad" o socialista de "Democracia" o socialista de cualquiera de los semanarios provincianos que ahora tanto comienzan a abundar, combatiéndose unos a otros, sino que todos nos sintamos simplemente socialistas. Para que se borre de todos la mala idea de la escisión. Para que el Partido Socialista Obrero Español siga siendo uno, indivisible e indestructible y de acuerdo con las normas y la trayectoria seguida desde su fundación, permanezca como el pilar más firme de las reivindicaciones sindicales y políticas del proletariado español. (pp. 13–14)

Further examples of the left-wing split are demonstrated later where a larger number of texts are examined. The Republican governments prior to and after the October Revolution also come under attack from the left wing. Maurín, who believes that the proletarian revolution, 'la toma del Poder político y económico por la clase trabajadora' (p. 46), is the only alternative left after the failures of the monarchy, the Dictatorship and finally the Republic, refers to the latter as 'un fracaso, casi espectacular, más rápido aún, más fulminante que el de la misma dictadura de Primo de Rivera' (p. 47), which, in less than four years, 'se ha desgastado completamente' (p. 45). Bergés, who takes a more moderate stance, considers the failure of the Republic as predictable:

> Lógico el fracaso, por timidez revolucionaria, debilidad humana, bondad doméstica y precaria, o cobardía remolona, de los primeros gobernantes de la República, inclusos los dirigentes socialistas. (p. 31)

She believes that the socialists, who were seeking a revolutionary solution to the critical socio-political situation faced by Spain, were wrong to form part of the Republican government, and the bourgeoisie, which dominated the government after November 1933, were careless to totally exclude socialist representation in the Cabinet, the only factor which could safeguard a peaceful compromise.[45] All in all, despite the hopes which had initially been placed on the Republic and the joy which had greeted it, these texts demonstrate that both sides soon became aware of its shortcomings. Hence its failure does not appear to come as a surprise, neither for the left nor for the right.

Due to their lack of details, the researcher using these texts as a single source will not acquire a complete vision of the events. In other words, knowledge of the course of the Revolution, the number of victims, the places where the battle was most intensely fought, and other such data are taken for granted. The texts are nevertheless interesting for other reasons, not only for the author and the contemporary reader but also for today's researcher. The authors aim to explain the causes of the Revolution, examining Spain's recent political history if necessary, and to criticize the way the Revolution has been handled, either for being too repressive or too lenient. Whether intentionally or not, however, they also manifest a series of characteristics which, apart from being interesting in themselves, are relevant to all the texts on the Revolution examined in this study. Firstly, they are a good source to turn to, particularly in the case of the autobiographical texts, in order to clarify some of the contradictory statements that emerge in the texts that are examined in later chapters. Thus — just to mention a few examples — in the final speech which he gives during his trial, transcribed in *Documentos Socialistas*, González Peña denies any involvement in the robbery of the Banco de España; Hidalgo explains why the Vega arms factory fell to the revolutionaries so quickly, an incident blamed on him; and Azaña's true escape from Barcelona, supposedly via the sewers of the Catalan Parliamentary building, is revealed.[46] The texts also provide information about each other: Valdivielso mocks Diego Hidalgo and his book,[47] examined here, while Bergés ridicules the newspaper which Valdivielso writes for, describing it as a 'curioso periódico medieval que realiza la estupenda broma de llamarse "El Siglo Futuro"' (p. 168). Although the reader at the time is only likely to have been interested in those books endorsing his own political position and providing the 'correct' interpretation of the events, for today's researcher a full study of all the texts should help to yield a fuller picture of the conflict.

Secondly, one of the factors which make the texts examined in later chapters more novelistic, or based more on the imagination, is the extent to which the episodes and anecdotes narrated are fictionalized. In the 'factual' texts in this chapter some of those incidents are referred to, and yet, although they appear to be less dramatized they are not necessarily more accurate. If we examine Maurín's unembellished account of Aida

Lafuente's heroic death and compare it to Taibo's version, as it appears in his exhaustive study of the Revolution, we find that Maurín, just as most writers of the time, claims that she died in combat.[48] Aware that he is contradicting the most popular version, Taibo rejects it and insists that she was executed along with seven other revolutionaries.[49] The usual unfounded claims of violence made by the right wing against the revolutionaries are also found in these 'factual' texts. For example, Valdivielso claims that the children of the Civil Guard had their eyes poked out by the revolutionaries in an act of revenge (p. 199), and he disseminates the story of the three young girls who were raped and shot dead by four miners (p. 209), who were later found to have been forced under torture to sign the confession.[50] The provenance of the revolutionary armament and the number of weapons which each of the fighting sides possessed are two of the most contentious issues. El Caballero Audaz is alone in asserting that the *Turquesa*, the boat which supplied arms to the revolutionaries, made eight trips to Asturias.[51] The superior number of fighters and weapons belonging to the revolutionaries is repeatedly given by the right wing as the explanation for their enemy's initial success. Accordingly, El Caballero Audaz alleges that while the government soldiers were very short of ammunition, thousands of revolutionaries had been able to acquire a weapon.[52] Similarly, the advantageous position of the revolutionaries is used by Karl to explain the ineffective action of the government forces:

> El trágico octubre. La fecha imborrable de los bárbaros. [. . .] La fermentida y canalla Revolución.
>
> A un lado, el Enemigo, con sus potros de apocalipsis: El Marxismo, el Anarquismo y la Masonería, bien armado; porque si una verdadera casualidad frustró, en parte, el alijo del *Turquesa*, se puso, en cambio, en las manos revolucionarias, nada menos que fábricas enteras repletas de dinamita, fábricas de fusiles, fábricas de cañones. [. . .]
>
> Al otro lado, un Ejército destruido por Azaña, aniquilado por sus leyes, "triturado" por su sistema, sin efectivos, sin ropa, sin dotación. ¡Casi desecho [*sic*]! (pp. 16–17)

Naturally, the information offered by Maurín is diametrically opposed to that of El Caballero Audaz and Karl:

> Las fuerzas del gobierno, dos compañías de guardias de asalto y una del ejército, disponen de toda clase de armas modernas, incluso de ametralladoras. Los revolucionarios utilizan principalmente la pistola, que resulta casi completamente inútil. (p. 151)

In fact, the revolutionaries were short of weapons until one of the Oviedo arms factories was taken, and even then, the shortage of ammunition was so acute throughout the Revolution that it is considered to have been one of the reasons for its failure.[53] Nevertheless, contrary to what Maurín writes, the government forces stationed in Asturias, despite being well armed, were initially few in number, leading to the already mentioned criticisms against the government and Diego Hidalgo in particular. These are just some of the many examples in which the original 'factual' texts give an inaccurate account of certain aspects of the Revolution when compared to recent historical studies. The inexactness of many of the details could be attributed either to unintentional misinformation or to the propagandistic objectives of the author. The exaggerated claims made by the authors against the enemy, characteristic of nearly all the texts from the most to the least fictional, suggest that the latter is the case. In these non-fictionalized texts the exaggerations, both against the enemy and in favour of their own side, are particularly prevalent in Maurín, Karl, El Caballero Audaz, and Cossío, in other words, in the most politically extreme texts.

Thirdly, due to their intentionally subjective nature, the texts in this chapter reveal the disbelief, sadness, disgust, and frustration felt by the authors which in turn convey the vexed and troubled situation in which Spanish society found itself following the Revolution. For example, Azaña mentions with sadness the slow disintegration and destruction of the Republic's institutions and laws, which he, as the first President of the Republic, was responsible for. Similarly, Hidalgo feels bitter at the fact that he is being accused of not dealing adequately with certain problematic situations which he believes he tackled to the best of his abilities; and in *Documentos Socialistas* A.G. expresses his concern about the constant bickering over party policy in the ranks of the Socialist Party. Azaña comments that in order to grasp the full significance of the Revolution the socio-political atmosphere, conveyed most convincingly by those involved in the events, must be taken into account:

> Quien pretenda escribir la historia de estos sucesos, no un cronicón anecdótico, ni un repertorio de insultantes polémicas, deberá, para dar a cada uno lo que es suyo, investigar a fondo el valor emocional de los antecedentes y la realidad psicológica a que aludo. (p. 101)

In this sense these texts provide a unique insight into the October Revolution.

The writers of these texts, most of whom are political figures or journalists, have set out not only to inform but also to provide political ammunition for those who seek to reinforce their version of the events. Thus, while Hidalgo and Azaña and the contributors of the *Documentos Socialistas* provide information and first-hand evidence, Bergés, and more so in the case of Karl, Maurín, Oliveros, and El Caballero Audaz, make use of selected information to formulate a political argument with which to arm the militant party ranks. The fact that the authors are explaining certain events and expounding certain arguments lead to texts in which logical and clear explanations are used, where theorists and similar historical precedents are referred to as examples, and in which the usual rhetorical devices are used, amongst them, rhetorical questions, repetition, and irony. Karl, who is the most satirical of the authors examined here, sarcastically criticizes the fact that Sargento Vázquez was executed while the socialist leaders were pardoned: 'La suprema autoridad del movimiento que costó tantas vidas a España y nos degradó ante el mundo, residía en el sargento Diego Vázquez Corbacho, del Regimiento de Infantería número 3. ¡Quién lo iba a sospechar!. . .' (p. 168). Karl, El Caballero Audaz, and Maurín are particularly inclined to satirize the enemy in their texts, so that when he describes Largo Caballero, Karl writes:

> Sin creer en la frenología, ni en las teorías de Lombroso, vamos a dar un pequeño retrato del célebre estuquista, afirmando que el mentón de Largo Caballero no es signo de *voluntad*, como pueden creer algunos discípulos de la antropometría, sino más bien que la barbilla del líder socialista es un maxilar aguzado y saliente a fuerza de horadar bajo la tierra, como los topos. (p. 148)

He also refers to Indalecio Prieto as 'don Inda' (p. 200) and to González Peña as 'Pancho Villa' (p. 157), while Maurín maintains that the government has been led 'por las señoras Samper y Salazar Alonso rodeadas de las otras damas de su corte de honor' (p. 124). In the most didactic works the authors directly address the reader, such as El Caballero Audaz who writes: 'Jamás, jamás, lo digo con la mano sobre el corazón, amable lector, me perdonaré haber sido la causa de tal alboroto' (p. 183), and Karl who calls on the readers to do something about the political situation: '¿Podéis dormir? ¿No se turba vuestro sueño? ¿No sentís el ramalazo crudo de la realidad? [. . .] ¿No veis cómo ruge la bestia delante de vuestros ojos? [. . .] ¿No la veis, durante vuestro sueño, en pesadilla horrible?' (p. 387). Typographical variations such as the use of italics and capital letters to highlight particular assertions are repeatedly found. Occasionally less subtle rhetorical devices are employed, such as by Karl when he introduces a question mark or a commentary in brackets to discredit an attribute conferred on a particular person: when he criticizes Horacio Echevarrieta he writes, 'ese hombre (?) pudo. . .' (p. 144), and when examining Largo Caballero, '. . .en el alma (?) del famoso señor Paco' (p. 149). The rhetorical dimension of these texts is particularly significant. As Bergés states, the extreme nature of the conflict and the deep divisions in Spanish society prevent any clear and logical explanation from being made:

La fogarata ha sido demasiado intensa para que en mitad de su llama pudiera nadie conservar la mirada serena y el juicio claro. Ningún español espiritualmente vivo ha dejado de arder en la pasión militante del movimiento revolucionario o de la resistencia contrarrevolucionaria. (p. 26)

Hence, there is no room for sympathy and the charges made against the enemy are unequivocal. The authors generate ridicule, disgust and horror and juxtapose them with the unduly positive attributes of their own side.

Clearly the complexity of the text, which can be calibrated in several ways, is an indication of the status of the reader to whom it is directed. Unlike many of the fictionalized texts studied later, where the style, register, and vocabulary used by the author to relate the course of the Revolution are simple enough to make them accessible to as wide a readership as possible, these political essays are written in formal registers, follow scholarly stylistic conventions, and employ specialized vocabulary, inscribing a certain level of abstract reasoning pertaining to the philosophical and theoretical dimensions of politics, rather than to the everyday consequences of voting for a given side. Similarly, the texts in this chapter refer to historical, as well as contemporary characters, thinkers, and events which would not be familiar to those not acquainted with this type of political discourse. Although, as indicated in Chapter 2, an increasing number of journals and newspapers of the time were ideologically committed and dedicated some space to divulging political theories, in these texts there are some references which only the most educated reader would recognize. Maurín, for example, refers to the Paris Commune and the Russian Revolution, and quotes from works by Lenin, Marx, Engels, and Trotsky, but he also refers to passages from European literary figures such as Oscar Wilde (p. 152) and Lissagaray [author of *Histoire de la Commune de 1871* (1876)] (p. 162), while Bergés refers to Voltaire (p. 52), and Cossío to Jovellanos (pp. 60–61), Oliveros quotes, amongst others, Victor Hugo (p. 375), and Karl cites Hitler (p. 154).

Some of the authors — namely Maurín, El Caballero Audaz, Karl, and Oliveros — vary their style depending on whether they are describing the Revolution or examining its causes and failure. For example, in his largely political text El Caballero Audaz describes at the start the spectacular mountain ranges of Castile and Leon: 'Braveza de las sierras, verdes, negras y azules en la lejanía, encinas y carrascales trepando hasta las nieves de las cumbres cual un ejército de negros soldados retorcidos' (p. 110). However, as El Caballero Audaz deals less with his journey to the affected regions of Asturias and concentrates more on presenting his point of view and on advocating the right-wing counter-revolutionary measures, so his descriptive efforts diminish. Because of their political and didactic nature there are few literary features of interest. Nevertheless, in those texts in which the Revolution is related to some degree, there are instances in which figurative language is used, especially metaphors, similes, symbolism, personification, and the already mentioned irony. The colour combination of the sky and the landscape blending in with the outline of the distant mountains is so evocative that Cossío compares the view which he enjoys with a painting:

A lo lejos empiezan a dibujarse las montañas de León, envueltas en luz. Luz de otoño, dorada, que subraya los azules, los blancos y los grises, afinando el perfil de la sierra con el trazo seguro de un experto dibujante. (pp. 27–28)[54]

When Maurín — in whose text the difference between the descriptive and the discursive narrative is most evident — describes the battles between the revolutionaries and the government forces, he selects the style and vocabulary that convey best the dramatic nature of the moment: 'La huelga corre y lo devora todo. Es irresistible. Para el volante, para la correa de transmisión, para la máquina. Para la ciudad' (p. 132). Although to comprehend the discursive sections some knowledge and understanding of politics is required, the vivid images which Maurín creates are easily visualized by any reader: 'Aquellos cíclopes saldrán, esta noche y mañana, de las entrañas de la tierra, y con sus barrenos, con sus picos, con sus cartuchos de dinamita, intentarán hacer saltar la Historia' (p. 149). There is a clear difference between the dramatic atmosphere conveyed in these sections, composed of short, concise sentences and powerful images: 'En plena lucha, detrás de una barricada. Los milicianos rojos combaten desde hace horas. Están rendidos de fatiga. Tienen hambre, sed, sueño. Y siguen firmes en su puesto' (p. 157), and the long-winded rhetorical discourse. Occasionally the descriptive and the rhetorical come together in the long lists which Maurín compiles and in which he makes use of anaphora in order to emphasize, as in the following example, the material as well as the spiritual strength of the revolutionaries:

En Mieres, lejos del fuego, se fabrican bombas de mano. Disponen de hierro, de acero, de dinamita, de maquinaria, de brazos, de deseos ardientes de ser útiles a la revolución. (p. 156)

For Maurín many of these symbolic images are just as powerful as his political statements, and for those who are not acquainted with the political terminology they are more meaningful.

However, not all of the writers vary the difficulty of the narrative as does Maurín. Oliveros, for instance, does not simplify the vocabulary or the style in the chapter in which he deals with the Revolution, as demonstrated in this example in which the critical situation lived by the Asturians is described:

Todo el horror de la tragedia. Días sin pan, sin luz y sin agua; días de espanto en los que la muerte, enseñoreada de la ciudad, surgía a cada instante; desaparecía y volvía a surgir, haciendo presa o soltándola, como en juego mefistofélico con la vida. (p. 397)

Neither does Azaña who, rather than deal with political theories, concentrates on his personal experience. Thus the core of the text is made up of his actions, his feelings, and what he sees, the latter being particularly prevalent when he deals with the boredom of his confinement aboard the prison ship *Galiano*. In the following example he gives a detailed and colourful description of the nearby hills and the distant horizon:

El país fragoso, no dejaba de ser apacible. Caminos de montaña, estrechados por la espesura de robledas y castañares, surcan las frondosas Guillerías, de formas tranquilas, sin la abrupta violencia de las sierras calvas. Una masía se enrisca, y el payés labra sus coles en los planos talados del monte. En lo hondo, un huerto, una era abastada de mies rojiza, un molino. Desde tal vericueto la banda gris del mar, muerto en la distancia, y cerrando un ancho valle, el alzamiento grandioso del Montseny, bermejo y malva, erguido sobre las nubes. (pp. 39–40)

Just as with Oliveros the images created by Azaña occasionally take a more elaborate form:

El *Uruguay* corta inmediatamente la visual por el lado de tierra: mole sin gracia, pesada, ventruda, detonante su bronca rojez sucia en las fluídas tintas azulencas del cielo y del mar. La nave inválida resuena con fragor de máquinas y eyacula por un ijar caudales de agua hirviendo. (p. 158)

For Azaña, literary effectiveness takes priority over the simplicity and readership accessibility that Maurín aims for. There are very few instances in which Azaña makes use of rhetorical figures or of blatant political propaganda, a factor which sets him apart from the other writers examined here. Nevertheless, it must also be taken into account that despite his later involvement in politics, Azaña, unlike the other writers, had a literary background.[55] In this sense Oliveros and Cossío's texts are particularly creditable for, although they are largely discursive and journalistic, they nevertheless incorporate an element of literariness, with their skilful use of evocative descriptions and figurative language. This is demonstrated, for example, in this bleak description of the horror and desolation of the city of Oviedo, offered by Cossío:

La vitrina de un fotógrafo, roto el cristal, muestra intactas las fotografías en esa forzada expresión de la instantánea, con el niño iluminado en colores y riendo, con los recién casados de tiros largos, mudos testigos de la tragedia, sin que les alcanzase una bala. (p. 57)

In addition, Azaña's objectives are different from the rest. His is a confessional text in which he defends himself; all the rest of the texts, apart from Hidalgo's, concentrate on defending a particular ideology or political position. Linked to this is the fact that Azaña targets a different sort of readership to the others. Whilst Maurín aims to persuade as many people as possible, from all backgrounds, Azaña hopes to convince the influential middle class and intellectuals of his innocence, as it is they who will determine his political future. Whereas the masses followed and voted for an ideology — be it communism, socialism, or anarchism — the years of Republican rule had demonstrated that it was the intellectuals who controlled the government and selected its representatives.

Throughout this chapter these texts have been referred to as 'factual' in order to distinguish them from the texts examined in subsequent chapters which, although not entirely 'fictional', arrange the narrated events into a plot and display a degree of characterization, typical of the novel or story. These 'factual' texts do not aim to relate the story of the October Revolution. They merely include this episode as part of a wider political discourse. I have chosen to examine all the 'factual' texts together in the same chapter in an attempt to demonstrate that despite their generic diversity — the confessional texts of Azaña and Hidalgo; the political treatises of Maurín, Bergés, Oliveros, El Caballero Audaz, and Karl; the collections of articles of Valdivielso and Cossío; and the *Documentos Socialistas*, a compilation of varying documents — they are all composed with the same priority in mind: to produce an interpretative instead of a descriptive discourse. The authors, who strive to get across their version of the events, use this to promote their opinion of the republican years (which are, for the most part, judged negatively by both sides of the political spectrum) and more generally, democracy and other political issues.

Despite their diametrically opposed ideological stance the authors tackle their factual discourse in a similar way. The pursuit of the readers' full confidence is of paramount importance for all of them, and various means are devised to ensure that this is achieved, techniques which are similar regardless of the political leaning of the text: mainly the use of corroboratory information, personal experience, or reliable witnesses, and rhetorical figures of speech. Other techniques can also be found. Azaña, for example, includes a letter signed by members of the Spanish middle class to underline the veracity of his claims, whilst some of the right-wing authors use investigative journalism to demonstrate that their claims have been thoroughly researched. Despite these techniques, the texts contain contradictory and inexact statements, highlighting the care that must be taken in believing the allegations and claims of truth of even these 'factual' texts. However impartial or objective they claim to be, the writers carefully select the information according to their political bias, predisposing them to a distinctly prejudiced view of the events and consequently to a one-sided interpretation of the Revolution. Save for the odd allegorical and figurative example, these largely political texts are of little aesthetic value. They should be considered on the whole didactic texts, with which the authors aspire to convince the readers that their opinion, interpretation or account is the correct one. More importantly, this corpus of works is vital for an overall assessment of the prose narrative of the October Revolution. The complicated nature of these works and the erudite references suggest that the mostly uneducated working class was not necessarily the intended readership, as was the case for particularly the left-wing texts examined in subsequent chapters. Nevertheless, the texts are indicative of the general socio-political atmosphere which dominated Spain at a time in which its political future was undecided, veering from one extreme political ideology to another. Whilst all of the narrative prose about the October Revolution demonstrates this, these eight texts, of which five are right-wing, show most clearly the ideological arguments and theories that were used to arm those who would subsequently communicate the 'facts' about the Revolution and the accompanying political messages.

The Texts of the Repression

While the Revolution had been quelled and its leaders were in exile, or had been imprisoned or killed, the repression which ensued provoked widespread condemnation of the government's reaction, ultimately leading to its demise and electoral defeat.[56] As pointed out by Manuel Aznar Soler, the repression was not only of political concern; it became an important theme in Spanish literature as writers and intellectuals had also fallen victim to the government backlash:

> Estos documentos y testimonios prueban la protesta colectiva de los intelectuales españoles contra la represión del octubre asturiano. Y es que la censura de prensa, la supresión de la autonomía catalana, la clausura de locales sindicales y políticos, las interpelaciones parlamentarias, las torturas, detenciones o fusilamientos [. . .] fueron hechos objetivos que convirtieron entonces el tema de la represión asturiana en columna vertebral de la vida política y en tema candente de la literatura española.[57]

Thus, despite the government's attempt to cover up the alleged ruthlessness and irrationality of its own forces of order, the repression became an issue discussed not only at popular level on the streets, but also in parliamentary and official circles, and in intellectual and academic spheres, such as in 'Ateneos', universities, and other cultural institutions.[58] The texts included here are written examples of precisely that range of responses.[59] Despite their different socio-political and professional provenance and their intended readers — parliamentary, intellectual, and popular — they all coincide in their outright condemnation of the repression.

The first of the written responses, a series of official reports which I have included here as one entity, is the result of a detailed inquiry carried out by the parliamentary deputy Gordón Ordás at the end of 1934, in which he investigated the repression which took place in Asturias, León, and Palencia, the regions most affected by the Revolution.[60] Ordás' 'tarea investigadora' (p. 227) gave rise to a number of written statements, circulated probably in the form of pamphlets: 'A la opinión pública. La represión en las provincias de Asturias, León y Palencia' (dated 22 December 1934); 'Por la salud pública' (11 January 1935); and 'Llamamiento a los intelectuales' (18 February 1935).[61] Incidentally, Ordás was not the only deputy to investigate the repression. Marco Miranda and Fernando de los Ríos also investigated and produced reports,[62] and the speech of another politician, Álvaro de Albornoz, is reprinted in a compilation of the speeches which he gave in the run-up to the electoral victory of the Frente Popular in 1936.[63]

Ordás' primary concern is to convince the government and, failing that, all responsible politicians, that an investigation into the repression and in particular the conduct of the police force and the army is required. His main report on the repression, 'A la opinión pública', was meant to be read by Alejandro Lerroux. It was only when the head of the government declined to debate the matter in Parliament that he decided to make public his controversial findings and the letters containing Lerroux's negative feedback, which were subsequently printed and distributed secretly.[64] In addition, aware of the influential role of the intellectuals, with his 'Llamamiento a los intelectuales' Ordás called on 'el corazón caliente y el cerebro jugoso de los escritores, de los artistas, de los filósofos, de los sacerdotes, de los letrados, de los ingenieros, de los arquitectos, de los sanitarios, de los investigadores, de los economistas, de los maestros y de cuantos profesionales sean capaces de percibir toda la intensidad trágica de estas horas enormes' (pp. 297–98) to join him in his demands.

As a politician Ordás has to explain to his readers why an investigation into the repression must be conducted and convince them of the need to uncover the real situation in the affected regions. In order to fulfil his objective he takes two considerations on board. Firstly, he manifests his impartiality by maintaining that he has never been in favour of the Revolution, regarding this as an unduly drastic measure:

> Nadie ha puesto [. . .] más voluntad que yo para procurar que se disipara la ilusión revolucionaria del proletariado, ni nadie ha sentido más en lo hondo de su alma que lo he [*sic*] sentido yo el dolor de la revolución. (p. 261)[65]

His allegiance in this matter is to the Republic, not to any specific left-wing parliamentary group. Similarly, because for him the concept of justice is basic to the Republic's founding principles: 'República es justicia o no es más que una palabra sin sentido' (p. 295), he also condemns the government's ruthless reaction. He denies and mocks the exaggerated allegations made by this sector, in particular Gil Robles, Cambó, Calvo Sotelo, and Fernández Ladreda, that this has been the worst Revolution ever in the history not only of Spain but of the world, describing it instead as 'el estallido de una revolución de gran ímpetu inicial y de menguado alcance, con los heroísmos y las ruindades propios de todas' (p. 262).

Ordás contests the alleged insensitivity and brutality of the revolutionary conduct.[66] He focuses on the need for the pursuit of the truth in order to achieve justice. If the masses are to continue to have faith in the Republic and its laws, regardless of whether it is led by the left or the right, the government must treat both sides equally.[67] Ordás goes one step further and warns that unless these issues are acknowledged and acted upon, Spain's future political stability is under threat; the social and political polarization in Spanish society will become so acute that it will be irreconcilable.

A second strategy which Ordás employs in order to appear impartial is to provide verifiable evidence so that the report on which the politicians are to act appears to be the result of diligent research and is completely reliable. He lends credence to his report by insisting on the accuracy of the allegations and the reliability of his sources: he quotes first-hand accounts and gives the names of countless witnesses and victims or, in those cases in which they choose to remain anonymous, assures the reader that he has a record of their names.

If he is to reach the moderate politicians, regardless of their political affiliation, Ordás has to tender a range of arguments which will be of interest to the left and the right. This is what he does in these pamphlets, making them so different from most of the other texts examined in this chapter. Aware of the suspicions which his writings will arouse amongst the right wing he offers them a legitimate reason why they should support his initiative, insisting that the false rumours against the government forces will cease once the secrecy surrounding the repression is cleared up. As a further consideration that he hopes will catch the attention of the more rational moderate right wing, Ordás argues that Spain's reputation as a developed, just, and civilized nation is at stake.

Rather than aim at a specific political group, Ordás calls on the 'republicanos auténticos' (p. 260), reminding them what the Republic stands for and warning them that it is under threat.[68] Ordás thus rejects both extreme positions: he repudiates the violent revolutionary approach as a political alternative (contemplated by both sides) and, equally, he censures the justification, indeed encouragement, of the excessively harsh reaction to the Revolution, and the hypocrisy of the right in general for having provoked it in the first place. While he agrees that war and crime must be punished (referring to that of the revolutionaries), he feels that this also applies to the repression that ensued. For Ordás the question boils down to this: anyone reluctant to uncover the truth about the repression and to bring those responsible to justice — in other words, those defending the government action — is clearly against the Republic. Consequently, those who espouse the principles behind this democratically elected system must denounce the repression and the government's attempt to cover it up. With regard to this issue, there is no middle ground and it applies both to the left and the right.

The second written response is an example of the intellectual interpretation of the repression. *¡Acusamos! El asesinato de Luis de Sirval* (1938) is a compilation of short pieces of writing, short and long, by different important writers, journalists, and politicians on Luis de Sirval, shot dead in suspicious circumstances while he was in prison.[69] According to Aznar Soler, Luis de Sirval 'constituyó para los intelectuales españoles la víctima simbólica del octubre asturiano' (p. 88).[70] Numerous intellectuals contribute to this text: Ovidio Gondi, Gabriel Alomar, Manuel Azaña, Luis Araquistain, Roberto Castrovido, Antonio Espina, Juan García Morales, González Peña, F. Gordón Ordás, J. G. Gorkín, A. Hermosilla, A. Pestaña, Indalecio Prieto, Angel Samblancat, R. J. Sender, Enrique Fajardo (Fabián Vidal), and Javier Bueno. It is not clear if the short pieces were composed for this compilation or if they had been published independently elsewhere and then gathered together at a later date. Neither are there any clear indications of the aims of the text although it could be the pamphlet which the 'Comité Luis de Sirval' published shortly after it was set up informing of its creation and its objective, namely 'exigir la depuración de las responsabilidades por su asesinato [el de Luis de Sirval]' (p. 57). In other words, it was written for intellectuals by intellectuals to prompt further action against the government. The Committee's manifesto, where a reference to the pamphlet in question is made, is transcribed at the end of the text as it appeared in *El Mercantil Valenciano*.[71]

In *¡Acusamos!* the contributors express their admiration for Sirval and criticize the way in which his assassination was investigated. It is an intellectual response to the repression, where the contributors are concerned with expressing how Sirval's death has affected them personally and professionally as fellow journalists and writers, and in which they denounce the detrimental effects which a restriction on the freedom of the press will have on the principles behind the Republic. The work is composed of a variety of items. It begins with Sirval's biography, written by an anonymous author (possibly his brother, Eduardo de Sirval). This is followed by a fairly detailed re-enactment of his final hours, as described by Ovidio Gondi who was with him up to the moment of his death. Gondi narrates Sirval's last moments and quotes their final conversation in the prison cell, immediately before Sirval was pushed out into the courtyard and shot dead. Thus, the evidence provided by Gondi and the introductory biography provide the necessary background information which will ensure that the largely didactic statements which follow have a moving and compelling effect on the reader.

In 'Juicios sobre el asesinato de Sirval', the middle section of the text, the intellectuals write about Luis de Sirval and his death. Some of these pieces take the form of letters, such as in the case of Manuel Azaña's and González Peña's, while other contributors, such as Luis Araquistain, Indalecio Prieto, and Ramón Sender, choose to tell anecdotes in which they reminisce about important episodes and key discussions held with the now absent journalist. The majority, however, such as Gordón Ordás, Angel Pestaña, J. Gorkin, Antonio Espina, and Angel Samblancat, centre their attention on the government's lack of interest in tackling the problem of the repression and in its reluctance to determine those responsible for Sirval's death and the motives for the crime.[72] A. Hermosilla indicates that Sirval's death constitutes a backward step in Spain's political progress, and Gabriel Alomar and Roberto Castrovido refer to the irony of the death of someone who believed in freedom and justice at the hands of the republican system which he had so resolutely promoted and helped to set up.

As examples of Sirval's most recent work the text includes his last, and unpublished, third article on the October events, and his notes written in pencil (a list of names of civilians who died, and other brief notes). These, along with the constitution of the 'Comité Luis de Sirval', the first of which was established in Valencia,[73] comprise the third and final part of *¡Acusamos!*.

There are some features which link this compilation as a whole to the texts already examined in this chapter. Clearly, most of the contributors place emphasis on their denunciation of Sirvals' death, criticizing not only the soldiers responsible for shooting the journalist but also, in Gorkin's words, 'quienes han armado el brazo', in other words, the government, firstly for provoking these crimes, and secondly for letting them go unpunished.[74] Gorkin goes as far as to declare that Sirval's death will be the death of the government: 'Sirval y los cuatro mil cadáveres de la represión asturiana, [. . .] serán los enterradores del régimen actual' (pp. 35–36). All of the authors extol Sirval for his talent and professionalism as a journalist and for his courageousness, and most attribute his death, referring to it as his martyrdom, to these qualities. For this reason Sirval's death is evocatively and symbolically described by some of the authors, such as Gabriel Alomar: '¡Que la sangre de Sirval fecunde a España y la regenere como un bautismo! ¡Que sea estigma rojo en la frente del Odio, y vino simbólico para la pacificación de España!' (p. 26).[75] Thus the contributors link explicitly and implicitly, directly and metaphorically, Sirval's death with the government's imperative to keep the repression secret.

Apart from their obvious allegiance to the Republic and to the truth, described by A. Hermosilla as 'la antorcha del derecho y de la justicia' (p. 36), few of the contributors openly support or ascribe to Sirval a defined political stance. Instead they prefer to separate ideology and political viewpoint from the matter in question which concerns Sirval's unjustifiable death. In this way the issue is given an ethical dimension and the denunciations do not appear to be motivated by a desire to promote any particular party line. Nevertheless, it is fully agreed on by all of the contributors that Sirval had not only been a keen supporter of the Republic, but had also been instrumental in its establishment. For this reason the intellectuals are urged to vindicate Luis de Sirval, their colleague and friend, and to take the initiative in condemning the repression.[76]

Los crímenes de la reacción española (1935) was a pamphlet published in Spanish, English, German, and French by the Sección Española of Socorro Rojo Internacional (S.R.I.), aimed at informing any concerned citizens.[77] The S.R.I. criticizes the repression and asks for donations to help the families of the victims of the Revolution and to combat fascism.[78] The first of the S.R.I. manifestoes is directed at '¡Trabajadores manuales e intelectuales de todas las tendencias!' (p. 114). According to this pamphlet the S.R.I. had three aims: to raise money through donations to help the victims of the Revolution; to campaign against the repression and the death penalty and press for a total amnesty; and to advocate the unity of all the left-wing political groups into a Frente Unico which would fight effectively against fascism.

Although the S.R.I. calls on everyone's contribution the actual number of intellectuals who sympathized with or were affiliated to the Communist Party (to which the S.R.I. was related) were few.[79] The S.R.I. would have been aware that most of their militants and supporters were workers and accordingly pays tribute to the solidarity and generosity of the working class who responded to their calls 'entregando unos céntimos de sus jornales de hambre para la ayuda de sus hermanos encarcelados y perseguidos' (p. 114). Thus, without ignoring the influential role of the intellectuals, the targeted readership of this pamphlet, and of the organization's propaganda in general, were the workers: 'Todos los trabajadores' (p. 98).

The pamphlet is divided into two parts, the first of which deals with the allegations of torture and murder committed by the forces of order, and the second offering details of the organization and its contribution to the relief of the victims of the Revolution. Unlike the other two texts already examined, right from the outset this one takes a political, combative, and critical stance, and the prologue is suggestive of the accusatory form the pamphlet will adopt. However, despite taking a more defined political stance, this text does not overlook the need to corroborate the information imparted. Before the individual cases of torture and death are dealt with, an 'Advertencia previa' warns that the text does not contain a detailed account of *all* the crimes committed during the repression, as many remain shrouded in secrecy. Two messages can be deduced from this: firstly that the crimes that are mentioned have been thoroughly researched and accurately documented; and secondly that the situation is even more alarming than it appears in the text as there are many more crimes still to be uncovered.

The S.R.I. assures the reader that there is no reason to doubt the veracity of the text:

> En la intención de dar a estas páginas sus calidades indiscutibles de sinceridad y de justeza, nos abstenemos de recoger todas aquellas versiones, que no han sido plenamente confirmadas aun cuando tuvieran claros síntomas de verosimilitud.
>
> Fieles a este criterio, los hechos que a continuación se describe, constituyen una pequeña parte del acerbo de crímenes perpetrados durante el período represivo que se inició en Octubre bajo la más violenta ferocidad, y que aún no se ha cerrado en España.
>
> Creemos, no obstante, que el presente relato es suficiente para forjarse una idea de los procedimientos utilizados por las fuerzas gubernamentales durante y después de la insurrección.[80]

The content of this pamphlet is attributed to reliable sources and comes either from witness reports of the victims and their families or from the more official investigations carried out by Gordón Ordás and Marcos Miranda, both of whom are republican but 'ajenos a la propia conmoción revolucionaria' (p. 5), as well as from the detailed information given to Eduardo Ortega y Gasset, the lawyer of many of the victims.

The inclusion of some photographs provide more direct visual evidence. These include pictures of those considered to be responsible for the repression (for example, Gil Robles, Lerroux, and López Ochoa), and portraits of many of the civilians killed by the Tercio, as well as more dramatic photographs of people leaving the towns as the troops advance, and of rows of dead civilians and revolutionaries strewn across the ground. Many of these are accompanied by a caption enhancing the effect of the image, such as '¡Rapiña, crímenes, violaciones! He aquí el «orden» de la reacción' written below a collage composed of photographs of the Moors, or 'Un ejemplo de las formas de «pacificación» de la barbarie reaccionaria. ¡El «orden» de la reacción!' written underneath the image of a row of dead revolutionaries. William Stott affirms that photographs are often used in propagandistic texts as they are (mistakenly) thought to be more impartial and, therefore, more persuasive than words: 'A photograph is made from ingredients in the world; writing is made of words. Actuality vouches for part of any photo; one may have what a writer says just on his say-so. And his word, or his words, may not be sufficiently impartial.'[81]

The inclusion of Ordás' and Miranda's researched and respected reports ensures the credibility of the allegations. However, the corroborated claims are merged with other accusations that do not appear elsewhere, and can therefore be considered to be less reliable. The most doubtful of these is the alleged conversation which was mistakenly broadcast on the radio between the Minister Eloy Vaquero and the under-secretary Sr Echeguren, during which they allude to the falseness of the news that they have just imparted (p. 9).[82] Antonio Jiménez Plaza, a soldier in the Foreign Legion, is quoted as stating that 'El general López Ochoa se tomó la libertad de fusilar a un obrero en el cuartel de Pelayo, con su pistola y por su cuenta y riesgo' (pp. 42–43). In addition, this 'testigo presencial' reveals other shocking acts of cruelty committed by the army, identifying each of the perpetrators: prisoners who were burnt or buried alive; soldiers who were given ten pesetas for every hand taken from a man killed by him; officers responsible for blowing open the safe of a bank and pocketing the money; and a captain who, after giving his troops alcoholic drinks, ordered them to machine-gun women and children and to rob everything they could. Jiménez Plaza's allegations are, to my knowledge, unique to this pamphlet and I would be inclined to think that, although the actual testimony may exist, the nature of the soldier's allegations, if not invented, are certainly exaggerated.

Most indicative of the exaggerated nature of the information contained in the pamphlet is the S.R.I.'s manipulation of the facts contained in Ordás' report. Whilst this report is used to guarantee the reliability of the information in the pamphlet, there are instances in which the data are altered without warning. The clearest example of this is the discrepancy in the number of men who were apparently driven from Sama police station to Carbayín, where they were brutally murdered by the Civil Guard. Whereas Ordás estimates that the number of victims was twenty, perhaps a few more, the S.R.I., basing their facts on this same report, raises this figure to forty-three. The credibility which is conveyed with the use of Ordás' report, as well as all the others, is put into serious doubt when these deviations emerge. (Ironically, it is this sort of exaggeration which Ordás claimed in his report he wanted to avoid.)

The first part of the text, entitled 'Características de la represión', provides information about several aspects of the repression. First of all the dubious backgrounds of those in charge of suppressing the Revolution are examined. Secondly, the instruments of torture are described, including the 'trimotor', the 'tubo de la risa', the 'rueda', the 'baño de María' and the 'cepo'. Finally, the names of the civilians who died at the hands of the army as it advanced into Asturias are listed and their deaths related, and details of numerous individual cases of prisoners tortured to death by the Civil Guard are given.[83] Further cases of brutality are listed in the extract from the report produced by the prisoners of the Cárcel Modelo in Oviedo, inserted after the 'Características'. This report, originally addressed to the Republic's Attorney General and dated 24 January 1935, is a denunciation of the unimaginable and inhumane conditions and practices in that prison.[84] Rather than a summary of the report, the pamphlet includes an exact copy (of an extract): 'Son ellos mismos, los propios torturantes, quienes describen los tormentos que han sufrido, mejor de lo que pudiéramos hacerlo nosotros' (p. 67). Eight pages containing the signatures of all those prisoners who ratified the report follow the extract.

Despite its own use of misleading information, the S.R.I. denounces the misinformation propagated by the government, both in the right-wing press, in particular the newspapers *El Debate*, *ABC*, *Informaciones*, and *La Nación*, and in a booklet, attributed to Víctor Gómez de la Serna, containing the 'official' version of the Revolution. The pamphlet argues that: 'Las autoridades gubernativas y la censura les asistían eficazmente en la obra de inventar los episodios revolucionarios más espeluznantes y difundir las calumnias más infames' (p. 8).[85] What is most worrying for the revolutionaries is the fact that they cannot answer the charges because of the censorship imposed, a situation which is just as pernicious and intolerable as the repression itself: 'El primer crimen de la represión ha sido la campaña de mentiras pavorosas' (p. 21). For the S.R.I. this clearly demonstrates the campaign which has been waged against the revolutionaries, and which has been a deliberate government manoeuvre designed to turn the population against the losing side. The S.R.I. takes the view that the government's use of the soldiers of the Tercio and their chiefs, known for their ruthlessness, was motivated by their desire to crush the revolutionary movement. Once the fighting is over and the strength of the masses has been shown to be invincible the right-wing government escalates its attempt to annihilate the working class, as an active social movement, and its political and syndical organizations.

The S.R.I. provides its own interpretation of the post-revolutionary situation and the true and unspoken objectives of the government. The repression is to act as a deterrent for those already attached to the revolutionary movement, while the censorship is aimed at discouraging any sympathizers or future revolutionaries. With these two drastic measures the government strives to solve two problems at once: to avoid any further revolutionary threats while at the same time securing the backing of the (misinformed) population. The pamphlet does not only relate those cases in which revolutionaries are victimized; it also accuses the army of stealing from middle-class houses, shops, and bars, and of mistakenly arresting government supporters. In this uncontrollable and blind persecution innocent children, women, and men also become victims. Thus, whereas Lerroux and his Ministers claim to act in the interests of Spain and for the defence of its citizens, the pamphlet argues that the violence and determination of the army's conduct, endorsed and encouraged by the government, is motivated to a large extent by hate and a desire for revenge.

Finally, *La cárcel por dentro* is a unique and intriguing book consisting of portraits, sketched by the socialist Luis Quintanilla, of some of the prisoners with whom he was jailed. These include both well known political figures, such as Amaro del Rosal, Santiago Carrillo, Largo Caballero, Benavides, Javier Bueno, Zugazagoitia, and Companys, and anonymous workers. Julián Zugazagoitia wrote the prologue to the collection in 1934 while in jail in Madrid. I have included this last work not so much for the important aspects which it reveals about the written representation of dramatic events, but because it is of singular documentary value as a pictorial depiction of the suffering and boredom of the jailed revolutionaries, highlighted by Zugazagoitia. With his drawings Quintanilla presents us with what could be regarded as a documentary report, 'una visión exacta de la cárcel'.[86] Zugazagoitia writes an interesting and telling discourse about how art can eternalize history. He begins by describing the passage of the prisoner from the hands of the sergeant at the police station to those of the judge in the courtroom. Because of the exceptional circumstances and despite there being no charges, he is sent to prison where he must await his release, delayed by red tape. It is precisely this situation and the gloomy prospect of long days in prison which are conducive to the creation and the reception of art: 'Cuando esa desgraciada metamorfosis se ha producido, el tiempo no tiene precio, la ilusión de la libertad se amortigua y la aspiración al arte hace, solapadamente, su aparición' (pp. 7–8). The emerging creativity — choral music, popular song, literary readings, as well as drawings such as Quintanilla's — relieves the prisoners of their boredom and despair.

For Zugazagoitia, however, the artistic initiatives stemming from critical stages in history and evocative of real-life experiences have wider implications. With Quintanilla's sketches, whose models are 'representativos': 'El minero y el periodista, el campesino y el bancario, el jornalero y el dependiente — los modelos de Quintanilla son siempre trabajadores' (p. 5), the impact which the October Revolution has had on ordinary people is accurately recorded. Thus the drawings have documentary as well as artistic value:

> Hay en ellos, conseguidos con el mismo esfuerzo, dos valores distintos: el expresivo, consecuencia de la objetividad del artista, y el poético, obra de su personal manera de sentir el trabajo. Esa doble valoración admite otra exégesis. Lo expresivo es, en definitiva, si lo aceptamos con fidelidad, periodismo, actualidad. Sólo la poesía — y me sirvo de esta palabra arbitrariamente — apunta a la eternidad. La actualidad de estos dibujos es una actualidad consignada a la historia. Las jornadas de octubre, de las que nacen en definitiva, no son una anécdota pasajera, sobre la que el olvido pueda actuar con celeridad, sino un punto de referencia dramático al que, en lo por venir, se otorgará incuestionable valor. (p. 8)

By providing a visual depiction of the revolutionaries, the artist ensures that future generations are reminded of this momentous period in Spanish history and have a true image of those involved.

This brief analysis of four of the texts of the repression has shown that, in spite of their limited subject matter, many of the features already identified in the 'factual' texts discussed in the main part of the chapter are also evident here. Generally speaking, Gordón Ordás writes for politicians; the members of the Comité Luis de Sirval for fellow intellectuals; and the Socorro Rojo Internacional for anyone who is intent on fighting fascism, particularly the working class where its impact is most acutely felt. Each of the texts bases its contents on the interests of the author, whether these are the predicament of the Republic and Spain's uncertain social and political future, the importance of a free and truly informative press, or the implacable hatred that the government feels for the working class and its political organizations. Regardless of whether the issue of the repression is to serve as a subject to be debated in Parliament or as a pretext for raising funds for the victims, in every text the author's/organization's outrage is foremost. The aims of the texts determine the tone in which they are written; and what emerges here is a progressive change from a narrative that is primarily informative to one in which blatant criticism and denunciation take priority. Whereas Ordás sets out to divulge the details of the repression, Sirval's colleagues reveal the journalist's personal and professional background *and* criticize the government's lack of interest in his death, and the S.R.I. are mostly interested in condemning the unjustifiable action of the army and the Civil Guard, endorsed by the government.

1. Joaquín Maurín, *Revolución y contrarrevolución en España* (Paris: Ruedo Ibérico, 1966) [original edition published in 1935 with the title, *Hacia la segunda República*]; *Documentos Socialistas* (Madrid: Indice, 1935); Consuelo Bergés, *Explicación de octubre: historia comprimida de cuatro años de República en España* (Madrid: Imp. Garcigay, 1935); Manuel Azaña, *Mi rebelión en Barcelona* (Madrid: Espasa Calpe, 1935); Antonio Oliveros, *Asturias en el resurgimiento español: apuntes históricos y biográficos* (Madrid: Imp. Juan Bravo, 1935); Francisco de Cossío, *Hacia una nueva España: de la revolución de octubre a la revolución de julio 1934–1936* (Valladolid: Castilla, 1936); Juan Simeón Valdivielso, *Farsa y tragedia de España en el 1934: un año de preparación revolucionaria vista desde mi "Mirilla"* (Oviedo: T. de la Presa, 1935); Diego Hidalgo, *¿Por qué fuí lanzado al Ministerio de la Guerra? Diez meses de actuación ministerial* (Madrid: Espasa Calpe, 1934); El Caballero Audaz [José María Carretero Novillo] *Traidores a la patria: la realidad sobre Asturias y Cataluña. ¡Los responsables!* (Madrid: Ediciones El Caballero Audaz, 1935); Mauricio Karl, *Asesinos de España: Marxismo, anarquismo, masonería* (Madrid: Ediciones Bergua, 1935). All page references are to these editions.
2. In addition to the works examined in detail, there are four political essays which refer briefly to the Asturian October Revolution. Marcelino Domingo, one of the founders of the Partido Republicano Radical Socialista, and Minister of Agriculture, Industry and Commerce (1931–33), wrote *La revolución de octubre: causas y experiencias* (Barcelona: [n. pub.], 1935); Antonio Ramos Oliveira, editor of *El Socialista*, wrote *La revolución española de octubre: ensayo político* (Madrid: [n. pub.], [1935]); Rafael Salazar Alonso, supporter of the right-wing Partido Radical and Minister of the Interior (1934), published *Bajo el signo de la revolución* (Madrid: Imp. Sáez Hermanos, 1935); and Alicio Garcitoral, *España y la Verdad* (Buenos Aires: Ediciones Anaconda, 1937).
3. The text deals mostly with Oliveros' experience in the Reformist Party and his worsening relationship with its leader, Melquíades Álvarez. According to the author, his text is directed at anybody who wants to know more about the conflict between the two men.
4. El Caballero Audaz is the pseudonym used by the journalist and writer José María Carretero Novillo. He published a book immediately before the Revolution, entitled *¡Viva la revolución!: los malhechores de la política. Opiniones de un hombre de la calle* (Madrid: Ediciones Caballero Audaz, 1934), in which he called for harsh measures to be taken against Azaña and the left-wing parties.
5. Azaña was arrested under the charge that he had held secret meetings in Barcelona with the Catalan separatists and revolutionary leaders in order to plan the forthcoming Revolution. Azaña maintained that in fact he had gone to Barcelona to attend the funeral of Jaime Carner, a former Minister in his government.
6. Unfortunately the only compilations available are those of right-wing journalists. The strict censorship which was imposed immediately after the events prevented the revolutionary side from expressing their point of view in the press.
7. The Asturian born Antonio Oliveros was editor of the Gijón newspaper *El Noroeste*, from 1917 to 1931, after having worked in numerous other magazines and newspapers in Cuba, where he had lived from when he was a child up to 1915. He was actively involved in politics and campaigned against the monarchy and the Dictatorship.
8. Francisco de Cossío y Martínez Fortún (1887–1975) was the editor of *El Norte de Castilla*. He was the president of the Confederación de Empresas Periodísticas de España from 1929 to 1936. He was also a literary critic and an occasional poet.
9. For example, Walsh argues that 'there functions in historical thinking a subjective element different from that which is to be found in scientific thinking, and [. . .] this factor limits, or alters the character of, the objectivity which the historians can hope to attain.' In William H. Walsh, *An Introduction to Philosophy of History* (Bristol: Thoemmes Press, 1992), p. 98. Similarly, LaCapra claims that the traditional 'objectivism' and 'relativism' (or 'subjectivism'), which differentiates history from novel, are 'false options'. In

Dominick LaCapra, *History and Criticism* (Ithaca: Cornell University Press, 1985), p. 21.

10. Such was the nineteenth-century conception of history which dictated that 'if one only eschewed ideology and remained true to the facts, history would produce a knowledge as certain as anything offered by the physical sciences and as objective as a mathematical exercise.' In Hayden White, 'The Fictions of Factual Representation', in *The Literature of Fact: Selected Papers from the English Institute*, ed. by Angus Fletcher (New York: Columbia University Press, 1976), pp. 21–43 (p. 27).
11. 'La actitud de los escritores de una generación frente al momento social de su pueblo y de su época es [*sic*] un tema fundamental que interesa siempre, y que interesa más cuando el momento es más agudo, más hondo y más extenso. Uno de los problemas más difíciles que se le ofrecen al escritor [. . .] es la actitud a tomar como actor y como definidor en la contienda' (p. 13).
12. P. 20.
13. The aims of the *Documentos Socialistas* are: 'Ofrecer una base de meditación [. . .] sobre la necesidad de no descarriar las normas y la trayectoria del Partido y de conservar indestructible y firme la unidad de éste' (p. 5). A. G. could be Antonio Gascón whose letter to Indalecio Prieto forms part of the *Documentos*.
14. P. G. Collingwood, *The Idea of History* (Oxford: Clarendon Press, 1946), p. 235.
15. John Hellman, *Fables of Fact: The New Journalism as New Fiction* (Urbana: Illinois University Press, 1981), p. 4.
16. 'Plumas más ágiles y entendimientos más despiertos llevarán seguramente a cabo esa misión saludable, pues la política ha de ser aprendizaje para gobernantes y gobernados, y las enseñanzas deben tener siempre como base la Verdad' (p. 13).
17. Some examples can be found in Azaña, pp. 119–20, footnote 1, pp. 121–22, footnote 1, and p. 130, footnote 1; Karl, p. 153; Maurín, p. 171; and Valdivielso, p. 177.
18. These make up a large part of Hidalgo's text and can also be found in, for example, El Caballero Audaz, pp. 148, 187–89.
19. For example, El Caballero Audaz, p. 146.
20. For example, Cossío, p. 65; *Documentos Socialistas*, pp. 11–12, footnote 1; Karl, pp. 266–69; Maurín, pp. 129–30; Oliveros, pp. 382, 392; Valdivielso, p. 179.
21. These make up a large part of Azaña's text; other examples can be found especially in *Documentos Socialistas*.
22. For example, Maurín, p. 153.
23. For example, Bergés, who refers to Gordón Ordás' report (pp. 194–95); Cossío, pp. 40–41, 55–56; Valdivielso, p. 209; Oliveros, pp. 401–02; El Caballero Audaz, pp. 120–26, 134–35.
24. These make up a large part of *Documentos Socialistas*; other examples can be found in Karl, pp. 238–39.
25. In El Caballero Audaz.
26. For example, Karl, pp. 361–84; Maurín, pp. 139–40, 154–55.
27. Some of the writers who signed the statement include 'Azorín', José Bergamín, Antonio Espina, F. García Lorca, Paulino Masip, Valle Inclán, and Alejandro Casona.
28. At the start of Part II of *Traidores a la Patria* El Caballero Audaz makes a clear distinction between what he considers to be the enemy and the defenders of Spain: 'De un lado, los rebeldes, los facciosos y los traidores a España, unidos a las masas alucinadas por los sectarios de la antipatria, por el internacionalismo marxista y los secuaces de la masonería extranjera. De otro, lo más compacto y viril de la espiritualidad del país: el pueblo todo de España, sin distinción de clases ni matices políticos, que se ponía en pie para defender la unidad de la Patria y la continuidad de sus gloriosos destinos' (pp. 107–08).
29. Although the sections are given a heading rather than a chapter number I have decided to refer to them as Chapters 1 to 9 for the sake of clarity.
30. Some of the figures he examines incluye Horacio Echevarrieta, Francisco Largo Caballero, Ramón González Peña, Sargento Diego Vázquez, Manuel Azaña, and Angel Pestaña.
31. Karl is not the only one to congratulate himself for his ability to predict the Revolution. Valdivielso is surprised with the prophetic value of the articles he wrote: 'Muchas de estas notas cobran por los sucesos posteriores valor de profecía y resultan, leídas ahora,

verdaderamente impresionantes' (p. 10). El Caballero Audaz goes as far as to predict what would have happened if the revolutionaries had won (pp. 169–79).

32. For example, the Revolution is mentioned in pages pp. 144, 147, and from 159–65 where González Peña and Sargento Vázquez's involvement is dealt with.
33. Valdivielso, p. 6. In a letter written on 14 October 1934 and incorporated into his text, Valdivielso doubts the effectiveness of democracy, about which he writes: 'Tan anacrónico e inútil como el miriñaque, en el orden de la indumentaria femenina' (p. 6). He later adds, 'Berlín o Roma, el fascismo en una palabra, es más bien que una doctrina, una táctica, y buscando afanoso la doctrina, la hallé pronto en la Comunión Tradicionalista. Tradición española frente al empuje del internacionalismo bolchevizante' (p. 7).
34. It is worth noting that, in contrast to many writers and intellectuals of the time, Bergés clearly indicates that, although she is pro-revolutionary, she does not agree with any dictatorial forms of government, be it communism or fascism.
35. Oliveros writes: 'Demasiado sabían los dirigentes socialistas y sus aliados que en España no había arraigado el fascismo. Que las derechas dirigidas por Gil Robles habían repudiado el fascismo, que no eran ni son fascistas' (p. 376).
36. According to Cossío: 'Una huelga revolucionaria [. . .] en el que aparecen turbias confabulaciones de elementos que hasta hace poco gobernaron nuestro país, y aun dieron muestras excesivas y crueles de gubernamentalismo' (p. 17).
37. Oliveros, p. 407. He adds: 'A este obrero se le estuvo intoxicando dos años con propagandas disolventes' (p. 398).
38. Cossío, p. 17.
39. Mirta Núñez Díaz-Balart, 'Javier Bueno, un periodista comprometido con la revolución', in *Periodismo y periodistas en la Guerra Civil*, ed. by Jesús Manuel Martínez (Madrid: Fundación Banco Exterior, 1987), p. 75. The regionalist sentiments of the Catalans were another source of negative feeling towards the 'Patria'.
40. El Caballero Audaz claims that the revolutionaries were not frightened of the government forces: 'Los vencidos atribuyen su fracaso a ineptitudes, al no aprovechamiento de oportunidades, a flaquezas y deserciones de los suyos [. . .]. Pero no a la acción definitiva, enérgica y aplastadora, de un poder avasallador inflexible, de una autoridad superior en inteligencia, en medios y en decisión' (p. 136). Much of this criticism is directed at Azaña's military reforms.
41. Pp. 182, 177, and 176 respectively.
42. El Caballero Audaz, who believes that the revolutionaries do not consider themselves as having been defeated, is of the same opinion: 'La derrota no les había afligido; para ellos [. . .] lo pasado no era el vencimiento, sino un episodio malogrado [. . .]. Al final, el triunfo sería suyo [. . .]. Se creían en una tregua, en un compás de espera' (p. 134).
43. In his conclusion Hidalgo states that the army 'está dotado de una magnífica primera materia: el soldado, que es valiente y sufrido; de un cuadro de oficiales disciplinados, estudiosos y bravos, y de unos jefes inteligentes y decididos' (p. 189). Other examples of acclamation are found in pp. 69–70, 84–85, and 97–100.
44. Marta Bizcarrondo, *Octubre del 34: reflexiones sobre una revolución* (Madrid: Ayuso, 1977), p. 49. Eventually all the left-wing groups came together to form the Frente Popular. The political developments of the Spanish left wing from 1934 to 1936 are examined in detail in Bizcarrondo, pp. 48–76.
45. According to Bergés: 'Cuando la representación del partido socialista fue arrojada, literalmente arrojada, de la participación en el Gobierno democrático de la República, los excluidos se apresuraron a declarar que desde aquel momento quedaban cancelados sus compromisos y rotas sus vinculaciones con el régimen' (pp. 76–77).
46. *Documentos Socialistas*, pp. 167–69; Hidalgo, pp. 41–49; Azaña, pp. 118–19.
47. 'Ahora lo que hace falta es que se decida a publicar un libro que se titule "Por qué fui nombrado ministro de la Guerra". Porque eso sí que no lo sabe nadie' (p. 208).
48. 'El Tercio va a tomar una de las últimas barricadas. Hay allí una ametralladora que dispara sin parar, despejando el área de su radio de acción. La maneja una muchacha. Moros y Tercio disparan con furia y van acercándose. La muchacha sigue, impertérrita, haciendo funcionar la máquina de guerra. Se acaban las municiones. Entonces, la heroína, sola, de pie sobre la barricada, arrancándose el corpiño y ofreciendo su pecho a las balas, grita: — ¡Tirad, canallas! ¡Viva la revolución!' (p. 163).

49. Taibo bases his version on the notes taken by the journalist Luis de Sirval, later shot by an officer of the Tercio, and corroborated by Alfonso Camín and Juan Ambou. In Paco Ignacio Taibo, *Asturias 1934*, 2 vols (Gijón: Jucar, 1984), II, 58.
50. Taibo gives a full account of the alleged story and the real happenings (II, 156–60). According to him, 'Tendría que levantarse la censura en 1936 para que las tres mujeres supuestamente asesinadas recobraran su identidad. De la primera, Aida Lafuente [. . .] su personalidad en el movimiento revolucionario es conocida, así como la forma en que murió. La segunda, la "verdulera", se encontraba viva y sana, tal como había intentado declarar su madre ante el juez militar de Oviedo, que no había aceptado su testimonio. La tercera, Josefa Álvarez, escribía en abril de 1935 una pequeña nota que no pudo hacerse pública hasta enero del 36 [in which she denied the claims made against the revolutionaries and thanked them for being so attentive when she was so frightened]' (pp. 159–60).
51. 'El vapor "Turquesa" recalaba de continuo en las costas asturianas, trayendo su bodega llena de fusiles y municiones. Hasta su octavo viaje no fue descubierto por la Policía el tráfico criminal' (pp. 130–31). The most reliable cotemporary sources and current historical studies agree that the boat made only one trip, the same trip that was discovered by the police and that El Caballero Audaz refers to.
52. Pp. 114–15.
53. Even the right-wing Oliveros alludes to the precarious position of the revolutionaries: 'Los mineros entraron en Oviedo armados los más malamente: un número menor portaba fusiles [. . .] la mayoría escopetas y pistolas, con cartuchos de dinamita en el cinto la generalidad' (p. 395).
54. Cossío's brother, Mariano de Cossío (1898–1960), was actually a well-known painter.
55. *La velada de Bernicarló* (1939), *El jardín de los frailes* (1927), *La corona* (1930) are some of Azaña's literary works.
56. In his detailed study Taibo asserts: 'Según todos los testigos que el autor ha podido entrevistar, [. . .] el caso es que todos recuerdan tan sólo, como centro de la campaña electoral, la *amnistía a los presos de octubre*. Junto a esta consigna, escucharon también repetidamente las llamadas al castigo de los torturadores, las peticiones de reapertura de locales y de volver a ocupar los Ayuntamientos. Los demás elementos del programa del Frente Popular desaparecieron por lo visto de la campaña electoral.' In *Asturias 1934*, II, 214 (author's emphasis).
57. Manuel Aznar Soler, 'La revolución asturiana de octubre de 1934 y la literatura española', *Los Cuadernos del Norte*, 26 (1984), 86–104 (pp. 89–90).
58. Ibid., pp. 88–90.
59. Felix Gordón Ordás, *Mi política en España*, 2 vols (Mexico: [n. pub.], 1962), II, 253–98 (where 'A la opinión pública. La represión en las provincias de Asturias, León y Palencia' [pp. 253–59], 'Por la salud pública. La represión en las provincias de Asturias, León y Palencia' [pp. 260–95], and 'Llamamiento a los intelectuales. La represión en las provincias de Asturias, León y Palencia' [pp. 296–98] can be found); *¡Acusamos! El asesinato de Luis de Sirval* ([Valencia: Ediciones del Comité Luis de Sirval, [n.d.]); *Los crímenes de la reacción española* (Madrid: Ediciones de la Sección Española del Socorro Rojo Internacional, 1935); Luis Quintanilla, *La cárcel por dentro*, with a prologue by Julián Zugazagoitia (Oviedo: Fundación José Barreiro, 1995). Further references to these editions are given after quotations in the text.
60. In his memoirs Ordás gathers these reports together in one chapter as they all deal with the October Revolution, and they are sequential. I have included them here as one for the same reasons.
61. Ordás explains in his 'Notas ampliativas' that he went incognito to Asturias to carry out his enquiry: 'Sin más precaución que viajar mezclado con el pueblo en vagones de tercera clase ni otro disfraz que tocarme la cabeza con una boina vasca recorría las zonas en que la represión estaba haciéndose con una fría y sistemática crueldad. [. . .] Oí calladamente las conversaciones entre personas de diversas categorías sociales y recogí abundantes datos aislados' (p. 307). According to Aznar Soler the second of these was a pamphlet, 'folleto' (p. 88), suggesting that the other two were also.
62. Marco Miranda went to Oviedo to investigate the claims of repression which had taken place there. On 4 December he finished his report on the killings of Tenderina, Villafría, el Caño, San Esteban de las Cruces and la Cabaña, all of these districts of Oviedo. The

report was sent to the Attorney General of the Republic and to representatives of all the parliamentary groups. Nevertheless the government quietened the scandal that it provoked. Similarly Fernando de los Ríos left on 1 January to visit Oviedo and Leon and wrote a report of his findings. He intentionally lost a copy of his report which ended up in the hands of the French press and was subsequently published there. Fernando de los Ríos' report is included in Margarita Nelken, *¿Por qué hicimos la revolución?* (Barcelona: Ediciones Sociales Internacionales, 1936). These reports, as well as Ordás', were ignored by the authorities and did not come to light until 1936. Taibo, II, 155.

63. Álvaro de Albornoz, *Al Servicio de la República: de la Unión Republicana al Frente Popular. Criterios de Gobierno* (Madrid: J. M. Yagües, 1936), pp. 155–76. The speech referred to was given in Valencia on 1 December 1935 in memory of Luis de Sirval. Before dealing with the death of the journalist, Albornoz criticizes the attempts to cover up the repression and the government's refusal to condemn it.
64. 'Ya de regreso en Madrid [. . .] denuncié por escrito las atrocidades que había descubierto, primero al Excmo. Sr. Presidente del Consejo de Ministros y después con todos los detalles a S. E. el Presidente de la República, quienes no reaccionaron como yo esperaba ante mis acusaciones contra un poder bárbaro que deshonraba a nuestro régimen. Lejos de atendérseme en tan justa demanda, pues el primero llegó incluso al extremo coactivo de impedirme que diera estado parlamentario a mis informaciones [. . .] se comenzó contra mis derechos una sorda y mal disimulada persecución, tratándome en realidad como si fuera un delincuente. Ante aquella insólita conducta de las autoridades decidí hacer público el documento que contenía mis denuncias oficiales, así como las cartas cruzadas entre el Jefe del Gobierno y yo y el llamamiento que hice a los intelectuales' (pp. 307–08).
65. Ordás took a number of measures to try and prevent the Revolution: 'Desde que en el mes de abril de 1934 quedó bien manifiesto el propósito mayoritario del Partido Socialista Obrero Español de realizar un movimiento revolucionario si se les encargaba del Poder a las derechas acaudilladas por el Sr. Gil Robles, sentí yo la apremiante necesidad de emplear a fondo todas mis energías para procurar disuadir a las organizaciones obreras de aquel proyecto, que me parecía insensato visto desde el propio interés de ellas y muy seriamente comprometedor para la vida misma de la República, sobre todo al considerar que también el Sr. Gil Robles había dado a entender en un discurso por igual fecha que sus elementos desencadenarían la revolución si a las derechas no se les entregaba el Poder, que en su opinión les correspondía' (p. 306).
66. 'Porque si es evidente que hubo en la revolución actos vituperables, que repugnan a toda conciencia sensible y que deben castigarse con la adecuada severidad, también lo es que hubo verdaderos actos heroicos, que enaltecen el espíritu humano, y en general es obligado reconocer que preponderó en la revolución un sentido generoso' (p. 258).
67. 'No he pedido ni pido impunidad, sino castigo, para los crímenes cometidos por algunos revolucionarios; [. . .] quiero igualmente castigo y no impunidad para los crímenes cometidos por algunas autoridades. Pero en ambos casos castigo dentro de la Ley, que debe ser soberana en el Estado democrático' (p. 297).
68. In his 'Notas ampliativas' Ordás gives the names of some of those from the right wing who supported him, such as Diego Martínez Barrio and 'una comisión formada por elementos muy derechistas del Cuerpo de Ingenieros de Minas' (pp. 309–11).
69. Ignacio Carral, *Por qué mataron a Luis de Sirval* (Madrid: Imp. Sáez Hermanos, 1935) is another work wholly devoted to the life, work, and death of Sirval. Carral dedicates his book to '[la] amistad de juventud de quince años' (p. 13) which he shared with the victim, as well as to 'el sentimiento de justicia del pueblo' (p. 13). As in *¡Acusamos!*, the author re-enacts Sirval's assassination and records the government's ambivalent reaction.
70. Although here I am referring to the 1938 edition of *¡¡Acusamos!!*, according to Taibo's bibliography the original copy dates back to 1935. In Taibo, II, 246. According to J. G. Gorkin, the title of the book is based on Zola's *¡Yo acuso!* (p. 35).
71. 'Este Comité se propone editar en breve un folleto sobre la vida y la muerte de Luis de Sirval. Este folleto, que será una verdadera acta de acusación, servirá de documentación y de propaganda a los Comités que se constituyan y a los partidos y organizaciones de izquierda que nos den su adhesión' (p. 59).
72. Although the literary value of these short pieces is not worth examining, there are a number of figurative images, such as Gabriel Alomar's symbolic depiction of the workers'

movement in Asturias: 'Una pululación de obreros subterráneos que podrían ser un día semillas de una humanidad nueva, en el surco ávido de luz y aguas del cielo' (p. 26).

73. The Comité de Sirval was made up largely of journalists of diverse ideologies from Valencia, the city where Sirval was born. Shortly after the Valencia committee was formed another one was set up in Madrid about which there was no news because of the censorship. (José Díaz Fernández, Antonio Espina, and Sender were some of the most renowned members of this Committee.)

74. P. 35. Ordás, who also contributes to *¡Acusamos!*, is most concerned about this, as revealed in his pamphlets on the repression. In his piece he states: 'Si está bien que se pida la responsabilidad de los ejecutores directos de los crímenes, mejor estará aún laborar por el gran proceso que enjuicie y castigue a los Gobiernos responsables de tanta barbarie' (p. 34).

75. There are other examples such as: 'Una mano criminal, cortando de raíz la vida del egregio periodista, privó a la Patria de la luz maravillosa de sus crónicas; tumbó para siempre al testigo que tenía que bordar las páginas de la Historia con los hilos de oro de la verdad' (p. 33) from G. Morales, and 'Murió entre los trabajadores, con los trabajadores cuya memoria trataba de salvar inscribiendo sus nombres en el corazón del pueblo' (p. 43), from Sender.

76. Their determination to do this and the influential status of the intellectuals unnerved the right wing and led to allegations that the intellectuals and journalists were responsible for poisoning people's minds, one of the most common features of the right-wing texts. Sirval's anonymous biographer denies these charges, 'Sirval no era un comerciante ni *un envenenador de conciencias*; era un hombre de ideas y hombre honrado' (p. 9, my emphasis), as does Gondi in his comments on a girl who looks at him on the train: 'Intenta convencerse a sí misma de que un incendiario o un asesino — ¡lo que dicen los periódicos! — puede llevar gafas de carey y traje de impecable corte inglés' (p. 12). Gondi also makes reference to the violent feelings felt by the soldiers against the journalists: The captain who arrested Sirval 'afirmaba que él dejaría en libertad a todos los mineros y que exterminaría a todos los periodistas de izquierda, envenenadores del pueblo' (p. 16).

77. Another similar pamphlet is *La represión en Asturias: reporte sindicalista* ([n.p.]: [n. pub.], [n.d.]), published immediately after the events by an anonymous author or organization clearly in favour of the Revolution.

78. 'El S.R.I. es una organización sin partido; en ella caben todos los que odien la reacción y el fascismo, todos los que quieren ayudar a los presos políticos y sociales y sus familias' (p. 98).

79. Regarding the state of the Communist Party, according to Taibo: 'El Partido Comunista se encuentra muy débil orgánicamente. [. . .] se encuentran en la mitad de los efectivos que tenían antes de la Revolución de Octubre. [. . .] Sin embargo, una de sus organizaciones periféricas, cobrará una extraordinaria importancia en Asturias dada la situación en la que se encuentra la región, y permitirá desarrollar profundamente la labor de los comunistas. Se trata del Socorro Rojo Internacional. [. . .] Con un millar de cotizantes y menos de doscientos militantes, el SRI depende absolutamente de los cuadros comunistas. [. . .] Gracias a esta labor de los militantes del SRI, la presencia del Partido Comunista, muy débil en los medios obreros en materia sindical, se extiende utilizando el prestigio del Socorro Rojo' (II, 179–80). As to the political affiliation of the intellectuals, Aznar Soler affirms: 'Sólo una minoría militaba ya en partidos políticos obreros y, por ejemplo, la nómina de escritores afiliados al Partido Comunista de España era, en octubre de 1934, tan exigua como prestigiosa: Rafael Alberti, María Teresa León, Emilio Prados, Joaquín Arderíus, Pascual Pla y Beltrán, César Arconada, a los que debemos añadir los nombres de simpatizantes tan cualificados como Arturo Serrano Plaja, Luis Cernuda o Ramón Sender' (p. 87).

80. P. 6. There are other instances in which the veracity of the text is assured: 'Estos son los principales episodios de la invasión de Oviedo. Hay muchos más. Pero sólo hemos recogido los que están perfectamente comprobados y avalados por el testimonio del diputado valenciano Sr. Marcos Miranda, perteneciente a la Izquierda Republicana de Valencia. El Sr. Marcos Miranda ha recogido sus datos en el propio lugar de los crímenes' (p. 40); 'De todo ello hay testimonios fehacientes' (p. 58).

81. William Stott, *Documentary Expression and Thirties America* (London: Oxford University Press, 1973), p. 32.

82. Eloy Vaquero was Minister of Labour, not of the Interior (Portela Valladares) as implied in the text.
83. For example, the deaths of Fernando González Fernández ('Moscón'), socialist councellor in Mieres; Francisco Dapena, socialist mayor in Barruelo de Santullán; Domingo Pellitero, arrested and beaten for owning a communist book and a photograph of Galán and García Hernández; Juan Suárez, arrested for not letting a friend of the Civil Guard hide his car in his house; and Eusebio Fernández, arrested after being accused of blocking the road, León-Asturias, and preventing the troops from advancing.
84. For contemporary historical research this text is interesting as the report of the prisoners of the Cárcel Modelo in Oviedo is not included in any of the other texts that I have consulted about the Revolution.
85. These allegations appear in nearly all the right-wing texts on the Revolution and include the carving up of the dead Civil Guard Alonso Nart; the orphans of the Civil Guards whose eyes were poked out; the priest hung up and sold as meat in a butcher's shop in Sama; and the rape and killing of the three girls.
86. P. 5. Although the pages in this book are not numbered I have resolved this by taking the page after the title page as the first and numbering the rest successively. Accordingly, pages 5 to 9 correspond to the prologue. All subsequent page references to this text have been determined in this way.

CHAPTER 4

NON-FICTIONAL ACCOUNTS OF THE REVOLUTION

So far I have dealt with the political response to the October Revolution in the historical context of the Second Republic and the more specific intellectual and popular response to the repression which took place after the Revolution (Chapter 3). This chapter will be the first of five to examine the narrative response to the Revolution itself, with each one considering increasingly dramatized and fictionalized versions of the events. In this chapter the non-fictional works selected have been classified into four separate categories: Government and Counter-Revolutionary, Military, Religious, and Revolutionary. The one feature that these texts have in common is that they relate the course of the Revolution with the stated aim of providing a reliable and, in most cases, conclusive version of the events.

As will be shown in due course, many of these texts contain dialogue and re-enacted episodes which serve primarily to subjectify the experiences of the narrators or their protagonists. These elements, which are more commonly associated with fictional writing, are nevertheless incorporated into the non-fictional and journalistic forms of reportage and chronicle. In this body of works we find texts which relate the experiences of some of the victims as told by a third person, such as that of Sergeant Vázquez (written by José Romero Cuesta) and the religious victims of Turón (written by an anonymous author), autobiographical testimonial writing, such as the texts by Aurelio de Llano Roza de Ampudia and Manuel Grossi Mier, and political and official statements providing purportedly objective information such as the government report on the Revolution, *La revolución de octubre en España*. Some of the authors choose to narrate the episodes chronologically while others, in order to overcome the initial difficulties of relating a series of episodes which are happening at once in different geographical points, choose to do so geographically. The length of these texts and the degree to which the authors go into detail also differ — some are mere pamphlets, such as in the case of the government report, while others are quite substantial such as Jenaro Geijo's and Ignacio Núñez's (which comprises two volumes). Similarly some deal with the Revolution nationally, while others deal with more specific aspects of the fighting and concentrate on Asturias. In essence, all the authors whose texts could be considered in this chapter (including those not examined here) strive to convince the reader that their version of the Revolution is the most reliable.

Government and Counter-Revolutionary Texts

This first subsection examines the government and counter-revolutionary versions of the Revolution. The main text which I will analyse is *La revolución de octubre en España* (1934), the official government report following the events, written by an anonymous author. In addition to this I will examine Ignacio Núñez, *La revolución de octubre de 1934* (1935), which chronicles the revolutionary events as they took place nationally, and devotes Chapter 10 to the events in Asturias, and José Romero Cuesta, *El sargento Vázquez* ([1936]), which gives details of the role played by this sergeant who joined the rebellion, and considers the reasons why he was executed while the more responsible leaders of the Revolution were not.[1] There is a fourth work which, although not dealt with here, is worth mentioning as it too is a right-wing political response to the Revolution. *Octubre rojo: ocho días que conmovieron a España* ([n.d.]) by Reporteros Reunidos is a compilation of up to fifty individual short written pieces, arranged chronologically and divided into five parts, starting with the 1931 elections ('Esperanzas en abril') and ending with the Revolution ('Escenas asturianas de la Revolución').[2] Despite the authorship being attributed to a group of reporters, the uniform style throughout the work strongly suggests that it was written by one person only. In addition, apart from their brevity, there is no indication that any of the forty-nine pieces were actually published in the press.

La revolución de octubre en España (1934) is a valuable text as it reveals the exact version of the Revolution which the government wished to disseminate, while the other two offer information and display characteristics which are interesting for this study. In order to demonstrate how the revolutionaries unjustifiably went on the rampage, targeting specific honourable and religious members of society, the three authors use a series of manipulative strategies, namely the selection of facts, the alteration of information, and the use of blatant lies. The authors employ each of these to different degrees, but the final political effect is the same. Although the government report's estimation of the effectiveness of the Republic as a form of government is more positive than in the other two texts, on the whole the conclusions reached by the three authors coincide: Azaña and his supporters were unable to accept their electoral defeat in 1933; the action taken by the miners was wholly unjustifiable; the intellectuals, with their use of propaganda and the press, were responsible for inciting the Revolution; the religious orders and innocent civilians were needlessly made to suffer; and finally, the government forces fought bravely and systematically during the fifteen days covered by the events.

Before examining in more detail the manipulative strategies employed in the three texts, I will first examine their content. *La revolución* (1934) is the official version of the Revolution, a fact which should be taken into account when examining it. Accordingly, it should be an objective and informative account, and yet in reality it is one of the most carefully manipulated as it is the means employed by the government to explain and justify its own decisions and actions. This text is a mixture of factual presentation and anecdotal representation. The author insists from the start, and continues to stress in the epilogue, that his account is objective, impartial, true to life, and based on documentary evidence, with the information and photographs taken from newspapers of all political allegiances and official archives; none of the data will be omitted or tampered with. Although the text deals relatively little with details of the actual fighting, the author relates particularly significant episodes, such as the killings of Turón and the violent attack on the barracks of the Civil Guard in Langreo, which serve not only to highlight the bravery and the tenacity of the Civil Guard and the soldiers and denounce the ruthlessness of the revolutionaries, but also to convey the dramatic nature of the Revolution. In addition to the graphic description of the fighting, the author is concerned with providing numerical details such as the number of victims in the government ranks, which buildings were destroyed, the number and type of weapons taken by the revolutionaries from the various arms factories, and the amount of money stolen from the banks. He devotes pages 54 to 59 to the treasures of the Cámara Santa (the Holy Chamber), describing each object in turn and the degree to which it has been damaged.

While the author is ready to deal with the destruction inflicted on Oviedo by the revolutionaries, he does not mention the plane bombardments, and although he does not explicitly attribute all of the devastation to the enemy his silence about who is responsible is just as effective a condemnation. It is interesting to note that in an attempt to discredit the apparent success of the revolutionaries, the author avoids alluding to their initial achievements and unwavering support among the working class. In this way the government makes this conflict appear to have been merely a larger and more violent version of the usual strikes, rather than a bold and momentous Revolution. To round off the text, an epilogue highlights once again the accuracy and veracity of the information and concludes that due to the unequivocal and, at the same time, humane and tolerant action taken by the Spanish government and its forces, the essence of European democracy has been saved. This epilogue, in which the author devotes four pages to outlining the lenient treatment of the revolutionaries, appears to be directed at those who accused the government of reacting too severely. However, the author also rejects the right-wing criticisms, similar to those of Núñez and Romero Cuesta, that it has acted too sparingly, stressing that the government is a parliamentarian and democratic institution, 'sereno y humanitario' (p. 72).

In the prologue to the second of the books examined, Núñez also stresses the violence of the Revolution especially against the Church, attributing the Revolution to an attempt on the part of Marxists and Jews to propagate atheism in Catholic Spain. He hopes his book will serve 'para llevar un rayo de luz a algunas inteligencias obcecadas y las mueva a buscar la verdad en la Iglesia de Jesucristo' (I,12). Despite the apparent religious bias of the text, Núñez concentrates on the general revolutionary action prior to and during the Revolution. Apart from dealing with the actual fighting, this extensive text tackles the background to the Revolution, including 'El separatismo catalán' (Chapter 2), 'El socialismo y el comunismo en Asturias' (Chapter 3), 'El separatismo y la revolución en las provincias vascongadas' (Chapter 4), 'Los móviles de la revolución' (Chapter 8), and 'El odio sectario' (Chapter 9). The political dimension of Núñez's text means that it is not as dramatic as *La revolución*. The political and analytical commentaries on the Revolution are separated from the anecdotes, which are taken from sources such as newspapers, letters, and witness reports, and included in an appendix accompanying each chapter. If we turn to his prologue, Núñez states that rather than relate the history of the Revolution he is merely going to gather together the information and reports already published up to that point (up to 8 December 1934 which is when the prologue is dated) as well as other accounts which he assures are 'completamente verídicos' (I,12). Therefore while stressing the veracity of the information which he does give, Núñez states that there is much which has yet to come to light; until this happens the whole story of the Revolution cannot be written. Unlike in *La revolución*, where the need for commentary is paramount due to the government's need to defend its actions, for Núñez this requirement is reduced as 'los hechos se comentan solos, ellos hablan y dicen más de lo que pudiéramos decir nosotros' (I,12).

Romero Cuesta's work is much more dramatic than either *La revolución* or Núñez's account of the Revolution due to the fact that it comprises numerous re-enacted key episodes in the life of the executed Sergeant Vázquez.[3] The opening chapters deal with the propagandistic preparations for the Revolution and the protagonist's introduction in revolutionary circles. The initial political concerns of the author means that the protagonist of the text, Sergeant Diego Vázquez Corbacho, does not appear until page 19, where his political outlook is revealed: he is anti-monarchical, republican, and pro-liberty, but according to the author lacks any defined political views. Vázquez's involvement in the Revolution is then examined, in particular his assault on the Cuartel Pelayo. Finally his trial and the attempts to overturn the death sentence are depicted, and Vázquez's last moments are re-enacted, including the conversation with his father and the confession to the priest before he is executed. The final chapter serves to criticize the fact that this man was executed while others which the author considers to have been much more responsible were not. Indeed the last chapters of the book once again return to the political discourse which predominates at the start and which is put aside during the descriptive depiction of the Revolution and Vázquez's role in it. Just like the other authors, Romero Cuesta constructs his portrayal of the events by borrowing bits and pieces from other sources, one way of guaranteeing the verifiability of his text. *El sargento Vázquez*, like *La revolución*, is a mixture of anecdote, document, and interpretation. Unlike the two texts already mentioned, however, there seems to be no consistent claim to objectivity or reliability; the fact that Cuesta is using primary sources makes this redundant.[4] Nevertheless, although he makes much use of quotations and documentary evidence, his sources are most often unspecified. Much of the data is verifiable, such as the decree outlining the seven objectives of the Revolution (pp. 32–33), and Diego Hidalgo's address to the government forces (pp. 47–49). However, there are other elements the accuracy of which is much more difficult to determine, for example the private conversation held between Amador Fernández and Vázquez (p. 20), and the speeches made by the revolutionary leaders in the local working-class gatherings (pp. 18 and 21). Indeed, I believe that the likelihood of the author having that information is questionable. Without indicating it to the reader, he appears to rely on what he supposes may have been said.

In this subsection on the government and counter-revolutionary texts I will concentrate on the propagandistic and interpretative effect which the rhetorical strategies employed by these authors — namely, the selection and omission of information, the inclusion of false information, and the stylistic manipulation — have on these semi-factual texts. Whilst all three texts use each of these to some degree, I have found that in *La revolución* the author is primarily selective, Núñez massages the facts to his own advantage, and Cuesta's use of style and vocabulary is determined by the desire to create an emotive effect which will influence the readers' response.

La revolución (1934) demonstrates how without necessarily manipulating the language of the narrative, but by selecting and omitting information, the author can subtly and effectively impose his biased opinion. While most of the text is composed of information backed up by documentary evidence, this has been selected to the author's liking in order to reinforce his point of view and, just as importantly, the government's competence. Unlike in many of the texts, in *La revolución* the relentless and unsubstantiated negative depiction of the revolutionaries and the contrasting positive attributes of the soldiers and religious martyrs do not abound. In those texts where this is the case, such as in the religious accounts which I will examine further on, where the Revolution is associated with evil, greed, and ignorance right from the start, the author refers to the revolutionaries throughout the text in negative terms using both figurative and rhetorical language as well as blatant direct accusations. In *La revolución* the author defends and substantiates his criticisms by providing accompanying, verifiable information. As the author himself explains the reader can corroborate the allegations by consulting the sources: 'En los archivos oficiales españoles quedan, a la disposición del historiador, los documentos demostrativos de cuanto vamos a narrar' (p. 5). Neither does the author of *La revolución* use the witness report as a main tool, like many of the other authors writing on the October Revolution; he quotes only the security guard who was imprisoned with Rafael del Riego and who recounts the cruel treatment received from the revolutionaries (pp. 39–40), and the owner of the factory in Campomanes where the soldiers were positioned during the fierce fighting in the southernmost front (pp. 44–46). Instead the author chooses to take his information from newspaper articles, speeches, letters, and a record of strategic instructions, objectifying his text and giving an illusion of independence.[5]

Despite his introductory remark that 'nada será omitido ni desfigurado' (p. 5), when it is convenient, in addition to selecting the information which will be included, the author of *La revolución* omits certain details. For example, when dealing with the 1933 right-wing electoral victory he insists that the socialists should have accepted the result given that the election was free and conducted according to the Constitution which they themselves had established in 1931. Indeed, all three authors examined here agree on this.[6] Although this is partly true, the authors do not mention other significant factors which led to the left-wing defeat, attributing this merely to a general change in the country's political allegiances. They fail to mention that for this election the right-wing forces had coalesced, and on the other hand the left-wing coalition, which had favoured the distribution of seats, had broken up. In addition, the right wing, with the Church actively supporting it, had bribed the working class and the peasants in some of the most impoverished regions into voting for them.[7] Similarly, the author of *La revolución* attributes the Revolution to the fact that the socialists had lost these elections when in fact, as I have explained in Chapter 1, the problem was more complex. The author reinforces this viewpoint by quoting some of the declarations made by socialist leaders (for example Largo Caballero, Prieto, and Azaña) and Catalan regionalists, which called for revolutionary measures; on the other hand, the violent exhortations of the CEDA and the right-wing military youth organizations are not alluded to.

Usually the manipulation is very subtle. For example, when describing the deaths of the Civil Guard in Sama during the assault on their barracks the author rightly states that many were killed and that the fighting was very violent. However, he fails to mention that the captain, Alonso Nart, was given the option to surrender and leave the building on several occasions. Similarly, the attack on the Ciaño barracks where all but one of the Guards, including Sergeant Dionisio Fernández and his wife, were killed is not fully explained. In reality the revolutionaries had persistently implored the Guards to surrender. When one of the revolutionaries attempted, in person, to convince them he was shot dead, thereby provoking the fierce revolutionary backlash.[8] Regarding the fighting in Vega del Rey, the author sidesteps the issue of the death of thirty revolutionaries at the hands of the Civil Guard. The information which he gives about the arrest of these men is from the start inaccurate. He claims that the prisoners were taken when they advanced on their stronghold with an aim to bomb it, while according to Taibo, the revolutionaries approached the position after seeing a white flag, suggesting to them that the Guards had surrendered. Once inside they were taken prisoner, tied together with a rope and placed in front of the firing line. Only five out of thirty-five men survived.[9] Finally, the author's notion of whether the action taken is commendable or not depends on which side he is writing about. For example, he admires the fact that the Civil Guard in Campomanes continued to fire, albeit carefully, against the revolutionaries who protected themselves behind a fellow soldier held captive. However, he regards similar action taken by the revolutionaries as callous and loathsome.

The second of the manipulative strategies which I have identified is the deliberate use of false information with an aim to engender a feeling of anger and disgust against the revolutionaries. The author, whose role is also to demonstrate that the government forces acted correctly at *all* times, disregards the accuracy of the sources when extracting the information on which he bases his text and his interpretation of the events. Thus, in spite of the author's reliance on verifiable sources such as newspaper reports, letters, and speeches, his credibility is questionable. This is especially relevant in the case of Núñez. For instance, when he deals with the revolutionary violence in Chapter 10, he inserts as supporting evidence of the enemy's ruthlessness the following extract from an article written by the Falangist poet Federico Urrutia for the newspaper *Informaciones* on 26 October:

> Paso, pues, a la Verdad, y oigan quienes quieran escuchar, como yo escuché de millares de labios.
>
> Aquí se han violado mujeres y aun niños de siete años.
>
> Se han asesinado a cuchilladas Hermanas de la Caridad.
>
> Se ha bombardeado la Cruz Roja, atestada de heridos.
>
> Se han asaltado y destrozado todos los domicilios y comercios.
>
> Se han sacado los ojos a sacerdotes.
>
> Se han tenido prisioneros durante seis días sin comer, bajo de la amenaza de la muerte continuamente.
>
> Se han despedazado guardias civiles, cuyos despojos han sido colgados en los ganchos de las carnicerías y cuyas cabezas han sido expuestas en los escaparates, en unión de carteles en que se anunciaba que se vendía «carne de cerdo».
>
> Se han quemado vivos, después de colgados, a mozalbetes seminaristas atados de pies y manos.
>
> Se han puesto a los detenidos por delante de las barricadas, amarrados en montones, para parapetarse de los disparos de las tropas leales a España.
>
> Se han volado edificios con dinamita, en cuyo interior estaban refugiados docenas de mujeres y de niños.
>
> Se ha intentado volar el edificio del Hospital, lo que no han podido realizar gracias al esfuerzo de los heroicos salvadores.
>
> Se ha fusilado sin cesar, día y noche, durante una semana eterna, a cientos de detenidos, y alguno a sido atado a las colas de caballos robados, después de ser rociado con petróleo y encendido.
>
> En pleno Parque de San Francisco han estado colgados de los árboles, durante cinco días, los cadáveres de varios carmelitas, carbonizados por los verdugos de las «checas» rojas. (II, 131–32)

Núñez's text demonstrates how, despite being based largely on primary information, a text may be inaccurate. Lars Sauerberg, examining the 'neutrality' of the historian, explains this succinctly:

> However neutral the historian considers himself in his transformation of research data into the learned article, his very use of language and the very act of writing, understood as the continuous process of formulating and editing, will already have corrupted the assumed neutrality. But the neutrality of the facts has actually been challenged long before the historian gets to work in his study. If he is dealing with textual material [in other words, peace treaties, correspondence and chronicles, as opposed to excavations, monuments and kitchen utensils which is nontextual material], a writing process will already have been at work interpreting the facts. [10]

Consistent with Sauerberg's theory, much of the data used by Núñez is already an interpretation of the events and this text is hence removed even further from the bare facts. As with Núñez, most of the misinformation in *La revolución* surrounds the activity of the revolutionaries, such as the allegation of the three raped women discussed elsewhere, a story which Taibo has subsequently shown to have been fabricated by the right-wing press and ratified in this official text, or the claim that the pre-Romanesque church of Santa Cristina de Lena was destroyed by the revolutionaries when in reality it appears to have been bombed by army artillery.[11] However, in addition the author of *La revolución* actually fabricates certain details, a tactic exposed and criticized by other authors writing on the Revolution, such as the right-wing Antonio Oliveros, examined in Chapter 3, and Llano Roza dealt with later on.[12] For example, in *La revolución* the author refers to the revolutionary allegation that Javier Bueno, arrested prior to the start of the Revolution, had been tortured in prison. He indicates that the wounds which appear in a widely disseminated photograph of the victim (and which the author reproduces in his own text) were the result of a medical condition, 'una forunculosis vulgar' (p. 33), a claim which Bueno denied while in prison and subsequently, once liberated. In order to hide any trace of enmity for the journalist, which might serve to explain why Bueno was subjected to such ill-treatment, the author adds in a footnote that Bueno 'ha sido siempre [. . .] hombre veraz y austero' (p. 33). In fact Bueno, as editor of the newspaper *Avance*, was considered to be an enemy by the right wing who accused him of inciting the Revolution by spreading propaganda, and his unpopularity is evident in most of the counter-revolutionary accounts of the Revolution.

The third rhetorical strategy, employed particularly by Romero Cuesta, is the manipulation of the reader's sentiments through the use of emotive language. In this way Cuesta succeeds in making Vázquez's situation seem more tragic than other texts on the Revolution suggest. The usual negative portrayal of the Revolution, as for example 'vahos de odio y barbarie' (p. 12), and the revolutionaries, 'las multitudes ofuscadas, embriagadas, bestializadas por la revolución' (p. 37), appear in this text. However, for the most part, the narrative is more personalized; it deals in detail with the life of an individual person, his character, relationships, and experiences, rather than with the general events and facts of the Revolution. He describes Vázquez's initial involvement in the Revolution and depicts melodramatically his last hours. Cuesta attempts to explain why the sergeant became so deeply involved and implies that his ambitious nature was taken advantage of. As Vázquez successfully leads the revolutionary troops during the first days of the Revolution he is further spurred on by the promise that in a new Spain an important military role will be conferred on him. Pity and criticism are conveyed in the following caricature of the sergeant leading a group of revolutionaries:

Va por las calles al frente de su grupo con la fanfarronería de un guerrero sioux... Se le ve [...] empuñando una pistola con la mano derecha y un silbato en la izquierda, vistiendo un pantalón de cuartel y un jersey rojo y ostentando en el pecho las más extrañas condecoraciones, diversos distintivos de metal y cintajos de colorines. (pp. 31–32)

However, the author also makes reference to Vázquez's positive attributes before his political involvement, highlighting both the damaging influence of the revolutionary propaganda and what made the protagonist vulnerable to such temptation: 'Su carácter franco, alegre y benévolo; su charla, siempre espontánea y pintoresca [...] abrían fácilmente brechas a la amistad de cuantos le trataban... Su puntualidad en el cumplimiento de las obligaciones militares le ganaban la confianza y la estimación de sus superiores' (p. 54). On a number of occasions the author insinuates that Vázquez did not entirely agree with the revolutionary procedures or objectives. At the end, when Vázquez is about to be executed, the author implies that the sergeant's heart-felt patriotism re-emerges as he realizes that his is the Spanish flag, not the revolutionary one:

Al pasar frente a la bandera se cuadró, giró los talones con impulso seguro y exacto, y se llevó la mano a la frente con el mismo ademán con que lo hiciera en una gran parada... Pero también con una extraña y entrañable emoción... Porque aquella era su bandera... *¡Su bandera!*... Lo comprendía entonces. (p. 80)

When he relates the trial in which Vázquez is sentenced to death, the author, writing in the present tense, uses short sentences and ellipsis, conveying the tense atmosphere lived in the court room. He exposes the arguments of the defence and the prosecution, and witnesses are gradually introduced who identify Vázquez as the military leader of the Revolution, adding an extra element of drama as the inevitable outcome becomes more and more apparent.

Vázquez, who spent his last hours in the prison cell with his father, his girlfriend (Engracia Menéndez), and his best friend (Hilario Fernández Rebaque), was, according to them, very calm and unafraid of dying. The last night is re-enacted using fictional narrative techniques, where dialogue is included, the feelings of the grief-stricken characters are revealed, and the moving parting scenes are illustrated, all against the background of the knowledge, of those acting in the story and those reading about it, that time for Vázquez is running out. Naturally, the last action of the convicted man before he is executed is his confession to Padre Arroyo; just as his patriotic fervour comes out in the end, so does his religious faith. The author, who reveals Vázquez's inner thoughts and feelings, effectively acts as an omniscient narrator, another characteristic of this text more commonly associated with fictional writing. This fictional device, however, lends the text a degree of reality which it may have otherwise lacked given the shortage of concrete documentary and recorded evidence which the other texts present. Hellman, who examines New Journalism and the presentation of journalistic material in the form of fiction, writes:

Various journalistic elements of the text are selected, arranged, and stylistically transformed so that they create an aesthetic experience embodying the author's personal experience and interpretation of the subject. Each author transforms his journalistic subject into a living text so that the reader does not merely read about events, but participates in the author's personal experience and interpretation of them.[13]

Thus, Cuesta creates a realistic effect by using fictional devices.

We should not make the mistake of thinking that Cuesta did not agree with Vázquez's execution, however. His point is that all of the revolutionary leaders should have been executed. The author continuously calls attention to the fact that Vázquez was not afraid to admit to his participation in the Revolution or to suffer the consequences, unlike González Peña and Largo Caballero who denied leading the Revolution and, in the case of the latter, that he even knew what had been planned. The detailed description of Vázquez's temperament and integrity, and the intricate re-enactment of his fate at the hands of the revolutionaries and then of the court of law, serve to highlight the contrasting cowardly and deceitful nature of the real revolutionary leaders.

Although the rhetorical strategies serve to influence how the events should be perceived, the authors are also concerned with evaluating the effectiveness and legitimacy of the Republic as a governing regime, as well as with establishing that the Revolution, over which the 'real' poor people had no control, should be attributed mainly to the greed of the miners and the self-interest of the intellectuals. Starting with the view of the government that emerges from these texts, the authors differ in their support for a republican regime and the extent to which its introduction should be held responsible for the ensuing Revolution. The authors agree that enthusiasm for the Revolution was forged during Azaña's two years in government throughout which time the left wing supposedly made arrangements to weaken the forces of order and undermine the influence of the Church. Hence, any doubt as to why Azaña carried out his reforms, which to the right wing seemed incomprehensible, are explained:

Deshecho el ejército, gracias a la trituración azañista; desarmados todos los ciudadanos amantes de la Patria, gracias a las disposiciones que dieron los gobernantes para privar del uso de las armas a los elementos de orden; armados los extremistas hasta los dientes con toda clase de pertrechos bélicos — armas, municiones en abundancia extraordinaria y dinero suficientes para una larga guerra —, convertidos en somatenes la mayor parte del hampa de todos los pueblos, y unidos todos por un odio a la religión, a Dios, a Jesucristo, a la Iglesia, a todo lo sagrado, odio que se pudo inspirar gracias a la libertad desenfrenada de una propaganda intensísima a la que no se puso coto alguno; desbordadas todas las pasiones: las de los rabassaires, legalizando su rapiña; las de los socialistas, azuzando el odio de clases; la de los anarquistas, prometiéndoles las «delicias» de un paraíso como el de Rusia, llega el momento en que se ciernen sobre España los cuervos que la acechan dentro y fuera, y estalla la revolución cuando creen que era el más oportuno para que triunfase.[14]

In *La revolución* (1934) the author examines the financial gains of the miners' unions, the newspaper *Avance*, and the cooperative mine of San Vicente and affirms that much of this money was spent on preparing the Revolution. These texts thus not only demonstrate that the Revolution had been prepared long before the 1933 electoral defeat but also that the Republican government of Azaña was involved in laying the groundwork. On the one hand, *La revolución*, as the official report, does not reflect on Lerroux's or Samper's responsibility to any extent and no consideration is given to the possible inadequacy of the Republic as a form of government. However, Núñez not only criticizes Azaña but also the right-wing Republican government, and especially the Governor of Asturias, Fernando Blanco, for being naïve and for not taking sufficient measures to prevent the revolutionary attempt when it was clear that something was being planned.[15] For Núñez, who holds the most extreme opinion of the three authors examined, the left-wing government's involvement in the Revolution and the subsequent right-wing government's failure to prevent it, make him question the reliability of a republican regime.

A close examination of these writings reveals that the authors tend to divide the revolutionaries into two groups: the leaders and the fighters, in other words, the intellectuals and the miners. The leaders, with their incessant use of propaganda, have encouraged the working class to rebel, and the greed of the workers makes them vulnerable to this encouragement. In *La revolución* (1934) the author insists that the miners live and work in enviable conditions and that therefore hardship was not the main motivating factor.[16] Indeed, it is generally accepted by the authors that given their relative economic wealth and advantageous working conditions the real desire of the miners was to be in control of the working class. The injustice of the Revolution is further emphasized by the fact that on many occasions the motives are personal, such as the need to feel superior, or a yearning to seek vengeance for past incidents. Núñez adds to these a criminal incentive:

Es en esa clase medio acomodada [. . .] en donde prenden más fácilmente las chispas de todas las teorías materialistas como las del socialismo y marxismo, por el ansia de gozar más, de subir más, de poseer más que tienen los que ya gustan el principio de ese goce material. Y como no tienen esperanzas de otros bienes superiores, y como el bienestar les da tiempo y ánimo para hacerse ilusiones, aspiran a más, y se lanzan a todas las revoluciones, porque en ellas siempre se pesca, como se vio en los saqueos de Asturias, o por lo menos se satisfacen los más viles odios o las más repugnantes pasiones que anidan en tales almas. (I, 97–98)

On the other hand, the people who are genuinely poor are dragged into the conflict and made to fight as their towns are gradually taken by the revolutionaries. Thus the revolutionary assertion that they are fighting for the benefit of the poor in society is challenged.

For their part, the leaders are consistently portrayed as power seekers prepared to influence and take advantage of the greedy, ignorant, and gullible masses. Núñez, who devotes much of his text to the part played by the socialists in inciting the Revolution, is particularly critical of the intellectuals and their means of reaching the working class and persuading them of the legitimacy of their objectives:

Hoy como siempre o aun tal vez más que nunca quien arrastra a las multitudes son los intelectuales. [. . .] La inteligencia puesta al servicio de la verdad crea apóstoles y produce santos; puesta al servicio del error engendra monstruos y provoca los cataclismos de las revoluciones sociales. [. . .] Las revoluciones modernas tienen su génesis en los ateneos, en las redacciones de los periódicos, en las aulas de los centros docentes y hallan eco en los medios culturales que dejan a un lado su fin y se dedican a la política. Desde el advenimiento del nuevo régimen, en el que tuvieron una parte tan notable literatos, filósofos y hombres de carrera, se han publicado muchísimos libros en que se pone de manifiesto su influencia y se aspira al menos a gozar las altas prebendas, los ministerios, las embajadas, los gobiernos civiles, etc., o a la participación siquiera del horror que cada cual quiere tener en el triunfo. (II, 186)

The capacity of the revolutionary press, and in particular *Avance*, for propagating socialist ideas is a determining factor in the Revolution, and for Cuesta it is evident in the fact that Vázquez, despite not being a communist or socialist, is persuaded by the rhetoric of the newspaper to become involved. Núñez maintains that the Asturian miner (the intellectual of the Spanish proletariat) is deliberately made to believe that he is fully acquainted with the revolutionary principles, and that it is his responsibility to instruct the other workers in them. On the other hand, Cuesta condescendingly disputes their intellectual ability by quoting mistakes from their speeches, such as the words '*cosciente*' and '*reinvindique*' (p. 17, author's emphasis). By means of a careful selection of key words and phrases the authors succeed in making the revolutionary claims which appear in articles and speeches seem exaggerated, irrational and, in some cases, ridiculous. This is true of most of the texts about October, both left- and right-wing, and is a way of discrediting the enemy. Apart from using the revolutionaries' own words to belittle their assertions, the authors add their own political commentaries, such as Cuesta who indicates his indignation and concern: 'En la tertulia se paladea golosamente la dulce envoltura de palabras que oculta el amargo veneno' (p. 20).

According to these texts, for the intellectuals the Revolution represents an armed revolt against Catholicism and the *Patria*, the overthrow of which would open the way for their own dominance. In order to achieve their all-important goal they are ready to expose their fighters to whatever action is required, regardless of the dangers and even if this results in the workers having to bear the brunt of the government backlash. This is the case of the leaders of the first Revolutionary Committee who run away when it becomes clear that the Revolution has failed in the rest of Spain. In other words, for these authors, the ordinary worker was persuaded into blindly fighting in the Revolution: 'Pobres hombres alucinados, casi irresponsables, que habían sido empujados a la revolución sin saber por qué', just like Vázquez.[17]

Military and Police Accounts

Amongst the texts which were written criticizing the Revolution we find a series of what I have called military or police accounts, versions of the Revolution which concentrate on the defence and attacking manoeuvres of the forces of order. The author of each of these texts may have been militarily involved in the Revolution or alternatively he may simply be interested in relating the experiences of a particular section of the forces. I stress this as in these texts the latter tends to be the case. Thus José Rubinat concentrates on the *zapadores*, General López Ochoa gives a day by day account of his military tactics as head of the army, and Jenaro Geijo chooses to focus on the defence of the Civil Guard.[18] On the other hand, Aurelio de Llano Roza de Ampudia gives a more generalized account of the military events. Here I will concentrate on Aurelio de Llano Roza de Ampudia, *La Revolución en Asturias. Octubre 1934: pequeños anales de quince días* (1935) and Jenaro Geijo, *Episodios de la revolución* (1935).[19] I have chosen these two texts as they offer a number of different features as far as content and style are concerned which lend themselves to a useful comparison. In the first place, Llano Roza is there during the Revolution as a witness while Geijo arrives eight days later and is witness to the aftermath; secondly, as mentioned already, Geijo concentrates on the Civil Guard while Llano Roza is more general; and thirdly, the academic status of each of the authors is different — Llano Roza is 'Académico correspondiente de la Academia de la Historia, de la de Bellas Artes de San Fernando y de la Española', according to the front cover of the book, while Geijo is a former Civil Guard and has a magazine, *Información*, to which he contributes regularly.[20] And yet, despite these fundamental differences, I will show that both texts are actually very similar. Both demonstrate the accomplishment and professionalism of the forces of order while condemning the revolutionaries. Linked to this, both show their political stand and give their opinion on the events even though their texts are not meant to be political.

Although the aims of these two authors are the same, the circumstances in which they write differ. Geijo arrives eight days after the Revolution has ended with the intention to see the aftermath and the destruction. He uses what he sees and the people to whom he talks, as well as other documentary evidence, to reconstruct the revolutionary fighting and recreate a series of episodes which he hopes will give the reader an idea of the extent and the horror of the Revolution. Llano Roza, on the other hand, stresses the fact that he has witnessed the events in Oviedo directly and that his version is based on the notes he has taken. Geijo, who has not actually witnessed the events himself, is at an apparent disadvantage. He has to overcome any possible doubts about the reliability of the provenance of his information. Thus in the prologue he states categorically that all his information comes from reliable witnesses and that it has not been exaggerated in any way:

> Nos han sido referidos personalmente, [. . .] por actores supervivientes de la catástrofe. Los datos de otros los hemos tomado de los partes oficiales, y en ambos casos hemos ajustado la narración que de ellos hacemos a la más absoluta y fiel veracidad. No hay, por lo tanto, en su exposición exageración alguna, ni son ficticios tampoco, ni abultados, ni amañados, los actos de crueldad. (p. 5)

In other words, he 'automatically provides some means of measuring the reliability of his work'.[21] Because his text is composed of episodes and witness accounts, some of which take up a substantial part of the text, Geijo warns that his text will not be an exhaustive history of the Revolution 'sino una colección de episodios de la misma' (p. 5).[22] In addition he incorporates photographs, quotations from newspapers, reports from witnesses, and statistical details such as the numbers of dead and injured.

Llano Roza's work initially takes the form of a diary as he explains the events in Oviedo.[23] However, given his decision to extend his account to the rest of Asturias, he is also forced to rely on 'investigación' and 'noticias dignas de crédito' (p. xi). Right at the start, where the author's attempt to establish the veracity of the text is particularly prominent, Llano Roza indicates the exact position from where he has witnessed the events:

> Se oyen en Oviedo los primeros tiros de la revolución. Y me entran deseos de ver algo de lo que ocurre en el contorno, para lo cual me sitúo a veintitantos metros de altura, en una ventana abierta detrás de la balaustrada de la cornisa del edificio núm. 3 de la calle de Cervantes, sito en uno de los puntos más elevados de la ciudad. [. . .] En aquella altura pasé los días de la revolución y muchas horas de la noche, tomando notas de cuanto veía, que fue mucho, provisto de buenos prismáticos.[24]

Thus this text is the product of Llano Roza's meticulous note-taking, with details as precise as the weather conditions on a given day, or the exact time at which the government planes flew over Oviedo.[25]

This diaristic account includes conversations between the author and the witnesses, as well as information from the author about his feelings of hunger and cold: 'Es tal la debilidad que tengo por falta de alimentación' (p. 91), placing him at the scene of the Revolution. By means of careful investigation he gathers other detailed information which he incorporates. For example, he has counted the bullet holes in a train engine: 'En la máquina Feijóo he contado ochenta impactos, que le hicieron desde la estación' (p. 23, footnote 1); he has taken the measurements of one of the trains: 'Lleva delante de sí dos vagones de hierro de doce toneladas. Sus cajas tienen siete metros y setenta centímetros de largo por dos cuarenta de ancho, y uno setenta de alto. Los he medido' (p. 57); and he has counted the cannon impacts on the Cuartel Pelayo: 'Total, doscientos veintiocho cañonazos, sin contar los del tejado. He contado los impactos' (p. 99). The author has even held in his hands one of the cannon shots, which he is able to describe (p. 22). He also inserts detailed numerical data of, for example, the number of troops accompanying Bosch (p. 184) and Ledesma (p. 185). Llano Roza provides extra information about the events in the footnotes which refer to the trials of the members of the government forces who allegedly acted incompetently.[26] Whilst the presence of such details should strengthen the credibility of the text, in the case of Llano Roza the result is counter-productive. The excessive attention to detail gives the impression that an omniscient narrator is at work, paradoxically lending the text a fictional appearance. For example, how would the author know the activities that took place in the revolutionary camp at such precise times?: 'A las dos y media de la mañana llegó un nuevo grupo de revolucionarios a incorporarse a la columna' (p. 8); or the exact words of the revolutionary chief, since he could not have heard them:

> A las doce del día, en la calle del Paraíso, frente a las puertas de la fábrica de gas, un jefe de grupo toca un silbato. Acuden sus guardias y dice:
> — ¡A ver, dos dinamiteros! Tú y tú, venid conmigo. (p. 41)

In the case of *El sargento Vázquez*, by Romero Cuesta, I argued that the presence of an omniscient narrator added an element of reality to the text. The effect produced in Llano Roza's work is different, however, as the appearance of this narrator is inconsistent with an autobiographical text: 'An autobiography is different from a novel in that its author claims to be recounting facts and not constructing fictions.'[27] Given that the eye-witness, in other words, Llano Roza, cannot see or know everything, all the extra details which he inserts to make his text appear more complete and thorough contradict his initial assertion that this text (at least the first part) is fruit of the notes he has taken and his own observations. Llano Roza's work demonstrates how the incorporation of extreme detail raises doubts about the authenticity of the information; rather than convey credibility it makes the data appear to be at least partly invented.

In the second part, in which he gives an account of the Revolution in the rest of Asturias, Llano Roza insinuates that although he has not witnessed the incidents directly, his information is based on what he has observed in the immediate aftermath. For example, in Gijón he claims to have seen the vestiges of the Revolution: 'Estuve en todos los puntos donde se levantaron estos parapetos' (p. 129), and in Turón he has seen the charred remains of the Civil Guard barracks: 'No quedaron más que las paredes. Lo he visto' (p. 170). In addition he refers to primary source materials, such as leaflets, printed manifestoes, public proclamations, rationing vouchers and booklets, and posters, as well as witness reports. In this way he attempts to reconstruct the events and illustrate what conditions must have been like in the revolutionary towns. Nevertheless, given the type of evidence available, apart from the section on Oviedo the narrative deals to a greater extent with the military manoeuvres and less with social and psychological issues.

Given that these are military discourses, it is not surprising that they should deal primarily with the tactics and experiences of the soldiers and the Civil Guard rather than with broad political questions. Llano Roza begins by examining the military manoeuvres of the government forces in Oviedo chronologically (from 5 to 17 October). According to him, his account was initially going to deal with the events in Oviedo as this is what he witnessed, and indeed the events which took place in the capital take up over half of the entire text. However, he decides to extend his study to the whole of Asturias so that Gijón, Avilés and all the other places affected by the Revolution are dealt with too. For his part, Geijo approaches his text geographically, taking each place in turn and describing the events there.[28] According to his introductory 'Objeto de esta obra' he is concerned with the fate of the Civil Guard, so many of whom were 'sacrificados en el ara santa del DEBER por las hordas revolucionarias' (p. 5, author's emphasis). Thus he examines how the Civil Guard defended themselves and how they were treated by the rebels in each place where the Revolution broke out. As expected, in both of these texts the government forces are praised in every possible way. Llano Roza, by stressing the fact that there were initially 30,000 revolutionaries fighting against 2500 soldiers and Guards, and that the former had powerful weaponry and many means at their disposal, including 'cinco líneas de ferrocarriles y toda clase de medios de transporte por carretera; camiones blindados [. . .]; cañones y armas automáticas; las fábricas de explosivos con grandes cantidades de dinamita; [. . .] los establecimientos fabriles, en los que podían construir cuanto necesitaban' (p. xiii), conveys the latter's proud performance. Similarly, at the end of a long paragraph in which he lists the material the revolutionaries possessed, Geijo remarks that 'ni con la superioridad del número, ni con la de pertrechos, lograron completo dominio de la ciudad' (p. 266), heightening the sense of accomplishment and professionalism of the forces of order. This is further demonstrated when, despite being at a disadvantage, the forces manage to resist the hordes of revolutionaries who attack their barracks and positions, as in this example taken from Geijo:

> Han disparado ya el último proyectil. Han hecho cuanto humanamente han podido. Han cumplido con su deber y han dejado bien puestos el honor de la Guardia civil. No pueden defenderse más. Les faltan medios materiales. El espíritu, en cambio, está incólume. (p. 162)

Because of their reverence for the *Patria*, in its defence the forces exert 'supremo heroísmo' (p. 202), 'admirable espíritu de sacrificio' (p. 15), 'titánica resistencia' (p. 161), and 'gran arrojo' (p. 190), displaying outstanding bravery and integrity.[29] Thus when Geijo refers to the victims on the government side he does so with praise and glory rather than with sadness and regret: 'En el pequeño pueblo de Campomanes [. . .] escribió la Guardia civil, con la sangre de una docena de sus mártires, una de sus acostumbradas páginas de gloria' (p. 198). The positive attributes conferred on the Civil Guard with Geijo's manipulative and heavily charged language are conveyed in a different way in Llano Roza's text. The following examples in which both authors describe the death of the sergeant of Ciaño and his wife demonstrate the differences in the factual, semantic and stylistic treatment of both narratives. Llano Roza writes:

> El cabo, con su mujer y un guardia, se repliegan a una habitación interior de la planta baja [. . .] de donde tienen que salir inmediatamente. Al llegar a la puerta de un patio central del edificio, el cabo y su esposa caen muertos el uno al lado del otro, con las armas en la mano; y cerca de ellos, el guardia. (p. 160)

In his account Llano Roza avoids using overly prejudiced wording. Geijo, on the other hand, is much more aggressive in his accusation:

> A *ellos*, gritaron algunos, y dispararon contra el cabo que cayó acribillado a balazos.
> — ¡Piedad para una madre sin amparo! — clamaba con los brazos en alto, la esposa aterrada.
> Y no hubo tampoco clemencia para ella. Las hienas mineras, incapaces de tan altos sentimientos, la asesinan a tiros y la pobre Julia cae exánime sobre el cuerpo agonizante de su marido. (p. 163)

Llano Roza's detailed and unembellished depiction of the forces in action and their success conveys, just as powerfully as Geijo's highly prejudiced account, the efficiency, courage, and honour of the troops. Indeed, for the reader merely searching for information about the events this extreme partiality is detrimental since all the claims made by the author begin to lose credibility. This is not the case with Llano Roza's text and to this extent it is more persuasive.

Because of the ideological nature of the events, politics cannot be completely ignored by these or any other author writing on October 1934. It is widely accepted that the military classes had a vested interest in a right-wing government and quite openly sided with the richer landowning and business classes in all those revolts in which the masses claimed the right to better working and living conditions.[30] This explains the political stance of these authors, whether declared or not. While indicating his intention of being accurate and truthful, Geijo does not make any allusion to his impartiality, unlike Llano Roza who claims to write free of any political prejudice:

> A esta obra quiero darle carácter imparcial. No estoy afiliado a ningún partido político. Esto, unido a la independencia que disfruto, y a mi modo de ser, me deja la pluma libre para escribir imparcialmente — como debe escribirse la historia — lo que ha ocurrido en los días de la revolución. (p. xi)

Both Geijo and Llano Roza concentrate on the causes of the Revolution, although each takes a different approach. While Geijo examines the socialist attitude to the 1933 elections, Llano Roza looks more deeply into the possible discontent of the working class and uses his conclusions to predict the future of Spain. The undersecretary of the Home Office, Eduardo Benzo y Cano, who writes the prologue to Geijo's text, refers to the reluctance of the socialists to accept their electoral defeat in 1933. For this reason 'se aprestaban con desenfadado cinismo a la conquista del poder por la fuerza' (p. 9), in other words, they set their sights on a Revolution as a means to take over power. Benzo criticizes the masses who, dissatisfied with their leaders' performance whilst in government and with the parliamentary process in general, supported this violent and destructive initiative, and implies that it is the result of their backward and reprobate nature: 'La inteligencia, la perseverancia, el esfuerzo moral y material se necesitan para construir' (p. 10). As part of his own political analysis Geijo refers to the socialist revolutionary preparations and in particular the spread of harmful propaganda: 'La propaganda subversiva, que se hacía con el mayor descaro, inoculando a los obreros el virus revolucionario' (p. 19). Geijo maintains that this propaganda not only lured the workers, but also frightened the feeble-spirited citizens who, facing the revolutionary threat, chose to hide rather than confront the enemy. He professes that had the revolutionaries won this battle Spain would now be 'un paraíso soviético a usanza rusa' (p. 19), or '[un] paraíso por el cual suspiraban con el mismo afán que los hijos de Mahoma por el lupanaresco edén que el profeta africano promete en el Corán a sus creyentes' (p. 20). Instead of remarking on the actual political programme of the socialists, Geijo merely ascribes to any future Spanish Socialist Republic a series of negative qualities which are enough to make any citizen feel threatened.

In Llano Roza's account the immediate antecedents to the Revolution are not given much consideration. Instead the author examines the roots of the discontent of the working class, and in so doing makes a pessimistic observation about future peace in Spain. Llano Roza declares that 'se ha roto el equilibrio social' (p. 87), and quotes a passage from *Encíclica sobre las condiciones de los oficios*, written by Pope Leo XIII, in order to explain the discontent of the workers:

> Los elementos del conflicto son inconfundibles; el incremento de la industria y los sorprendentes descubrimientos de la ciencia; la alteración sufrida por las relaciones entre patronos y obreros; las enormes fortunas individuales y la pobreza de las masas; la creciente confianza en sí mismo y la natural unión cada vez más estrecha que se advierte en la población obrera; y finalmente el general desgaste moral. (p. 88)

Having asserted that this conflict is just the beginning of the greater and more important battle which is still to come — 'Será el prólogo de una tragedia que se desarrollará más adelante en un escenario de gran extensión' (p. 87) — Llano Roza ends his text with the following words:

> En el aire de las cuencas mineras flotan ciertas inquietudes difíciles de calmar. . . El día 14 de agosto de este año, la guardia civil de Sama de Langreo encontró, en una cueva sita en un monte de aquel concejo, ciento sesenta fusiles mosquetones nuevos, seiscientos peines de ametralladora y doscientos cartuchos de dinamita. . . (p. 210)

By ending with an ellipsis the author leaves the 'story' unfinished; it is up to the reader to make sure that another violent Revolution does not take place.

As might be expected, the criticism directed at the socialists is much more prevalent when the authors deal with the actual fighting. Not only are the revolutionaries considered to be disloyal, but they are also accused of acting irrationally and cruelly. In Geijo's text the references to the savagery of the revolutionaries and the harshness of the Revolution recur constantly. The Revolution is described as catastrophic ('la hecatombe' [p. 253]) and is compared to '[un] ciclón' (p. 19): 'El viento de locura [. . .] soplaba ya imponente y devastador por toda la Península' (p. 26). Similarly the revolutionaries are depicted in a number of negative ways: as beastly ('la jauría revolucionaria aúlla' [p. 162], 'las sanguinarias fieras revolucionarias' [p. 165], and 'insaciables buitres' [p. 172]); vandals and thieves ('los vándalos del siglo XX' [p. 23], 'la destructora ola roja' [p. 182], and 'los desenfrenados saqueadores' [p. 251]); vengeful; drunk; greedy hypocrites, especially with regards to the availability of food and the distribution of money ('Otros de los establecimientos saqueados fueron los Bancos Herrero y Asturiano, en los que *abolieron*, guardándoselo cuidadosamente, todo el dinero contante y sonante' [p. 237]); and, worst of all, as bloodthristy criminals ('Las vejaciones, los atropellos, los latrocinios, los crímenes, los asesinatos, los martirios dantescos de que Oviedo fué víctima, durante su novenario de pasión' [p. 260]; 'Restos despedazados de su heroico teniente don Fernando Halcón, a quien la jauría revolucionaria arrastró hasta aquel paraje, después de muerto, para hacer explotar en su boca, aún sangrante, un cartucho de dinamita y amputarle, a cuchilladas, ambas piernas' [p. 205]).[31] The cruelty of the revolutionaries goes hand in hand with the cowardice that distinguishes them from the heroic and brave Civil Guard: 'Pero la cobardía del enemigo, que en cuanto veían caer a dos o tres de los suyos, se agazapaban y no daban la cara, nos evitó llegar a ese sacrificio, que desde luego hubiésemos hecho' (p. 297). The women, many of whom were 'vestidas de encarnado o con trajes masculinos' (p. 275), are also criticized. Finally, Geijo censures the socialist leaders, whom he considers to be uncultured and selfish, and whose propaganda and press, 'el germen de la rebelión' (p. 156), has resulted in this deplorable situation: 'Vivas y mueras electrizados por los latiguillos sediciosos de Largo Caballero e Indalecio Prieto' (p. 27).

In Llano Roza's text, as in Geijo's, there are many examples of bias against the revolutionaries, although these are more subtly expressed. For example, the weapons at the hands of the revolutionaries take on a monstrous appearance: 'Está [el cañón Schneider] pintado de minio, cuyo color y tamaño le dan el aspecto de un monstruo rojo, enorme' (p. 34). However, are these not the same weapons that the soldiers had? In the same way the author criticizes the revolutionary attack on the cathedral claiming that they were about to destroy a valuable and magnificent example of Gothic architecture: 'Si continúan cañoneando, deshacen la aguja de la torre, aquella aguja espiritual, esculpida sutilmente por el cincel gótico, que se remonta gallarda por encima de la ciudad' (p. 31). On the other hand, the author does not consider the fact that the soldiers, having chosen the cathedral as a position from where to attack the revolutionaries, may also have failed to contemplate its historical and artistic significance. The revolutionaries felt they had no alternative but to destroy this military safe haven which was proving to be a lethal stronghold.

By not being so explicitly condemnatory, Llano Roza's critical depiction of the revolutionaries is much more credible than Geijo's. Even though he also accuses the revolutionaries of cruelty, thieving, and hypocrisy, Llano Roza endorses his earlier claims of impartiality by occasionally remarking positively on their actions. This is the case in this example in which a nun describes how they were treated by the revolutionaries: 'Hablaron con nosotras y no pasaron del portal ni nos han molestado. Un día nos trajeron pan, que buena falta nos hacía' (p. 17).[32] It should be noted, however, that most favourable comments about the revolutionaries are immediately invalidated by a negative observation. For example, the author refers to Belarmino Tomás's pledge to remain in Asturias until the Revolution had come to an end, only to contradict this honourable assertion by affirming that he went abroad as soon as it had been defeated, thereby avoiding all the repercussions:

> Belarmino Tomás, le dijo al ingeniero señor Laine:
> — Para evitar desmanes, no saldré de aquí hasta que vea entrar en el pueblo el primer soldado.
> Así lo cumplió. Y luego se marchó al extranjero. (p. 202)

This tactic, whereby criticism is implied and not directly stated, is Llano Roza's preferred means of transmitting his negative view of the Revolution. Often the author has preconceived ideas about the revolutionaries which he implicitly passes on to the reader. For example, when the author relates the episode in which a law student is killed in Oviedo he adds, 'Es el único estudiante que murió a manos de los revolucionarios' (p. 25). This almost positive remark hides a negative supposition — that the revolutionaries may have intended to kill more students. Although Geijo and Llano Roza specify that their texts will depict the fate of the soldiers and Civil Guard, the fact that the 'enemy' was involved in taking violent and insurrectionary action against an apparently democratically elected government impels the authors to consider certain political issues. Furthermore, given that in the hostile environment of a Revolution the forces of order and the rebels have a political value attached to them, it is inevitable that the texts produced should be biased, as in the case here.

The scholarship and erudition of the authors is the third factor which I consider to be influential in the composition of these works. Geijo, an ex-Civil Guard who writes for a magazine called *Información*, warns the reader not to expect too much as far as the quality of the narrative is concerned, reminding him that he is only 'un mediano aficionado a las letras' (p. 6). Nevertheless for Benzo, Geijo's background makes his writing all the more sincere and compelling:

La prosa sabia y cuidada de Jenaro G. Geijo nos cautiva y emociona, tanto porque el relato es certero y veraz, como porque mueve la pluma de un guardia civil, de todo un Guardia Civil, con lo que queda hecho su mejor elogio, pues el cese de la vida activa no ha entibiado su espíritu de Cuerpo ni ha eclipsado sus virtudes acrisoladas. (p. 15)

Clearly, the magazine *Información,* 'Espejo de aspiraciones, guía de perfeccionamiento corporativo y altavoz de hechos que no deben permanecer en el olvido' (p. 15), from where Geijo championed the unforgettable exploits of the Civil Guard, is a propagandist publication. Given that this is Geijo's main focus, it is not surprising that *Episodios de la revolución* adopts a biased stance.

In the case of Llano Roza, his status as a historian and academic should in principle be a guarantee of the objectivity of his narrative.[33] As I have demonstrated above, on the surface this may appear to be true, but in reality it is far from being so. What does stand out is the hybrid and, at the same time, contradictory nature of the text; the objectivity so important to Llano Roza is compromised by the dramatic re-enactment where the temptation to invent or embellish must be greater. This switch from academic to dramatic writing is most clearly seen when the author deals with 'La destrucción de Cámara Santa' on the eleventh day of the Revolution in Oviedo. Llano Roza recounts the attack of the revolutionaries, which began at five o'clock in the morning, and the ensuing military response. When the author considers the bombing of the Cámara Santa he gives a detailed account of the history and architectural features of this part of the cathedral, illustrating his explanation with numerous photographs (pp. 69–81). Once he has described all the treasures which have been damaged or ruined, Llano Roza opts for a dramatized narrative form to depict the experiences of a group of nuns.[34] He re-enacts the conversation between the nuns and the revolutionaries when the former are forced to leave their convent. Regardless of whether he was actually present or not, the author lends his eyes to the reader who subsequently witnesses the events for himself. The fact that there is no intermediary step between the depiction of the 'story' as it takes place, and its rendering by the reader (in other words, that there seems to be no narrator to shape the course of events) results in the episode coming to life and confers on the text not only a sense of reality, but also an apparently unmediated view of the events.

Occasionally the apparent authenticity of the scenes depicted is further enhanced with the author's strategic use of colloquial language and dialect, as in the following example in which the author transcribes the distressing account of a witness:

Escasea la comida, y a las fuerzas se les hace imposible la estancia en las casas. De esto da idea la narración que me hizo una mujer de Vega del Rey, Leonarda González, al oscurecer de un día de mayo de este año, delante de la casa donde tuvo el general Boch su Cuartel General.

— ¿Qué tal lo pasaron ustedes por aquí? — le pregunté.

— ¡Ay, señor! Mal, muy mal. No quiero acordame de ello. Los rapacinos estaben acurrucadinos en los rincones, llenos de miedu: pero, ¡bah!, miedu todos los vecinos lu teníamos.

Los soldaos pasaben de una casa a otra per unos furacos que ficieron nes paredes. Ni de día ni de noche cesaben de tirar tiros, ¡probinos! (p. 195)

Given that colloquial speech is associated with the less educated, in other words, the lower class, the author's choice of witness is determined by the need to sustain his seemingly impartial view of the events. The fact that these claims about the difficult circumstances faced by the soldiers come from the mouth of a 'mujer sencilla', as opposed to that of an officer of the army, or a business man, or any other obvious right-wing member of society, heightens the relevance and credibility of the information contained in the statement; a working-class woman (for whom the government forces of order are traditionally her enemy) would not make such allegations if they were not true.

After comparing the narrative style of the two authors, in my view Llano Roza's superior writing ability is evident in that he considers stylistic issues more commonly of concern to the novelist. This skilfulness is further reflected in his use of literary language, which is also present to some extent in Geijo's text. It tends to be limited to those parts where violence is portrayed given that the sight of destruction lends itself particularly well to a dramatic and creative rendering. Geijo, for example, describes the bombing of Oviedo in the following terms: 'El lúgubre eco del bombardeo, que como llamada de trompa guerrera rueda por el angosto valle y trepa hasta el picacho nevado de las montañas cercanas, ha hecho tender su vuelo hacia el poblado a los buitres de la revolución' (p. 202). However, as a spectator, Llano Roza's description of the gradual destruction of the city is more evocative as he effectively relates the images and sounds which he witnesses directly:

¡Qué espectáculo estoy presenciando! Lo contemplo con intensa emoción. Las llamas de los incendios enrojecen el cielo. Las mujeres salen de las casas incendiadas y huyen despavoridas con sus hijos en brazos. Y el populacho se acerca a los comercios gritando:

¡Al asalto! ¡Al asalto!

Los dinamitazos resuenan en las calles. Los aviones bailan una danza macabra; sus bombas, al percutir en el suelo, forman surtidores de metralla que se desparrama en todas direcciones segando vidas. El ruido continuado de los cañonazos asemeja el bramido de las olas en una noche de tormenta. Y los "tableteos" de las ametralladoras parecen aplausos infernales. (p. 87)

Due to the informative and documentary nature of the texts, apart from Llano Roza's dramatic depiction of the scenes he witnesses in Oviedo, and Geijo's figurative description of the revolutionaries, typical of most right-wing accounts and already examined here, there is very little in the way of literary language to comment on.

These two works, selected from a group of relatively similar texts, deal with the experience of the soldiers and the Civil Guard, and the military tactics undertaken. They depict the patriotism, bravery, resistance, and professionalism of the forces of order, and their accomplishment in the face of their alleged material disadvantage. While the authors extol the virtues of the forces, the revolutionaries and their socialist leaders are subjected to an interminable barrage of criticism from which their unpatriotism and cruelty stand out. I have identified a number of factors which determine the content and style of these texts. Firstly, the sources on which the authors base their accounts differ: Llano Roza's text is based largely on his own notes taken as he witnessed the events, while Geijo's is almost entirely based on witness reports and documentary evidence. Secondly, Llano Roza is an erudite academic and historian, while Geijo is an ex-Civil Guard turned journalist, a distinction which to a large extent explains the differences between their approach to the narrative. Llano Roza's *anales* are a hybrid of academic scholarship and dramatic re-enactment, while Geijo's text, as the title suggests, is an episodic account of the events throughout which the narrative style is even and uncomplicated. However, Llano Roza's inclusion of overly detailed intricacies and anecdotes which he could not possibly have witnessed, as well as some of the inaccuracies in the information which he gives, cast doubt on the reliability of his text. In the case of Geijo, the facts he uses are based on documentary evidence and witness accounts, while the descriptive portrayal and justifiability of the events rests on his own biased opinion.

Religious Accounts

I have included in this category the texts that deal exclusively with the suffering and death of members of the clergy and religious orders in Asturias. Whilst Rucabado, *Los mártires de Asturias* (1935) and the book published by the Asociación Católica Nacional de Propagandistas (A.C.N.P.), *Asturias roja* (1935), is concerned with all those religious persons persecuted, arrested or killed in Asturias during the Revolution, *Langreo rojo* (1935) by Noval Suárez, *Los mártires de Turón* (1935), and *Episodios de la revolución en Asturias* (1935) concentrate on the experiences of a particular group: the victimized clergy in Langreo, the Lasallian brothers (Hermanos de la Salle) killed in Turón, and the Passionists

(Pasionistas) persecuted in Mieres, respectively.[35] A wide selection of texts has been included in order to show the extent to which the clergy were eager to disseminate their own interpretation of the events. What stands out in this group of religious tracts is the similarity in the language used, the political view, and the moral attitude adopted, all of which are determined by the religious status of the authors.

Before examining the similarities in these texts I will briefly summarize them. Rucabado's, subtitled: 'Homenaje a los eclesiásticos que dieron la vida por Cristo en la región asturiana durante la revolución socialista y anticlerical de octubre 1934' is an account of when, where, and how each of the religious figures was killed. While Rucabado is the only contributor to his text, in the book published by the A.C.N.P. different authors write under the editorship of the journalist and Chief State Prosecutor José María Rodríguez Villamil. *Los mártires de Turón* and *Episodios de la revolución en Asturias* are the most interesting texts as the experiences of the protagonists are related in detail from the moment in which the Revolution breaks out to the point at which they are killed or liberated. In the case of *Los mártires de Turón*, the anonymous author describes how on 5 October, while in the middle of mass, the armed rabble forced their way into the convent in Turón in search of arms hidden there by the Catholic youth organisation (the Juventud Católica). When no arms turned up the eight brothers were arrested and taken to the *Casa del Pueblo*, allegedly for their own protection. However, on the night of 8 October the prisoners were taken to a cemetery where two large pits had been dug out. There the eight brothers, a visiting Passionist priest from Mieres, and two riflemen were executed and buried. In addition to the main story, an appendix reports on how the bodies were disinterred and transferred to their final burying place, and a series of photographs illustrate the exhumation, the funeral entourage as it entered the city of Palencia, and the procession to the cemetery.[36] In the case of *Episodios*, the Passionist community in Mieres, most members of which survived the ordeal, relate their experiences themselves — their escape from the convent, the verbal and physical abuse from the general public, the means used to escape from the revolutionaries, their imprisonment, and their feelings and thoughts during those moments. The text covers the period from the eve of the Revolution to the entry of the government troops in Mieres, and the last chapter deals with the retrieval and burial of the three dead friars, ending with a prayer in their tribute. In the final text, Noval Suárez begins his account before the other authors examined here, describing the peaceful atmosphere which reigned before the revolutionary problems began. According to the Introduction, the Church in Langreo had been harassed throughout the two-year left-wing republican period.

Noval Suárez refers to the preparations and the violence in the run-up to the Revolution. He examines the fate of each of the religious practitioners in the district of Langreo, beginning with the death of the priest in Sama, an episode mentioned to some degree in nearly all the texts dealing with the Revolution by both revolutionaries and counter-revolutionaries, either to show how the government and the press manipulated the information or to depict the brutality of the miners.

The objectives of these texts fall into three categories: to respond to the requests from the general public to relate their experiences; to pay tribute to those who have died at the hands of the revolutionaries; and to provide an accurate record of the suffering endured by the religious orders for future generations. In *Episodios de la revolución en Asturias* the rector of the Passionist community in Mieres explains to the reader that the book was composed after the many petitions received for news about the harrowing experiences of the friars. He also points out that instead of a collection of 'relatos' embellished with 'invenciones novelescas de fantasía' (p. viii), the reader will find written accounts which have not been novelized in any way and which, as a result of the number of contributors, are written in different styles, 'son tantas las plumas como las narraciones' (p. viii). In fact, on close examination, there are only slight differences in the style of each of these accounts suggesting that the text in general has been subjected to the editor's scrutiny. It is therefore not clear how much of the *Episodios* are exact depictions of their authors' experiences, written solely by them. The resulting composition does manifest, however, a desire to pay tribute to those who have died. In *Los mártires de Turón* this objective takes priority and is evident in the appendix where the author transcribes the 'testimonios de afecto al Instituto de los Hermanos de las Escuelas Cristianas, recibidos por los Superiores con motivo del vil fusilamiento de los Hermanos de Turón' congratulating that religious community for the fact that those 'sacrificed' were members of the religious order of La Salle. According to José Cuesta, prologuist to Noval Suárez's text, this author has a constructive aim in mind — to provide a valuable future record of the events:

> Cuando todos [. . .] vayamos aportando datos, noticias, hechos comprobados y fidedignos, y será hoy una crónica, mañana un folleto, aquí unas fotografías, allí un comentario, más allá un proceso, hasta que podamos ofrecer a las generaciones venideras la historia definitiva y documentada de aquella locura que tantas lágrimas y sangre generosa ha costado y aun costará en lo sucesivo. (p. iv)

For his part, Sabino Gendín, the Secretary of the A.C.N.P., affirms: 'Nuestro libro *Asturias roja*, queremos que a la par de tributo de los hombres a los sacerdotes y religiosos mártires [. . .] sirva de ejemplo a los demás mortales para morir con el tesón y valor espiritual que lo hicieron ellos' (p. 9). Hence, through religious veneration a moral example is set. Indeed, regardless of their initial objectives, ultimately all of the authors want to convey the importance of practicing religious sentiments and values, demonstrated in the way the suffering and martyrdom of these men have been perceived by both protagonists and observers.

As with most of the works examined in this chapter, the authors here stress the veracity and accuracy of their texts. Hence, Noval Suárez assures the reader that 'en el relato que va a leerse no haya ni una sola palabra que no fuese una realidad, ni de cuya veracidad no certifique' (p. 1). In addition they include transcribed documentary evidence as well as photographs of the protagonists, of the sites where the martyrs died, and, in the case of *Los mártires de Turón*, of the exhumation of the bodies. The author of this particular text includes a substantial appendix in which extra background information is provided, such as a summary of the history of the religious order of La Salle, or details of the Asturian countryside. Most of the accounts which comprise these texts are autobiographical. However, other witnesses are used to provide additional information. So, continuing with the example of *Los mártires de Turón*, the gravedigger responsible for burying the eight Lasallian brothers describes what he witnessed, and some of the declarations made by the leader of the revolutionary firing squad are quoted at the end of the text. The reliability of the text will also have a decisive influence on the credibility of any political message conveyed, as indicated by Villamil, in charge of compiling the A.C.N.P. text, who acknowledges that the evidence will serve to demonstrate unequivocally the anti-Catholic intentions of the Revolution:

> En este libro, pues, encontrará el lector [. . .] una serie de relatos, cuya veracidad avalamos por ser recogidos de testimonios de testigos presenciales, que sin formar, [. . .] una descripción sistematizada del sectarismo antirreligioso de la revolución roja asturiana, sirvan para edificación del que leyere y al mismo tiempo para presentar al movimiento marxista tal como él es en el aspecto religioso, esto es, esencial y fundamentalmente antirreligioso y anticristiano y, más concretamente, anticatólico. (p. 14)

Hence, just as with the military accounts, these religious texts also engage in political discussion, adopt the same political and moral stance, and have a similar hidden agenda: the unconditional allegiance to the C.E.D.A. and the controversial newly-formed government, admiration for the courage and competence of the forces of order, and the outright condemnation of the Revolution and in particular the socialist and communist leaders. Any action taken against the right-wing government and the *Patria* is necessarily an attack on Catholicism as it is this institution which poses a threat to the dominant influence of the revolutionary leaders, and their false expectations, over the working class.

The popular support for the Revolution is alluded to in these texts, although the contributors do not agree on its extent. Contradicting the general view that the Revolution was anxiously awaited for by most, Noval Suárez and many of the contributors writing in *Episodios* maintain that only a minority of the population of Asturias endorsed the Revolution. In *Episodios*, for example, the view that predominates is that the majority of people suffered needlessly at the hands of a small group of rebels. Accordingly, given the Church's popularity, the religious figures are portrayed as having many friends willing to help them during those threatening days by hiding them, guiding them through unknown terrain, and providing them with food. Noval Suárez informs the reader that the towns were taken by a rowdy minority while the rest of the population remained hidden and frightened inside their houses. Even within this text, however, the question of the degree of revolutionary support is inconsistent. Noval Suárez inserts an account written collectively by the Dominican monks (padres Dominicanos) in La Felguera, in which they describe those attacking their church as being in their thousands and claim that most awaited the Revolution with eagerness:

> Un día [. . .] entre un grupo de obreros que salía del trabajo, decía uno de ellos: "la revolución está en puerta, y será la más sangrienta que se ha conocido". Este obrero traducía en sus palabras los presentimientos de la casi totalidad de la población. Unos, quizá un noventa y cinco por ciento, la esperaban con ilusión, hasta con regocijo, como se esperan los faustos acontecimientos. (pp. 135–36)

Indeed, this is how most of the religious figures regarded the Revolution, contradicting the equally popular belief that the Church enjoyed the support of a large section of society. To overcome this inconsistency an explanation must be found as to why most people refused to help them and, in most cases, turned against them. As already mentioned, some of the authors claim that those wealthier members of society who were not actually involved in the fighting refused to help the imperilled clergy as they were frightened of reprisals being taken against them and their families, an excuse by and large criticized for being hypocritical. For those who actually persecuted the clergy other explanations must be sought, the most common of which is the view that the masses were brainwashed by the revolutionary leaders and their propaganda and press. Thus in *Los mártires de Turón* a communist praises a Lasallian brother who had once been his teacher demonstrating that he must have been brainwashed into acting against the Church; in *Episodios* the ideology behind the Revolution is described as 'la gran mentira marxista' (p. v); and in *Langreo rojo* those who are most criticized are the press for persuading the masses. Occasionally, instead of the persuasion argument, the author goes a step further and alleges that the workers were simply forced to fire against the clergy and the fleeing monks and friars.

Although the revolutionaries are persistently portrayed in these works as a threat to society, there are instances in which they appear to act compassionately. For example, in *Los mártires de Turón* the revolutionaries are accused of banqueting on the food stolen from the brothers, and of taking their clothes and beating up their dead bodies once they have been shot, confirming their greed, materialism, and cruelty.[37] On the other hand, in the first chapter of this same text the author describes how the brothers were protected from the angry rabble by the armed revolutionaries. Most of the authors here relate similar situations. In *Episodios* the author naturally criticizes the revolutionaries with the predictable depictions of evil and cowardly violence ('los caníbales rojos' [p. 208]), thieving ('bandidos' [p. 31]), and rowdiness ('berreaban con más estridor que el bronco pitorro de la maquinaria' [p. 64]), and the women of brazenness and indecency ('una joven rojilla, de carnes enjutas, un poco vinagre y un mucho de precocidad' [p. 69]). Nevertheless, as in *Los mártires de Turón*, the revolutionaries safeguard their prisoners from the uncontrollable population, the 'multitud furiosa' (p. 98). Noval Suárez's text actually distinguishes between different types of revolutionary:

> Entre los revolucionarios hemos podido distinguir tipos de muy diferente catadura. La chusma obraba con descoco, pero siempre tímida ante la mirada de los jefes. Los fusileros, procaces y atrevidos, como quien tiene conciencia de su poder. Los directivos, relativamente sensatos y moderados y deseosos de evitar atropellos innecesarios. (p. 139)

He also claims that the revolutionary leaders prevented the bloodshed and pillage from being more widespread.[38] These texts are not so inconsistent in how the Revolution as a movement should be regarded, however. They all coincide in their unconditional condemnation, such as in *Los mártires de Turón* where the religious view of the Revolution in Asturias is summarized in the following way:

> Durante cerca de quince días, la parte de la provincia dominada por los rebeldes vivió sometida al régimen del terror, y en nombre de la libertad y redención del pueblo, se cometió toda clase de crímenes y se asesinó sin compasión. (p. 95)

Similarly, in *Episodios* the Revolution is described as one of the worst tragedies in history, and it is compared to a fierce storm, 'huracán revolucionario' (p. 11), and an earthquake with its 'sacudidas de muerte y de destrucción' (p. v).

In order to ensure the reader's rejection of the Revolution a number of manipulative strategies are adopted. All of these texts insist, or at least insinuate, that the religious figures were particularly targeted and that the revolutionaries took particular pleasure in tormenting them. However, Noval Suárez stresses this victimization further by exaggerating the suffering of the religious persons in those instances where it might not even have existed. Although only one priest in Langreo was killed, the author describes the ordeal each one of them underwent as if they too had been about to be executed when in fact most of them were only imprisoned and some were even allowed to go free. This attack on the deep-rooted authority of the Church and its practitioners, influential at every level of society, is portrayed in such a way as to turn the reader's mind against the Revolution. This, along with the depiction of the suffering and hardship of the brave forces of order and innocent population, ensures that the reader will not want to identify himself with the thieving, vicious, and insatiable revolutionaries, and will reject those who have tried to persuade him to commit such barbarities.

Further biased comments and rhetorical techniques enhance the revulsion felt toward the revolutionaries. For example, in the text published by the A.C.N.P. Villamil compares the miners to the Moors:

> Nosotros deseamos que a todos nos sirvan de provechosa lección para que, rectificando conductas, no vuelva a ser necesario que aquellos contra quien se alzó Pelayo hace doce siglos vuelvan a España y a ¡Asturias! a librarnos de la morisma interior que renace al pie de las montañas de Covadonga. (p. 14)

Given that most Asturians will be acquainted with the story of the Reconquest, whether in its historical or legendary form, the analogy drawn between the quashing of the Revolution before it spread across Spain, and Pelayo's defeat of the Moors, preventing them from conquering Asturias, acts as an incentive. In *Los mártires de Turón* the extent of the Revolution is portrayed as having been greater than it really was. While this justifies the severe criticism against the revolutionaries, it also serves to heighten the effective action undertaken by the forces of order which defeated such a massive insurrection. Noval Suárez bases much of his text on the prejudiced versions of the press and the government and although he refers to the inaccuracy of many of the allegations of revolutionary violence and crime, he fails to state categorically that these have been invented or exaggerated. The contributors to *Episodios* enhance the strength of their allegations by addressing the reader directly and by employing irony. Finally, the vivid description of the sight and sound of the bombing and in particular the dynamite explosions, accompanied by the portrayal of tragic and heart-rending anecdotes, convey the horror experienced by the clergy and the religious orders and stress even further their suffering:

> Cuentan lo que han visto y oído, lo que ellos mismos han vivido y padecido, y lo hacen en estilo ingenuo, sencillo, en ocasiones descuidado, efecto de la emoción con que se escribe y *casi* siempre sin arreos literarios, como deben ser escritas estas crónicas [. . .] desnudas de ropaje poético que pudiera desvirtuar la magnitud de la tragedia. (pp. iii–iv, author's emphasis)

The dramatic nature of the events is used by Cuesta, in the prologue to *Langreo rojo*, to explain the lack of literary language. The experiences themselves are powerful enough without having to embellish them.

The notion that the Revolution is an attack against Catholicism and that therefore the suffering of its practitioners is comparable to the suffering of Christ at the hands of the Jews, emerges in all the works. Thus José Cuesta, in the prologue to *Langreo rojo*, claims that although the Revolution was expected nobody thought it would be taken to such extremes, with the Church suffering worse calamities during October than when it was first founded. According to Noval Suárez, although the majority of the population acknowledge the Church's important contribution to society, the fear of retribution prevented the clergy from being fully supported by the people. In those cases in which individuals chose to help certain religious persons, such as the 'muy piadosa, muy caritativa, muy afecta a la Iglesia' (p. 31) Señorita María Castañón, they too were targeted as enemies of the Revolution. Noval Suárez is particularly concerned with outlining how the Church has participated in Spain's social and educational progress. Similarly, according to the author of *Los mártires de Turón*, the brothers 'ponían a los hijos de los obreros en disposición de ganarse honradamente un decente vivir, y de conquistar el reino eterno de los cielos' (p. 84), their main objective being 'procurar el bienestar de los obreros y la cristiana educación de los niños' (p. 86). This is why their death by precisely this sector of society is all the more reprehensible, and why the authors and all those sympathetic to the Church regard the deaths as martyrdom.[39]

Given that the majority writing in these texts are members of the clergy and the holy orders it comes as no surprise that they are replete with allusions to Catholic thought and doctrine, invocations to God, the Saints, and the Virgin, and quotations from and references to the Bible. In *Episodios*, for example, the Passionists explain how in the most difficult of circumstances they felt they were being protected by God, and in some cases they regard their survival against the overwhelming odds as a miracle. It is also interesting to observe that occasionally scenes from the Bible are compared with equally harrowing episodes from October 1934: '¡Qué bueno fue Dios con nosotros! ¡Qué a tiempo nos proporcionó casa y acompañantes seguros y nos sacó, como a otro Lot del fuego de Sodoma, de tan inminente y gravísimo peligro!' (pp. 46–47). Although literary language is very rarely used, when metaphors and symbolism appear they are placed in a religious context and expressed with liturgical terminology, such as in this example taken from *Langreo rojo*: 'Rezaban formando un murmullo que parecía un aletear de los Angeles del Cielo que traían mensajes de fe y aliento para fortalecerles' (p. 90). For the religious community this first fortnight of October 1934 is another of the milestones in the history of the Catholic Church. For that reason the violent death of these men is considered as a sacrifice for which, according to the author of *Los mártires de Turón*, the Lasallian brothers were ready: 'Estaban dispuestos al sacrificio' (p. 122). The suffering of the clergy and religious orders is comparable with that of Jesus Christ and, equally, they must forgive those who acted against them, just as Christ did those who acted against him.

It is clear that the dominant concern of these texts is to underline the sacrifice of the religious martyrs. Beneath this noble guise, however, there lies an equally important agenda: an outright condemnation of the Revolution and the backing of the governmental and military handling of the conflict. The authors embrace the pro-*Patria* flag and stress the fact that the Catholics were the primary target of the Revolution without examining why this may have been the case. They heighten the negative perception of the revolutionaries by mentioning the good deeds of the Church and these religious persons in particular. The resulting text is one which appears to be just as biased as the political texts examined at the start of this chapter.

Revolutionary Works

I have selected two texts from the many revolutionary non-fictional responses to October 1934 studied: N. Molins i Fábrega, *U.H.P.: la insurrección proletaria de Asturias* (1935) and Manuel Grossi Mier, *La insurrección de Asturias* (1935).[40] Molins, a Marxist journalist, was not involved in the revolutionary fighting; instead his work is the result of his investigations during a visit to Asturias following the events. His original plan was to write a series of articles, but the sheer volume of information which he gathered prompted him to set his sights on something more ambitious. According to Wildebaldo Solano, this work, originally written in Catalan, is one of the most interesting and yet one of the least well-known texts on the October Revolution. It was so popular that when it first appeared it sold out in a few months.[41] On the other hand, Grossi Mier's diaristic account is written from the point of view of someone who took part in the events, as the representative of the Alianza Obrera in the Revolutionary Committee in Mieres. Grossi's book was written while he was in prison in Mieres after the revolutionary defeat; in a note written by the author to the 1978 edition he explains how the pages were secretly smuggled out of the prison and eventually gathered together to form this book. The differences in the narrative form and style of these two texts, a result of amongst other things the contrasting conditions under which the authors wrote, make them ideal for comparison.

I will concentrate first of all on the claims of objectivity which, as already established, will influence the whole of the text, interesting in the case of Molins as no attempt is made to hide the bias which so frightens most of the other writers studied in this thesis. Secondly, unlike most of the revolutionary writers, who support a given political party, Molins and Grossi write from the point of view of supporters of the Alianza Obrera. Thirdly, one of the issues which the left and the right most disagreed on is the degree to which the Revolution was supported, on the one hand, by the population at large, and on the other, by the forces of order. Both of these texts examine this in some detail and, as to be expected, conclude that the masses were very much in favour of the Revolution. Finally, just like all the other revolutionary texts, Molins and Grossi praise their own side and criticize the enemy; they allude to episodes which they claim have been erroneously represented to the detriment of the revolutionary side and depict others to condemn the measures taken by the government forces, all of these substantiated with witness reports and documentary evidence. Both Molins and Grossi have an ultimate goal in mind: to divulge the true details of the fighting and, at the same time, afford a series of lessons for the future. As Grossi Mier writes in 1978: 'Cierto que la lección ha sido muy dura y sangrante, pero también altamente educativa para la juventud revolucionaria' (p. 16).

One of the first striking features of Molins's work is the explicit statement that he is not going to be objective as his aim is to purposefully influence the working class and demonstrate the lessons which he believes must be learnt from the October Revolution. He takes the issue of objectivity further when he considers if it is possible for any author writing on these events to be impartial, claiming that deeds and ideas are perceived by man and are therefore interpreted according to his beliefs: 'Unos hechos, unas ideas, son siempre vistos por un hombre y este hombre los ve y los interpreta a su manera. El es objetivo, pero lo es en relación a sí mismo, nunca en relación a los demás' (p. 19). Aware that this might influence negatively the credibility of his text, Molins confesses that it has been written for a particular group of people (the working class) and with a particular aim in mind ('obtener una lección política').[19] Indeed, according to the author, if his text were not to be useful to someone he would not have any reason for writing it: 'No podría escribir si supusiera que mi libro no ha de tener utilidad para alguien y, en este caso, este alguien es la clase trabajadora' (p. 19). Therefore he turns what is initially a negative aspect of the work into a fundamental priority.

Given his didactic aim Molins warns the reader that his text is not going to be 'un reportaje absoluto de los hechos' (p. 19) or even 'un relato demasiado amplio' (p. 19), admitting that he has only included that information which best suits his objectives. Nonetheless, he does not believe that a detailed study on the Revolution can be conducted until a few years have passed: 'Un estudio completo de los hechos de la insurrección española de 1934 no se podrá hacer hasta que dentro de unos años la perspectiva histórica haya desbrozado la visualidad de partidos presos inmediatos que pueden desenfocar la visión de la realidad' (p. 19), admitting the dangers of immediate representation and intrepretation of events. Grossi, on the other hand, does not tackle the issue of objectivity until the end of his text, at which point he states that his work is necessarily impartial as his only aim is to tell the truth. Thus in the second last paragraph he writes:

> El único propósito que perseguía creo que lo he alcanzado: decir la verdad, la áspera y cruda verdad. [. . .] Mi relato, mi informe, a falta de otros méritos, tiene al menos ese, para mí el más valioso: el de la imparcialidad y el de la objetividad. (p. 130)

Grossi, whose text was composed in adverse conditions, limits himself to a descriptive account of what he has witnessed, according to him enough to verify the credibility and impartiality of his text.

Both texts draw attention to roughly the same lessons, although the way these are presented differs. The lessons can be divided into two categories: the politically relevant issues of exactly how committed the political parties actually were to the Alianza Obrera and the Revolution; and the practical question of military tactics where the manoeuvres which proved to be detrimental to the insurrection are revealed and examined. While Grossi offers impulsive and spontaneous advice whenever his narrative allows it, Molins's enlightening and instructive considerations are carefully and methodically placed in the text where they will have the greatest effect.

Whereas Molins produces a thorough analysis of the Revolution in which he examines critically the decisions taken by the revolutionary leadership, Grossi presents a descriptive account of the events and seeks to justify his judgement and actions. Thus Grossi's text deals relatively little with theoretical political questions. For this the author relies on the prologue, written by Joaquín Maurín, dated 5 July 1935, which gives a résumé of the working class movement in Spain from 1909 to 1934, and the epilogue by J. G. Gorkin, dated July 1935, which examines the origins of the revolutionary fight in Spain in which 'Octubre de 1934 no es sino la culminación histórica de todo un proceso revolucionario, iniciado en 1909' (p. 133), and concludes that the Asturian Revolution is 'el preludio de la gran revolución triunfante, una especie de ensayo general' (p. 135), in other words, the beginning of the final victory of the proletariat.

Molins also concentrates on politics in the prologue, where he examines the antecedents to the Revolution, and in the last chapter, where he indicates why the Revolution failed. His political concerns, much more important to the text than in Grossi's case, are threefold — why the Revolution was successful in Asturias and not in Catalonia; the reasons for the socialists' reluctance to support the armed insurrection; and, influencing these two factors, the importance of the Alianza Obrera in uniting the working class. Given that Molins campaigned for the Alianza Obrera and taking into account his self-admitted political bias, the arguments which he uses naturally endorse his viewpoint and vindicate the alliance's objectives. He gives various reasons why the Alianza did not succeed at a national level: although the bourgeoisie government in Catalonia initially supported the Revolution, they were more concerned with the issue of Catalan independence than with working-class discontent. Whilst in Asturias the Revolution was seen as a means to put in power a proletarian government, in Catalonia the leaders merely aimed to return to the political situation of April 1931. Any revolutionary success like that proposed by the Asturians would mean an end to the bourgeois government, in power since 1931. This proved to be the main obstacle as far as the Revolution in Catalonia is concerned. In addition, the anarchists, the most influential workers' force in that region, not only refused to join the Alianza Obrera but went as far as to boycott the Revolution (precisely because it was supported by the Catalan bourgeoisie).

As for the situation in the rest of Spain, Molins claims that the lack of action in Madrid, where the weapons available were not distributed, confirms his belief that the Socialist Party were just as wary of the Alianza Obrera and the Revolution as the Catalans: 'La falta de preparación para la lucha, la descohesión creada a conciencia en Madrid, ignorando a la Alianza Obrera y negándole el derecho a intervenir en la insurrección, demostraron la poca o nula voluntad revolucionaria' (p. 23). Instead of deriving from the preparations and guidance of the established political parties, the insurrection was the result of the constancy and fighting spirit of the Asturian working class. However, despite their resolute and unshakeable faith in the Revolution, according to the author numerous incidents, and in particular the disastrous situation in Gijón, demonstrate that even in Asturias the Revolution had not been properly prepared by the socialist leadership which was more concerned about its control over the armed working class than about the insurrection itself. The socialists espoused revolutionary action in the belief that the threat would be enough to make the reactionary groups which were now part of the government withdraw. According to Molins far from feeling threatened, Gil Robles had deliberately provoked this hostile reaction on the part of the left wing in order to defeat the revolutionary working class before they were ready to fight nationally against the right-wing forces. Once it became apparent that the Revolution had really broken out the socialist leaders were no longer interested. Nevertheless, while in the rest of Spain the socialists did not recognize the Alianza Obrera and merely considered it to be 'un mal menor' (p. 222), in Asturias this alliance became a reality. Faced with the chance to realize their revolutionary aspirations, the Asturian working class, whose final objective was 'la instauración de la República Obrera española' (p. 24), did not hesitate and imposed their desires on their leaders. In the last chapter, 'Asturias y Cataluña, dos insurrecciones distintas', Molins examines in greater detail the constructive role played by the Alianza Obrera in Asturias where it was most influential. And yet, despite its obvious and valuable contribution he laments that there continues to be resistance to its existence.[42]

The Alianza Obrera, which arose from the need of the working class to unite, was effective in bringing together workers of different and sometimes conflicting political allegiances, contradicting the right-wing claim that there was little enthusiasm for the Revolution. Molins affirms that the left-wing political leaders had to yield to the revolutionary demands of their followers or, alternatively, face losing their support. Thus, his first anecdote from the Revolution depicts a worker taking the initiative and control in the fight for the railway station in Oviedo. The initial passive attitude of the socialist leadership did not deter the determined and enthusiastic workers of Asturias:

> La fe era la revolución. Discutir era derrotismo. Ya lo discutiremos después. Si nuestros líderes fallan, como decís vosotros, los incrédulos, los fusilaremos. Nuestra fuerza, una vez puesta en marcha, no tiene freno. Ni la traición de los líderes ni vuestras dudas pueden derrotarnos. Queremos la victoria, y la obtendremos. Abridnos paso, vosotros los cobardes que teméis a la revolución y dejaos de discusiones bizantinas los que no tengáis confianza en vuestros líderes. ¿Queréis la revolución? ¿Sí? Pues aquí tenéis un arma: en el extremo de vuestros brazos hay unos puños potentes para conquistar, cuando haga falta, una más. O venís con nosotros, o caeréis primero que nuestros enemigos como traidores.
>
> Este espíritu de revolución era el que azotaba el alma del proletariado, de todas las masas trabajadoras.[43]

According to the two texts, despite their material disadvantage and lack of preparation, the conviction that they were fighting for a just cause occasioned among the workers a feeling of hope and absolute devotion to the Revolution. Indeed, the revolutionary cause for the miners is occasionally depicted as a religion. Contrary to the right-wing assertion that only a small number of people backed the Revolution, Grossi argues that 'la casi totalidad de los trabajadores asturianos se han puesto ya al lado de la revolución' (p. 52), while Molins goes further and contends that even men from higher social backgrounds were keen to join, such as in Turón and Mieres:

> Los hombres que nunca habían tomado un fusil, hombres que nunca habían pensado en luchar por la revolución proletaria, incluso gente de clase media conocidos más que nada como enemigos de la clase trabajadora, empujados por el ambiente, con el puño en alto iban a ofrecerse a los comisarios para los servicios que hicieran falta. (p. 126)

This author also examines the degree to which the forces of order intended to collaborate with the revolutionaries, an issue which remains unclear today. He explains how the pilots at the León airbase and the marines aboard the first war ship which anchored in Gijón's port waited in vain for the revolutionary aid promised to them. These missed opportunities were especially regrettable as the plane and ship bombardments destroyed not only revolutionary positions but also morale.

Both Grossi and Molins agree in their view that one of the most critical mistakes committed by the leadership at the start of the Revolution was their failure to realize the significance of taking the city of Gijón, especially important for its port. Indeed Molins dedicates the whole of Chapter 8, 'Gijón en la insurrección', to the fiasco of the Revolution in this city, attributed elsewhere in the text to 'un resultado directo de la falta de confianza de los anarquistas y de los celos de los socialistas' (p. 80). The considerations he makes are too detailed to present here but essentially Molins claims that the revolutionaries in Gijón were indecisive, and by neglecting to call a general strike on 5 October, they allowed the government forces to prepare themselves. When they did finally make a move they lacked the arms to take any effective action. The fact that the socialists and the anarchists were divided in Gijón, so detrimental to the Revolution, is attributed to their rejection of the Alianza Obrera, highlighting the importance of this coalition.[44] Grossi indicates that even in Oviedo, where the revolutionaries were eagerly united, the initial hesitation of the leadership, along with the resilient military defence, meant that the city became a tough target. This author, actively involved in the fighting, makes a series of observations to be taken into account in any future revolutionary movement: Firstly, thieves and criminals taking advantage of the disarray caused by the revolutionary situation must be severely punished: 'En los lugares donde reprimimos a esta escoria con mano dura, todo va bien; por el contrario, nuestra negligencia en hacerlo en otros sitios, nos acarrea toda clase de males. Es esta una lección que es preciso tener siempre en cuenta' (p. 36). Secondly, the importance of discipline: 'Durante la batalla hemos observado en nuestro frente la falta de disciplina en la dirección. Cada camarada ha disparado caprichosamente, se ha movido a su guisa sin esperar órdenes de los jefes y del Comité. Es preciso corregir enérgicamente estos defectos que ponen en riesgo la causa de la insurrección' (p. 35). Thirdly, the revolutionary leaders must be united and well-organized, unlike in Oviedo at the start, and Avilés and Gijón throughout the insurrection: 'Se observa [. . .] en el frente la falta de unificación del mando. Cada jefe de grupo actúa con plena independencia, lo cual constituye una falta grave que decidimos subsanar lo antes posible' (p. 38). Finally, the availability of arms and ammunition must be strictly controlled: 'El no haber impuesto un rígido control en la distribución y en el uso de las municiones ha construido uno de nuestros más graves errores' (p. 51).

For Molins, one of the major lessons to be learnt from the fight concerns the preservation of the cathedral tower, according to him '[una] obra de arte puesta como siempre al servicio de los enemigos de la clase trabajadora' (p. 64). He criticizes the artistic grounds for the leadership's reluctance to bomb this military safe haven from where the government forces were causing many revolutionary casualties. This same group of leaders, who headed the first Revolutionary Committee, come under further severe criticism later on in Molins text when he rebukes them for secretly running away knowing that the insurrection 'estaba tocada de muerte' (p. 162). Each of the two authors views this incident differently. It must be remembered that Grossi formed part of the Committee criticized by Molins. In his text Grossi justifies the move and makes claims which contradict the information given by Molins. Molins criticizes the arbitrary decision taken by the Committee and claims that the leaders ran away in the mistaken belief that faced with no leaders, the fighters would also give up and go home. Instead a second Committee was set up and the absconded members of the first were regarded as traitors by the more extremist revolutionaries. Molins considers if the revolutionary tactics after the first Committee ran away were the best ones. He claims that it was clear at this point that the Revolution had failed throughout Spain, although the information fed to the revolutionaries affirmed that it had been successful, and that before long it would inevitably come to an end in Asturias too. Molins laments that the revolutionaries did not surrender at this point as the severity of the government backlash was undoubtedly due to the unremitting resolve of the fighters; had they given up at this point the consequences would not have been as catastrophic. Instead, those socialists who remained loyal to the Revolution (and who probably did not know the extent of its failure in the rest of Spain) formed a final Committee, composed of four socialists and two communists.

For his part, Grossi, who attempts to justify himself, explains that contrary to the communist allegations that the decision to flee had been made by the cowardly socialists, in fact it had been a measure backed by every political party represented on the Committee.[45] He acknowledges that this act must have deeply affected their followers, who continued to fight on, and accepts their anger: 'No cabe duda alguna que la marcha de los Comités tenía que decepcionar grandemente a los trabajadores que con tanto valor y heroísmo habían emprendido la lucha revolucionaria en la madrugada del 5' (p. 88). Grossi was one of those from the first Committee who later served in the third and last Committee. However, despite returning to the Revolution, for Grossi the idea that victory was still possible was absurd and reckless, thereby agreeing with Molins on this point:

> Morir por morir con las armas en la mano, sin que esto reporte ventaja alguna para la causa de la emancipación obrera, nos parece completamente absurdo. Una vez perdida la batalla lo revolucionario es el repliegue estratégico, con el fin de salvar la mayor cantidad de elementos posibles para la preparación de las futuras batallas revolucionarias. (p. 88)

Accordingly, Grossi states that had the revolutionaries surrendered on 12 October, the day after the surrender of the first Revolutionary Committee, there would probably have been fewer victims.

The fact that Molins aims to provide a set of lessons and therefore concentrates on the injudicious aspects of the Revolution does not mean that this text lacks praise for the revolutionaries. Indeed, this is far from the case. Many of the accusations made by the right wing against the revolutionaries are contested by Molins. While the leaders are for the most part criticized, Molins praises the fighting revolutionaries for their heroism, initiative, and kindness. Contrary to the right-wing claims that the revolutionaries were well-armed, Molins and Grossi stress that at the start of the Revolution they had few effective weapons: Grossi states that at the beginning the revolutionaries had to fight with 'escopetas y [. . .] aperos de labranza' (p. 25). After the assault on the factory of La Vega there was no longer a lack of arms. However, there was still a shortage of ammunition. Although, the contraband from the *Turquesa* included many rounds of ammunition, according to Molins 'unos 115.000 cartuchos de fusil mauser' (p. 72) were among the material confiscated by the police. Even the cannons expropriated from the factory in Trubia were useless given that the necessary component to make the shell explode had been removed by the guards defending the factory before surrendering.

Nevertheless, the fall of these factories, although of limited practical value, were psychologically important for the revolutionaries. The author insists that the enthusiasm of the revolutionaries prevailed over the material superiority of the government forces:

> Uno de los ejércitos tenía a su favor la coordinación de la jefatura, la disciplina, la superioridad de las armas, el terror a un código severísimo. El otro ejército en presencia puede decirse que no tenía nada de todo esto. Estas ventajas, que en una lucha armada realmente lo son, eran superadas por el entusiasmo, el valor, la fe en el futuro y la necesidad sentida por todos de cambiar el orden de cosas existente. Aquello, que en unos era superioridad material, en los otros estaba suplido por la superioridad moral. (p. 47)

Thus, in spite of their limited military supplies, the revolutionaries were able to put up a heroic resistance. The only 'weapon' which the revolutionaries had in large quantities was the dynamite from the mines. Molins acclaims the effective and careful use of this potentially dangerous and destructive substance which, according to the right wing, should not have been employed. Both authors give the dynamiters a special mention for their bravery and their contribution to the Revolution, and Molins compares how they were perceived by both fighting sides: '[Los dinamiteros] eran vistos como semidioses por el pueblo obrero y como diablos escapados del averno por los burgueses y por los enemigos de la revolución' (p. 49). Dynamite also has a symbolic presence in Molins's text: Up to the October Revolution it had been considered as a killer of the miners, and yet it now becomes an indispensable instrument in the forging of a new Spain: 'Aquella misma dinamita asesina de obreros, a fuerza de vivir juntos se ha hecho amiga y les sirve para anunciar las grandes solemnidades y los grandes días proletarios' (p. 76).[46]

Grossi, whose text is more a chronicle than an in-depth analysis of the Revolution, is less critical of the forces of order, and not as adulatory of the revolutionaries as Molins. Nevertheless, he does express his admiration for several aspects of the revolutionary effort. For instance, he pays tribute to the fact that the revolutionaries were willing to die for the sake of the Revolution: 'No se conoce el miedo. Los obreros dan pruebas de una decisión y un valor inconmensurables. Sus ojos están fijos en la victoria. Por alcanzarla están todos dispuestos a sacrificar la vida' (p. 28). However, Grossi focuses on the efficient running of the factories under revolutionary rule, such as the one at Trubia, rather than on the actual physical fighting:

> El orden y la disciplina dentro del trabajo no han sido nunca tan perfectos. Los obreros no trabajan ya para el armamento y defensa de la clase enemiga; trabajan para sí, para la victoria de su causa. Las máquinas les obedecen. [. . .] Sólo hay lugar para la emulación y el ejemplo en el trabajo y en el sacrificio. Todos los obreros constituyen una sola familia, trabajando por la emancipación colectiva. (p. 66)

Related to this, Grossi gives details of the arsenal manufactured by the revolutionaries, including armoured trucks and trains, bombs, cannons, and rocket launchers, which enabled them to resist as long as they did. Indeed, he affirms that even the enemy was astounded by the revolutionary skill and resourcefulness.

Molins and Grossi regard favourably the social and economic organization put in practice during the revolutionary period, and both use Sama as the best example. According to Molins life in the revolutionary towns 'era completamente normal' (p. 138) and the rationing introduced ensured that during the revolutionary period 'ni en una sola casa faltó lo más imprescindible para vivir' (p. 42). In order to disprove the allegations that the members of the various Revolutionary Committees had more food at their disposal than everyone else, he quotes a wealthy witness, 'un vecino acomodado de Turón' (p. 140), who declares that the revolutionaries had just as much as they did. For Molins, the threat of severe punishment confirms that they would not have dared to steal. Instead, the clothes and shoes that were taken from the shops were for the use of the badly equipped fighting men. To rebut further these allegations, Molins depicts a number of episodes in which the revolutionaries help the old, the sick and wounded, and the hungry, even when these are from the bourgeoisie. Other scenes display their compassion, courage, and kindness, as highlighted by Molins:

> De episodios como éstos, llenos de ingenuidad, de heroísmo sereno, de humanidad, la insurrección de Asturias nos ofrece a millares. El entusiasmo de la victoria no embriagó a aquellos que sólo habían vivido pensando en aquel instante, finalidad de su vida; al contrario, les dio una serenidad y un sentido de la responsabilidad. (p. 70)

On one occasion, the revolutionaries put their own lives at risk saving the nuns from the Convento de San Pelayo, set on fire by the government forces. This humane action jeopardizes their own military strategy as the government forces take advantage of the time employed to strengthen their positions in the Gobierno Civil, preventing the revolutionaries from ever taking it. In other words, for Molins the integrity of the revolutionaries occasionally worked to their detriment.

This contrasts with the infinite claims of brutality and inclemency which form a major part of the right-wing texts, including the lies about the friar burnt alive in the Parque San Francisco, the dead priest hung up in the butcher's shop, the children of the Civil Guard whose eyes were poked out, and the rape of the three girls,[47] these being made known in the right-wing press who invented horrific stories in order to hide the vicious acts of their own side. As far as the deaths of the Civil Guards in the mining valleys are concerned, Molins insists that they were always given a chance to surrender and only after their continuous refusals were they attacked. While the right-wing reports regard the son of one of the Civil Guards in Murias, who died as a result of his participation in the defence of the barracks, as a hero, Grossi remarks about the same boy: 'Ha tenido la imprudencia de intervenir en la lucha' (p. 26), highlighting how each side has its own idea of what is to be considered as heroic.[48] In addition Molins denies that civilians were used in the attack against the Cuartel Pelayo, or that all of the destruction was caused by the revolutionaries. Unlike the right-wing and religious texts, Molins is positive about the contribution of women, 'aquellas chicas abnegadas y heroicas' (p. 184), to the Revolution. Grossi gives this more consideration and examines the different ways in which women were involved: they were nurses to the sick and wounded, and assistants to the doctors; they provided the front with provisions and ammunition; they encouraged the fighters and cheered for them enthusiastically; and sometimes they even took part in the fight. He affirms that despite his initial doubts, 'después de la experiencia de la Comuna asturiana tengo que reconocer que la mujer obrera puede jugar un papel tan importante en la revolución como el de los proletarios. Su valor sobrepasa incluso, a veces, al de los trabajadores' (p. 101). Both authors quote enemy prisoners (such as the director of Duro-Felguera, Antonio Lucio) who claim that they were well treated by the revolutionaries, and Grossi maintains that this was deliberate so as not to tarnish the principles behind the Revolution. Finally, Molins rejects the widespread belief that the revolutionaries sought revenge, affirming that: 'La revolución no puede estar a merced de venganzas ni de preferencias personales' (p. 124). On the other hand, the degree of repression exerted by the government forces, and especially the arbitrary killing of innocent men at Carbayín on 24 October, induces a feeling of revenge, effectively described by Molins and worth quoting in its entirety:

> Las fuerzas reaccionarias ya sabían que se hacían al querer destruir físicamente a todos los obreros asturianos, pero aunque lo hubieran conseguido no habrían evitado esta venganza ni el triunfo de la revolución. Tanto lo uno como lo otro viven en el ambiente, se respiran en el aire, están impregnados en la tierra calada de sangre, se deslizan en el agua de los ríos, salen con la vaharada húmeda de la mina. Matarían a todos los obreros de Asturias que han conocido la tragedia, y los que los suplirían sentirían cómo el viento, el aire y los árboles y los mismos pájaros que vuelan por el cielo de Asturias les indicarían el camino que habían de tomar para la venganza y el triunfo. (p. 203)

The government forces with their severe backlash have unsuspectingly secured the continuation of the revolutionary struggle.

Consistent with all the texts on the Revolution, in these left-wing accounts the authors' high-esteem for their own side goes hand in hand with their condemnation of the enemy. Just as in his appraisal of the revolutionary tactics, Molins directs his criticisms at the military leadership of the right-wing forces whom he depicts as cowardly, especially when compared to their own soldiers.[49] The sergeants of the Civil Guard are often portrayed as irresponsible, such as in the case of Alonso Nart in Sama who is accused of forcing his men to fight despite the desperate situation, leading to the death of many of them. Molins occasionally alludes to the bravery of the soldiers in the government forces, especially when he describes their vehement defence of certain positions such as the Comandancia de Carabineros: 'Este episodio de la Comandancia de carabineros de Oviedo fue uno de los más sobresalientes de la defensa de la ciudad por las fuerzas del Gobierno' (p. 52).

Most of the time, however, the authors are critical of the army and Civil Guard and centre their attack on three areas — their pillaging, destructiveness, and cruelty, as Grossi succinctly writes: 'Se asesina. Se roba. Se incendia' (p. 92). Molins alludes on several occasions to the robbing perpetrated by the soldiers, especially on the part of the Tercio and Regulares who were promised by their chiefs that they could do so. He also criticizes the destructiveness of the forces who, in an attempt to demoralize the revolutionaries, provoked the first fire of the Revolution by setting alight the *Casa del Pueblo*, where the printing presses of the newspaper *Avance* were located. Grossi actually alleges that all of the vandalism and the fires, including the one in the Cámara Santa, were caused by the forces of order. Molins refers with indignation to the tactic of placing civilians in front of the army in order to protect the troops, a strategy which according to Molins and other left-wing authors explains López Ochoa's easy entry into Oviedo. He includes as evidence the declaration taken from 'un tal González' who verifies the allegations made against López Ochoa: 'A las dos de la tarde, el general, viendo que no podía avanzar, ordenó que fuésemos puestos en línea de fuego para servir de defensa a los soldados' (p. 172).[50] The heavy plane bombardments in Mieres and Oviedo, many of the victims of which were women and children, is also regarded with revulsion and sadness by Molins, and even more so by Grossi who points out that anyone could fall victim to the bombs: 'Las bombas asesinas no eligen sus víctimas. Matan en serie' (p. 65). The authors give many examples of the cruelty perpetrated by the Tercio and Regulares, described as bloodthirsty animals by Grossi: 'Los soldados del Tercio parecen chacales ávidos de sangre. Matan sin miramiento. Matan lo mismo a hombres que a mujeres y niños' (p. 81). According to a government soldier, interviewed by Molins in Chapter 13, these troops had boasted to him that they had buried people alive. In addition Molins examines in detail the death of the civilians in San

Esteban, Villafría, and Las Arenas, and in the hospital of Oviedo where according to him two hundred people were killed.[51] Unlike Grossi, he deals with the policy of repression which the government implemented after the Revolution, and by using investigative journalism, proves that, despite the denial of the authorities, such as in the case of Javier Bueno, the use of torture was widespread.

The positive depiction of the revolutionaries and the negative depiction of the government forces form part of the manipulative strategies employed by the authors, which in turn serve to determine the reader's response to the events. This is especially true in the case of Molins whose text has been composed more carefully, as outlined above. I will give five examples from this text which demonstrate the ways in which Molins manipulates his narrative. Firstly, in the same chapter in which he deals with the attack on the Civil Guard barracks in Sama, Molins bitterly reminds the reader of their punitive and pitiless treatment of the workers and peasants in the past:

> Más de un guardia al ver un compañero agonizando en un rincón, al encontrarse con la mujer y los hijos llorosos que le suplicaban con los ojos humedecidos, debía pensar en las otras veces que él había tenido así, también acorralados, familias de obreros o de campesinos miserables que habían cometido el delito de no querer conformarse con morir de hambre ni con ser tratados como bestias. (p. 85)

The author does this deliberately to stop the reader feeling moved by the suffering and death of the Civil Guard which he goes on to describe. In addition, to prevent the revolutionaries from appearing to be callous, the death of the Guards must be made out to be their own fault. Thus Molins stresses that the revolutionaries constantly pleaded with them to surrender, a call met with refusal: 'El [Nart] y sus hombres perdieron la vida a causa de su ceguera y tozudez' (p. 87).

The second example emerges in the paragraph which Molins devotes to the Turón deaths. While initially admitting that the revolutionary shooting of the brothers was unwarranted, he goes on to argue that on the other hand the deaths among the forces of order were justifiable as they had been killed in battle, unlike many of the revolutionaries who died after surrendering, without a chance to defend themselves:

> En Turón se produjo el fusilamiento de nueve frailes; fusilamiento que, revolucionariamente, no está del todo justificado. [. . .] No podemos decir lo mismo con relación a los guardias civiles muertos. Estos, como casi la totalidad de los que murieron en Asturias, lo mismo que soldados y guardias de asalto, cayeron en lucha. ¡Si pudiéramos decir lo mismo con relación a los revolucionarios! (p. 127)

Thus, not only does Molins casually dismiss the issue in question, avoiding having to account for this controversial and unjustifiable revolutionary action, but he also manages to change the subject, subtly drawing attention once again to the suffering of the revolutionaries. Grossi's account of the Turón deaths is interesting too. Contrary to the claims from both left and right that the order for the execution was given by the Mieres Revolutionary Committee, of which Grossi was a member, he claims that this execution was decided on by individual revolutionaries. In addition, although he regrets it having taken place he adds that, taken in a wider context, compared to the violence of the Tercio and Regulares this act is insignificant.

The third way in which Molins manipulates the narrative is evident in his use of witness reports and diaries, such as the 'diario de operaciones del comandante militar de la plaza de Gijón' (p. 93) which he quotes to demonstrate the indecisiveness of the miners. Even when using the diaries to supply information to the reader, Molins does not hesitate to make remarks aimed at influencing how the diary should be interpreted, and where he disagrees with the diarist the disparity is attributed to the misinformation of the latter. Thus, despite using primary sources Molins challenges whatever facts he objects to and adds others which he believes the diarist 'omite voluntariamente' (p. 95). Indeed, given his initial claims in the prologue that his work will be biased it seems paradoxical that he should find the need to investigate and incorporate verifiable evidence in order to provide an objective view. In this respect, it seems Molins is working on the supposition that his bias is true, a characteristic applicable to many of these writers.

The fourth example demonstrates how Molins uses a technique widely employed by authors on the left and right, which consists of regarding a seemingly unsuccessful or mistaken manoeuvre as a deliberate tactic. For example, Molins tries to explain why the revolutionaries did not attack the Cárcel Modelo in Oviedo or why the prisoners did not attempt to take the prison from the inside, attributing it to a decision taken by the revolutionaries rather than to the effective defence of the forces of order. Similarly, in his text Grossi claims that in the important front of Campomanes the revolutionaries would certainly have been capable of beating their enemy if they had launched an all-out attack against them. However, worried that the victims would be too numerous, the leaders *choose* not to attack. In the fifth and final example, Molins rejects the allegation that the revolutionaries purposefully targeted the library of the University of Oviedo because of their hatred for books, reminding the reader that the workers valued the libraries highly, demonstrated by the fact that they set one up in many villages and towns:

En Oviedo, como en todo Asturias, los únicos que saben lo que significa y cuesta una biblioteca son los obreros, los únicos que han llenado de ellas el país, que han montado una en cada pueblo con la más grande desesperación de los burgueses. (p. 168)

When he describes how the forces of order reduced to ashes many books from the library in Sama, Molins claims that it was in the belief that the ignorance of the working class guaranteed the dominance of the bourgeoisie: 'En la ignorancia de los obreros está la garantía de la permanencia de su dominación' (p. 193).

In the prologue to his text Molins states that he will attempt to write 'lo más frío posible' (p. 19) when he carries out his political analysis. However, he also admits that when relating the experiences of the revolutionaries the narrative will inevitably and necessarily be dramatic, just like the events:

La insurrección asturiana ha costado demasiada sangre obrera para poder hablar siempre con absoluta serenidad, y los intereses de la clase trabajadora son demasiado sagrados para dejar que el ánimo se caliente demasiado al hacer aquella parte de crítica de los actores de la tragedia. (pp. 19–20)

The dramatic description of the countryside and the atmospheric settings which Molins evokes serve an additional purpose. It is another means used by the author to influence the reader's response to the Revolution and to the subsequent repression. Through his poignant and impassioned writing Molins manages to induce sadness and disappointment, indignation and impatience in the reader. I have chosen two from the many examples available to demonstrate how the author effectively dictates the way the reader will view the situation he relates by basing the description on subjective feelings rather than on objective facts. In the first example Molins describes how a final revolutionary effort is made:

Y las montañas de Sama sintieron cómo un pueblo congregado despedía a su ejército al canto de la *Internacional*. Las voces de los que se iban y de los que se quedaban eran firmes, de hombres decididos a luchar, a morir luchando, de hombres que sabían que en la lucha estaba su vida y la de los suyos, y en la cobardía, su muerte. Ni una madre, ni un hijo, ni una esposa no incitó a ninguno de los suyos a no seguir al ejército revolucionario. (p. 177)

While evoking the inherent sadness of a scene in which a large group of men leave to fight to their death, and their mothers, wives, and children bid them farewell perhaps for the last time, Molins expresses to the reader the determination of the revolutionaries to fight to the end, and their conviction that only a victorious outcome is acceptable. In this example there is an initial intimation that the countryside reflects the mood which reigns over Asturias as the revolutionaries make a last desperate effort, a stylistic device more fully developed in the second example, in which the author sets the scene for the civilian deaths of Carbayín:

Derrotada la insurrección, el terror planea sobre los hogares obreros de Asturias. Sus alas negras de cuervo oscurecen el cielo y tapan el horizonte. [. . .] Las iglesias, ¡lugares sagrados!, se han convertido en cárceles, en lugares de tortura para los vencidos; las escuelas en cuarteles; las Casas del Pueblo, en fortines de la reacción; los caminos en calvarios; los barrancos, en cementerios que ofrecen cadáveres a la lluvia, a las aves de rapiña. [. . .] Aquellos niños que habían presenciado cómo su padre era fusilado, cómo su madre era maltratada, cómo su hermano era torturado, cómo su hermana era mancillada por los bárbaros. Aquellos ríos que bajaban al mar contando los secretos de los hombres mantenidos en sus aguas frías horas y días. Aquel aire que nunca más podría hacer otra cosa que llevar de un lado a otro de la tierra los gemidos y blasfemias que había escuchado día y noche. El aire se había vuelto viento alocado, y ya nunca más sabría acariciar la hierba ni peinar pinos y castaños. Corre, corre, dando vueltas a la tierra, huyendo de los gritos de dolor, de los chillidos de espanto, de las exclamaciones de rabia. No sabe dónde dejar su carga monstruosa, en el mediodía de Francia arranca árboles, en el Mediterráneo destroza barcos, en Asia central derriba casas, en el Japón provoca incendios. ¡Volverá, volverá aquel aire que, loco, se ha vuelto viento! (pp. 196–97)

The resentment and bitterness of the workers is metaphorically manifested in the elements (in this case the wind), where it will remain for centuries to come and prevail over future generations. For his part, Grossi is not as dramatic or atmospheric in his portrayal and prefers to communicate concrete facts rather than emotive descriptions. For example, although he too refers to the singing of the *International* by women and children, and the emotion which he feels as he watches them, the language which he employs is, in comparison, plain and matter-of-fact. Thus, in his text the reader's response will be influenced by the drama conveyed by the facts, not the style, of the narrative.

I will conclude my analysis of the revolutionary accounts with another stylistic consideration, by drawing attention to a particularly interesting characteristic of Molins's text which, in addition, distinguishes it more than any other feature, from Grossi's: its hybrid nature. The former is a mixture of anecdotal examples, combined with documentary evidence and descriptive language. There is also an element of fiction at the start of the text when Molins depicts a gathering of a group of middle-class friends: In Chapter 1 the author introduces 'nuestro buen burgués', a fictional character appearing only in this chapter, who thinks back to the discussions held with his friends, 'dos alamacenistas, un comandante, un capitán y un burócrata como él [the protagonist of this meeting]' (p. 28), prior to October about a possible Revolution. The characters are specifically chosen to represent the bourgeoisie and military class of Oviedo, and the author goes from one person to the next analysing their views. The fictional aspect gets more pronounced as the author goes on to describe their physical appearance, thereby constructing real-life characters as opposed to mere opinions. Rather than explain the outlook of those who were to condemn the revolutionary attempt, Molins enacts it. Another characteristic occasionally employed by Molins and more often associated with fictional writing is dramatic irony, produced by narrating the events as if the outcome were unknown. Other dramatic elements which form an essential part of the text can be found in the re-enactment of certain episodes of the Revolution, for example, when the author describes the actual fighting, in the depiction of the interview between López Ochoa and Belarmino Tomás, and in the sensitive descriptions of the atmosphere in certain places at given critical moments which prompt a specific response from the reader. Along with the fictional and dramatic aspects of the text, there are the purely factual which take two forms — as documentary evidence, such as transcribed edicts, diaries, letters, and police reports, and as political digressions, for example when the author examines critically the socialist-anarchist conflict in Gijón. The fictional, dramatic, and factual come together in this text providing the reader a series of lessons from which Molins highlights three: 'Preparación revolucionaria, voluntad de vencer y audacia son la única garantía de victoria' (p. 25).

Grossi's text is not as complicated. Instead of a mixture of narrative forms it is a diaristic report of the Revolution, starting on 3 October with the crisis of the Samper government, and ending on 18 October, the day on which the author is arrested. Grossi gives an account of the events as experienced by him and, having witnessed the results of the Revolution, while interned in the prison in Mieres, muses about the action which has taken place, providing a series of lessons which he thinks must be taken into account for the future. Although at first sight the spontaneous nature of the text and the near absence of investigative recourse appear to invalidate its credibility,[52] Joaquín Maurín, who writes the prologue, claims that its diaristic form and the lack of literary and elaborate writing make the text more real as the author provides 'una traducción tan próxima de la acción' (p. 21):

> Grossi nos aporta un documento de un valor excepcional. No se trata de un reportaje hecho por una pluma brillante. Grossi durante los días de la sublevación no manejaba la pluma, sino el fusil, la bomba y la ametralladora. [. . .] Sus páginas, secas, pero fuertemente emocionantes a veces, son un reflejo interesantísimo de aquellas jornadas cargadas de electricidad e iluminadas por las explosiones de la dinamita. (p. 21)

In the epilogue the author's lack of literariness is once again alluded to by J. G. Gorkin who also claims that this is a positive characteristic of the text:

> Lo primero que verá el lector es que no ha sido hecho por un escritor. Está exento de galas literarias. Es una obra sin pulir. [. . .] Esas notas breves, directas, como

aguafuertes, tienen un sabor de cosa vivida de verdadero documento humano. Es el diario de un combatiente rojo que, en el silencio carcelario, va rememorando las escenas vividas durante la lucha. (p. 134)

Grossi himself, in the penultimate paragraph of his diary, indicates his objectives and insists that his ultimate aim is to tell the truth about the Revolution. Regardless of the quality of the language, he believes that he has achieved this: 'Soy un minero y un revolucionario, sin otra cultura que aquella que he podido adquirir a fuerza de sacrificios. El único propósito que perseguía creo que lo he alcanzado: decir la verdad, la áspera y cruda verdad' (p. 130).

These two authors write with the same goal in mind, to provide a series of lessons which workers and revolutionaries will be able to refer to in the future in order to guide them to victory. Nevertheless, the methods with which they do this differ due to the different circumstances in which they write. Molins, with the advantage of writing freely, produces a text which is more carefully structured, researched, and overall better written than Grossi, who has to write his text secretly in prison with all the disadvantages which that entails. And yet the core message is conveyed just as effectively in both texts, namely that in order to ensure the organization, discipline, and determination necessary the Alianza Obrera must be accepted as the overall unifying force.

In this chapter I have examined a series of texts in which the authors present different accounts of the Revolution, whether writing down their own experiences or relating those of others. With the government and political texts, by comparing *La revolución*, and the texts written by Ignacio Núñez and José Romero Cuesta, I have drawn attention to three different manipulative strategies which may be employed by authors who wish to convey a specific message to the reader. In the case of the military accounts, the text by Aurelio de Llano Roza, who wrote his account as a direct witness of the Revolution, and that by Jenaro Geijo, who investigated the events after they took place, demonstrate the differences which arise depending on how close the author is to the events and the extent to which he has experienced them. The religious texts examined show the degree to which their religious status influenced the content and style of their accounts. Finally, the revolutionary works reveal the two different approaches used by Manuel Grossi Mier and Narciso Molins i Fábrega, writing from the point of view of the losing side, who aim to disseminate a series of lessons, suggestions, and political messages in spite of their defeated position.

Whilst I have shown that each of these texts presents a set of features which are unique to their category, there are also parallels between the texts in one category and another, including the use of manipulation and rhetoric, the introduction of documentary and witness evidence, their didactic purpose, as well as semantic and stylistic similarities. Ultimately these texts aim to tell the story of the October Revolution from beginning to end. In doing so, three main features are particularly influential in determining the content, the point of view, and the style of all of these works — the ideological stance, the professional status, and the revolutionary experience of the authors. In other words, the authors establish what political stand they will take and write according to this. This, is in turn, is influenced by their professional status, explaining, for example, the religious rhetoric and imagery in the religious texts, the emphasis of patriotism and bravery in the military accounts, the irony used against the left wing in the political texts, and the symbolism of the miners in the revolutionary works. These two elements, the political and professional viewpoint of the author, are merged with his experience of the Revolution which inevitably adds the dramatic element to the narrative — the fighting is described, the tragic death of the victims is related, and the suffering of the innocent is stressed. The authors aim to relate to the reader the course of the Revolution and in the process, in their interpretation of the events, transmit a set of ideological and religious beliefs which ultimately have a propagandistic purpose. However, these are neither political discourses nor purely descriptive accounts; rather than possess any marked literary distinction it is clear that they come closer to informative journalism. It is evident, therefore, that however specific and detailed a text is, whether the events have been personally witnessed by the author or the evidence has been gathered from other sources, or whether the text is written from the point of view of a historian or a journalist, a Civil Guard or a fighting revolutionary, a priest or a government supporter, the driving force behind these strategies is the author's desire to make his version the most believable and to convey his political view to the reader.

1. *La revolución de octubre en España: la rebelión del gobierno de la Generalidad. Octubre 1934* (Madrid: Bolaños y Aguilar, 1934); Ignacio Núñez, *La revolución de octubre de 1934*, 2 vols (Barcelona: José Villamala, 1935); and José Romero Cuesta, *El sargento Vázquez* (Madrid: Gráficas Aglaya, [1936]). References to these editions are given after the quotations.
2. Reporteros Reunidos, *Octubre rojo: ocho días que conmovieron a España* (Madrid: Imp. Vallinas, [n.d.]).
3. There is, in addition, another work dealing with Vázquez's involvement in the Revolution: Ignacio Barrado, *El sargento Vázquez: reportaje* ([n.p.]: [n. pub.], [1936]).
4. The edition consulted has the first chapter missing and starts on page 9, preventing me from stating categorically that there is a definite absence of any claim on the part of the author professing the reliability of his text. Nevertheless, in other texts the initial claims

are accompanied throughout the text by further assurances and in Romero Cuesta's these secondary assurances do not appear. This leads me to deduce that this must not be a priority.

5. Quotes from newspaper articles can be found in pp. 6, 13, 14, and 19; speeches are transcribed in pp. 6, 10, 11, and 12, including a radio bulletin on pp. 24–25; and sections of a document with the revolutionary 'instrucciones tácticas' can be found in pp. 15–17.
6. It is typical of the right-wing texts to stress that the Revolution was an attack against a constitutionally elected government, thereby implying that the socialist leaders went against the wishes of the Spanish electorate.
7. Paco Ignacio Taibo, *Asturias 1934*, 2 vols (Gijón: Ediciones Jucar, 1984), I, 5.
8. Ibid., I, 149–51. According to Taibo the revolutionary killed was Juan Freigedo, brother of Julia Freigedo who was the wife of Sergeant Dionisio Fernández.
9. Ibid., I, 247–48.
10. Lars Ole Sauerberg, *Fact into Fiction: Documentary Realism in the Contemporary Novel* (London: Macmillan, 1991), p. 59.
11. Taibo deals with each of these incidents in II, 155–60 and II, 245 respectively.
12. Llano Roza states about the government report that 'en esto, como en otros datos, tales como el sitio por donde comenzaron los incendios, nombres de calles, fechas históricas, etcétera, ha padecido errores' (p. 15, footnote 1).
13. John Hellman, *Fables of Fact: The New Journalism as New Fiction* (Urbana: Illinois University Press, 1981), p. 25.
14. Núñez, II, 53–54.
15. 'Al frente del gobierno de la provincia estaba un hombre que por lo menos se ha de calificar de inepto, pues no quiso ver la tragedia que ya se mascaba, aunque más de una vez se le intentó hacer que la viese. Y para colmo de desdichas, era presidente del Consejo de ministros un hombre de funesta memoria, el señor Samper, cuya negligencia sólo es comparable a la del señor Blanco, gobernador de Asturias, reos ambos, por omisión, de la tragedia asturiana y cooperadores, conscientes o inconscientes, de la política de Azaña' (I, 96).
16. According to Núñez: 'La clase minera es una clase que puede llamarse rica entre las clases trabajadoras, pues los sueldos de los mineros en Asturias son muy altos, de 15, 20, 25 y hasta 50 pesetas diarias. Familias había en Asturias en que entraban más de dos mil pesetas mensuales por su trabajo. Creían algunos que las doctrinas del marxismo no pasarían de teorías entre gente minera que manejaba dinero, que lo gastaba sin privaciones, que lo disfrutaba hasta con lujos y que hasta llegó a lavarse las manos con champán' (I, 97).
17. Romero Cuesta, pp. 50–51.
18. José R. Rubinat, *Héroes y mártires: los Zapadores y la Revolución de Octubre* (Oviedo: Imp. Emiliano, [1935(?)]). This is a pamphlet dedicated to and about the '8° Batallón de Zapadores Minadores', based in Gijón, whose help in the fight against the revolutionaries in Oviedo was crucial, and about who there was very little written: 'Para todos hubo menciones muy merecidas, y, por imperdonable olvido, no la hubo para los bravos Zapadores, que fueron quienes arrostraron los primeros peligros, llegando a Oviedo cuando nuestra ciudad era una inmensa hoguera, para plantar a sus puertas, con el sacrificio de varios compañeros, la primera palma del martirio patriótico' (p. 9). Eduardo López Ochoa, *Campaña militar de Asturias en Octubre 1934* (Madrid: Ediciones Yunque, 1936). In the prologue (written in Barcelona in October 1935) López Ochoa writes: 'Transcurrido un año de aquellos sucesos [. . .] he estimado de oportunidad y conveniencia [. . .] narrar de una manera clara y terminante los pormenores, tácticos y episódicos de aquella breve campaña militar' (p. 8).
19. Aurelio de Llano Roza de Ampudia, *Pequeños anales de quince días:* la *Revolución en Asturias. Octubre 1934* (Oviedo: Talleres Tipográficos Altamirano, 1935), and Jenaro G. Geijo, *Episodios de la revolución* (Santander: Tipografía de la Librería Moderna, 1935). References to these editions are given after the quotations in the text.
20. Despite extensive research I have been unable to track down any issue of or reference to *Información*. Consequently, I have been unable to determine whether Geijo was the editor or merely a contributor to this publication.
21. Ronald Weber, *The Literature of Fact: Literary Non-Fiction in American Writing* (Ohio: Ohio University Press, 1980), p. 53.

22. For example, the report of one of the Guards who survived the killings in Sama and who relates the events which took place there (pp. 165–75), or that of another Guard describing his experience in Oviedo (pp. 290–97).
23. Llano Roza himself occasionally refers to his notes as a diary: 'Son las dos de la mañana. Llueve — lo tengo anotado en mi diario de la revolución' (p. 194).
24. P. xi. At the end of his account of the events in Oviedo the author once again reminds the reader that he has witnessed all that which he has described: 'Anoche he terminado de tomar notas desde el punto que he citado arriba tantas veces, donde durante nueve días [. . .] he vivido la revolución, presenciando un espectáculo terrible, devastador' (p. 116).
25. Some of the details are extremely accurate and unnecessary: 'Un pequeño grupo de casas situadas a los lados de la carretera, cuya pendiente en este punto es de 16 por 100' (p. 4).
26. For example, of those in La Vega factory who did not remove the bolts from the guns (p. 40); a colonel for not leaving his office in the Gobierno Civil (p. 119); and the officers of the Civil Guard who surrendered in Pola Lena (p. 182).
27. Tzvetan Todorov, *Genres in Discourse*, trans. by Catherine Porter (Cambridge: Cambridge University Press, 1990), p. 18.
28. Geijo's text deals with the whole of Spain but I am concentrating on the chapters which deal with the events in Asturias.
29. All of these examples are taken from Geijo.
30. According to Michael Alpert: 'It had been usual for governments in Spain to use the army at times of public disorder and, though the Republic had tried to avoid this by creating a corps of Republican police — the Assault Guard — this was also paramilitary and commanded by officers seconded from the army. The declaration of states of siege, which brought troops onto the streets, was often judged less provocative than bringing in the ruthless and better trained Civil Guards.' He adds: 'In conservative circles, the Republic was seen as impermanent and most officers could feel no emotional loyalty to it. They clung instead to the ideals of loyalty to the army and the territorial integrity of Spain.' From Michel Alpert, 'Soldiers, politics and war', in *Revolution and War in Spain 1931–1939*, ed. by Paul Preston (London: Methuen, 1984; repr. London: Routledge, 1993), pp. 202–24 (p. 208).
31. These are only a selection from the many examples available and not included for lack of space.
32. Further examples of the nuns speaking positively about the revolutionaries can be found on pp. 51, 61, and 82.
33. Aurelio de Llano Roza de Ampudia (1868–1936) specialized in archaeology and folklore. In addition he published articles in *El Carbayón* and in *El Correo de Asturias*, and founded the Centro de Estudios Asturianos (1920). In the text Llano Roza refers to his own book, *Bellezas de Asturias de Oriente a Occidente* (1927), on several occasions (pp. 77, 191).
34. Other academic explanations include the description of the foundation of the University and its quad (pp. 107–10); information about the pre-Romanesque church of Santa Cristina (pp. 190–91); demographic, geographical, and historical details of the valleys of the Nalón (p. 158), Turón (p. 169), Aller (p. 173) and Mieres (p. 176); and historical details of the cannon factory at Trubia (p. 18).
35. R. Rucabado, *Los mártires de Asturias: la escuela mártir de Turón*, 2nd edn (Barcelona: Catalunya Social, 1935); Asociación Católica Nacional de Propagandistas, *Asturias roja (octubre de 1934): sacerdotes y religiosos perseguidos y martirizados* (Oviedo: Moderna Imprenta Trufero, 1935); *Los mártires de Turón: notas biográficas y reseña del martirio de los religiosos bárbaramente asesinados por los revolucionarios en Turón (Asturias)* (Madrid: La Instrucción Pública, 1935); *Episodios de la revolución en Asturias: los pasionistas de Mieres (Asturias) y la Revolución de octubre de 1934* (Santander: El Pasionario, [1935(?)]); and Senén Noval Suárez, *Langreo rojo: historia del martirio y persecución de los sacerdotes en el arziprestazgo de Langreo, durante los sucesos revolucionarios de 1934* ([La Felguera]: Imp. la Torre, 1935). References to these editions are given after the quotations in the text.
36. According to the text the bodies were transferred to Bugedo on 26 February 1935. On the way — in Ujo, Pola de Lena, Palencia, Burgos, Briviesca, and finally Bugedo — the funeral entourage was met by lay and religious people.
37. Pp. 64, 45, and 72 respectively.

38. Evidence of this is available according to Taibo, II, 28–32.
39. On 21 November 1999, Pope John Paul II declared the Passionist priest shot in Turón and the eight Christian brothers of La Salle martyrs of the Catholic Church.
40. N. Molins i Fábrega, *U.H.P.: la revolució prolètaria d'Astúries* (Barcelona: Atena, 1935), and Manuel Grossi Mier, *La insurrección de Asturias* (Barcelona: Ediciones La Batalla, 1935). I have used the later editions of these texts: *U.H.P.: la insurrección proletaria de Asturias*, trans. by Carmen García Ribas (Gijón: Jucar, 1977) and *La insurrección de Asturias* (Madrid and Gijón: Jucar, 1978). Page references are given after the quotations. Ignotus [Manuel Villar], *El anarquismo en la insurrección de Asturias: la C.N.T. y la F.A.I. en octubre de 1934* (Valencia: Ediciones Tierra y Libertad, 1935) and Fernando Solano Palacio, *La revolución de octubre: quince días de comunismo libertario en Asturias*, 3rd edn (Barcelona: [n. pub.], [1936]) could also have been included here. However, Molins's and Grossi's texts bear more resemblance and deal more with the actual fighting of the Revolution, while the other two works (both of which are anarchist) are more concerned with the political dimension of the Revolution.
41. Wildebaldo Solano, who writes the introductory 'Presentación' to the 1977 edition of Molins's text, gives a biographical sketch of the author, and summarises what led Molins to compose this work and how it was received by the public. He informs the reader that Molins 'no vivió personalmente los acontecimientos, puesto que se encontraba en Barcelona, militando en el seno de la Alianza Obrera y trabajando en *La Humanitat* en octubre de 1934' (p. 17).
42. Molins corroborates this by transcribing a letter written by Largo Caballero, dated 30 April 1935, in which the leader of the Socialist Party writes: 'La Unión General no tiene nada que ver con los trabajos que en ésa puedan realizar las Alianzas Obreras, toda vez que nosotros sólo estamos en contacto directo con nuestras secciones y Federaciones. No sostenemos ni hemos sostenido correspondencia con ellas ni les hemos dado órdenes de ninguna naturaleza. Ello quiere decir que nuestros compañeros en ésas y en las demás localidades de España deben realizar la propaganda necesaria dentro de los Sindicatos para llevarlos por el camino que a nuestras tácticas conviene. Sin confusionismos que entorpecerían nuestra labor y sin quebrantamientos de nuestra clásica disciplina' (p. 224).
43. Molins, pp. 35–36.
44. Molins writes: 'La multiplicidad de organizaciones había retrasado la acción; era necesario añadir a la indecisión de los dirigentes la mala voluntad o la poca comprensión por su parte de la consigna que había cohesionado hacía tan poco a toda la clase obrera asturiana y que, en realidad, la mantenía cohesionada moralmente: la Alianza Obrera.' (p. 101).
45. Grossi writes: 'Todos los componentes del Comité, socialistas, comunistas y anarquistas, llegaron a ponerse de acuerdo. Conviene hacer esta advertencia porque hay un partido político obrero que trata de llevarse los laureles de la insurrección asturiana en detrimento de los demás partidos obreros y, sobre todo, del Partido Socialista. Folletitos se han publicado en que se acusa de cobardes a los camaradas designados por el Partido Socialista para dirigir la acción. Yo no pertenezco al Partido Socialista ni estoy de acuerdo con la trayectoria política que ha seguido este partido. Pero a pesar de ello tengo que decir con toda franqueza, con toda lealtad, que mientras ha durado la lucha, todos los compañeros socialistas, lo mismo los directivos que los de la base, han dado pruebas de valor y de abnegación, como corresponde a verdaderos revolucionarios' (p. 87).
46. In Ignotus, *El anarquismo en la insurrección de Asturias*, one of the texts not examined here, dynamite also has a symbolic presence: 'Los estampidos, propagándose de pueblo en pueblo y de valle en valle, eran la señal de que la revolución se extendía victoriosa por toda Asturias, envolviéndola en sus rojas llamaradas. Emergiendo de los pozos llenos de sombra, trocando la herramienta de producción por el arma que había de permitirles realizar y garantizar la conquista de su libertad, los mineros se lanzaron como titanes a la desigual contienda' (p. 68).
47. Pp. 57, 82, 82, 214–19 respectively.
48. For example Geijo writes that the boy 'se había distinguido notablemente en la defensa del destacamento' (p. 225).
49. Examples can be found in pp. 41, 49, 64, 73, and 81. An example can also be found in Grossi, p. 72.

50. According to the author this is how the anarchist representative in the Alianza Obrera, Bonifacio Martín, died (p. 172).
51. Pp. 179, 181–82, 182–83, and 185 respectively.
52. It is true however that Grossi quotes primary documentary evidence, including a substantial part of an article from *Ahora* about the Campomanes front (pp. 56–57), various of the proclamations and edicts disseminated by the revolutionaries (pp. 68, 70, and 79), and the surrendering speech made by Belarmino Tomás in Sama (pp. 123–25). Incidentally, the fact that this evidence is included suggests that the text must have been edited before being published as Grossi would not have had these sources with him in prison.

CHAPTER 5

ON THE BORDER BETWEEN FICTION AND NON-FICTION (I)

The texts included in the following two chapters belong to that uncertain range of narrative types which are not clearly identified as fiction or non-fiction. While they do deal with factual events, the way in which they are presented resembles fictional prose narrative. Thus, in determining the generic types of these texts, we have to take into account the evident crossing of borders from the factual to the fictional realm of literature, where re-enacted and dramatized episodes are merged with factual reports and documented accounts; or where one real experience is related employing literary devices more commonly associated with fictional or novelistic writing.

The first of the four texts is Francisco Prada, *Asturias la desventurada: caminos de sangre* (1934), which I have classified as 'dramatized vignettes' as in it the author collects a series of independent episodes which he dramatizes and re-enacts in order to relate the experiences of a wide range of people. He then combines these with 'objective' and informative political and military accounts of the Revolution. Secondly, *El sindicato católico de Moreda y la revolución de octubre* (1935), is an account written in the first person in which the miner and Secretary of the Catholic Trade Union (Sindicato Católico de Obreros Mineros Españoles), Vicente Madera, relates in chronological order his own experiences as he leads a group of men in the defence of his trade union centre and, subsequently, as he escapes to the mountains and hides from the revolutionaries. Continuing with the theme, in Chapter 6 I have included Adro Xavier [pseud.], *Sangre jesuita. Asturias 1934: Padre Emilio Martínez y H. Juan B. Arconada* (1938), a novelized biography in which the author relates the life story of the two religious figures and the way in which they were killed by the revolutionaries. I will compare Adro's text with a more essayistic version of the same story and on which it appears to be based. I will leave the most interesting and at the same time the most complex of these four texts till last, Alfonso Camín Meana, *El valle negro: Asturias 1934* (1938). Alfonso Camín's text is a collage of many narrative styles pertaining to the realms of both creative and fictional writing and documentary and historical reports.

Dramatized Vignettes of the Revolution

In this text, *Asturias la desventurada: caminos de sangre* (1934), Francisco Prada provides us with a series of twenty-eight separate and unrelated episodes, each of which tells the experience of a particular person or family, or some other anecdote of the Revolution.[1] The separate vignettes take different forms. The majority are dramatized episodes where the author relates the suffering of the innocent victims. In these the action takes place in the private realm of the victim or his or her family, whether this is a living room or a hospital bedside. In addition, three of the vignettes are transcriptions of the experiences of a witness. The remainder are simple accounts of the revolutionary situation in one place or another, such as Mieres or Oviedo, which resemble journalistic reporting.

Before examining the actual style, contents, and other details of the narrative, a brief glance at the overall structure of the text provides the first indication of its hybridism. The prologue leads into the twenty-eight short vignettes, which are followed by numerical details of the dead, the injured, and the disappeared in the government forces. In the dramatized episodes, most of which are at the most three or four pages long, the reader is plunged straight into the heart of the action as the author provides a window through which the reader can observe the protagonists of each individual story expressing their grief, anxiety, anger, and hope. In this way the author, by means of conversing characters and the omniscient narrator, relates eighteen separate stories and experiences of the Revolution, all of which have the suffering innocent as a common denominator. In the journalistic episodes the reader is provided with a more seemingly objective and informative political and military account of the Revolution; specific personal experiences are not referred to and instead an overview is given of how the Revolution progressed in a number of Asturian towns. Thus, as with many of the authors examined in the previous chapter, Prada chooses to employ two very different narrative approaches to relate the different aspects of the Revolution: the personal, humane, subjective and sentimental real-life experiences which evoke what the Asturian Revolution has meant for the civilians, and the impersonal and strategic political and military accounts which provide the background information to the course of the Revolution and is necessary in order to place the dramatized episodes in their real-life context. Unlike in the texts examined in Chapter 4, however, even the informative accounts take on dramatic qualities and use fictional techniques which, taken together with the dramatized episodes, produce a text which is more fictional and novelistic in nature. Integrated into the representation of the Revolution is the author's interpretation of it, and although in the prologue he argues that he will be impartial and truthful, the clear bias which emerges at the beginning is further reinforced throughout the text. However, this is an issue which I will deal with after examining the narrative characteristics of this text.

In the first set of episodes the author effectively and realistically depicts the tense and frightening situation lived by the civilians by means of the language and style he employs. These purposefully enhance the dramatic mood required of the text in order to convey the drama and atmosphere of the circumstances. In the first vignette, 'La angustia por el que no vuelve', which relates the first of the dramatic episodes, Prada describes a scene in which a family awaits anxiously for the father to arrive after leaving the previous day in search of food. The episode concentrates on the fears and anxieties of each of the family members, and only at the very end of the last page does the father finally appear safe and sound. The family is comprised of the man's wife, his elderly mother, and his two young children. It would seem plot-wise, that this story is slight. Different from most of the other texts dealing with the Revolution, there seems to be nothing tragic about this particular episode — nobody dies and no one is imprisoned or subjected to verbal or physical abuse, and the father does turn up at the end only slightly injured by a stray bullet. However, in my view, Prada does not include this episode to provide evidence of the violence of the Revolution, or information about the strategies followed by either side. Rather, it sets the scene. Apart from serving a chronological purpose and demonstrating the initial effects of the Revolution, Prada is attempting to demonstrate how, regardless of tragic and sad stories, the mere presence of the Revolution affected *everyone*, ordinary people included. However, I do not think that it is mere coincidence that the ordinary people which appear in this episode should be particularly vulnerable: two women, one of them elderly, 'una viejecilla casi impedida de ochenta y tantos años' (p. 5), and two young children, in other words, blameless victims of the social circumstances. By choosing to start with an episode involving these very specific characters the author transmits to the reader from the start a feeling of disgust and sadness towards the Revolution, before any tragic and regrettable events are even described or any explicit biased stance has been taken. Thus Prada sets the historical as well as the sentimental scene to the revolutionary days.

The dramatic representation of the episode and the appropriateness of the characters involved (the latter more likely to be picked up by the critic than the lay reader) may create the impression that the story has been invented by the author. However, Prada insists that 'de labios de estos testigos [. . .] hemos escuchado' (p. 5). He is thus merely relaying the information which he has been told by those who lived it. And yet it is very clear that whereas the basic facts of the story could certainly have originated in a witness report (most probably that of the wife, although not actually stated in the text), the author's use of the narrative voice influences the way that this information is served to the reader. The manner in which the story is told is as influential as the story itself.

The author, whose only available tool is his use of written language, resorts to succinct descriptions and images which evoke to the reader the sentiments demonstrated by the interviewee. The witness, for example, may have suggested to the author through gestures or verbal intonation, or other means which cannot be expressed textually, the uncertainty and fear felt as communications and lighting were cut off and darkness set in on the night the Revolution broke out: 'La noche había cubierto la capital de Asturias con sus negros mantos' (p. 5). With this metaphor, evoking how darkness and silence set in on the region, the author is reinterpreting what the witness felt, or what he would like us to think she felt. There are several more instances where the author uses this technique. For example, when one of the little boys speaks his voice is described as 'la voz sentenciosa de un hombrecito' (p. 6). Surely the narrator is responsible for this description and not the boy's mother. Similarly, when the start of the Revolution is related, the imaginative and evocative metaphor 'la muerte había iniciado su danza infernal' (p. 7) is more likely to originate with the narrator than with the witness who is giving a spontaneous and not a carefully thought-through verbal account of the events. When describing the sunrise of the next morning the narrator takes some time to describe not only the increase in the amount of light, but also the reliability of nature which cannot be subjected to the influence and manipulation of man:

> La claridad de un nuevo día empieza ya a iniciarse en el firmamento. La luz que fabrican los hombres para dar claridad a la sombra en la noche, pudieron los hombres adueñarse de ella y destrozarla y anularla y romperla, pero la fuerza divina que impulsa al sol en su camino, ésa no está al alcance de los hombres. (pp. 7–8)

Thus the author not only uses the power of the narrator to create a tense atmosphere shrouded in suspense but also to impart implicit messages, as will become evident further on. Half way through the episode the author–narrator appears once again, as if Prada were reminding the reader that he is relating a story which has, in turn, been related to him by the witness:

> En la casa de nuestros amigos crecía por momentos la desesperación y la angustia. ¡El marido ausente seguía sin volver!. . . ¿Estaría sobre el pavimento de alguna calle

> de la ciudad con el corazón destrozado por alguna bala certera?... ¿Habría conseguido encontrar un refugio antes de llegar a su casa?... ¿Estaría en poder de las turbas revolucionarias?... (p. 7)

I have quoted the whole of this paragraph as it reveals an interesting feature: the author-narrator forsakes his omniscience (Prada will have been aware of the happy outcome at the time of writing) as he worries about the fate of the father, thereby putting himself in the place of the mother and wife who wonder what has become of him.[2] Thus, instead of statements questions are used. The author conveys to the detached reader not only the uncertainty which faced the family as they lived those episodes, but the degree of their anxiety which he, as interviewer, perceived.

These feelings of anxiety and foreboding, crucial to this introductory vignette and enhanced by the author's reminders that what he is depicting is a truthful re-enactment of a witness account, are further enhanced in a number of ways. The most evident way is with the title of the episode, 'La angustia por el que no vuelve...', which provides the first inkling of what the story will be about and what emotions it will provoke in the reader. The author, far from being frightened about giving the plot away, is preparing the reader for what is to come. There are other more subtle ways in which anxiety and tension are generated and for which the author resorts to techniques commonly associated with fictional writing: the figurative depiction of the passing of time, and the detailed and re-enacted representation of the emotional state of the characters. This first episode begins on the 4 October as large numbers of miners reach Oviedo and the town begins to grow restless and uneasy. Night falls and while the revolutionaries take over the city, in one of its suburbs a family, the collective protagonist of this episode, awaits anxiously for the head of the family to return. The passing of time is linked to the increasing anxiety of the members of the family, so that 'cada minuto que pasaba era como un puñal que se clavaba en el corazón de la esposa y de la madre' (p. 6). As time passes the man's absence becomes more pronounced; instead of feeling every minute he is away the women are reminded with each tick of the old clock in the sitting room, compared by the narrator to each beat of their heart: 'Y el reloj en su vieja caja de madera seguía latiendo y los corazones de las dos pobres mujeres parecían que iban a escaparse al galopar de sus latidos' (p. 7). The women feel the man's absence increasingly as they face the ever likely prospect that something must have happened to him. Their hope gradually fades away as the night hours pass, until 'el reloj da cuatro campanadas' (p. 7), at which point an exclamation from both of the women that the man is not going to return ('¡¡No vuelve!!' [p. 7]) announces that all hope has been lost. It is not until the next morning that the husband arrives and the story ends. Apart from the physiological reaction of the women (in other words, their increased heart rate as panic sets in), their anxiety is also conveyed through their psychological and emotional response. The mother of the man feels the anxiety of one who has lived the Carlist War, and fears that this other 'guerra civil' has taken her son away from her. For her part, the wife is sad not only about her husband's absence but at the sight of her distraught children who ask for their father and seek reassurance from the adults that he is not dead: 'La madre, cubriendo la carita del ángel con sus besos y con sus lágrimas, sentía que le rasgaban el corazón' (p. 6). Thus, the combined depiction of the stunned mother, the anxious wife, and the upset children, lend a tragic picture to a distraught household, representative of many families during that first night of the Revolution. In the morning, when the wife draws open the curtains and sees the pavement covered with dead bodies, she lets out a scream of shock as the likely fate of the husband confronts her head-on. Nevertheless, at that point there is a knock at the door and as the husband walks in she shouts once again but this time with joy.

The ending of this first vignette is also worth drawing attention to. When the man does finally arrive at the house, only the immediate relief and happiness of the wife is depicted. In the sentences which follow this happiness disappears and the narrator states that 'la angustia sigue viviendo en aquel hogar' (p. 8). This pessimistic ending can be explained if we consider the theme and the message that runs through this vignette. The author is depicting the harrowing and anxious moments lived by the civilians and this is just the first night; there are many more to follow, and each night will be lived just as anxiously as the first. The father hugs and kisses his two sons relieved that he has once again been able to see them, yet the episode ends with the pessimistic statement: 'Y la ciudad sigue consumiéndose en el volcán de sus locuras. . .' (p. 8). There is nothing positive to be seen in the Revolution or in this particular episode even though the man has arrived safely to his awaiting family.

The second of the chosen episodes, vignette number twenty-one, 'El azahar de la novia se ha teñido de sangre', also takes place on the first day of the Revolution, 'la madrugada del 5' (p. 70), although, unlike the first, this one does have a tragic ending. Its title also functions as a summary and the reader knows before he has begun to read the main narrative that this will be a tragic episode. And yet the author begins the episode with the happy image of a young and beautiful girl, living in an idyllic village, putting the finishing touches to the dress which she will be wedded in on 7 October. The first news of the Revolution is brought by a neighbour who claims that her husband, a miner, has left that evening armed with a gun to fight for the revolutionary side. The initial fears of the bride-to-be are dispelled as she chats with her elderly and nearly senile aunt who recalls how beautiful she looked on her wedding day all those years ago. When she finishes sewing the brilliant white corsage of orange blossom on to her dress she tries it on. While she waits for her fiancé to arrive, anxious to show him how beautiful she looks in the dress, a loud explosion is heard, followed by gun-fire. At this point the happiness depicted in the narrative suddenly ceases with an ellipsis. The row of asterisks which goes on to divide the vignette announces the start of the tragedy: 'De pronto se rasgó con un alarido de tragedia el silencio de aquella noche sin estrellas' (p. 74). The girl, alarmed by the noise outside, goes to close the window. She falls down dead on the floor as a stray bullet reaches her. The elderly aunt cries over her dead body, dressed in the bloodstained wedding gown. Adding to the tragedy of the episode, the boyfriend arrives at the house at that moment and breaks down when he sees his beloved dead on the floor. The reader has been taken through the careful and tender tailoring of the girl's dress, the eagerness felt when she has tried it on, and her excitement about the approaching wedding in the knowledge that sooner or later, according to the title, the dress will end up stained with blood, in other words, that the episode will end in tragedy. The author's use of dramatic irony is further enhanced as the girl and her aunt choose not to take seriously the neighbour who warns them of the impending Revolution.

The author chooses to recreate rather than simply report the events and as a result much of the vignette is made up of conversations between the characters. Given that the narrator is unlikely to have witnessed these he insists that 'nos contaron [esta narración]' (p. 73), although the person who did so is not identified. The fact that the information is transmitted in the form of dialogue does not make the messages imparted by the author any less valuable. According to Leech and Short: 'The conversations between the characters are ultimately a part of the message from author to reader' (p. 269). In this vignette there are many examples of this, aimed at influencing how the reader should perceive the Revolution. Although she will be the one most affected by it, the young girl's only declared attitude towards the Revolution is her naïve and simple view that it must be the result of the madness of men. On the other hand, the character who is most responsible for feeding the negative messages against the Revolution to the reader is the neighbour. It is ironic that it should be her, the wife of a revolutionary, who, through her gossipy conversation, should kindle the negative feelings which will, at the end of the vignette, be confirmed by the deeds themselves. She suggests that her husband is a drunkard, fitting in with the idea of the drunken miner turned revolutionary which appears in most of the right-wing texts. She is also worried that her husband, easily persuaded, has been dragged into the conflict:

La vecina, angustiada, añade:
— Estoy atemorizá. Mi marido es muy bueno, pero se deja arrastrar por el primero que llega.
— Esa es la perdición de muchos hombres — dice la viejuca — , que se dejan arrastrar por los que juegan con las vidas de los demás sin exponer nunca la suya. (p. 71)

The important message of this short extract of conversation is that the revolutionaries seem to be unsure about what their aims are and that the revolutionary propaganda has been very successful in rounding up ignorant men to fight for a cause which will be of real benefit to only a few. In addition, the neighbour's allusion to her husband's belief that once the Revolution has succeeded he will become 'por lo menos Comisario del pueblo, como en Rusia' (p. 71) not only reinforces the idea that the miners (and workers in general) were bribed under false pretences into fighting, but it also highlights the altruistic aims of the revolutionaries. As the aunt points out, who will work in the mines if all the miners are to become commissars? The indirectly informative exchanges between the characters, and the ensuing violent events depicted, finally culminate in the narrator's assertion: '¡Ya había prendido la llama siniestra de la revolución!' (p. 75). However, the story is not over yet. Just to heighten the tragedy of the episode, and thereby the Revolution, the boyfriend, who is not involved in the Revolution and who works in the office of a mining company, as opposed to down the pit (note the author's implicit link of the man's profession and his rejection of the Revolution), arrives at the house and is greeted with this sorry sight. In the final scene of the vignette: 'Los labios del zagal al besar los azahares de la novia, se tiñeron de sangre. . .' (p. 75). Without the explicit assertion of the narrator, associating the Revolution with evil or violence, the perception which is nevertheless created through the dramatic re-enactment is that the life of an innocent young girl has been unnecessarily cut short due to the circumstances produced by men such as the drunken miner who has been talked into fighting in return for being given the opportunity to leave his job down the pit. In addition, the lives of the boyfriend and the aunt have also been destroyed by this ignorance and greed. Not only does the author depict the suffering of the innocent, as in the first vignette, but also, with this one specific scene the author is imparting a view on the Revolution in general.

In vignette number six, '¡Hospitales de sangre!', after describing the merit and worthy deeds of the doctors, nurses, and nuns looking after the wounded soldiers, the author focuses on the story of one young patient. It is interesting to note the way in which the author has come to know about this story, according to him, the result of 'casualidad' (p. 21). Indeed, on reading it this certainly seems to be the case. It appears that, eager to include a section on the injured soldiers, the narrator has gone to a hospital to investigate the experiences of some of these brave men. Initially, the likelihood of fulfilling his investigative exercise seems uncertain as access to the injured is very limited: 'Las órdenes de no hablar con los heridos son rigurosísimas. Por ello tenemos que desistir de nuestro propósito de interrogar a algunos aquí en Asturias' (p. 21). However, as luck would have it, he witnesses the following episode which forms the basis of this vignette. He sees a soldier, recently operated on and tucked up in bed, talking to one of the nurses. The intrepid narrator gets closer to the bed:

> Nos acercamos un poco más hasta la cama donde reposa el soldadito de los grandes ojos azules que miran asustados, pero no nos atrevemos a romper la consigna severísima y no le hablamos, pero estamos tan cerca que si él hablara podríamos oírle. (p. 22)

Thus the author–narrator is witness to what he is going to relate. He sees two women enter the ward, the mother and the girlfriend of the soldier in question. The happiness of the mother who feared that her son was dead is depicted. She assures her son that soon he will be discharged and he will be able to carry on with life as normal, work in his vineyard and dance with his girlfriend as in the good old days. While the mother carries on talking joyfully, the girlfriend reads in her beloved's eyes that there is something wrong, 'una mayor tragedia' (p. 23), the first indication to the reader that this vignette, like most of the others, will end tragically. Indeed, when the mother tells her son to hug her like he used to when he was a child the soldier weeps bitterly. The mother pulls down the covers slightly and lets out a scream when she sees that her son has had both arms amputated. The vignette ends dramatically with the exclamation: '¡Su hijo ya no tiene brazos!. . .' (p. 23). Any happiness which may have emerged from this episode is, as in the first, short-lived and immediately dissipated.

As in the two vignettes already examined, the author depicts the suffering of the innocent, and the protagonist, or 'soldadito', as the narrator prefers to call him, must be portrayed as being particularly vulnerable. Thus he is described as having 'una cara de niño, muy pálida, con unos grandes ojos azules que miran asustados' (p. 21). His youth is confirmed when his mother reveals that he is 'de servicio' (p. 23), in other words, that he is doing military service. This young man, whose bad luck it was to be carrying out the obligatory military service at this precise moment, is now badly maimed and marked for life. A similar case is related in vignette number twenty-four, '¡Vida entre sombras!', in which a soldier, blinded by a dynamite explosion, regrets not being able to look at his beautiful girlfriend ever again, and worse still, not being able to see when other men look at her: '¡Ni podrá verla a ella, ni saber si algún otro hombre la mira!. . .' (p. 83). In other words, both men, neither of whom will be able to enjoy their girlfriends as they used to, feel that their manhood has been taken away from them and that their youth has come to an abrupt end.

These four vignettes demonstrate the author's desire to focus on the suffering of the innocent people, affected by the Revolution. Whilst most of the texts dealing with the Revolution depict the fighting, the advances of the army generals and the (lack of) military strategies followed by the revolutionary fighters, the bombing of key positions by both sides, and the population's favourable or critical reaction to either side, this text concentrates on the human dimension of these issues: how the victims suffer in the hospital bed, and their families at their bed side; the anxiety produced by the deafening sound of bombs, the tragic sight of dead men lying on the ground, and buildings destroyed; and the lives which are devastated by death and injury. Thus harrowing scenes are depicted in which a soldier awaiting his first child is shot dead before he has a chance to meet his daughter (vignette number fourteen); a mother who kneels down and cries inconsolably at the site where her young son has been killed by a dynamite explosion (vignette five); more mothers whose sons have been badly injured (vignette six) or killed (vignette seven) while in battle and who try to come to terms with the tragedy; and children who have been maimed (vignette eight) or whose life has been put at risk because of the lack of food (vignette three). Even the revolutionaries are represented as victims as they have to endure the repercussions of their thoughtless and reckless actions (vignette twenty-six).

The impact of these scenes, as pointed out above, is enhanced by having the 'characters' themselves re-enact the dramatic and tragic episodes which they have suffered. This narrative approach serves an additional purpose, however. The author gives the impression that the characters themselves are telling the story, distancing the role of the narrator and, seemingly, his influence on the events depicted. On the other hand, in order to prevent the reader thinking that he is reading a piece of fiction, a fair supposition given the narrative techniques the author has chosen to employ, Prada includes a prologue in which he writes: 'El más intenso dramatismo palpita en estas páginas que hemos arrancado de la misma realidad, puesto que de unas fuimos testigos presenciales y otras nos las relataron quienes vivieron la tragedia' (p. 3). Thus Prada insists that the information on which the episodes are based is verifiable and has been witnessed by him or by trustworthy people whom he has personally interviewed. The author finishes his guarantee of the book's truthfulness with a warning ('Debemos *advertir* previamente' [my italics]) that this text 'ni es tendencioso, ni es apasionado, ni es político' (p. 3). Instead it is 'un juicio sereno de cuanto ha ocurrido' (p. 3). This 'warning' is merely a means used by the author to hide the biased point of view which he so claims to reject.

Another means used by the author to distance himself from the events narrated is by transcribing directly what he has been told. He does this on three occasions: vignettes four, 'La espantosa odisea del gerente del banco asturiano', sixteen, 'Cómo se hicieron dueños de Oviedo las tropas del Ejército', and twenty-eight, 'Los pájaros de acero'. If we look at one of these in detail, in the fourth vignette, the author transcribes the allegations made by Alas Pumariño about his time as a prisoner of the revolutionaries. Amongst other acts of cruelty he relates two incidents of imprisoned men being killed by the revolutionaries. Instead of the narrator accusing the revolutionaries of any cruel deeds, he lets the well-respected bank director who has witnessed them reveal these acts. However, in his effort to present the human dimension of the conflict more fully than many of the other authors, Prada inevitably, implicitly and explicitly, passes judgement on the revolutionary events themselves. The vignettes examined above demonstrate that in the re-enacted episodes the author rarely criticizes the miners directly, preferring instead to present a series of situations in which a number of negative attributes are conferred on the revolutionaries and the Revolution, a technique used by some of the authors previously mentioned in Chapter 4 of this thesis. The following vignettes, different from the ones examined above, demonstrate how the revolutionaries and the Revolution are denounced without the author appearing to take a blatantly political stance.

Vignette number twenty-three, 'La lección del maestro', depicts the first day back at school after the Revolution. The teacher's chosen lesson for that day is not Arithmetic or History, but 'lección de Humanidad' (p. 79). With this specially tender scene the author's wider goal is clearly to convey to the reader what sort of behaviour is acceptable. In order to achieve a rapport with his readership, necessary if the message is to get through successfully, the contents of the episode must be interpreted and evaluated in an appropriate way. By alluding to the importance of teachers as bolsterers of morality and integrity ('No hay título más noble que el de maestro' [p. 78]), the author not only generalizes that all teachers are alike, but that they all share the same opinion (that is, his opinion). The virtues of this particular teacher are stressed even further:

El maestro de nuestra narración es un hombre de nobles virtudes, de acendrado patriotismo, de corazón sano y generoso, que ha procurado siempre inculcar en sus pequeños discípulos la idea de la hermandad, del bien, del amor a la patria y a los hombres. (p. 78)

Having established the importance of teaching as a profession and the virtues of this particular individual, there is no room for doubting the legitimacy of the teacher's beliefs. The teacher directs his attention especially at one young boy who has lost his father in the Revolution and who, according to the narrator, 'Se cuentan de él algunas escenas sanguinarias' (p. 80). Thus the teacher has taken it on himself to 'moldear el alma de aquel niño' (p. 80), of course, in such a way that is acceptable to him: 'Sólo hace falta que seas para tu patria como el mejor hijo y para los hombres, para todos, como el mejor hermano. . .' (p. 80). When the narrator states that the teacher wants to arouse in the boy 'los más altos, los más generosos pensamientos' (p. 80) and that he wants to instil in the class in general 'un sentimiento de hermandad' (p. 79), he is taking for granted that the school teacher's perception of these is the only valid one.

Vignettes number thirteen, '¡Ha bajado un lobo de la montaña!' and twenty, 'La tiendecita del indiano' concentrate on the actions of the revolutionaries and provide examples of the author's depiction of these ignorant, and in some cases cruel, men. Hence, in number thirteen a young and recently married couple is taken by surprise as a group of revolutionaries force their way into their house and shop. They eat and drink everything that they fancy and finally force the husband to take a rifle and fight on their side. In his absence the wife is kissed (raped?) by one of the revolutionaries guarding the shop. Whilst the couple beg the revolutionaries not to take all of their merchandise, the shop being their only means of making a living, one of the miners exclaims that they have a right to as under revolutionary rule everything belongs to everyone. In this way the author links the couple's misfortune with the egoistic revolutionary ideals, effectively making a mockery of the latter. This reaches its most serious implications as one of the revolutionaries uses it as an excuse to rape the wife; he claims he has a right to as '¡Todo es de todos!' (p. 43). This person is given a fictional name: 'El Rojizo — le llamaremos así — [. . .]' (p. 42). Apart from contradicting the author's initial assertion that all the information in the text is real, the negative connotations inherent in this name are quite evident (precisely the reason why it has been chosen) and are further reinforced by the beastly descriptions of the same man: 'La clava [a la mujer] sus garras y mancha los labios con un beso de monstruo' (p. 43), and further on: '¡Aquel monstruo con forma humana, es un reptil con figura de hombre!' (p. 44). El Rojizo is the character most damningly criticized in the whole of the text; not all of the revolutionaries are portrayed in this monstrous way. Indeed, the comrade also in charge of guarding the shop and a witness to the sexual assault exclaims that he feels deeply embarrassed to fight alongside elements like El Rojizo. It is worth pointing out, as Leech and Short argue, that in order for a text to be taken as realistic it must be credible.[3] For Prada it is enough to depict one revolutionary in such harsh terms; to depict any more would be stretching the credibility of the episode and of the text in general. Instead he chooses to base his criticisms on the violence and destruction caused by the revolutionary movement as a whole and its effects on the innocent people, as explained above.

Vignette number twenty, 'La tiendecita del indiano', is not as violent as the one just examined, although it is just as dramatic. There is no re-enactment of the revolutionaries forcing their way into the house and confiscating goods or harming anyone. Rather, the narrator relates the story of a fifteen-year-old boy who emigrates to South America in search of a better life. He returns years later, after much hard work, with the money he has saved, which the narrator stresses is 'una pequeña fortuna que no la había hecho engañando a nadie, que no la había heredado de nadie' (p. 68), to care for his now aged parents. A break in the vignette represents the passing of a number of years, during which time the *indiano* has bought a shop and the house above it. With his father now dead, his small business provides for him and his mother. The Revolution only makes an appearance at the end of the vignette, after all the essential contextual information has been provided, when the narrator reveals that the shop has been ransacked and the *indiano*'s home destroyed. Ironically, after yearning to return to Asturias, the fruits of his hard work and the effort expended in a far-off foreign land have been taken away from him or destroyed in his home country:

> Toda su labor perseverante de años y años, todas sus privaciones, todo el esfuerzo de su juventud y de su trabajo ha sido destruidas. ¡Cuanto ganó en toda una vida y en otras tierras, lo ha perdido en la suya, a la que vino a hacer ofrenda de cuanto tenía! (p. 69)

For the author, the Revolution generalizes people's class and socio-economic position, failing to recognize individual effort — not all shops and businesses are run by ruthless money-makers. Instead, the revolutionaries take by force, in the name of 'the Revolution', what rightfully belongs to others and has been earned after much work and sweat, regardless of the social and economic implications for these people and their families.

In the vignettes which I pointed out at the beginning as being more journalistic, Prada leaves to one side the individual tragic stories and concentrates on the material destruction and on the contribution of certain groups (not all necessarily military) to the defence against the revolutionaries. These vignettes are presented as more factual and provide more concrete objective information about the Revolution. For example, number fifteen, 'Algunas de las obras de arte destruidas', which resembles a list, deals, as the title indicates, with the works of art destroyed in the many fires of the Revolution, 'entre la voracidad de las llamas' (48). Other information provided includes the exact numbers of police and military forces in Oviedo when the Revolution broke out and where they were stationed (vignette seventeen), the names of the soldiers who took part in the fighting in Asturias (vignette twenty-seven), and the streets and buildings destroyed in Oviedo (vignette twenty-five). Some of these contain a moral message, such as in the case of number fifteen where the narrator ends:

> Hay que enseñar a los hombres a ser humanos para que no se maten los unos a los otros; hay que infundirles una cultura que, en las mayores tragedias, en las convulsivas revoluciones, les lleven a respetar los inagotables tesoros artísticos. (p. 49)

Nevertheless, Prada very rarely blames the destruction depicted on one side or the other. Instead he merely acknowledges that it took place. Thus in vignette number nine, 'Oviedo', he writes: 'El fuego, la destrucción y la muerte, sobre sus tres caballos apocalípticos, han cruzado por la hermosa capital de Asturias' (p. 30). After exposing other difficult and dramatic moments which Oviedo had been through since the sixteenth century, the narrator, as if addressing the city itself, regrets the implications which the destruction will have on Oviedo on this occasion:

> En 1934 hay que escribir una nueva página de luto en la historia de esta magnífica ciudad. El esfuerzo de todos volverá a darte lo que perdiste, tus edificios destruidos, tu riqueza destrozada, tus campos deshechos; pero ni los tesoros de arte que han sido destrozados, ni las vidas que en la lucha civil se perdieron de tantos de tus hombres, podrás recuperar ya, Oviedo, la ciudad hoy envuelta en negros crespones. . . (p. 31)

The negative feelings which are produced via the re-enacted episodes, in the way outlined above, ensure that all the injurious actions in the text (including those described in the journalistic accounts) are attributed to the revolutionaries. This in turn ensures that the moralistic messages are interpreted 'correctly'. Thus, the two types of narrative act in conjunction. The dramatic episodes frame the state of mind of the readers, and determine how we will perceive the journalistic accounts. On the other hand, the facts recorded in the accounts are not information for their own sake but provide a context for the suffering revealed in the dramatized episodes.

It is interesting to note that although the author wants the reader to feel anger and disgust toward the Revolution, there is very little reference to ideology and actual political parties and their leaders, so that the communists, the socialists, and the anarchists, as well as the right-wing groups, are not mentioned at all. Only a few references are made to Russia and the Soviet-style organization implanted in some of the revolutionary towns in Asturias, such as Turón (vignette number ten). In spite of the absence of explicit support of right-wing politics or even of praise for the government's handling of the situation, Prada does devote a few vignettes to those who helped in the defence against the revolutionaries. For example, in vignette nineteen, 'El cuerpo de telégrafos da una prueba más de su patriotismo y abnegación', the author examines how the workers in the telegraphic services continued to work and attempted to keep the telephone lines working so that Asturias would not be cut off. Vignette twenty-two, 'La defensa de la catedral' relates the difficult situation of those troops defending the city from the top of the cathedral tower; and vignette seventeen, 'Los primeros defensores de Oviedo' depicts the bravery of the forces of order defending Oviedo in the first instances of the Revolution. In addition to these three vignettes Prada transcribes Yagüe's declaration of how he advanced into Asturias (vignette six) and the air force operations, explained by a pilot (vignette twenty-eight).

The unusual structure of Prada's text begs the question of why he chose to employ this hybrid and, if we take into account that the vignettes are not arranged in any thematic or chronological order, chaotic approach. As readers we are not sure if this text should be read like a documentary report, as the author in the prologue insists we should do, or as a fictional creation which is what the text resembles at times, especially in the case of the re-enacted episodes. Regardless of the decision of the author to merge these two types of narrative in order to create a balance between the dramatic and the informative, and to use the opportunities presented by the vignettes to transmit an, at times, subtle and personal opinion on the revolutionaries and the Revolution, I think we should take into account more practical considerations. A long, continuous narrative can be just as dramatic as the episodes concisely depicted in Prada's text, as I will show in the next chapter. However, to produce this, the writer requires not only more expertise, but also more time. Prada was not a well-known professional writer (at least after extensive research I have found no other bibliographical references) and to recreate effectively the October Revolution textually in a long artistically polished and at the same time documentary piece of writing, with all its chronological and spatial complexities, in such a way that the necessary information is provided, the crucial issues raised, and the human dimension conveyed, would require considerable expertise. In addition, in order to have its full impact the text needed to be published shortly after the events, when the consequences of the conflict were still in the news and while people were still interested to learn more about the circumstances and experiences lived by the Asturians. This of course was not only important for publication concerns, the text would after all sell better if written in the heat of the moment, but it was also important in the reigning political atmosphere where writers hoped to influence the reader into adopting one position or another. Because this text was published very soon after the events, in a matter of months, there would have been little time to polish up a long narrative, explaining perhaps why there were so few of these.[4] As for the disorderly structure of Prada's text, it can be simply explained by the fact that he merely inserts the vignettes into the text as he collects them. By so doing he avoids the arduous task of deciding in what order they should be placed and at the same time he provides variety and to a certain extent the impression that he is indeed collecting these testimonies and stories as he travels around Asturias after the events.

Relato in the First Person

Clearly the easiest option when choosing to write about an event is to relate your own experiences and the events you have personally witnessed. You do not have to worry about searching for data, and can assure the reader that the information your witnesses give is reliable, since you yourself *are* the witness. In *El sindicato católico de Moreda y la revolución de octubre* (1935), Vicente Madera relates how he and his fellow colleagues at the Catholic Trade Union (Sindicato Católico de Obreros Mineros Españoles) defended themselves in the trade union centre until, faced with increasing dynamite explosions and their depletion of ammunition, they were forced to escape to the mountains where they were hunted down by the socialists and communists during the remainder of the Revolution.[5] Once in the mountains, unsure of the revolutionary situation, due to the lack of news, and with no place to go, they face a harsh survival, exposed to the elements and weakened by the lack of sleep and food. Although there is no denying that, as far as the contents are concerned, relating your own experiences is easier than investigating someone else's, there are stylistic and rhetorical considerations which Madera, just like Francisco Prada and Adro Xavier, has to take into account and which are determined by the narrative's didactic aim. Before analysing Madera's text further I will give a brief résumé of the history of the Catholic Union and point out why it was targeted by the revolutionaries. This will explain the point of view taken by the author and will help to identify the social and political messages transmitted through the words and actions of the author–narrator and the characters. As a final consideration, I will argue that the author's means of representing his story and his message grants this narrative a number of fictional properties which place it on the border between fiction and non-fiction.

According to Adrian Shubert this episode was used by the right wing to make Madera a symbol of working-class resistance to socialism and a prototype of the Catholic and patriotic worker.[6] Thus on 11 December 1934 the Confederación Nacional de Sindicatos Católicos Obreros organized a theatrical representation in Madrid in honour of the workers of Moreda, and on 3 February 1935 Madera was paid tribute to and given 35,000 pesetas, collected from public donations, in an act held in the Teatro de la Zarzuela in Madrid. Despite Madera's indisputable courage, evident in the text, the fact that this group was so isolated during the October Revolution is indicative of the failure of Catholic trade unionism in Asturias, first established in 1918. Although initially it had a substantial following, according to Shubert 10,897 members (while the socialist Sindicato Minero Asturiano had 10,000 in its first year), this number rapidly declined so that by 1932 they had 1139 members. By October 1934 'no quedaban sino los "restos" del Sindicato Católico'.[7] Shubert explains this rapid decline. While Catholic trade unionism, initially an idea of the progressive Maximiliano Arboleya, was meant to deal with social issues, the more reactionary influence, especially from the Marqués de Comillas, owner of the mining company Hullera Española, came to predominate over the ideas of Arboleya. The Catholic Unions were established and financed by company directors who, far from being in favour of the defence of working-class interests, were reluctant to tolerate the idea of a true trade union, whatever ideology it followed. Instead they used moralistic and religious rhetoric to hide their real objective which was to prevent the expansion of the worker's movement, or in Shubert's words: 'Servir de profiláctico del movimiento obrero'.[8] Juan José Castillo quotes the Jesuit Narciso Noguer who affirms that the fight against the socialists and the working-class movement 'ha sido en la práctica la fundamental o, si parece demasiado, una de las fundamentales (razones) para la formación de sindicatos católicos de obreros'.[9]

However, the history of this trade union only partly explains why Madera and his men were so fiercely targeted by the revolutionaries. The second reason lies within the Revolution itself. The revolutionaries had managed to make the Civil Guard and the police force retreat from their different positions in the valley of Aller, of which Moreda is a town. Despite the revolutionary victory, Madera, the General Secretary of the Catholic Union, had entrenched himself with his men (twenty-seven of them and one woman) in their trade union centre, most of them armed. This was a clear act of provocation, recognized by Madera himself in his text: 'Tan metido teníamos en el alma que no debíamos permanecer con los brazos cruzados ante el peligro inminente que nos rodeaba, que desde catorce días antes de la revolución veníamos haciendo guardia todas las noches en nuestra casa social de Moreda' (pp. 9–10).[10] Their provocative action was an indication that the Catholic Union would not accept the revolutionary victory and, while most of the revolutionaries went to fight in other parts, four hundred men stayed to fight in Moreda in an attempt to take the centre and the men defending it.[11] In addition, whilst Madera insists in his text that the revolutionaries began to attack first, forcing his men to respond, in another contemporary version of the Revolution, the anarchist Fernando Solano Palacio claims that the first shots came from the centre when Madera's men shot dead a worker who was walking past with a handful of detainees. Following this aggression the revolutionaries responded with fury.[12]

Madera's political stance determines the information which he includes in his text. Thus, he makes no reference to the fact that the revolutionaries, having already beaten the Civil Guard, viewed his aggressive resistance as deliberately provocative. Instead, according to him, a decision was taken by the defenders to act only if the revolutionaries attacked them first: 'Se dio una orden terminante de no hacer uso de las armas hasta que no comenzaran a hostilizarnos' (p. 14). In other words, Madera and his men, although prepared for an attack, would not be the first to shoot. The episode which Madera goes on to describe is thus blamed on the revolutionaries. Needless to say, Madera only rarely alludes to the historical social conflicts between the two trade union movements and concentrates instead on the immediate effects of the Revolution. While this prevents him from digressing too much, it is also a way of depicting, once again, the revolutionary attack as an unfair act of provocation and avoiding having to deal with other contentious issues which might distract the readers' attention away from his terrible experience of the Revolution and his resulting legitimate perception of the revolutionaries.

Madera's motives for writing are important in determining how he writes (stylistically) and what about. The first declared aim is to describe his experiences to the population at large. The résumé of the historical context of this text reveals a second and more politically propagandistic aim not alluded to by the author whereby, through the narration of his experiences, Madera hopes to inculcate a particular point of view into his reader or reinforce a stance already shared. The first aim is clearly explained in the Prologue, written by Manuel García[13] with an addition written by Madera himself. According to the author, like many of the religious accounts already examined in Chapter 4, his fifty-page pamphlet is a response to the petitions from many people who want to know about his experiences during the Revolution. Instead of style and elegance,

Madera states that in his text he provides the truth, for him just as important to a text:

> Le ofrezco la verdad. Lo que aquí se narra son hechos vividos por los compañeros leales y valientes y por el autor de estas líneas, que pone toda su buena voluntad para contar con exactitud lo que tal vez se resistan a creer muchos lectores. (p. 7)

While Madera explains what drove him to write the book, Manuel García deals with the narrative style employed by the author and in particular the lack of literariness in the text. He admits that the reader will not find 'lo que suele llamarse literatura' (p. 5). This, however, should not be taken as a drawback, he goes on to argue, as literature is sometimes used to describe and forge dead ideas. What is important is the idea or, in Madera's case, the act, not the literariness of the language in which it is expressed: 'Cuando se trata de realidades sangrantes, ellas solas se bastan y no necesitan ropaje literario' (p. 5).

Nevertheless, it is quite evident that Madera is also eager to convey his political view to the reader as an integral part of his experience. Throughout the text there are numerous very clearly biased comments, from which I will select only a few examples. Straight away in the opening paragraph of the first chapter Madera indicates his perception of the Revolution: 'Si la revolución triunfaba, las consecuencias para la religión, la familia, la propiedad (bien entendida, como nuestra doctrina la define), y, lo que es también importantísimo, la misma clase trabajadora, serían funestísimas' (p. 9). Thus Madera, as the Secretary of the Catholic Union believes in the family, religion, property, and 'la Patria', the last three of which are associated with conservative and traditional ideals. However, perhaps even more telling is his view in the next chapter that his men quite happily went down the mine to 'cumplir con su deber de trabajadores' (p. 13), highlighting the compliant attitude of the Catholic Union, and the clear influence of the proprietors who were keen to disseminate their idea of a passive working-class association, and end in this way the expansion of the combative left-wing workers' movement. Referring back to the first paragraph, to round it off, Madera, after listing the terrible consequences of the Revolution, indicates who was responsible and why: 'El socialismo no tenía otra salida, después de haberse comprometido descaradamente a propagar y desencadenar la revolución' (p. 9). Thus, unlike Prada, Madera explicitly points his finger at a concrete political group. By failing to mention any of the revolutionary social and economic objectives Madera implies that there were none, an example of the deliberate omission of information, a manipulative strategy discussed in Chapter 4. Initially Madera alleges that he did not expect the revolutionaries to act against him and his men as they had helped the socialist miners financially on several occasions during past strikes (he does not give any dates). He uses this charitable action of the Catholic Union along with their brotherly perception of their colleagues, and the 'cruel' action of the revolutionaries to compare the two movements: 'Esos elementos [socialistas] no saben ser agradecidos ni honrados; devuelven mal por bien. Son el reverso de la doctrina social católica' (p. 16). Indeed, Madera considers himself and his men as the 'tan codiciada presa' (p. 17) of the revolutionaries.

In Madera's text, just as in the vast majority of right-wing versions of the October Revolution, the negative depiction of the revolutionaries extends beyond ideological concerns. Besides their greediness, and their rage and reluctance to admit Madera's superiority, which he demonstrated by surviving against all the odds, the majority of criticisms involve allegations of cruelty. Most of these, however, are suppositions about how they would have been treated had they been caught by the revolutionaries. For example, Madera's reason for not surrendering when first given a chance is that he and his men would have been cruelly murdered. Similarly Madera claims that if he is ever captured by the revolutionaries 'ellos pondrán todo su empeño en verme hecho una piltrafa' (p. 23). Thus, whereas initially he claims that due to his Union's charitable gestures he did not think he would be attacked, on the other hand here he is quite certain of the working-class hatred felt towards him and his organization. On their escape from the building to the mountains, Madera and his men cross a cemetery where a large hole has been dug. The author is certain that it was done by the revolutionaries to bury him and his men: '[Una] fosa enorme, que no sabemos quién, aunque lo suponemos, mandó abrir para, en el momento oportuno, arrojarnos en ella sin ningún trabajo y de cualquier manera' (p. 28). However there is no other indication in the text to suggest that this was the case and even if it were true there is no way that Madera would have known since he did not come into contact with the revolutionaries. Finally Madera claims that the revolutionaries hunted them down while they were in the mountains, anxious to 'exhibir nuestras cabezas como trofeo' (p. 35). The significant thing about these allegations is that many of them are based on supposition: 'Quizá traiga' (p. 17); 'suponíamos que' (p. 28); 'sospechamos que' (p. 35); 'al parecer' (p. 49). The criticisms which Madera directs at the revolutionaries and the tense atmosphere which he depicts as he describes what could have happened are based largely on assumptions, not on real acts.

According to Elizabeth Bruss, in reporting something to his readership, an author 'delimits the scope of what ostensibly they already know. He makes assumptions about their ignorance and their need, if not actually their desire, to be acquainted with some fact'.[14] Given that this book is directed primarily at all those who want to know of Madera's experiences during the Revolution, his text appeals to the sympathy and belief of his readership. A reader who trusts Madera would believe the author's suppositions. Because these are not questioned they eventually become certainties. There is therefore no need for the author to present concrete evidence that something is true. Except for four of the men who died defending the union building, and the priest who was executed, there is no concrete indication in the text of any innocent person dying or coming to any harm.[15] There is one instance in which Madera admits that not all of the revolutionaries were cruel with their prisoners. However, he attributes this to the fact that they knew they would lose the Revolution and suggests that it was a deliberate strategy to prevent the forces of order from being too aggressive in the inevitable backlash: 'Les convenía tratar bien a los prisioneros, para que esto les sirviese después de atenuante' (p. 42). To make the cruelty of the revolutionaries appear to be set off by their greed and cowardice, and not to be the result of frustrated bravery, towards the end Madera portrays the pathetic image of their retreat: 'Cómo abandonaban sus puestos a paso ligero aquellos infelices que, en su mayoría, no sabían ni tener las armas que hombres de mala fe, cobardes y sin entrañas, les habían facilitado' (p. 44). Of course the sorry, pathetic, greedy and cruel depiction of the revolutionaries contrasts with the exemplary behaviour of Madera and his men.

The only criticism that Madera directs at his own side involves the organization of the defence against the Revolution. Firstly, he suggests that the forces of order were disorganized and claims that if they had been better prepared and had relied more on him and his men, the Revolution would not have lasted as long. Secondly, he criticizes those who, despite being against the Revolution, refused to give him their arms, preferring to keep them so that they could defend themselves, an attitude which proved to be imprudent and risky as the revolutionaries confiscated the guns and eventually used them against their owners and against Madera. Madera's Catholic faith is also clearly evident in the text. For example, he wonders on occasions whether his luck is actually due to a miracle, such as when the fire in their centre suddenly ceases for no apparent reason: '¿Fue un milagro? No lo sé, pero lo parecía. El hecho indiscutible es que, cuando se intentó atajar el fuego en aquella madera de pino y seca, no se pudo, y poco después se apagaba él solo' (p. 20). When the men prepare to escape from the building they ask to confess and are absolved by the priest who is trapped with them. This serves to calm and encourage the men: 'Nos sirvió de gran consuelo y nos dio ánimos para todo' (p. 23). In the final example of the religious nature of the text, when Madera and his men contemplate saving one bullet each so that, rather than be caught by the revolutionaries 'y que hiciesen con nosotros ignominias' (p. 24), they can commit suicide, they decide that this is irreligious and instead propose that when their time to die arrives they will let themselves be shot by the revolutionaries. The religious fervour that emanates from Madera's text is more attuned to the religious texts than to the workers' versions.

The anti-revolutionary and pro-Catholic patriotic presence in the text is embodied by Madera himself. This is especially significant if we consider that Madera was both a miner and a Catholic. He portrays himself as the leader of the group, not only militarily but also psychologically and morally; when decisions have to be taken his is the final say. In addition he is fair, warning his men that the fight will be long and bloody; caring, concerned that all his men escape safely from the Union building; and brave and heroic, such as when he suggests that he will give himself up to the revolutionaries to give his men time to escape:

> Voy a salir yo solo, y cuando estén entretenidos conmigo cesará el asedio, porque yo trataré de vender cara mi vida, y ellos pondrán todo su empeño en verme hecho una piltrafa. Os aprovecharéis rápidamente de la confusión y griterío salvaje que ha de armarse y salís por las puertas contrarias. Así os podréis salvar, si no todos, la mayoría de vosotros. (pp. 23–24)

The men reject this honourable gesture outright. Fully in touch with the situation Madera relates a number of occasions in which he is able to predict correctly the outcome of the Revolution, implying that all his other suppositions, dealt with above, can be taken seriously.

In case there is any doubt as to the moral message of the text, Madera includes in his last chapter three paragraphs summarizing what the Revolution should have taught the working class, placing particular emphasis on his view that 'los trabajadores jamás mejoraremos, ni moral ni materialmente, por medio de la violencia y de las revoluciones armadas' (p. 48). However, he not only wants to discourage the workers from becoming involved. He also wants to spread the virtues of his own Catholic Union in an attempt to gather support at a time when the socialist trade unions and the working-class movement in general has been pushed underground following their defeat. Hence he writes:

> ¡Compañeros de trabajo! Sólo hay un medio para conseguir nuestro mejoramiento moral y material; ese medio eficaz por excelencia es la Organización seria y honrada, que trabaje por capacitar y ennoblecer a la gran familia trabajadora y lleve a la práctica paulatinamente, pero de un modo firme y estable, la justicia social que predican los Pontífices y anhelan los sindicalistas católicos. (p. 49)

Thus Madera uses the excuse that he is merely responding to the inquisitive desires of the reader to relate his story about the revolutionary events, and in the process to impart a political message: His story would not be adequately complete without the political message to round it off; and the political message without the accompanying true-to-life story would certainly not have as much impact. W. Gallie, on examining the role of the conclusion in any story, writes:

> Admittedly, when we are first introduced to the main characters of a story and begin, so to speak, to live in them and with them, we are willing to go with them, to follow them, in almost any direction. They interest us, and all we ask is 'What will happen to them now?' and 'What will happen to them next?' But very soon these questions are replaced by one that expresses a much more serious concern, namely: 'How will things turn out for them *in the end*?' [. . .] Thus the conclusion of a story is the main focus of our interest before we know what that conclusion is going to be.[16]

The political lesson is considered by Madera to be the best conclusion to his text. After describing how he and his men have arrived safely at their home, he provides the reader, who is at this point most receptive to any message, with an example from someone who has lived the situation, who is experienced in such matters, and thus who knows what he is writing about. The heroic and brave Madera not only provides an exciting and at the same time informative narrative but also a didactic tract.

The author does not indicate at any point how he wants his text to be considered generically and, although the prologuist García defines it as 'un diario de campaña' (p. 6), there are elements which, in my view, make it more than a mere diary. The easiest option would be to consider it an autobiography: the author writes about his own experiences in the first person. Nevertheless, the text cannot be categorized as such for a number of reasons, the most obvious of which are its length and the short time span it covers. In addition Weintraub indicates a number of basic ingredients which a conventional autobiography should contain and which Madera's text lacks.[17] The most important of these is the fact that Madera's experiences do not reflect on his personality. It is interesting to note that his depiction of the events is limited to how he acted, what decisions were made, and what the result of these were at a practical level. Madera does not analyse how his actions or decisions influenced his character in the long term, an impossible task given the proximity of the event and his rendering of it. Hence there is no degree of character development except for the shallow feelings of the author–narrator at a given time, a phenomenon quite distinct from the inner developing character referred to by Weintraub.[18] Madera's priority is not the ingenuity or the literariness of the narrative but rather its immediate effectiveness. Hence he includes only those elements which ensure this, omitting any other ingredients which might distract the reader from his real objective — to influence him to react and, in consequence, to act in a determined way.

In choosing the term *relato* to define this text we should not be mistaken into believing that it is purely non-fictional. True, there is no literary or figurative language, or complicated and intricate stylistic devices. Neither is there any character development, either in the case of the author–narrator, as established above, or in the rest of the participants in the text. Indeed, these are not even physically described and, in the case of Madera's men, only their obedience and their bravery are referred to. However, there is a plot; the text takes a clear direction, a characteristic lacking in many of the texts already examined in Chapters 3, 4, and 5 which appear instead to be a random body of recollections and experiences from a selected group of witnesses. The text begins with Madera and his men preparing for the revolutionary attack (Chapters 1 and 2), follows through the defence of the Catholic Union's building (Chapters 3 and 4), and concludes with the men's escape into the mountains until the Revolution ends (Chapters 5 and 6), at which point so does the narrative. Thus it conforms to Aristotle's requirement (taken in a very broad sense) that a plot should have 'a beginning, a middle, and an end, and that its events should form a coherent whole'.[19] Another way in which Madera's text resembles a fictional narrative is in his reporting of speech. There are occasions, especially at the beginning of the text, in which Madera chooses direct speech over reported speech. Madera's reason for employing one or the other form may be found in Bruss's definition of the two forms:

> By using direct discourse and separating reported speech from his own discourse by quotation marks, a writer purports to transmit the original speech without interference, reproducing both the manner and the matter [. . .]. Indirect discourse allows for greater distortion of reported material. The embedded speech has been fully assimilated, with no quotation marks or shift of tense to set it off as an autonomous act. (p. 28)

Madera is keen to communicate the 'exact' wording of a conversation when its context is important.[20] Thus direct speech is largely limited to those significant episodes related in the text. For example, when the priest attempts to convince Madera to give up and the latter gives his reasons for refusing while knowing that the lives of two men are in his hands and are pending on his decision; when Madera tells his men to escape while he bears the brunt of the revolutionary fury, and his men's rejection of the proposal; or when he tries to convince Florinda (who was to remain with them in the building) to leave and her determination to stay, highlighting that it was her own choice. These are all key decisions which have repercussions on how the reader will perceive Madera, and which could be deliberately (or not) misinterpreted. Thus Madera provides the ultimate proof — the exact words of the conversations. As the narrative progresses and the number of crucial decisions declines, so does the use of direct speech; in the last chapter where the decisions taken are limited to material issues of where they should sleep, or where they may be able to find food, no direct speech is used. For example, Madera describes how occasionally the men laughed at the situation they were in:

A ratos nos reíamos de nuestra situación, [. . .]. Cuando de mejor gana lo hacíamos era siempre que Corsino, en sus cosas de chico, añoraba las *fabadas* que había comido en otros tiempos. Ponía tal gracia en la descripción de la comida que parecía que la estaba saboreando. Secundino (Garrafa), de genio opuesto, se encargaba de echar por tierra los apetitosos recuerdos de Corsino. Aunque rara vez nos acompañaba la risa, no podíamos menos de reírnos con los graciosos diálogos de estos dos compañeros, que amenizaban en lo posible aquellas largas horas de nieve y de cabaña. (p. 45)

This scene could easily lend itself to dialogue, where the author would merely have to reproduce the jokes, giving in the process a humorous touch to the narrative. However, by using indirect report the writer limits himself to providing a summary of the speech act and, in general, of that relatively insignificant aspect of the experience (it is significant enough to be included, but only as a summary). In this scene the important message is that the men, despite their difficult circumstances, managed to cope; what is superfluous are the actual jokes told. And yet even in the later chapters when direct speech is reduced to a minimum, the 'story-like' essence of the narrative remains, maintained by the author's continuous provision of exciting, sad, humorous and, above all, humane anecdotes which feed the reader's desire to discover how Madera's predicament is finally resolved.

Another aspect which differentiates this text from any 'factual' text examined so far is the absence of verifiable or substantiated information. There is no documentary detail apart from the photograph of each of Madera's companions trapped inside the building, and a list of their names integrated naturally into the narrative (as opposed to being provided in the form of a table or a diagram). There are no quotations or transcriptions from source material, or the appearance of any eye-witnesses except for the participants. The only evidence that the reader is provided with is Madera's word and the knowledge that he is relating his own experience.

1. Francisco Prada, *Asturias la desventurada: caminos de sangre* (Madrid: Castro, 1934). Subsequent quotations are cited parenthetically in the text.
2. This narrative device is used by many writers, as pointed out by Geoffrey N. Leech and Michael H. Short, *Style in Fiction: A Linguistic Introduction to English Fictional Prose* (London: Longman, 1980).
3. Leech and Short define credibility as 'the likelihood, and hence believability, of the fiction as a "potential reality", given that we apply our expectations and inferences about the real world to fictional happenings. A fiction tends to be credible to the extent that it overlaps with, or is a plausible extension of, our "real" model of reality'. Leech and Short, p. 157. Although these comments are directed at fiction I apply them to Prada's text as, although non-fictional in nature, it is written in a way that is usually associated

with fictional writing. The fact that Prada's text must be taken as real, as it (presumably) *is* real, only stresses the claims made by the two critics.

4. There is another text which has the same narrative characteristics as Prada's, which is also episodic: Un Testigo Imparcial, *Revolución en Asturias: relato de la última guerra civil* (Madrid: Castro, 1934).
5. Vicente Madera, *El sindicato católico de Moreda y la revolución de octubre* (Madrid: Imp. Sáez Hermanos, 1935). Subsequent quotations are cited parenthetically in the text. Other *relatos* written in the first person which I have not examined are Eraclio Iglesias Somoza, *Episodios de la revolución: asedio y defensa de la Cárcel de Oviedo* (Vitoria: J. Marquínez, [1935(?)]), and Julián Orbón, *Avilés en el movimiento revolucionario de Asturias: octubre de 1934* (Gijón: Tip. La Fé, 1934).
6. Adrian Shubert, 'Entre Arboleya y Comillas: El fracaso del sindicalismo católico en Asturias', in Gabriel Jackson, et al., *Octubre 1934: cincuenta años para la reflexión* (Madrid: Siglo XXI, 1985), pp. 243–52.
7. Ibid., p. 245. In his article Shubert provides information about the rise and fall of Catholic trade unionism. Elsewhere, Frances Lannon summarizes succinctly why the Catholic Church was so unpopular: 'Whatever the technically apolitical stance of the Church as an institution, Catholic politicians and Catholic voters behind them spelt out the equation in deeds: defence of the Church equals the defence of landed property rights, whatever the social cost, which in turn equals rejection in real terms of the necessarily reforming Republic.' Frances Lannon, 'The Church's crusade against the Republic', in *Revolution and War in Spain 1931–1939*, ed. by Paul Preston (London: Methuen, 1984; repr. London: Routledge, 1993), pp. 35–58 (p. 45).
8. Shubert, p. 247.
9. Juan José Castillo, 'Sindicalismo católico, sindicalismo amarillo', in *Sindicalismo y movimientos sociales*, coord. by Manuel Redero (Madrid: UGT, Centro de Estudios Históricos, 1994), pp. 147–53 (p. 153).
10. In addition Madera claims that he had been promised one hundred rifles (p. 10). He does not mention by whom but Taibo supposes that it must have been from the company Hullera Española. Paco Ignacio Taibo, *Asturias 1934*, 2 vols (Madrid: Jucar, 1984), I, 143.
11. Taibo, I, 143. According to Madera the number of revolutionaries attacking the centre was two thousand, an underestimate according to witnesses he cites which put the number at four thousand (p. 16).
12. Fernando Solano Palacio, *La revolución de octubre: quince días de comunismo libertario en Asturias*, 3rd edn (Barcelona: [n. pub.], [1936]), p. 88. According to J. Bécarud and E. López Campillo, *Los intelectuales españoles durante la II República* (Madrid: Siglo XXI, 1978), this book was brought out as a response to the government banning and withdrawal of the issue of *Revista Blanca* of 15 December 1936, in which reports of the government's repression against the miners were published.
13. Manuel García is probably Manuel García y García, the chaplain of the Hullera Española de Caborana. The only other information I have found is that he was a poet, according to Constantino Suárez, *Escritores y artistas asturianos: índice bio-bibliográfico*, 7 vols (Madrid: Imp. Saez Hermanos, 1936; Oviedo: Instituto de Estudios Asturianos, 1955–59), IV (1955), 100.
14. Elizabeth W. Bruss, *Autobiographical Acts: The Changing Situation of a Literary Genre* (Baltimore: Johns Hopkins University Press, 1976), p. 27.
15. Madera claims that the priest of Moreda, Tomás Suero Covielles, was sent by the revolutionaries to convince those resisting in the Catholic Union to surrender under the threat that they would execute two well-known fascists they had taken prisoner. Despite the priest's attempt Madera refused to surrender and the priest decided to remain in the Union building. He managed to escape but was eventually arrested by the revolutionaries and executed. Taibo, referring to Solano Palacio's anarchist text, claims that the two fascists, Villarín and Mata, were sent as part of the first attempt to convince Madera to surrender, but as they approached the building they were shot by mistake by someone inside, leading to the death of one of them. The priest was sent in a second attempt. He decided to stay with Madera, explaining his eventual execution when he was arrested. Taibo, I, 143–44, and Solano Palacio, pp. 88–89, deal with the events in Moreda.

16. Walter Bryce Gallie, *Philosophy and the Historical Understanding* (London: Chatto & Windus, 1964), pp. 28–29, author's emphasis.
17. Karl J. Weintraub, 'Autobiography and Historical Consciousness', *Critical Inquiry*, I (1975), 821–48.
18. 'Real autobiography is a weave in which self-consciousness is delicately threaded throughout interrelated experience. It may have such varied functions as self-explication, self-discovery, self-clarification, self-formation, self-presentation, self-justification. All these functions interpenetrate easily, but all are centered upon a self aware of its relation to its experiences.' Weintraub, p. 824.
19. Chris Baldick, *The Concise Oxford Dictionary of Literary Terms* (Oxford: Oxford University Press, 1990), p. 171.
20. Some critics, such as Leech and Short, pp. 159–66, argue that an exact representation of conversation is impossible, firstly because one cannot possibly remember every word said, and secondly because in a real act of conversation there are pauses, fill-in-words, and other features which are not reflected by the author.

CHAPTER 6

ON THE BORDER BETWEEN FICTION AND NON-FICTION (II)

Novelized Biography

In *Sangre jesuita: Asturias 1934*, Adro Xavier narrates the life story of two martyrs of the Revolution, Padre Emilio Martínez and Hermano Juan B. Arconada.[1] The narrative takes the form of a biography, as defined in the *Oxford English Dictionary*, 'The history of the lives of individual men, as a branch of literature', although with its dramatized reconstructions of incidents it adopts a novelized appearance. Adro's story of the Padre and Hermano, both of whom are made out to be extraordinary and exemplary followers of Christianity, starts with the beginnings of their religious vocation and recounts the professional career of the two men. They help the young, the sick and the needy. P. Martínez is praised for carrying out many good deeds, both in the humanitarian and in the religious fields, while H. Arconada is just as highly praised for serving the ecclesiastics, as coadjutor. Their role in spreading the Catholic faith among children, and particularly those from working-class areas, is specially highlighted. The precise course of events which leads up to the death of the two men are described in detail: the brief trial and dramatic sentencing, the long hours prior to their death, the trip to the place where they will be executed, and even the conversations of their captors. All the while the two protagonists remain calm and unafraid of dying, in the knowledge that their sacrifice will be in the name of God.

A close chapter-by-chapter examination of the text will reveal how, in line with the Church's predominant attitude, Adro's right-wing, traditional and patriotic stance are gradually but systematically conveyed. Just as in Madera's text, examined above, Adro praises the Civil Guard, criticizes the left-wing Republican government before 1933 for inciting the revolutionary movement, and its right-wing counterpart after 1933 for being ineffectual in controlling it. However, although important, these concerns are only part of the larger and primary issue of the text, that is, the essential role of religion and its practitioners in society, as demonstrated by the exemplary action of the two men depicted in the text. Along with the explicitly stated propaganda, Adro's text contains much more figurative language than any of the texts examined so far. Apart from fulfilling a literary role, this is aimed at eliciting the reader's sympathies and thereby influencing his political allegiance. Hence in this text it will become apparent that the use of literary language has, above all, a propagandistic role. By comparing this text to Francisco Martínez's much more essayistic *Dos jesuitas mártires de Asturias: el P. Emilio Martínez y el H. Juan B. Arconada* (1936), from where I will later suggest that Adro Xavier's text mostly stems from,[2] I will argue that a text which is more literary in nature does not necessarily have to be less propagandistic. Of course, this leads to the deeper issue about the nature of propaganda in literature which admittedly cannot be given the full attention it deserves in the short space provided in this chapter, and which will therefore be touched on, although briefly, further on in the final Conclusion.

Any doubt as to the political stance of the text is dispelled from the outset in the Prologue, written by Adro Xavier himself (and dated May 1936). It begins with a quote from the 'insigne' Calvo Sotelo about the Revolution — 'Acontecimiento inconmensurable en su misma grandeza trágica' (p. 3) — and affirms that it was a copy of the French and Russian Revolutions, and incited by communist ideology: 'Asturias en 1934, bajo el trapo rojo, machacada fieramente por el martillo de la impiedad, segada por la hos [*sic*] de odios sociales' (p. 3).[3] The author laments that the religious orders have had to go through the dramatic episode of October 1934, in which they have been specially targeted and crushed, at a time when they were getting over their lowest moments due to the official and popular attacks. These attacks refer to the Church reforms during the Republic which aimed to reduce (initially to erase completely) the influence of the Church in society through measures such as the introduction of a state system of education, the prohibition of all members of congregations from teaching, and the disbanding of the Jesuit order (of which the author was a member), all of these referred to and criticized by Adro.[4] Indeed, the efficiency of religious schooling is demonstrated throughout the text in the various re-enactments of the two men at work and in the respect and affection which their pupils have for them.

Apart from providing the historical context, the author divulges information about himself. He explains that he was in exile during the Asturian Revolution, where he heard about the deaths of these two religious figures, the violence exerted and the degradation of a once healthy Spain infuriating him. At the same time he wonders how and why the population can have been so easily convinced into hating the Church given its evident and constantly demonstrated generosity and sacrifice: 'Generosidades tan fosforescentes, de sacrificios tan solemnnes y austeros'

(p. 5), laying the blame on the 'escrófulas intelectuales' (p. 6), in other words, the propaganda spread by intellectuals on both sides of the political spectrum, many of whom despised the Church. Nevertheless, given that 'hay quienes saben justipreciar la historia pasada, quienes conocen los caminos de la virtud' (pp. 6–7), he believes that Christianity will win the day and the legions of Jesuits '[se lanzarán] por llanadas y alcores, villas y ciudades, dando la mano de salvación a la misma raza hispana que los maltrató' (p. 7). And so begins the spiritually edifying story of the two martyrs which will serve to highlight the importance of the Church and the intolerable and unjustified nature of the action taken against it, generating in the process hope for the future.

The narrative starts off in 1923 during a Geography class given by Padre Martínez in which he is shown to capture the full interest of his pupils, even the most troublesome ones. Hermano Arconada, in the same school in Valladolid, devotedly looks after one of the Padre's pupils who has fallen ill in one of his classes. Through the conversation between the coadjutor and the boy the reader learns some of the scant background information provided about the older of the two religious men:

> Yo ya tenía mucha más edad que tu tienes ahora, y aún no sabía casi leer, y mucho menos de cuentas y otras cosas, porque mis padres son labradores muy buenos, pero pobres, y cuando Dios me dio la vocación para jesuita ya tenía dieciocho años, y aún no había estudiado lo necesario para poder empezar a estudiar la carrera de Cura. . . Sólo sabía muchas cosas muy buenas de cultivar los campos y cuidar las gallinas y las vacas. . .[5]

However, most of this first section, entitled 'Intimidad de la vida', deals with P. Martínez, about whom there seems to be much more information. We learn that after his time in Valladolid, in 1924, P. Martínez goes to the Monastery of Oña where he studies and teaches religion to children and adults, and where he is ordained in 1927. Thus, this first chapter[6] serves as an introduction to the lives of the two martyrs, in which their positive attributes, such as patience, kindness, devotion, helpfulness, and seriousness are highlighted throughout.

Chapter 2, 'Barrio sin lindes', begins with the appearance of Cardinal Segura travelling to France on a train.[7] The narrative jumps back in time in order to explain Segura's visit. P. Martínez had sent him a letter asking for help in the task of providing religious teaching for neglected Spanish immigrants living and working in Southern France, according to him prime targets of communist propaganda: 'Como carne de cañón se les consideraba en los centros marxistas' (p. 26). A number of anecdotes follow in which P. Martínez's brave, patient, and persistent action and nature are portrayed in, for example, the conversion of one adamantly atheist girl on her death bed. He visits a coal mine where, for the first time, he perceives the terrible difficulties faced by the working class: 'Todo el problema gigante de la clase proletaria le descubre de repente sus entrañas' (p. 33). For the priest the problems faced by the miners, far from relating to their working or living conditions, pay, or any other socio-economic factor, lies in their inability to find comfort in religion which would help them cope: 'Los pechos desgraciados de sus compatriotas que, huérfanos de todo bien humano, ni disfrutan en lo hondo de sus penalidades de la luz consoladora de la religión. . .' (p. 33). Driven by his newly-realized vocation P. Martínez declares a propagandistic war on the communists in the Spanish working-class districts of Grenoble and Lyon. Segura is included in these plans which end up being a success and with which the conversion of many is accomplished.

Chapter 3, 'Páginas sueltas', is set in 1931. H. Arconada and, in particular, P. Martínez's initiatives in attracting children to the Church by founding religious schools and holding prayer meetings are praised. Their work is made much more difficult by the anti-religious measures of the new Republican government, a factor very much criticized and the consequences of which are alluded to, such as the fact that 'unos 60.000 (*sesenta mil*) hijos de obreros quedan sin la enseñanza gratuita que recibían en sus escuelas nocturnas y patronatos' (p. 44, author's emphasis), while old men, 'Hombres heroicos que habían consagrado su vida a una clase de Geografía o Algebra, durante cinco, quince. . . y veinte años' (p. 44), are forced to wonder the streets aimlessly, 'con los ojos arrasados de lágrimas' (p. 44), and with no place to go. In line with its propagandistic aims, only the negative aspects of the republican reforms are alluded to by the narrator, and on no occasion does he refer to the criticisms directed at the Church of which there were many.[8] The author devotes the beginning of this chapter to describing the feelings of loss and isolation when the members of religious orders are forced to abandon their residences and communities and, as a result, are forced to live in hotels and in people's homes, dependent on their charity. Nevertheless, P. Martínez continues to carry out his charitable acts, taking children to old people's homes and visiting the sick. The chapter concludes with the children's procession to Covadonga on the 25 June 1934 organized by P. Martínez, its picturesque and poignant nature depicted by the narrator. According to a witness ('quien le ayudó activamente' [p. 68]) and a newspaper where most of the information regarding the procession is quoted from (and identified only as 'la prensa asturiana' [p. 68]), the gathering was very successful and emotional, and for the narrator it was symbolic as it marked 'la despedida solemne del apóstol de los hijos de los obreros de su Madre Santísima' (p. 72).

The Revolution does not break out until Chapter 4, 'Camino grana'. The two protagonists are not in Asturias. Instead they are on a train travelling from Castile to Gijón where they are expected to hold a mass the next day. As they enter the region, due to an attack on the railway tracks, they are forced to leave the train and seek refuge in nearby Ujo, where they find somebody willing to help them. The circumstances which result in the two religious men being involved in the revolutionary episode are not attributed by the narrator to bad luck but to God's wish: 'Es, por consiguiente, la mano de Dios, inconfundible, la que traza el rasgo fundamental de este cuadro orlado con palmas martiriales' (p. 89). On 6 October the revolutionaries arrive at the house where P. Martínez and H. Arconada are hiding in search of arms. Fearing that they will be found and that revenge will be taken on the kind family, they leave and, in the company of another of the passengers, Junquera, head for Oviedo. P. Martínez, weak and sick, is too frail to go the whole way and the three men stop at Santullano, where the chapter ends. The narrator signals that this will be the two martyrs' last port of call — having reached that town he exclaims: '¡Han caído!' (p. 94).

From the start this chapter is replete with descriptions of the scenery, the sky, the sunrise, and the elements (particularly the mist):

> Amanece. El sol — rubí flamígero — enciende todo el paisaje inmenso con sangre de cambiantes fantásticos.
>
> [. . .] Un mar enloquecido de nieblas golpetea los costillares titanes de las sierras que la vigilan. Sus taludes perpendiculares hunden sus bases en hoyadas inundadas por las brumas. El astro sol — tristón, enfermizo — se asoma tembloroso en el horizonte, dejando sanguinolentas pinceladas espesas en los riscos duros que flotan sobre las nieblas arremolinadas.
>
> Cielo y tierra, todo, llora lágrimas de sangre. . . (p. 73)

Many of these elaborate descriptions, in which elements of the countryside (such as the mountains, rivers and valleys) take on symbolic colours and expressive textures, characteristics and moods, presage the tragedy: 'Matices rojos anunciando desgracias' (p. 76), or express hope when the situation seems to have been saved: 'En el horizonte ennegrecido, se rasgó de pronto una línea azul y blanca' (p. 80). Thus red, symbolic of blood and communism, and black (including dark and grey tones) associated with death and tragedy, are the dominant elements in the scenery: 'Un día plomizo' (p. 85); 'cayó la noche temprana' (p. 85); 'amanecer de sangre' (p. 86); and '[la] sangre de sol tiñe las sierras y picachos' (p. 74). It is worth noting that the anarchist flag and many of the banners that were undoubtedly being waved during those days would have been precisely these colours — red and black — adding to the author's negative association.

In Chapter 5, 'Armas antiespañolas', P. Martínez and H. Arconada are shot. Having reached Santullano they are immediately taken prisoner and imprisoned in the *Casa del Pueblo* in Mieres where their fate is uncertain and where they are practically sentenced to death by the angry anti-religious mob. The two men are taken back to Santullano where they are condemned to death and where they remain that night. On the way to Santullano the mob, eager for the execution of the two religious men, force the red guards to shoot them but they are saved on this occasion by a woman who rejects that the executions should take place against her garden wall. A friend of Junquera, the companion of the two protagonists, who manages to save him, is unable to do the same for the Jesuits. That night P. Martínez and H. Arconada are driven to the entrance of a mine on the road to Mieres where they are shot. The situation of the two religious men is compared to that of Christ: 'Han detenido a los fugitivos. Empieza su pasión. Como a Cristo, gentuza armada prende ahora a los jesuitas' (pp. 94–95).[9] Much of the chapter concentrates on the illiteracy, and uncouth, aggressive, and beastly behaviour of the revolutionaries, 'antiespañoles', whose minds have been taken over by Russian propaganda, and the unjust system which they abide by, mediated by their Marxist beliefs. Naturally, every aspect of the Revolution and its proponents is depicted as unjust, irrational, and cowardly, especially compared to the Jesuits who, despite their suffering, cold, and hunger, show their integrity, heroism, and generosity right to the end, in the case of P. Martínez by writing a safe-conduct for Junquera on behalf of the illiterate revolutionaries. The two men irradiate peace, calmness, and saintliness: 'Con paso firme se colocan donde les dicen. Allí, ante la mina, en medio del marco profundo de negruras indefinidas, sus dos figuras resplandecen con irisaciones de cosa santa' (p. 110). As the title of the final chapter indicates, 'Religión y Patria', in this final section the Church and the Civil Guard are linked. For the narrator, the fact that P. Martínez and H. Arconada have been buried in the same grave as the Guard Tomás Escribano is symbolic of this union. He takes the concept further by suggesting that these two institutions are the only solution to the advance of communist immorality, corruption, and barbarity:

> Un mismo puñado de tierra abrazó los representantes ilustres de las dos instituciones españolas que simbolizan — una en el mundo de las almas, y la otra en el del orden social — los esperontes más avanzados contra la barbarie roja: La Compañía de Jesús y la Guardia civil. (p. 113)

The official burial, which takes place after the exhumation of the bodies on 23 October, is described and the narrative ends as the three souls wait to go to heaven.

On comparing Adro's narrative with the text written by Francisco Martínez, P. Martínez's real (as opposed to religious) brother, and also published in 1936, there are striking similarities in the contents, especially when the death of the two men is related, where even the wording of non-quoted passages are alike. According to this second text, F. Martínez, along with his younger brother, Adrián, went to Asturias shortly after the Revolution had been defeated to investigate the deaths of their brother and his assistant, taking photographs and speaking to eye-witnesses. In the case of Adro, who was not present either during the events, the information for his text also seems to come from the written and oral testimonies of a wide range of witnesses, as well as from verifiable sources such as newspaper reports, leaflets, and letters. The information on which the final hours of the two men are based comes from Junquera who survived the Revolution. Unlike Francisco Martínez, however, Adro does not explain how he gathered this information; it is merely absorbed by the narrative. Indeed, the origin of his data and the identity of who has given it to him does not seem to be one of Adro's main concerns; he does not give the name of the newspaper he quotes from and only sometimes gives the names of the witnesses he uses, preferring instead to refer to them abstractly, such as 'una de las maestras' (p. 57); '[un] testigo ocular' (p. 47); 'un testigo fidedigno' (p. 56); and 'quien cooperó en sus trabajos' (p. 57). In fact, when examining closely both texts it becomes clear that much of the information used by Adro is found (in some cases word for word) in Martínez's text. The fact that Adro mentions on one occasion Martínez's text (vaguely, in passing, and inadequately, given the amount of information which he appears to take from it) suggests that the more essayistic text, in other words Martínez's, was published first: 'En una conferencia escrita con cariñosa inspiración por un hermano carnal del Padre Emilio, nos hemos topado con este delicado párrafo' (p. 87). What follows is a quoted description of the emotional state of the two men while they were hiding from the revolutionaries in the house of Señor Muñiz which also appears in Martínez's text. There are extracts which, although not directly quoted, are based on the earlier text. Compare, for example, the following two extracts, the first taken from Adro and the second from F. Martínez:

> Consideraciones enérgicas sobre sus inocencias, y sobre los bienes que el Padre hacía a la clase obrera educando sus hijos en la caritativa fundación de Revillagigedo, y sobre los desinteresados ministerios de los dos jesuitas entre los rapaciños de los barrios obreros de Gijón, al fundarles escuelas y catecismos. (p. 106)

> Don José Iglesias se interesó también por los dos sentenciados. Dijo que le constaba que no se les podía tachar de nada y que el Padre Martínez se dedicaba a enseñar

obreros en la fundación Revillagigedo y también a los hijos de obreros en escuelas que tenía fundadas en los barrios de trabajadores. (p. 48)

This is just one of the many examples.

Elsewhere Adro presents the information as his own, such as when he quotes information which, according to him, 'El padre Irala nos dice' (p. 37) while in the second text the same quotation is extracted from a letter sent by Irala to Adrián Martínez from Fachang, China where he is a missionary, and transcribed in its entirety (pp. 23–24). The significance of this similarity in the data can be perceived on examining the Prologue to F. Martínez's text, where Enrique Herrera Oria, reveals that when considering the form which the text should take, or more specifically, whether, given the dramatic nature of the episode it relates, the investigative data should be rendered more literarily, he opted in the end for keeping the essayistic form chosen by F. Martínez to record the results of his research: 'Hemos pensado mucho si convendría retocar la relación y darla un carácter literario; pero siempre nos dio pena arrancar a tan precioso documento histórico su frescura nativa' (p. 3). Thus, except for the headings added at the start of each section the text takes its original form. What is interesting is that Adro, on the other hand, takes this same information and converts it into a literary experience, thereby carrying out what Herrera Oria had originally contemplated.

Adro re-enacts many of the situations and conversations described by F. Martínez, and introduces much literary language, especially in the form of figurative and symbolic images. Leech and Short write:

> When a writer creates a fiction, he has to make decisions on such matters as how much information to give, what kind of information to give, and in what order to present the information. These are the sorts of decision which also have to be made in non-fiction reporting. (p. 154)

If we apply this statement to these two texts, it is not strange to find that although based, and therefore reliant, on Matínez's text, Adro stresses particular information, some of which is not included in the original text and the provenance of which is uncertain. For example, F. Martínez describes the office of the local communist leader:

> Aquel recinto de la Casa del Pueblo, cuya visión posterior no se nos olvidará. Suelo sucio, en cantidad; ambiente limitado y, sin duda, entonces, enrarecido con demasiados alientos y humos de infierno; bancos junto a las paredes; una mesa como de café y dos prolongaciones laterales de madera. Sobre esta presidencia un cartel con *¡Abajo la guerra!* y una figura humana, cuya espalda desnuda están descuartizando. (p. 53)

Compare this description in which (allowing for the supposition 'y, sin duda, entonces') the author describes what he has seen in his investigative trip, with Adro's, who places the same furniture in the same room but who, without altering the facts provided by Martínez, conveys more effectively the filth and oppressive atmosphere:

Un edificio estrecho y alto esconde en su piso bajo el cubil socialista. La habitación es angosta, y está rodada de bancos acoplados a la pared, como los pesebres en las cuadras y pocilgas. El suelo inmundo, saturado de polillas yríspidos salivazos. Las ennegrecidas paredes encierran un ambiente reducido y una atmósfera fétida.

Allá, en el fondo, una mezquina mesa de cafetín con dos alargamientos de madera hacen de mesa al tribunal. Encima, en la pared, un letrero que haría sonreír irónicamente si no estuviese teñido con sangre de miles de españoles

«¡ABAJO LA GUERRA!»

A un lado, una realista figura humana, cuyas espaldas están descuartizadas despiadadamente. (pp. 101–02)

Leech and Short go on to write:

In deciding what to include, the author, unlike the detective, would have artistic criteria of relevance. On the one hand he might omit information [. . .] in order to leave to the reader the task of guessing, inferring, or imagining 'what actually took place'; on the other hand, he might include circumstantial information on the natural environment, the behaviour of the onlookers, the dress of the principal characters, etc: matters which would be of little interest to the detective, but which might be important to bring out thematic contrasts or symbolic relationships, for example. (p. 155)

If, as argued above, Adro's main aim is to highlight the importance of the Church and the very necessary role it fulfils in society in general, then the details and language of this text must convey this. As summed up by Aristotle, the function of literature is to express the universal through the particular. Thus Adro very carefully chooses his images, for example when he describes the two men bleeding after being shot:

Un hilo fino y encarnado mana de los pechos abiertos. . . y al mezclarse con el regajo de cristal, camina y anda por breñas y campiñas, fecundizando la tierra astur, la gran patria española. . . *Sanguis martyrum semen christianorum*. La sangre de los mártires es semilla de cristianos. (p. 112)[10]

In addition, many of the details (such as the descriptions of the scenery or the 'characters'), which may be of secondary importance to the documentary text, provide a fuller picture complete with the necessary context, and give the reader the sense that he is an observer or a participant:[11]

Zigzagueando entre frondas policromadas, saltando entre rincones de fantasmagórico colorido y bañándose los pies en los regajales de cristal, sube, sube lenta y arriscadamente hasta caer de rodillas a los pies de la Reina *pequeñina* y *galana* de los asturianos, la Madre que vela la cuna de su hija España, la española Virgen de Covadonga.

Treinta autocars [*sic*] — inmensos, chatos — embragan y aceleran cuesta arriba. Caminan jadeantes, sudorosos. Piden limosna, ánimos y alegría a los dos mil gárrulos chiquillos que abarrotan sus interiores.

Una vuelta repentina. Todos los ojos se elevan.

Entre un claro del bosque, encima, allá arriba, alta, sobre el fondo de un cielo azul metálico, la basílica de paredes doradas se yergue cual gigantesca corona real en las sienes floridas de la monumental montaña.

El primer segundo de emoción anuda las gargantas. . .

Otro, y un atronador, nervioso, delirante grito, retumba por los profundos hondones, y choca contra las agabas gris perla y los roquedales rojos:

Bendita la reina de nuestra montaña
que tiene por trono la cuna de España
y brilla en la altura más bella que el sol
es Madre. . . y es Reina. . .

Y las vocecitas atipladas de los niños, llegan agudas, afiladas, a la roca sagrada, al trono pequeño y grande, sencillo y sublime de la *Santina*. (pp. 66–67)

The author describes the gradual appearance of the Basilica of Covadonga, hidden in the mountains, and, through the depiction of their singing, their sighs and their facial expressions, the reader perceives the excitement and awe which this produces in the children taking part in the procession. At the same time, however, the colourful and intricate description of the mountains and the church lend the narrative a more novelistic aspect. The same effect is produced in this literary, novelistic description of P. Martínez's face which depicts vividly and transmits to the reader his love for children: 'El Padre, a todos sonríe. Sus ojos son dos surtidores de cariño. Su boca, concha que vierte cascadas de dulzura. No es exageración ni hipérbole' (p. 10). As pointed out at the beginning of this chapter when dealing with Prada, *Asturias la desventurada*, the re-enactment of speech can also, on the one hand, contribute to the novelization of the narrative and, on the other, impart a realistic effect, as the actual words exchanged between the characters along with their described attitude, tone of voice, or any other information of the physical response give life to the text and make the participants more palpable. In order to show this I will quote an extract from both texts, in which F. Martínez quotes a statement made by a witness, while Adro places the same information in a conversation. When the former relates D. Juan Iglesias's attempts to free the two Jesuits he writes: 'Contestaron que estos no eran maestros, sino "embaucadores del pueblo", y por esto había que matarlos' (pp. 48–49). Adro, on the other hand, re-enacts the situation:

— ¡Cállate!, que te será mejor. ¿Conque ésos son maestros? ¡Ay, pazguato, si estás engañado! Embaucadores, embaucadores sin un pelo de vergüenza; unos descastados. . .

Y gritos y amenazas probaron cumplidamente las acusaciones. (p. 106)

Here I have merely pointed out the paradox of the two contradictory effects of both descriptive language and re-enacted episodes, and its significance to the propagandistic aims of the author. Because of the significance of these issues to this study in general I will leave it to the final Conclusion to discuss in more detail, where some of the texts examined in other chapters will be referred to.

To finish off my analysis of Adro Xavier's *Sangre jesuita*, I will consider an equally important issue, that is, its seemingly ambiguous literary status. In order to highlight what differentiates Adro's narrative from Martínez's I refer to Sauerberg who argues that it is the author's aim (in this case Adro's) to 'produce the right "feel" of the situation, not merely to reproduce a set of physical circumstances'.[12] As already established this text takes the form of a biography in which the lives of specific men are related. While the problems of a biographer are similar to those of a historian, in that he has to interpret documents, letters, eye-witness reports, and other such information, while also deciding on its trustworthiness, biography is nonetheless the nonfictional genre considered closest to the novel, sharing many characteristics with narratives of fiction.[13] In addition Sauerberg makes yet another relevant statement which can be applied to Adro's dramatization of Martínez's information, and which brings us nearer to identifying the literary status of this problematic text: 'The biographical novelist does not have to choose time and time again between the quotation from a letter or some other publication and a paraphrase of it. Whatever is essential from such sources is simply dramatized' (p. 153). While the majority of his descriptions are unoriginal and the symbolism predictable, both of these clearly influenced by his propagandistic aim, Adro does employ a certain degree of figurative language which reveal a degree of literary concern and ability. For example, 'Largas lenguas rojas delataban en varios puntos los incendios criminales' (p. 84). This metaphoric depiction of the flames, allegedly caused by the revolutionaries, is one of the many examples provided in Adro's text which support my belief that the more literary text is not necessarily the least propagandistic. Thus, Adro uses the biographer's approach together with the novelist's techniques to communicate a message, in this case a religious, patriotic, and anti-revolutionary propagandistic message. Indeed, nearly all of the quotations extracted from Adro's text manifest its blatantly biased nature and add further evidence to support the idea that he had a propagandistic aim in mind. By comparing it to Martínez's account, I have demonstrated when a factual account can be considered to be a novelized narrative and what the results are. As a biographical novelist, Adro is free to resort to imagery and other literary effects. As a propagandist, he will merge his message into the literary language.

COLLAGE

Alfonso Camín Meana's extensive hybrid work, *El Valle Negro*, can be briefly described as a collection of impressions from a wide range of people about the Asturian Revolution.[14] As the last gunshots are heard in Madrid, Camín, a well-known journalist and poet, sets off on a journey from the capital city to Oviedo with a mission to try to reconstruct the events which took place. Accompanied by two friends, Corso and Rufo, Camín drives north to León, crossing the city and reaching the mountains which divide Asturias from the rest of the Peninsula. They retrace the steps of the government troops, from León to Oviedo, passing through those towns and villages which were caught in the middle of the fighting between the soldiers and the miners. Once he reaches Oviedo the rest of the chapters are randomly added, without following any chronological order. Although the journey begins in Madrid, the text deals mostly with Asturias. It is divided into thirty-five short, unnumbered episodes (which for the sake of clarity I will call chapters) where the experiences of particular witnesses are related (both in first person and by the author–narrator) and the events in the affected areas described. Camin's text is unique in that it does not side with any political group whether left or right. Instead he prefers to dwell on the effects of the Revolution on the population at large, for him the crucial issue. *El Valle Negro* takes the form of a collage where the author makes use of ready-made materials, such as diaries, letters, and reports, and where the witnesses themselves provide their own experiences. These are then combined with Camín's own findings, the result of his investigation, and the descriptive and figurative writing which lend the text its literary appearance. It is the mixture of fictional and non-fictional elements which grants this work an ambiguous generic status, situating it on the border between fiction and non-fiction.

Unlike in most of the other texts where there is a prologue or an introduction, written by either the author or someone else, and where the ideological stance and other aspects of the text — such as its structure, its origins, and its veracity — are first referred to, in Camín's text the introductory function is fulfilled by the first chapter, 'El Turquesa'. This chapter sets the scene and serves as a forewarning of the war and the suffering which will be depicted and re-enacted throughout the narrative. It does not deal directly with the revolutionary events and instead it is used to describe the political background to the conflict. Rather than an objective summary of this, however, what emerges is Camín's scepticism of all political parties, a feeling which will be constant throughout the text. In dealing with the issue of the *Turquesa*, an essential contributing factor to the Revolution — 'El "Turquesa" nos da la clave' (p. 11) — Camín refers to the general political situation in Spain.[15] The man in charge of furnishing the *Turquesa* and of organizing the transportation of armament to Asturias, Egocheaga, is compared with many of the government figures whom Camín considers responsible in some way or another for the outbreak of the Revolution.[16] The latter are made out to be incompetent, such as Niceto Alcalá Zamora and Ricardo Samper; hypocritical, as in the case of Manuel Azaña; or malicious such as Alejandro Lerroux and José María Gil Robles. Not even the revolutionary leaders are exempt from the criticisms, and except for Pablo Iglesias, Manuel Llaneza, Indalecio Prieto, and Julián Besteiro, 'los demás portavoces del proletariado en España, incluyendo a Largo Caballero, están cien codos por debajo del mérito, de la honradez y del tesón obrerista de este gran guerrillero asturiano [Egocheaga]' (p. 14). He adds:

> En todas las revoluciones, después de las arengas populares, de las descargas cerradas o de las guerras mayores, los altos representantes del movimiento obrero, o se lavan las manos como Pilatos, o se disculpan de sus hechos, o ganan a zancadas la frontera. No les falta el colchón de lana fina, el buen plato, el buen cheque. (pp. 14–15)

As part of his recent historical summary Camín, as narrator, refers to the important political conflicts which in his view have had an impact on Spanish society and which have ultimately provoked the outbreak of the Revolution, namely Gil Robles's meetings in Covadonga and El Escorial, the right-wing election victory in November 1933, and, the final spark, the introduction of the three anti-republican CEDA members into the cabinet of Lerroux on 3 October. Indeed, Camín goes as far as to blame Gil Robles for the bloody events: 'Esta era la cosecha del acto de Gil Robles. Poner en pie los odios del paisaje' (p. 20). Thus Camín begins with a factual and political chapter in which, through his allusion to the two most influential factors which will pave the way for the Revolution, in other words, Gil Robles's politics which provided the socio-political incentive, and the availability of armament which enabled the revolutionaries to take action, he unveils his political point of view, without admitting at any point in the narrative that he is being partial. And so the Revolution and Camín's journey begin in the next chapter: 'Así comienza la tragedia española del 34' (p. 21).

Camín's narrative can be divided into three main blocks. From Chapters 2 to 11 he describes his journey from Madrid to Asturias, passing through León; Chapters 12 to 21 deal with the events in Oviedo; and Chapters 22 to 34 relate the fighting in other parts of Asturias. Camín concludes with his 'Ultimas palabras' which, I will later suggest, were added to his text at a later date. The thread which runs through all of the separate chapters, joining them together, is the detailed description of Camín's journey through Asturias. In this manner, Camín tackles the difficulty of relating the events in some sort of order, when in fact, the scenes which he describes in many cases took place at the same time, during the twenty days of Revolution. Within this carefully delineated framework, Camín incorporates the fruits of his investigation in a diverse manner. He does not attempt to modify the data in order to construct a continuous, coherent and uniform narrative, where the events are told by the same narrator employing the same language throughout. Instead Camín employs a number of different narrative styles. While he occasionally includes the research material in its original form — such as when diaries or witness reports are transcribed — elsewhere he re-enacts episodes of the Revolution, while in other chapters he describes what he sees, in the aftermath, and combines it with what he has been told by the witnesses to reproduce the events which took place. This diversity leads to a complex text with many narrative points of view, including the first-person narrator in the witnesses' primary sources, the third-person narrator in the re-enacted episodes, and the author–narrator as Camín relates the progress of his investigation and his own perceptions on the events. However, all of these seemingly independent points of view, as well as the subject matter included, are chosen and controlled by Camín, and are determined by the clear populist and anti-political party message which he wants to convey: 'Las revoluciones las hacen siempre los pueblos. Jamás los partidos políticos' (p. 25).

Camín's narrative strategies can be more easily identified by examining each of the three blocks separately. Once this has been done we can consider why Camín opts for such a complex narrative style given that his aim is to inform the reader of the facts of the Revolution and provide data which he will be able to compare with official and revolutionary accounts. This issue will in turn determine how the text is designed to be read. If we examine the first block of chapters, from Chapter 3 ('Noche en León') to Chapter 12 ('De cómo Don Suero de Quiñones llega a las puertas de la capital asturiana'), Camín works his way into Asturias, and deeper into revolutionary territory, passing through 'Pola de Gordón' (Chapter 4), 'Alto Pajares' (Chapter 5), 'Campomanes' (Chapter 6), 'El frente del sur' (Chapter 7), 'Vega del Ciego' (Chapter 8), 'Pola de Lena' (Chapter 9) and 'La cuenca del Caudal' (Chapter 11). He describes the bloody encounters which the miners had in each of these places, first of all with the Civil Guard and, once the government troops arrived, with the army. Each of these chapters is made up of data from different sources. Camín narrates his journey to the town or village which he will deal with, portraying the landscape, the ruined buildings and the depressed people which he sees on the way. He adds to his own impressions a brief outline of the revolutionary events in that particular place, often concentrating on one significant incident or the experiences of one particular person. For example, Chapter 7 concentrates on the stalemate in Pola de Lena between the army and the revolutionaries, and Chapter 4 relates the death of five men, prisoners of the Civil Guard, in Pola de Gordón. Thus the clashes described may be those which took place during the Revolution, in which case the actions of the revolutionaries and more particularly of the miners are the main focus of attention, or the repression which ensued, anecdotes in which the army are the protagonists. In this way Camín describes the effects of the Revolution as he sees them (in the present tense), and the violence of the fighting as it is described to him by its witnesses (in various forms of the past tense) as they recollect their experiences.

In Chapter 6, where the revolutionary fighting in Campomanes is depicted, the author first presents the version which the owner of the pasta factory provides about the needless slaughter of the soldiers defending that position, and then goes on to give his own account, based on the data which he has collected and the evidence which he has seen: 'Mi opinión, producto de los datos recogidos sobre el barro y la sangre' (p. 59). He concludes that the soldiers were killed because they fought fiercely (and heroically) against the revolutionaries. Thus here we have an example where Camín uses witness evidence in order to challenge it and present his own carefully reasoned argument. At other times Camín also makes use of flashbacks so that past events are described in the present tense. Given the complex nature of the narrative — it is frequently difficult to identify exactly when the events referred to take place, or the narrative voice of a particular story — Camín occasionally imposes some order into the narrative by recapping the events which he has just been dealing with, thereby limiting the confusion felt by the reader. For example: 'Ya hace varios días que se encuentra sitiado el general Bosch en Vega del Rey; ya sucedió la tragedia de la Guardia Civil en Campomanes; ya han venido soldados de refuerzo desde la parte de León y son pocos, según el cerco que va poniendo el enemigo' (p. 65).

Camín finally arrives in Oviedo at the end of Chapter 11, and Chapters 12 to 21, which constitute what I have called the second block of the text, deal with the events in this city. These nine chapters are more varied narrative-wise than the first twelve. The story is no longer centred on Camín's trip. Instead, the author relates numerous versions of the events, obtained first-hand from the mouths of a wide selection of witnesses representing all sectors of society. Through these personal stories Camín conveys the difficult days lived in Oviedo, relates the suffering of the most innocent, and demonstrates how the citizens coped with this violence. As stated above, Camín is not interested in offering a political view of the events or supporting the allegations of one side or the other. He concentrates on depicting the human suffering which accompanied the Revolution. For him what is important are those personal experiences which tell the truth of the situation as lived by the people. This helps to explain the diversity of the contents and style of the chapters in this second block which I will now examine.

Chapter 14 ('El Gobernador y yo') is a straight one-to-one interview with Fernando Blanco, the Governor of the Asturian government, who, guided by Camín's questions, gives his version of the events. Camín gives his friend Blanco an opportunity to defend himself, in the face of accusations of incompetence from central government and growing criticism from the public, by revealing data which partly contradicts official records and which the reader can compare with the widely and freely disseminated government accounts.[17] Apart from his friendly intention, this chapter serves to add weight to Camín's belief that the official government and revolutionary reports cannot be relied on. In contrast to this 'factual' question-and-answer chapter in which the author interviews the subject, in Chapter 15 ('El General y Belarmino') the peace negotiations between Belarmino Tomás and General López Ochoa are re-enacted. Nevertheless, even here the author-narrator makes an appearance, albeit at the very end: 'Corso me ha dejado durante unos días. Ha ido a Pola de Lena, vio a Rufino y me trae unos datos' (p. 166). Camín thus reminds the reader that he, as investigative journalist and despite the change of narrative voice and style in the chapter, is responsible for the information presented here too. Chapter 16 ('Episodios de Oviedo'), composed of thirty-one clearly separate anecdotes of life in Oviedo during the fighting, resembles the text *Asturias la desventurada: caminos de sangre*, by Francisco Prada, examined above. In this chapter Camín resorts even further than in the previous to using novelistic techniques; the author–narrator disappears altogether and Camín opts instead for an omniscient narrator. With this pot-pourri of individual, re-enacted stories, the author effectively humanizes and portrays the larger social situation. For Chapters 17 ('San Pedro de los Arcos') and 18 ('El Naranco') Camín returns to the strategy employed in the first chapters where he collects information from various sources and merges them together in order to give a seemingly reliable insight into one aspect of the Revolution, the life and death of the well-known Libertaria Lafuente in Chapter 17, and the positive experiences of the priest of El Naranco in Chapter 18. Camín merges what he hears, sees, and smells as he tours Asturias with what he is told by the witnesses, in the case of Chapter 17 incorporating into this a detailed account of Libertaria's involvement in the fight and her re-enacted execution. In Chapter 18, in addition to these elements, a historical summary of the Moorish defeat during the Reconquest serves as a comparison with the action of the Moors during the Revolution. In the historical version the Moors were fought against by the authorities, while in 1934 they are given the freedom to act as they please. Thus the historical addition serves an ironic as well as an informative purpose.

In Chapter 19 ('Dimitri Ivanoff') Camín resumes his journalistic and investigative task and sets out to find out information about Dimitri Ivanoff, responsible for the death of the journalist Luis de Sirval. He describes how he searches for him in the bars of Oviedo and the subsequent interview in which Ivanoff provides his version of Sirval's death. However, Camín's own ensuing (re-enacted) version contradicts the information given by the Bulgarian solider and, after a brief biographical sketch of the journalist, Camín concludes that Ivanoff's fear of Sirval's investigative zeal was exaggerated, thereby implying that his violent death was unwarranted. In Chapter 20 ('Los Moros en Villafría') Camín employs a new narrative technique for depicting the murderous, horrific and ransacking actions of the Moors, proper of a tragedy. Thus at the start, the chapter takes the form of a theatrical piece in three acts:

> Como las guitarras trágicas, este paisaje tiene también tres tiempos, tres matices, tres actos completos, como las obras enterizas en los teatros formales. Primero, el ejército minero [. . .].
> [. . .]
> Segundo acto: El sargento alucinado. Pedro, con la espada en la vera de Cristo, creyendo más en los fusiles que en las parábolas, recoge por las cuencas a los últimos combatientes, ascuas del gran incendio, y vuelve a las puertas de Oviedo, trabando combate feroces con el Tercio y los moros [. . .].
> [. . .]
> Acto final: Represión y este desierto que vemos [. . .]. (pp. 251–53)

It is interesting to note that elsewhere in the narrative Camín compares the Revolution to a Shakespearean tragedy: 'Es Corso — de nuevo — quien se recuesta sobre la silla, tira la boina a un lado y nos cuenta la historia que es más bien un pasaje de las tragedias shakespirianas. La sombra del "Rey Lear" clamaba en estas soledades' (p. 45).[18] For the remainder of Chapter 20, to ensure that this dramatic reconstruction is not misinterpreted as fictional (and therefore make-believe), Camín makes his way around the houses of Villafría, many of which are now empty, unfolding to the reader what happened to the inhabitants of each of them and how they fared with the Moors.

The last chapter in the second block, Chapter 21 ('Por ella me fui yo al Tercio'), narrates the tragic story of a young woman who loses her husband in the Revolution. It is impossible to know for certain whether this episode is factual or fictional. Although we assume that it is factual, given the informative priority of the rest of the text, the manner in which this particular chapter is narrated resembles that of a fictional story. The fact that Camín does not make any attempt to clear up this ambiguity leads me to surmise that for the author this is an unimportant and irrelevant concern. Although it may be fictional as regards the concrete data, it conveys the 'real' tragic moments of the Revolution and the suffering of the innocent population — precisely what I believe the author is striving to depict. Thus, the stories presented here and in the 'episodios' in Chapter 16, although possibly fictional (we will never know for sure in the majority of cases), illuminate the 'truth' of the human dimension of the Revolution, just as imaginative literature can illuminate the sense of history.[19]

Once Camín has examined a great many aspects of the Revolution in the capital he moves on to the surrounding mining valleys, concentrating on the events in the Valle del Nalón (Chapters 22 to 27), Turón (Chapter 28), the Valle de Aller (Chapter 29), and Pola de Siero (Chapter 31). Chapters 32 and 33 deal with the two most important cities of Asturias apart from Oviedo, Gijón and Avilés, the citizens of which did not play a significant role in the course of the fighting. With few exceptions, the narrative style of the chapters in this third block takes the form of those in the first. In the case of Chapter 32 ('Los episodios de Gijón') and Chapter 34 ('Anecdotario asturiano'), Camín employs the same device as in 'Episodios de Oviedo' in order to depict as wide as possible a range of experiences. In the former the anecdotes are based in Gijón, while in the latter they deal with parts of Asturias not yet dealt with, such as Grado, Taverga, Las Regueras, Bernueces, and Posada de Llanes. Chapters 22 ('Diario de un hombre pacífico') and 31 ('Las memorias de Xuacu') are diaristic accounts. The former is a diary written by an unknown person, while the latter is a day-to-day account of events as lived by Xuacu and related by Camín.

The nature of Chapter 22 raises several very interesting issues, some of which can also be applied to Chapter 31. This interpolated diary gives an account of the events from 5 to 22 October. It is an interesting chapter for the issues it raises question the reliability of Camín's use of the witnesses throughout the narrative and ultimately Camín's overall purpose. The implied author of the diary is anonymous; the only information we are given about him is that he lives in Pando, near La Felguera, and that he works in 'Los Hornos de Cok'. He relates how he leaves his home and his family when he finds out that the revolutionary army are conscripting men from the countryside and towns to fight on their side. He returns to his village, Pando, on 9 October, after having been away for four days, during which time he writes about the Revolution as he witnesses it. The Revolution continues while he is in Pando and he writes about its development, its ups and downs, conveying the feeling of desperation of the revolutionaries as their situation looks increasingly precarious: 'Los ánimos del pueblo decaen por las aceras' (p. 290).

There are a number of characteristics which suggest to me that Camín may have written this diary himself. For a start, the chapter begins and ends with the diary; Camín does not appear anywhere explaining, for example, where he obtained the diary from. The rest of the evidence lies with the diarist and his work. The diarist is a factory worker. Even if Camín had edited the diary for spelling and punctuation mistakes, would he really have been able to write in such a stylistically polished manner? It is possible that Camín is making use of a set of notes and that he is writing the diary himself, inevitably influencing the style and the contents of the narrative. A close look at the style reveals that it is very similar to that of the rest of the text. The diarist, just like Camín, employs imagery: 'El día también es triste. Parece que en las victorias de los primeros días estalló en luz y que ahora el mismo horizonte opaco va señalando la derrota. Un horizonte cansado, que parece inclinarse de hombros por la fatiga' (p. 288). This personification of nature is one of the clearest features throughout the text, as I will later demonstrate. In addition Camín refers very often to the advantage which nature gave the government troops, just as the diarist does: 'Parece que hasta el sol es un desertor más y amigo de los fuertes' (p. 289). Biblical and classical references are employed by both writers: 'Por aquí todavía andaba Virgilio soñando con las esquilas' (p. 280). If Camín influences the contents of the diary, we can assume that any criticisms which arise here should coincide with those in the rest of the narrative. This is indeed the case. For example, the diarist criticizes those who flee from the Revolution:

> En realidad, los campesinos, a pesar de ir unidos en la bandera de la contienda, no tenían ningún sentido ni afán de guerra. Estaban a la que se caía. Pero en cuanto se les indicaba que hacían falta unos huevos o unas gallinas y que era necesario que el mozo de casa tomase un fusil, se escapaban o lo hacían a la fuerza. Porque estos hombres que huyen, son casi todos labradores disfrazados de obreros. Se aprovechan de la mina, pero no olvidan su sentido de pequeños propietarios del agro asturiano. (p. 284)

It is evident, thus, that rather than a 'real' diary this may simply be another literary device employed by Camín to transmit the human dimension of the Revolution. Accordingly, the diarist expresses his desire for peace and the difficulties in remaining uninvolved in a fight of this nature where everyone becomes a victim: 'No creí que costaba tanto ser un hombre pacífico' (p. 279); 'Que no me vea en otro aprieto semejante, porque yo tiro para una o para otra cuneta. Es demasiado molesto hacer de árbol solitario entre dos vientos enemigos' (p. 279).

In the case of Chapter 31, Xuacu's testimony is told from the point of view of someone who has returned to Asturias after having emigrated to Cuba (incidentally mirroring Camín's own situation). In this way Camín depicts how the Revolution was lived by yet another sector of society. Whereas in Chapter 22 the author–narrator does not appear, here Camín is clearly present performing the role of interviewer. Nevertheless, when Xuacu's story is actually related the interview format, and with it the author–narrator, disappears altogether. The same coincidence in the style and contents that were pointed out for Chapter 22, and the fluency of the narrative, suggests that rather than a direct transcription, Camín gives his own rendering of Xuacu's testimony. By highlighting and omitting certain aspects he is able to manipulate the substance of the personal testimony, again with an aim to convey most effectively the human dimension of the conflict.

Having examined the medley of narrative styles and points of view used by Camín, we need to explore why he complicates his task so much and why he does not just relate the effects of the Revolution straightforwardly in the third person. The first and most basic explanation is that it introduces variety, avoiding the possible monotony in a work of this length (over five hundred pages long). Secondly, in his definition of 'collage', Hutchinson writes that the author may use this technique as a form of game where the reader is challenged to 'determine what is actually happening [in the narrative] and to follow its course' (p. 72).[20] I do not think this is the case in *El Valle Negro*, although it could be argued that, by producing a confusing effect on the reader, Camín attempts to depict the havoc present during the days of the Revolution. By referring to his last chapter, 'Ultimas palabras', further explanations can be sought. This chapter, in which Camín refers to those who were involved in the Revolution of 1934 and examines their position during the start of the Civil War in 1936, may have been included as an epilogue in the original narrative or it may have been added on for this particular edition, published in 1938. Camín refers to his aims and throws light on why he chose to depict the Revolution in this way, drawing attention to the fact that he does not want his text to resemble or be associated with the heap of biased reports and novels published shortly after the events (many of which are examined in this thesis). The vast majority of these texts concentrate on the *political* aspects of the Revolution, siding with either the government or the revolutionaries, and not the human suffering which everyone, irrespective of their ideological stance, was subjected to. For Camín the most important task is to tell the reader about those 'facts' that, given the restricted political focus of the other accounts published, he could not easily learn otherwise. However, rather than offer dry historical data (which would undoubtedly fail to convey fully the atmosphere and feelings which reigned) Camín resorts to narrative devices where his sympathy for the victims will be transmitted to the reader. Thus, through the dramatized and re-enacted episodes and through witness testimonies Camín does not merely tell the reader of the human suffering, he actually depicts it.[21] The author is effectively ensuring that the reader becomes involved in the predicament of the victims. In addition, he presents to the reader the information in the same way that he learns about it, explaining why in some chapters he transcribes interviews while in others he merely describes the sights and people which he sees in the aftermath. Without stating it Camín is relying on the fact that his actual presence in Asturias and the conversations held with the witnesses will make his text reliable. While the objective data which he provides is verifiable, and for the most part accurate, for Camín it only serves to contextualize the human suffering, which is his main concern.

It is important to consider how much after the Revolution Camín actually wrote *El Valle Negro* as the accuracy of the information he provides can become questionable if the book was composed long after his journey and the events. If, as Camín himself claims, the object of the book is to clear up any contentious points of the Revolution and to tell that truth which no other book has told, this is a serious issue. While Camín writes in the last chapter that his book was published in 1938, Albino Suárez insists that it was first written in 1934, even though it was not published until 1938 in Mexico.[22] If, as Suarez claims, the book was written in 1934 (indeed, the directness and freshness of the text would support this), he may have waited so long that it was still unpublished by the time the Civil War had broken out. If this was the case, Camín would not have been able to publish it until he was in exile in Mexico, during which time I believe he may have added the last chapter. Occasionally Camín's remarks give the impression that he is composing the narrative as he advances through Asturias: 'Corso me ha dejado durante unos días. Ha ido a Pola de Lena, vió a Rufino y me trae unos datos' (p. 166). On the other hand, there are times when he appears to have composed the book well after he has carried out his interviews: 'Por aquellas fechas, aún se ignoraba la suerte y el paradero del sargento Vázquez' (p. 315). The following observation sets the composition of the work from the actual dates of the Revolution even further apart: 'El General López Ochoa, dentro de unos días, no estará en su puesto' (p. 165). Rather than composing the work whilst he is travelling I believe it is a product of the notes which Camín has collected. By the time he transcribes the notes and writes the narrative the aftermath of the Revolution becomes apparent, hence the use of the future tense to explain what will happen.

Having established that most of the information has been collected shortly after the events, we should consider its reliability given that much of it is based on witness testimonies which, in a politically conflictive situation such as this, are unlikely to have been impartial. Although Camín interviews a wide range of individuals, from villagers to miners, the Civil Guard and the Moorish troops, archaeologists, landlords, and even the protagonists of the Revolution such as the Governor of Asturias and Dimitri Ivanoff, the stories which the witnesses tell Camín are subject to ideological manipulation, an issue which Camín is aware of and takes into account, such as in the case of the owner of the pasta factory mentioned earlier. I have further argued that many of the dramatized stories and the anonymous characters which appear in them may not be real in form but in essence. This is the case when Camín describes the death of many innocent citizens who step outside their houses in search of bread and water:

Y sobre la acera, en actitud de haber querido ganar la plaza, se ve a un pobre niño muerto — once años que corta el plomo — con las manos abiertas y los ojos al cielo. Las dos hogazas de pan duro que traía entre las manos brillan a un lado, mientras se ensancha la sangre de la criatura en la acera. (p. 143)

Camín describes this scene as if he were witnessing the death of this child. This is impossible, given that he does not arrive in Asturias until after the Revolution. However, Camín is using his own imagination in order to depict what he 'knows' happened in the streets of Oviedo during the fighting, based on what eye-witnesses have told him. Of course, although Camín may reach his own conclusions about the events (based on his investigation) there is no absolute guarantee that what he claims is anything more than a reasonable personal opinion. In the case of the transcribed interviews, there is evidence to suggest that the author manipulates the witnesses' responses in his own rendering. For example, in Chapter 18 the priest of El Naranco describes the sad events:

— ¡No estaban organizados! [. . .] Tenían cinco objetivos, a base de tomar de noche y por sorpresa a Oviedo. [. . .] ¡Pero no estaban organizados!

Las milicias de Oviedo ocuparían las bocacalles. [. . .] ¡Pero no estaban organizados!

Cuatro fábricas de armas. [. . .] ¡No estaban organizados!

[. . .] Toda esta parte del Naranco estaba cubierta de hombres que andaban de un lado para otro con la consigna de U.H.P. ¡Pero no estaban organizados! [. . .] ¡No estaban organizados! (pp. 228–29)

Surely this is an example in which Camín manipulates the answers of one of his witnesses and, by so doing, emphasizes particular issues (in this case that the revolutionaries were not prepared for the Revolution).

Whilst it is difficult to determine the authenticity of some of the characters which appear in the text, there are other characters who are clearly identifiable. Camín refers to important and well-known collaborators of the Revolution, figures whom the readers will be able to identify, including military and political leaders on both sides. In the same way Camín incorporates into his work extracts of documents and other verifiable data: he reproduces a letter written to the wife of Manuel Pedregal, the ex-minister of Hacienda, by the Revolutionary Committee (p. 463); the medical report which claims that Javier Bueno was suffering from ulcers when in fact he had been tortured while in jail (p. 490); a copy of Belarmino's peace talk, calling for the miners to put down their arms (p. 312); biographical details of some of the important participants of the Revolution, such as González Peña in Chapter 30 ('González Peña') and Luis Sirval in Chapter 19 ('Dimitri Ivanoff'); and even a song from the Revolution (p. 341). All these are pieces of documentary evidence which are verifiable. Amongst the documentary information included we can find specific press reports and official government documents Camín believes have been used to mislead people. He criticizes the right-wing press for spreading political propaganda and for deceiving the people:

> Apartamos los ojos del paisaje, cuyo silencio es más trágico y elocuente que todos los gorigoris de tantos escarbamientos de la prensa negra, plañideras del Madrid estrecho y barato, como han salido a comentar la guerra de Asturias, con negros plumeros de potros de entierro y destemplados maullidos de gatos de luna y teja. (pp. 89–90)

The witnesses he interviews also allude to the press lies, including one doctor who worked in a hospital during the Revolution who rejects the press claims (fed by right-wing political and religious groups) that the priest in Sama was killed and put on display in a butcher's shop; or the priest, don Pepe Villanueva, whose obituary was printed in the newspaper *El Cruzado Español.* Don Villanueva, the chairman of the 'Liceo Asturiano' and a respected member of society, condemns the press lies and the Church's endorsement of such lies: '¡La mentira y el fango quieren subir hasta el trono de Dios! ¡Y por nuestras propias escalas!' (p. 193). Camín's point of view, backed up by doctors, priests, and other important personages, is given more moral weight, and consequently his judgement on the events becomes more influential.

The press is not the only source of information criticized. Camín also refers to the government's official information, most of which is divulged in the 'folleto oficial' (p. 74), in other words, *La revolución de octubre en*

España: la rebelión del gobierno de la Generalidad. Octubre 1934 (1934), examined earlier on in Chapter 4. Camín not only points out and criticizes the biased information, such as that which blames the miners for the destruction of the Ermita de Santa Cristina, calling in the process for '¡Menos hipocresías domésticas, eclesiásticas y oficiales!' (p. 74). He also complains of the inaccuracy of some of the concrete data contained in a report which is supposed to provide information about the events and which is instead used as yet another tool to propagate ideological concerns, leaving aside the real issue which is the human suffering.[23]

Given the human focus of his text it is not surprising that Camín concentrates on delving into the psychology of man and of the *pueblo* in this work. He examines the temperament and attitudes of the miners, and he is more positive towards this group of people than any other. He is sympathetic towards those who fought in the Revolution, encouraged by their dire working and living conditions: 'En Matallana los rebeldes mataron al cura párroco. El cura quería darles dinero. Pero lo rechazaron. Para los hombres de este ideario rebelde tiene poca importancia el dinero. Les importaba más el cura, que no bajaba a la mina' (p. 31). On the other hand they respect the priest and the people of La Felguera, their reasons being, 'a quien hace el bien, con bien se responde, ya se trate de un cura o de un anarquista' (p. 348). The revolutionary army is made up of peasants most of whom are forced to fight and villagers who are frightened or who feel they have something to gain from the Revolution. Thus, the only real revolutionaries are the miners: 'Los revolucionarios auténticos. Los convencidos de que iban a una lucha social de redención humana' (p. 86), whom he goes on to praise:

> Los mineros han sido los que se lo jugaron todo, lo mismo en Campomanes que en todas partes donde fue necesaria su presencia. Los mineros estaban donde había tiros y había sangre. Creían en un nuevo ideal. En la redención de una clase de hombres. En lo que puede creer el que está siempre en el fondo de la tierra. [. . .] Como la sombra sueña con la luz — con el otro extremo — , los verdaderos revolucionarios soñaban ayer y soñarán mañana con la Virgen de la Anarquía. Con lo que ellos llaman nuestra Señora, con el mismo fervor con que otros creyentes sueñan con nuestra señora del Carmen o la Virgen de la Esperanza. Por eso ellos sabían que marchaban a la guerra. Y no les espantaba morir. Iban a la guerra con un ramo de bombas entre las manos, como pudieran ir con un ramo de flores. Era la ofrenda negra para la "Virgen trágica" de sus sueños. [. . .] Sólo cuando se hacían fuertes los mineros, quedaban detrás los grupos agazapados en espera de la victoria para reclamar su parte en este botín de la muerte. (pp. 86–87)

In some cases Camín examines the background of some of those who were involved in the Revolution, searching for factors which may have determined their conduct. He does this for example when he considers the reasons which led to the massacre in Turón, in which Rafael Riego, his friend and the owner of the mine there, two guards, and eight monks and a priest were shot by the revolutionaries. The gravedigger who was on call the night these men were killed is interviewed by Camín and he explains to the author why he believes these three institutions were targeted:

> Cualquier tirano es menos peligroso para la causa que un hombre bueno, puesto en la acera de enfrente [about Riego]. [. . .] Raro es el hombre del pueblo que no recuerda sus miedos, la bofetada, la paliza o la dureza de las esposas en las dos manos [about the Guardia Civil]. El cura, por todo el Norte, está clasificado como el fartón de cada pueblo o de cada casa rica, como el servidor del cacique en la política, en la economía y hasta en los asuntos conyugales. (pp. 374–75)

Rather than those particular individuals, the killers felt rage towards the employers, the Church, and the Civil Guard. They take their rage out on these twelve men. Camín criticizes society in general for having fostered that hatred which encourages such acts of violence. Poverty is one of the factors which encourage the miners to join the Revolution. In order for the reader to comprehend this Camín describes a number of scenes of utter poverty and compares them to the luxurious living conditions which the bosses and the owners live in:

> Ujo se compone de una porción de casas misérrimas, engarabitadas unas en otras, tristes y antihigiénicas, de cuyas ventanas cuelgan las ropas pobres. Son las casas de los mineros de Ujo. Hay un silencio trágico en ellas. En sus ventanas y pasadizos se ven niños descalzos y escuálidos, mujeres paupérrimas con la piel color de ladrillo, flacas, enfermizas, deshilachadas. (pp. 103–04)

The working class have always felt a special hatred towards Oviedo — 'Esa ciudad ociosa y haragana' (p. 135) — because of what it has stood for, explaining why it becomes one of their prime targets. As he walks around Oviedo, Camín despises the sight of the wealthy of this city who appear only once the Revolution has been defeated: 'Estoy frente al espectro de Oviedo. En la calle de Uría [. . .] encuentro gentes conocidas, ovetenses que no han hecho más que vivir ociosos a la sombra de la ciudad señora, en el tresillo del casino, la maledicencia de las tertulias aseñoritadas y la cómoda especulación banquera y minera' (p. 133). This criticism of lack of involvement, however, is also applied to the more humble citizens of Gijón, whom Camín accuses of cowardice, and Grado where, according to Camín, the people supported the Revolution for the sake of convenience: 'En Grado, unos, por simpatía, los menos, por miedo y los más, por adoptar una postura cómoda, todo el pueblo era rojo, menos unos cuantos. Lo mismo que al fracasar la revolución, menos unos cuantos, todos han vuelto a ser sacristanes' (p. 487).

Camín provides his own opinion of the events from the start of the text, opinions which are very clearly and explicitly expressed, although more often than not they are embellished through elaborate metaphoric language. He is very critical towards politics in general, 'la política, que es lo más bajo del pensamiento, cambia a su gusto las conductas' (pp. 364–65), and he denounces politicians of both sides. As early as in the first chapter Camín criticizes the members of the various Republican governments whom he believes are responsible for the events. He blames the Revolution categorically on Gil Robles: '¡Esto que veis, don Gil, es vuestra obra!' (p. 134). Even the socialist leader Teodomiro Menéndez is criticized: 'Mientras se trató de argumentos civiles y de asambleas de badulaques, todo lo encontraba bien, pero [. . .] en cuanto oyó cómo estallaba la dinamita se metió en casa' (p. 176). Instead he supports the people and their desire for Revolution, insisting that the initiative must come from them and not from the politicians:

> Las revoluciones las hacen siempre los pueblos. Jamás los partidos políticos. Un partido político puede asaltar el Poder. Puede hacer de su capa un sayo, hasta que el pueblo, formado de todas las capas sociales, de arriba y de abajo, se ponga en marcha. Ese día desaparecen los partidos políticos para aparecer las verdaderas revoluciones. (p. 25)

Along with his criticism of the political leaders, Camín reveals throughout his text his bias against the Church, the employers (and their capitalist system), and the army. The Church is generally depicted as hypocritical, money-grabbing, and unsympathetic to the sorry situation of the workers and their aspirations for improvements. It is also accused of consenting to the violence exerted by the government forces. The employers are accused of being irresponsible and of ignoring the dire conditions which their workers live and work in, while they enjoy countless luxuries. The conditions suffered by the miners, including their dangerous work, the constant police surveillance which they are subjected to, the total absence of home comforts, and the lack of dignity and education, are described in detail and with indignation by Camín who underlines this issue throughout the narrative, such as in this example in which he describes the living conditions of those who live near the mines at Figaredo:

> Doblando por Santullano a la derecha, rumbo a Turón y al Valle Negro, con las aguas del Caudal a la izquierda, hieren la vista unas chozas de piedra, agrupadas entre algunos hórreos en ruina: viviendas ceñudas, destartaladas, unas sobre otras, auxiliándose las vigas y las paredes, como si temieran irse de bruces sobre el camino. En las puertas de estos desvanes, sin bisagras ni cerraduras, en las callejas sucias de estos cubiles, sobre las cercas de piedras amontonadas, en los corredores de maderas podridas por el viento y la lluvia, entre los árboles tísicos de las huertas estrechas donde cuelgan harapos, rotos y limpios, como banderas rebeldes de la miseria, se ven niños famélicos, roídos por la atmósfera viciada de los carbones; madres anémicas con las caras mustias, pelos pajizos, los senos flágidos, en los que muerden los hijos, como lobeznos, chupando la sangre y el tuétano; mozuelos de ojos turbios, desmedrados, de ánimo rencoroso, que hace tiempo no encuentran trabajo en la

mina; sombras humanas que todo lo han dado a los tajos mineros y que a los cuarenta años, parecen viejos; paisanos con aspecto de mendigos que ellos mismos dan sus puntadas gruesas al chaquetón remendado; "rapazas" descalzas que bajan al río con ropas y calderos, y en los ojos esa tristeza de las mozas en ciernes que no tienen zapatos nuevos, ni pan, ni libros de escuela. Rematan el cuadro dos o tres cabras que triscan hierbas ralas por los vericuetos y desmontes, y el soliloquio de alguna vieja, que descarna en el huerto las últimas hojas a las berzas, que ya son troncos frente al camino. Toda la tierra es barro, piedras y escoria negruzca. (pp. 361–62)

In comparison with this image of absolute poverty Camín describes the luxury enjoyed by their bosses: 'Las famosas minas de Figaredo, cuyos accionistas, herederos y mandatarios, faltos de cultura y de esfuerzo, ocupan el mejor palacio de las afueras de Gijón y forman la aristocracia económica asturiana, sin otros timbres de nobleza que los millones heredados' (p. 362).

Apart from the working-class response to the Revolution, Camín examines why it broke out in the first place. He suggests that the miners were antagonized by the Church and the employers. He insists that as long as these antagonisms remain the possibility of another Revolution is likely:

Si los de arriba proceden con esta intransigencia, no pidamos cordura de los de abajo. Si atruenan las campanas con este júbilo escandaloso sobre la tumba de la Casa del Pueblo, cerrada con doble llave, no será extraño que si mañana vuelven a alzar la frente los humillados, enmudezcan las campanas y rueden las cabezas de los campaneros. (pp. 362–63)

Camín harks back to the idyllic past of Asturias, when the peaceful atmosphere of the countryside influenced people's characters positively:

El pueblo de Bóo, compuesto de gentes pacíficas, de hombres que siempre llevaron en los ojos la paz del campo y de mujeres que, antes de llegar por aquellos contornos el aire grueso de la mina, no sabían de más ruidos que los de las esquilas y el canto de cortejo del mozo, el responso del agua molinera y la flauta del mirlo en el álamo, el bronce alegre de las campanas y el saludo temprano de los vecinos. . . (p. 382)

Thus, he blames the businessmen too for creating such a dehumanized situation, by turning the idyllic countryside of Asturias into busy towns such as Turón: '¿Quién trajo las masas a Turón? Las Empresas. [. . .] No se puede cobrar la renta de un rascacielos y exigir a los vecinos que se alumbren con candiles' (pp. 363–64). Camín argues that if there are businessmen who wish to introduce mines, factories, and therefore progress, they must understand that what is traditional becomes outdated, including the important role which the Church plays in society and more particularly in education, clearly a republican stance. Finally, the army chiefs are accused of being incompetent and violent, and many are portrayed as having little control over their soldiers. Camín highlights the danger of this: 'Un crimen no justifica otro crimen. La anarquía no es el Estado. Y cuando el Estado procede como la anarquía, deja de ser Estado. Es una fuerza ciega más peligrosa que las rebeliones mineras' (pp. 38–39). While Bosch blames his ineffective action on his assumption that what was required of him was to control a strike, Camín suggests that the problem lay with his incompetence and cowardice. The Civil Guard are also accused of being cruel and of using torture, in particular during the repression.

In an attempt not to commit the same mistake as most of the accounts and reports which he criticizes, Camín tries to create some sort of balance by not generalizing. Thus he shows a positive attitude towards certain individuals belonging to each of these three groups, and highlights the exceptions to the general rule. In the case of the Church, Camín emphasizes that he is not against religion in general, but rather the abuse of power by Church dignitaries. He condemns the politicians' use of religion to excuse their violent actions and to reach the masses, and believes that politics and religion must not be confused:

> Gil Robles agita sus banderines viejos en todas las fortalezas político-militares. Anuncia su viaje a Covadonga, confundiendo lo político con lo religioso. Las negras pasiones humanas, con la limpia Cruz de los Angeles. Quiere que también la "Santina" tome partido. Va más allá que los mineros. Porque los mineros, que también se quitan la boina frente al Santuario de Covadonga, nunca le han dicho a la Virgen galana que hay que votar por González Peña. (p. 19)

In Chapter 18 ('El Naranco'), where Camín interviews the priest who has been living alongside the revolutionaries throughout the conflict, he alludes to those characteristics which differentiate him from other priests and religious figures: He donates all his time, patience, and material goods to the poor, and he carries out the duties that a priest should carry out. In the same way, not all the employers are cruel and selfish. In the case of the owner of the Turón mines, Rafael Riego, killed by the revolutionaries, Camín, who knew him, describes him as 'noble de corazón, alto de inteligencia, trabajador sin horario, visitas a puerta abierta, sin distinción de clases ni de asuntos, caballero romántico y sin tacha, a quien se debe toda la canción de progreso y de vida, de bienestar y de esfuerzo que llena el Valle asturiano' (p. 364). Despite their later actions the Civil Guard are initially praised for their bravery: 'No veremos ningún aspecto de tropa en guerra en las defensas de la Guardia Civil con los mineros. Han dado el pecho como ellos. Y el saldo ha sido ése: caer como los mineros, luchando a la descubierta y el rostro a las balas' (p. 58). He admires 'el esfuerzo heroico de la Guardia Civil' (p. 30) who, at the start of the Revolution put up a brave fight in many places against the miners who vastly outnumbered them without the help of those whom they were defending: 'La Guardia

Civil se bate sola. El resto del pueblo, que, regularmente no está formado por obreros, sino por propietarios de casas, dueños de tierras, hombres de carrera y comerciantes, se mete en su hoyo, como el grillo en su cueva' (p. 26). Naturally Camín mentions those army officials and soldiers who, opposed to the government actions, joined the revolutionary side, most importantly Sargento Vázquez and Teniente Torrens.

There are, however, no exceptions to the cruelty of the air force or the Moors. The action of the air force is condemned throughout the text, first of all for taking advantage of the confusion over what side they were going to be on and secondly for the arbitrary bombing in many villages and towns which led to many deaths and much destruction. For their part, the Moors are depicted as the bestial invaders of the Asturian countryside, executing an act of revenge: 'La Media Luna no pierde ocasión de entrar a saco en los hogares y de teñirse en sangre española, aprovechando este momento de revanchas históricas' (p. 111). They are responsible for most of the looting in the region, 'Los moros entran en la casa de "El Gordo", que tiene un comercio en la esquina. No le dejan chorizo ni prenda. Hasta el traje de novia de la hija' (p. 441), and for most of the bloody violence:

> ¡Villafría, Villafría! Turbantes moriscos saltando en la niebla, igual que fantasmas de antroxo. ¡Carnestolendas de la muerte! Vampiros con las alas llenas de sangre. ¡Vendimiadores trágicos con las pezuñas rojas! Casas que son sepulcros, cercas que son cadalsos, praderías que son mortajas, huertas que son cementerios, hondonadas que son osarios, árboles desnudos de hojas, crucificados como los hombres y hombres crucificados como los árboles. (p. 251)

Here Camín uses heavily charged language with an unequivocal critical purpose to convey to the reader the fear felt at the sight of the advancing Moors (and the planes flying overhead) in their governmentally consented rampage.

In the same way that Camín does not criticize all priests, employers, and soldiers, he does not praise all revolutionaries. On the one hand, he stresses the politeness and kindness of many of them: When they find an injured Civil Guard the revolutionaries try to help him, ' —¡A curarlo en seguida! Está herido y hay que atenderlo. El luchó desde su puesto como nosotros desde el nuestro. Y lo curaron con esa ternura que ponen los hombres buenos cuando un pájaro se parte un ala' (p. 50). The teacher in Campomanes describes the miners' actions with the young children:

> — Lo mismo niños que niñas — me dice con tono evangélico —, a todos me los sacaron de la mano hasta ponerlos en lugar seguro. Cada minero llevaba dos, uno de cada lado. Para que no tuvieran miedo los iban contentando por el camino: "No te pasa nada, neñín, no te pasa nada". "No tengáis miedo, que ahora vais con los padres. Estas manchas son de carbón. Es que venimos de la mina. En casa también tenemos unos niños como vosotros". (pp. 60–61)

Even the nuns in the convents of Oviedo praise the miners:

> El primero de noviembre de 1934, dice la Madre Superiora [del Convento de las Adoratrices], con su lengua celeste de paloma evangélica:
> — No lo crea usted. No todos son lobos. Los hay muy buenos. Cuando llegaron al Convento, no pasaron del portal. Comprendieron que nosotros sentíamos miedo. [. . .] "¿Les hace falta algo?", me dijeron con voz fuerte y, en apariencia, mal encarados: "Por ahora, no", les dije. Así volvieron dos o tres veces. Un día nos trajeron pan. (p. 186)

Nevertheless, there are also exceptions to the praise of the revolutionary side: 'También entre los mineros hay lobos' (p. 369). Camín criticizes some aspects of their conduct and the lack of control of some of the revolutionaries leading to unnecessary violence. He criticizes those individuals who gave the revolutionary side a bad name for taking advantage of the uprising to exact revenge on their enemies, instead of fighting for the revolutionary cause.

On reading the text, apart from the issues raised and the information provided, what stands out is the very elaborate language in which it is written. Metaphors and imagery predominate throughout. Camín occasionally plays with words and expressions to produce comic effects, and at other times sarcastic innuendoes or a sense of horror, all of these at the service of his underlying purpose. According to Albino Suárez, 'Dícese que una de las facetas más brillantes de nuestro personaje [Camín] es la sátira, la burla y el sarcasmo'.[24] Accordingly, in *El Valle Negro* some of the characters are caricatured. The most extensive example of a parody can be found in Chapter 12, 'De cómo don Suero de Quiñones llega a las puertas de la capital asturiana', in which López Ochoa, on his march to Oviedo, is depicted as Don Suero, the character which Cervantes parodied in order to create his *Don Quijote.*[25] López Ochoa, who repeatedly states: ' — Yo "desencantaré" la ciudad' (p. 131), takes on the characteristics which Don Quijote is famous for:

> — Yo vengo a desencantar ciudades como Jerusalén, como la Imperial Toledo cuando Alfonso VI penetra, entre sangre y laureles, por la gran puerta de Visagra. [. . .]
> Y dicho esto, López Ochoa cruzó con la espada en alto — como Don Suero la vieja Puerta de Orbigo. (p. 127)

Just like Don Quixote, he also suffers from hallucinations: 'En vez de hombres que le presenten la cara, vuelve a topar con árboles tumbados en la carretera. Manda apartarlos con asco: — ¡A mí con Molinos!' (p. 127); 'Lo mismo que Don Suero, lo mismo que Don Quijote, viene dando tajos en la noche contra los hombres, contra la sombra, contra los árboles. No siente ni el golpe de los batanes, ni el ruido de las aspas de los molinos que se le quiebran en el pecho' (p. 130). As he enters Oviedo on 11 October, he is not afraid of anything because of his state of madness: 'Arden los edificios. ¡No se inmuta! Piensa que son antorchas que se le encienden al paso' (p. 132). Even the site of the dead does not repel him: 'El General sonríe por las calles llenas de muertos' (p. 132). He is living in another world. Camín chose the figure of Don Quijote purposefully. He is a well-known literary character with certain traits which make him appear to be mad but which, at the same time, make him liked. Indeed, López Ochoa, is depicted moderately well compared to the rest of the generals. He was one of the most liberal-minded generals, responsible for negotiating with Belarmino Tomás the terms for the withdrawal of the revolutionaries.

Further examples of satire can be found in the first chapter where the members of the Government are caricatured. Don Niceto Alcalá Zamora is described: 'Tarambana, estallante, desmemoriado, ya no se acuerda ni de la palabra ni de las armas' (p. 12); Samper 'no es más que un cartucho vacío. Se le puede poner una etiqueta. Llenarlo de resina o de pólvora. Enano de Velázquez: el de Corias, el de Vallecas' (p. 12);[26] and Azaña is described as 'carigordo, medita con la mano rechoncha en la barba' (p. 12). Camín opts to make fun of these three figures by basing his caricatures on their bodily characteristics and the effect, as well as derogatory, is humorous. Finally, in Chapter 33 ('La comedia de Avilés') the narrator conveys in a farcical depiction the panic and indecisiveness which made the Revolution in this city a shambles:

> Unos hombres [. . .] cogen unas escopetas de caza, prenden a Pedregal en su finca, echan cuatro tiros al aire, corren en calcetines siete señores sin hacienda, ocho navieros sin naves, seis frailes sin vocación, dos impresores de esquelas mortuorias, un juez sin causas, un abogado sin pleitos, un notario sin escrituras y un alcalde sin presupuestos, contaminan con su nerviosismo a la Guardia Civil, se meten todos en el Ayuntamiento y dejan en mano de los sublevados el pueblo, el campo y la ría.
>
> Los rebeldes tampoco saben qué hacer con todo aquello en las manos. Primero, se sientan por las terrazas, toman el sol, bien apretada a las piernas la carabina. (pp. 457–58)

In the same way that Chapter 20 ('Los moros en Villafría') resembles a tragedy, so this literary interpretation resembles a comedy, more specifically a satire. According to Scholes and Kellogg, satire is the most extreme attempt of the author trying to control the reader's response.[27] Thus, Camín exposes the cowardice of the ruling classes and the passivity of the revolutionaries to ridicule, conveying both amusement and indignation.

Camín includes some very effective descriptions, similes, metaphors, and images which not only add to the literary value of the text but which also convey to the reader the horrific events of the October Revolution. The following are just some of the literary devices which Camín employs in his text. Many of the images are of nature and the elements. They may be simply descriptions of the beautiful scenery which Camín encounters: 'Se ve la nieve colgando de las faldas de los montes, como si los hogares solitarios tendieran la ropa del año prado abajo y monte arriba. Las nubes bajan a besar la nieve' (p. 44). However, in most cases nature is used as a metaphor to convey the destructiveness and violence of the Revolution. In the following example nature is personified: 'Como avanzamos nosotros, la niebla avanza en contrario. Viene hacia nosotros como diciéndonos: Atrás. Paso cerrado. Parece que no desea que veamos tanto dolor más allá del Pajares' (p. 24).[28] The force of the miners is compared to the force of a river:

> La revolución minera tiene mucho de instinto geográfico. Parten del nacimiento de los ríos, de más arriba de La Nalona y de los manantiales primerizos [. . .] que dan nombre al Caudal en la otra cuenca. Por esta de Langreo, empezaron los hechos más arriba de Ríoseco, vienen hasta la Pola de Lavina y Los Barredos, toman fuerza en Sotrondio, se agrandan en Ciaño, se acumulan en Sama. Bajan creciendo como el Nalón y sin dejar la vera del río. Cuanto más avanza el Nalón, más aguas lleva. Cuanto más avanza la invasión minera, más se agranda el torrente de hombres. Cuando en las cercanías de Olloniego se abrazan al Nalón y el Caudal, también se abrazan las masas mineras de las dos cuencas: Langreo y Mieres. Son dos corrientes caudalosas que llevan el curso y la fuerza del río hasta formar el cinturón de Oviedo. Allí las aguas de los dos ríos tienen un solo nombre: El Nalón. Tampoco hay hombres de Sama y de Mieres. Son una sola fuerza. Un solo nombre: mineros. (p. 353)

The wind and the rain are used to describe the destruction and havoc caused by the war: 'La revolución minera se divide en tres tiempos, igual que los torrentes vigorosos: lluvia, torrentera, y estrago. Primero, se sublevan las cuencas; después, se lucha con la tropa, y más tarde, las consecuencias que presentan los hogares vacíos' (p. 105). Thus, he uses the natural elements to develop a series of metaphors combining nature, man, and war, such as in this extensive example, in which he describes the scenery of the mountains of the León-Asturias border:

> El agua, el lobo y el hombre moverán sus naturalezas a ritmo con el paisaje. Si el lobo está harto de carne, no bajará a la llanura. Si el torrente no viene herido por los peñascos, azuzado por el viento y ahogado por lluvias gruesas — extrañas a sus limpias vetas de cristal nativo —, no dejará su cauce para arrasar las siembras. *Si el hombre no viviera en el pulmón de las montañas, de espaldas a la luz y de cara a la muerte, no saldría tampoco, hoy, mañana, pasado, arrasando el camino y las veredas, estremeciendo el día con los rencores de la dinamita.* A flor de surco revientan las semillas y se transforman en frutas, granos y rosas. Pero *del fondo de la tierra, de esa entraña dura de roca, hierro y carbón, no pueden salir más que monstruos* en el torrente, en el lobo, en el reptil o en el hombre. Procurad que todos los hombres vivan sobre la tierra, de cara al día, que el lobo no tenga hambre y que la lluvia no enturbie los manantiales. Y el lobo no atacará, aunque paséis por su vera, ni a los hombres ni a los rebaños. Y el agua, en vez de torrente, será un hilo de agua clara que brindará su pureza a los labios del caminante. Y el hombre será bueno, porque

verá delante la montaña como si fuera una novia. Y no como un cadáver que lleva encima, bajo un cielo entoldado, lleno de cuervos. (p. 44, my emphasis)

The above quotation shows that animals and birds become symbolic. Elsewhere in the work Lerroux and Gil Robles are compared to crows and vultures: 'Don Alejandro, el buitre, chochea con las piltrafas en la boca sin dientes. Don Gil es como un cuervo que no perdona un cadáver. Atrae el trueno y la lluvia' (p. 166). Wolves are used to describe the soldiers while the revolutionaries are compared to bears, native to Asturias. In another example, violence and death take the form of a horse galloping from one place to another, creating havoc wherever it passes: 'El recuerdo inmediato de la muerte, que pasó con sus cascos de potro suelto, relinchando de un lugar a otro, de ésta a aquella ladera, con estruendos de bombas y la crin invisible de las balas que iban cortando igualmente las ramas de los árboles y la voz de los hombres' (p. 80). Nature is thus linked throughout the novel with violence, war, and death.

Death can also be the subject of more matter-of-fact descriptions:

Algunos habían mascado las cuerdas con los dientes antes de la agonía. Otros, tenían los ojos saltados, los brazos arañando la tierra, las piernas encogidas, la boca llena de espuma roja, los sesos saltados, los vientres fuera. Muchas cabezas estaban materialmente separadas del tronco. Otros, antes de morir, se habían quedado sin un brazo. Otros tenían en el pecho tres puntazos con los bordes llenos de sangre coagulada. (p. 334)

Por la vera del Nalón se ven sillas deshechas, maderas antes voladas, boinas sueltas, ropas deshilachadas de hombre y de mujer a flote sobre las aguas y restos de carne humana que marchan río abajo. Algunos miembros humanos, carnaza flotante y roja, aparece tan desfibrada, que da la impresión de una escoba deshecha empapada de rojo. (p. 292)

Blood is often compared to wine — 'Entre el barro que estuvo borracho de sangre y ahora viene a adecentarlo la lluvia de los días anteriores' (p. 54) — drunk by the river or by the earth. In the same way the excess of dynamite, death, and suffering is described as drunkenness: 'Borrachera de pólvora, de dolor, danza de astillas y de piltrafas' (p. 355). Dynamite is also used in metaphorical descriptions,[29] and religious imagery is often used when violence is being described.[30] Although some of the descriptions such as the ones already illustrated above are complex, there are other occasions when Camín opts for short, concise sentences, each one illustrating a specific image which, taken together with the rest of the images, conveys a wider picture: '. . .escombros, dolor, cenizas. Y los escarabajos del odio. Y el espionaje sombrío. La sangre, mal lavada en las aceras. El llanto, seco en los ojos. Y los hogares sin hombres. Y los niños sin padre. Y las mujeres de luto' (p. 134). With each short sentence the description becomes increasingly tragic and desolate. Another common technique used is to make a statement which is subsequently expanded with further comments all of which deal with the same issue — a paragraph in many cases is a list of sentences which essentially say the same thing but in a different way. In Chapter 13, for example Camín uses a list of synonyms to describe the 'escombro' which he sees: 'Bloques de piedra desdentados, techumbres medio rotas que aún claman, solitarias, su dolor a las nubes. Capiteles deshechos. Columnas blancas de cal y ciegas de pólvora, revueltas con la escombrera' (p. 141).

In his work Camín puts into practice the principle of collage, where he makes use of ready-made material and texts and combines them with others of his own invention in order to produce his own rhetorical design. He is concerned most of all with conveying the suffering which the Revolution produced. He condemns most politicians, from both the left and the right — the left for promoting a fratricidal and ludicrous civil war, which although legitimate, was entered into with insufficient preparation; the Government and its right-wing allies, along with the consent of the Church and the help of the army, for unleashing an exaggerated response and a fierce repression. Ultimately, the ones who suffer are the innocent masses who are inevitably caught up in a political conflict that, far from solving their very real problems, only serves to accentuate them. In order to depict his indignation and sadness Camín makes use of various literary devices, many of which are usually associated with novelistic or creative writing, and others which are more suitable for documented and historical accounts, thereby producing this unusual hybrid narrative. Camín sets out to interview a wide rage of witnesses who have been involved in the Revolution (on either side) or who have seen how it has progressed and its effects. The information which he gathers is subsequently rendered in various ways. Whilst sometimes he transcribes the interviews, at other times he dramatizes or re-enacts certain events, based on that information which he has collected. In many of the chapters which deal with stories of human suffering, however, Camín sets loose his imagination and produces anecdotes which are harrowing, horrific, and evocative of what was lived by ordinary people at that time. While in essence the atmosphere, the devastation, and the human reactions and feelings are real — there was bloodshed, buildings were ruined, people did suffer, and families were tragically broken — it is unclear if the actual stories are true, if those particular characters are real, and if the man who was allegedly robbed by the Moors actually exists. For Camín, however, this is unimportant. He knows that the reader knows that the Revolution is real, and he wants to depict the suffering which he has seen and which people have expressed to him on his travels around Asturias, which so perturbed him. Thus we find in this narrative a mixture of dramatized episodes told by alternating narrative voices and in a range of tenses, where Camín makes use of caricature, satire, literary descriptions of, for example, the landscape, and other devices associated with imaginative writing. Given that he is depicting an important historical event, in line with the documentary nature of the text, Camín also makes use of verifiable data, such as letters, leaflets, speeches, and interrogation reports. He transcribes interviews and offers the reader the information which he has revealed after arduous investigation. Along with his consideration for the suffering masses, Camín concentrates on what led him to reject most of the other versions of the Revolution and produce his own, pointing out that these were too concerned with political issues to consider what really mattered — the human dimension and the effects of the Revolution. These other writers are too busy, according to Camín, figuring out how to make the faction which he supported appear to be the rightful victor, on one side, or the sacrificed victim, on the other. Through his informative and, at the same time, expressive depiction, Camín suggests that everyone was a victim.

I have reviewed in Chapters 5 and 6 four texts which, because of their narrative style and structure, are difficult to define categorically as fiction or non-fiction. Prada combines re-enacted episodes with factual details in a series of miscellaneous chapters in which he concentrates on the suffering of the innocent. Similarly, Camín sets out on a journey with a mission to reconstruct the events which took place in Asturias, focusing on the human dimension of the conflict; he leaves to one side the political debate and ideological favouritism and concentrates on the people, or *pueblo*, whom he believes have been ignored in other written accounts despite being the clearest losers. Madera and Adro take a different approach. Through a continuous narrative, as opposed to a medley of chapters dealing with a wide-ranging set of subjects, these two authors concentrate on one single story, or experience. Thus, there are two opposite narrative strategies at work, and while the factual element in these four texts is constant, namely that they deal with a real historical event, the imaginative, creative, and artistic ingredients which give them their fictional appearance differ. In their re-enacted episodes, Prada and Camín depict the dialogues between their characters, bring to light dramatic experiences, and illustrate atmospheres and moods figuratively. Clearly, these are characteristics which are found in fictional writing, drama, and cinema. However, by bringing to life real people — by describing their physical appearance, and focusing on their fear and anxiety, and their exhausted mental state — and the real surroundings of the city or the countryside, altered by the violence and destruction of the Revolution, the authors effectively produce a non-fictional, or factual, rendering of the events. For their part, the narratives written by Adro and Madera manifest a different set of features, including a linear chronology, a well-formed plot, with a beginning, a middle and an end, a number of characters which remain constant throughout the text, and an unchanging narrative voice. Whilst these elements — 'plot', 'narrative voice', and 'character' — are more commonly associated with fictional writing, they are also indispensable in any historical or journalistic discourse, where the writer's handling of historical time, the events, the participants, and the objectivity of the author–narrator, influence the historical and documentary value of the work.

The political priority of the four authors examined here also varies. Although Prada claims in his prologue that he will be impartial and truthful, and despite the fact that he does not refer to any specific political group, a clear bias against the revolutionaries emerges from the start and is reinforced throughout. Madera, as Secretary of the Catholic Trade Union, is eager to rally members from the working-class sector, demonstrating in the process his unequivocal support of the Church and the government forces. Adro's right-wing, religious and patriotic stance is gradually but systematically conveyed, although his primary concern is to advocate the essential role of religion and its practitioners in society. Contrary to the other three writers, Camín rejects any political interpretation of the October Revolution, arguing that more often than not, this perspective fails to accommodate the human dimension of the conflict and the suffering of the population at large, irrespective of ideological allegiances. Clearly the structural differentiation in the texts is insignificant, for all four texts function similarly in the way that they manipulate the contents, namely by oversimplifying the issues at stake and by denigrating the enemy and proving their own side morally and politically right. Even in the case of Camín, who has his own non-political agenda, he uses a full and effective range of rhetorical devices to pursue and promote his stance. He is therefore no different from the other three writers, or indeed anyone else, who wrote about the Revolution.

1. Adro Xavier [Alejandro Rey Stolle], *Sangre jesuita. Asturias 1934: Padre Emilio Martínez y H. Juan B. Arconada* (Bilbao: El Mensajero del Corazón de Jesús, 1938). Subsequent quotations are cited parenthetically in the text. Alejandro Rey-Stolle Pedrosa (Santiago de Compostela, 1910–?), was a historian, essayist, and novelist who entered the 'Compañía de Jesús'. He published more than fifty works, including biographies, novels, and historical essays.
2. Francisco Martínez, *Dos jesuitas mártires de Asturias: el P. Emilio Martínez y el H. Juan B. Arconada* (Burgos: Imprenta Aldecoa, 1936). Subsequent quotations are cited parenthetically in the text.
3. Later on in the text he quotes the *falangista* Ramiro de Maeztu (p. 45).

4. These were the three most radical constitutional reforms which were passed against the Church and its members. Others included the introduction of civil marriage and divorce, and the gradual ending of the State's subvention of the clergy. V. Palacio Atard, 'La Segunda República Española (1931–1936–1939)', in *Diccionario de Historia Eclesiástica de España*, ed. by Quintín Aldea Vaquero, et al. (Madrid: Instituto Enrique Florez, Consejo Superior de Investigaciones Científicas, 1972), II, 1179–84, and Frances Lannon, 'The Church's crusade against the Republic', in *Revolution and War in Spain 1931–1939*, ed. by Paul Preston (London: Methuen, 1984; repr. London: Routledge, 1993), pp. 35–58 (pp. 41–53).
5. p. 17. Other details that arise include his age (thirty-three) at the time of the conversation, that is 1923 (p. 16); that he was a member of the congregation before his novitiate (p. 19); and that he is originally from Carrión de los Condes (p. 19). We also learn that P. Martínez's family is from Navarre but that he was born by chance in Ahedo de los Pueblos, a small village in the province of Burgos (p. 19).
6. I have numbered the sections 1 to 6 and will refer to them as chapters for the sake of clarity.
7. As Cardinal of Toledo, Cardinal Segura was the highest Church authority in Spain. Adro Xavier describes him favourably as 'figura austera y espiritual del insigne purpurado' (p. 24) who, later in time, 'en virtud de un decreto hijo del izquierdismo y del odio, cruza la frontera entre una pareja de guardias con fusiles terciados' (p. 44). In reality he was forced to leave Spain after his assertions defending the monarchy a few months after the Republic had been proclaimed. He had openly praised the monarch for conserving traditional values and defending the Catholic faith during his reign. Segura was forced to leave Spain after the outcry caused by his declarations. On 10 May 1931 he left Toledo and on 13 May he began his journey to Rome. From Vicente Cárcel Ortí, 'La iglesia durante la II República y la Guerra Civil (1931–1939)', in *Historia de la Iglesia en España*, ed. by Ricardo García Villoslada (Madrid: Editorial Católica, 1979), pp. 331–94.
8. According to Lannon, Catholic organizations never faced the widespread misery of the southern *latifundio* areas, preferring instead to side with the landowners, and Catholic intervention in industrial relations did not fare any better. Indeed, Catholics had gained a reputation as enemies of democracy. Adro Xavier writes that 'la única democracia [. . .] es la de la Iglesia' (p. 35). Although there were Catholics with progressive ideas (such as J. Bergamín and his *Cruz y Raya*, Angel Ossorio y Gallardo, J. M. Gallegos Rocafull, and Maximiliano Arboleya), the majority held traditional, conservative, and reactionary views.
9. This comparison continues throughout the chapter and the rest of the text: 'Aquí les esperan las agonías de la flagelación' (p. 101); 'Los mártires, a imitación de Cristo en la flagelación, sufren en silencio, orando' (p. 108); 'Nace lúgubre el viernes santo de nuestros dos jesuitas' (p. 86).
10. The same image, although not as descriptive, arises in F. Martínez's text: 'Las balas, primero, y los golpes, después, hicieron brotar de los dos cuerpos abundante sangre, que allí quedó fundida como sello sublime de firme perseverancia cristiana' (p. 56).
11. All these issues about how language is used in fiction to depict fact are dealt with by Geoffrey N. Leech and Michael H. Short, *Style in Fiction: A Linguistic Introduction to English Fictional Prose* (London: Longman, 1980), pp. 155–59.
12. Lars Ole Sauerberg, *Fact into Fiction: Documentary Realism in the Contemporary Novel* (London: Macmillan, 1991), p. 69. He is referring here to Norman Mailer's *The Armies of the Night* (1968), covering the 1967 protest march on the Pentagon, which offers 'two parallel narratives — a novel and a history' (p. 69).
13. Sauerberg, p. 141.
14. Alfonso Camín Meana, *El Valle Negro: Asturias 1934* (Mexico: Editorial Norte, 1938). Subsequent quotations are cited parenthetically in the text. Camín was born on 12 August 1890 in Roces, Gijón. His father worked in a stone quarry and at the age of ten Camín joined him, being forced to leave school as a result. He made his first journey to South America in 1905, when he went to Cuba, where he began to write poetry. From then on begins a lifetime of constant travel between the two continents, during which time Camín publishes numerous novels and books of poetry, eventually becoming well-regarded as a writer. Some of these books include, *Adelfas* (1913), *Crepúsculos de oro* (1914), *Cien sonetos* (1915), *La moza del castañar* (1923), and *Entre volcanes* (1928).

Whilst in exile in Mexico, following the Spanish Civil War, Camín made the conflict and his exile subjects of his work: *España a Hierro y Fuego* (1938), *Romancero de la Guerra* (1939), *Últimos cantos de la Guerra* (1948), and *Retorno a la Tierra* (1948). During his lifetime he also wrote many articles in newspapers, both in South America and in Spain. In 1967 Camín returned to Spain where he died on 12 December 1982.

15. Details of the *Turquesa* are given in Chapter 1 of this study.
16. The Asturian Eladio Egocheaga coordinated the *Turquesa* operation and according to Taibo was 'hombre legendario durante las huelgas mineras de Río Tinto'. Paco Ignacio Taibo, *Asturias 1934*, 2 vols (Madrid: Jucar, 1984), I, 82.
17. In his text Camín describes Fernando Blanco as his friend: 'Conozco a Fernando Blanco desde hace mucho tiempo' (p. 150).
18. Again in p. 332.
19. This is the case of the historical novel. Avrom Fleishman writes: 'In the historical novel, the generic properties of plot, character, setting, thought, and diction (in Scott, even song) operate on the materials of history to lend esthetic form to historical men's experience.' Avrom Fleishman, *The English Historical Novel: Walter Scott to Virginia Woolf* (Baltimore: Johns Hopkins University Press, 1971), p. 8. The resemblance between history and the novel is also taken up by, amongst others, Hayden White and Dominick LaCapra in their discussions of the increasingly eroding boundaries of fiction and fact. For example in Hayden White, *The Content of the Form: Narrative Discourse and Historical Representation* (Baltimore: Johns Hopkins University Press, 1987), and Dominick LaCapra, *History and Criticism* (Ithaca: Cornell University Press, 1985).
20. Peter Hutchinson, *Games Authors Play* (London: Methuen, 1983).
21. This distinction is drawn by Wayne C. Booth, *The Rhetoric of Fiction*, 2nd edn (London: Penguin, 1991), p. 202.
22. Albino Suárez, introduction to Alfonso Camín, *Poemas: antología* (Oviedo: Biblioteca Caja de Ahorros de Asturias, 1990), p. 19.
23. The erroneous information deals mainly with the allegations of atrocities committed by the revolutionaries, and the military manoeuvres.
24. Albino Suárez, p. 17
25. In fact Camín would later write a book, *Don Suero de Quiñones o el Caballo Leonés (De cómo encontró Cervantes la figura de Don Quijote)* (1967), in which Camín demonstrated, according to Suárez, 'su erudición histórica y amplio conocimiento en torno a Don Quijote'. Ibid., p. 19.
26. Camín refers to the paintings of the dwarfs *Bobo de Corias* and *Niño de Vallecas*, by Diego de Velázquez.
27. Robert Scholes and Robert Kellogg, *The Nature of Narrative* (Oxford: Oxford University Press, 1966), p. 82.
28. Further examples can be found in pp. 335 and 414–15.
29. Such as in pp. 34, 93, and 142.
30. Such as in p. 36.

CHAPTER 7

THE NON-FICTIONAL NOVEL (I)

From Chapter 3 on, each chapter has dealt with works in which the fictional or novelistic element has been more pronounced, and in which the documentary aspect although equally important makes a less obvious appearance. The works in these final two chapters could belong to a number of literary genres or sub-genres including the 'novela político-panfletaria',[1] 'novela social', historical novel, or documentary novel. Other critics have used different generic terms to describe novels of this kind, including 'novel of the recent past'; 'non-fiction "fiction"'; and 'creative reportage'.[2] However, I have chosen to call them non-fictional novels, for reasons I will outline before examining the following four works in detail: *La revolución fue así: octubre rojo y negro* (1935) by Manuel Benavides, *¡¡Asturias!!: relato vivido de la insurrección de octubre* (1934) by Alejandro Valdés, *Heroínas* (1935) by Federica Montseny, and *Octubre rojo en Asturias* (1935) by José Díaz Fernández.[3] The authors of these works sought to render their interpretations of the events in a variety of forms which, by virtue of being more fictional, differed from those adopted by the majority of the writers I have already examined. However, although they are novelistic in their creativity and structure, they are clearly not so in content. In addition, since the didactic considerations are of central importance to the authors, the political and rhetorical characteristics of their works take on a special significance.

After dealing with the longer non-fictional novels, I will examine briefly five short stories, by Concha Espina, María Teresa León, César Arconada, and Ramón Sender. There are, in addition, another three novels which I have decided not to include in my detailed analysis for several reasons: *¿Por qué Oviedo se convirtió en ciudad mártir?: película* (1935) by Gil Nuño del Robledal, *Sangre de octubre: U.H.P.* (1936) by Maximino Álvarez Suárez, and *Los presos del "Manuel Arnús": novela* (1935) by Tomás Verdal. Robledal's is an overtly right-wing text (indeed, the only right-wing novel of all the texts examined here) which, apart from displaying the characteristics of the right-wing socially committed novel of the 1930s, lacks literary interest. The work of the communist militant Álvarez Súarez has already been examined by Manuel Aznar Soler,[4] and I am concentrating on works which have not been studied to any great extent. Finally, the novel by the socialist Tomás Verdal deals with the revolutionary events in Barcelona and I am focusing on the events in Asturias.[5]

Benavides's is the most problematic text as far as genre is concerned and its narrative structure will be discussed in order to demonstrate why I have incorporated it into this chapter. There is no doubt that the other three texts examined are non-fictional novels. I will concentrate on how Valdés's communist stance influences the way he depicts the Revolution; how Montseny's anarchist beliefs and her status as a woman condition the story and the facts which make up the plot; and how Díaz Fernández's last novel demonstrates much more incisively than any of the other works the merging of literary and aesthetic principles in vogue in the 1920s with the politically committed themes of the 1930s. The fact that the short stories, whose authors are renowned, are also prose narrative justifies their brief analysis. Politically the four novels I have chosen are revolutionary in ideology, although they take different points of view. Montseny is an anarchist, while Valdés is a communist, Benavides a socialist, and Díaz Fernández a supporter of Izquierda Republicana. This selection of texts represents nearly all of the political persuasions which, though not necessarily united, were nevertheless involved in the Revolution. This will enable me to compare the texts in order to demonstrate how their different ideological stances influence the narrative strategies.

As stated, the emphasis so far has been on works in which the documentary aspect has been a primary consideration for the authors. In these works primary sources and verifiable information are quoted in an attempt to appear as truthful and accurate as possible in the proposed interpretation of the events. Thus, so far I have identified texts which fall into the following generic categories: political discourse, confession, journalistic response, political pamphlet, non-fictional accounts and tracts, dramatized vignettes, *relato* in the first person, collage, and novelized biography. In the remaining two chapters I dwell on authors who compose texts in which fictional protagonists act in real settings during a real event, namely the Revolution. These works exhibit particular features for which they may be associated with the novel, normally considered a fictional genre. Summarizing what has already been stated in the Introduction, in general terms, a novel is usually expected to include a predominant use of realism; at least one character shown in stages of change and social relationship; a plot, or some arrangement of narrated events; use of dialogue, point of view and/or interior monologue; and a development of scenic depiction rather than historical summary.

I will refer to the works discussed in this chapter as non-fictional novels despite the fact that this term did not exist in the 1930s and is being applied retrospectively.[6] What may be considered the non-fictional element occurs because, in an attempt to be accurate and truthful, the authors introduce historically verifiable data. Unlike the novel, a generic definition usually applied to works of narrative fiction, it can be argued that the works examined here are, in as much as it is possible to be accurate, factual accounts of historical events. According to Lodge the term 'non-fictional novel' was first coined by Truman Capote to describe his book *In Cold Blood* (1965), an account of a brutal multiple murder committed in Kansas in 1959.[7] The similarities between the novels written in North America in the late 1950s and 1960s and the group of novels examined below make the term 'non-fictional novel', of common currency these days, particularly appropriate. A number of critics discuss the genre in detail.

The Non-Fictional Novel

John Hollowell, for example, discusses the term in the context of the New Journalism in the 1960s.[8] According to him, this type of novel arose as novelists complained about the difficulty of writing fiction in a period in which 'daily events seemed to preempt the possibilities of the novelist's imagination' (p. 4). The momentous political circumstances meant that writers favoured documentary forms, eyewitness reports, and personal testimonies in order to explore issues of public concern, a preference shared by those writing about the Revolution. Hollowell defines the New Journalists as reporters who 'have experimented with fictional techniques by rebelling against the conventional standards of "objective reporting"' (p. 11). If we turn this definition around, non-fictional novelists are writers who incorporate conventional strategies associated with 'objective reporting' into their fictional writing. Using Hollowell's own words: 'Together these writers have generated a new kind of nonfiction that defies our usual classifications of "fiction" and "nonfiction" since they combine elements of both genres in a variety of ways' (p. 11). This critic identifies more than six features which are common to realistic fiction and are central to the New Journalism: (1) portraying events in dramatic scenes rather than in the usual historical summary of most articles;[9] (2) transcribing dialogues fully instead of the occasional quotation or anecdotes of conventional journalism; (3) recording the 'everyday gestures, habits, manners, customs, styles of furniture, clothing, decoration by which [people] experience their position in the world'; (4) using point of view in complex and inventive ways to depict events as they unfold; (5) the presence of interior monologue or the presentation of what a character thinks or feels without resorting to direct quotations; and (6) composite characterization, or the 'telescoping of character traits and anecdotes drawn from a number of sources into a single representative sketch' (pp. 25–26).[10] Hollowell adds to these other literary techniques, such as powers of social observation, eye for minute details, ability to convey the subjective atmosphere of an experience, as well as flashbacks, adumbration, and other stylistic and figurative techniques employed to achieve the vivid and colourful writing usually found only in fiction.

According to Sauerberg, who also undertakes a critical analysis of the non-fictional novel: 'Nonfiction "fiction" supposedly turns into narrative a segment of documentable reality without interfering with it'.[11] When comparing traditional realism and documentary realism he states that whilst both employ the kinds of discourse commonly used for the communication of fact, only the latter relates verifiable events and figures, and 'explicitly or implicitly acknowledges borrowing "directly" from reality, that is, from kinds of discourse intended for nonliterary purposes' (p. 3). He argues that as conventional realism and factual accounts such as history, reporting, and biography bring into play the same type of expository prose (a major concern of realism is to pose as reality), the encounter between the fictional and the factual is distinguishable in the narrative only if a specific source is indicated for the latter. In the texts where this is not specified the documentary element can be appreciated 'only as a consequence of the reader's ability to distinguish between fact and fiction in the linguistically unified texture of the narrative' (p. 6). For the critic, the difference between documentary realism and history is a matter of the degree to which the conventions of narrative are allowed to shape the text. Fact may be incorporated into documentary realism in two ways, either by introducing obviously factual material in the form of, for example, footnotes or references into the narrative's otherwise fictitious realm, or by adapting a 'wholly factual series of events to a traditionally fictional narrative pattern' (p. 7). Both of these are evident in the texts of the Revolution examined in this chapter, where sometimes a combination of both is used. Sauerberg, who criticizes the premises on which fictional and factual texts are normally distinguished, identifies a number of elements which are common to both historical accounts and fictional narratives and which bring the two types closer than might at first appear to be the case. For example, he claims that, as in literature, the presence of flashbacks and anticipations demonstrate that historical accounts are 'seldom marked by strict adherence to the calendar' (p. 61). In his view, a purely chronological progression would contradict the historian's stated claim of accounting for historical events: 'To proceed chronologically without consideration of causality would hardly amount to more than mere compilation of phenomena linked only on sequential conditions' (pp. 61–62). It is worth noting that, contrary to Sauerberg's assertion, Hollowell maintains that the non-linear use of time is a feature alien to history and borrowed by the non-fictional novel from fictional writing.

Robert Smart points out that the non-fictional novel has both personal and subjective material in it, as well as actual historical and factual material. For him the non-fictional novel is a modernist development of the traditional novel. He stresses that 'the nonfiction novel does have a type of plot movement, does interpret material, does present facts from a subjective point of view, and it is definitely a subgenre of the novel form'.[12] In defence of this sub-genre, Smart claims that 'the overwhelming quality and urgency of the historical event justifies the novelist's abandonment of the traditional novel form' (p. 17). Whilst non-fictional writers cannot alter the facts, they can capture and present them more dramatically. Geoffrey Ribbans, who refers to the similarities between history and the novel points out that 'all writing is interpretation, organisation, selection',[13] and this applies to historiography as much as it does to creative literature. However, he also adds that fiction allows 'a much wider scope for variation of the narrative mood or voice, for intertextuality, for the utilization of symbolic or mythological material, for metonymic or metaphorical patterns, for ironic presentation, for self-reflexive analysis, and so forth' (p. 21).

The rise of mass political movements in the nineteenth and twentieth centuries led to a corresponding evolution in the function of literature, and in an atmosphere in which the social and political situation was changing constantly any issues considered to be important had to be dealt with in an immediate manner. Celia Fernández Prieto, who examines the Spanish historical novel, discusses the 'novel of the recent past', a sub-generic term coined by Kathleen Tillotson[14] and used when classifying those novels which do not fit in the category of the historical novel because of the proximity of the events to their rendering.[15] Fernández Prieto examines the ways in which the novel of the recent past differs from the traditional historical novel of the distant past. Firstly, the reader and the writer share much more information; this forces the author to pay particular attention to the documentary evidence used. Secondly, because the author and many of the readers will have experienced, directly or indirectly, the events, 'los acontecimientos del pasado cercano ejercen un mayor impacto emocional sobre autores y lectores o son objetos de polémicas o de enfrentamientos ideológicos muy crispados' (p. 190). In other words, the ideological position of the author and the reader becomes particularly important. Thirdly, the 'plot' (the episode being related) is still developing in reality as the author writes. Thus, by providing a further interpretation of the events the author is contributing to the creation of history. Indeed, Fernández Prieto argues that the novel is a useful aid to historiography as it offers the possibility 'de *completar la historia* llegando hasta donde ella no puede llegar: los detalles de la vida privada, los acontecimientos menudos, las costumbres, etc.' (p. 89, author's emphasis).

Although referring to another genre, the comments which Fernández Prieto makes are applicable when comparing the historical novel with the non-fictional novel. In order to appear credible and to be more persuasive the author must pay particular attention to the data which he or she uses; the ideological stance of the author will determine to a great extent the way in which the events will be interpreted and also the way in which the reader will approach the work; and the belief that the struggle is far from over and the hope that the revolutionary defeat may one day be overturned are expressed in these non-fictional works in which the writers offer practical advice and messages in order to boost the morale of the combatants of the future. In Andrew Barker's words: 'Faced with the reality of history', the authors are 'concerned to show the ways in which the workers can draw strength and encouragement from the disaster of defeat'.[16] Another critic, William Stott, who examines the documentary non-fiction of the 1930s in America, points out that social documentary deals with facts that are 'alterable'. It has an intellectual imperative to make clear what the facts are, why they came about, and how they can be changed for the better. However, its emotional dimension is usually more important; 'feeling the fact', or sharing the experience being related by the author, may move the reader to want to change it: 'To right wrongs, to promote social action, documentary tries to influence its audience's intellect and feelings.'[17]

La revolución fue así. (Octubre rojo y negro.): Reportaje by Manuel Benavides

La revolución fue así. (Octubre rojo y negro.): reportaje was written by Manuel D. Benavides in 1935. The text is divided into three main sections, each of which deals with a different aspect of the Revolution. Part I, 'El disco rojo', considers the advent of the insurrection and moves on to examine the revolutionary action primarily in Madrid, as well as in other parts of Spain such as Barcelona, Andalusia and Bilbao. Part II, 'La revolución de los mineros', deals entirely with the insurrection in Asturias. Finally, Part III, 'La República del oficial Ivanoff', examines the repression which the army, following government orders, carried out against the revolutionaries. In this way, Benavides gives an overview of the confrontation — its prelude, its course, and the consequences.

This text is not a conventional third-person historical account of the October Revolution of 1934. Instead, Benavides combines a number of styles and alternates between the first and the third person narrative. At least three main styles can be identified: a straightforward documentary account of events; a series of dramatized and re-enacted anecdotes; and, given the political nature of the subject-matter, ideological tracts in which the social, political, and economic situation in Spain is analysed and evaluated. Although all the chapters incorporate characteristics which are usually found in non-fictional and historical accounts, and others which are commonly associated with fictional works, it is evident that from Part I to Part III, the narrative becomes less novelistic as Benavides quotes and refers increasingly to primary source material (mainly newspapers and speeches) and as he interrupts the narrative more often with political digressions in which he often asserts his own personal opinion. In the very last chapter, which I will deal with in a little more detail, the narrative once again returns to the fictional narrative in order to express symbolically the fate of the working-class movement in the face of the October Revolution. I will examine how these three narrative styles combine with a view to determine how they contribute to the literariness of the text and how they frame the political and didactic message of the author.

Clearly the non-fictional essence of the text is present in its historical nature — the narrative deals with the October Revolution, a real event; it refers to historical episodes, such as the peasant strike and the proclamation of the Republic; and it includes names of well-known political and social figures, such as Alejandro Lerroux and Antonio Goicoechea. Often the historical information is clearly demarcated from the rest of the text. For example, half-way through Chapter 1 of Part I, where a military training session of new revolutionary recruits is depicted, Benavides interrupts the narrative in order to offer an outline of the origins of the Revolution — 'La revolución de octubre de 1934 tiene en su preparación varias fases que pueden determinarse perfectamente' (p. 29) — and in two pages and eight 'fases' he summarizes the political events from the proclamation of the Republic in 1931 to the introduction of the three anti-republican and pro-CEDA members into the cabinet of Lerroux. In Chapter 3 of the same part the narrator describes how the different revolutionary forces in Madrid united, thereby giving the reader information vital to the understanding of the development of the conflict. As in the previous example the presentation of the facts is uncomplicated and concise, aimed at informing the reader:

El 4 de octubre se hizo la fusión de las milicias socialistas con las M.A.O.C., milicias antifascistas obreras y campesinas (organizaciones comunistas). Llevaron las gestiones los directivos de los dos Partidos, asesorados por militares afiliados, y acordóse que un representante técnico de las M.A.O.C. ingresara en el estado mayor de las milicias socialistas, aunque sin mando directo. Se hizo, por último, un acoplamiento y recuento de fuerzas y redujéronse a cuatro los cinco sectores: Palacio-Universidad, Buena Vista-Chamberí, Congreso-Hospital y Latina-Inclusa. (pp. 45–46)

In Chapter 3 of Part II, before he goes on to depict a conversation between a group of miners who expectantly await the black-out, the signal that the Revolution had started, the narrator provides information about the distances between the various mining towns and Oviedo and gives details of how the miners were to advance (pp. 188–89). In a final example, taken from Part III, in Chapter 4, after quoting the government's spurning of the reports on the repression investigated by Marco Miranda, Gordón Ordás, and Álvarez del Vayo, rejected in the belief that they were 'fábulas', the narrator lists the different forms of torture which were used by the Civil Guard and the army against the revolutionaries (pp. 438–45).

These factual accounts are often substantiated by newspaper extracts or other forms of documentary evidence intercalated into the text by Benavides. In Chapter 10 of Part II, for example, the narrator refers to Diego Hidalgo's parliamentary speech, given on 6 November, in which he, as Minister of War, explains the decision to use the Tercio and Regulares. A large portion of this is transcribed by the author. Thus, as in *El valle negro* by Alfonso Camín, examined in the previous chapter, this text is made up to a degree of a collage of ready-made pre-existing texts. Occasionally Benavides quotes whole sections of newspaper reports and argues against the claims made. Such is the case in Part III where the author refutes the charges made by the right-wing press, including *ABC*, *El Adelantado de Segovia*, *El Nervión* (Bilbao) and *La Unión* (Seville), against the revolutionaries, exposing crimes which they had committed, so as to justify the repression. Naturally the objectivity of the information provided by Benavides is questionable, as I will later demonstrate. Both the 'truth' of the evidence which he provides to substantiate his informative summary of the Revolution, and the 'falseness' of the press allegations which he criticizes and which he claims are based on invented data, are determined by two factors: Benavides's choice of one piece of evidence over another, and the reader's own perception of the events and ideological point of view. Benavides will have to select that information which he believes is 'correct' and which will bolster his interpretation of the events; on the other hand, the reader, if he is a fascist or a fervent Catholic, will not believe Benavides however much 'factual' data he includes in the narrative. This, of course, relates to the didactic purpose of the narrative, but before discussing this I will identify the fictional characteristics of Benavides's text.

In *La revolución* Benavides employs a series of stylistic and linguistic devices not normally associated with works of a purely factual and informative kind. First and foremost, this text contains the basic elements which make up a conventional novel, namely a plot, a setting, and characters. The significance of these varies for each of the three parts. Part I, which deals mainly with the Revolution in Madrid, relates how the leading members of the 'Juventudes' prepare, as far back as 1933, for the forthcoming insurrection. The political characters — Lino Cuesta, Broca, Luis Romeral, and Luciano Ortiz, amongst others — do not appear in any of the encyclopaedias or political dictionaries I have consulted. Thus their names are probably pseudonyms hiding the identity of the real participants. These are joined by other secondary characters, such as Antonia, 'la vieja', and 'el chiquillo', who are clearly fictional. Although in this same part the author digresses in Chapters 6 and 7 in order to inform about other places in Spain, in the last chapter, Chapter 8, in which the defeat of the Revolution is recounted, he returns to the main characters and reveals their fate. It is this constant presence of the same characters which makes this first part more novelistic in appearance than the other two. Through the narrator's descriptions of the characters' actions, speech, and physical appearance, and their response to the critical situation facing them, the reader perceives the tension of the moment, as the following example demonstrates:

> Estaban los cinco J.D. y los dos comunistas junto a un aparato de radio. Consumían su impaciencia con tragos de humo. Se aspiraba el tabaco en largas fumadas; la brasa de los cigarrillos se corría hacia las bocas y simulaba una pupila sangrienta entre los ojos contraídos para evitar los arañazos del humo.
> "Ahora, señores, música de baile" — anunció la radio.
> Entró un enlace:
> — Se ha acabado el pan en todo Madrid — dijo —. Comienzan a formarse las colas. . .
> Latían en el aire cruzado de ondas las melodías de la música de baile. Entre esas melodías se fraguaba el presagio revolucionario. Cesó la música.
> "No lo olviden ustedes. La felicidad de los niños se logra con los polvos Calber. ¡Polvos Calber!"
> — ¡Que idiota! — exclamó Lino Cuesta.
> Y redujo la dimensión de la onda. (pp. 54–55)

While the historical setting is real, the atmospheric and detailed depiction of the charged ambience in the room, conveyed by the anxious drags taken from the cigarettes and the impatience with which the radio broadcast is listened to, introduce into this text elements which are unimportant and irrelevant to a purely historical account.

In Parts II and III characterization is not as relevant. However, the combination from beginning to end of different narrative voices (including different forms of the third-person and the first-person narrator), styles (most significantly, historical, rhetorical, and literary), and tenses (the present and forms of the past) is not usually found in historical or documentary works where these tend to be kept consistent throughout. On the other hand, in fiction writing this is not uncommon. For example, if we refer to Chapter 3 of Part II, most of the information about the advance of the revolutionaries into Oviedo is related in the third-person and in the past tense. The narrative, however, alternates from straightforward, documentary, and purely factual, to literary and dramatic, with one style often merging into the other:

> La orden de Dutor para las milicias armadas en San Esteban de las Cruces era la de que esperasen a los autocares de Mieres, que los detuvieran a su arribo y se concentraran todos en la ciudad del Naranco.
>
> Hacía frío. Los muchachos paseaban arma al brazo. Un silencio denso envolvía la ciudad. Se movían las sombras. Tardaban los autocares. Consultóse el reloj: las doce. (p. 189)

In addition, in this chapter, and throughout the work, an intrusive narrator provides the most explicitly propagandistic interpretation of the events: 'Lo que el revolucionario mata es lo que el guardia representa, el Estado de que es servidor y que le ha dado un uniforme. Pero el guardia no comprende una cosa tan sencilla y el revolucionario se ve en la necesidad de matar al guardia para destruir lo que el guardia representa' (p. 194). Elsewhere in other chapters the past and present tenses are combined, such as half-way through Chapter 4 of Part II where the action in Sama is suddenly related dramatically in the present tense. In Chapter 1 of Part II even the first-person is used: 'Prosigo por mi cuenta el relato' (p. 168). This is also the case in Chapter 3 of Part III where, on this occasion like in a journalistic report, the narrator refers to the questions he asked during an interview which he supposedly held with López Ochoa: 'Yo le pregunto al general López Ochoa, sin esperanzas de que me conteste' (p. 416). This, however, like the phenomenon of the intrusive narrator, will be dealt with further on when I consider the rhetorical and didactic dimension of Benavides' work.

There are other more specific characteristics, involving the author's use of figures and imagery, syntax and diction, which novelize the work. For instance, the work is replete with tropes, most notably metaphors, similes, symbolism, personification, and irony, of which the following are just a few of many examples. While some of the metaphors denote routine actions, such as the act of writing: 'Su lápiz, fuerte guión entre los dedos, calzóse los esquís de unas líneas y deslizóse por el papel' (p. 18); every-day things: 'El autobús colorado arrastra el vientre por la calle Ancha' (p. 84); or environmental or weather conditions: 'Estaba clara la noche; retazos de nubes, henchidas pechugas de plumones blancos, bogaban por el cielo' (p. 165), others are more elaborate and are associated with the political context of the text:

> Cae la candela entre la hierba seca; es una llamita que yergue su cabeza de víbora y muerde las puntas de los tallos, oscila, se tiende, se alarga, se muere, revive, se esconde — era una llama, son dos; eran dos llamas, son cuatro. . . (p. 458)

In this example, Benavides describes metaphorically how, despite attempts to keep it a secret, the information about the deaths of twenty-four men at the hands of the Civil Guard at Villafría slowly spreads. Other metaphors and similes are clearly symbolic of the Revolution and are repeated not only in this work but in other texts dealing with the Revolution, as is the case with 'el disco rojo', a signal that, taken literally, opens the way for a train and, metaphorically, for the Revolution; and the red dawning or sunset which symbolizes a new era for the proletariat and the peasants: 'Cuando disparaba el fusil, cada disparo le parecía que horadaba la noche de una aurora nueva. En la boca de su fusil podía estar el amanecer de los trabajadores del mundo' (p. 338).[18] The Revolution appears personified on various occasions, as in this example: 'Otra vez se le escapa a la vieja la revolución. La ha visto rondar y desaparecer súbitamente. ¿Dónde se había metido? Andaba suelta por Eibar, por Barruelo, por Villarrobledo, por Teba.' (pp. 76–77). Irony is present in particular in the description of real political figures, such as Lerroux:

> La orina del jefe del Estado era más dulce que la del presidente del Consejo, tenía menos presión arterial también y, en el sistema de vasos comunicantes del torrente circulatorio, produjo una rarefacción del gaseoso y patibulario frenesí que dilataba las cholas de D. Ale y sus ministros. (p. 461)

It also arises when the military generals justify their ineffective action, such as that taken by López Ochoa:

> — Una fuerte concentración revolucionaria — me dice López Ochoa — me recibió con un fuego muy vivo.
>
> La fuerte concentración revolucionaria la formaban siete muchachos — 7 — apostados tras de unas rocas. (p. 316)

In addition to employing figurative language to create a literary narrative, Benavides exploits syntax and diction for the same purpose. In the following example the narrator describes the oppression felt by any man when he is confined to a prison cell:

> Impresión de que el cuerpo es una armadura, un encierro más dentro de otro encierro, como esas cajas que se guardan unas en otras: las paredes de la Dirección general formaban la caja que guardaba las restantes: los sótanos; el calabozo dentro de los sótanos; el detenido dentro del calabozo; el pensamiento dentro del detenido y dentro del pensamiento, el cansancio. (p. 389)

The gradual homing-in on the prison, the prisoner and, eventually, his feelings is effectively conveyed in this long and fragmented sentence in which each image (similar to a cinematic zoom shot), separated by a semicolon, focuses increasingly on the human suffering; the description concludes with an illuminating perception of what the primary feeling of these men is — exhaustion, physical and psychological. Repetition is another device used by the author to place particular emphasis on the valuable or critical aspects of a particular action or scene:

> Ocho horas escasas de lucha fueron suficientes para vencer a Cataluña. Está mal dicho. Ocho horas escasas de lucha fueron suficientes para rendir la Generalidad. Tampoco está bien así. Ocho horas escasas de lucha fueron suficientes para agotar las fuerzas de resistencia de un partido político. Ni aun eso está bien. Ocho horas de lucha fueron suficientes para poner término al predominio de un hombre: Dencás. . . Demasiadas horas. (p. 150)

Here repetition has a didactic and sententious function, as Benavides conveys the pathetic insurrectionary action in Barcelona, and in particular Dencás' performance. In the following example it provides a striking and slightly humorous, and, at the same time, tragic depiction of what the bored prisoners could see from the cells which looked out on to the street:

> Empezaba la noche. Por delante de las gateras enrejadas de los sótanos los pies cortados de los transeúntes hacían su camino; pies calzados con botas, grandes pies de guardias o de curas; pies anchos y en zapatillas de porteras; pies ágiles y menudos de jovencitas; pies limpios y pies sucios; pies de viejos que arrastran arenas y pies de automovilistas que apenas conocen el piso de la calle. . . Todos ellos atraían las miradas de los detenidos. (pp. 386–87)

Finally, Benavides uses colloquial language and takes advantage of the regional dialect of Asturias in the dialogues between the participants, especially when the Revolution in the mining valleys is depicted, such as in Chapter 2 of Part II:

> El jefe de la columna le dijo:
> — Déixame que yo lleive un poco el caxón.
> Plantóse el hombruco:
> — Este caxón no lu dexo yo a naide. Con él pienso entrar en Uvieo faciendo trastaes. (p. 247) [19]

Naturally, as in the case of the author's use of narrative point of view, the choice of words, grammar, and sentence structure, as well as the use of imagery and figures of speech, is determined by the style which the author chooses to give any particular part of the work, whether this be rhetorical, informative, or literary.

Given the political theme of the work and the biased objectives of the author, the prevalent didactic nature of the narrative should not come as a surprise. Throughout the work Benavides explicitly manifests his political stance in a number of ways. As mentioned above, he employs different narrative voices. One of these is the first-person narrator, used most often when Benavides directs the narrative straight at the reader: 'No crean ustedes que todos los ferroviarios' (p. 116), 'Voy a contaros ahora' (p. 119), and 'Caminemos ahora en busca de' (p. 102); or at the characters: 'Vea usted, D. Melquíades [Álvarez]' (p. 187), 'Vosotros, guardias salvados por los revolucionarios' (p. 208), and 'Usted, D. Diego Hidalgo, usted sí que es un tópico y un novelero' (p. 343). Secondly, the third-person intrusive narrator, which appears in the political digressions interrupting the main narrative at least once in every chapter, provides general moral commentaries as well as more specific criticism on ideological issues:

¡Mineros!

Vigilantes de rampas, picadores de carbón, entibadores, barrenistas, caballistas, camineros, vagoneros, ramperos y peones. . .

Las entrañables riquezas de la tierra son tuyas, minero.

Minero que abres la galería a filo de filón, perforas la roca y cargas los tiros. Minero que pones el cuadro para conservar la mina, y tú, que lo reparas, y los que picáis el carbón y enmaderáis el tajo. . .

Bajo la tierra, el hierro y el acero de los martillos de aire comprimido, estremecen al hombre y sacuden la galería. Cae el pico con su tin-ton entre los hastiales. . .

. . .Y el minero salió de la mina y sobre la tierra perforó la roca de un Estado afrentoso, puso el cuadro que encerrara como en un molde un mundo de libertad, de pan y de trabajo, y quiso picar y extraer los ricos metales de una existencia nueva. . .

¡Mineros! (pp. 201–02) [20]

The intrusive narrator also directs his assertions at the characters, as can be seen in this last example, and often uses rhetorical questions, aimed at persuading the reader, rather than as a genuine request for information. Thus the author separates the facts (seemingly objective information) from the political interpretation (subjective personal opinion) by using the omniscient third-person narrator for the former, and the first-person and intrusive narrators for the latter. In this way Benavides hopes that the facts which he includes to strengthen his argument do not appear to be influenced by ideology, thereby making them more credible. Having said this, there are at least two examples in which the narrator admits that what he provides is his version of the events: 'Prosigo por mi cuenta el relato' (p. 168), and 'Rectifiquemos aquí la version dada por los corresponsales' (p. 224). In the second example Benavides gives his version of how Captain Nart left the barracks and met his death, correcting the account given by the 'corresponsales', supposedly of the right-wing press.

The title of the work, *La revolución fue así*, suggests that no other interpretation of the events is possible — this version is the only genuine one: 'Vean ustedes ahora la diferencia que existe entre la verdad oficial y la verdad verdadera' (p. 236). He identifies and highlights the government reports as 'official' and, therefore, inherently false, and offers his own alternative and true account. In the same way he criticizes any historical interpretation of the events:

> Los historiadores suelen enriquecer, en los momentos culminantes de su historia, la biografía de sus personajes con frases bien trabajadas, frases terminadas en punta, que se clavan con facilidad en los meollos. Yo no soy historiador; no necesito por lo tanto trabajar frases. Yo soy un periodista que aspira a la fidelidad en sus reportajes, aunque la fidelidad perjudique a la retórica. (p. 369)

For Benavides a historian's intentions are suspect as he provides a neat, polished and text-book style rendering of the events, where textual form and clarity are all-important. In addition, in line with the precepts of historiography during the first half of the twentieth century, in the interest of scientific objectivity the historian would have remained distant from the events and their implications. Thus, Benavides may be concerned that a historian's account would concentrate on concrete and limited aspects of the Revolution, namely the actions of the important participants, and the detailed numerical data of, for example, the dead and injured, without delving into their relation to other events and contexts. All of the documented information would have been biased as the data registered in the official reports would have themselves been partial:

> The tendency of professional historians [is] to see texts as documents in the narrow sense of the word and, by the same token, to ignore the textual dimensions of documents themselves, that is, the manner in which documents "process" or rework material in ways intimately bound up with larger sociocultural and political processes. Historians often read texts as simple sources of information on the level of content analysis.[21]

Unlike the historian, Benavides is concerned solely with the journalistic task of recounting the events, according to him without being subjected to any external influence. Despite the writer's assertions, however, there is, of course, no absolute guarantee that what he says is anything more than a reasonable personal opinion.

Even though Benavides appears to use objective evidence, such as extracts from newspapers, speeches, radio bulletins, letters, and official reports, he has a clear criterion of selectivity. Out of all the documentary evidence available to him he selects that which best serves his purpose. Thus, his ideological message is implicit in the use of these sources. In Chapter 2 of Part III, Benavides examines the right-wing newspaper reports in *ABC*, *El Debate*, and *La Nación* in which the journalists call for the merciless repression of the revolutionary forces. He suggests that these writers are biased, really searching for the annihilation of the now popular

Socialist Party by killing and incarcerating their leaders. The author takes each one of the newspaper extracts he has selected and undermines the claims it makes. In another example of how he manipulates the evidence which he selects, Benavides transcribes Gil Robles' 'confession', where the leader of the CEDA admits that, 'En aquellos momentos en que yo veía la sangre que se iba a derramar, me hice esta cuenta: [. . .] ¿Revienta la revolución? Pues entonces, que estalle, antes de que caiga sobre todos nosotros, antes de que nos ahogue. Y eso fue lo que hizo Acción Popular. Imponer el aplastamiento implacable de la revolución' (p. 34), in order to strengthen his previous speculative declaration that the revolutionaries were actually on the defensive, and that the attack was an initiative taken by the Church. Further on he quotes Lerroux's speech in which the latter states that 'Según unos, el señor Oreja [Elósegui] fue fusilado por la espalda, y según otros, fue asesinado por las turbas' (p. 101), in order to deride Lerroux and his 'incapacidad para enterarse' (p. 102). According to Benavides, the death of this important businessman took place when the troops arrived as there was 'una colisión y, en el tiroteo, cayó muerto Oreja' (p. 101). In a final example, Benavides quotes Dencás' pronouncement on the radio that 'los extremistas han iniciado una agresión contra la fuerza pública y han cometido algunos desmanes que hay que evitar' (p. 137), only to state that hours later he was asking these same extremists for help. On the other hand, when he uses pro-revolutionary sources to criticize the government action he does not question their reliability or credibility. For instance, he transcribes a letter written by a police captain, 'soldado del ejército rojo', to reveal what happened in Valencia and suggest why the Revolution failed there (p. 120). When dealing with the causes of the Revolution, he refers to a manifesto, signed in Paris on 15 January 1935 by the President of the Federación de Obreros Mineros de España and the President of the Sindicato Minero de Asturias, which he transcribes in its entirety (pp. 178–79). Finally he refutes the government's claim that the allegations of torture were fabricated by the revolutionary side by providing a record of Gordón Ordás' report on the methods of torture used by the forces of order (pp. 441–46).

As a committed socialist Benavides praises the revolutionaries, in particular the miners, and despises the Church, the army, the government and the bourgeoisie.[22] The miner is described as 'puro', candid, honest, humane, and brave, while the enemy are greedy, ruthless, and cowardly. By comparing the two sides Benavides accentuates these traits:

> Las fuerzas de Bosch tenían una moral floja. Luchábase con ellos sin encono. Nadie podrá señalar en Vega del Rey un acto de crueldad cometido por los mineros. Si alguna vez se transgredieron las leyes de la guerra, esas transgresiones, como más

adelante veremos, hay que incluirlas en la cuenta de los guardias que iban con los soldados. (p. 299)

Many of the other pro-revolutionary texts censure at least one of the political groups which formed part of the Alianza Obrera: In *Octubre rojo en Asturias* (1935), José Díaz Fernández blames the anarchists; in *Heroínas* (1935) the anarchist Federica Montseny criticizes the socialists and the communists; and in *El valle negro* (1938), Alfonso Camín criticizes members of all the political parties. Rather than criticize the communists and the anarchists, however, Benavides criticizes sections of his own party. For example, he suggests that the left-wing republicans lost the 1933 elections because of the split which Julián Besteiro and Trifón Gómez were responsible for bringing about in the Socialist Party.[23] Far from doubting the effectiveness of the Alianza Obrera, he praises collective action:

No son, sin embargo, las Alianzas las que deciden el movimiento. La revolución la desencadena el Partido Socialista y la U.G.T. Ahora bien, fue la obra de todos y su gloria corresponde por igual a los socialistas, a los comunistas y a los sindicalistas. (p. 182)

According to him, it is the lack of this unified action which led to the failure of the uprising in other parts of Spain, most notably in Madrid and Barcelona. Disorganization and impatience, of which all the political sides throughout Spain were guilty, are also mentioned as factors which hampered the positive outcome of the Revolution. Despite being an intellectual, Benavides implies in the first part of his work that some individuals were only involved in debating the issues behind the conflict and predicting what a future socialist Spain would be like, whilst they left the practical and vital military planning to others. Thus, in Chapter 1, while the leader of the revolutionary forces in Madrid is planning the revolutionary attack on the capital city, in an adjacent room a group of 'contertulios' argue about theoretical and philosophical issues which the narrator deems of little consequence at that point in time:

En la puerta de cristales había renacido la sombra peripatética con un libro en las manos; de sus páginas alzábase el vuelo de una lectura.

— Lo difícil es que persista a través de los hechos. Esa concepción lleva consigo una fuerza disociadora en cada una de sus bases individuales. El instinto natural conduce al aislamiento. La unión organizada sale de un razonamiento. La razón debería, pues, estar siempre en actividad. De otro lado, no hay que olvidar la traición de la fatiga. . . (p. 16)

However, this does not imply that Benavides rejects cultural and intellectual activity; he has no doubt about everyone's right, the middle class and the proletariat alike, to have access to culture and education: 'Libros, conferencias, proyecciones cinematográficas, sanatorios. . . Eso es lo que ellos [the miners] esperaban de la República socialista' (p. 110).

As far as the allegations of lack of control and brutal behaviour on the part of the revolutionaries are concerned, Benavides does not mention at any point that the revolutionaries were responsible for any arbitrary violence, again differing from other pro-revolutionary authors, such as N. Molins i Fábrega who, in *UHP: la insurrección proletaria de Asturias* (1935), criticizes the killing of nine monks in Turón, or Manuel Grossi Mier who, in *La insurrección de Asturias* (1935), denounces the theft which took place in some of the towns taken by the miners. In this sense *La revolución* resembles the pro-government accounts which exonerate the government forces from any blame for the destruction. All revolutionary violence is depicted in the text as a reaction to social discontent, and Benavides excuses it by alleging that the poor sectors of society had been provoked: 'En Azuaga había un contrato de trabajo, en el que se estipulaba el jornal y la comida. Como no se estipulaba la bebida, un propietario tapió el pozo de su finca para que los segadores no pudieran beber' (p. 87). In order to excuse the murder of monks and friars Benavides gives examples of these shooting against the revolutionaries. The Church as an institution and its hierarchy are denounced for providing the army with a haven from where they could shoot, such as the cathedral. According to the narrator: 'Fueron los primeros en aprobar que se convirtieran en fortaleza sus torres con la cruz en lo alto, una cruz que sólo abre sus brazos para acoger a la guardia civil' (pp. 283–84). In contrast, the town and village priests are, for the most part, applauded for being in touch with and occasionally on the side of the people.

One of Benavides' main concerns is to incite the reader to fight for the Revolution. For the author, although disorganization, impatience, and political divisions have stalled the revolutionary process, this lull is only temporary. His very last chapter, the most rhetorical and didactic, acts as a conclusion in which the essential message of the whole work is imparted. Here the reader is urged never to forget the dramatic events which have taken place nor the brave men who have died in the name of the revolutionary cause:

> Hay que sustraerse al terror y no olvidar. Por los días de los días, aticemos el recuerdo de Octubre y avivemos la llama de nuestra esperanza y de sus promesas. Porque España estará para siempre encerrada en esa fecha generosa, como si no tuviera antes. La historia empieza en Octubre de 1934, el mes tremendo. (p. 477)

This will revive the revolutionary aspirations which motivated the fighters in October, and the determination to realize the Revolution, described metaphorically as 'una sinfonía incompleta' (p. 484). In the chapter three prisoners, a communist, an anarchist, and a socialist, are discussing the aims and achievements of the Revolution while they lie in pain in their prison cell after having been tortured. One of the men, a miner, describes the Revolution as a rock fall inside a mine: although the landslide has killed some of the men and the situation seems desperate, the rest of the survivors have formed a chain which will help save them. The chain is an allegory of a united proletariat revolutionary front. As one of the prisoners die, he calls out: 'Mantengamos nuestra Alianza hasta en la muerte' (p. 484). The dialogue ends with another of the prisoners pronouncing:

> — Tú te partes los riñones hasta dejarlo llano, llano. . . Del otro lado del camino está nuestro mundo. Para llegar a él, trabajas, trabajas. . . Como los de Trubia, como los de La Felguera, como los de Turón. . . en Octubre. . . Sin chistar. "¡Animo, muchachos!. . . El ingeniero pedía seiscientas toneladas. . . Pues nosotros, para nosotros, le arrancaremos a la vena dos mil. . . ¿Tienes hambre? Aguántatela un poco. . . Hemos de terminar el camino, abrirnos paso a nuestro mundo. . . Y cuando el camino esté listo, llamas a tu mujer y le dices: "Suelta el hijo, que su padre le ha hecho un camino. . ." ¿Comprendéis bien? Hacer el camino ha sido nuestra tarea. . . (pp. 485–86)

Thus the text ends with a clear message: these men have cleared the way for the Revolution and it is now up to the new generations to take the initiative; the Revolution must continue.

In considering its generic status, should we regard Benavides' work as historical or literary? If we apply to *La revolución* the condition stipulated by Baldick that a text, in order to be considered literary, must relegate history to a secondary role and be based on imagination and creativity, its status as a literary piece becomes rather tenuous. The three parts which make up the work tackle three different subjects, all linked to the general theme of the Revolution of 1934. The first part deals with the Revolutionary Committee in Madrid and their preparations for the Revolution in the capital city; the second relates the action in Asturias and includes individual anecdotes offering dramatic scenes of the insurrection; and the third describes the efforts of the government and the Church to lay the blame for all the destruction and violence on the revolutionaries, thereby justifying the repression. Within these three parts Benavides employs three narrative styles, each of which has its own function — to inform, to instruct, and to entertain. Benavides relates the causes and course of the Revolution and the reasons for its failure, with an aim to reveal what mistakes were made in its organization and execution, and persuade the reader of the need for the revolutionary process to continue, using a range of rhetorical and literary devices that ensure, at least some of the time, that the narrative is exciting, dramatic, and emotive, as well as literarily valuable on those occasions on which the author chooses to be creative.

If *La revolución* were a conventional novel then we would legitimately expect a fictionalized version of the events. However, this is not what we get in this work. Benavides himself provides in the title an indication of how he believed his work should be considered: a 'reportaje'. In other words, a 'trabajo periodístico, cinematográfico, etc., de *carácter informativo*. Referente a un personaje, suceso o cualquier otro tema' (my emphasis).[24] Benavides wrote for those who wished to read a 'reportaje', an accurate, journalistic account of the events. By defining the work from the outset in the title, he selects the reader and determines how the text must be read. As a critic, however, I am inclined to view the text somewhat differently. As I have shown above, the text contains features which are associated with different generic types making its classification problematic. What is indisputable is that the text is a hybrid of the novel and historiography. On the one hand, it resembles a fictional prose narrative in that certain key moments are extracted from the story of the Revolution, re-enacted, and related with varying degrees of figurative language and imagery. On the other hand, the work is replete with historical and documentary references. Indeed, the documentary aspect of *La revolución* is of central importance, given that the text is based on a concrete historical event. Because of this historical emphasis — history is present not just in the form of factual details regarding, for example, the military manoeuvres, the type of weapons confiscated by the revolutionaries from the factories, or the number of dead and injured, but also in the setting and the characters — I regard this work as a non-fictional novel, in which the author, in addition, employs a range of rhetorical devices in order to promote his political agenda.

¡¡Asturias!! Relato vivido de la insurrección de Asturias by Alejandro Valdés

Alejandro Valdés composed his text, *¡¡Asturias!! Relato vivido de la insurrección de Asturias*, nine months after the events, in other words in mid 1935; a relatively long period of time had passed and the immediate repercussions of the Revolution had taken place. His work is divided into two phases, the first of which, twelve chapters long, deals mainly with the taking of Oviedo and the near revolutionary victory, and the second, six chapters long, with the shift of the revolutionary action to the mining valleys, once Oviedo had been retaken by the government forces, and the final withdrawal of the revolutionaries. The text also includes an Introduction, 'Algunas palabras de Introducción' (pp. 5–9), in which the author justifies the composition of his text and in which he insists on its factual nature; both of these features correspond to most of the texts I have examined, whether fictional or documentary. The author provides the necessary background information in the first two chapters in which he examines the workers' movement in Asturias, and more generally in Spain, prior to the events of October. He examines the significant political events which took place in September 1934, including the demonstrations in support of the right wing and the CEDA and the strikes called for by the working-class groups in response. Chapter 2 takes a small step forward in time and deals with the political events immediately before the outbreak of the Revolution. It also serves to summarize the October events in the rest of Spain. Chapter 3 depicts an intensive debate, held on 4 October by the future leaders of the Revolution, regarding the preparations for the fight and the manoeuvres which should be employed. The protagonist, Ríos, makes his first appearance and the lack of organization, one of the major themes that run through the text, comes to the fore. The Revolution finally breaks out in Chapter 4. The action in the mining valleys has got fully under way but will not commence in Oviedo until the following day, 6 October, related in Chapter 5. The narrative follows a linear plot so that once the Revolution has broken out in Chapter 4 the narrator describes the revolutionary victories and subsequent defeats in chronological order. The Revolution reaches its climax on 10 October (Chapter 10): 'La lucha ha alcanzado su grado culminante. Diríamos mejor que en lo que respecta a Oviedo ha superado la curva ascendente e inicia el descenso' (pp. 253–54), and from this moment on the strong revolutionary position rapidly deteriorates, culminating in defeat. The ending of the last chapter, Chapter 6 of Part II, serves as a final conclusion for the whole of the work. By depicting a debate between Ríos and a socialist comrade, the author makes some didactic comments on how the revolutionary fight must proceed.

Unlike most of the authors discussed in these final two chapters, for instance, José Díaz Fernández, Manuel Benavides, and Federica Montseny, Alejandro Valdés is not known to have written any other literary or political work, or any significant journalistic piece, dispelling the possibility that we may be dealing with a novelist, essayist, or journalist. Further careful research in the major national as well as regional bibliographies and encyclopaedias has failed to unearth any clues as to his identity, and his absence from historical and political books about Asturias indicates that he was not an important figure in the field of politics. I am inclined to believe that the author was one of the many witnesses of the Revolution who felt the need to record the events for future reference, or that Alejandro Valdés is the pseudonym of the real, and as yet unidentified, author, a risky assertion which is not supported by the text itself and which no other critic, to my knowledge, has proposed.

Amid the uncertainty about the identity of the text's author, one irrefutable fact which emerges from the very beginning of the narrative is the author's unconditional communist stance and his fervent support of the Revolution.

This text's interest lies in its political emphasis, and it is on this that I will focus. It does not display the narrative intricacies of Manuel Benavides' work, where the author employs different points of view, verb tenses and other literary techniques in order to convey its message. Instead it is one continuous narrative, told in chronological order, by an omniscient narrator, where the author concentrates on the actions of Ríos and his comrade Bravo, both of these fictional members of the revolutionary leadership in Asturias. The bias towards communism is present from the start and is indeed instrumental in determining the work's contents (the themes which the author chooses to deal with, the characters involved, and the nature of the evidence and verifiable sources which he presents to corroborate his arguments), and the style, where the use of rhetorical devices and figurative language is aimed at reinforcing the work's ideological message. The Communist Party's objective to 'capitalizar al máximo tanto la propia intervención como los errores e insuficiencia de las demás formaciones, para demostrar el acierto de la línea seguida por el partido antes y después de la insurrección' is thus reflected in the post-revolutionary analysis undertaken in *¡¡Asturias!!*.[25]

The themes that emerge from Valdés' treatment of the subject matter are present in most of the other texts examined, and can be divided into three main areas: praise for the action of the revolutionaries; criticism of the government, the army, and those sectors of society supportive of the counter-revolutionary measures; and suggestions on how tactics must be improved in order to ensure a future victory. Starting with the first of the themes, when he extols the virtues of the revolutionary side, the author depicts above all the heroism and bravery displayed by the fighters. These are heightened as the Revolution progresses successfully and the workers sense that the ideals which they are fighting for are nearer to being realized. The first of the revolutionary advances described by the narrator is that which takes place at daybreak on 6 October at San Esteban de las Cruces, on the outskirts of Oviedo, as the miners descend on the capital of Asturias: 'Entre las panas de las chaquetas se quiebran en rojo trechos de camisas socialistas y el azul de los jerseys [*sic*] comunistas. Es todo su uniforme. Son todas sus cruces' (pp. 73–74). The image of the advancing revolutionaries, although dominated by the lack of equipment and uniform, is a colourful and striking one which induces respect, as the narrator conveys with the emotive, categorical affirmation: 'Son los mineros' (p. 74).

As they approach the city and the fighting intensifies, the revolutionaries become more determined and enthusiastic and perform increasingly heroic deeds. The lack of weapons and ammunition forces them to seek alternative, and often dangerous, means of attack, such as the use of dynamite. For example, in the battle for the Cuartel de Pelayo, unafraid of dying for their ideals and for the revolutionary cause, the miners, 'que se lanzan ciegos, corajudos, temerarios, al asalto' (p. 236), drop their rifles and advance unprotected in order to hurl the cartridges of dynamite at their enemy. This bravery and enthusiasm is sustained to the end. When their fortunes take a turn for the worse and the Revolutionary Committee, faced with the realization that the movement has failed everywhere else in Spain, considers giving up, the miners insist that they should continue:

> Comprenden que el deber, su deber revolucionario, su deber de proletarios que han intentado destruir para siempre un sistema odioso y crear un nuevo régimen, es luchar, derramar hasta la última gota de sangre en aras de su ideal emancipador, por el triunfo definitivo de los explotados y oprimidos. (p. 259)

Thus when the first Committee takes flight and many workers flee in panic, thousands more remain in Oviedo fighting. This continues to be the case even when they are warned by their comrades of the army's repression in Oviedo. Even if the revolutionaries lose the battle on this occasion, the fight will not cease:

> La batalla no cesa. No puede cesar. El proletariado en armas luchará mientras conserve el fusil en sus manos, mientras tenga un solo cartucho. Y luchará para defender las conquistas de la Revolución y para extender su influjo a todo el ámbito del país. Aun cuando las fuerzas enemigas, superiores en número y mejor pertrechadas les obliguen a retroceder o a rendirse, y sus esfuerzos de seis días se malogren momentáneamente, no por ello habrá terminado la lucha. (pp. 259–60)

When it becomes clear that the only alternative is to withdraw, and after their initial indignation when faced with the prospect, the revolutionary zeal wins through; they look upon this situation as a pause in the fight which will continue and eventually conclude successfully. The proletariat have not yet been beaten, 'El proletariado pierde una batalla con la reacción, pero no queda vencido' (p. 357), and the seed of the Revolution has been planted:

> Sí, son muchos los muertos. Sí, son muchos los camaradas torturados. Sí, son muchos los hermanos de clase encarcelados. Pero también son muchos, legiones que crecen sin cesar, los que forman bajo los pliegues rojos de la bandera revolucionaria, los obreros hartos de una vida miserable e indigna, los campesinos hambrientos y esquilmados por la reacción enquistada en el Poder. (p. 372)

As the miners head off to the mountains, once the government forces reach the mining valleys, the narrator stresses that it is not the withdrawal of a defeated group: 'No es la caravana sombría de los vencidos. Es la retirada de los luchadores a templar horas más favorables de batalla, de victoria y de muerte' (p. 368). Thus, the courageous reputation acquired by the miners remains valid right up to the end of the narrative.

In addition, Valdés refers to the discipline, honesty and humaneness of the revolutionaries and goes as far as to depict them as saviours and freedom fighters, 'libertadores de Oviedo' (p. 80). The narrator suggests elsewhere that the humane attitude of the revolutionaries partly explains their defeat against an enemy much more violent than them. Despite having the chance to shoot government soldiers responsible for the death of some of their comrades, they restrain their anger and follow their leaders' orders to take them prisoner. The revolutionaries do not seek vengeance and, contrary to their expectations, the bourgeoisie in the revolutionary zone live in a relatively peaceful environment. Valdés relates two episodes in which the revolutionaries, putting their own lives at risk, save people trapped in their houses near the bishop's palace and in the Hotel Covadonga, after these have been set alight, in the first case, by the revolutionaries, and in the second, by the army. What makes this all the more commendable is the fact that they are risking their lives to save people who regard them as their enemies. Altruism is another key virtue of the revolutionaries. Ríos is impressed by his men who, despite being hungry, refrain from taking the food and money requisitioned for revolutionary use: 'Junto a los escaparates, abarrotados de viandas, los soldados de la Revolución palidecían de apetito incapaces de traicionar el sentido sagrado de los bienes comunes' (p. 99). For the narrator this is clearly demonstrative of 'la honradez proletaria' (p. 140). Thus, when referring to the thieving which the revolutionaries were accused of, the narrator claims that it was only a measure taken to feed the hungry revolutionary soldiers whose conscience stopped them from robbing: 'Llevaban horas y horas extenuados por la lucha, enervados por días enteros de combate, resistían el acoso del hambre a las puertas mismas de los almacenes de víveres, quizá con un excesivo respeto, que no les imponía nadie, que sólo se lo dictaba su conciencia de clase' (p. 100).

Although the government forces are the eventual victors, owing largely to their superiority in numbers and equipment, initially it appears as if the Revolution will succeed. This is attributed to the fact that the revolutionaries are driven by strong motives, such as hunger, misery, and inequality, while the soldiers, who are generally not concerned about any specific ideals, are merely carrying out their job of defending the privileges of the bourgeoisie. However, in spite of the criticisms directed at the government forces, the narrator is reluctant to blame the ordinary soldiers, most of whom are conscripts, as opposed to professional (like the Civil Guard).

The revolutionaries consider these men as brothers who are unfortunately, through misinformation or physical pressure, forced to fight against them.[26] The government and military chiefs are initially unsure whether their men will remain loyal or rebel, and the troops, escorted at the outset by a police guard, are prevented from coming into contact with the workers, who cheer for the 'Ejército del pueblo'.[27]

Although Valdés presents the humaneness of the revolutionaries as a positive attribute he distinguishes between unnecessary cruelty and necessary wartime aggressiveness. He gives examples of instances in which they prove their capacity for being ruthless when the situation demands it, such as during the first attacks on Oviedo: 'Es preciso seguir, arrollar a todas las fuerzas reaccionarias de la población, perseguirlas en sus propias madrigueras, vencerlas a tiros y con bombas de dinamita y hacer prisioneros a los guardias que queden con vida' (p. 82). References to revolutionary repression and violence are scarce, and where they do exist they are explained rationally by the narrator. For example, in the case of the execution of the manager of the explosives factory of La Manjoya, the narrator justifies the revolutionary act: 'Era éste un hombre al que los obreros odiaban de antiguo' (p. 191). This individual was a known reactionary who had forced his employees to go to church, had established his own catholic union, and worst of all had drawn up a black list according to which none of the workers who appeared could find work in Asturias.

The heroism of revolutionary women is also highlighted, in particular their role as nurses and carers of the wounded revolutionaries. However, their contribution went further than this. Occasionally these women had to pick up their patients' guns and take their place until the ambulance arrived. Valdés points out that there were whole women's battalions involved and that their action was just as meritorious as the men's. Indeed, he goes as far as to suggest that they are an intrinsic part of men's achievements:

> Siempre, al lado de los luchadores, hay una legión de compañeras, armadas muchas de ellas, que disparan a su lado, pero que en el momento que es herido o muerto algún camarada, le cogen y le proporcionan cuidados maternales, llevándole al hospitalillo más próximo. (p. 139)

They are able to switch from their traditional feminine and motherly responsibilities to their role as combatant members of the revolutionary forces, depending on what is required. Only one specific woman is referred to, Aida Lafuente, but she represents the ideal revolutionary proletarian woman. She is first introduced in Chapter 7 helping a wounded miner, and is further praised in Chapter 8 when her death is described: 'Murió con valentía ejemplar, a la entrada en Oviedo de las tropas del Tercio y Regulares. Contra ellas disparó, hasta el último instante, una ametralladora' (p. 182).[28] Valdés aims to spread the message that the participation of women, both as nurses and as fighters, is crucial if the Revolution is to be successful, and for which they will be remembered in the future.

Similarly, the author pays tribute to the peasants and small farm tenants. As early as Chapter 2, he comments on the lack of peasant participation and forewarns that it will be one of the main reasons for the revolutionary defeat. Indeed, according to Marta Bizcarrondo the communists criticized the socialist focus on urban support, forgetting to include the all-important peasant class in the revolutionary movement.[29] Although, prior to the insurrection, they continue to fight and rebel, their action is isolated: 'Las masas campesinas no vibran a tenor del proletariado' (p. 25). Only some parts of Asturias could count on their support during the October Revolution, and this contribution consisted mainly of supplying the revolutionaries, 'sus aliados naturales contra la opresión y el bandidaje burgués-terrateniente' (p. 136), with provisions. The plight of the peasants is described in greater detail in Part II in which the harsh living and working conditions of the families living in small rural villages are depicted, evidence that hardship was not faced only by those living in large industrial towns. The landless labourers realize that the revolutionary proposal presented to them by the miners is the only alternative to their desperate situation and see this Revolution as an opportunity to free themselves from the landowners and the Civil Guard.

The second of the three themes which Valdés deals with revolves around his condemnation of the ruthless military action and those sectors of society supportive of the counter-revolutionary measures. As with all the other left-wing texts, Valdés makes numerous references to the repressive measures taken by the forces of order, namely the plane bombardments, the advance of the Tercio and Regulares as the government tried to regain control of the region, and the bad treatment of the revolutionary prisoners. The reactions of several middle-class individuals who regard these attacks as extreme and unwarranted are quoted:

> — ¡Horrible, horrible! — clama un farmacéutico — . Esto es un crimen ignominioso. No me extrañaría, ni puede extrañar a nadie, que estos hombres, justamente exasperados, tomen la venganza por su mano. [. . .]
> — Tiene usted razón, don Joaquín — corrobora otro industrial — . A esto no hay derecho. Yo no soy revolucionario. Ni quiero la Revolución. Pero hay que comprender que va mucha diferencia de cómo proceden los obreros a cómo lucha esta gente que envía la aviación para arrasarlo todo. ¡Canallas! (p. 252)

Similarly, a reactionary Catholic shopkeeper, supporter of the right-wing Acción Popular, criticizes the conduct of the government soldiers. Thus, even the bourgeoisie are critical of the governmental repressive measures. In this way the allegations made by the author (and the witnesses quoted in the narrative) of the violent and cruel action of the government forces gain credibility and appear to be less politically motivated. The repression exacted by the Tercio and Regulares is first mentioned at the end of Part I. The use of the Moors, whose violence during the Moroccan Wars still remains fresh in people's minds, engenders a sense of panic amongst the revolutionaries as well as the innocent population of Asturias. These mercenary soldiers, who have been instructed by the capitalists to crush the Revolution, ruthlessly attack anyone whom they consider to be guilty. They are even allowed to plunder as an incentive. As the troops advance people's houses are destroyed by cannon shots and innocent villagers are victims of barbaric acts. As the action moves to the mining valleys, in Part II, the Tercio and Regulares do not ease their repression, unleashing an implacable attack against the villagers in Villafría and San Lázaro, massacres which are referred to in most of the texts dealing with the Revolution. The inhabitants of these villages report to the revolutionaries the horrific results of the Moorish advance: 'Las casas humildes devastadas, los cadáveres de mujeres despanzurrados y de niños mutilados pudriéndose en charcos de sangre' (p. 344).

By the same token, López Ochoa is criticized for breaking the promises which he made '«por su honor»' that the Tercio and Regulares would not be involved in the advance on the mining towns and that no revenge would be exacted on the revolutionaries prior to their arrest and trial. His ruthlessness and callous nature is illustrated earlier on in the narrative, for example, when he avoids heavy casualties on his side by using prisoners on the front line of his advancing troops to stop the revolutionaries from firing against their comrades. Whilst this proves to be a successful measure, the same tactic employed by the revolutionaries does not have the desired results. When Ochoa's troops see their colleagues on the front line they pause. Nevertheless, Ochoa orders his soldiers to open fire. The violence perpetrated personally by the general is particularly focused on and denounced: 'El general López Ochoa se encuentra satisfecho. Esta vez ha ganado honores y algún apreciable ascenso. Le mancha las polainas de charol la sangre que vierte el cadávar [*sic*] de un hombre. Jamás desaparecerá de sus botas la sangre obrera en que las ha hundido para siempre' (p. 287). The narrator converts an image into an extended metaphor in which the blood of one man is the blood of all the proletariat. Despite their aggressive attitude, however, the Civil Guard and the military chiefs prove to be cowardly and inept, especially compared to the bravery and competence of the revolutionary soldiers. Even López Ochoa is depicted as feeble and fearful when he is startled by cannon shots.

The author not only differentiates between the two armies. The population is also divided into two large groups which are treated in a different way depending on whether they support the revolutionaries or the government. What is clear is that everyone must take sides, and quickly: 'Hay que decidirse con rapidez' (p. 81). As the citizens of Oviedo wait for the revolutionary troops, their preferences are plainly visible: 'Los obreros, radiantes de alegría. Los burgueses, los curas, los guardias, el gobernador, el jefe de la policía y las damas de la alta sociedad, con un supremo miedo, como quien espera la mayor de las catástrofes' (p. 67). For the workers the miners are their saviours, while for the enemy they are to be feared for their bravery. The comparison between one group and the other is made from the beginning of the narrative. While the workers, regardless of the risks posed by the flying bullets, meet, and in some cases join, the revolutionary army as they advance on the regional capital, the bourgeoisie and wealthy sector of Oviedo flee from the city abandoning their property and possessions. Those who choose to stay are terrified by the apparent imminent victory of the revolutionaries. Both the bourgeoisie and landowners, responsible for the hardship faced by the disadvantaged lower classes, and the Civil Guard, traditionally guilty of crushing any move to end with that hardship, dread the approach of the workers and peasants. They not only fear for their lives but also face gloomily the prospect of their possessions being confiscated and put to the use of the Revolution, and the certainty that they will no longer enjoy their privileged position in society. The author depicts the two-faced attitude of the wealthy, reactionary classes. Whilst the bourgeoisie freely change political sides the workers remain loyal to their cause; they do not beg for pardon when they have been defeated and are subjected to torture. In contrast, when López Ochoa enters Sama with his troops the narrator refers to the hypocritical attitude of those who welcome the general and who, a few days earlier, had welcomed the revolutionaries with the same enthusiasm: 'Todas las «gentes de orden» se apresuran a lamer las espuelas del militarote. Como, en culminación de su pánico, hubieran lamido el cáñamo de las suelas de los revolucionarios' (p. 370).

Religion, the Church, and the priests are also negatively represented, although unlike other texts, the Church does not figure to any great extent. Whenever it is mentioned it is severely criticized, both explicitly and at a symbolic level. It represents backwardness and injustice: 'Proyectando su sombra siniestra, ahí está, incólume, más amenazadora que nunca, peñasco interpuesto en el camino del progreso y de la libertad, la Iglesia, el clero, exhalando su hedor feudal' (p. 390). The cathedral tower from where a group of government soldiers effectively defended the centre of Oviedo is made a symbol of the Church's repression, and the bullets which originate from the bell tower are described by the narrator as 'balas ungidas de religiosidad' (p. 201). The Church's hypocrisy is further highlighted as the narrator reminds the reader of its support for the side which is making use of Muslim troops against its own Christian congregations. For the author the execution of religious persons by the revolutionaries is justifiable and inevitable given that many priests and monks physically fought on the side of the government forces. Thus, the Church, which was already considered to be on the side of the wealthy classes, actively demonstrates its support for the economic inequalities and class system in force.[30] The hypocrisy attributed to the army, the bourgeoisie and the Church suggests an absence of honesty and a lack of ideals and values, while at the same time it reinforces the claims of cowardice and weakness levelled at the enemy elsewhere in the narrative. The author generalizes the anecdotal material in order to convey the nature of a class of people which he personally despises and which he feels are politically corrupt, avaricious, and detrimental to society as a whole.

The third issue dealt with in this work revolves around the lessons which must be learnt from this failed revolutionary attempt in order to ensure a future victory. The first of these is to secure the inclusion of women and peasants in any insurrectionary plan, both of these groups having demonstrated their indispensable contribution during October. However, the central concern, and one of the main issues running through the text, is the confusion and disorder which, according to the author, most hampered the revolutionary side. The author stresses that the defeat of the Revolution was not the result of a lack of enthusiasm on the part of the workers but rather attributable to the misdirection of their leaders, all the more inexcusable when taking into account the number of victims. In the summary to the background of the Revolution, Valdés refers to the lack of arms and ammunition which was one of the most serious consequences of the disorganization and which arises as a problem as early as the second day of the insurrection. In Madrid, for example, the workers back the strike unanimously but, due to the lack of weapons, cannot set in motion an armed insurrection. As I will later demonstrate, this lack of organization is almost entirely blamed on the socialists who, right from the start, were indecisive as to how the action should proceed. In the first meeting between the socialists and communists, in Chapter 3, Ríos is informed that the revolutionary plan has been drawn up and that he, as representative of the communists, has to accept it as it is. Whilst the communists are hesitant at the start of the Revolution, before any action has been taken, in the belief that the matter has not been properly thought about and that the proposed offensive is too hurried, the socialists, who initially insist that a military campaign must be launched as soon as possible, hesitate once the fighting has commenced. When it appears that the Revolution will be defeated, the socialist leaders retreat, arguing that it is not the best moment to embark on revolutionary action, and concentrate instead on finding a hiding place. The lack of communication between the two political groups, which accounts for much of the confusion, is evident before the fighting has even begun. When the insurrection breaks out at midnight on 5 October, it takes the communists by surprise. From this moment on Ríos' main feeling is that the movement has been largely improvised. He constantly meets fighters who complain that they do not know what their next moves should be. They feel isolated and desperate, and frustrated enough to consider giving up. Thus the disorganization, apart from having negative effects on the course of the Revolution, is responsible for much of the demoralization.

Just as the themes reveal and are determined by the political stance of the author, so the characterization of the protagonists is indicative of his ideological manipulation.[31] The characters in Valdés' work are divided into three categories: the factual characters who are given their real names; the factual characters who are referred to by a pseudonym; and the fictional characters. In the case of the first group, those characters who are referred to by their real name, we find the figures who either supported the right-wing government forces or individuals on the left who rejected the radical revolutionary position, such as Francisco Ladreda (a right-wing CEDA politician), Alas Pumariño (chairman of the Banco Asturiano who claimed to have been badly treated by the revolutionaries), Teodomiro Menéndez (the socialist who gave the go-ahead for the Revolution to commence from Madrid but who, being on the right of the Socialist Party, did not support the Revolution and was not involved any further), and Julián Besteiro ('reformista' of the Socialist Party and openly against an armed insurrection). In this group we also find José María Martínez (representative of the anarchist CNT in the Alianza Obrera and Revolutionary Committee) who was mysteriously killed during the conflict; Sargento Arturo Vázquez, who deserted the army and joined the Revolution and was executed shortly after the conflict; and Aida Lafuente who was killed during combat. Since these characters are dead, they have nothing to lose by being referred to by their real name. Furthermore they are well-known figures and heroes of the Revolution and easily identified by the readership. In the second category, composed of real figures referred to by a pseudonym, we find the majority of the revolutionary leaders and protagonists, including Carlos Ríos and José Bravo. By using pseudonyms Valdés avoids giving any information that may be used against those involved in the Revolution. The true identity of many of the characters can be easily determined: Ramón González Peña (Antonio

Peinado) arrives late to El Naranco and Bernardo Torres (Belarmino Tomás) meets López Ochoa to draw up the pact which will end the Revolution; Carlos Ríos is Carlos Vega, Juan Bravo is Juan José Manso, and José Deogracias is Martínez Dutor.

In the third category we find the fictional characters, most of whom are anonymous, who represent the fighting revolutionaries as one single entity. For the most part, the narrator refrains from going into a deep psychological analysis and only occasionally describes the physical attributes of those characters who appear only once in the narrative and disappear shortly after without a trace. This third group of characters collectively represents the camaraderie, the bravery, the enthusiasm and initiative of the improvised army which in a disciplined manner sets out to defeat the government forces. This phenomenon of the collective protagonist is referred to by Fulgencio Castañar in his study of the 'novela comprometida'. He indicates that there are 'personajes desdibujados que se pierden en la masa', while 'solamente aparecen como más completos aquellos que van a ser los exponentes de las ideas que defiende el autor'.[32] As Valdés writes in the Introduction to his book, he does not wish to have protagonists in the narrative — all the revolutionary fighters are protagonists: 'El protagonista del libro es el proletariado en armas, es Asturias, son los mineros, los trabajadores, la Revolución. El protagonista del libro es el Poder Obrero y Campesino de Asturias que perfiló en quince días los trazos de la nueva sociedad' (pp. 6–7). The extreme conditions accompanying the Revolution makes the best of each man come out, especially in the case of the communists — the brave fighter finds the words to give a speech, and the orator finds the courage to physically fight. This is the case of Sabi, a communist miner who is wounded in an attack on the arms factory of La Vega, and whom Bravo regards with admiration: 'Sabía de su actividad, de sus especiales condiciones para la oratoria, para captar conciencias para la Revolución, pero no le conocía en la lucha tal como se le había presentado hoy, en un arranque de valentía y heroísmo inigualables' (p. 169).

The key individuals who represent the author's point of view are Ríos and Bravo. The author uses these two characters to structure the narrative; Ríos guides the reader through the revolutionary episode, while Bravo represents the ideal communist combatant. As the narrator indicates, the October events are told as witnessed and experienced by Ríos: 'Paso a paso, palabra a palabra, se sigue la actuación de un militante comunista, Ríos, miembro del primer Comité revolucionario y figura destacadísima en el movimiento' (p. 6). Ríos has only witnessed the Revolution in Oviedo and the central mining valleys, and somebody else briefly describes the situation in Campomanes to him. This is why the events in Gijón,

Avilés or any of the other fronts are not dealt with. For him the October Revolution is a move from 'las luchas intermitentes a las jornadas decisivas' (p. 42). He thinks back to the class struggles in which he has taken part unveiling both his political background and Asturias' past class struggles, of which the October Revolution is merely a continuation. On this occasion Ríos, as member of the Revolutionary Committee, has the opportunity to make a real contribution to the workers' movement. On the other hand, his condition as a Committee member limits the degree of his decision-making as he has the obligation to take into account the views of the other colleagues on the Committee, whether he agrees with them or not.

Valdés highlights Ríos' leadership qualities as well as his skill in the use of oratory. He gives speeches throughout the narrative in order to incite the revolutionaries who, in this way, remain enthusiastic, even during the most difficult moments. In one speech he invokes popular enthusiasm for the revolutionary victory and calls for bravery on the part of the fighters: '¡No vamos a la muerte, sino a la victoria! Pero si alguno de nosotros cae, moriremos como los valientes, como muchos de nuestros hermanos asesinados por la burguesía. Moriremos gritando: ¡Viva la Revolución! ¡Viva el Gobierno Obrero y Campesino!' (p. 126). The speech has the desired effect on the revolutionaries: 'El puño cerrado y el brazo en alto saludan las últimas palabras del orador y el grito de «¡Viva la Revolución!» retumba en el espacio y expande el eco por las montañas. [. . .] Al rojo vivo está el espíritu de lucha' (p. 126). The didactic messages expressed in the speeches given by the key characters in the text spill out over the boundaries of the narrative and are directed at the reader, making their effectiveness all the more important. The narrator insists on the importance of communication between the leaders of the movement and the revolutionary soldiers by illustrating the effects which Ríos' speeches have: 'Los revolucionarios oyen en silencio, apretados de emoción, hombro con hombro, las palabras de Ríos. Este es otro lenguaje. Este es el lenguaje de la Revolución' (p. 298). He is also depicted as being brave, shrewd, full of initiative, and willing to do anything for the Revolution, virtues which seem to be inherent in all communists. Apart from fight, coordinate the new social organization based on a system of soviets, and liaise between the Committee and the fighters, Ríos is in constant touch with his men, and is capable of spurring them on and keeping up morale. He remains an exemplary leader right to the end. While the rest of his colleagues in the first Revolutionary Committee escape with the money seized from the Banco de España, Ríos, determined that this money should be set aside for the families facing poverty as a result of the failed Revolution, refuses to follow them and continues to fight alongside his men to the end.[33]

In the characterization of Bravo, the *real* communist, the author focuses on a different set of values. As well as being brave and honest, and an effective leader, he adheres strictly to his party's principles. Thus he insists that the fight should continue to the end and that the enemy should not be spared. Bravo does not appear in the narrative until Chapter 6, and after this point does so regularly. He is Rios' comrade in the Communist Party and a worker at the Trubia cannon factory on which he leads a successful attack. The narrator depicts Bravo as the ideal revolutionary proletarian:

Hombre joven y fuerte, Bravo tiene todo el aspecto del auténtico proletario de fábrica. Ríos reconocía en él al compañero que simboliza la inteligencia joven, dinámica, y la fortaleza robusta del proletariado revolucionario. Inteligente sin ser impetuoso, y contundente en sus juicios, Bravo es el tipo del comunista consciente de su misión como conductor de muchedumbres proletarias. En el concepto de Ríos y de todos sus camaradas, Bravo es un bolchevique, suprema dominación que no todos los comunistas merecen. A los veintiséis o veintisiete años de edad tiene bien probado su temple de acero, como el que sus manos trabajan en la fábrica, como el de los cañones. Conocedor de los principios y la táctica de su partido, la aplicaba con justeza en el radio de acción donde desarrolla sus actividades revolucionarias. Su conducta de luchador infatigable había sido premiada por la confianza que le dispensaron millares de obreros que con él trabajaban. (p. 117)

Unhappy with the way the Revolution is being led, Bravo repeatedly affirms that he is prepared to break with the rest of the forces in the Revolutionary Committee and consequently in the Alianza Obrera. He distances himself from the Revolutionary Committee following a series of disagreements, the greatest of which concerns the destruction of the cathedral bell tower. Bravo finds it inconceivable that the artistic attributes of the tower should be deemed more important than the lives of those workers willing to sacrifice themselves for their ideals. Despite the increasingly precarious situation of the revolutionary side, Bravo remains optimistic throughout the fifteen days of fighting and shortly before Oviedo is finally taken by the troops he is still hopeful of a victorious outcome. Far from considering Bravo an idealist, Ríos admires his energy, strength, and clarity of judgement when he proposes the steps that they must take to prevent the army from entering Oviedo. In one of Bravo's last appearances the narrator once again refers to his unique revolutionary qualities: 'José Bravo, cuya superioridad organizadora, su prestigio revolucionario intachable, su valor y su inteligencia excepcionales, la diafanidad de sus juicios y lo ejecutivo de su conducta, merecían el mayor crédito de los trabajadores' (p. 340), conveying the great respect and admiration which his actions have engendered.

The rhetorical and figurative language employed by Valdés is also influenced largely by the ideological message which he wants to transmit, as well as by the military nature of the narrative. The work is full of imagery of devastation and violence, and the effects and sounds produced by the weapons and heavy artillery: 'Hierve ahogado en el hondo del valle el fragor de la metralla' (p. 332). Destructive and inanimate objects are personified: 'La boca redonda, reluciente, del cañoncito «Arellano», parece sonreír ante las miradas cariñosas de los revolucionarios' (p. 128); 'El cañón comienza a hablar' (p. 166); 'Hay ametralladoras que no tienen alimento y fusiles callados' (p. 169); 'La tartamudez vertiginosa de las ametralladoras' (p. 76); when referring to the bombs falling from the planes, the 'pájaro de acero' (p. 196), the narrator describes it as 'el fuego vomitado de las nubes' (p. 249); and when depicting the urgency of a motorbike to get to its destination: 'El corazón de la motocicleta bate con latido loco contra el viento' (p. 163). The cathedral, from where much of the machine-gun fire proceeds, is described in a number of ways: 'Casi cubre el edificio [the Ayuntamiento] la sombra fatídica de la catedral. ¡La catedral, magnífico cetro negro, repulsivo, monstruo envuelto en negruras infernales que vomita plomo, acero y proyectiles explosivos por entre sus filigranas ojivales sobre las calles y tejados adyacentes!' (p. 101); or 'La torre maldita, monstruosa, podrida de arte, reventando de orgullo estilista en las ojivas prodigiosas que escupían balas' (p. 164). The ideological force of the Revolution is described in this elaborate metaphor which compares the political circumstances to a sea which gradually gets rougher: 'Navegando en un mar encrespado. La nave es agitada por el oleaje de la lucha de clases llevada a su más extrema tensión' (p. 25). This extended metaphor continues in the next page as the narrator describes the growing instability of the political situation: 'Las medidas represivas [. . .] no puede contra esta corriente que amenaza ahogarles al propio tiempo que al régimen que defienden' (p. 26).

The portrayal of the proletarian working for the Revolution is inspiring: 'Cuando salen de la reunión centenares de obreros abandonan la fábrica. Negros de hollín, brillantes de sudor, traen una alegría insólita del trabajo. De sus músculos tensos, de su pericia exacerbada, de su esfuerzo titánico acaban de producirse las armas y municiones de su liberación' (p. 311). The dramatic nature of the conflict and the sheer number of revolutionary combatants involved is conveyed by the author: 'Un bosque de brazos en alto rematados por un puño crispado' (p. 13); 'Se rasga, se despedaza, se hace bronce batido por un titán el grito de millares de trabajadores' (p. 318). Indeed, the revolutionary calls are so energetic that they spread throughout Asturias like an echo: ' — ¡Viva la Revolución! El grito ronco se pierde por el hondón del valle hasta partirse contra la montaña. De allí un eco inextinguible debía llevarlo por toda la región' (p. 294). On the other hand, silence, and hence the lack of action, is portrayed as negative, such as when the end of the Revolution in Sama is described: 'Al amanecer de este día de octubre, el pueblo parece muerto. Cegadas todas sus ventanas, todas sus puertas. Las calles desiertas, frías, sin más rumor que el taconeo de la lluvia en las losas' (p. 369). The author contemplates the atmosphere inside the proletarian houses once the revolutionaries admit and accept that the Revolution is over: 'Trajinan las mujeres en sus hogares y destruyen los vales de las cooperativas, las proclamas revolucionarias. . . Aprietan el puño y secan con él una lágrima salada de odio, de impotencia y de rabia' (p. 357). The sense of failure and the feeling that their hope for a better life has been dashed, engender a mood of despair and pessimism.

Symbolic imagery forms an integral part of this didactic and political text. At the very beginning, the funeral procession of Joaquín Grado is described metaphorically:

> Sobre los cuatro hombros rudos, el peso del camarada muerto en el estuche del féretro. Hoy pesa más. Es un peso que cala el hombro y busca calenturas en el corazón. Un peso de muerte; un peso que sólo tendría alivios de venganza, que gravitará siempre cada día con más fuerza, aun después de arrojado al vientre de la tierra, en el hombro, en la frente, en el pecho de los trabajadores. (p. 14)

The weight felt by the coffin bearers is present in the hearts of all those who are out to demonstrate against the government repression. There are several examples of how the colour red, traditionally symbolic of socialism, blood, violence, and anger, is linked to the Revolution:

> Rojo como el signo de la tarde proletaria, como la canción de los camaradas, como el corazón de los obreros, como la sangre recién vertida, el disco de la estación.
>
> Rojo, acabado de encender, el horno de la locomotora. (p. 318)

In the final paragraph of the main body of the text, before the concluding pages, the narrator explains that the workers have hidden the revolutionary flag which the army cannot find. The flag, which represents the hopes of the revolutionaries, is still in their own hands: 'No han podido encontrar los oficiales del Gobierno la bandera roja que tremoló durante doce días sobre el pueblo, como signo del poder del proletariado en una de las revoluciones de entre las más intensas y gloriosas. . .' (p. 371). It will once again be brought out, and the revolutionary hopes realized, when the workers are finally victorious.

Time and its passage are also portrayed figuratively. The obstacles that accompany the night time are metaphorically described: 'Las sombras. Todas las calles y las casas están envueltas en el hule mate de la noche. Es el enemigo de esta hora: la oscuridad insondable de la noche' (p. 71). As dawn sets in on day two of the Revolution, the favourable position of the revolutionaries is conveyed in the positive connotations of the image of the sun rising: 'Oviedo sube la pendiente de la madrugada del día 6 de octubre' (p. 71). By the last day, however, the colour of the sky at dawn has changed: 'Por la cima de los montes apunta el azul sucio de la madrugada' (p. 355), coinciding with the desperate situation facing the revolutionaries on the last day of their armed revolt. The passing of time is most effectively described as the Revolution draws to a close and time for the revolutionaries has run out: 'El corazón de los trabajadores registra el latido de cada segundo' (p. 355). The uneasiness which they feel as they wait for their leaders to pact with the government forces is conveyed:

> Están tensos los nervios del pueblo. Millares de ojos se clavan en la carretera en la impaciencia de avizorar una luz. Las agujas del reloj del Ayuntamiento realizan su viaje circular con más pereza que nunca. Cada campanada bate el bronce en el pecho de los revolucionarios.
>
> [. . .] Llueve. Hace frío. La lluvia está helada y pronto cuaja en una nieve menuda que traspasa la ropa. Más lentas, cada minuto que transcurre, las horas de la espera, desconfían ya. (p. 355)

The time factor is just as important at the start of the Revolution when speed and coordination are crucial. The anxiety felt by the Committee members, as they wait on the night of the 5 October for the clock hands to reach 1:30am and the power to be cut off, is vividly depicted:

> Los cinco miembros del Comité revolucionario, presos de una terrible ansiedad, cuentan los minutos. Su vista no se aparta del reloj. ¡La una y media! Esperemos. . ., no hay que ser muy exigentes. Los camaradas habrán encontrado alguna dificultad imprevista. El minutero ha dado una vuelta completa a la esfera del reloj. Una hora más. . . ¡Y no se apaga la luz, ni Peinado llega con los mineros! Transcurre otra hora. Se oyen algunas detonaciones y el alumbrado empieza a oscilar. (p. 56)

This description of the passing of time increases the expectation and the tension felt by the reader and is one of the stylistic techniques employed to capture and maintain the attention of the reader. Another means, typical of the 'novela por entregas' of the late nineteenth century, is to end the chapters with a problem or situation which is not resolved until the following chapter; Valdés ensures that the reader's curiosity will not be satisfied unless he reads on.[34] The suspense is enhanced by employing a series of ellipsis at the end of key chapters in which the revolutionary action reaches a dramatic point. In this way, Chapter 9 ends on Tuesday 9 October, 'con la amenaza de un ataque a la ciudad [. . .] si antes no le cerraban el paso los obreros armados. . .' (p. 221). This ellipsis give rise to a degree of suspense as to what will happen the following day, and in the next chapter. The most basic device, however, is through dramatic irony — while the characters, convinced that they will defeat the government, debate the best way to advance, the reader is aware of the true and tragic outcome.

As with the themes, the characters, and the style, the fictional and non-fictional material employed in the narrative is determined by the ideological message of the author. A close examination of the text reveals that the material comes from three sources. First of all there is the documentary evidence, the material which can be corroborated, for example, the recommendations published by the Communist Party for a successful outcome of the Revolution (p. 18); a section of the transcribed speech of Dolores Ibárruri given in Madrid at the Monumental Cinema and published by the Seville weekly journal *La Verdad* (14 June 1935) (pp. 182–83); or the text contained in the leaflets dropped by the planes ordering the revolutionaries to surrender (p. 196).[35] The second source of material are slightly altered versions of popular anecdotes and significant events which appear in other contemporary texts and historical accounts, such as Bernardo Torres' (Belarmino Tomás) speech informing the crowds that the revolutionaries must withdraw (p. 355); the destination of the money of the Banco de España (p. 300); and the fight for the Cárcel de Oviedo (pp. 270–71).[36] Finally, there are anecdotes and dialogues which, although fictional, capture the fear and hate, enthusiasm, relief, and happiness dominating the atmosphere. For example, at the beginning, in the imaginative recreation of the procession during Joaquín Grado's funeral in Madrid, the chief of the police force, under the orders of the Minister of the Interior, Salazar Alonso, tells the demonstrators not to raise their fists or he will be forced to shoot at them. These, far from taking any notice, begin instead to sing the *International*:

> Paso marcial. Puños, más puños. Brazos, más brazos. Los pies, encerrados en alpargatas, en zapatos rotos o simplemente deslucidos, golpean el pavimento. Tras los milicianos, mujeres, muchas mujeres, millares y millares de mujeres. Tras éstas, hombres de todas edades, con enérgica expresión en el rostro. (p. 14)

In a re-enacted conversation between the two policemen their fear and anxiety at the sheer force of the marching workers is conveyed. This in turn demonstrates the power of a united proletariat.

Along with the details of the battles, which are for the most part precise, there are stories of individual heroism which the author either invents or adapts from real stories. For example, the author recreates the unsuccessful assault on the civil government building, which did actually place.[37] However, he focuses on the contribution of one particular communist miner, Ricardo Llaneza, who fights heroically and with determination, and continuously manifests his integrity, altruism, and humaneness.[38] Llaneza's action in life and his attitude to death serve as an example to others. Thus, his death in combat is not to be lamented as, according to the narrator, he had always understood that the revolutionary fight was accompanied by sacrifice: 'Varias veces había pensado que la lucha revolucionaria está sembrada de sacrificios y de muerte, que la liberación de los oprimidos había de llegar sobre ríos de sangre' (p. 83).

The work is partly fictional and partly non-fictional; the author places in real settings imaginary characters representative of the ideal revolutionary fighter and with whom the reader will want to be identified. Similarly, when the reader sees how the bourgeoisie and the government supporters act in other episodes in the work, where they display their cowardice, selfishness, and hypocrisy, the wisdom of his chosen ideological stance will be reinforced. Thus, the episodes which the author chooses to re-enact and the characters which take part are determined by the aims of the work. This selection procedure ensures that the revolutionaries are praised while the government supporters are denounced and rejected.

Given its historical and documentary nature it is interesting to note the discrepancies which exist between this work and the right-wing texts, especially if we take into account that most of them claim to be truthful. There is a striking difference between the official governmental accounts and the revolutionary version of the events, and the narrator refers on a number of occasions to the misleading press reports which were biased toward the government, the army, the Church, and society's most reactionary wing. The narrator does not lay all the blame on the press, however, and admits that occasionally the false allegations published originate with the inaccurate reports of individuals who had been taken prisoner by the revolutionaries, such as in the case of the director of the Banco Asturiano, Alas Pumariño. Although Pumariño was released a couple of hours after he was arrested, he claimed that the revolutionaries had tried to kill him. His false accusation was, according to the author, one of many and these untruthful allegations, published in the press, eventually found their way into the longer right-wing narrative accounts. Many of the discrepancies between the two sides involve the extent to which the government soldiers and the ordinary citizens were willing to join the revolutionary side. For example, when the guards from the factory of La Manjoya are used to convince the soldiers at the Cuartel de Pelayo to give up, according to Valdés the guards volunteered, while right-wing texts insist that they were forced at gunpoint to talk their colleagues into surrendering. Another example relates how four prisoners, who have escaped from the Cárcel de Oviedo after being sent by the guards in search for water, arrive at the revolutionary headquarters. The men in Valdés' account give a different picture of the living conditions inside the prison and the success of the revolutionary attempts to take it, from that given by the director of the prison, Eraclio Iglesias Somoza, in his autobiographical account.[39] The most extensive example of government and press misinformation is illustrated in Chapter 10, 'La contrarrevolución incendiaria', dedicated almost exclusively to the arson attacks blamed on the revolutionaries and, according to Valdés, caused by the government forces. The narrator offers evidence which, in his opinion, demonstrates that the fires in the Teatro Campoamor, the Hotel Covadonga, and the Audiencia Nacional, were deliberately started by the army, and that the widespread destruction of the city was the result of the plane bombardments. The narrator attempts to discredit further the press by suggesting that journalists, driven by avarice, were often guilty of fabricating first-hand reports, which were more sought-after and better paid by the newspapers. Thus, the search for what really happened came second place to the hunger for money, reinforcing the unreliability of the right-wing versions.

However, just as the counter-revolutionary reports were guilty of giving out exaggerated, and in many cases, false reports, so some of the accusations made by Valdés are hard to believe:

> Un jefe de Regulares puso precio al más lujoso collar de orejas cristianas.
>
> Y a los presos, a los heridos, a los muertos, los moros mercenarios, con sadismo brutal, les cortaban las orejas y las ensartaban en un fino alambre para ofrecerlo al miserable cotizador de este salvajismo.
>
> Por todo el barrio se paseó uno de estos defensores del orden con las cabezas de dos trabajadores sujetas al cinto. Trofeos de la victoria. (pp. 346–47)

The author is relying on the terror and dread felt by the population towards the Moorish soldiers, stemming from the time of the Moroccan wars, and on their knowledge (based on real-life experience or on rumours) that they did act violently in Asturias, to make plausible the severity of the allegations. On the other hand, the narrator chooses to ignore episodes of revolutionary arbitrary violence and repression, and he seldom refers to the many Civil Guards which were killed in the mining towns, or to the shooting of the monks in Turón. The extreme violence of one side and the pacifism of the other serve to set both parties further apart. This characteristic is present in nearly all of the works examined throughout this study and clearly indicates that both left and right-wing interpretations of the course of events are ideologically manipulated. Whilst for today's readers this confusion makes difficult an objective and panoramic view of the Revolution, for the contemporary reader, who sought above all to consolidate his political beliefs, it was expected.

The important role played by propaganda, fundamental to the communist revolutionary preparations, is highlighted by the narrator: 'La propaganda tenaz, el sacrificio de un año y otro daba ahora sus frutos en la unión de todos los obreros, [. . .] La unidad se había impuesto por necesidad histórica, pero esta necesidad histórica había llegado en el vehículo de la tesonera propaganda' (pp. 43–44). As already indicated, the author of this text is himself carrying out a propagandistic exercise by comparing the action of the different revolutionary sides.[40] Naturally, in *¡¡Asturias!!* it is the communist leaders and fighters who are most favourably represented, mainly for their organizational abilities during those stages in which confusion prevails. The Communist Party is represented as the most efficient, adept and organized, and the group that ultimately should lead the revolutionary battle. They appear in the text as the natural allies of the working class, as the *real* revolutionaries, and thus as the obvious leaders of the workers' movement. Their positive attributes, referred to throughout the text, are often compared to the socialist untrustworthiness and indecisiveness. The arguments used by Valdés correspond to the communist interpretation of the events, as pointed out by Marta Bizcarrondo who writes: 'El comportamiento del propio partido es presentado como un bloque sin fisuras, a modo de polo positivo frente a la negatividad que caracteriza a las direcciones de las otras formaciones obreras, justificando una vez más la estrategia del Frente Único'.[41] Although the immediacy of the events impedes them from making any alterations to the socialist plan, the communist short-term aim is to take over the leadership of the Revolution. According to the narrator, the initiative of the communist fighters on the front line explains the successful attacks on the government-held buildings and consequently the initial revolutionary success. Ríos' greatest regret is that despite the heroism and the enthusiasm of the workers, the incompetence of most of their leaders nullifies any possible chance of victory. For this reason he feels that although it is important for the communists to fight in the front line they should also be involved in the decision-making, especially given the lack of determination and energy of the socialist-dominated Revolutionary Committee, whose members act 'con excesiva cautela' (p. 55) and take 'innecesarias precauciones' (p. 55). Equally, although Ríos forms part of the Revolutionary Committee, he severely criticizes his colleagues for knowing less about the situation than most workers. For their part, the fighters, socialist and communist alike, criticize the fact that few of the Committee members are seen physically fighting, or even liaising with those heading the military action.

The direct hands-on approach favoured in the narrative is indicative of the author's political posture, as is the use of military terminology, such as 'columna', 'regimiento'. For the communists, the fighting revolutionaries were regarded as a workers' army, 'el Ejército de la Revolución', subject to the same discipline and organization as a regular army. The narrator highlights on more than one occasion that although these are mere workers their actions are like those of a real, professional army:

De esta libre iniciativa, de entre estas masas que, armadas de fusil y de escopeta, de ametralladora y dinamita, emergen los guerrilleros extraordinarios, los héroes anónimos que causan el asombro, por su pericia, por su arrojo, de la multitud y de cuantos conocen sus hechos. Los que en plena batalla, como jefes innatos de rebeliones, dan órdenes seguras y firmes como las de un general. Y verdaderos comandantes del incipiente ejército rojo de Asturias, son estos jefes de grupo, comunistas y socialistas en su gran mayoría, y también anarquistas y obreros sin partido. No son militares de profesión. (p. 155)

The equally important belief that power should be taken by force is also expressed by the narrator: 'El Poder no se pide, sino que se toma. Y se toma de la única manera posible: revolucionariamente' (p. 28). This contrasts with the attitude of the socialists who, shortly before the Revolution broke out, were naive enough to suggest to the Minister of the Interior, Alcalá Zamora, that they should head a new government. Thus, while the socialists waste their time with inane and meaningless political moves the communists are busily preparing the masses.[42]

The criticisms directed at the anarchists centre on their reluctance to follow orders. The anarchist rejection of discipline is alluded to and criticized as early as the first chapter during the funeral of Joaquín Grado. When a mass of demonstrators are instructed by their leaders to form in rows of six the anarchists protest. Nevertheless, one anarchist obeys the order, serving as an example to others: 'Y el camarada anarquista forma al lado del camarada socialista, y los dos al lado del camarada comunista. ¡Adelante el ejército de la revolución!' (p. 15). A little further on in the text, in Chapter 2, in which the narrator examines the events in Catalonia, hampered by the reluctance of the anarchists to join the insurrection, he goes as far as to describe the anarchists as Lerroux's agents.[43] Their boycott of the strike action led to the revolutionary defeat in Barcelona and consequently in nearly all of Spain. Regardless of whether this allegation is legitimate or not, the narrator fails to mention that the reason for the anarchist inaction is thought to have been prompted by the indifference and inertia exhibited by the communists and the socialists towards their own previous revolutionary initiatives. The narrator limits himself to blaming the defeat of the Revolution on the anarchists: 'Si se afirma que principalmente a quien se debe la transitoria derrota de octubre es a los jefes de la F.A.I. y de la C.N.T., se está en lo cierto' (p. 32).

In line with communist theory, Valdés, while not fully criticizing the Republic, alludes to its incompletion and the need for a revolutionary movement to set in motion and secure the socio-political measures which had only partly been established in 1931. The aims of the Revolution are presented in a metaphor: 'Cambiar la fachada del edificio político, como se hizo el 14 de abril de 1931, no es lo mismo que derruir el viejo caserón, cobijo de un régimen, para levantar sobre sus cimientos un palacio amplio que sirva de hogar colectivo a sus habitantes' (p. 173). Rather than as a transitional stage, the October insurrection is described by the narrator as 'la destrucción violenta de un régimen para levantar sobre sus escombros otro régimen nuevo' (p. 173). The rhetorical way in which Valdés denounces the middle-class attitude, based on historical and social arguments, is unique to this text, making it particularly interesting.[44] According to the narrator, the success of the Revolution and the final change in Spain's social order are only a matter of time. At the same time, the narrator explains that in all Revolutions great sacrifices have to be made in order to end with the 'infierno permanente que es el régimen de producción capitalista, con los asesinatos constantes, con la guerra, con el hambre y la desolación' (p. 175). Halfway through the narrative, in an ideological discourse in which the narrator opts for the future as opposed to the past and tradition, represented by the ruling classes and the bourgeoisie, he explains that, in the same way that the middle-class finally triumphed over the aristocracy and the feudal lords, the victory of the proletariat is inevitable. As in other European countries, the bourgeoisie, faced with the increasing threat of being unseated as the dominant class by the workers, look to fascism.[45] This reactionary political movement is the alternative to communism, the ideology of the Asturian revolutionaries who search for freedom: 'Su causa es la causa de la humanidad, la causa de los que todo lo han producido, de los que han roto las cadenas de la esclavitud en un acto de fuerza indomeñable' (p. 103), and it must be passionately fought against. Therefore the revolutionary casualties and destruction must be blamed on the bourgeoisie who fail to accept their destiny.

The greatest concentration of explicit ideological messages can be found in the final chapter, composed of a political discourse which sets the Revolution in its worldwide political and social context, uncovers what the next step of the workers' movement must be, and summarizes the measures which must be taken in the future. Here the narrator argues that the Communist Party, and in particular its demands for a united front, the Frente Unico, have gained in popularity following the October Revolution. In order to distance the Socialist Party from the revolutionary acclaim, the author introduces a dialogue in which a socialist asks Ríos to explain his criticisms of the Socialist Party. In the dialogue that ensues Ríos argues that due to the pressure exerted by their supporters, the socialist leadership had been forced to become more radical and to cease collaborating with the government. However, he adds that it had been the propagandistic initiatives of the communists which had determined the change in the workers' mentality and the radicalization of their opinions:

> La actividad de nuestro partido, poniendo ante los ojos de los obreros socialistas, y de todos los trabajadores, la experiencia de la colaboración ministerial, proclamando siempre que no era la colaboración con la burguesía la que convenía a los intereses del proletariado y aduciendo ejemplos sobre el fin de esta táctica tradicional de la socialdemocracia, que nos llevaba de la mano al fascismo [. . .] (p. 381)

Ríos explains to the inquisitive socialist that his Party's acceptance of the revolutionary road was motivated not by a genuine belief in the revolutionary cause, but by a desperate attempt to preserve their influence among the working class; had the Socialist Party not radicalized itself, many of their supporters would have shifted to the Communist Party. He warns the socialist not to be deceived by the apparent change of heart and resourcefulness of his party as many of their policies have been taken directly from the communist manifesto, and reminds him that despite their assurances, when it comes to deeds, the Socialist Party have in the past supported the bourgeoisie and collaborated with their repressive measures. Ríos concludes that 'si bien el Partido Socialista habíase visto empujado por la situación y su dirección por la radicalización de las masas, no por ello había aceptado con todas sus consecuencias la necesidad indiscutible de ir a la Revolución' (p. 386). Consequently, when the Revolution breaks out in October the socialists are unprepared and disorganized, and during the fighting hesitation prevails. On the other hand, the commitment to the Revolution in Asturias, and its subsequent success, is attributed to the fact that the Communist Party was strongest in this region. Despite the confrontation between the two left-wing factions, however, the narrator wants to make us believe that both parties still remain a united force:

> Cada cual hace su apreciación sin que los lazos de la cordialidad se desaten. ¡Son camaradas de lucha! Juntos ofrecieron sus pechos a las balas del enemigo. Juntos vieron caer a camaradas de uno y otro partido. Juntos recorrieron el camino del triunfo. (p. 388)

As the narrator brings the narrative to an end he emphasizes once again the importance of unity and the need for a united front: 'Luchar unidos hoy, mañana, siempre, hasta la victoria definitiva. [. . .] En nombre del proletariado: unidad en lucha, identidad de pensamiento para la acción, conjunción de esfuerzos frente al enemigo común' (p. 389). This is the main message which Valdés wants to impart — the most immediate concern is the defeat of the fascist and capitalist enemy, and for this to be realized all the workers and peasants need to be united in one single revolutionary force, led by the communists.

With this work, in which the October Revolution in Asturias, as lived by a communist member of the Revolutionary Committee, is recounted by an omniscient narrator, Valdés has two objectives in mind. Firstly, he blames the government and the bourgeoisie for provoking and sustaining the increasingly desperate socio-economic situation, in which the workers are forced to fight to survive, and the army and forces of order for protecting the privileges of the wealthy and for their extreme and unjustified counter-revolutionary response. Secondly, he presents the Communist Party as the left-wing faction best prepared to lead a future revolutionary force. Valdés, who evidently sets out to argue a personal conviction rooted in ideological affiliations, is open about his objectives. The work militates in favour of the unity of the proletariat and the peasants under the leadership of the communists, in other words, the Frente Unico. This in turn determines how the story and the facts are presented. The political slant of the work is established in Chapter 2, at the end of which the author has extolled the communists for being brave, organized, and foresighted, and denounced the socialists for being disorganized and naïve and lacking in initiative, and the anarchists for being disobedient, cowardly, and traitors. From here on the comments and observations made about the political groups will serve to reinforce the characteristics which the author confers as the main constituents of the Alianza Obrera. Apart from censuring the capitalist and fascist enemy and paying tribute to the revolutionary combatants, Valdés goes out of his way to expound the errors committed during this insurrectionary attempt so that in the future — the Revolution continues beyond the text — they will be better prepared and victory will be guaranteed. Although Ríos dominates the narrative and the plot follows his steps as member of the Revolutionary Committee, the author stresses the experiences of all Asturian men and women who fought heroically, regardless of their political affiliation. These had to face defeat and all its repercussions due to factors which were out of their control, such as the lack of arms and the poor organization, for which their leaders should have been responsible. Valdés provides information, instructions, and propaganda with the aim of encouraging new revolutionary fighters and raising the morale of those who took part in the most recent struggle, and of justifying or rectifying the negative allegations made by the reactionary population. Thus, the contents, characters, and style which form part of this work are the result of a deliberate selection procedure according to which communist doctrine and its followers come out unsurpassed.

1. Joaquín Marco, 'En torno a la novela social española', *Insula*, 202 (1963), 13.
2. Kathleen Tillotson's generic classification is referred to by Avrom Fleishman, *The English Historical Novel: Walter Scott to Virginia Woolf* (Baltimore: John Hopkins University Press, 1971), p. 3; Lars Ole Sauerberg, *Fact into Fiction: Documentary Realism in the Contemporary Novel* (London: Macmillan, 1991); and Ronald Weber, *The Literature of Fact: Literary Non-Fiction in American Writing* (Ohio: Ohio University Press, 1980), respectively.

3. Manuel D. Benavides, *La revolución fue así: octubre rojo y negro* (Barcelona: Imprenta Industrial, 1935); Alejandro Valdés, *¡¡Asturias!!: relato vivido de la insurrección de octubre* (Valencia: Verdad, [1935]); Federica Montseny, *Heroínas*, in *Novelas breves de escritoras españolas (1900–1936)*, ed. by Angela Ena Bordonada (Madrid: Editorial Castalia, 1989), pp. 423–97; and José Canel [José Díaz Fernández], *Octubre rojo en Asturias*, intro. by José Manuel López de Abiada (Gijón: Silverio Cañada, 1984). All quotations are taken from these editions and are cited parenthetically in the text.
4. Manuel Aznar Soler, 'La revolución asturiana de octubre de 1934 y la literatura española', *Los Cuadernos del Norte*, 26 (1984), 86–104.
5. Tomás Verdal's novel is set on board one of the prison ships which were used to jail those arrested after the October events. In this novel a number of prisoners relate their experiences during the Revolution in Barcelona and Tarragona.
6. Although the generic term 'non-fictional novel' was new in the 1930s, the mixture of history and fiction was not a novel idea and had been used by Benito Pérez Galdós in his *episodios nacionales*, a series of seven novels written from 1873 to 1879. Geoffrey Ribbans examines the way in which recent history is presented in Galdós's novels in *History and Fiction in Galdós's Narratives* (Oxford: Clarendon Press, 1993).
7. 'Every detail of this book is "true", discovered by painstaking research. [. . .] Yet *In Cold Blood* also reads like a novel. It is written with a novelist's eye for the aesthetic possibilities of his *donnée*, for the evocative and symbolic properties of circumstantial detail, for shapeliness and ironic contrast in structure.' David Lodge, 'The Novelist at the Crossroads', in *The Novel Today: Contemporary Writers on Modern Fiction*, ed. by Malcolm Bradbury (London: Fontana Press, 1990), pp. 87–114 (p. 94).
8. John Hollowell, *Fact and Fiction: The New Journalism and the Nonfiction Novel* (Chapel Hill: University of North Carolina Press, 1977). Hollowell focuses on Truman Capote, Norman Mailer, and Thomas Wolfe. John Hellman, *Fables of Fact: The New Journalism as New Fiction* (Urbana: Illinois University Press, 1981) also concentrates on New Journalism, and Ronald Weber, *The Literature of Fact* deals with literary non-fictional writing in North America.
9. Ribbans, who refers to Gérard Genette's *Narrative Discourse* (1980), distinguishes between 'scene' and 'summary': 'Summary is fast-moving, apparently objective, a narrative account of the past from one who claims to know what is happening; scene is slow (its discursive time is the same as story time), reveals the subjective feelings of the characters, is unmediated and simultaneous with the action'. Ribbans, p. 21. For his part, Lee Gutkind, in *The Art of Creative Nonfiction: Writing and Selling the Literature of Reality* (New York: John Wiley and Sons, 1997), writes: 'Scenes (vignettes, episodes, slices of reality, and so forth) are the building blocks of creative nonfiction — the primary factor that separates and defines literary and/or creative nonfiction from traditional journalism and ordinary lifeless prose. The uninspired writer will *tell* the reader about a subject, place, or personality, but the creative nonfiction writer will *show* that subject, place, or personality in action' (p. 33). He adds: 'To make scenes seem authentic and special, writers attempt to include memorable small or unusual details that readers would not necessarily know or even imagine' (p. 47).
10. Hollowell goes on to examine each of these six basic features in more detail, pp. 26–34.
11. Sauerberg, p. 2.
12. Robert Smart, *The Nonfictional Novel* (Lanham: University Press of America, 1985), p. 17.
13. Ribbans, p. 21.
14. See note 2 above.
15. According to Chris Baldick in the historical novel 'the action takes pace during a specific historical period *well before* the time of writing [my emphasis]'. In other words the term is not suitable for those texts which deal with an event which has only become historically significant in retrospect. Chris Baldick, *The Concise Oxford Dictionary of Literary Terms* (Oxford: Oxford University Press, 1990), p. 99.
16. Andrew Barker, 'Anna Seghers, Friedrich Wolf, and the Austrian Civil War of 1934', *MLR*, 95 (2000), 144–53 (p. 152).
17. William Stott, *Documentary Expression and Thirties America* (London: Oxford University Press, 1973), p. 26. He goes on to explain that social documentary tries to persuade in two ways, directly (where the facts are put as incontrovertibly as possible before the

audience who will consequently commit themselves to change them) and by example, or indirectly (where the reactions of a character in the text to the facts is as influential as the facts themselves).

18. The metaphor of the 'disco rojo' can also be found in, for example, Alejandro Valdés, *¡¡Asturias!!*, pp. 318–19, also examined in this chapter. It may have originated with Julián Zugazagoitia who wrote an article in *El Socialista* (3 January 1934) entitled 'Atención al disco rojo', in which he calls for: '¡Guerra de clases! Odio a muerte a la burguesía criminal. ¿Concordia? Sí, pero entre los proletarios de todas las ideas que quieran salvarse y librar a España del ludibrio. Pase lo que pase, ¡atención al disco rojo!'. Paco Ignacio Taibo, *Asturias 1934*, 2 vols (Gijón: Jucar, 1984), I, 14. In the case of the dawning metaphor, it appears in nearly all of the texts written from a revolutionary stance, both fictional and non-fictional.
19. In actual fact, the dialect which Benavides employs in these dialogues is not that of the mining valleys. In his article on the use of language in Asturian literature during the 1920s and 30s, José Bolado refers to Isidoro Acevedo's use of dialect in *Los Topos* (1930), and identifies the main traits of the vocabulary and grammar of the Asturian mining valleys. These do not always coincide with those used in *La revolución fue así*. José Bolado, 'Atitúes diglósiques ejemplares na práutica cultural del movimientu obreru asturianu, nos años 20 y 30', *Lletres asturianes*, 17 (1985), 11–15.
20. The intrusive narrator is a term identified by Baldick, p. 112.
21. Dominick LaCapra, *History and Criticism* (Ithaca: Cornell University Press, 1985), p. 38. La Capra goes on to write: 'Rarely do historians see significant texts as important events in their own right that pose complex problems in interpretation and have intricate relations to other events and to various pertinent contexts.' On the other hand: 'The multiple roles of tropes, irony, parody, and other "rhetorical" devices of composition and arrangement generate resistances to the construal of texts in terms of their "representational" or narrowly documentary functions' (p. 38).
22. 'Miembro del PSOE. Durante la contienda [the Civil War] fue comisario de la flota republicana. En 1938 asistió, con José Bergamín y Quiroga Pla, a la Conferencia Extraordinaria de la Asociación Internacional de Escritores para la Defensa de la Cultura. [The Conference actually took place in 1937.] Acabada la guerra marchó a Méjico. Allí militó en el grupo Jaime Vera, del PSOE, pero poco antes de morir se pasó al PCE.' José Esteban and Gonzalo Santonja, *Los novelistas sociales españoles (1928–1936): antología* (Barcelona: Anthropos, 1988), p. 303. Benavides himself refers to his socialist point of view: 'Los socialistas no *podemos*' (p. 80, my emphasis).
23. Besteiro was against direct revolutionary action, unlike Largo Caballero. The latter put forward a proposal to the UGT by which this trade union would adopt a revolutionary plan, already agreed to, if the CEDA ever reached the government. Besteiro, Saborit, and Trifón Gómez formed an alliance and defeated the proposal.
24. *Real Academia Española. Diccionario de la lengua española*, 21st edn.
25. Marta Bizcarrondo, *Octubre del 34: reflexiones sobre una revolución* (Madrid: Ayuso, 1977), p. 64. Bizcarrondo examines the communist response to the October Revolution (pp. 191–225).
26. The army and the Civil Guard, as well as the *Guardias de Asalto*, a paramilitary police force created by the Republican government to tackle public disorder, were used to crush the workers' movement. Whilst the officers in the army came from the middle class, the regular soldiers were conscripts, for the most part from the poorest sectors of society, who were forced to fight on the 'wrong' side. According to Michael Alpert: 'It was the working class which bore the brunt of the conditions of military service. Recruits were taken away from families which depended on their earnings'. Michael Alpert, 'Soldiers, Politics and War', in *Revolution and War in Spain 1931–1939*, ed. by Paul Preston (London: Methuen, 1984; repr. London: Routledge, 1993), pp. 202–24 (p. 204).
27. According to Valdés, the soldiers defending the Cuartel de Pelayo were forced at gun point to resist by their chiefs. There are occasions in which the soldiers do join the revolutionaries, such as those guarding the explosives factory of La Manjoya.
28. The narrator places emphasis on the extent of Aida's bravery by referring to an article published in the magazine *Estampa* in which a sergeant of the Tercio claims to have witnessed the heroic episode (p. 182). Aida's heroism and popularity is further stressed by the author in a quotation from a speech given by Dolores Ibárruri at a meeting held

by the Communist Party in the Monumental Cinema, and published in the Seville weekly journal *La Verdad* on 14 June 1935, in which the communist militant refers to Aida and her sister, María. Ibárruri describes the heroic actions of these two women in order to demonstrate, not only to other women but also to men, that women are just as capable of fighting as their male counterparts. In her speech, Ibárruri insists that the revolutionaries should not ignore the potential of a woman's militia force (pp. 182–83).

29. Bizcarrondo, p. 67.
30. The only exception in the text to the criticisms against religion and its practitioners is the priest of the village of Quirós who joined the revolutionary cause: 'Los revolucionarios ríen satisfechos de contar en sus filas con aquel sacerdote bravucón que tiraba mejor que nadie a los bolos y se echaba un pulso con Dios' (p. 296). It is interesting to note, however, that this priest leaves his priesthood to become a revolutionary; the two are incompatible.
31. According to Fulgencio Castañar, regarding how the author presents his characters to the reader: 'En la forma de hacer la enunciación de cada uno de ellos subyacen matices ideológicos'. Fulgencio Castañar, *El compromiso en la novela de la II República* (Madrid: Siglo XXI, 1992), p. 315.
32. Ibid., p. 330. Hollowell refers to these characters as 'composite characters' (p. 30).
33. In fact, if, as I have argued, Ríos is Carlos Vega, the author's claims are inaccurate as the communist leader did use money from the Banco de España in order to reach Russia. Taibo, II, 187.
34. Jean Francois Botrel, *La novela por entregas: mitad de creación y consumo* (Castalia: Madrid, 1974).
35. Others include the decree drawn up by the Sama local Revolutionary Committee on 16 October introducing measures for the conscription of men to fight in the Revolution (pp. 335–37); an edict brought out by the Revolutionary Committee on 9 October attempting to stop burglary and crime (pp. 212–13); and a report published in the newspaper *Estampa* in which a Sergeant of the Tercio claims to have witnessed the death of Aida Lafuente (p. 182).
36. All of these episodes are related in detail in Taibo, II, 95–96, 187–89, and 4, respectively. They are also depicted in many of the contemporary texts. For example, the speech given by Belarmino Tomas and its impact on the revolutionaries is recounted by Manuel Grossi Mier, *La insurrección de Asturias* (Gijón: Jucar, 1978), pp. 125–26, and Ignotus [Manuel Villar], *El anarquismo en la insurrección de Asturias: la C.N.T. y la F.A.I. en octubre de 1934* (Valencia: Ediciones Tierra y Libertad, 1935), p. 103; the episode of the fight for the Cárcel de Oviedo is described by N. Molins i Fábrega, *UHP: la insurrección proletaria de Asturias*, trans. by Carmen García Ribas (Gijón: Jucar, 1977), p. 58, and Eraclio Iglesias Somoza, *Episodios de la revolución: asedio y defensa de la Cárcel de Oviedo* (Vitoria: Tip. J. Marquínez, [1935(?)]); and the money 'robbed' from the Banco de España is referred to by Jenaro G. Geijo, *Episodios de la revolución* (Santander: Tipografía de la Librería Moderna, 1935), pp. 279–80, and *La revolución de octubre en España: la rebelión del gobierno de la Generalidad. Octubre 1934* (Madrid: Bolaños y Aguilar, 1934), pp. 31–32.
37. It is recounted in Taibo, II, 1–13.
38. I take Ricardo Llaneza to be a fictional character as there is no trace of anyone, with or without that name, who undertook the same activities in any of the other contemporary texts or historical books consulted.
39. Eraclio Iglesias Somoza, *Asedio y defensa de la Cárcel de Oviedo* (Vitoria: Tip. J. Marquínez, [1935(?)]). Firstly, whilst Valdés claims that the officers ate and lived much better than the prisoners, Somoza insists that everyone lived in the same harsh conditions. Secondly, in *¡¡Asturias!!* the prisoners appear to support the Revolution while in the right-wing text the prisoners are depicted as being against it. Finally, Valdés relates an episode surrounding a revolutionary advance on the prison: 'Hace dos días nos hicieron objeto de una provocación criminal. Sacaron una especie de bandera blanca encima del tejado. Nuestros compañeros creyeron que se entregaban y avanzaron confiados. Estaban ya próximos a las puertas cuando, de improviso, hicieron una descarga cerrada y asesinaron así, de manera tan cobarde, a seis u ocho camaradas. . .' (p. 271), while Somoza makes no mention of this would-be significant incident.

40. Once the defeat of the Revolution is evident an anarchist comments to Ríos: ' — Yo estoy desengañado. Sin organización no se va a ninguna parte. Peor aún que con mala organización. Los únicos que podrán hacer algo son los comunistas' (p. 358), a propagandistic comment on the part of the narrator hoping to convince any anarchist reading the text to join the Communist Party. Another man, this time a socialist, agrees: 'Los comunistas han sido los mejores combatientes y, sobre todo, los más acertados en sus consejos y decisiones' (p. 358). Ríos, having listened to these two men has his belief further reinforced that the Communist Party is 'el Partido de la Revolución' (p. 358).
41. Bizcarrondo, p. 65.
42. Bizcarrondo writes: 'Frente a la conducta socialista, la táctica comunista de agitación y movilización, impulsando las huelgas en un sentido de preparación revolucionaria, es presentada como el prólogo imprescindible para el comportamiento revolucionario' (p. 65).
43. According to Bayerlein: 'La acusación de traición que se les hace a los anarquistas es una constante en la política del PCE en toda la etapa posterior [a Octubre]'. Bernhard Bayerlein, 'El significado internacional de Octubre de 1934 en Asturias: La Comuna asturiana y el Komintern', in G. Jackson et al., *Octubre 1934: cincuenta años para la reflexión* (Madrid: Siglo XXI, 1985), pp. 19–40 (p. 31).
44. Although this idea is not often expressed in these texts, it was an issue debated at the time. According to Mainer, who examines the development of literature at the turn of the century: 'De repente [. . .] la burguesía no es ya la clase revolucionaria y [. . .] la protesta obrera amenaza la preponderancia conseguida por el orden burgués'. He goes on to quote Galdós who witnesses the first of the 1 May celebrations, in 1890: 'Los tiranos somos ahora nosotros [. . .], los que antes éramos víctimas y mártires, la clase media, la burguesía que antaño luchó con el clero y la aristocracia hasta destruir al uno y la otra con la desamortización y la desvinculación. ¡Evolución misteriosa de las cosas humanas! El pueblo se apodera de las riquezas acumuladas durante siglos por las clases privilegiadas. Con estas riquezas se crean los capitales burgueses, las industrias, las grandes empresas ferroviarias y de navegación. Y resulta que los desheredados de entonces se truecan en privilegiados. Renace la lucha, variando los nombres de los combatientes, pero subsistiendo en esencia la misma'. José-Carlos Mainer, *La Edad de Plata (1902–1939): ensayo de interpretación de un proceso cultural*, 4th edn (Madrid: Cátedra, 1987), p. 98.
45. He proceeds to denounce this dictatorial system, which he describes as hell-like and uncivilized, and detrimental to everyone except the rich: 'El infierno fascista. El régimen que implanta el capitalismo para aplastar la Revolución e intentar el hallazgo de una salida por medio del crimen de la guerra y de la infamia del hambre a su crisis de fondo. Un régimen que es la negación de la civilización. Un régimen que aborrece la cultura, que somete — como la Inquisición — al fuego los libros, el producto de la inteligencia, el compendio del progreso de siglos. Un régimen donde sólo puede vivir el gran tiburón capitalista, el gran terrateniente y los verdugos fascistas. Un régimen que arruina a los pequeños propietarios, que sume en el hambre y en la desesperación a los modestos industriales y comerciantes, a los funcionarios, a los ciudadanos de profesiones liberales, que cierra toda perspectiva de vida útil a la juventud escolar, que condena a la inactividad forzosa y al hambre a la juventud obrera, que esclaviza aún más a la mujer' (p. 176).

CHAPTER 8

THE NON-FICTIONAL NOVEL (II)

HEROÍNAS BY FEDERICA MONTSENY

Heroínas, a short novel written by the well-known anarchist activist, Federica Montseny, was published in the collection *La Novela Libre* (1929–37) some time between 1935 and 1936.[1] According to Ena Bordonada, the actual year of publication does not appear in the original edition and she makes a rough estimate, taking into account the historical contents of the plot. What is transparent is that the text must have been written shortly after the Asturian Revolution, using this historical setting as a backdrop. Although Montseny was not in Asturias during the Revolution, she did take a tour shortly afterwards round the places most affected, talking to witnesses and seeing the destruction for herself. According to Bordonada, *Heroínas* is a tale wholly representative of Montseny's beliefs and literature; for her, just as for a growing number of young writers in Spain during the 1920s and 1930s, politics and literature were inextricably linked. I will examine how Montseny's work fits into the wider literary panorama where the novel, according to Esteban and Santonja, came to be regarded as a means of analysing society and contributing to change it.[2] In addition, few of the texts about the October Revolution were written from the point of view of a woman.[3] Federica Montseny, as a woman and an anarchist, therefore provides an interesting angle and a seldom alluded to interpretation of the events which took place in Asturias on October 1934.

Federica Montseny was born into a politically active family. Her father was Juan Montseny (better known as Federico Urales), editor, writer, and a prominent figure in the history of Spanish anarchism, and her mother Teresa Mañé (otherwise known as Soledad Gustavo), a teacher, writer, and one of the pioneers of Spanish feminism. They both exerted strong influence on Federica. She was born in Madrid in 1905. Up to the age of eighteen her only teachers were her mother and her books. She became interested in literature and in politics more or less to the same degree from an early age, writing philosophical and literary articles in, for example, *La Revista Blanca* (1923–36). In 1922, when she was seventeen years of age, she started to contribute to anarchist publications, writing a weekly column for the CNT theoretical journal, *Solidaridad Obrera*, a year later. She also contributed to the various collections edited by the group 'Ediciones de la Revista Blanca', founded by her parents: *La Novela Ideal* (1925–37), *La Novela Libre* (1929–37), and *El Mundo al Día*.[4] In addition, she published a number of novels including *La victoria* (1927) and *El hijo de Clara* (1927), both of which dealt with the freedom of women, and a year later *La indomable* (1928), an autobiographical novel. In 1923 Montseny joined the CNT and participated in many political acts, meeting at the same time many figures who were to be very influential in her life such as Max Nettlau, Teresa Claramunt, Salvador Seguí, and Angel Pestaña, to name but a few. Despite her love for literature she opted during the Civil War to set aside her literary aspirations in favour of her political activities. At the start of the Civil War Federica Montseny joined the FAI (Federación Anarquista Ibérica) and in November she became the Minister for Health in Largo Caballero's cabinet, becoming the first woman minister in Europe.

Before examining Montseny's work in closer detail I will explain why I regard *Heroínas* to be a non-fictional novel, even though at first sight it does not seem to conform to the specifications outlined at the start of Chapter 7. Unlike in the works by Benavides and Valdés, where the Revolution of October 1934 is mentioned as such, and the battles which take place are depicted as they happened (or as the author maintains they happened), in their real location, and the protagonists clearly correspond to real participants whose identities have been disguised to protect them, in *Heroínas* the conflict depicted is not referred to as the Asturian Revolution, the place names are invented, as are the protagonists, and the story related probably did not take place.[5] However, on closer examination, the historical setting, the place names, and the characters are easily identifiable. The historical setting is obvious as Montseny deals with a controversial and violent episode which was very significant at that time and probably still remained in people's minds. Thus, when she refers to the miners and the factory workers, the 'pacto' between the socialists and the anarchists (the Alianza Obrera), and the violence of the Moorish troops, she is picking out the most salient aspects of the Revolution that lead the reader to immediately associate this story with the real historical event. Montseny, who sets her novel in Cantabria, transfers all the action to the neighbouring region. However, two of the place names, Girón and Vetusta, are easily identifiable as Gijón and Oviedo. Girón, a suggestion made by Bordonada,[6] refers to the town Gijón, while Vetusta, the setting of Clarín's *La Regenta*, refers to Oviedo. The other place names which are mentioned in the work do not appear on any map or in any regional encyclopaedia and are therefore most likely to have been made up by the author. Nevertheless, given that Montseny toured round the affected towns and villages in Asturias (including Mieres, La Felguera, Gijón, Oviedo, Avilés, Ciaño, and some of the coastal towns) shortly after the Revolution, it is very possible that she has those places in mind, even though she disguises the real place names with fictional names. In her autobiography Montseny admits that she was greatly affected by her visit to Asturias:

> Recorrimos los pueblos donde las brutalidades de la represión gubernamental se habían ejercido con mayor dureza. Por ejemplo, Ciaño, Santa Ana y Mieres, donde las fuerzas del general Franco habían entrado a sangre y fuego, matando a muchos obreros en el dintel mismo de sus casas, encarcelando y torturando a muchos más, para hacerles confesar dónde estaban las armas y el resto de [*sic*] guerrilleros.[7]

The bulk of the action takes place in a small mining town called Orbejo. Given the physical attributes of Orbejo, 'pequeño', 'el centro de una activa producción hullera', 'el centro a que afluían numerosas aldeas aún más pequeñas' (p. 425), it could represent any of the small towns in the mining valleys which had taken part in the fighting. María Luisa and the 'soldados de la guerrilla' (p. 481) cross a number of villages and natural landmarks, such as Ventisquero, Plandio, and La Cabeza del Perro, places which, if not fictional, are not well known. Keeping in mind the policy of repression which was still in force in Asturias following the insurrection, Montseny will not want to implicate any of the villages. In addition, by not referring to any specific village the novel could be referring to anywhere in Asturias; the fate of Orbejo and of those living there encompasses the fate of Asturias and of the Asturians in general.

As far as the characters are concerned, Montseny uses fictional characters (the main protagonists of the novel, in other words, María Luisa, Pereda, Salcedo, and Carmen) and non-fictional participants (such as Largo Caballero, Besteiro, Saborit, and José María Martínez) who help contextualize the plot. Finally, the villagers, the members of the guerrilla, and the committee members of the local CNT, most of whom are not even given names, represent all those who fought. Despite the inclusion of purely fictional characters, however, some of these are based on the real protagonists of the Revolution, for example, Carmen and Libertaria Vetusta seem to have been inspired by the real Aida Lafuente. Carmen's heroism is described by one of the revolutionaries: '¡Qué mujer! Defendía como una leona ella sola la entrada de una calle. Con una ametralladora en la mano, la disparaba con tanta precisión, que donde ponía el ojo, segaba al enemigo' (p. 468). Anybody acquainted with the Revolution would be able to identify these brave deeds with this heroine. Although María Luisa also exhibits some of the features which characterize

Libertaria Lafuente, for example, her middle-class status and her courageousness, she seems to have been based on the real life anarchist figure Louise Michel whom Montseny greatly admired.[8] During an interview in which she was asked about the people who were most influential in her life, Montseny describes Louise Michel, author of *La Commune* (1898). Her description of the anarchist heroine bears resemblance to María Luisa's characterization:

> Físicamente no era hermosa. [. . .] No obstante, los que la conocieron de joven afirmaban que, si no era lo que puede decirse guapa, tenía un extraño encanto. Sus ojos eran muy hermosos y se desprendía de ella una tal impresión de bondad y dulzura que raras fueron las personas que no se sintieran atraídas por ella.[9]

In addition Michel felt 'pasión por entregarlo todo a los demás, su amor a los animales'; she was 'literalmente una santa', giving the poor lodging and food; and in Paris she was known as 'la buena Luisa'.[10] The similarity between María Luisa and Louise Michel is therefore evident. If we define in a very general sense the non-fictional novel as a re-enactment or a literary rendering of a real event (with real characters acting in real places), Montseny's work, taken at face value, hardly complies. However, in its generic labelling we should also take into account that the contents were determined by the unique and difficult political circumstances in which Montseny was writing. In order to avoid censorship and retribution against anyone implicated, she chose not to refer directly to Asturias and its Revolution. Whereas this fictional rendering enabled Montseny to overcome the hurdles facing her, for today's reader it must be seen as another version of the revolutionary events, in which the author focuses on those aspects which most interest her, namely the role of women during the Revolution, and the political differences between the socialists and the anarchists, paying tribute in the process to the contribution of the latter.

We should situate *Heroínas* within the tradition of anarchist and proletarian literature which developed in Spain between the end of the nineteenth century and the beginning of the twentieth century, stretching as far as the thirties as in the case of *La Novela Proletaria* (1932–33).[11] Certain recurring themes characterise this politically-motivated literature: attacks against the Socialist-Republican government (after 1931) accompanied by accusations that it was frustrating the revolutionary process by allowing the recovery of the right-wing element in politics, and betraying people's expectations; criticism of the Church; resentment at those individuals who having once been against the Republic were now in favour of it; disapproval of the manipulation of the press against the working class and the revolutionary cause; and condemnation of the Civil Guard for interfering in workers' disputes. In addition, Fulgencio Castañar identifies four characteristic traits of anarchist art which I will apply to this novel.[12] Firstly, 'el arte ha de tener un ideal' (p. 111), in other words, life must be reflected in the novel and, in turn, the novel must be a means of changing society. Secondly, 'El arte es un fenómeno más social que individual' (p. 112), and the principles of liberty, equality and fraternity must be disseminated not only in newspapers and pamphlets, but in all art forms such as the novel and theatre.[13] Thirdly, 'El arte ha de ser expresión de la vida' (p. 113), and the problematic social situations depicted in the novel must be solved so as not to engender a feeling of pessimism among the readership. Finally, art is envisaged as 'la expresión de la libertad y de la rebeldía', meaning, 'la ausencia de una normativa sobre la creación artística' and 'la falta de un magisterio cuyas ideas han de ser seguidas fielmente'.[14]

Many of these features appear in Montseny's work, suggesting that the work should be situated within the context of the traditional anarchist novel. It is set, as already mentioned, around the time of the 1934 October Revolution in Asturias, in which the CNT took a significant role, hence Montseny's interest. The protagonist is a young middle-class female teacher, María Luisa Montoya, who, despite everybody's expectations, chooses to teach in a newly opened school in the mining town of Orbejo. Unhappy to teach in a state school, María Luisa opts, as soon as she finishes her teacher training, to try out her newly learnt skills in an 'escuela racionalista',[15] a school founded by the anarcho-syndicalist association (the CNT) in the village. Here she can employ innovative and radical teaching methods which pay particular attention to the relationship between man and nature, far removed, therefore, from the traditional religious educational programme found in most of the schools at the time. A year after working in Orbejo María Luisa meets an old acquaintance, the socialist Alejandro Pereda, who asks her to help him gather anarchist support and aid for the forthcoming Revolution which his party have planned. From here on María Luisa becomes further involved in the political situation. When she tells the CNT committee in Orbejo about Pereda, the President, Menéndez, sends her to Vetusta to ask the influential figure Luis Salcedo for his opinion. Salcedo and his wife Carmen, both as individuals and as a couple, make a great impression on her. María Luisa spends a few days in Vetusta with them, during which time she becomes further acquainted with anarchist ideology. Salcedo's advice is to join in the Revolution. With the anarchist help having been conceded to the socialists the Revolution breaks out. María Luisa's story as a fighter does not begin until after the October Revolution — she learns of the death of her dearest friends, Salcedo, Carmen, and Pereda, and witnesses the massacre of innocent people in the village where she lives and teaches. She directs a guerrilla force composed of a group of revolutionaries hiding in the mountains, ready to attack any business, military, or government convoy that comes their way, taking revenge at whatever cost.

The plot itself is uncomplicated, dealing primarily with the fate of a number of characters. The events narrated in the novel, and in particular in Chapter 6 ('La Revolución'), parallel real historical events: a definite date is given, the night of 4 October, during which strong offensive action will be taken. This chapter, which, unlike all the rest, is divided into three parts, is particularly important as it relates the revolutionary episode. In the first part María Luisa bids farewell to Salcedo who accompanies her to the train station, in the knowledge that she will never see him again. In the second part, on 4 October, Pereda visits her to say goodbye before leaving Orbejo to take up his position in the revolutionary forces. Again María Luisa expresses her 'tristes presentimientos' (p. 463). These two parts take the form of the rest of the narrative, where dialogue is re-enacted, thoughts are revealed, and the narrator clearly follows the plot. The beginning of the third part, however, takes the form of a documentary account in which the progress of the Revolution is briefly reported. The narrator gives a quick summary of the events in Catalonia and then of the slow defeat of the revolutionaries in Cantabria (Asturias). She makes references to what she believes are the most important details of the Revolution and introduces them into her short summary. These include the taking of the arms factories by the miners; the vital role played by the women; the misinformation and confusion which reigned over the revolutionary side; the death of the union leader, José María Martínez; the aerial bombardments; the slow advance of the government troops and the barbarities committed by the African legion; and the final day of the insurrection in Vetusta (Oviedo). In the last pages of Chapter 6 Salcedo's execution and Pereda's arrest are referred to and María Luisa's reaction to the news is depicted: 'Sentía como si todo se hubiera desplomado a su alrededor, como si la vida se escapara de sus venas; sentía también como un fuego que le abrasaba las entrañas; un furor sobrehumano poseerla' (p. 469). However, in line with the anarchist literary precepts outlined above, this pessimistic outlook is not sustained, and instead it signals the moment at which María Luisa decides to actively join the fight.

As the protagonist of the work, María Luisa is endowed with all the essential personal and ideological qualities of the anarchist. From the beginning of the novel Montseny describes her physically and intellectually, emphasizing the value of the latter traits:

> Era María Luisa alta, robusta, de hermoso pelo negro y ojos de un castaño luminoso, profundos y pensativos. No podía ser considerada hermosa, pero había en su

persona tal aire de distinción y de inteligencia, una elegancia natural tan discreta y tan señora, que pocos hombres dejaban de encontrarla atractiva. (p. 424)

Following her studies at Madrid University, during which time she lived in a student residence, María Luisa lived for a while in the city of Girón. Thus, Montseny confers on her protagonist a highly cultured status which few women enjoyed. Unlike most other middle-class educated women, however, María Luisa chooses to go and teach in a small mining village where initially she is received sceptically, 'produciendo en él una revolución' (p. 424). The lack of confidence is expressed in the narrative by one of the mining engineers: 'Una muchacha que viene sola a regentar una escuela laica; que vive sola, etc., etc. ¿Quién no piensa mal?' (p. 431). This distrust dissipates as people learn about her modern and successful teaching methods. Although she starts off with twenty children in her classroom, the number of pupils increases to one hundred after one year, with non-anarchist parents choosing to send their children to this celebrated school, once their initial doubts about lay education are seen to be unfounded. The narrator compares the traditional and backward teaching methods of the 'maestra nacional' to the modern and progressive approach of the 'maestra racionalista'. The latter aimed to instil into the children love and respect for people, animals, and nature. Most radical of all, however, was the fact that boys and girls were taught together, unthinkable in religious schools.

According to her autobiography, as a child Montseny lived in a number of farms and her family bred animals, helping to explain the sense of affinity with the countryside in the novel.[16] Also influential, one of the basic principles of the 'escuela racionalista' was that children should be in touch with nature.[17] Thus, many of the lessons depicted in *Heroínas* are taught outside in the open-air:

Las lecciones las daba al aire libre, en largos paseos a los montes y fuentes cercanos. Cantabria, tan rica en naturaleza, le brindaba mil ocasiones de enseñar a sus pequeños, mostrándoles la maravilla viviente de la vida. (p. 425)

María Luisa, who shares the Rousseauian vision that men are equal and innocent until they are integrated into society,[18] believes that the urban environment is responsible for bringing out the worst in children:

Y no fue poco su trabajo, hasta encauzar bien aquellos temperamentos desordenados, en los que existía — contagio del medio ambiente — el deseo de la violencia y del atropello de los más débiles; la tendencia a la burla y a los juegos más brutales. (p. 426)

Thus, she regards the countryside as the best surroundings for them to learn how to be unprejudiced, civilized, thoughtful, and decent. As a result, the children seem to be better behaved and better educated.

María Luisa's role as a teacher is on a par with the guiding role of an apostle on a mission, 'en busca de almas que modelar, de existencias que dirigir, de conciencias que formar' (p. 427). Her influence extends beyond the classroom to the village, and she is respected by both men and women. The life of María Luisa, who, leaving self-interest to one side, devotes herself to teaching, is idealized, nearly to the point of mythification:

A través del dialogo, el alma de María Luisa se transparentaba, mostrándose con toda su altivez sencilla, en su misticismo innato, en aquel desinterés por sí misma, que era el mejor y más extraordinario adorno de su carácter. (p. 453)

She is given mystic qualities from the start where, 'con todo su ser entregado generosamente a la obra' (p. 427), she is compared to the women in the Middle Ages who renounced and sacrificed their lives to become nuns. María Luisa's ascetic lifestyle extends to the sphere of amorous relationships. The novel could potentially have developed into a love story: an attractive woman who falls in love with two men, each of whom arouses different sentiments in her. Nevertheless, the only instance in which the possibility of romance is alluded to emerges when María Luisa meets Pereda and he tries to caress her. After initial doubts about whether to consent to Pereda's moves, she pushes him away. She fends off his desirability ('Alejandro era guapo, joven, varonil, atrayente como hombre' [p. 440]) with the firm conviction that her emotions should not be governed by sexual attraction. Thus, when she is threatened with the love of a man she is able to control herself: 'Renacía en ella aquel orgullo íntimo que era la garantía de su pulcritud, de la pureza valerosa y abnegada de su vida' (p. 440). When she meets Luis Salcedo in Vetusta she feels spiritually attracted to him; he is the 'símbolo de la justicia y de la fuerza' (p. 438) which she yearns for. His working hands have an alluring beauty and she compares him to Pereda:

Veía en su frente ancha y contraída el cerebro poderoso, la mente lúcida que dominaba por la inteligencia y el prestigio limpio de sus manos productoras.

E involuntariamente le comparó con Pereda. ¡Qué diferencia había del uno al otro! La idea leal, desinteresada, noble; la entrega generosa a una causa que no podía darle beneficios en éste; en el otro, la ambición, el deseo de poder y de mando, la creencia en su alto destino, el engreimiento del pastor de multitudes. (p. 453)

Whereas with Salcedo 'podía amársele con el alma y con el cuerpo', Pereda 'era la tentación de los sentidos' (p. 458). He is married, however, and indeed there is never any doubt that María Luisa wishes he was not, especially as she grows equally fond of his wife. Yearning for the domestic bliss of Carmen and Salcedo, she hopes that some day she will find somebody similar to Salcedo for herself, an ideal man:

Veía el comedor de casa de Salcedo; le veía a él y a Carmen tan amantes y tan unidos. ¡Oh, una cosa así, ideal y pura; un amor completo, del cuerpo y del espíritu; una compenetración total; una vida de amor eterno, leal y simple; esto es lo que ella ambicionaba! (p. 458)

That is, until the Revolution has transpired and she takes up arms, at which point love is no longer an issue.

Anarchism's parallel with lay religion is very interesting. References to mysticism and spiritual connotations can be found throughout the work. María Luisa's dedication is compared to that of a saint or a martyr: 'Cenó frugalmente y acostose, de nuevo serenada, de nuevo reintegrada a su existencia de olvido de sí misma, de trabajo y de desintegración de sí propia' (p. 440). María Luisa admits herself that she is not the same as other women. When Pereda comments on how pretty she is and declares his love for her she replies: 'Ya sabe usted que soy muy rara y que a mí no puede tratárseme como a las demás mujeres' (p. 429). Nevertheless, when she meets Carmen and Salcedo she realizes that she still has some way to go to deserve the same high regard as the committed couple:

El mundo desconoce tanto esfuerzo noble, tanto sacrificio, esta dignificación de la vida que vosotros representáis. Digo vosotros, porque aún me siento fuera de este mundo. Vengo de otro muy distinto, sin más guía que mis inquietudes y mi buena voluntad. (p. 455)

María Luisa's ultimate sacrifice is her initiative in the formation of a guerrilla force, and her leadership of this small group of resistance fighters. Unlike her fellow comrades, many of whom have suffered the loss of loved ones, her austere and solitary lifestyle prevents her from losing anything or anybody (apart from her dear friends). Level-headed, María Luisa realizes that the onus is on her to guide these men in their search for revenge. In order to hold out in the mountains for as long as possible María Luisa insists that they must act ruthlessly: 'El que caiga, ha de caer para no levantarse jamás' (p. 482). The men admire how, despite her utter exhaustion, and sore and bleeding feet, she treks through the mountains without complaining. Nevertheless, in line with her anarchist beliefs and in spite of her comrades' insistence, she refuses to be considered as their leader. Instead she prefers to be regarded as the person responsible for both the successful and failed actions of the rebellious force:

— Todos somos iguales; no hay ni debe haber jefes entre nosotros. Pero sobre alguien ha de caer la responsabilidad de las iniciativas que tengamos. Quiero que esa responsabilidad recaiga sobre mí, como sobre mí recaerá la gloria de las acciones. (p. 482)

From her respectable standing as a teacher, she has become the equally respected leader of the rebellious group hiding in the mountains. However, according to the narrator, she seems to have been destined to lead this life: 'Su vida, tan seria y tan austera, veíase coronada por aquella resolución trágica, por aquel destino trazado e impuesto por las circunstancias cruentas' (p. 479). Indeed, the force of Destiny is all-powerful in this novel as the narrator reveals towards the end:

> El Destino era esto: Salcedo y Pereda, muertos, confundidos en el mismo fin y el mismo hoyo; ella allí, símbolo de Venganza y de Rebeldía eterna, victoriosa aún, enfrentada con el mundo, aceptando el *destino impuesto* [emphasis mine], con su juventud desviada de su cauce y su vida sobrehumanizada. (p. 496)

By introducing Destiny into the narrative Montseny does not dwell on the reasons for the revolutionary defeat and its repercussions, suggesting, instead, that they were inevitable. What she does emphasize, however, is the bravery and the commitment of those who fought: 'Ha sido éste un movimiento único; puede decirse que el pueblo lo desbordó todo, pasó por encima de todo y fue más lejos de lo que unos querían y otros habían previsto' (p. 462). This is one of the principle messages which Montseny wants to impart to all those who took part and who will take part in the future: a message of support.

Although the male characters take a secondary role, it is a fundamental one as far as the development of the plot is concerned. It is only after the Revolution has taken place and María Luisa has experienced all the ensuing horror and sadness that she decides she must dedicate the rest of her life to the revolutionary cause. Up to that point, apart from illustrate and eulogize the virtues of the 'escuela racionalista', for which the protagonist works, and reveal how haphazardly the Alianza Obrera was constituted, by conferring on María Luisa the role of messenger between Pereda and the CNT, Montseny uses this character, her trustworthy judgement and intuitive feelings, to compare two alternative revolutionary stands, represented by Pereda and Salcedo. The comparison which María Luisa makes between these two male characters is also crucial for the elaboration of the political message which Montseny wishes to convey, whereby anarchism is extolled and socialism is denounced. According to Bordonada: 'El co-protagonismo masculino se desdobla en dos personajes [Alejandro Pereda and Luis Salcedo], oponiendo unos valores positivos frente a unos valores negativos'.[19] Thus, the two male co-protagonists are compared throughout the narrative. Pereda is a single middle-class socialist lawyer, striving to be a powerful politician. Salcedo, on the other hand, is a working-class anarchist whose only ambition is social equality for all men and women, and who is married to Carmen, also an anarchist factory worker.

The positive portrayal of Salcedo demonstrates Montseny's anarchist tendencies, while Pereda's unfavourable depiction is indicative of her doubts regarding the true intentions motivating the socialists. When

María Luisa asks the latter on one of their first meetings exactly what he and his party are planning Pereda only declares his yearning for political power. Thus his revolutionary ambitions revolve around his own personal gain and aggrandizement. At their very first meeting since their years at University, Pereda asks María Luisa if she does not have any political ambitions, like his hopes to hold a seat in Parliament. She replies that she prefers her anonymous status as a teacher: 'Esas glorias no me conmueven. Me contento con la obra anónima de formar conciencias, de modelar almas de niños' (pp. 430–31). While Pereda had gone to study law, María Luisa, contrary to the wishes of the rich aunt who had paid for her studies, chose teaching instead of the more prestigious profession: 'María Luisa [. . .] por rectitud de carácter y bondad de alma, sentía invencible repugnancia por la abogacía, carrera de oportunistas y para la que se requerían condiciones que ella no reunía' (p. 432). By unveiling the personal aspirations of the main characters, Montseny reveals the contrasting essential qualities of anarchists and socialists: while Pereda wishes to be 'un hombre público' (p. 430), María Luisa is quite content with her 'obra anónima'. Pereda's ambitious intentions are such that he sees himself as a dictator: 'Se vio dictador, dueño absoluto de la Confederación Española de Repúblicas Socialistas' (p. 464). On the other hand, Luis Salcedo is portrayed as an honest man, ready to join the revolutionary fight whenever he is called to. Although he foresees the defeat of the Revolution which he is being asked to join, he believes it is his responsibility to support it:

> Creo que vamos a ir a un fracaso, pero que no podemos dejar de ayudarles, si se lanzan al movimiento. Fracaso, tanto si ganan como si pierden. Las ideas quedarán ahogadas por la marejada autoritaria de los jefes y sólo en contadas regiones los anarquistas podremos llevar la revolución adelante. Pero se trata, realmente, de algo serio y que no puede ser desechado Mi opinión, [. . .] es: si los Socialistas se lanzan al movimiento, debemos secundarles y procurar que la revolución no quede detenida en una dictadura o un socialismo de estado. Partiendo de la base de que los obreros han de tener sus consignas propias y no han de dejarse dominar ni dirigir por los caudillos comunistas, ni socialistas, ni sindicalistas. (pp. 452–53).

Salcedo intuits the socialist quest for dominance over the new government if these succeed in the insurrection, the same monopoly of power which Pereda dreams of.

The critical portrayal of Pereda ceases, however, after the defeat of the Revolution, when he is imprisoned. He is no longer compared to the anarchists, or criticized by the characters and the narrator. Instead he blames himself. Regretting the outcome of the revolutionary attempt, he writes a letter to María Luisa before he is executed in which he holds himself and the leaders of the insurrection responsible for the unfortunate events. He laments the deaths and suffering which he and his party's ambitions have occasioned. He admits that under the socialists the miners would not have been free; they would have simply been 'encadenados con distintas cadenas' (p. 493), as María Luisa affirms at the start of the novel. The narrator stresses that Pereda is unlike other socialists, however, and attributes his new perspective to a change of attitude regarding the Revolution, an attitude which draws closer to the anarchist conception of the movement:

> Se había portado como un valiente, batiéndose a la desesperada, cuando vio la revolución perdida. Al lado de la cobardía de los jefes principales del partido, la arrogancia del mozo, que representaba un nuevo sentido revolucionario dentro del socialismo, sorprendía y admiraba. (p. 485)

Pereda's stance contrasts sharply with that of the socialist leaders who formed part of the first Revolutionary Committee and who ran away when it became obvious that the Revolution was lost. In addition, the third Committee, composed of socialists and communists, without anarchist representation, was responsible for drawing up the terms of surrender. Both of these acts were regarded by the anarchists as defeatist and cowardly.

As indicated at the beginning of the chapter, this is one of a handful of texts on the Revolution written by a woman, and consequently one of the few examples in which the author relates the events from a feminine point of view and concentrates on the outstanding contribution made by the female revolutionaries. Most of the main characters which appear are women: Carmen, Juana, Gertrudis, and Libertaria Vetusta; all of them brave fighters and supporters of the Revolution. Significantly, Montseny does not dwell on the physical beauty of any of her female characters without emphasizing also their intellectual capacity or personal virtues. Thus, she avoids 'el idealizador canon de belleza perfecta'.[20] María Luisa herself, in order to be an effective leader, has to renounce certain aspects of the traditional feminine role:

> María Luisa cambió pronto su vestido de lanilla por unos pantalones de pana y una chaqueta de hombre. Su cabellera, corta y ensortijada, escapábase de las alas de fieltro del sombrero que llevaba. Cargó con una pistola y un arma larga. (p. 475)

She does not reject her femininity outright and thanks a fellow rebel, Juana, for fetching her some underwear: 'Llenó una mochila con ropa interior y una serie de prendas íntimas que habían de serle necesarias' (p. 477). Montseny, rather than reject femininity, demonstrates that external appearance is unimportant; what matters is the person's willingness to commit him or herself to the social-revolutionary cause, whether man or woman, rich or poor, teacher or mine-worker. For this reason the novel should not be mistaken for a feminist text. In an interview for the magazine *Cuadernos para el Diálogo*, Federica Montseny declares that the feminist fight comes second to the anarchist fight; she defends everyone not just her own sex: 'Creo que si liberamos el género humano habremos liberado a la mujer.'[21] When considering this aspect of the novel, Bordonada writes in her introduction:

> En la maestra racionalista-guerrillera, Federica Montseny proyecta, además de sus ideales sociales y políticos, el modelo de mujer, culta, moderna, independiente, con capacidad de decisión, defensora de sus derechos, entre los que, tal vez, el más importante es la libertad.[22]

The only instance in which the voice of the first-person author–narrator appears in the narrative, Montseny expresses her regret that the part played by women in the Revolution has not been paid all the attention that it deserves, explaining the plot of her novel: 'Es esta epopeya de las mujeres en Cantabria la que no se ha escrito y quisiera *yo* escribir algún día' (p. 466, my emphasis). Montseny declares to the reader that although her characters are invented, her work is an attempt to convey the importance of female participation which, nevertheless, must be properly documented sooner or later.

As already indicated in the introduction, *Heroínas* was to form part of the collection *La Novela Libre*, published by Ediciones de la Revista Blanca, which aimed to expose and promulgate anarchist ideology. According to Castañar, one of the main characteristics of these novels was the illustration of 'paradigmas de comportamiento para que los lectores supiesen cómo actuar en determinadas circunstancias'.[23] Thus, given the large number of copies which would have been published, according to Alcalde around 20,000,[24] Montseny's objective would have been to disseminate to a large readership her anarchist view about the revolutionary events and politics in general. Being what we could call a 'propagandistic novel', it is interesting to see the political issues which are tackled in *Heroínas*. The most obvious concern, the October Revolution, is present from Chapter 2 to the end, whether it be at the preparatory stage, during the fighting, or in its aftermath. The first time that revolutionary action is mentioned is in Chapter 3 when Pereda visits María Luisa and tells her that he is preparing 'una misión especial' (p. 434), and further on when he comments on '[el] hecho revolucionario que se está gestando' (p. 435). Nevertheless the Revolution becomes an intrinsic part of the plot from the start of the novel when Pereda admits to María Luisa that he is searching for anarcho-syndicalist support. Unlike in many of the other texts already examined, except for the repression exerted by the Moorish troops, right-wing participation in the Revolution is hardly mentioned or criticized.

Instead the characters discuss their political ideas (in particular anarchists and socialists, whose stances are juxtaposed), and the political approach of the CNT is contrasted with that of the UGT. Thus, it is this difference between the socialists and the anarchists which dominates the text. These are most clearly brought up in the constitution of the 'pacto', or Alianza Obrera, where the priorities of both factions differ and hinder the effectiveness of the movement.

The author criticizes in particular the Socialist Party and the political ambitions and quest for power of those in it. This criticism relates to the Republican government of 1931–33, a government made up of 'intellectuals' which was expected to do much more than what it did.[25] When Pereda asks María Luisa why the anarchists do not trust the socialists, she replies:

> No tienen motivos para confiar mucho en las promesas de los socialistas. Habéis traicionado todos los movimientos y vuestro paso por el Poder no es ninguna garantía de libertad ni de beneficio para los trabajadores. (p. 444)

As support for her arguments against the socialists, Montseny falls back on the many occasions on which they failed to take part in the anarchist insurrections. María Luisa summarizes the hypocrisy of the socialists: they want to be the leaders of a strong government but in order to achieve this they need the support of the anarchists who will get nothing in return. Thus, through the protagonist, Montseny very clearly expresses her own political beliefs. She, being a fervent supporter of anarchism, is very much against the socialists and the idea of a strong government, believing instead that people should rule themselves. Montseny also imparts essential messages to the reader, such as at the end of *Heroínas*, in María Luisa's closing speech to her comrades. She explains to them that those who choose to continue to resist by her side must be prepared to kill themselves if caught alive by the authorities, in order to prevent (accidentally) betraying the rest of the fighters. For those not willing to accept this drastic condition, it is their chance to withdraw. The men unanimously turn down this opportunity, prompting María Luisa to give a speech:

> Al fin, la victoria será nuestra. Porque, muertos, seremos más fuertes que nunca. ¿Acaso no es la muerte el símbolo mismo de la vida eterna? Somos ya una leyenda heroica; seremos pronto un mito vivo: la religión de las muchedumbres, que aman a los héroes y a los mártires, que necesitan la fuerza de la sangre para verse fecundadas por las grandes ideas. Dormid tranquilos, muertos queridos; miles de seres inmolados: el mañana es todo nuestro. El triunfo nos espera. [. . .] Lo mejor de nosotros sobrevivirá, como han sobrevivido a sí mismos todos los mártires y todos los héroes. (pp. 496–97)

If we apply Castañar's assertions, pointed out above, to Montseny's novel, this closing paragraph professes one of the 'comportamientos' which the reader should adopt; it is the same message which Valdés imparts to his communist partisans, and Benavides to his socialist followers — that the fight must continue and that those who have died for the revolutionary ideals (as understood by the author) will live on in people's memories.

According to Gareth Thomas, the aesthetic danger inherent in all rhetorical narrative is that it destroys creativity. He affirms that 'instead of exploring ideas and emotions the novelist resorts to ready-made analyses and slogans which are the negation of literature'.[26] How does *Heroínas* fare against this accusation? According to Castañar: 'El novelista [anarquista] no se cuida de trabajar con un *corpus* coherente, exhaustivo y riguroso de ideas estéticas sino que parte de unos principios generales en los que fundamenta su visión del arte'.[27] For the anarchists, and all socially committed novelists, language and style had to be at the service of the author's message and not used for the sole purpose of creating a literarily valuable work. As already summarized in the four points identified by Castañar, and quoted above, for the anarchists, art (in this case the novel) and life were not to be viewed as distinct and unrelated; instead art had to reflect society and the difficult situation of those living in it, and, in the process, suggest how it could be changed. In order for these propositions to reach a wide (mostly uneducated, working-class) readership the plot had to be uncomplicated and the language simple to understand. Thus, as Castañar points out, the stylistic aspect of the work takes second place to its contents (if indeed it is considered at all).[28]

In Montseny's novel, the contents are largely dominated by the characters. Much of the descriptive writing is concerned with the feelings and physical and psychological traits of those who participate in the Revolution: the men who return from the fighting in Vetusta are described as 'hombres cubiertos de sangre y de lodo, con la mirada de locos' (p. 467); and those witnessing the carnage in Orbejo 'miraban atónitos, con los ojos desorbitados' (p. 471). Montseny pays particular attention to the description of the fictional characters: Gertrudis is 'alta, desgarbada, con la cara arrugadísima, prematuramente envejecida por años de explotación en la cuenca mortífera; con los ojos pitañosos. Físicamente un verdadero adefesio' (p. 484), while Salcedo is 'alto, recio, de rostro bronceado y enérgico. [. . .] Daba la sensación de ser fuerte e inteligente, una de esas naturalezas privilegiadas que surgen por generación espontánea entre el pueblo español' (p. 450). In addition, the characters depict much of the action which takes place in the novel through dialogue, enhancing reality.[29]

The repression which follows the Revolution is more effectively conveyed through the use of images, and in Chapter 6 the narrator describes the impact which the death of Salcedo and all the other victims has on María Luisa: 'La silueta de Salcedo, esfumada en aquel crepúsculo de sangre y humo; perdida para siempre en la muerte, había de quedar como ahogada por aquél montón horrendo de cadáveres que crecía, crecía, crecía' (p. 469). There are a few more examples of figurative language, mainly in the form of symbolism. For example, the mine is given maternal qualities: 'La mina Mayor, la más antigua, prolífica como una buena madre, que aún vaciaba hulla de sus entrañas fecundas' (p. 428). The mine is clearly an essential part of life for those living in Orbejo. Apart from being an inexhaustible source of coal, as a good mother is traditionally a continuous source of children, the mine (where men work and earn money) rears the families by providing them with something to eat. In this example, it is evident that Montseny does not employ figurative language to create a literary or descriptive image which is there merely for its artistic value. She hopes that, with her use of symbolism, the ideological messages which she is disseminating will reach the reader more easily:

> Con los símbolos lo estético adquiere una dimensión profunda pues se aúna, junto a la belleza de la imagen utilizada, el alcance del mensaje que puede penetrar hasta los rincones más profundos del lector de una manera subliminal.[30]

When considering Gareth Thomas' claim that the aesthetic danger of socially-committed writing is that it destroys creativity, we should first and foremost take into account what motivated this type of composition. As already argued in Chapter 2, the authors, for the most part, were not attempting to be literary or creative; during this momentous socio-political period they had a different order of priorities where persuasiveness, eloquence, clarity, and encouragement were all-important. Thus, when valuing the creativeness of Montseny's work this factor must be taken into account. Consequently, any figurative or literary device she uses is for the sole benefit of her message, and not for the sake of the literariness of the work itself.

In conclusion, there are two things that stand out in this text, the events of 1934 and a woman's response to them, as told by a female author. The essential issues which the text focuses on are those same issues addressed by Spanish society in the 1930s: the disparity in the ideological principles of the left-wing political parties and groups, and in particular the conflicting philosophies of the anarchists and socialists; the causes and repercussions of the October Revolution; and woman's role in the Revolution and more generally in society. In her non-fictional novel, Montseny analyses these issues and, by depicting a story in which the events, the characters and the places are easily identified as real, she suggests to the readers how they can change the unfair society in which they are living. *Heroínas* is representative of Montseny's anarchist beliefs and literature. The protagonist, María Luisa is compared to a saint, and her closest comrades to martyrs, stressing what anarchism should be all about — devoting your life to the social revolutionary cause, not just to satisfy a limited number of individuals, which is how the socialists perceive the revolutionary attempt, but for the good of society. Montseny keeps the plot and the style uncomplicated so that her message will be fully understood. To illustrate the difference between the two stands Montseny creates two male protagonists, Salcedo and Pereda, each representative of a different position. Naturally, it is the anarchist Salcedo who comes out favourably in the work, and even Pereda, the fervent socialist, admits prior to his execution that his conception of the Revolution was erroneous. As in all of the socially committed novels examined previously, she encourages those who have fought in the recent Revolution as well as those youngsters who have yet to fight their first. Monseny's main objective is to explain the unsuccessful outcome of the Revolution and to suggest a way forward. She imparts her belief, as convincingly as possible, that as long as there are workers who desire a new restructured society based on anarchist principles, and victims to avenge all the wrong that has been done during the Revolution and in the past, the continuation of the fight is ensured. Hence the novel ends on a positive note.

Octubre rojo en Asturias by José Díaz Fernández

José Díaz Fernández was born in Aldea del Obispo, a village in the province of Salamanca, on 20 May 1898, and died while in exile in Toulouse on 18 February 1941. Although born in Salamanca, he always considered himself a native of Asturias where he had gone to live at an early age. This connection with Asturias largely explains the sensitivity with which he writes in *Octubre rojo en Asturias*. Díaz Fernández started his journalistic career by writing for the newspaper *El Noroeste* (Gijón). He became literary critic for another newspaper *El Sol* (1917–39), wrote in *Crisol* (1931–32), *Luz* (1932–34), *Política* (1935–39), and *Post-Guerra* (1927–28), and founded and edited *Nueva España* (1930–31) along with Joaquín Arderíus and Antonio Espina. In view of the censorship to which the press was subjected, *Post-Guerra* was suspended and Díaz Fernández, along with Joaquín Arderíus, José Balbontín, R. Giménez Siles, and Juan Andrade, created *Ediciones Oriente*, the first publishing house devoted to translations of foreign socially committed novels. As well as a journalist he was a novelist. From September 1921 to 1922 he had had to fight in

Morocco as a conscript in the expeditionary force, a harrowing experience which he wrote about in the novel *El blocao* (1928), for which he won first prize in a literary competition organized by the newspaper *El Imparcial.* Although Díaz Fernández's literary works dealt with social problems, the influence of the avant-garde tradition is evident in, for example, *La Venus mecánica* (1929), a novel which he wrote while in exile in Lisbon. In 1930 he published *El nuevo romanticismo*, a collection of theoretical essays in which he argues his opinions about the development of literature.[31] Politically, Díaz Fernández was a committed moderate left-wing republican. He had declared himself against Primo de Rivera's dictatorship, taking part in the 1930 Jaca rebellion led by the republican captains Fermín Galán and García Hernández, and was closely bound to the Partido Radical Socialista and later to Azaña's Izquierda Republicana. In 1931 Díaz Fernández was elected as deputy for the Cortes. However, with the 1933 right-wing election victory, he withdrew from active politics until 1936, at which point he became a member of the Popular Front government.

As indicated in Chapter 2, Díaz Fernández showed with the publication of *El nuevo romanticismo* not only that he was a successful journalist and popular novelist,[32] but also that he had very clear ideas about the course that literature should take. However, during the 1930s it became evident that many writers were distancing themselves ever more from the avant-garde characteristics which Díaz Fernández had at one time hoped to merge into the socially committed novel. Instead they opted for a more direct style with less linguistic complexity in order to reach a wide and politicized readership. Boetsch suggests that it was this extreme politicization of literature which drove Díaz Fernández to search for another way of expressing his committed stance. His final literary contributions, before writing *Octubre rojo*, were *La largueza* and 'Cruce de caminos', both of these published in 1931.[33]

The Asturian Revolution of October 1934 provided Díaz Fernández with an incentive strong enough to break that literary silence, although he still stood by the conviction that a work of art should not be composed solely for the purpose of propaganda.[34] He was very much in touch with the political situation in Asturias and had personal and emotional ties with the region. The prologue to his work helps to explain why Díaz Fernández decided to make this one-off literary contribution:

> Yo he sentido, como el que más, el dolor de ver correr la sangre por aquel país que es mío, que está unido a la intimidad de mi corazón, porque en él se han mezclado mis luchas y mis triunfos. Las calles devastadas de Oviedo, sus ruinas innumerables, sus árboles destrozados y sus torres caídas, pesan sobre mi alma, porque, además, todo eso va unido a los recuerdos de mi primera juventud. Pero me duele tanto como

eso la injusticia que pudo hacer posible la revolución; me conmueve el heroísmo de esos mineros que, sin pensar si van a ser secundados, se lanzan a pelear por una idea que va dejando de ser una utopía, sin pensar si son bien o mal dirigidos, ofreciéndole a la revolución la vida, porque es lo único que tienen. (pp. 23–24)

Octubre rojo en Asturias, a novel which gives an account of the events in Asturias from 5 to 20 October 1934, was first published in 1935.[35] The novel is composed of fifteen independent but related chapters which generally follow the chronology of the Revolution, starting with the events in Mieres in Chapter 1 ('Mieres inicia la revolución') and ending with the flight of some of those revolutionaries involved, in Chapter 15 ('La huída'). There appear intermittent chapters within the chronological framework in which the action of specific characters during particularly critical episodes is highlighted. In addition, a prologue, signed by Díaz Fernández, sets the scene.

Díaz Fernández's principal objective is, on the one hand, to expose the heroism with which the Asturian miners fought, and, on the other, to criticize the naivety and irresponsibility of those who had thought that this was a suitable moment to embark on a revolutionary campaign, knowing that the strong military and governmental opposition would react ruthlessly to crush it. He was amongst those in the left-wing ranks who were critical of the Revolution, claiming that the difficult economic circumstances of the workers and their desperate need for social and political change had been taken advantage of, and the revolutionary forces had been encouraged to fight in a battle which had not been carefully prepared, materially or strategically, and which had not been properly directed. He is even more critical of the more militant left-wing groups, namely the communists and the anarchists, for pretending that the situation in Asturias and the rest of Spain was successful and lying to the revolutionaries in order to encourage them to carry on. What is particularly interesting about this work is the way in which Díaz Fernández imparts his ideological point of view. As I have already shown, he was reluctant to completely ignore the aesthetic and literary dimension of the work for the sake of the ideological message. And yet he clearly desired to convey his interpretation of the revolutionary events unequivocally. Thus, in the composition of this work there are two obvious key considerations — the expected aesthetic requirements of the novel, and the clarity of the message imparted. I will examine first of all the rhetorical and narrative strategies which Díaz Fernández employs in order to ensure the truthfulness of his account and the persuasiveness of his interpretation. Secondly, I will examine the political, social, and revolutionary issues which he deals with and which are determined by his own ideological stance. Finally, I will give examples of some of the figurative language which he uses and which demonstrate that he was still concerned about the aesthetic value of his work.

The prologue of *Octubre rojo*, signed by José Díaz Fernández, is of indispensable value when examining the work's narrative point of view. Here the author writes: 'Este relato está hecho sobre el manuscrito de un testigo de la revolución' (p. 23). Díaz Fernández provides the prologue to the work of 'José Canel' which is based on the manuscript of an anonymous miner. José Manuel López de Abiada suggests that Díaz Fernández deliberately used a pseudonym to hide his real identity. In the introduction to the 1984 edition of *Octubre rojo*, he copies an article written by the author, entitled 'Los contrarrevolucionarios', published in *El Liberal*, on 10 August 1935, in which he reveals that he is the true author of the work. The opening sentence of the article is: 'Con motivo de un libro que acabo de publicar sobre la revolución de Asturias'.[36] The issues raised in this article are tackled in a similar way as in the novel. For example, he condemns the lies which were propagated about the action of the revolutionaries by precisely those individuals who remained hidden away at the time of the fighting and failed to come out in support of their political beliefs. Similarly, in *Octubre rojo* a number of characters fit perfectly the profile of the cowards and hypocrites Díaz Fernández denounces in his article. There are various reasons why he may have chosen to use a pseudonym. On a practical level, he may have feared persecution, not only by the government forces, but also by the revolutionary participants and groups, many of whom he criticizes. As I have shown, many interpretations of the Revolution were written and published, but few are as openly critical towards the leadership of both of the fighting sides.[37] Secondly he may not have wanted the reader to sense that his version of the historical events have been determined by his personal political view (although, admittedly, the prologue by Díaz Fernández will certainly be an indication of the general ideological stance of the work). Naturally, the apparent presence of a manuscript distances Díaz Fernández even further from the rendering of the events.

It is interesting to note that Díaz Fernández is the only writer, out of all of those examined, to use the verifying device of a manuscript. According to Fernández Prieto, who examines the use of the manuscript in historical novels: 'El narrador tiene que justificar su saber acerca de estos sucesos que han tenido lugar en el pasado',[38] making it the ideal means of proving the truthfulness of the facts presented. This assertion can also be applied to *Octubre rojo*. In the case of most of the other authors examined, they either claim to have witnessed the events directly or to be relying on information provided by eye-witnesses. In this work, the manuscript which has supposedly been used belongs to a revolutionary miner. While

Díaz Fernández affirms that 'no se cuenta [. . .] más que lo que el autor del documento ha visto por sus propios ojos' (p. 23), he also warns the reader that, in order not to falsify facts, only the well-grounded and irrefutable information of an eye-witness will be included, even if this means omitting important episodes: 'Por eso se omite algún episodio resonante, pues nada se quiere contar de memoria, y es preferible pasar por alto algún hecho antes de falsearlo' (p. 23). Stressing further his concern that the truth about the Revolution be known, he writes: 'A la revolución de Asturias hay que juzgarla generosamente, con arreglo a un criterio histórico, sin ocultar sus errores ni añadirle crueldad' (p. 23), a comment which is directed at the left just as much as to the right wing, and which explains the emphasis given throughout the narrative to the mistakes committed by the revolutionary leadership and fighters during the Revolution. In line with the claims made in the prologue, we would expect the narrator to relate the experiences as lived, witnessed, and interpreted by the miner. If the work is indeed based solely on this primary source, and is a faithful rendition of the manuscript, the personal opinion of the author–narrator should not intrude on the narrative. And yet there is evidence throughout the work of the presence of the narrator's own voice, sometimes taking the form of an omniscient narrator who provides information which the miner, as eye-witness, could not have possibly known and which would not have been recorded in the original text.

It is easy to identify those sections which are based on the information provided by the manuscript, namely when the course of events is related, and those parts which clearly originate with the narrator. The narrator's intrusion is discernible when he comments in general terms on the miners, of which the manuscript writer was one. For example, on one occasion the narrator gives his own opinion about what motivated the miners: 'El dominio político implicaba en sus almas simples la conquista de todo lo que hasta entonces les había sido negado. La palabra "revolución", que trepidaba dentro de ellos, como un motor, quería decir sobre todo acceso a una existencia hasta entonces vedada' (p. 88). Evidently, this is his own interpretation of the feelings which the miner conveys in his manuscript. There are instances in which the narrator describes a real situation, probably depicted in the original text, but in his own figurative and rhetorical way: 'A la luz de las bujías, las caras de los mozos mineros, desencajadas por la fatiga, se les aparecían a los pacíficos habitantes de Oviedo como rostros monstruosos chamuscados por el fuego infernal' (p. 94). The narrator's omniscience is evident when he describes situations in which the real manuscript writer would not have been present, such as during private conversations, or when the inner thoughts of the characters are revealed. For instance, when he describes the last meeting held by Peña with his friends before the revolutionary committee decides to run away, at which the miner would not have been present (unless he was a friend of the revolutionary leader): 'En la última conversación que tuvo Peña con sus amigos de Mieres, declaró terminantemente que él abandonaba la lucha' (p. 152). He also portrays the tense atmosphere and the conversation inside the car in which Belarmino Tomás escapes from the city of Oviedo (pp. 168–69). In a final example in which he demonstrates his omniscience, the narrator describes the feelings of Teodomiro Menéndez when he becomes a target of the revolutionary troops who accuse him of treason:

> El que durante muchos años quiso la salvación de los parias, en aquel momento, mientras tronaban las explosiones y silbaban las balas de las ametralladoras enloquecidas, solo pedía la salvación de su compañera de siempre, de aquella mujer humilde y laboriosa que ahora respiraba dificultosamente en el lecho, con los ojos semicerrados por la fiebre. (p. 158)

It is unlikely that the miner was present in the bedroom of the sick woman, and less still that he should know Menéndez's thoughts. Thus, although Díaz Fernández insists in his prologue that 'José Canel' has omitted that information which is not absolutely verifiable from his account, there is evidence that the version which emerges is to a large extent 'Canel's' own interpretation of the miner's eye-witness account and, further still, that he seems to add data of his own.

The use of a pseudonym distances Díaz Fernández from the depiction of the events, while the use of the manuscript makes the work appear to be real as it is based on the experiences of an eye-witness. These are both rhetorical strategies employed by the author to make his text more factual and consequently more persuasive. According to Stott, by reading about the experiences of real people in real circumstances the reader will react by wanting to ameliorate their predicament.[39] He will be more inclined to accept the author's notion about how the situation has originated and how it can be changed for the better, or in the case of *Octubre rojo*, how it can be prevented in the future. Accordingly, he will be more susceptible to the author's (implicit or explicit) suggestion that by adopting his politically committed stance he can help resolve this unfair and inadmissible state of affairs.

By introducing real and popular figures the author heightens the factual appearance of the contents, a device used by most of the other authors examined. Whilst it is difficult to determine the authenticity of some of the characters which appear in the novel, Díaz Fernández includes important and well-known collaborators of the Revolution, for example, Teodomiro Menéndez, Belarmino Tomás, Ramón González Peña, General López Ochoa, José María Martínez, and Aida Lafuente 'La Libertaria'. Some of the right-wing figures referred to include Pedregal, Don Nicanor, and Alonso Nart. In addition the narrator refers to exact dates, times and other details such as the available arsenal ('Algunos de estos artefactos eran verdaderas máquinas infernales. Contenían dos paquetes de dinamita — unos cuarenta y dos cartuchos — y diez kilos de metralla hecha con recortes de varillas de acero' [p. 33]), which can be substantiated by consulting other sources. All of these verifying strategies, which aim to make the work credible, are a crucial element in the work if we take into account that Díaz Fernández was writing in order to impart a specific ideological message.

In the prologue to *Octubre rojo*, signed by Díaz Fernández, a summary of the events is provided, in which the factors that led to the armed insurrection are outlined. The opening paragraph, in which Díaz Fernández affirms that the socialists were mistaken in the timing of the Revolution, as society was not prepared and the bourgeois forces were too strong, clearly presents a partial stance. Thus, he is not concerned about demonstrating his impartiality, and whereas for the novel he is keen to hide his identity as the author, this is not the case for the prologue. For Díaz Fernández, 'los hechos históricos [. . .] son consecuencia siempre de hechos anteriores' (p. 9), justifying the historical résumé which he provides here. He begins with the downfall of Primo de Rivera and the monarchy, and goes on to explain the dominance of the moderate forces in the interim government before the Republic, attributing this mainly to the fear of Bolshevism; the 1931 elections which led to the left-wing republican majority; the failed agricultural and Church reforms of the Republican government, put down to the lack of courage of the socialists; the election of Alcalá Zamora as President of the Republic (highlighting in the process that he, as member of the Cortes, proposed an alternative candidate); the President's naming of Lerroux as head of the government in an attempt to lessen the influence of the left-wing majority; and the elections of 1933. He refers to the coalition of the right wing and the division of the left which led to the victory of the former, and the ensuing dismantling of the socialist reforms of the previous two and a half years. He recounts how the CEDA ended up being part of the government. Finally he explains how, following their election defeat, the socialists suddenly adopted a revolutionary attitude, one of the factors he most criticizes:

> Los socialistas habían reprimido con energía las reclamaciones impacientes de comunistas y anarquistas. Con un intervalo de muy pocos meses, los socialistas, no sólo rectificaban a fondo su táctica de siempre, sino que proclamaban la necesidad de la revolución social y trataban de improvisar el frente único proletario. Este frente único, en tales condiciones, era pura utopía. (p. 16)

In the second part of the prologue Díaz Fernández summarizes how the Alianza Obrera was formed, highlighting the fact that the anarchists were not willing to get involved except in Asturias and explaining why the revolutionary forces in many parts of Spain did not have the necessary support. In addition most of the socialist supporters were not used to revolutionary action and were thus unprepared. What Díaz Fernández censures most with regards to the leadership of the Revolution is the absence of a clear objective. When describing it, he examines why it only succeeded in Asturias:

> El minero asturiano es un obrero que, reuniendo las características del trabajador industrial, posee también el empuje primitivo del montañés. En las Casas del Pueblo está en contacto con las ideas revolucionarias, que llegan a través de la lucha de clases, pero no es de todos modos el obrero urbano que disfruta de algunas ventajas de la civilización; [. . .] Ignora lo que es el peligro, porque vive en el fondo de la tierra, expuesto al grisú y manejando a diario la fuerza devastadora de la dinamita. [. . .] Esto, unido a una gran disciplina sindical, adquirida en los viejos Sindicatos, hizo que la rebelión adquiriese una magnitud única. (pp. 20–21)

According to him, whilst at the start the revolutionaries successfully took many important towns, the lack of armament and clear military leadership prevented their absolute victory, a situation worsened by the increasingly divergent position of the individual revolutionary factions. He claims that the allegations of revolutionary destructiveness are false and that acts of cruelty were an exception. Finally, apart from criticizing his own side, Díaz Fernández denounces the depravity and selfishness of the reactionaries in society, the real traitors of the Revolution, who took advantage of the revolutionary defeat to gain control over the political power which they had not won legitimately during the elections:

> Frente a ellos [the real heroes of the Revolution], están sus calumniadores, los mismos que en octubre, temblando de pánico, se disfrazaban y se escondían, para después surgir blandiendo la venganza y la delación. Esa burguesía indigna que pide penas de muerte y hace de ellas un programa político, no puede despertar en las clases populares otra cosa que odio y repulsión. Hemos visto a ciertos hombres y ciertos partidos aprovechar la revolución de octubre para apoderarse de los Ayuntamientos, de la Diputación, de los organismos que el voto popular en su día les había negado y reponer en él al más viejo, inmundo y desacreditado caciquismo. Estos son los verdaderos saqueadores de la revolución. (p. 24)

Thus, the four dominant themes dealt with in the main narrative are brought up in the prologue: the bravery and integrity of the revolutionaries; the lack of preparation which hampered their efforts; criticism for the idealism and irresponsibility of the revolutionary leadership; and the greediness and hypocrisy of the wealthy and bourgeois right wing, who live in enviable conditions compared to the working class.

Acts of bravery abound in this novel. Paralleling real historical events, the narrator begins relating the Revolution as it spreads from Mieres, Campomanes, and Langreo to Oviedo. In Chapter 2, 'La lucha en Campomanes', we are introduced to the first of the characters, Gerardo Monje, in charge of the railway station at Linares where a train full of supplies is waiting to be requisitioned by the local Revolutionary Committee. As the first of the revolutionary characters to be portrayed, Monje displays many of the virtues conferred on the revolutionaries, including courageousness, determination, and rectitude. Conscious of the scarcity of food in Linares and in other nearby villages, Monje proceeds to distribute some of the food among the hungry villagers before handing the rest of the supplies over to the Committee. Three days later Monje decides to capture an enemy cannon which up to that point had been responsible for the deaths of many of his men. The chapter deals mostly with Monje's obsessive drive to silence the cannon, and indeed the miner dies in the process, failing to take it: 'El cañon [. . .] continuaba en lo alto de la loma, confabulado con los aviones de bombardeo para batir a los pueblos en armas' (p. 51). In this chapter pessimism already sets in: 'Los mineros presentían que el final de la lucha no podía ser otro que la derrota' (p. 43) a feeling which continues in the next chapter, 'Sabían que el total fracaso de la revolución les pisaba ya los talones' (p. 61), and throughout the account. And yet the narrator declares that there were many men who were willing to face death in the name of the Revolution: 'Había pelotones de jóvenes mineros con valentía y arrestos para enfrentarse con la muerte y ofrendar sus vidas a la revolución' (p. 44).

Once the Revolutionary Committees were established in Mieres and in Langreo, the politically symbolic Oviedo, regarded as the most important city in Asturias by the revolutionaries, became the focus of the fighting. Although after the first day of fighting the revolutionaries controlled a large part of the city, they had to endure four days of street fighting before being able to take the central core and reduce the defenders to a few isolated pockets: the barracks, the jail, the civil government building and the cathedral. The narrator depicts the heroic fighting in Oviedo in Chapter 6 ('Avance sobre Oviedo') by concentrating on the actions of another character, a miner called Feliciano Ampurdián, a 'dinamitero'.[40] This violent chapter recounts the taking of the town hall and the surrounding area, heavily defended by government soldiers. With the help of a number of volunteers and his dextrous use of dynamite, Ampurdián reaches the town hall. However, as he ascends the flight of steps to the first floor he is shot and killed. Despite being mortally wounded, 'Arrojando sangre por la boca, con la cara destrozada' (p. 91), the brave miner spurs on his comrades. His encouraging calls ensure the seizure of this key position: 'El grupo, lleno de rabia, subió disparando sus mosquetones. Varios guardias perecieron en la defensa y otros huyeron por las puertas laterales' (p. 91). Once taken, the town hall becomes the revolutionary headquarters.

As part of the positive depiction of the fighting revolutionaries, the narrator defends their justness during the Revolution, rejecting the right-wing claims that they were responsible for acts of cruelty and that they deliberately aimed to destroy the city. This is the case in Chapter 7, 'Oviedo en llamas', in which the narrator explains why the revolutionaries set alight some of the buildings. For example, in the case of the Banco Asturiano, the army were causing heavy casualties on the revolutionary side leading to the decision to set it on fire:

> Exasperados por estas bajas, los revolucionarios arrojaron contra el Banco, que estaba a una distancia de ocho o diez metros, latas de gasolina que entraban por las ventanas. Después lanzaron bombas cubiertas de algodón, también empapadas en gasolina. Al explotar las bombas, se inflamó la gasolina y así se produjo el incendio del edificio, que se propagó a toda la manzana. (p. 100)

In the case of the destruction of the University library, the narrator's explanation is especially interesting as it accommodates both the right and the left-wing versions of the explosion, a characteristic rarely observed in these texts:

> No se sabe si por la dinamita de los revolucionarios o por las bombas de los aviones. Una versión dice que una bomba aérea cayó en un laboratorio y produjo el incendio. Otra asegura que fue una explosión casual de la dinamita que los revolucionarios habían acumulado allí. (p. 101)

However, at no point does the narrator contemplate the government claim that the University was purposely blown up by the miners.[41] When he does admit unacceptable behaviour he attempts to justify it. For example, the pillaging and theft is justified by the hunger of the people, especially towards the last days of the Revolution: 'Muchos de los saqueos de aquellos días tuvieron su origen en el hambre y la impaciencia de las masas' (p. 42). Rather than present cruelty as a dominant trait of the revolutionary action, the narrator claims that the citizens of Oviedo, expecting to be on the receiving end of the brutality of the Marxist miners which the press had reported, were pleasantly surprised by their politeness and in some cases their kindness. Similarly, rather than kill the soldiers and Guards the revolutionaries choose to take them prisoner: ' — Al fin y al cabo — decía un minero —, sufren como nosotros' (p. 49).

Despite the bravery of the revolutionaries, their efforts were hampered by the lack of preparation and clear leadership, an issue which the narrator broaches from the start of the work, and the second of the main themes which he deals with. In nearly every chapter the narrator comments on this, whether it be regarding the lack of co-ordination, the shortage of armaments and military expertise, or the ineffectual control over the revolutionary troops. When describing the start of the mobilization on 5 October, the narrator depicts the frantic search for weapons in Mieres. Thus, as early as in Chapter 1 there is a reference to the lack of firearms, a problem which will be alluded to again and again as an indication of how badly prepared the Revolution was. When they take the factory of La Vega the miners are finally provided with plenty of weapons, 'armas largas, fusiles, mosquetones y rifles' (p. 102). However, their lack of control means that much of the ammunition is wasted, and yet again they face the same impossible situation in which they have nothing but dynamite to attack the army with. In Chapter 2 the narrator criticizes further the lack of organization: 'Los obreros luchaban desordenadamente, sin una organización regular, actuando por propia iniciativa. Apenas funcionaban los servicios de guerra más elementales' (p. 39). It is interesting to note that whereas Valdés, in his text, praised the individual initiative of the revolutionaries, Díaz Fernández affirms that this hampered the success of the Revolution, an example of how the varying political views of the authors are reflected in their interpretation of the events. Both men agree, however, that in spite of the lack of material, there were plenty of men willing to fight against the government forces, explaining the initial success of the insurrection. According to Díaz Fernández, the inadequacy of the organization meant that the fighters were faced constantly with the uncertainty of what would happen next, itself an obstacle: 'Aquello era la guerra, quizá más horroroso que la Guerra, porque faltaba la organización rígida de los ejércitos y todo denunciaba la improvisación trágica, la sorpresa alucinante, el no saber en ningún instante qué es lo que va a ocurrir' (p. 101). Due to the absence of clear leadership, arguments arise between the revolutionaries about the best course of action ('discutían furiosamente sobre lo que convendría hacer' [p. 57]), leading to improvisation, chaos, and delay.

The third theme of the work, also concerning the revolutionary leadership, is the criticism of its confidence that the Revolution would be successful. The narrator condemns those leaders who had encouraged the miners to fight without being aware of the catastrophic situation which was to occur, and the extent to which both revolutionaries and innocent people would suffer. He objects to the fact that the revolutionaries were told lies about their situation in the rest of Spain, both before and during the fighting, in order to encourage them to continue to fight.[42] The Asturian proletariat were made to believe that they really had a chance of winning the fight against the government and struggled hard to succeed.

Consequently, they had to face the crackdown which followed, while the political leaders and the members of the various Revolutionary Committees, who had incited them in the first place, were able to escape and avoid the backlash. The hopes of the fighters were raised to such an extent that, when the Revolution seems finally to have been defeated, after encouraging the masses to fight, nobody dares to tell them to surrender: 'Se había hecho creer que la revolución constituía el fin de sus dolores y sus miserias' (p. 152). The few criticisms directed at the revolutionary fighters arise when the narrator relates the creation of the second Revolutionary Committee in Chapter 12, 'Momentos difíciles'. According to him, following this: 'Los revolucionarios actuaban por su cuenta y toda iniciativa cuanto más temeraria y extremada que fuese, era bien recibida' (p. 164). Indeed he calls this stage of the Revolution 'el periodo del terror' (p. 164) as, exasperated, the miners become increasingly irrational and instead of using dynamite to fight with they use it to destroy the city so that the army will only find rubble. However, this is presented as only a symptom of their desperation and frustration kindled by the promises of their leaders.

The fourth and final issue dealt with by the author concerns the forces of reaction, and is present in all left-wing versions of the Revolution. The narrator criticizes the unfair socio-economic situation prior to the Revolution which provoked the miners into rebelling, as well as at the attitude of the bourgeoisie after the Revolution. Right from the beginning he illustrates the landscape and the difficult living conditions in which the miners, the workers and the townsfolk live:

> [Mieres] es un pueblo grande y negro, diseminado en la falda de una montaña, desde la cual le anuncia un resplandor rojo, el de las fábricas metalúrgicas. [. . .] Allí están también las casas obreras, pintadas de bermellón, donde al atardecer hormiguean los hombres vestidos de mahón, las mujeres despeluchadas y asténicas, con los grandes ojos enrojecidos por la temperatura del taller y de la escoria, y los chiquillos sucios, desgarrados, hostiles. (p. 29)

The essence of this description is repeated in other chapters dealing with places in which the Revolution had a great impact, such as in Chapter 5, 'Langreo':

> Langreo es un inmenso valle, a orillas del río Nalón, que corre sucio, desgarrado y espeso, en medio de unos pueblos apretados y oscuros, desparramados al azar en la falda de la montaña llena de caries y de túneles. [. . .] Desde Sama hasta Sotrondio, corre una inmensa prole de pequeños pueblos, donde se amontonan las casas estrechas, sucias, pitañosas, morada de numerosas familias obreras. (pp. 77–78)

These descriptions of poverty and overcrowding contrast enormously with that of Oviedo in Chapter 6, 'Avance sobre Oviedo', where the narrator explains the irresistible attraction of the forbidden city of Oviedo to the miners: 'La gran ciudad brillante y atractiva [. . .] Aquel foco de lujo, de comodidad, de vida fácil' (p. 87). The majestic city provides everything which the mining towns lack; indeed it is even described as the holiday place of the rich professional men, such as the engineers, the same men who make the miners' lives a misery and who do not have to bear the conditions which they themselves have helped to create. In the chapter on Langreo, the narrator refers to the novel written by Armando Palacio Valdés, *La aldea perdida* (1903), in which the author expresses his horror at the imminent industrialization of precisely the same area, Langreo, and of the negative repercussions which this would have on the peasant population. Palacio Valdés criticizes in his novel the violence and the drunkenness caused by the visits to the bar that had resulted from, according to him, the increased amount of money that the workers had to spend. On the other hand, in *Octubre rojo*, the narrator suggests that the living conditions of these families were so appalling, especially the overcrowding, that the men rather than go home after work preferred to congregate in the bar. It is precisely here where the miners and workers' solidarity has its origins: 'Los mineros aprendían los rudimentos de la solidaridad social' (p. 78). By concentrating on the huge differences between the living conditions of the wealthy and the poor, Díaz Fernández is hopeful that the reader will take up the politically committed stand which will eradicate this injustice and the political system which makes it possible and sustains it.

Díaz Fernández focuses on the distress which the Revolution caused on the innocent civilian victims, regardless of their political leanings, who were inevitably dragged into the fighting as their towns and villages were included in the battle zone. Along with the chapters which relate the course of the Revolution, there are others randomly introduced which provide anecdotal evidence of the horror of the confrontation. These episodes provide some interesting details about the fighting and the harrowing effects it has on the population. The first of such chapters is 'El tren blindado' (Chapter 3). Because of the number of enemy troops arriving in Asturias, the revolutionaries decide to send fresh troops to Campomanes in an armour-plated train. As there is no train driver who voluntarily agrees to drive the train, the revolutionaries call around the village houses until they find someone capable of doing the job. They force the unfortunate victim, married and with children, to drive the train and therefore join the Revolution, a move which the narrator criticizes and which sparks off the more general criticism of the way in which innocent individuals were forcibly enlisted.

The chapter which best conveys the situation faced by the innocent people is Chapter 4, 'En el hospital'. The wounded in Campomanes are taken to the hospital in Mieres, manned mainly by doctors and nurses in favour of neither fighting side, except for one socialist doctor, Patricio, who despite his political leanings, treats everybody equally. In this chapter the narrator describes the horrendous situations faced by some families as they or their family members are taken to hospital. He concentrates on the fate of seven victims, each one of which offers a different but equally tragic story. The first victim ends up in Mieres after a long and desperate search for her husband, a wounded Civil Guard. The narrator describes the woman's feelings towards the revolutionaries when she sees a group of them by the road side on the way to the hospital: 'Eran, sin duda, los que habían dado muerte a su esposo, los enemigos implacables de los guardias, los que habían dejado a su hijo a merced de la orfandad y la miseria' (p. 68). The lady does not consider whether the miners are right or wrong; what she is most worried about, like most other victims, is the fate of her husband as a human being, as a husband and as a father, and not as a soldier. She does not find her husband. Facing desperation, she tries to commit suicide by throwing herself over the edge of the banister in the hospital. The second victim is a small boy (eight to ten years old) who has a fever. His house was caught in the middle of a shooting range in Campomanes, where he lived with his parents. The family left their home and found shelter in a nearby house which was eventually also bombed. The boy has lost a leg, his father has died and his mother who is badly injured eventually dies: 'La madre murió en una de las salas bajas del edificio, sin saber que su hijo, suspirando por ella, estaba gravemente herido en una sala del piso superior' (p. 70). The third victim is a mother who comes in with her two children; she has been injured by machine-gun fire while she queued for bread. The fourth victim is a beggar called Pedro whose feet have been crushed by some falling rubble. The fifth story is that of a miner who has gone mad and who tries to bite his hands to shreds. Despite attempts to hold him down he continues with the 'espantosa autofagia' (p. 71). The sixth victim is Lucero (nineteen years old and a socialist) who was driving various revolutionaries to Mieres. One of these, convinced that they are being followed by the enemy troops, insists that Lucero drive quicker. Lucero cannot go any faster and as a result the revolutionary slits his throat. The revolutionary runs away in a fit of madness and Lucero drives on to the hospital in Mieres where he dies. He has bled to death. The seventh and final victim is Bautista. He takes his wife and two sons to the hospital. All three have been injured by an aeroplane machine gun. One of the sons eventually dies, leaving the father shocked ('quedó como petrificado' [p. 73]).

Clearly, these small individual stories are effective in humanizing a larger social situation. Most of the characters presented in this miscellaneous chapter are anonymous, and none of them have a face or a history. They are representative of a whole cluster of people involved in the conflict. The stories of all the characters which Díaz Fernández creates could be those of any of the many victims of the Revolution, making the conflict in Asturias universal and heightening the tragedy of the event. This is also the case of the fictional characters who make a more prolonged appearance in the work, such as Gerardo Monje (Chapter 2), 'El Roxu' (Chapter 3), and Feliciano Ampurdián (Chapter 6), who live and die within the boundaries of the chapter in which they appear. Along with the themes, the treatment of the non-fictional and fictional characters is representative of the ideological stance of the author. Although most of the characters appear only briefly in the account there are other characters which the narrator focuses on to a greater extent. For example, in Chapter 8, 'El médico rural', the protagonist is Ramón Tol, a non-fictional character who was not only a young doctor but also a socialist soldier and propagandist. The figure of the rural doctor who joins the revolutionary fight and instructs the peasants about the need to fight for their rights is present in other socially committed novels of the 1930s, such as César Arconada's *Reparto de tierras* (1934). Before the Revolution Tol spread information about Lenin and Marxism in the villages where he practised. He had helped the peasants in many different ways and was very popular among the villagers:

> Su marxismo era quizá puramente sentimental; pero soñaba con un mundo nuevo y una justicia superior. Cuando encontraba a los aldeanos, trabajando la tierra o cuidando el ganado, les gritaba:
> — ¿Sabéis que se va acabar la renta? Las tierras van a ser vuestras.
> Los aldeanos hacían un gesto escéptico, pero en el fondo pensaban que algo raro estaba ocurriendo cuando el médico, un señorito, hablaba de aquel modo. Estos aldeanos le amaban como nadie. Porque el médico, no sólo les acompañaba al Ayuntamiento y al Juzgado de la villa, para arreglarles sus asuntos y reñir, por ellos, con los curiales, sino que no les cobraba las visitas. (p. 120)

The general impression which the reader gets is that of an idealistic young man full of utopian ideals who is willing to do anything for the Revolution, a character profile which is reinforced in subsequent chapters dealing with the doctor. After the Revolution we are told that Tol was kept in hiding by the same peasants he had once helped until he managed to find his way to Portugal (the adventures are related in the last chapter of the novel, 'La huida').

Other chapters have less worthy characters as their protagonists. For example, Chapter 9, 'Prisioneros y fugitivos', gives a very sarcastic portrayal of Don Nicanor,[43] the chairman of one of the many banks destroyed. While Ramón Tol is described as being young and energetic, 'de aire optimista', intelligent, loved by the peasants, and willing to do anything for the Revolution, Don Nicanor is described in a derisory manner. When he is offered some biscuits and milk by the revolutionaries: 'Se lanzó sobre las galletas y alternándolas con grandes tragos de leche no daba paz a la boca' (p. 133). This chapter is worth elaborating on as it indicates what Díaz Fernández thought of the bourgeoisie. Don Nicanor is taken prisoner after a ruthless plane bombardment. When the head jailer orders the bank chairman to go and see him Don Nicanor thinks, along with the rest of the prisoners, that the time has come for their execution. He is pleasantly surprised however when he is offered the biscuits and milk. There is very little food to go round the prisoners and the prison guards; everybody is hungry. The head of the prison asks Don Nicanor to join the revolutionary side as they are in need of intellectuals who will endorse the Revolution, bribing him further with a cigar. He goes back to the cell and tells the rest of the prisoners what has happened, adding that he has been asked to collaborate with the new regime, a plea which Don Nicanor accepts as, after all, 'a última hora, uno es un técnico' (p. 134). In other words, the narrator is demonstrating the hypocrisy of the enemy side; they do not know what they are fighting for, and businessmen are concerned only about their own interests. When the prisoners hear that they too will receive some food, they think well of the revolutionaries. The banker once again manifests his greediness: 'A los pocos minutos las viandas se habían agotado, distribuídas [*sic*] equitativamente por Don Nicanor, entre los prisioneros' (p. 134). The one who has just helped himself to as much food as he wanted has now made himself responsible for distributing what is left. Another non-fictional character dealt with in detail is Teodomiro Menéndez who is arrested by the second Revolutionary Committee accused of attempting to escape and of treason. The narrator criticizes the persecution to which Menéndez was subjected and praises him for his warm-heartedness. Menéndez is one of the few leaders of the Revolution whom Díaz Fernández does not criticize as he too was against the Revolution.

There is one episode in particular in which Díaz Fernández manipulates his characters in order to praise the side which he supports. In Chapter 6 a fighting miner helps the sick son of a soldier who is fighting on the enemy side. He brings him a doctor and some milk and the boy recovers. One day he fails to visit the boy as he had done every day up to then. When the mother of the boy asks after him a colleague informs her that he had been shot that morning. It is interesting to note that in another contemporary account already examined in Chapter 5, *Caminos de sangre. Asturias la desventurada* (1934) written by Francisco Prada, a right-wing supporter, this same episode is related in a slightly different way. Instead of the man who brings the milk to the boy being a revolutionary, he is a Civil Guard.[44] We will never be certain which of the versions is the truthful one. Nevertheless, what is interesting about this episode is the fact that each individual author confers on his characters, even those which are supposedly real, a set of traits which are determined by the ideological stance of the work. In this way, 'a través de la perspectiva elegida el narrador orienta la actitud de los lectores hacia los personajes y las fuerzas que los mueven'.[45] The reader will be sympathetic towards Teodomiro Menéndez, while he will despise the hypocrisy of Nicanor; he will admire Ramón Tol's practical nature, compared to the irresponsible and naïve attitude of the communist leaders; and the compassion of the miner who saves the child's life by finding him milk will be held in high esteem, making the vindictiveness of the upper and middle classes who seek revenge after the Revolution all the more incomprehensible.

The final aspect which remains to be examined is the literariness of *Octubre rojo*, especially having established at the start that this is an important aspect of this work. Díaz Fernández includes some very evocative and effective descriptions, metaphors and images which not only add to the literary value of the text but which also help the reader imagine the horrific incidents witnessed by all those present in Asturias during October 1934. Thus he describes the destruction and the horrific scenes witnessed by the population: 'Un olor denso, donde el de la pólvora y los gases se mezclaba al de las calles, sucias de detritus, de cadáveres sin enterrar, de sangre coagulada, dominaba la atmósfera' (p. 100). Occasionally he shows the horrors of the war by focusing on the serious wounds sustained by the fighting men: 'Se llevó una mano a la cara y con su propia sangre se hizo una máscara espantable. Era la imagen viva del horror de la guerra' (pp. 104–05). The miners and the natural elements surrounding them are inextricably linked, so that when one miner dies the natural world also metaphorically suffers: 'Se le enterró en el monte, cerca de un arroyo, cuyas aguas bajaron muchos días mezcladas con sangre' (p. 48). This image is one which will crop up again and again throughout the account. Indeed it is one with which the account ends:

> Otros revolucionarios, que también habían huído por el monte, no tuvieron tanta suerte. La Guardia civil les persiguió incesantemente. Unos cayeron combatiendo y otros fueron capturados. Rotos, hambrientos, desamparados, fueron sucumbiendo sin gloria ni heroísmo. El Nalón y el Caudal, los dos ríos mineros, astrosos y lentos, llevan desde entonces en sus aguas la sangre de los parias, mezclada con la escoria y el carbón de la mina. (pp. 204–05)

Thus, the author ends with a sombre and pessimistic image which brings together coal (the mining industry and the miners), blood (the Revolution), and nature (the landscape), all emblematic elements of Asturias.

Nature is used to create other striking images, for example: 'Mientras el sol iba limpiando de oscuridades las montañas' (p. 45); 'El alba rompía la última tela de la noche otoñal [. . .] Los gallos rompían el cristal del aire con sus kikirikíes metálicos' (p. 200). The forces of nature are also used to describe the destruction and havoc caused by the war: 'La cuenca entera estaba en armas, desmandada, como un río en crecida que todo lo arrasa' (p. 31); 'La madrugada turbia, cenicienta, horrible, encontró amontonados aquellos falsos cadáveres que permanecieron allí muchas horas, mientras caían en las calles otros combatientes para no levantarse más' (p. 163); 'En el atardecer bituminoso, los rescoldos humeantes de los incendios, el paso asustado de algunos transeúntes, las esquinas estranguladas, las casas sangrando por sus flancos, todo ofrecía un aire pavoroso y cruento' (p. 187); 'Los montes estaban encharcados, los caminos convertidos en lodazales y el cielo lo surcaban nubes negras, hidrópicas, que amenazaban encallar sobre los campos desteñidos y pálidos' (p. 199). Animals and insects are also used: 'Seguido por los aviones que pretendían hincar sus granadas en el convoy como sus uñas dos pájaros de presa' (p. 61); 'En época normal los trenes mineros entran y salen en las explotaciones, como alimañas en sus madrigueras' (p. 77). The descriptions of some of the characters are striking: 'No era un hombre [Felicino Ampurdián], sino un monstruo, un aquilón mítico que sacudía el suelo como un terremoto' (p. 90), the narrator is comparing the action of the dynamite which Ampurdián uses with the miner himself. The Church is also the subject of Díaz Fernández's creative images: 'La sangre corría hacia las puertas santas en cuyos herrajes rebotaban las balas isócronamente' (p. 114); 'Esa torre, que llevaba siglos presenciando el paso pacífico de las nubes, de los vencejos y de los canónigos; sus piedras son los únicos testigos de los comienzos de la nacionalidad' (p. 114). Although, as pointed out by Castañar, the socially committed works, of which the revolutionary literature examined here forms part, were very much influenced by the political language used, there were a few which stood out for their creativeness and their literary merit. Clearly, while keeping in mind that Díaz Fernández wanted above all to provoke the reader to act rather than to reflect on the literary merit of his work, its literariness makes it one of these exceptions. While Díaz Fernández dealt with a topic which he felt especially strongly about, his sensitive use of figurative language and imagery are evidence that he kept in mind the literary value of his work just as he had proposed in *El nuevo romanticismo*.

These final two chapters conclude this study of the textual representations of the Asturian Revolution of 1934, in which I started off by examining the political texts (Chapter 3), followed by the testimonies and versions of the politicians, the military, the religious, and the revolutionaries (Chapter 4), and ending up with those works in Chapters 5 and 6 which, due to their style and contents are not easily defined as fiction or non-fiction, but are certainly more creative and novel-like than the texts in the first two chapters.

The versatility of the novel and its ability to adapt to different themes and styles means that the works dealt with here can be said to be a type, or sub-genre, of the novel. I have argued that they can be classified as non-fictional novels, a generic term used to classify certain novels written in North America in the late 1950s and 1960s, which I have defined and which can be described briefly as the fictional rendering of real events. Although I regard the four works studied as fictional in, amongst other things, their use of point of view, scenic reconstruction, and literary creativity, they are clearly not so in that they depict and inform about real events, which is why I have argued that they cannot be called novels (of the traditional kind). The basic critical problem with non-fiction material cast in the form of fiction is credibility; because these works reconstruct events instead of describing them and because they draw on a variety of techniques associated with fiction, questions about the writer's commitment to fact are invariably raised. For the novels of the Revolution this is an important consideration as the authors' power of conviction is based partly on the information which he or she presents. The authors' concern for the documentary and historical value of their work is evident and a number of strategies are employed to convince the reader of the truthfulness and reliability of the revolutionary account which they are providing, including the insertion of primary source material such as newspaper articles, references to interviews and conversations held with witnesses, and the incorporation of real characters and events easily recognized by the readership. The concern of the writers to express their political point of view is an equally important element of these works. In this respect the four novels examined here are particularly interesting as they each represent a different left-wing stance within the revolutionary side, making possible a comparison of how the events are manipulated or interpreted according to different political views.

Short Stories

Within the corpus of narrative texts dealing with the October Revolution there is a group of four left-wing stories, two by María Teresa León, 'Intelectual' and 'Liberación de octubre', one by César Muñoz Arconada, 'Xuan, el músico', and 'El guaje' by Ramón Sender, and, written from an ideological perspective which is diametrically opposed to these three authors, 'El Dios de los niños' by Concha Espina.[46] As well as dealing with the actual violence, in this group of short stories the Revolution is used as a backdrop for considering the injustices faced by women and other vulnerable sectors in society, such as children and the physically disabled. In the case of León, Arconada, and Sender the expected condemnation of a thoroughly unjust society is intensified by the denunciation of the defencelessness and lack of future prospects of these particularly vulnerable individuals. On the other hand, Concha Espina longs for the times when Asturias was a predominantly rural and agricultural society with a strong community spirit. Despite her right-wing stance, she is critical of Spain's increasing industrialization and the individualism that accompanies capitalism.[47] While the three left-wing authors look to the socialist Revolution as an answer to the problems of the proletariat, Concha Espina turns to religion and traditional patriotism as an answer to the problematic social situation, which she calls a 'trastorno social' (p. 38). The fact that these stories were composed in 1936, in the case of the left-wing texts and a bit later, 1938, in the case of Concha Espina,[48] may explain why the authors deal first and foremost with the general issues, as opposed to the more specific details of the Revolution. What is important at this moment in which the authors are writing, with the Civil War if not already broken out then about to, is to present their ideological credentials. However, although the October Revolution is not the salient issue, the fact that it is chosen as the backdrop reflects its importance as a historical and political event in the minds of the authors. So, in 'Liberación de octubre', Rosa, a bored and childless housewife finds in the Revolution a chance for freedom; in 'Intelectual' Paco, a school teacher who lives with his aging spinster sisters, sees the Revolution, just as Rosa does, as a way to liberate himself from his dull and monotonous life, joins it and is finally executed; Xuan, in 'Xuan, el músico', is also executed for playing the *International* on his harmonica, his only means of earning a living following an accident when he was a miner in which he lost an arm; and the boy in 'El guaje' although forced to live an adult life is too young and innocent to fear for his life and oblivious to the fact that unless he runs away he will be executed. On the other hand, 'El Dios de los niños' relates how a group of children attending a religious school miraculously survive an explosion, and how, due to the dramatic circumstances triggered off by the Revolution, two complete strangers, Xuaco, a peasant, and Julia, a widow, are brought together — another miracle. Concha Espina offers the point of view of a traditionalist, a monarchist, and above all a Christian who attempts to find a positive side to the regrettable violent episode.

While the documentary nature of many of the longer narrative texts makes their fictional status questionable, in the case of the short stories examined here all except for Sender's are clearly invented. 'El guaje' resembles the longer texts more than the other short stories as Sender converts an anecdote, which he claims to have been given by a witness,[49] into a story (albeit brief), complete with descriptions and dialogue, making it more realistic and consequently more shocking. Indeed, the everyday issues which form part of these stories, and which are applicable to the lives of many of the readers, makes them more striking and more accessible. Although the specific details are not necessarily true to life, the familiar feelings that are elicited, along with the very real revolutionary backdrop, make the stories and the experiences of the characters more credible. Thus, the authors' analyses of the characters enable the reader to see them as real people, not just as fictional beings, and to understand and sympathize with their feelings. In this way, Rosa's concerns as she confronts her barrenness and faces rejection by her husband, aggravated by the fact that she is getting older and will not be fertile much longer, are feelings that some women may have identified with. Certainly every woman reading this story would be aware of the importance of a woman's childbearing capacity. Similarly, most Spanish men, fruit of a predominantly male-chauvinist society, would have understood why Ramón's inability to make Rosa pregnant could have occasioned his sense of failure. The fact that this story (as well as the others) deals with wider issues reflects the belief that the October Revolution and the Civil War were prompted not only by hunger and poverty but also by a search for a change in the political and social structure of the country. Accordingly, the main message which runs through this story is that with a new revolutionary government brought about by the worker's movement, in which women need to have participated, not only will the class struggle have been won but also the battle for women's liberation.

The second of León's stories, 'Intelectual', also has important female characters, although the issue of women's liberation is not the primary concern in the story. Here, León tells the story of two lonely spinster sisters, Amada and Florentina, who live with their brother, Francisco. Whilst the first of León's stories deals with the liberation of women, the second of her stories is more concerned about Paco's liberation from his two pious sisters who, isolated from the world outside and from politics, misunderstand what the Revolution is about and merely associate it with fear and an absence of food: 'Aisladas, el miedo y la angustia se habían sentado con ellas. Se acabó la harina y requisaron su cosecha de castañas. Estas fueron sus relaciones con la revolución' (p. 54). Tragically, despite their non-involvement the government soldiers senselessly kill the two women. Unlike Rosa in the first of León's stories, who joins the Revolution, Florentina and Amada are victims of the Revolution, perhaps because of their reluctance or inability to understand it.

The vulnerability of certain groups in society is one of the constant themes in all of these short stories. Sender and Arconada deal with the innocent status of children and the physically disabled respectively. Sender's story, based on real events, tells how government soldiers in the village of Villafría arrest a group of men. Amongst these is a boy about fifteen years old. As the soldiers prepare to execute the men, the boy tells the officer in command that his baby brother is at home alone. The officer, who feels sorry for the boy, tells him he has eight minutes to take the baby to a neighbour, hoping that on the way he will escape. Nevertheless, the boy returns, calmly and fearlessly, 'con esa serenidad que se tiene a los quince años para lo trágico' (p. 101): 'Entonces apareció bajando por la colina, con el paso seguro y tranquilo, el «guaje». Había oído las descargas, estaba viendo transportar los muertos y rematar los heridos. Y seguía avanzando, impasible' (p. 102). The boy is finally shot along with the other men. Sender demonstrates how this boy, who works down the mine and looks after his baby brother in the absence of his dead mother and father, has been forced by the circumstances to be treated like an adult. Ironically, his innocent and childlike character becomes evident when he fails to comprehend the dangerous situation he is in and misses the only opportunity he will have to save his life. On the one hand, Sender draws attention to the callousness of the soldiers who are even prepared to execute a fifteen-year-old boy, and to the severity of the repression which many workers, whether actually guilty or merely suspects, were subjected to. On the other hand, he touches on the more general issue of the difficulties faced by the poor and disadvantaged in an unjust society in which young children need to work down the mine in order to subsist.

Also vulnerable, Arconada's protagonist is an old ex-miner who, after losing an arm in a mining accident, has had to find another means of survival. Xuan now depends fully on the charity of other people to feed his wife and three children and earns money by playing the harmonica in bars and fiestas at the request of the clients. While initially he is asked to play folk songs and jigs as time passes by and the Revolution gets closer the *International* becomes the favourite request. Xuan plays the communist anthem, even though he is aware of the possible grave consequences, as it is his only livelihood. The sight of all his friends going off to fight eventually convinces the ex-miner of the significance of the Revolution. However, because of his disability he cannot physically contribute and chooses instead to play the emblematic song for his absent friends: 'De día y de noche, en la casa o en la huerta, Xuan tocaba, tocaba continuamente, sin fin y sin descanso, como si con ello tratase de comunicarse con los lejanos amigos que luchaban más allá de las montañas' (p. 205). Despite his absence from the battlefront two soldiers, who hear him play the *International*, feel that this defiant gesture signals his support for the Revolution, warranting his execution.

For Concha Espina the whole of the working class, exposed to the inhumane capitalist system and ignored by a government which has forgotten 'la práctica generosa del puro Cristianismo' (p. 14), is vulnerable to the propagandistic initiatives of the revolutionary movement: 'Hay demasiadas criaturas envenenadas por la perfidia negra de otros muchos hombres' (p. 17). Essentially, Espina believes that the Revolution, carried out by ignorant people, has been incited by greed and vanity and is therefore an act against Christianity:

> Muchos saben que los hombres malignos [. . .] excitan la ignorancia de los hermanos insolventes para que imaginen unas vanidades tremendas. Y procuran realizarlas con los procedimientos más viles: sacrificar, demoler, destruir la historia y la civilización, erigir el odio en las almas. (p. 24)

The brainwashing power of communist ideology, 'los mandamientos emperatrices que anulan su [the miner's] conciencia' (p. 29), is also alluded to in some of the longer right-wing texts and it is the counter-revolutionary way of explaining why the majority of workers decide to join the Revolution. Accordingly, Espina accuses the political parties of cheating on the workers and refers to the hypocrisy of the revolutionary leaders who leave the workers to bear the brunt of a situation that they have incited. At the end of 'El Dios de los niños' the narrator relates how Xuaco sees a fat man in a luxurious car drive off with his pocket full of cheques, 'un «señor» gordo y cobarde, con largos cheques en el bolsillo' (p. 45). This is a reference to González Peña, the socialist 'generalísimo' of the Revolution.

While Espina believes that working-class support for the Revolution is a negative result of people's vulnerability to the propagandistic initiatives of the political parties, León demonstrates in her stories the important role of propaganda in informing the workers of the need for a proletariat revolution. For León the fact that all workers and intellectuals should join the Revolution is of the utmost importance. In both of her stories she deals with the resentment felt by those who belong to one particular social class and who wish they belonged to another. In 'Liberación de octubre' the cause of Ramón's bitterness is his failure to become an engineer and consequently of enhancing his social status by moving up the social ladder, 'su derrota de aspirante a la pequeña burguesía' (p. 10).[50] According to León what is important is an understanding of the revolutionary movement. Thus, when Ramón's wife joins the Revolution she is not only liberating herself from the traditional woman's role, but also from the resentment felt towards her working-class status, caused by her political ignorance. At the end of the story Rosa realizes that she belongs to the proletariat and this allows her to take a positive stance and join the Revolution, changing in this way her up to then pessimistic outlook on life. León implies that if Ramón had understood the revolutionary movement he would not have yearned to move up the social ladder. On the other hand, in 'Intelectual' Paco, a teacher, belongs to the middle class. This apparently advantageous social position turns out to hinder his involvement in the Revolution as he does not know how to shoot a rifle or how to handle dynamite like the other revolutionaries. After the frustration of not being able to take part in the fight, 'tan necesitado de revoluciones como los otros, tan proletario, tan valiente' (p. 59), Paco is finally given a chance to contribute by writing political pamphlets. Thus León's portrayal of Paco contrasts sharply with Espina's image of the evil propagandist intent on poisoning vulnerable minds.

Although I have concentrated primarily on aspects which differentiate these short stories from their longer narrative counterparts, it is also important to note that there are clear similarities, the most obvious of which are the ideological insinuations that arise in the texts. For the communist authors the revolutionaries are heroic and the Revolution a chance to free the proletariat from the grasp of greedy capitalists and the Church, while for Concha Espina the miners are monsters who have been convinced to destroy everything in society and everyone not on the side of the Revolution, which is in turn an attempt by the satanic communist forces to dominate Spanish minds. Most works written around this conflictive period, be they long or short, prose or poetry, recognize the importance of political commitment — refuge cannot be found in neutrality. For one side, the mere fact of belonging to the working class or the peasantry is enough to deem you a revolutionary in the eyes of the government and the repressive forces, whilst the other side maintains that the bourgeoisie, the Church, and the forces of order are the favourite targets of the evil revolutionaries. José Zapata, the Mexican who writes the Preface to León's collection, refers to the growing need to choose between the political sides in the increasingly polarized Spanish society,[51] a consideration that was specially relevant on the advent of the Civil War. The split in Spanish society is especially discernible in the left-wing stories in which the notion of 'ellos' and 'nosotros' emerges. For example, Rosa is finally convinced by the idea of 'nuestra libertad', while Xuan's wife Martina refers to the revolutionaries as 'nuestros' and to the government soldiers as 'ellos': '«Ellos» eran la muerte que llegaba, los tiros hechos personas, el horror hecho fuerza gubernamental' (p. 206). It is also interesting to note that apart from dividing Spanish society into two, this use of possessive and personal pronouns serves an additional purpose, that is, to include the reader in the revolutionary group and ensure that the latter identifies with the messages conveyed.

As with the longer novels, the short stories refer to and are critical (or laudatory) of the Church and the army, the Church for its negative (or positive) influence on the background of the characters, and the army for its repressive (or liberating) action during the Revolution. If we deal first with the representation of the Church, in 'Liberación de octubre' the narrator accuses the Church of ruining Ramón's ambition to become an engineer, alluding to the more general criticism of the Church's control over people's lives. Rosa's religious experience has not been altogether positive either. She has a flashback in which she remembers her priest during confession having no objections to her licking his hand, 'las únicas manos blancas entre tantas terrosas como lagartijas en medio del sol de las eras' (p. 13). León criticizes the easy life that the village priests enjoy in comparison with their congregations and, at the same time, demonstrates their vulgarity and lack of morality, dismissing the values of the Church as hypocritical. Whilst for León the Church destroys lives, for Concha Espina God and Christianity help to create them, such as when the children trapped in the collapsed school miraculously survive.

The misconduct of the army also provides the left-wing authors with a source of criticism, especially in the stories that touch on the revolutionary defeat. In 'Xuan, el músico' and in 'Intelectual' the Moorish soldiers and Foreign Legion are represented as horrific and cruel. Arconada describes the soldiers who arrive to take Xuan away as 'dos tíos fuertes, foscos y mal encarados, como criminales en una encrucuijada' (p. 206), whilst in 'Intelectual' León describes how Amada is stabbed to death as she holds on to the soldier's shoulders and neck:

> Sintió un calor húmedo resbalarle por los costados [. . .]. Las manos seguían ciñendo el cuello, los brazos colgaban cortados sobre el pecho del hombre que los tiró violentamente a un rincón. Ella se sintió vaciar y notó cómo desaparecía de la vida. (p. 62)

In Sender's story, the sight of the young boy arouses the compassion of the officer in charge, 'esa voz que cuida de establecer en todos los casos, dentro del más ruin, las gradaciones de la vileza, habló a sus sentimientos' (p. 101). However, his initial clemency is overridden by his sense of duty and the boy is finally executed along with the other men. Espina does not deal directly with the army, but in the introduction to her collection she clearly demonstrates her support for the armed forces when she praises their performance in the Civil War.[52] Indeed, she blames all the destruction, which she so effectively describes in her story, on the action of the bombs and dynamite of the miners and claims that as the battle gets more desperate for the revolutionaries, 'Las últimas faenas de los rebeldes adquirían un satánico frenesí. [. . .] sacerdotes asesinados, autoridades quemadas a fuego lento; bibliotecas, aulas y joyas destruídas. . .' (p. 27). Accordingly, the violence and savagery of the revolutionaries are alleged to be the cause of the repression that ensued after the Revolution:

> Y los vencidos, que huyen, dejan paso a un clamor de loca impaciencia, a unas lamentaciones punzantes, mezcladas de improperios y augurios del castigo, profecías salvajes contra el malhechor; que así reacciona el pueblo acometido, para defenderse como un animal selvático. (p. 34)

Espina, who writes in 1938, is thus excusing the repression that was so fiercely criticized by influential intellectuals throughout 1935 and 1936.

What stands out in all of these short stories is their uncomplicated nature, which does not mean that they are lacking in literary value. The stories tend to have few characters and linear plots. Any background information, for example regarding the characters' past, is integrated into the storyline by means of flashbacks, economising in this way on the space, which is essentially limited in the case of the short story. In this way, although 'Liberación de octubre' is set on the night of 4 to 5 October, without the storyline leaving the night the Revolution breaks out, the reader is informed of Rosa and Ramón's background, explaining their outlook on life.[53] In her other story León interpolates in the story of the two sisters, which spans one day, that of Paco which reveals his background as a teacher and his more recent contribution to the Revolution. The two subplots do not converge until the end, with the death of the three characters. Arconada, who chooses to start his story before the Revolution, sketches out Xuan's impoverished life following a mining accident. Halfway through the story Xuan's apolitical attitude changes with the start of the Revolution, which finally claims his life. One striking similarity in these three left-wing stories is the despondency felt toward the Revolution by the protagonists and their subsequent relief and sense of accomplishment when they choose to join it. Espina's story is slightly different in that she begins with a descriptive summary of Oviedo's foundations in order to illustrate the change that the city and its citizens have undergone throughout the ages and explain the current conflicts in society. After her ideologically charged résumé, Espina's story, which deals with a concrete incident within the Revolution, also follows a linear plot that spans no more than a few days.

Apart from their uncomplicated structure, the stories are concerned with real people and with human predicaments which every reader will able to identify with. For example Espina is careful to introduce into her group of characters a peasant, a schoolteacher, and two working mothers, thereby implying that those on the side of the government forces are not necessarily all middle- and upper-class citizens; she hopes to round up support from the working class too: 'La indignación y el desaliento combaten al auditorio, compuesto de burgueses trabajadores y sencillos, con añadidura de algún proletario de orden, que también los hay, y muy abundantes por la gracia divina' (p. 18). Dialogue is used by these authors, thereby bringing the characters to life. In addition, the dialogue on many occasions is colloquial and shows elements of Asturian dialect: Xuan says to those who want him to play the *International* on his harmonica, 'Vosotros queréisme mal, muchachos. ¿Y si óyenme?' (p. 204), and in 'El Dios de los niños' a woman asks Julia when she screams, 'Pero, ¿qué ye nena? ¿Duélete mucho?' (p. 26). In this way the authors hope that their readers will identify more fully with the characters and the story in general.

One thing that stands out in these short stories is their literary quality, in which metaphors, imagery and figurative language abound. We must of course keep in mind that while some of the longer texts were not necessarily composed by professional writers, these five stories are the creation of famous and critically acclaimed authors. Arconada and Sender, whose stories are shorter, wrote theirs for the newspaper *Ayuda*.[54] León's story is included in a collection probably composed before the Civil War[55] and Espina included her story in a collection written towards the end of the Civil War. The urgency of the first three authors, as politically committed writers, to add their voice to the escalating criticisms directed at the socio-political situation, is less relevant in the case of Espina who wrote 'El Dios de los niños' towards the end of the Civil War, when the victory of the Nationalists was almost certain. This accounts for the sometimes complicated literary technique which Espina employs and the detailed information which she includes, such as the historical details of Oviedo and the various biblical references, all of which indicate, if not careful research, then at least ample general knowledge.[56] In most parts in which Espina makes use of this knowledge, the syntax and vocabulary become more complicated, as demonstrated in this example:

> Y sólo un número selecto de individuos siente y ve con diafanidad las verdades augustas de la vida. Que aún fluye la secular Fuencalada en el pecho de las calles modernas, igual que una voz de perenne rumbo, con la Cruz de la Victoria en el ápice de sus once siglos.
>
> Alguien se inclina, todavía, con fe, a escuchar en el quedo son de tales aguas un eterno manantío de salud, una bendita promesa a los que cumplen los mandamientos de Dios. (p. 15)

In these cases the story's accessibility to a wide readership is reduced. The complexity, however, is limited to the descriptive sections and the plot remains simple and, for the most part, accessible to most.

Both León's and Arconada's stories merge the revolutionary literary style with the avant-garde techniques, in vogue in the twenties and practiced especially by the latter. While the metaphors are not banished altogether, they are simplified and made more intelligible in order to reach the desired audience. In this example Arconada personifies the earth: 'Un desprendimiento de tierras, dentro de una mina, se había llevado su brazo derecho arrancándoselo de una dentellada, con esa ferocidad que la tierra cabada [*sic*] y agujereada tiene para los mineros' (p. 203). The terms of reference are accessible, familiar, and rooted in everyday social life. All four authors treat the descriptions of the countryside and the elements delicately, and sometimes link them to the violence, such as in this example, taken from 'El Dios de los niños':

> La tarde solar, al extinguirse, pone en las nubes un bello color ambarino, como el zumo fresco de las manzanas. Acaso miles de quintales de pomas fermentan su caldo en el cielo porque ya no quede en el país un campo libre y dulce para la mies de los licores. (p. 28)

In others the mere description of the countryside, the sky or even the sea is meritorious, as in this example from 'Xuan, el músico':

> Entonces, cuando ya no podía trabajar, se fue hacia la costa, en busca del mar y el límite, donde el agua azul de los confines trae constantes y amplias músicas de misterio. La costa y el horizonte abierto y la luz sin umbrales terminaron por enterrar aquello que en él había de negrura, de tenebrosidad, de fondo triste de mina. (p. 203)

Occasionally the difference between silence and noise is highlighted, with silence not necessarily being the most welcome of the two:

> Por la noche, aún más, [los tiros] golpeaban el silencio en todo el ámbito, haciendo ladrar a los perros y llorar a los niños. Algunas veces se oían como pisadas por las piedras resbaladizas de lluvia y musgo. Y voces. Y gritos y llantos ahogados, perdidos, hundidos en nuevos silencios pavorosos.[57]

The story that incorporates the least literary resources is that of Sender, mainly because of its brevity and the nature of the story, based on a real account. However, even here there is literary merit to be found. In this example Sender describes the hands of the soldiers as they meet the trigger: 'Cuando las manos de los «regulares» bajaron por el cañón hacia el cerrojo y los fusiles buscaron la horizontal' (p. 101).

An important element of figurative language, used by the authors to convey their ideological message, is symbolism. For example, in León's 'Liberación de octubre' the narrator confers a special significance on the drunkard whom Rosa sees shouting revolutionary slogans and who, in an attempt to climb a lamp-post, falls and bangs his head, leaving a puddle of blood around him. In my view this is symbolic of the Revolution and in the story acts as a premonition of what will happen. The slogans shouted by the man are those shouted by the working class during the revolutionary days, the climbing up of the lamp-post represents the initial revolutionary success, with the final fall of the drunkard being that of the revolutionary movement. The blood spilt by the drunkard is, in that case, representative of that spilt by all the revolutionaries in the ensuing repression. 'El Dios de los niños' also contains elements of symbolism. In line with the religious slant given to the story, for Concha Espina, the *pueblo* represents Jesus Christ, both of which have been sacrificed: 'En Asturias se incendia, se roba y se asesina. Después los cobardes tratarán de esconderse, y el pueblo quedará crucificado y vendido como Jesús en el Gólgota' (p. 24). In the same way, the children who miraculously survive are represented as angels, 'querubes o pájaros aselados milagrosamente en las ramas oscuras del terremoto' (p. 37). The narrator describes what witnessing this 'resurrection' has meant for Xuaco, again using the religious terminology that abounds in the story:

> Sólo aquella luz blanca del cielo le da un poco de estímulo, porque la relaciona con la ráfaga de candidez puesta en la oscuridad como un efluvio celeste durante el salvamento maravilloso de los colegiales.
>
> Imagina el hombre haber asistido en aquel episodio a toda una glorificación del bien y la salud. Era que los capullos nuevos renacían de la pestilencia humana sobre las cenizas y los estertores de la muerte. La ciudad agónica y convulsa daba a luz una esperanza inefable. (p. 40)

The use of symbolism is one way in which the authors can manipulate the literary language and create meaningful messages. For this reason most of the images which appear in these stories are symbolic.

Essentially, what these short stories show is that, just as with the longer narrative texts, the ideological position of the author determines the contents and, to a certain extent, the style of the story. In these stories the Revolution appears as the backdrop to the more general socio-political concerns, while in the longer, and for the most part earlier, texts the opposite is the case; the general issues appear as essential elements but within the main subject of the Revolution. The five stories examined are tragic, where the central themes are the fight for survival and the class struggle. For Concha Espina, religion, patriotism, and tradition are of paramount importance, and her short story, in which a miracle forms the crux of the plot, praises the value of the Church and criticizes the brainwashing power of the communists and the unfortunate greed which the growing industrialization of the once peaceful region of Asturias has brought. The other three authors deal with more human aspects in which the trials and tribulations of women, men and children who live in a society which is governed by an unjust class structure are revealed. The ideological beliefs of the authors are transparently clear, obvious when taking into account that the purpose of these texts is to praise the heroes and criticize the enemy. Although some of the short stories do not openly advocate revolutionary, or counter-revolutionary action, they do insist on the political commitment of the reader and, as clearly demonstrated by León, allude to the dangers of not embracing a defined political stance in those days of conflict in Spain.

1. The collection *La Novela Libre*, of which *Heroínas* formed part, was edited by 'Ediciones de la Revista Blanca', directed by Montseny's parents.
2. José Esteban and Gonzalo Santonja, *La novela social 1928–39: figuras y tendencias* (Madrid: Ediciones La Idea, 1987).
3. The titles which I have so far come across are: Dolores Ibárruri, *¡A la cárcel los verdugos de octubre!* (Madrid: Ediciones Prensa Obrera, 1936), which I have been unable to find in any library; María Luisa Carnelli, *UHP: mineros de Asturias* (Buenos Aires: Talleres Gráficos Weiss, 1936); Consuelo Bergés, *Explicación de octubre: historia comprimida de cuatro años de República en España* (Madrid: Imp. Garcigay, 1935), examined in Chapter 3; Margarita Nelken *¿Por qué hicimos la revolución?* (Barcelona; Ediciones Sociales Internacionales, 1936); and Elizabeth Leah Manning, *What I Saw in Spain* (London: Victor Gollancz, 1935).
4. *La Novela Ideal* started off with a print-run of 10,000 copies every week, increasing to 20,000 and later on to 50,000. The novels were against religion, and contained libertarian propaganda in favour of free love and against social prejudices. *La Novela Libre*, a monthly publication, was founded later and managed to have a print-run of 20,000 copies. *El Mundo al Día* was an illustrated magazine.
5. Indeed, about the guerilla forces, Taibo writes: 'No hay noticias de acciones defensivas y mucho menos de acciones ofensivas. Más que intentar mantener núcleos de resistencia guerrillera, los huidos trataron de ganar tiempo antes de esconderse, de ganar tiempo a la represión en las montañas mientras se podía organizar el escondite o la huida, o descendía el furor de la represión.' Paco Ignacio Taibo, *Asturias 1934*, 2 vols (Gijón: Jucar, 1984), II, 100.
6. Federica Montseny, *Heroínas*, in *Novelas breves de escritoras españolas (1900–1936)*, ed. by Angela Ena Bordonada (Madrid: Editorial Castalia, 1989), pp. 423–97 (p. 426, footnote 4).
7. Federica Montseny, *Mis primeros cuarenta años* (Barcelona: Plaza y Janes, 1987), pp. 79–80.
8. Louise Michel (1830–1905) was an anarchist who fervently preached social revolutionary ideals. She fought with the National Guard defending the Paris Commune against the Versailles troops in 1871. Her influence on Federica Montseny is described by Montseny herself during an interview recorded in Toulouse and transcribed for the prologue of the Spanish edition of Louise Michel's *La Commune*. The whole transcription can be found in Carmen Alcalde, *Federica Montseny: palabra en rojo y negro* (Barcelona: Editorial Argos Vergara, 1983), pp. 38–45.
9. Ibid., p. 41.
10. Ibid., pp. 39, 43, and 42 respectively.
11. Many of the collaborators of *La Novela Proletaria* were anarchist militants, such as Angel Pestaña, Eduardo Guzmán, Mauro Bajatierra, Emilio Mistral.
12. Fulgencio Castañar, *El compromiso en la novela de la II República* (Madrid: Siglo XXI, 1992), pp. 110–16.
13. Castañar quotes J. Llanus: 'La necesidad sentida de que las ideas de emancipación obrera traspasasen los límites del periódico de combate, del folleto y aún del libro en forma didáctica presentada, para invadir el terreno de la novela, del teatro, del esparcimiento en todas sus manifestaciones, a fin de difundir en ellas las ideas de libertad, igualdad y

fraternidad humanas que deban señalar el avance de los pueblos hacia su perfeccionamiento moral, material e intelectual, verdadera síntesis del progreso y de la civilización.' Castañar, p. 113.

14. Ibid., p. 114.
15. The 'escuelas racionalistas' were founded in 1901 by the anarchist pedagogue Francisco Ferrer i Guàrdia, who was executed following the events of the 'Semana Trágica' of Barcelona, in 1909.
16. In her autobiography Montseny writes: 'Siempre he querido mucho a los animales, y perros y gatos me han costado muchas lágrimas. En ellos, por lo demás, encontré siempre una extraordinaria correspondencia de sentimientos.' Federica Montseny, *Mis primeros cuarenta años*, p. 34.
17. Two of the other most important principles were education free of political and religious dogma, and mixed classes where boys and girls were taught the same lessons.
18. In his *Discours sur l'Origine et les Fondements de l'Inégalité parmis les hommes* (1755) Rousseau claims that the original man, while admittedly solitary, was healthy, happy, good, and free. The vices of men, he argues, date from the time when men formed societies.
19. Bordonada, introduction to *Novelas breves de escritoras españolas*, p. 24.
20. Ibid., p. 23.
21. Soledad Gallego-Díaz, 'Entrevista en Toulouse, con Federica Montseny', *Cuadernos para el Diálogo*, 29 (1976), 15–17 (p. 17). Carmen Alcalde refers to another interview, by Antonia Rodrigo, for the book *Mujeres de España* (Barcelona: Planeta, 1979), in which Montseny reveals the qualities which she admires most in a woman and in a man: 'De los hombres admiro la honestidad, la rectitud y el valor personal. De las mujeres, el espíritu de iniciativa, la rebeldía, y el afán de no ser sometidas, de no ser demasiado dóciles y admiro también las que saben encontrar un equilibrio entre lo que podemos llamar nuevas ideas y un cierto mantenimiento de la femineidad que, en cierta manera, es consustancial a la naturaleza de la mujer: el amor a los hijos, el gusto por la vida, por la casa, el saber hacer comidas, en una palabra, saber hacer la vida agradable a las personas que te rodean.' Alcalde, pp. 26–27.
22. Bordonada, p. 50
23. Castañar, p. 114.
24. This was the number of copies printed of each weekly issue of *La Novela Libre*, of which *Heroínas* was one.
25. According to Bécarud and Campillo, after 1933, anarchist writing expressed its mistrust of the intellectuals: 'Considerado como un traidor de clase potencial, [. . .] se procura no sólo minimizar su papel en la futura sociedad libertaria, sino hacerlo desaparecer radicalmente suprimiendo la distinción entre trabajo manual e intelectual, fuente de la reestructuración de la dominación.' J. Bécarud and E. López Campillo, *Los intelectuales españoles durante la II República* (Madrid: Siglo XXI, 1978), p. 96.
26. Gareth Thomas, *The Novel of the Spanish Civil War (1936–1975)* (Cambridge: Cambridge University Press, 1990), p. 26.
27. Castañar, p. 111.
28. 'Todos optaron por no llamar la atención sobre su estilo, sino hacia el contenido, con la esperanza de que ayudarían a sus conciudadanos a vivir mejor.' Castañar, p. 405.
29. According to Lee Gutkind: 'In real life [. . .] people communicate with spoken words.' Therefore, 'by recording conversation, the creative nonfiction writer captures reality'. Lee Gutkind, *The Art of Creative Nonfiction: Writing and Selling the Literature of Reality* (New York: John Wiley and Sons, 1997), pp. 21–23.
30. Castañar, p. 422.
31. José Díaz Fernández, *El blocao* (Madrid: Historia Nueva, 1928); *La Venus mecánica* (Madrid: Renacimiento, 1929); and *El nuevo romanticismo* (Madrid: Zeus, 1930).
32. Shortly after the first edition of *El blocao* was published a second edition had to be brought out due to its popularity.
33. *La largueza*, in *Las siete virtudes* (Bilbao: Espasa Calpe, 1931) and 'Cruce de caminos', *La Novela de Hoy*, 462 (20 March 1931). Both of these works appear in Díaz Fernández's bibliography included in José Esteban and Gonzalo Santonja, *Los novelistas sociales españoles (1928–1936): antología* (Barcelona: Anthropos, 1988), p. 307.

34. Castañar quotes from an interview with Díaz Fernández, published in *Letra* (8 February 1935), in which he affirms: 'Del mismo modo que hube de reaccionar contra aquella epidemia de los «ismos» que tantos estragos hizo en nuestra juventud, rechazaré el exclusivismo de este arte proletario que nos quieren pasar un poco de contrabando quienes no son artistas ni proletarios. Ni con los narcisos del futurismo, ni con los barrenderos de la propaganda staliana [*sic*]. Un realismo contenido, de formas sencillas y universales, espejo de nuestras luchas. Una literatura lo más humana posible.' Castañar, p. 406.
35. The original edition is 'José Canel', *Octubre rojo en Asturias*, prol. by José Díaz Fernández (Madrid: Imp. Marsiega, 1935).
36. José Manuel López de Abiada, introduction to José Díaz Fernández, *Octubre rojo en Asturias* (Gijón: Silverio Cañada, 1984), p. xlv.
37. Another example is Alfonso Camín, *El valle negro: Asturias 1934* (Mexico: Norte, 1938) in which the author is very critical of the violence which both sides employ.
38. Celia Fernández Prieto, *Historia y novela: poética de la novela histórica* (Pamplona: EUNSA, 1998), pp. 203–04.
39. William Stott, *Documentary Expression and Thirties America* (London: Oxford University Press, 1973), p. 26.
40. Those miners who used dynamite in the fighting were regarded as heroes by the revolutionaries and as villains by the government supporters, as Molins i Fábrega explains: 'Los dinamiteros eran los que formaban la avanzada de las columnas revolucionarias delante de las cuales, con sólo sentir su proximidad, muy a menudo las fuerzas de la reacción abandonaban las posiciones. Eran vistos como semidioses por el pueblo obrero y como diablos escapados del averno por los burgueses y por los enemigos de la revolución.' N. Molins i Fábrega, *U.H.P.: la insurrección proletaria de Asturias* (Gijón: Jucar, 1977), p. 49.
41. Taibo claims that the University blew up when a bomb dropped by one of the government planes fell on a box full of dynamite (II, 243).
42. One example of a communiqué which was sent from Madrid to Asturias to encourage the miners on 7 October: 'Podemos asegurar que el triunfo de nuestra clase está muy cerca. En Asturias particularmente, los obreros que han triunfado y se constituyeron en poder en Mieres y Langreo están a punto de apoderarse de Oviedo y Gijón dentro de muy pocas horas. Las noticias que tenemos de Vizcaya, Cataluña, Aragón, Levante, Valladolid y otras muchas provincias, son parecidas a las de Asturias. En Madrid tenemos a raya a las fuerzas reaccionarias'. Quoted by N. Molins i Fábrega, p. 137.
43. Although Don Nicanor does not appear in Taibo's detailed study, *Asturias 1934*, I am assuming that he is a real character as he appears in at least another three accounts on the Revolution in Asturias: Francisco Prada, *Asturias la desventurada: caminos de sangre* (Madrid: Castro, 1934); *La revolución de octubre en España: la rebelión del gobierno de la Generalidad (octubre 1934)* (Madrid: Bolaños y Aguilar, 1935); and Alfonso Camín, *El valle negro: Asturias 1934* (Mexico: Norte, 1938). The details of the episode in which Don Nicanor figures change depending on the account.
44. Other differences between the episode of the revolutionary soldier/ Civil Guard who takes milk to the child include the sex of the child (in Díaz Fernández's account it is a boy, in Prada's it is a girl) and the circumstances surrounding the death of the soldier/ Guard (while the mother in Prada's account witnesses the shooting of the Civil Guard, in Díaz Fernández's account a colleague of the soldier is responsible for informing the mother).
45. Castañar, p. 314.
46. María Teresa León, 'Liberación de octubre', in *Cuentos de la España actual* (México: Editorial Dialéctica, [1936]), pp. 7–21; María Teresa León, 'Intelectual', in *Cuentos*, pp. 48–62; César Muñoz Arconada, 'Xuan, el músico', in *Los novelistas sociales españoles (1928–1936). Antología*, ed. by José Esteban and Gonzalo Santonja (Barcelona: Editorial Anthropos, 1988), pp. 203–08; Ramón Sender, 'El guaje', reproduced by Manuel Aznar Soler, 'La revolución asturiana de octubre de 1934 y la literatura española', *Los Cuadernos del Norte*, 26 (1984), 86–104 (pp. 101–02); Concha Espina, 'El Dios de los niños', in *Luna roja: novelas de la Revolución* (Valladolid: Librería Santarén, 1939), pp. 13–45. All page references quoted parenthetically in the text are to these sources.

47. When she relates the process of industrialization that Asturias has undergone she writes: 'Empezaron los hombres a ponerse muy tristes, especialmente los mineros ennegrecidos con el polvo siniestro de la hulla, quejosos y miserables en sus arriesgadas faenas. Pedían, con razón, un organismo social que les garantizase las ventajas imprescindibles de la vida. Y los amos del tesoro no se ponían de acuerdo para originar aquella justa ley' (p. 14).
48. Although Concha Espina's collection was published in 1939, the prologue is dated August 1938.
49. Sender begins his story: 'En un viaje a Asturias hemos hecho acopio de anécdotas y de sucedidos', and claims that the boy can be identified: 'Hay quien tiene su nombre e incluso su fotografía' (p. 101).
50. According to Radcliff's table, 'Occupations by status category', as an electrician, Ramón would have belonged to the skilled manual working class; as an engineer he would have moved up to the upper middle class. In Pamela Beth Radcliff, *From Mobilization to Civil War* (Cambridge: Cambridge University Press, 1996), pp. 322–25.
51. José Zapata writes: 'Si la U.R.S.S. se levanta como afirmación del proletariado construyendo una nueva y magnífica tesis de la humanidad, Italia y Alemania se alzan como una odiosa antítesis que niega lo mejor del hombre invocando una cultura de epidermis, de razas y limitaciones nacionales. Corren y se agitan por el cuerpo de Europa estas contrarias energías.' In León, *Cuentos*, p. 4.
52. In the introduction to her collection Concha Espina writes: 'Y con profundo anhelo, también, de seguir al invicto Ejército de Franco por la margen azul de José Antonio, las cinco flechas sobre el corazón. Siquiera con el trabajo y el sentimiento [. . .] para llevar y traer unas pocas emociones hasta el fondo de las trincheras y los cuarteles, como quien brinda a los defensores de la Civilización el homenaje más puro de su alma' (p. 9).
53. The flashbacks in 'Liberación de octubre' include Ramón's expulsion from the religious school (pp. 9–10); an episode in which Rosa gets drunk during the christening of a neighbour's niece (p. 11); and the scene in which Rosa licks the priest's hand (p. 13).
54. *Ayuda* was published in Madrid from 8 February 1936 to 22 December 1938. It was edited by Socorro Rojo Internacional, and its subtitles were 'Órgano de la solidaridad', and later on 'Semanario de la solidaridad'. Its first director was María Teresa León, and Isidoro Acevedo, president of the S.R.I., took over this on 15 June 1936. Amongst its regular contributors were Luis Araquistain, Álvarez del Vayo, Dolores Ibárruri, Ramón J. Sender, Rafael Alberti, Margarita Nelken, César M. Arconada, Esteban Vega, Luis de Tapia, Armando Bazán, Antonio Machado, Emilio Prados, and Serrano Plaja. From Esteban and Santonja, *Los novelistas españoles*, p. 314.
55. The collection describes the tensions and terrible inequalities in Spanish society around the second half of the Second Republic which would ultimately trigger off the Civil War. Given that the prologue is composed in November 1936, the stories must have been written prior to this. Indeed seeing as the collection was published in Mexico where, shortly after the October Revolution, León was speaking about the events which had taken place and the ensuing repression which the revolutionaries were being subjected to, she may have composed the stories while she was there.
56. For example, Espina, born in Santander, refers to the origins of Oviedo as a Benedictine monastery founded by Fromestano (p. 13); various of the monuments in Oviedo such as the Foncalda fountain, the only civil architectural monument from the reign of the Asturian kingdom to survive (p 15); and the symbolic importance of the old oak tree in Oviedo, *El Carbayón* (p. 15).
57. Arconada, p. 206.

CONCLUSION

This study has brought to light a number of prose narrative responses to the Revolution which took place in October of 1934 in Asturias and which, with few exceptions, have not been examined previously in any detail. The works examined here are important for three main reasons.

Firstly, they provide extensive information about the causes, the course, and the consequences of the Revolution. More importantly than this, however, since the details often contradict each other, these works offer an insight into the harrowing, impassioned, and tense atmosphere which prevailed over the region prior, during, and in the aftermath of the Revolution. They reveal how the population at large reacted to the workers' revolt and later on to its defeat. More specifically, they show how the politicians and intellectuals responded. A common characteristic which emerges is that *all* of the authors examined use their writing as a weapon in defence of not only their position as regards the events but also to expound their views about politics and society in general. Hence, these texts demonstrate, for example, how different political sides perceived the Republic as a system of government, set up three years prior to the Revolution, and the reformist legislation which had been introduced during this time, or how they responded to the lack of such legislation. It becomes apparent that, reflecting society in general, many of these works champion extreme political tendencies, in which the right is attracted to fascism, a political philosophy rapidly growing in popularity throughout Europe, while the left is drawn to communism, consolidated in the Soviet Union. Just as in society, where political neutrality is rare, so few of the authors examined here choose to sit on the fence.

Secondly, these texts denote a stage in the development of Spanish literature from the avant-garde to the social and politically engaged writing of the 1930s which would become most ideologically charged during the Civil War. Avant-garde concern with form was shelved as authors focused their attention on social issues rather than on the aesthetic concerns which had predominated in the 1920s and early 1930s. The increasing popularity and availability of literary magazines with a socio-political agenda, translated political works (especially from the Soviet Union) and pacifist novels, and politically committed social novels written by Spanish authors and published by newly established publishing houses, indicate that not only were authors' priorities changing, but so were those of the readers. The Revolution moved many prominent writers and intellectuals to an almost immediate reaction. Hence, the literature which resulted from the 1934 Revolution contributed to the politicization of literature as intellectuals felt that an absence of political engagement was inappropriate in such a climate.

Thirdly, I have demonstrated how these texts confound the critical distinctions commonly drawn between fiction and non-fiction. The usually clearly identifiable boundaries between a factual and a fictional text become blurred when the author draws on fictional devices to convey most effectively the atmospheric background, while at the same time referring to verifiable data, a practice more commonly associated with factual discourse; in other words, when he applies fictional narrative techniques to non-fiction, and vice versa. The authors, under pressure to provide their interpretation of and opinion about the Revolution as quickly as possible and for the widest readership possible, draw on both fact and fiction to some extent. By analysing these works an insight into some of their narrative strategies, whereby factual reporting and fictionalized storytelling are merged, can be gained, ensuring a better understanding of the relationship between their historical subject-matter and literary form. In the light of the preceding chapters I would like to return to some of these issues.

Although Manuel García, in the prologue to Vicente Madera's *El sindicato católico de Moreda y la revolución de octubre* (1935), writes that: 'Un profesional de la pluma hubiera explotado con habilidad este episodio de la revolución de octubre vivido por un puñado de jóvenes valientes, estirándolo en reportajes de fantasía' (p. 5), in fact, the Asturian Revolution did not prompt as many novelized responses as the Civil War would do. Although some of the generic terms which arise in Maryse Bertrand de Muñoz's extensive study of the Civil War novel are applicable to the prose narrative of the Revolution — for example, 'relato en primera persona'; 'autobiografía novelada'; 'biografía novelada'; and 'biografía de un personaje ficticio' — there are very few novels where the plot, although based on real events, and the characters are purely fictional.[1] Frederick Benson affirms, about Civil War literature, that the novel cannot be written quickly because of the attention to detail which is required.[2] This assertion is even more relevant to the literature of the Revolution where the duration of the conflict is shorter and the sense of urgency felt by the writers to render their interpretation of the events more acute. The types of narrative and the content of most of the texts conform to a well-defined model and are therefore similar and predictable. I argue that this repetitiousness is an interesting feature of these works. The reason for it lies in the fact that the Revolution only lasted a fortnight at the most (much less in most places) and was limited to certain industrial and mining towns. Thus, the authors pick up on the same anecdotes which occurred in the same places and involved the same people. However, although many of these anecdotes are repeated from one text to the next, their interpretation, as I have demonstrated in Chapters 3 to 8, usually differ. By comparing the same anecdotes from different texts I have been able to show how the writings are determined by the political viewpoint of the authors and the issues which they most want to emphasize. This is equally true for the texts on the left and the right of the political spectrum, in which the authors manipulate many of the same elements but in a diametrically opposed manner.

Because one of the most salient characteristics of these works is their blend of documentary detail and fictional reconstruction, they have been classified generically in categories that range from factual discourse to the non-fictional novel. I began by examining the journalistic works and essays which tackle the Revolution only as part of a more general analysis on politics. I then focused my attention on the counter-revolutionary, military, religious, and pro-revolutionary discourses, where the authors concentrate on the Revolution from each of these specific viewpoints, providing a range of factual (but biased) interpretations which are interesting to compare. The works examined in Chapters 5 and 6 lie on the border between fact and fiction. In other words, they are clearly intended to be factual, although the authors often draw on techniques associated with fictional writing, such as plot, characterization, and dialogue. The final two chapters deal with those texts which I have chosen to call non-fictional novels, in which the author describes and depicts a real event (the Asturian Revolution) in a fictional manner, resorting to a wide range of novelistic techniques. Despite the seemingly factual accuracy of all the situations and dialogues portrayed, in these works the narrative reads more like a novel than a historical account.

Once arranged into their respective generic categories, we can identify a series of features which are common to most of the works. At the heart of these similarities lie the writers' attempts to convince the readership, principally through the use of various manipulative strategies, examined in detail in Chapters 3 to 8. Firstly, the events related by the authors are filtered through their own ideological viewpoint and prejudices. Fulgencio Castañar summarizes this most succinctly:

La estrecha relación que se establece entre narrador y lector lleva consigo el que este último siempre ve la realidad novelesca a través del prisma que le pone el narrador ante sus ojos. Nunca percibe la historia desde el ángulo que él quiere, sino que la perspectiva viene fijada por la palabra creadora del narrador.[3]

Thus, the author selects and arranges the facts, and emphasizes certain issues over others to lend power to specific aspects of his interpretation. Even if he does not tamper with the historical evidence, he does inevitably select it, modify it, and rearrange it, as a function of the feelings he hopes to arouse and the message he wants to convey. However, as Helmut Gaus indicates, the only tie from which the author cannot escape is the familiarity of the readers with the situation depicted.[4] Thus, whether the circumstances depicted have the desired effect-producing quality depends not only on the author but also on the reader's own assumptions and his receptiveness and unquestioning acceptance.

Secondly, if we continue with Castañar's quotation, cited above:

Siempre el narrador va a colocar un filtro ante el lector para que no vea a los personajes por sí mismo, sino por la deformación que favorece la propagación de la forma de ver la sociedad que el novelista quiere difundir por medio de la acción novelesca y, más directamente, por la manipulación que de los personajes hace el narrador. (p. 319)

Just as with the facts included and the scenes recreated, the author chooses his characters (from the long list of individuals who took part) and the attributes conferred on each of them. As W. H. Harvey affirms, the author is both 'omnipotent and omniscient' as he selects the characters and what traits they will display.[5] This explains why certain real characters appear to be, for example, kind in some works and cruel in others. The physical, moral, and behavioural characteristics which they adopt are determined in the vast majority of cases by the ideological stance which they represent. Thus, in a pro-revolutionary text the left-wing characters take on virtuous and irreproachable qualities, while the right-wing are depicted as, among other things, cowards and villains. Similarly, in the counter-revolutionary texts the military and religious protagonists are favourably portrayed, while communists and supporters of other left-wing political tendencies are criticized through the negative and condemnatory depiction of the revolutionaries and their leaders.

A third shared characteristic of these texts is their claim to objectivity, truth, and reliability, and in some cases, impartiality, although, as I have shown, the authors make less of an effort to insist on these in the more fictionalized works examined in Chapters 5 to 8. These writers clearly go to such lengths to record their objectivity in order to appear the most reliable and therefore the most convincing. Of course, in most cases, despite these assurances, the biased undercurrent of the works and explicit subjective remarks made by the authors cancel out any of these alleged commitments. Although the key to the reliability of these texts lies in the research performed by the authors and the value and availability of eyewitness evidence, it has been shown that the acquisition of data is just as susceptible to bias and manipulation as the wording of the narrative itself. It is for this reason that I argue that objectivity is impossible, especially in those works in which the subject-matter is essentially political. The authors shape the facts and manipulate the reader's response to the characters described and events depicted. Therefore, despite the claims made by most of the authors that they have scrupulous adherence to the facts, these texts are mere *versions* of the same event.

In Chapter 7 a number of works in which the distinction between fact and fiction is blurred were selected and compared to the non-fictional novels written in North America during the 1960s. The close parallels which could be drawn prompted me to apply the same generic term. Ronald Weber points out that at this time deep social concern over certain issues meant that morally charged matters could not be written about in a neutral fashion.[6] Similarly, in the works examined in this study, the people who had witnessed the Revolution and its aftermath felt the need to record what they had seen for themselves or heard about from others, not only as a means to inform and convince but also to satisfy the need to share their tragic experiences and alleviate their distress.

Just as Weber maintains, the reporter is never a totally neutral figure and something of the personal inevitably creeps into his work. James Agee's assertion is equally relevant:

> Objectivity within any text [. . .] is impossible within the subjective structure of manmade art. Words do not fall together meaningfully outside of human consciousness and without human effort, because language is the building substance invented by man to convey and affirm value and order.[7]

The selection and the shaping of the facts and the manipulation of the reader's responses to the characters and events described are indicative of a lack of objectivity. The details included in each work are by their very nature charged with meaning and their inclusion is determined largely by the ideological credentials of the author, thereby making neutrality impossible. According to John Mander, because every artist is committed to something, the idea of a wholly uncommitted art is a contradiction in terms.[8] This makes exact descriptions of past events unattainable; although these texts are based on one single event and relate many of the same anecdotes, these are given different interpretations. Nevertheless, it is also true that despite the disparities in the facts and figures, when a selection of these works is read in conjunction, the overall sense of the atmosphere that prevailed can be perceived.

Accompanying their claims of objectivity, the authors stress the truth value of their work, to which the same complex issues apply. Stephen

Spender argues: 'A truth which gives comfort to the enemy is a kind of lie, and [. . .] a lie which serves your own side is a kind of truth'.[9] In other words, the traditionally accepted notion of truth and lie is altered in these circumstances in which the reader prefers to have his ideas confirmed rather than challenged. This provides further evidence that in the configuration of these texts the author's ideological outlook is decisive, affecting at every level the way they are written.

After considering in the Introduction the differences between factual and fictional prose writing (history and the novel), I have indicated how these have been combined in the works examined here. In the factual discourses of Chapters 3 and 4, fictional devices are used, and similarly, in the increasingly fictionalized works of Chapters 5 to 8, factual features are present. For instance, most of the texts incorporate dialogue, a literary device, and real and verifiable documentation in the form of, for example, quoted speeches and newspaper articles. Indeed, there are critics who maintain that sometimes things are explained and understood better when they are depicted fictionally. The authors want these books to be read with the interest and excitement that a reader would read a novel, where plot, drama, and characters have a crucial part to play, but always keeping in mind that this is a real event; they merge the 'impeccable accuracy of fact *and* the emotional impact found only in fiction'.[10] Lee Gutkind insists that non-fictional novelists cannot alter the facts but they can capture and present them much more forcefully.[11] They utilize some of the literary techniques available to the fiction writer in order to render his or her story as dramatically, appealingly, and compellingly as possible. Thus, in the last set of texts, in Chapters 7 and 8, the author uses fiction to communicate fact, since 'fiction is the type of writing that provides the most effective means of dramatising the complexities and ambiguities of experience'.[12]

Throughout this study I have argued that the scenic reconstruction of the events together with characters' actions create a realistic and objective portrayal of the Revolution as the reader seemingly learns about it in the same way as the author — by viewing (metaphorically) the events as they take place, without the intrusion of the narrator. This enables the reader to judge and interpret the situation for himself. As well as being a characteristically fictional device, the use of dialogue enhances the sense of reality and establishes action since it eliminates the possible interference from a reporter or narrator attempting to sound authentic while maintaining objectivity. Even when the language of the author appears to be at its most tendentious it seems that he is recalling faithfully the words of real people in real settings. However, a narrative which is re-enacted seems more fictional because its form reminds the reader of the novel, or even drama or cinema, and because the writing impinges on the creative writer's terrain of fictional discourse. On the other hand, events which are recounted in an indirect, or 'reportorial', narrative mode[13] seem more reliable as they remind the reader of the (assumed) trustworthiness of written history. However, because the narrator is relaying, summarizing, and analysing the course of events, the information is susceptible to his influence, whether intentional or not. Faith in the narrator is therefore imperative. Thus, a significant paradox of these texts is that some of the authors choose to render their interpretation of the events in a manner usually reserved for writing of an imaginative kind, while others prefer to give a historical or documentary account. And yet, both of these methods have their drawbacks as all texts are subject to the author's manipulation. The range of choices taken by the authors highlight their quest for the maximum credibility in the belief that the most credible is the most persuasive.

I have indicated that many of the features common to these works are largely determined by the expectations of the reader and the author's intention to instruct and convince, or in David Caute's words, 'infuriate, activate and mobilise public sentiment'.[14] We must add to these another influential factor, that is, the proximity of the event to its rendering. In order to serve the immediate cause the texts would have necessarily been composed in great haste. The authors were aware that they would be more persuasive while the events were still fresh in people's minds, the political atmosphere still unsettled and charged with feelings of anger, bitterness, and resentment, and the Revolution still fiercely debated in Parliament and on the streets. The author would have wanted to reach the greatest number of people with the greatest simplicity and immediacy. Because there had to be no confusion about what side he supported and why, the language used is straightforward, transparent, and explicit. This explains why the literary value and the complexity of the plot, characterization, and style of even the more novelized works are slight. We should point out that the urgency faced by these authors meant that in producing their texts they had little time to double-check their data. This leads predictably, in certain cases, to accidental misinformation and occasional discrepancies.

Clearly, propaganda is one of the main constituents of these works. As Álvaro de Albornoz affirms: 'Hermosa es la palabra cuando conmueve, pero todavía es más hermosa cuando convence.'[15] Because of the political significance of the events which the authors are writing about, their works convey their ideological stand during this troubled time. Unable to remain passive in such heated socio-political circumstances, rather than strive to create an aesthetically pleasing work, they aim to discuss those issues which most concern them. That is why many of the texts deal to some extent with other political questions besides the Revolution. This is most obvious in the first category of works, dealt with in Chapter 3, where the authors analyse the political situation in general and only refer to the Asturian Revolution in passing. However, it is also evident in the works examined in the last two chapters where the communist, socialist, and anarchist conceptions of society are embodied in their interpretation of the Revolution.

Gareth Thomas identifies two types of propaganda: rational and irrational propaganda. Rational propaganda is based on facts, statistics, economic data, and technical descriptions, while irrational propaganda is aimed at manipulating the feelings and passions of the reader.[16] According to Thomas, given the extreme polarisation of views, in the novels of the Civil War there is a heavy reliance on the irrational element of propaganda. This assertion is also applicable to the works on the Asturian Revolution. Those with the most extreme political ideas, whether on the left or right, tend to employ more intemperate and sententious language. The calls from the left range from justice for those who suffered imprisonment and torture during the repression, to the dismantling of the bourgeois state, the dissolution of the Church, and the creation of the Frente Unico. On the other hand, the right criticizes the Republican government for failing to prevent the Revolution, and demands the elimination of communism and other left-wing parties and organizations, and the establishment of a fascist regime or a monarchy (depending on the author), where the *Patria* and the Church, the two most important institutions, must be vehemently defended. In general the task of those authors taking a revolutionary stance was not only to survey the collapse of the revolt but also to draw from it possible lessons for the future. They are upholders of the class struggle, defending the revolutionary path which will eventually ensure that power is given to the workers. For their part, right-wing authors warn their readers of the dangers of a proletarian revolution and the destruction and havoc which Marxism would engender, and most reject egalitarian ideas on the grounds that they go against human nature.

Contemporary critics warn that the danger in propaganda lies in that it destroys creativity; instead of exploring ideas and emotions the writer resorts to ready-made analyses and slogans which are the negation of creative writing. In addition, the non-fiction writers' commitment to the authority of fact is, in Weber's words, 'at once their strength, in a historical sense, and their limitation in a literary sense'.[17] Although traditionally propagandistic writing has tended to be viewed sceptically and aesthetically unworthy I have identified a number of tropes and figures of speech which are legitimate and effective from a literary point of view, especially in the last set of works, that is, the non-fictional novels. However, having established that the aim of the authors was not to create an exceptional work of enduring literary value, this issue becomes somewhat irrelevant and is therefore not central to my study. What is interesting is the way in which the style is determined by their propagandistic objectives. For example, recurring metaphors become politically symbolic; colours, weather patterns, and the landscape take on a special significance; and weapons are personified and their capacity for destruction described in minute detail.

In conclusion, this study of the literary response to the Asturian Revolution reveals how a wide range of authors from all strata of society chose to represent the critical historical circumstances in their work. Without proposing a definitive definition of the non-fictional novel, this study demonstrates that the type of writing that emerged is a hybrid of documentary reporting and literary creativity, and even in the most factual and fictional works both traits are evident. More importantly, however, within the framework of what has been said about prose writing in Spain up to the Civil War, I have traced the evolution and shifts which occurred, highlighting in the process that the Asturian Revolution was crucial in this development, and shown that something particular and new emerged in the context of Spanish prose in the mid 1930s. Clearly, as critics, we do not view these works in the same way that the author or reader did at the time of composition or publication. The author would have been impelled by the urgency of the situation to produce a text as quickly and as compellingly as possible. Similarly the reader would have been expecting this, not a refined novel. He would have felt confident that his opinions would be supported and his ideological views reinforced in the content and by the message of the text. Clearly no right-wing reader would have chosen to read a left-wing text, or vice versa. The readership and the purpose of the text are therefore well defined from the outset. Most would have known what its content and the ideological leaning were and would have been drawn to it precisely because of this. I have taken this study to 1938. Of course everything that the intellectuals of the 1930s made of the Asturian Revolution, on the one hand, and the development of literature, on the other, was truncated by the Civil War. The fact that this discussion has been brought to an end here does not mean that the issues raised ceased to be relevant. It is to be hoped that some intrepid student will examine them in other contexts.

1. *La guerra civil española en la novela: bibliografía comentada*, 2 vols (Madrid: José Porrúa Turanzas, 1982).
2. *Writers in Arms: The Literary Impact of the Spanish Civil War* (London: University of London Press; New York: New York University Press, 1968), p. 42.
3. *El compromiso en la novela de la II República* (Madrid: Siglo XXI, 1992), p. 319.

4. *The Function of Fiction: The Function of Written Fiction in the Social Process* (Gent: E. Story-Scientia, 1979).
5. 'Character and the Context of Things', in *Perspectives on Fiction*, ed. by James Calderwood and Harold Toliver (New York: Oxford University Press, 1968), pp. 354–73 (p. 356).
6. *The Literature of Fact: Literary Non-fiction in American Writing* (Athens, OH: Ohio University Press, 1980).
7. James Agee's assertion is referred to by Robert Smart, *The Nonfiction Novel* (Lanham, London: University Press of America, 1985), p. 59.
8. *The Writer and Commitment*, 8th edn (London: Sacker and Warburg, 1961).
9. *The Thirties and After: Poetry, Politics, and People (1933–75)* (London: Fontana, 1978), p. 31.
10. John Hollowell, *Fact and Fiction: The New Journalism and the Nonfiction Novel* (Chapel Hill: University of North Carolina Press, 1977), p. 70, author's emphasis.
11. *The Art of Creative Nonfiction: Writing and Selling the Literature of Reality* (New York: John Wiley and Sons, 1997).
12. John Hellmann, *Fables of Fact: The New Journalism as New Fiction* (Urbana: Illinois University Press, 1981), p. 18.
13. This literary term is referred to in Ross Murfin and Supryia Ray, *The Bedford Glossary of Critical and Literary Terms* (Boston, MA: Bedford Books, 1998), p. 134.
14. *The Illusion: An Essay on Politics, Theatre and the Novel* (London: Panther, 1971), p. 53. According to Caute these are 'ideologies of change', while 'ideologies of conservatism' aim 'to pacify, refract and divert public opinion' (p. 53).
15. Álvaro de Albornoz, *Al servicio de la República: de la Unión Republicana al Frente Popular. Criterios de Gobierno* (Madrid: [n. pub.], 1936), p. 155.
16. *The Novel of the Spanish Civil War (1936–1975)* (Cambridge: Cambridge University Press, 1990).
17. *The Literature of Fact*, p. 49.

BIBLIOGRAPHY

This bibliography is divided into five sections: Primary sources (with two subsections, the first of which includes those works examined in detail, and the second all other contemporary prose works about the Revolution); Bibliographical sources; Books and articles on the history of Spain from the Second Republic to the October Revolution of 1934; Books and articles on Spanish literature from the avant-garde to the Civil War; and Books and articles on literary and genre theory.

A. Primary Sources

The following list represents those works on the Asturian Revolution which I have been able to track down and consult.

Works examined in detail

¡Acusamos! El asesinato de Luis de Sirval ([Valencia]: Comité Luis de Sirval, [n.d.])

Adro Xavier [Alejandro Rey Stolle], *Sangre jesuita. Asturias 1934: Padre Emilio Martínez y H. Juan B. Arconada* (Bilbao: El Mensajero del Corazón de Jesús, 1938)

Arconada, César Muñoz, 'Xuan, el músico', in *Los novelistas sociales españoles (1928–1936): antología*, ed. by José Esteban and Gonzalo Santonja (Barcelona: Editorial Anthropos, 1988), pp. 203–08

Asociación Católica Nacional de Propagandistas, *Asturias roja (octubre de 1934): sacerdotes y religiosos perseguidos y martirizados* (Oviedo: Moderna Imprenta Trufero, 1935)

Azaña, Manuel, *Mi rebelión en Barcelona* (Madrid: Espasa Calpe, 1935)

Benavides, Manuel, *La revolución fue así: octubre rojo y negro* (Barcelona: Imprenta Industrial, 1935)

Bergés, Consuelo, *Explicación de octubre: historia comprimida de cuatro años de República en España* (Madrid: Imp. Garcigay, 1935)

Caballero Audaz, El [José María Carretero Novillo], *Traidores a la patria: la realidad sobre Asturias y Cataluña. ¡Los responsables!* (Madrid: Ediciones El Caballero Audaz, 1935)

Camín Meana, Alfonso, *El valle negro: Asturias 1934* (México: Norte, 1938)

Cossío, Francisco de, *Hacia una nueva España: de la revolución de octubre a la revolución de julio 1934–1936* (Valladolid: Castilla, 1936)

Díaz Fernández, José, *Octubre rojo en Asturias* (Gijón: Silverio Cañada, 1984 [1st edn 1935])

Documentos Socialistas (Madrid: Índice, 1935)

Episodios de la revolución en Asturias: los pasionistas de Mieres (Asturias) y la Revolución de octubre de 1934 (Santander: El Pasionario, [1935(?)])

Espina, Concha, 'El Dios de los niños', in *Luna roja: novelas de la Revolución* (Valladolid: Librería Santarén, 1939), pp. 13–45

Geijo, Jenaro G., *Episodios de la revolución* (Santander: Tipografía de la Librería Moderna, 1935)

Gordón Ordás, Félix, *Mi política en España* (Mexico: [n. pub.], 1962)

Grossi Mier, Manuel, *La insurrección de Asturias* (Madrid and Gijón: Jucar, 1978 [1st edn 1935])

Hidalgo, Diego, *¿Por qué fui lanzado del Ministerio de la Guerra?: diez meses de actuación ministerial* (Madrid: Espasa Calpe, 1934)

Karl, Mauricio, *Asesinos de España: Marxismo, anarquismo, masonería* (Madrid: Ediciones Bergua, 1935)

La revolución de octubre en España: la rebelión del gobierno de la Generalidad. Octubre 1934 (Madrid: Bolaños y Aguilar, 1934)
León, María Teresa, 'Intelectual', in *Cuentos de la España actual* (México: Editorial Dialéctica, [1936]), pp. 48–62
——, 'Liberación de octubre', in *Cuentos de la España actual* (México: Editorial Dialéctica, [1936]), pp. 7–21
Los crímenes de la reacción española (Madrid: Ediciones de la Sección Española del Socorro Rojo Internacional, 1935)
Los mártires de Turón: notas biográficas y reseña del martirio de los religiosos bárbaramente asesinados por los revolucionarios en Turón (Asturias) (Madrid: La Instrucción Publica, [1935(?)])
Llano Roza de Ampudia, Aurelio de, *Pequeños anales de quince días: la Revolución en Asturias. Octubre 1934* (Oviedo: Talleres Tipográficos Altamirano, 1935)
Madera, Vicente, *El sindicato católico de Moreda y la revolución de octubre* (Madrid: Imp. Saez Hermanos, 1935)
Maurín, Joaquín, *Revolución y contrarrevolución en España* (Paris: Ruedo Ibérico, 1966 [1st edn 1935])
Molins i Fábrega, N., *UHP: la insurrección proletaria de Asturias*, trans. by Carmen García Ribas (Gijón: Jucar, 1977 [1st edn 1935])
Montseny, Federica, *Heroínas*, in *Novelas breves de escritoras españolas (1900–1936)*, ed. by Angela Ena Bordonada (Madrid: Editorial Castalia, 1989)
Noval Suárez, Senén, *Langreo rojo : historia del martirio y persecución de los sacerdotes en el arziprestazgo de Langreo, durante los sucesos revolucionarios de 1934* ([La Felguera]: Imp. la Torre, 1935)
Nuñez, Ignacio, *La revolución de octubre de 1934*, 2 vols (Barcelona: José Vilamala, 1935)
Oliveros, Antonio, *Asturias en el resurgimiento español: apuntes históricos y biográficos* (Madrid: Imp. Juan Bravo, 1935)
Prada, Francisco, *Asturias la desventurada: caminos de sangre* (Madrid: Castro, 1934)
Quintanilla, Luis, *La cárcel por dentro* (Madrid: [n. pub.], 1936; repr. Oviedo: Fundación José Barreiro, 1995)
Romero Cuesta, José, *El sargento Vázquez* (Madrid : Gráficas Aglaya, 1936)
Rucabado, R., *Los mártires de Asturias: la escuela mártir de Turón*, 2nd edn (Barcelona: Catalunya Social, 1935)
Sender, Ramón, 'El guaje', reproduced by Manuel Aznar Soler, 'La revolución asturiana de octubre de 1934 y la literatura española', *Los Cuadernos del Norte*, 26 (1984), 86–104 (pp. 101–02)
Valdés, Alejandro, *¡¡Asturias!!: relato vivido de la insurrección de octubre* (Valencia: Verdad, [1934])
Valdivielso, Juan Simeón, *Farsa y tragedia de España en el 1934: un año de preparación revolucionaria visto desde mi 'Mirilla'* (Oviedo: T. de la Presa, 1935)

Other works

Includes other prose works about the Revolution published between the years 1934 to 1938 which have not been studied in detail but which have been consulted.

Albornoz, Álvaro de, *Al servicio de la República: de la Unión Republicana al Frente Popular. Criterios de Gobierno* (Madrid: [n. pub.], 1936)
Álvarez Suárez, Maximino, *Sangre de octubre: U.H.P.*, 2nd edn (Madrid: Cenit, 1936)
Barrado, Ignacio, *El sargento Vázquez: reportaje* ([n.p.]: [n. pub.], [1936])
Caballero Audaz, El [José María Carretero Novillo] *¡Viva la revolución!: los malhechores de la política. Opiniones de un hombre de la calle* (Madrid: Ediciones Caballero Audaz, 1934)
Carnelli, María Luisa, *U.H.P.: mineros de Asturias* (Buenos Aires: Talleres Gráficos Weiss, 1936)
Carral, Ignacio, *Por qué mataron a Luis de Sirval* (Madrid: Imp. Sáez Hermanos, 1935)
Domingo, Marcelino, *La revolución de octubre: causas y experiencias* (Barcelona: [n. pub.], 1935)
Fernández, Manuel, *Gijón en 1934* (Gijón: La Versal, 1935)
Garcitoral, Alicio, *España y la verdad* (Buenos Aires: Ediciones Anaconda, 1937)

Iglesias Somoza, Eraclio, *Episodios de la revolución: asedio y defensa de la Cárcel de Oviedo* (Vitoria: J. Marquínez, [1935(?)])
Ignotus [Manuel Villar], *El anarquismo en la insurrección de Asturias: la C.N.T. y la F.A.I. en octubre de 1934* (Valencia: Ediciones Tierra y Libertad, 1935)
La represión en Asturias: reporte sindicalista [no publication details]
López Ochoa, Eduardo, *Campaña militar de Asturias en Octubre 1934* (Madrid: Yunque, 1936)
López-Rey y Arrojo, Manuel, *Un delito de asesinato: el caso Sirval* (Madrid: Imp. Helénica, 1936)
Manning, Elizabeth Leah, *What I Saw in Spain* (London: Victor Gollancz, 1935)
Martínez, Francisco, *Dos jesuitas mártires de Asturias: el P. Emilio Martínez y el H. Juan B. Arconada* (Burgos: Imprenta Aldecoa, 1936)
Nelken, Margarita, *¿Por qué hicimos la revolución?* (Barcelona: Ediciones Sociales Internacionales, 1936)
Nuño del Robledal, Gil, *¿Por qué Oviedo se convirtió en ciudad mártir?: película* (Oviedo: T. de la Presa, 1935)
Orbón, Julián, *Patriotismo y ciudadanía: lo que destruyó la revolución roja del mes de octubre en Asturias* (Gijón: Tip. La Fé, 1935)
——, *Avilés en el movimiento revolucionario de Asturias: octubre de 1934* (Gijón: Tip. La Fé, 1934)
Ramos Oliveira, Antonio, *La revolución española de octubre: ensayo político* (Madrid: [n. pub.], [1935])
Reporteros Reunidos, *Octubre rojo: ocho días que conmovieron a España* (Madrid: Imp. Vallinas, [n.d.])
Rubinat, José R., *Los Zapadores y la Revolución de Octubre: héroes y mártires* (Oviedo: Imp. Emiliano, [1935(?)])
Salazar Alonso, Rafael, *Bajo el signo de la revolución* (Madrid: Imp. Sáez Hermanos, 1935)
Sender, Ramón, *Crónica del pueblo en armas* (Madrid, Valencia: Ediciones Españolas, 1936)
Socorro Rojo de España, *Asturias: octubre 1934–1935* [no publication details]
Solano Palacio, Fernando, *La revolución de octubre: quince días de comunismo libertario en Asturias*, 3rd edn (Barcelona: [n. pub.], [1936])
Testigo Imparcial, Un, *Revolución en Asturias: relato de la última guerra civil* (Madrid: Castro, 1934)
Verdal, Tomás, *Los Presos del 'Manuel Arnús': novela* (Reus: Librería 'La Gráfica', 1935)

B. Bibliographical Sources

Some of those works included in section D have also provided bibliographical details.

Álvarez Calleja, José, *2000 fichas de bibliografía asturiana* (Salinas: Ayalga, 1976)
Bertrand de Muñoz, Maryse, *La guerra civil española en la novela: bibliografía comentada*, 2 vols (Madrid: José Porrúa Turanzas, 1982)
Ruiz de la Peña, Álvaro, *Introducción a la literatura asturiana* (Oviedo: Biblioteca Popular Asturiana, 1981)
Suárez, Constantino, ed., *Escritores y artistas asturianos: índice bio-bibliográfico*. Tomos I–III (Madrid: Imp. Saez Hermanos, 1936); Cachero, José María, ed., *Escritores y artistas asturianos: índice bio-bibliográfico*, Tomos IV–VII (Oviedo: Instituto de Estudios Asturianos, 1955; 1956; 1957; 1959)

C. History of Spain from the Second Republic to the October Revolution

Aviv, Aviva and Isaac, 'Ideology and Political Patronage: Workers and Working-Class Movements in Republican Madrid, 1931–34', *European Studies Review*, 11 (1981), 487–515
Bizcarrondo, Marta, *Octubre del 34: reflexiones sobre una revolución* (Madrid: Ayuso, 1977)
Blinkhorn, Martin, ed., *Spain in Conflict 1931–1939: Democracy and Its Enemies* (London: Sage, 1986)
Brenan, Gerald, *El laberinto español: antecedentes sociales y políticos de la guerra civil* (Barcelona: Plaza y Janes, 1996)

Brugos, Valentín, and Gaspar Llamazares, *Los comunistas en Asturias (1920–1982)* (Gijón: Trea, 1996)
Cárcel Ortí, Vicente, 'La iglesia durante la II República y la Guerra Civil (1931–1939)', in *Historia de la Iglesia en España*, ed. by Ricardo García Villoslada (Madrid: Editorial Católica, 1979), pp. 331–94
Castillo, Juan José, 'Sindicalismo católico, sindicalismo amarillo', in *Sindicalismo y movimientos sociales*, coord. by Manuel Redero (Madrid: UGT, Centro de Estudios Históricos, 1994), pp. 147–53
Colectivo Febrero, 'Federica Montseny: una entrevista con la historia', *Tiempo de Historia*, 31 (1977), 4–19
Fernández, Alberto, 'Octubre de 1934: recuerdos de un insurrecto', *Tiempo de Historia*, 17 (1976), 11–21
Gallego-Díaz, Soledad, 'Entrevista, en Toulouse, con Federica Montseny', *Cuadernos para el Diálogo*, 29 (1976), 15–17
González Muñiz, Miguel Ángel, *Los asturianos y la política* (Salinas: Ayalga, 1976)
Ibárruri, Dolores, *El único camino* (Mexico: Ediciones Era, 1963)
Jackson, Gabriel, *The Spanish Republic and the Civil War 1931–1939* (New Jersey: Princeton University Press, 1965)
Jackson, Gabriel, et al., *Octubre 1934: cincuenta años para la reflexión* (Madrid: Siglo XXI, 1985)
Joll, James, *The Anarchists*, 2nd edn (London: Methuen, 1979)
Juliá, Santos, 'Rastros del pasado', *El País*, 25 July 1999, p. 15.
Laso Prieto, José María, 'La epopeya asturiana de octubre de 1934', *Agitación*, 2 (1994), 8–10
Mosse, George, 'Introduction: The Genesis of Fascism', *Journal of Contemporary History*, 1 (1966), 14–26
Palacio Atard, Vicente, *Cinco historias de la República y de la Guerra* (Madrid: Editora Nacional, 1973)
——, 'La Segunda República Española (1931–1936–1939)', in *Diccionario de historia eclesiástica de España*, ed. by Quintín Aldea Vaquero, et al. (Madrid: Instituto Enrique Flórez, Consejo Superior de Investigaciones Científicas, 1972), II, 1179–84
Peirats, José, *The CNT in the Spanish Revolution*, trans. by Paul Sharkey (Hastings: The Meltzer Press, 1996)
Peyroux, Celso, *Seronda roja: el movimiento obrero revolucionario de octubre de 1934 en el concejo de Teverga* (Teverga, Asturias: Ayuntamiento, 1991)
Preston, Paul, ed., *Revolution and War in Spain. 1931–1939* (London: Methuen, 1984; repr. London: Routledge, 1993)
——, 'Spain's October Revolution and the Rightist Grasp for Power', *Journal of Contemporary History*, 10 (1975), 555–78
Radcliff, Pamela Beth, *From Mobilization to Civil War: The Politics of Polarization in the Spanish City of Gijón, 1900–1937* (Cambridge: Cambridge University Press, 1996)
Rosal, Amaro del, *1934: Movimiento revolucionario de octubre* (Madrid: Akal, 1983)
Ruiz, David, *Insurrección defensiva y revolución obrera: el octubre español de 1934* (Barcelona: Editorial Labor, 1988)
——, *El movimiento obrero en Asturias* (Madrid, Gijón: Jucar, 1979)
——, *Asturias contemporánea (1808–1936)* (Madrid: Siglo XXI, 1975)
Shubert, Adrian, *Hacia la Revolución: orígenes sociales del movimiento obrero en Asturias, 1860–1934*, trans. by Agueda Palacios Honorato (Barcelona: Editorial Crítica, 1984)
Taibo, Paco Ignacio, *Asturias 1934*, 2 vols (Madrid: Jucar, 1984)
Thomas, Hugh, 'The Hero in the Empty Room: José Antonio and Spanish Fascism', *Journal of Contemporary History*, 1 (1966), 174–82
Trotsky, Leon, *The Spanish Revolution (1931–1939)* (New York: Pathfinder Press, 1973)
Woodcock, George, *Anarchism: A History of Libertarian Ideas and Movements* (Harmondsworth: Penguin, 1975)

D. Spanish Literature from the Avant-Garde to the Civil War

Includes books and articles on the avant-garde, 'literatura de avanzada', and political and socially engaged literature; politically committed social novels written during the second Republic; and articles and books about relevant authors.

Abellán, José Luis, 'Las "obras políticas" de Ortega y Gasset', *Ínsula* (January 1970), p. 6
Alberti, Rafael, *Poeta en la calle (obra civil)* (Madrid: Aguilar, 1978)
Alcalde, Carmen, *Federica Montseny: palabra en rojo y negro* (Barcelona: Editorial Argos Vergara, 1983)
Arconada, César Muñoz, *Río Tajo* (Madrid: Akal, 1978 [1st edn 1938])
——, *Los pobres contra los ricos* (Madrid: Izquierda, 1933)
——, *La Turbina* (Madrid: Ediciones Turner, 1975 [1st edn 1930])
Arribas, Jesús, *Ciges Aparicio: la narrativa de testimonio y denuncia* (Madrid: Editorial Novecientos, 1984)
Aub, Max, *Discurso de la novela española contemporánea* (Mexico: El Colegio de Mexico, Centro de Estudios Sociales, 1945)
Aznar Soler, Manuel, *I Congreso Internacional de Escritores para la Defensa de la Cultura (Paris, 1935)*, 2 vols (Valencia: Generalitat Valenciana, Consellería de Cultura, Educaió i Ciència, 1987)
——, 'La revolución asturiana de octubre de 1934 y la literatura española', *Los Cuadernos del Norte*, 26 (1984), 86–104
Bécarud, Jean, *Cruz y Raya (1933–1936)* (Madrid: Taurus, 1969)
Bécarud, Jean, and Evelyn López Campillo, *Los intelectuales españoles durante la II República* (Madrid: Siglo XXI, 1978)
Benavides, Manuel, *El último pirata del mediterráneo: reportaje* (Barcelona: Tip. Cosmos, 1934)
Benson, Frederick, *Writers in Arms: The Literary Impact of the Spanish Civil War* (London: University of London Press; New York: New York University Press, 1968)
Bergamín, José, 'Hablar en Cristiano', *Cruz y Raya*, 28 (1935), 73–83
——, 'El estado fantasma y ¿en que país vivimos?', *Cruz y Raya*, 25 (1934), 127–33
Bizcarrondo, Marta, *'Leviatán' y el socialismo de Luis Araquistain: estudio preliminar para la reedición de 'Leviatán'* (Liechtenstein: Verlag Detler Auvermann, 1974)
Blanco Aguinaga, Carlos, Julio Rodríguez Puértolas, and Iris M. Zavala, *Historia social de la literatura española (en lengua castellana)*, 3 vols (Madrid: Castalia, 1979)
Boetsch, Laurent, 'Una aventura de la otra generación de 1927: Díaz Fernández, Arconada y la literatura de avanzada', *Bazar*, 4 (1997), 144–49
——, *José Diaz Fernández y la otra Generación del 27* (Madrid: Editorial Pliegos, 1985)
Bolado, José, 'Atitúes diglósiques ejemplares na práutica cultural del movimiento obreru asturianu, nos años 20 y 30', *Lletres asturianes*, 17 (1985), 11–15
Borque López, Leonardo, 'Las Misiones Pedagógicas en Asturias', *Los Cuadernos del Norte*, 11 (1982), 83–87
Borrel, Jean François, *La novela por entregas: Mitad de creación y consumo* (Castalia: Madrid, 1974)
Brihuega, Jaime, *Manifiestos, proclamas, panfletos y textos doctrinales: las vanguardias artísticas en España, 1910–1931* (Madrid: Cátedra, 1979)
Buckley, Ramón, 'Francisco Ayala y el arte de vanguardia: hacia una nueva valoración de la generación de 1927', *Ínsula* (January 1970), pp. 1, 10
Buckley, Ramón, and John Crispin, *Los vanguardistas españoles 1925–1935* (Madrid: Alianza Editorial, 1973)
Butt, John, *Writers and Politics in Modern Spain* (London: Hodder and Stoughton, 1978)
Caba, Carlos y Pedro, 'La rehumanización del arte', *Eco*, 9 (1934), 1–5
Cano Ballesta, Juan, *La poesía española entre pureza y revolución (1920–1936)* (Madrid: Siglo XXI, 1996)
Carrasquer, Francisco, *'Iman' y la novela histórica de Ramón J. Sende*r (Amsterdam: University of Amsterdam, 1968)
Castañar, Fulgencio, *El compromiso en la novela de la II República* (Madrid: Siglo XXI, 1992)
——, 'La novela social durante la II República', *Tiempo de Historia*, 36 (1977), 60–69
Caudet, Francisco, 'Arturo Serrano Plaja: Apostillas a algunos de sus ensayos', in *Homenaje a Arturo Serrano Plaja*, ed. by J. L. Aranguren and A. Sánchez Barbudo (Madrid: Taurus, 1984)
——, 'Los intelectuales en la Guerra del 36', in *Actas del Sexto Congreso Internacional de Hispanistas: Celebrado en Toronto del 22 al 26 de agosto de 1977*, dir. by Alan Gordon and Evelyn Rugg (Toronto: Department of Spanish and Portuguese, University of Toronto, 1980), pp. 176–78

——, ed., *Hora de España: antología* (Madrid: Ediciones Turner, 1975)

Cobb, Christopher, *La cultura y el pueblo: España 1930–1939* (Barcelona: Editorial Laia, 1980)

Crispin, John, 'Antonio Sánchez Barbudo, misionero pedagógico', in *Homenaje a Antonio Sánchez Barbudo: ensayos de literatura española moderna*, ed. by Benito Brancaforte, Edward Mulvihill and Roberto Sánchez (Madison: University of Wisconsin, 1981)

Dennis, Nigel, 'César Arconada at the Crossroads: *La Turbina* (1930)', in *Hacia la novela nueva: Essays on the Spanish Avant-Garde Novel*, ed. by Francis Lough (Oxford: Peter Lang, 2000)

Díaz Castañón, Carmen, 'Introducción', *La Esfinge Maragata*, by Concha Espina (Madrid: Editorial Castalia, 1989), pp. 4–20

Díaz Fernández, José, *El nuevo romanticismo o polémica de arte, política y literatura* (Madrid: Zeus, 1930)

——, *La Venus mecánica* (Barcelona: Editorial Laia, 1980 [1st edn 1929])

——, *El blocao*, prologue by José Esteban (Madrid: Viamonte, 1998 [1st edn 1928])

Esteban, José, 'Editoriales y libros de la España de los años treinta', *Cuadernos para el Diálogo*, 32 (1972), 58–62

Esteban, José, and Gonzalo Santonja, *La novela social 1928–39: figuras y tendencias* (Madrid: Ediciones la Idea, 1987)

——, *Los novelistas sociales españoles (1928–1936): antología* (Barcelona: Anthropos, 1988)

Ferreras, Juan Ignacio, *La novela en el siglo XX (hasta 1939)* (Madrid: Taurus, 1988)

Foard, Douglas, 'The Forgotten Falangist: Ernesto Giménez Caballero', *Journal of Contemporary History*, 10 (1975), 3–18

Fuentes, Víctor, *La marcha al pueblo en las letras españolas (1917–1936)* (Madrid: Ediciones de la Torre, 1980)

——, '«Post-Guerra» (1927–1928): una revista de vanguardia política y literaria', *Ínsula* (November 1976), p. 4

——, 'Los nuevos intelectuales en España: 1928–1931', *Triunfo* (28 August 1976), pp. 38–42

——, 'La novela social española (1931–1936): temas y significación ideológica', *Ínsula* (November 1970), pp. 1, 4

——, 'La novela social española en los años 1928–1931', *Ínsula* (January 1970), pp. 1, 12, 13

——, 'De la literatura de vanguardia a la de avanzada: en torno a José Díaz Fernández', *Papeles de Son Armadans*, 54 (1969), 243–60

García Aznar, José María, *Confinado: novela política cómico-dramática* (Oviedo: Talleres Tipográficos Altamirano, 1934)

García de la Concha, Víctor, ed., *Época contemporánea: 1914–1939*, in *Historia y crítica de la literatura española*, ed. by Francisco Rico, 9 vols (Barcelona: Editorial Crítica, 1979–), VII (1984)

Gide, André, *Defensa de la cultura*, trans. by Julio Gómez de la Serna (Madrid: S. Aguirre, 1936)

Gil Casado, Pablo, *La novela social española (1920–1971)*, 2nd edn (Barcelona: Seix Barral, 1973)

Haro Ibars, Eduardo, 'La "Generación del 27": todo el espíritu de una época', *Tiempo de Historia*, 34 (1977), 38–47

Harris, Derek, ed., *The Spanish Avant-garde* (Manchester: Manchester University Press, 1995)

Hoyle, Alan, 'Ramón Gómez de la Serna and the Avant-Garde', in *Changing Times in Hispanic Culture*, ed. by Derek Harris (Aberdeen: University of Aberdeen, 1996), pp. 7–18

——, *El humor ramoniano de vanguardia*, Manchester Spanish and Portuguese Working Papers, 2 (Machester: University of Manchester, 1996)

Lechner, J., *El compromiso en la poesía española del siglo XX* (Leiden: Universitaires Pers Leiden, 1968)

Literatura y compromiso político en los años 30: homenaje al poeta Juan Gil-Albert (Valencia: Diputación Provincial de Valencia, 1989)

López de Abiada, José Manuel, 'José Díaz Fernández: la superación del vanguardismo', *Los Cuadernos del Norte*, 11 (1982), 56–65

Mainer, José Carlos, *La Edad de Plata (1902–1939): ensayo de interpretación de un proceso cultural*, 4th edn (Madrid: Cátedra, 1987)

Mañá, Gema, et al., *La voz de los náufragos: la narrativa española entre 1936 y 1939* (Madrid: Ediciones de la Torre, 1997)

Marco, Joaquín, 'En torno a la novela social española', *Ínsula* (September 1963), p. 13
Marrast, Robert, *Rafael Alberti en Mexico (1935)* (Santander: La Isla de los Ratones, 1984)
Montseny, Federica, *Mis primeros cuarenta años* (Barcelona: Plaza y Janes, 1987)
Nantell, Judith, *Rafael Alberti's Poetry of the Thirties: The Poet's Public Voice* (Athens, London: University of Georgia Press, 1986)
Núñez Díaz-Balart, Mirta, 'Javier Bueno, un periodista comprometido con la revolución', in *Periodismo y periodistas en la Guerra Civil*, ed. by Jesús Manuel Martínez (Madrid: Fundación Banco Exterior, 1987)
Ortega y Gasset, José, *Ideas sobre el teatro y la novela* (Madrid: Alianza, 1995 [1st edn 1925])
——, *La deshumanización del arte*, 10th edn (Madrid: Alianza, 1996 [1st edn 1925])
Osuna, Rafael, *Las revistas españolas entre dos dictaduras: 1931–1939* (Valencia: Pre-Textos, 1986)
Pérez Bowie, José Antonio, 'Militancia obrera y literatura: la obra novelística de Isidoro Acevedo', *Studia Zamorensia*, 1 (1980), 217–24
——, 'La temática minera en la novela de los años 30', *Studia Philologica Salmantincensia*, 2 (1978), 197–217
Pérez Firmat, Gustavo, *Idle Fictions: The Hispanic Vanguard Novel, 1926–1934* (Durham: Duke University Press, 1993)
Pino, José M. del, *Montajes y fragmentos: una aproximación a la narrativa española de vanguardia* (Amsterdam: Rodopi, 1995)
Rebollo Sánchez, Félix, *Periodismo y movimientos literarios contemporáneos españoles (1900–1939)* (Madrid: Huerga y Fierro, 1998)
Rebollo Torio, Miguel Angel, 'Los lenguajes de la derecha en la II República española', *Tiempo de Historia*, 20 (1976), 12–20
Romeiser, John (ed.), *Red Flags, Black Flags: Critical Essays on the Literature of the Spanish Civil War* (Madrid: José Porrúa Turanzas, 1982)
Santonja, Gonzalo, *Las Novelas Rojas* (Madrid: Ediciones la Torre, 1994)
——, *Las obras que sí escribieron algunos autores que no existen: notas para la historia de la novela revolucionaria de quiosco en España, 1905–1939* (Madrid: La Productora de Ediciones, 1993)
——, *Del lápiz rojo al lápiz libre: la censura de prensa y el mundo del libro* (Barcelona: Anthropos, 1986)
Schwartz, Kessel, *Studies on Twentieth-Century Spanish and Spanish American Literature* (Lanham: University Press of America, 1983)
Sender, Ramón, *Mr Witt en el Cantón* (Madrid: Alianza Editorial, 1995 [1st edn 1935])
——, *Siete domingos rojos*, 4th edn (Buenos Aires: Editorial Proyección, 1975 [1st edn 1932])
——, *Imán*, intro. by Marcelino C. Peñuelas (Barcelona: Destinolibro, 1997 [1st edn 1930])
Soldevila Durante, Ignacio, *La novela desde 1936* (Madrid: Alhambra, 1980)
Suárez, Albino, 'Introducción', *Poemas (Antología)*, by Alfonso Camín (Oviedo: Biblioteca Caja de Ahorros de Asturias, 1990), pp. 5–20
Thomas, Gareth, *The Novel of the Spanish Civil War (1936–1975)* (Cambridge: Cambridge University Press, 1990)
Trapiello, Andrés, *Las armas y las letras: literatura y guerra civil (1936–1939)* (Barcelona: Editorial Planeta, 1994)
Vallejo, César, *El arte y la revolución* (Lima: Mosca Azul Editores, 1973)
Wesseling, Pieter, *Revolution and Tradition: The Poetry of Rafael Alberti* (Valencia: Ed. Albatros Hispanófila, 1981)

E. Literary Theory

This final category includes works dealing with various theoretical aspects of fiction, fact, and history, and their relationship; studies on ideological discourse and propaganda; and texts which tackle the issue of generic classification.

Bakhtin, M. M., *The Dialogic Imagination: Four Essays*, ed. by Michael Holquist, trans. by Caryl Emerson and Michael Holquist (Austin: University of Texas Press, 1996)
Baldick, Chris, *The Concise Oxford Dictionary of Literary Terms* (Oxford: Oxford University Press, 1990)
Baquero Goyanes, Mariano, 'Sobre la novela y sus límites', *Arbor*, 8 (1949), 271–83

Barker, Andrew, 'Anna Seghers, Friedrich Wolf, and the Austrian Civil War of 1934', *MLR*, 95 (2000), 144–53

Booth, Wayne C., *The Rhetoric of Fiction*, 2nd edn (London: Penguin, 1991)

Bowra, C. M., *Poetry and Politics 1900–1960* (Cambridge: Cambridge University Press, 1966)

Brumm, Ursula, 'Thoughts on History and the Novel', *Comparative Literature Studies*, 6 (1969), 317–29

Bruss, Elizabeth W., *Autobiographical Acts: The Changing Situation of a Literary Genre* (Baltimore: Johns Hopkins University Press, 1976)

Bulhof, Ilse, 'Imagination and Interpretation in History', in *Literature and History*, ed. by Leonard Schulze and Walter Wetzels (Lanham: University Press of America, 1983), pp. 3–25

Butterfield, Herbert, *The Historical Novel: An Essay* (Cambridge: Cambridge University Press, 1924)

Calderwood, James, and Harold Toliver, eds, *Perspectives on Fiction* (New York: Oxford University Press, 1968)

Caute, David, *The Illusion: An Essay on Politics, Theatre and the Novel* (London: Panther, 1971)

Cohen, Ralph, ed., *New Directions in Literary History* (London: Routledge and Keegan Paul, 1974)

Collingwood, P. G., *The Idea of History* (Oxford: Clarendon Press, 1946)

Cruttwell, Patrick, 'Makers and Persons', *Hudson Review*, 12 (1959–60), 487–507

Duff, David, ed., *Modern Genre Theory* (Essex: Longman, 2000)

Fernández Prieto, Celia, *Historia y novela: poética de la novela histórica* (Pamplona: EUNSA, 1998)

Fleishman, Avrom, *The English Historical Novel: Walter Scott to Virginia Woolf* (Baltimore: Johns Hopkins University Press, 1971)

Foley, Barbara, *Telling the Truth: The Theory and Practice of Documentary Fiction* (Ithaca: Cornell University Press, 1986)

——, 'Fact, Fiction, and "Reality"', *Contemporary Literature*, 20 (1979), 389–99

Foulkes, A. P., *Literature and Propaganda* (London: Methuen, 1983)

Fowler, Alastair, *Kinds of Literature: An Introduction to the Theory of Genres and Modes* (Oxford: Clarendon Press, 1982)

Gallie, Walter Bryce, *Philosophy and the Historical Understanding* (London: Chatto & Windus, 1964)

Gaus, Helmut, *The Function of Fiction: The Function of Written Fiction in the Social Process* (Gent: E. Story-Scientia, 1979)

Gay, Peter, *Style in History* (New York, London: W. W. Norton & Co., 1974)

Gorgoza Fletcher, Madeline, *The Spanish Historical Novel 1870–1979* (London: Tamesis Books, 1973)

Gossman, Lionel, *Between History and Literature* (Cambridge, MA: Harvard University Press, 1990)

Gutkind, Lee, *The Art of Creative Nonfiction: Writing and Selling the Literature of Reality* (New York: John Wiley and Sons, 1997)

Hawkes, David, *Ideology* (London: Rouledge, 1996)

Hayward, Malcolm, 'Genre recognition of history and fiction', *Poetics*, 22 (1994), 409–21

Heirbrant, Serge, 'Historical Novels and the French Revolution', in *Tropes of Revolution: Writer's Reactions to Real and Imagined Revolutions 1789–1989*, ed. by C. C. Barfoot and Theo D'haen (Amsterdam and Atlanta: Rodopi, 1991), pp. 305–19

Hellmann, John, *Fables of Fact: The New Journalism as New Fiction* (Urbana: Illinois University Press, 1981)

Herrnstein Smith, Barbara, 'On the Margins of Discourse', *Critical Inquiry*, 1 (1975), 769–98

Hicks, Malcolm, and Gill Hutchings, *Literary Criticism: A Practical Student's Guide* (London: Edward Arnold, 1989)

Hollowell, John, *Fact and Fiction: The New Journalism and the Nonfiction Novel* (Chapel Hill: University of North Carolina Press, 1977)

Howe, Irving, *Politics and the Novel* (Freeport, New York: Books for Library Press, 1957)

Hutchinson, Peter, *Games Authors Play* (London: Methuen, 1983)

Johnson, Scott, *The Hero and the Class Struggle in the Contemporary Spanish Novel: An Essay on the Role of the Proletariat in Twentieth Century Spanish Literature* (New York: Gordon Press, 1977)
Labanyi, Jo, *Myth and History in the Contemporary Spanish Novel* (Cambridge: Cambridge University Press, 1989)
LaCapra, Dominick, *History, Politics, and the Novel* (Ithaca, London: Cornell University Press, 1987)
——, *History and Criticism* (Ithaca: Cornell University Press, 1985)
Lamarque, Peter, and Stein Olsen, *Truth, Fiction and Literature: A Philosophical Perspective* (Oxford: Clarendon Press, 1994)
Lange, Victor, 'Fact in Fiction', *Comparative Literature Studies*, 6 (1969), 253–61
Leech, Geoffrey N., and Michael H. Short, *Style in Fiction: A Linguistic Introduction to English Fictional Prose* (London: Longman, 1980)
Lerner, Laurence, *The Frontiers of Literature* (Oxford: Basil Backwell, 1988)
Lodge, David, 'The Novelist at the Crossroads', in *The Novel Today: Contemporary Writers on Modern Fiction*, ed. by Malcolm Bradbury (London: Fontana Press, 1990), pp. 87–114
——, (ed.), *Modern Criticism and Theory: A Reader* (London: Longman, 1988)
Lukacs, Georg, *The Theory of the Novel* (London: Merlin, 1971)
——, *The Historical Novel* (London: Merlin, 1962)
Mailer, Norman, *The Armies of the Night: History as a Novel: the Novel as History* (London: Weidenfeld & Nicolson, 1968)
Mander, John, *The Writer and Commitment*, 8th edn (London: Sacker and Warburg, 1961)
Manzoni, Alessandro, *On the Historical Novel*, trans. and intro. by Sandra Bermann (Lincoln: University of Nebraska Press, 1984)
Mills, Sara, *Discourse* (London: Routledge, 1997)
Mink, Louis, 'Narrative Form as a Cognitive Instrument', in *The Writing of History: Literary Form and Historical Understanding*, ed. by Robert H. Canary and Henry Kozicki (Madison: University of Wisconsin Press, 1978), pp. 129–49
Murfin, Ross, and Supryia Ray, *The Bedford Glossary of Critical and Literary Terms* (Boston, MA: Bedford Books, 1998)
Nieto, Ramón, 'El lenguaje y la política', *Cuadernos para el Diálogo*, 111 (1972), 11–14
Panichas, George A., 'The Writer and Society: Some Reflections', in *The Politics of Twentieth-Century Novelists*, ed. by George A. Panichas (New York: Hawthorn Books, 1971), pp. xxiii–liv
Ribbans, Geoffrey, *History and Fiction in Galdós's Narratives* (Oxford: Clarendon Press, 1993)
Roberts, Thomas J., *When is Something Fiction?* (Carbondale: Southern Illinois University Press, 1972)
Rowley, Brian A., 'Journalism into Fiction: Erich Maria Remarque, *Im Western Nichts Neues*', in *The First World War in Fiction: A Collection of Critical Essays*, ed. by Holger Klein (London: Macmillan Press, 1976), pp. 101–11
Sauerberg, Lars Ole, *Fact into Fiction: Documentary Realism in the Contemporary Novel* (London: Macmillan, 1991)
Scholes, Robert, 'Language, Narrative, and Anti-Narrative' *Critical Inquiry*, 7 (1980–81), 204–12
Scholes, Robert, and Robert Kellogg, *The Nature of Narrative* (Oxford: Oxford University Press, 1966)
Scott, Walter, *Waverley* (London: Penguin Books, 1972)
Shaw, Harry, 'The Historical Novel', in *Encyclopaedia of Literature and Criticism*, ed. by Martin Coyle, et al. (London: Routledge, 1991), pp. 531–43
——, *The Forms of Historical Fiction: Sir Walter Scott and his Successors* (Ithaca and London: Cornell University Press, 1983)
Smart, Robert, *The Nonfiction Novel* (Lanham, London: University Press of America, 1985)
Spang, Kurt, Ignacio Arellano, and Carlos Mata, eds, *La novela histórica: teoría y comentarios*, 2nd edn (Pamplona: EUNSA, 1998)
——, *Géneros literarios* (Madrid: Síntesis, 1996)
Spender, Stephen, *The Thirties and After: Poetry, Politics, and People (1933–75)* (London: Fontana, 1978)
Stock, Brian, 'Literary Discourse and the Social Historian', *New Literary History*, 8 (1976), 183–94

Stott, William, *Documentary Expression and Thirties America* (London: Oxford University Press, 1973)

Swales, John, *Genre Analysis: English in Academic and Research Settings* (Cambridge: Cambridge University Press, 1990)

Tillotson, Kathleen, *Novels of the Eighteen Forties* (Oxford: Clarendon Press, 1954)

Todorov, Tzvetan, *Genres in Discourse*, trans. by Catherine Porter (Cambridge: Cambridge University Press, 1990)

——, 'The Origin of Genres', *New Literary History*, 8 (1976), 159–70

Tuñón de Lara, Manuel, 'La historiografía de ayer y hoy', *Triunfo* (13 May 1972), pp. 38–41

Urey, Diane Faye, *The Novel Histories of Galdós* (New Jersey: Princeton University Press, 1989)

Villanueva, Darío, *El comentario de textos narrativos: la novela* (Gijón: Ediciones Jucar, 1995)

Walder, Dennis, ed., *Literature in the Modern World: Critical Essays and Documents* (Oxford: Oxford University Press, 1990)

Walsh, William H., *An Introduction to Philosophy of History* (Bristol, Thoemmes Press, 1992)

Weber, Ronald, *The Literature of Fact: Literary Non-Fiction in American Writing* (Athens, OH: Ohio University Press, 1980)

Weintraub, Karl J., 'Autobiography and Historical Consciousness', *Critical Inquiry*, 1 (1975), 821–48

Wellek, René, and Austin Warren, *Theory of Literature*, 3rd edn (New York: Harcourt Brace, 1956)

Wesseling, Elizabeth, *Writing History as a Prophet: Postmodernist Innovations of the Historical Novel* (Amsterdam and Philadelphia: John Benjamins Publishing Co., 1991)

White, Hayden, *The Content of the Form: Narrative Discourse and Historical Representation* (Baltimore: Johns Hopkins University Press, 1987)

——, 'The Value of Narrativity in the Representation of Reality', *Critical Inquiry*, 8 (1981), 5–27

——, 'The Fictions of Factual Representation', in *The Literature of Fact: Selected Papers from the English Institute*, ed. by Angus Fletcher (New York: Columbia University Press, 1976), pp. 21–44

Williams, Raymond, *Keywords: A Vocabulary of Culture and Society* (London: Croom Helm, 1976)

INDEX

ABC newspaper, 110, 247, 253
Acción Española magazine, 65
Acción Popular, 264
Acción Republicana, 19, 59
Acevedo, Isidoro, 69
!Acusamos! El asesinato de Luis de Sirval (compilation), 105–07
Adro Xavier (pseud.), 175, 190, 202–12, 236, 237
  right-wing stance, 202
A.G. (possibly Antonio Gascón), 85, 93, 96, 114 n13
agrarian reform, 60
Agrupación al Servicio de la República, 60
air raids and bombardments, 142, 157, 163, 189
Alberti, Rafael, 66, 68, 69, 70, 72–73
Albornoz, Álvaro de, 103
Alcalá Zamora, Don Niceto, 19, 20, 25–26, 39, 214, 232, 279, 309
Alfonso XIII, King, 17, 60
Alianza Obrera, 17, 29, 153, 310
  censure in pro-revolutionary texts, 255
  pact and terms, 27–28, 288
  political issues/support, 154, 282
  and Revolution, 31–37
  and socialist hostility, 156
  supporter for, 80, 255
  as a unifying force, 169
  and working class, 155
Alianza Republicana, 59–60
Alomar, Gabriel, 105, 106, 107
Altolaguirre, Manuel, 73
Álvarez del Vayo, Julio, 39, 69, 70, 71
anarchists, 93, 287–88, 290–91
  art/literature, 290–91, 299
  boycott of Revolution, 155, 157, 279
  censure for Revolution failure, 255
  parallels with lay religion, 295–96
anarcho-syndicalists, 29
Antuña, Graciano, 23
Araquistain, Luis, 66, 105, 106
Arboleya, Maximiliano, 191
Arconada, César M., 57–58, 64, 68, 70, 240, 321–32
Arconada, Hermano Juan B., 202–12
  imprisonment and death, 207
Arderíus, Joaquín, 52, 53, 57, 68, 69
Las Arenas, 164
arms and weapons
  provenance and supplies, 95–96
  of revolutionaries, 95–96, 122, 135, 136–37, 140, 159–61, 261, 312–13
  Turquesa incident, 30–31, 95
army, 93, 109, 327–38
  see also government forces; repression
Arnedo revolt, 62
Arriba magazine, 65
Arroyo, Vicente, 28–29
Asesinos de España (Karl), 80
Asociación Católica Nacional de Propagandistas (A.C.N.P.), 144, 145, 146–47
Association des Ecrivains et Artistes Révolutionnaires (A.E.A.R.), 69, 70
Asturian Revolution (1934)
  textual representations, 320–31
  see also October Revolution
!!Asturias!!: relato vivido de la insurrección de octubre (Valdés), 240, 258–82
Asturias en el resurgimiento español (Oliveros), 80
Asturias la desventurada: caminos de sangre (Prada), 175, 176–90, 211, 217, 318–19
Asturias roja (A.C.N.P.), 144, 150
Ateneos, 102
  Madrid, 60, 62
atrocities
  during repression, 37–38, 108–10
  during Revolution, 37, 70–71, 95, 128, 145–46
Aub, Max, 47, 69
autobiographical/biographical texts, 94–95, 120, 135–36
  La insurrección de Asturias (Grossi Mier), 152–70, 256
  La Revolución en Asturias. Octubre 1934 (Llano Roza), 133–44
  see also novelized biography
Avance, 24, 28, 31, 71, 128, 131, 132, 163
avant-garde literature, 45–51, 57–59
  criticism of, 52
Avilés, 33, 136, 158, 219, 270
Ayala, Francisco, 47, 54, 60
Ayuda newspaper, 329
Azaña y Díaz, Manuel, 62, 71, 126, 130, 214
  electoral defeat/success, 21, 40, 121
  post-Revolution writings, 80–81, 86, 87–88, 94, 96, 100–01, 105, 106

Republican allegiance, 19, 59
Azor magazine, 65
Azorín, 71

Bacarisse, Mauricio, 57
Balbontín, J. A., 52
Balmes, General, 33
Barcelona, 34, 70, 81
La Barraca mobile theatre, 63
Basque Country, 25
Benavides, Manuel, 64, 71, 110, 255, 260, 301
Benzo y Cano, Eduardo, 138, 141
Bergamín, José, 64, 70, 71, 73–74
Bergés, Consuelo, 80, 84, 93–94, 96, 98
Bernueces, 219
Bertrand de Muñoz, Maryse, 337
Besteiro, Julián, 22, 66, 71, 214, 255, 268
biography *see* autobiographical/biographical texts
Bizcarrondo, Marta, 264, 278
Blanco, Fernando (Governor of Asturias), 131
BOC (Bloc Obrer i Camperol), 27, 28, 35
Bosch, General, 33, 88, 135, 229
bourgeoisie, 93–94, 280, 310, 314, 318, 326
Bueno, Javier, 24, 71, 105, 110
  supposed torture, 128, 164, 224

El Caballero Audaz, 80, 85, 88, 89, 91, 92, 96, 97
  literary style, 98
  on *Turquesa* incident, 95
Caballo Verde para la Poesia magazine, 65
Calvo Sotelo, José, 81, 104, 203
Cámara Santa destruction, 122, 142, 163
Camín Meana, Alfonso, 1, 175–76, 213–36, 237, 247, 255
  narrative strategies, 215–16
Caminos de sangre. Asturias la desventurada (Prada), 318–19
Campoamor, Clara, 39
Campomanes, 31, 126, 165, 216, 269, 315–16
Cansinos-Assens, Rafael, 45
Capote, Truman, 6
Carbayín, 166–67
La cárcel por dentro (Quintanilla), 111–12
Carranque de Ríos, Andrés, 64, 68, 70
Carretero, J. M., 58
  see also 'El Caballero Audaz'
Carrillo, Santiago, 111
Casa del Pueblo, 145, 163
Casas Viejas revolt, 62
Castilblanco revolt, 62
Castrovido, Roberto, 105, 106
Catalonia, 25, 27, 34, 279
  independence issue, 155
  statute of autonomy, 60
Catholic Church, 62, 123, 133
  attacks on buildings, 128, 140–41, 142
  criticism of, 256, 266–67, 327
  left-wing opposition to, 130, 147–48, 326
  reforms, 203
  youth organization (Juventud Católica), 145
  see also Christianity; clergy and religious orders
Catholic Trade Union (Sindicato Católico de Obreros Mineros Españoles), 175, 190–91, 194
  and revolutionaries, 191–92
CEDA (Confederación Española de Derechas Autónomas), 21, 22, 23–24, 25, 26, 40, 126, 147, 214
  demonstrations/support, 259
  and Lerroux cabinet, 246, 309
CEDA — Radical Party coalition, 40
Cernuda, Luis, 66
Chacel, Rosa, 47
Christianity
  and communism, 73–74
  and the Revolution, 325
the Church *see* Catholic Church
Ciaño barracks attack, 126, 137
Cienfuegos, Casimiro, 73
Ciges Aparicio, Manuel, 68
Civil Guard, 36, 38–39, 136, 137, 223
  Adro's praise for, 202
  attacks on barracks, 122, 126
  criticisms of, 163, 229
  defence tactics, 133, 136
  and Geijo's account, 136
  repression atrocities, 109–10
Civil War *see* Spanish Civil War
Claridad magazine, 65
clergy and religious orders
  attacks on, 144, 148
  criticism of, 266–67
  and local population, 148, 151
  persecution of Passionists, 144–45
  Turón murders of Lasallian brothers, 37, 144, 145, 164–65
  victimization of, 146, 148, 150
CNT (Confederación Nacional del Trabajo), 22, 27, 35
coal mining industry, 18, 131
  see also miners
'Colección Valores Actuales', 47
collages, 175–76
  La revolución fue así (Benavides), 247
  El Valle Negro (Camín Meana), 213–36, 247, 255
Comité Luis de Sirval, 105, 112
communism/communists, 29, 68–69, 93, 325
  and Church/Christianity, 73–74, 190
  and October Revolution, 203, 264
  propaganda, 277–78
Communist Party, 25, 28, 66, 107, 278
  integration into Alianza Obrera, 28–29

Valdés' portrayal of, 260, 271, 275, 280–82
Companys, Luis, 34, 111
Confederación Nacional de Sindicatos Católicos Obreros, 191
Congreso Internacional de Escritores para la Defensa de la Cultura (First and Second), 69–70, 71, 73
La Conquista del Estado magazine, 65
Cossío, Francisco de, 80, 81, 83, 85, 86, 91, 96, 98
descriptive writing, 100
Cossío, Manuel, 62–63
Covadonga, 214
Basilica, 211
creative writing, 176
Los crímenes de la reacción española (S.R.I.), 107–10
Cruz y Raya magazine, 64, 66, 73, 74
Cuartel Pelayo assault, 124, 135, 162, 261, 276
Los Cuatro Vientos magazine, 65

El Debate newspaper, 110, 253
Díaz Fernández, José
journalistic career, 303–04
literary career, 44, 52, 53, 54, 55–57, 66, 68
Octubre rojo en Asturias, 240, 241, 255, 259, 303–21
'El Dios de los niños' (Espina), 322, 325–32
documentary genre, 7, 12, 240
Documentos Socialistas (compilation), 80, 85, 94, 96
Dos Passos, John, 6
Doval, General, 93

Echevarrieta, Horacio, 97
Ehrenburg, Ilya, 66
Empirical to Fictional narrative continuum, 6–7
Episodios de la revolución en Asturias (El Pasionario), 144, 145–52
Episodios de la revolución (Geijo), 133, 144, 145, 146, 147, 148–49, 150, 219
Ermita de Santa Cristina, 225
Espina, Antonio, 46–47, 53, 55, 60, 105, 106
Espina, Concha, 240, 322–32
essays, 98
La deshumanización del arte (Ortega), 48–49, 56
Ideas sobre la novela (Ortega), 48, 49–50
El nuevo romanticismo (Díaz Fernández), 56, 57
Estévez, Edmundo, 88
Europe, 53, 61, 98
intellectual movements, 68–70

fact/fiction genres: definitions, 6–8, 11–12
FAI (Federación Anarquista Ibérica), 36, 288
Falcón, César, 52, 53
Farsa y tragedia de España en el 1934 (Valdivielso), 80
fascism/fascists, 61, 70, 80, 92
manifesto, 59
and S.R.I., 107, 112
F.E. magazine, 65
Federación de Obreros Mineros de España, 254
Federación Socialista Asturiana, 23
La Felguera, 33, 35–36, 148, 219
Fernández, Sergeant Dionisio, 126
Fernández Ladreda, José María, 104
fiction genre, 176
definitions/characteristics, 6–7, 11–12, 236
fiction/non-fiction texts: analysis
author bias, 177, 193, 227–28
author–narrator technique, 179, 183, 221
author–reader messages, 181, 182
biblical/classical references, 220
biographical form, 202, 212
categorization, 197–98, 212, 219, 222–23
characterization, 177–78
descriptive language, 178, 206, 211–12
dialogue/direct speech, 181–82, 198–99
diaristic accounts, 219–20
dramatic representation, 176–78, 182–83
factual/documentary style, 176, 187–88, 189–90
fictional/novelistic techniques, 176–77, 179, 189, 211, 212
literary techniques/devices, 203, 209, 220–21, 232–35
metaphors and symbolism, 178, 209–11, 212, 220, 231–35
narrative styles, 176–78, 184, 189–90, 193, 215–16, 218, 219–21, 236
plots and settings, 177, 198
politics and propaganda, 203, 212, 221–22, 223, 237
prologues, 184–85, 192, 203–04, 209
transcription technique, 185, 189
verification/sources, 199, 208–09, 224, 236
witness evidence, 178–79, 199, 216, 219, 223–24
fiction/non-fiction texts: collage, *El valle negro: Asturias 1934* (Camín Meana) 175–76, 213–36, 247, 255
fiction/non-fiction texts: dramatized vignettes, *Asturias la desventurada: caminos de sangre* (Prada), 175, 176–90, 211, 217, 318–19
fiction/non-fiction texts: novelized biography, *Sangre jesuita. Asturias 1934* (Adro Xavier), 175, 202–12
fiction/non-fiction texts: *relato* in the first person, *El sindicato católico de Moreda y*

la revolución de octubre (Madera), 175, 190–99, 337
FNTT (Federación Nacional de Trabajadores de la Tierra), 23
Franco, General Francisco, 37, 91, 93
Frente Popular, 71, 103
see also Popular Front
Frente Único, 278, 280, 282
Futurist manifesto publication, 48

La Gaceta Literaria, 54, 57, 61
Galán, Fermín, 53, 54, 55
El Gallo Crisis magazine, 65
García Lorca, Federico, 60, 63
García, Manuel, 192, 193, 197, 337
García Morales, Juan, 105
Geijo, Jenaro, 120, 133–44, 169
Gendín, Sabino, 146–47
Germany
literary influences, 53–54
political influences, 61
Gide, André, 66, 69, 73
Gijón, 33, 34, 35, 136, 155, 219, 269
socialists/anarchists division, 157, 158, 168
Gil Robles, José María, 40, 92, 156
and CEDA, 21, 25, 26, 214
'confession', 254
and repression, 108
and Revolution, 104, 214, 227
Gil-Albert, Juan, 73
Giménez Caballero, Ernesto, 46, 54, 57, 58, 61, 63
Giménez Siles, R., 52
Glaesar, Ernst, 53
Gómez de la Serna, Ramón, 46, 47–48, 54, 57
Gómez de la Serna, Víctor, 110
Gómez, Trifón, 255
Gondi, Ovidio, 105, 106
González Peña, Ramón, 39, 81, 94, 97, 103, 106, 130, 224, 308, 325
González Tuñón, Raúl, 73
Gordón Ordás, Félix, 39, 71
repression investigation/report, 103–05, 108, 109, 112, 254
Sirval assassination, 105, 106
Gorki, Máximo, 66
Gorkin, J., 106–07, 155, 168–69
government forces, 220, 262–63, 326
collaboration issues, 157
defence organization, 195–96
Foreign Legion involvement, 33, 37–39, 327
left-wing allegations against, 88, 162–64
military actions/manoeuvres, 133, 136, 250, 264
and patriotism/*Patria*, 137
Tercio and Regulares, 108, 247, 264–65
trials of members, 135
troop numbers, 135, 136
see also Civil Guard; Moorish troops; repression
Grado, Joaquín: funeral, 25, 273, 275, 279
Grado (town), 219
Grossi Mier, Manuel, 35, 120, 152–70, 256
'El guaje' (Sender), 321, 322, 323

Hacia la segunda revolución (Maurín), 79–80
Hacia una nueva España (Cossío), 80, 81, 83, 85, 86, 91, 96, 100, 101
Halcón, Fernando, 140
Haz magazine, 65
Hellman, John, 86, 130
Hermosilla, A., 105, 106, 107
Heroínas (Montseny), 240, 255, 287–303
historical novels, 3–6, 50, 240, 244–45
historiography, 5
and novels, 9–10, 244
report writing, 176
history (historia/Historia)
and art, 111–12
definitions, 12, 81–82
historians' neutrality, 127
and literature, 4–10
as mix of myth and reality, 82–83
new historicism, 83
Hoja Literaria magazine, 59
Horizontes magazine, 65

Ibárruri, Dolores, 29, 68
Iglesias, Pablo, 214
Información magazine, 133, 141, 142
Informaciones newspaper, 110, 127
La insurrección de Asturias (Grossi Mier), 152–70, 256
'Intelectual' (León), 321, 323–24, 327–32
intellectuals
communist sympathizers, 107–08
imprisonment, 71–72
political engagement of writers, 84–85
and propaganda, 122, 204
role in politics, 59–62
role in Revolution, 70, 130, 133, 255–56
Sirval trial and written response, 71, 105–07
socio-political convictions, 64–65
Ivanov, Dimitri Ivan, 38, 71, 218, 223
Izquierda Comunista, 27, 28
Izquierda Republicana, 241

Jarnés, Benjamín, 46, 54, 60
Jesuits, 207, 211
Jiménez, Juan Ramón, 71
Jons magazine, 65
journalism/journalists
accounts of Revolution, 79, 80, 81–89, 176
censorship, 39, 52, 53, 71, 110, 111

journalistic style of vignettes, 176, 187–88
and politics, 98
and reality, 86
Juventud Católica, 145
Juventudes Socialistas, 23, 34

Karl, Mauricio, 80, 84–85, 87, 88, 91, 95, 96, 98
and fascism, 92
satirical comments, 97

Lafuente, Aida ('La Libertaria'), 94–95, 217–18, 268, 289–90, 308
Laín Entralgo, José, 23
Langreo, 31, 311, 315
attack on barracks, 122
victimization of clergy, 144, 145–46
Langreo rojo (Suárez), 144–52
Largo Caballero, Francisco, 18–19, 20, 21, 22, 23, 111, 214
cabinet, 288
post-Revolution criticisms, 93, 97, 126, 130, 140
Ledesma Ramos, Ramiro, 57, 61, 63, 65, 135
left-wing politics
conflicting ideologies, 302
government, 59, 62, 202
moderates, 80
and patriotism, 92
splits and divisions, 92, 93, 255
see also Alianza Obrera; Popular Front; Socialist Party
León, 103, 157
León, María Teresa, 66, 68, 240, 321–32
Lerroux, Alejandro, 19, 21, 23, 26, 39, 72, 214, 246
post-Revolution criticism, 92, 131, 279
and repression, 103, 105, 111
Letra magazine, 65
Leviatán magazine, 65, 66–67
'Liberación de octubre' (León), 321, 322–33, 325–32
El Liberal newspaper, 71, 72
La Libertad newspaper, 72
Libertad (warship), 33
Linea magazine, 65
'literatura de avanzada', 44, 51–59
literature
and creativity, 301, 302
definitions, 7–8, 11–12
and political movements, 244–45
prose, 44, 45–46, 64–65, 67
rhetorical narrative, 301
socially committed, 302
see also Spanish literature
Llanera, 33
Llaneza, Manuel, 214
Llano Roza de Ampudia, Aurelio de, 120, 128
Revolution account, 133–44, 169
López Ochoa, General, 33–34, 38, 108, 109, 133, 163, 217, 232, 250, 269, 308
criticism of, 265
La Lucha magazine, 65
Lukàcs, Georg, 2, 4

Machado, Antonio, 59, 60, 66, 70
Madera, Vicente, 175, 190–99, 202, 236, 237
as miner and Catholic, 193, 196
motives for writing, 192–93
political stance, 191–92
Madrid, 34, 69, 70, 191, 255
lack of support for Revolution, 155
Maeztu, Ramiro de, 61
Magazines, 45–46, 64–65, 67
Mailer, Norman, 6
La Manjoya execution, 32, 263, 276
Manzoni, Alessandro, 2, 4–5
Marinetti, Filippo Tommaso, 48
Martínez, Francisco, 203, 208, 211
Martínez, José María, 27, 308
Martínez, Padre Emilio, 202–12
Los mártires de Asturias (Rucabado), 144, 145
Los mártires de Turón (Anon.), 144, 145, 146, 147, 148, 150, 152
Marxism/Marxists, 59, 123
Mas, José, 68
Maura, Miguel, 19, 20
Maurín, Joaquín, 26, 36, 79, 80, 85, 90, 93, 94–95, 98
on arms and forces, 95–96
descriptive/discursive style differences, 99
Prologue to Grossi Mier's account, 154, 168
Menéndez, Teodomiro, 23, 39, 268, 308, 318–19
Mi rebelión en Barcelona (Azaña), 80
Michel, Louise, 290
Mieres, 31, 32, 33, 35, 153, 176, 313, 316
bombing, 163
persecution of the Passionist community, 144–45, 146
Revolutionary Committee, 165, 311
military, 36, 136
reports/texts, 120, 133–44, 321
miners, 146, 165, 230–31
instigation of/devotion to Revolution, 90, 122, 130, 157
and socio-economic situation, 314–15
surrender, 38
Miranda, Marco, 39, 103, 108, 109, 247
Misiones Pedagógicas, 62–63
Molins i Fábrega, N., 152–70, 256
Montseny, Federica, 240, 241, 255, 259, 287–303
anarchist beliefs, 287–88, 300, 302–03
background and childhood, 287–88, 293

Moorish troops, 33, 218, 223, 230, 265
brutality of, 37–88, 109, 288, 327
Moroccan wars, 54, 55, 265
Mundo Obrero magazine, 65

La Nación newspaper, 110, 253
narratives
definition, 12
see also post-Revolution narratives
New Journalism, 86, 130
definition, 242–43
non-fiction genre
concepts and definitions, 6–7, 11–12, 14, 240
generic categories, 241
see also non-fictional accounts; non-fictional novels; short stories
non-fictional accounts: analysis
authenticity and credibility, 136, 144
authors' scholarship/erudition, 141–44
bias and prejudice, 138, 139–41, 142, 144, 150, 152, 153
diaristic accounts, 134–35, 152–53, 165, 168, 169
fabrication and misinformation, 127–28
ideological/political stance, 147, 155, 170
investigative journalism, 164
manipulative strategies used, 121–22, 126–30, 150–51, 165–66, 170
narrative styles, 129–30, 143–44
objectivity issue, 153–54, 169
omissions and selective devices, 125–26, 132–33
propagandistic effects, 124, 170
rhetorical techniques, 125, 128, 130, 150
use of descriptive/emotive language, 128, 166–67, 170
use of first-person relating, 190–99
use of literary language, 143, 151, 152, 166, 168
verification and sources, 125–26, 143, 144
see also government and counter-revolutionary accounts; military and police accounts; religious accounts; revolutionary accounts
non-fictional accounts: government and counter-revolutionary
Octubre rojo: ocho dias que conmovieron a España (Reporteros Reunidos), 121
La revolución de octubre de 1934 (Núñez), 121, 123, 124–33, 169
La revolución de octubre en España (government report), 120, 121, 122–23, 224–25
El sargento Vázquez (Romero Cuesta), 121, 123–24, 135
non-fictional accounts: military and police
Episodios de la revolución (Geijo), 133, 134–44
La Revolución en Asturias. Octubre 1934 (Llano Roza), 133–44
non-fictional accounts: religious
Asturias roja (A.C.N.P.), 144, 146–47, 150
Episodios de la revolución en Asturias (El Pasionario), 144, 145–52
Langreo rojo (Suárez), 144–52
Los mártires de Asturias (Rucabado), 144, 145
Los mártires de Turón (Anon.), 144, 145, 146, 147, 148, 150, 152
non-fictional accounts: revolutionary works
La insurrección de Asturias (Grossi Mier), 152–70, 256
U.H.P.: la insurrección proletaria de Asturias (Molins), 152–70, 256
non-fictional novels: analysis, 6, 14, 240, 241–45, 321
analysis and definition, 243–44
author objectives, 305, 308
categorization of texts, 241, 249, 258, 288–89, 291
characterizations/pseudonyms, 248–49, 268–69, 288–90, 292–94, 301, 306, 308
collages, 247
data selection and omission, 247, 253–54
dialogues/colloquialisms, 251, 257, 280–81
documentary/historical aspects, 246, 247, 253, 258, 276, 288, 311
fictional characterizations, 247, 260, 268–71, 289–90, 317–18
figurative language and imagery, 249–51, 271–72, 273–74, 302, 305–06
ideological/political bias, 241, 251–52, 253–54, 260, 268, 271–72, 275, 276, 278–79, 299–301, 305–06, 320
literariness, 319–20
manipulation of evidence and characters, 254–55, 318–19
metaphors and symbolism, 249–50, 273–74, 319–20
narrative/rhetorical structure, 241, 246, 250, 257–58, 260, 301, 305–06
narrator strategies (verbal tense/person), 246, 249, 252, 275, 299
plots and themes, 244, 259, 260, 264, 267, 292, 296, 310, 313–14
selection/omission of data, 277
stylistic/linguistic devices, 248, 251, 299
verification devices, 275, 306–09
non-fictional novels
¡¡Asturias!!: relato vivido de la insurrección de octubre (Valdés), 240, 258–82
Heroínas (Montseny), 240, 255, 287–303
Octubre rojo en Asturias (Díaz Fernández), 240, 255, 303–21

La revolución fue así: octubre rojo y negro (Benavides), 240, 245–58, 253–55
Nosotros magazine, 53
'Nova Novorum' series, 46–47
Noval Suárez, Senén, 144, 146, 147, 148, 150, 151
novel genre, 4–10, 240, 321
  biographical, 212
  development, 46–51, 52–53
  First World War influence, 53–54
  and historiography, 9–10, 53–54
  metahistorical, 7
  novela comprometida, 269
  pacificist, 53–55
  pseudofactual, 7, 14
  socio-political influences, 67–68
La Novela Libre (Ediciones de la Revista Blanca), 287, 299
La Novela Proletaria (1932–33), 290
novelized biography, 175, 202–12
  comparison of texts, 208–09, 211–12
novelized biography texts
  Dos jesuitas mártires de Asturias: el P. Emilio Martínez y el H. Juan B. Arconada (Martínez), 203, 208–09, 211–12
  Sangre jesuita. Asturias 1934: Padre Emilio Martínez y H. Juan B. Arconada (Adro Xavier), 175, 202–12
Nuestro Cinema magazine, 65
Nueva Cultura magazine, 58, 65
Nueva España magazine, 53
Núñez, Ignacio, 120–33
Núñez Díaz-Balart, Mirta, 92

October Revolution, 31–37
  air raids/bombardments, 142, 157, 163, 318, 328
  atrocities and violence, 37, 70–71, 95, 128, 145–46
  casualties/deaths, 36, 37, 38–39, 40, 71, 121, 122
  and Catholicism, 147–48, 151
  causal factors, 138–39, 155, 203, 226, 246, 254, 257–58, 314–15, 323
  civilian sufferings and traumas, 70–74, 180–81, 184, 213, 216–18, 266, 282, 315–16
  destruction accounts, 36–37, 100, 122, 142–43, 187–88
  effects on vulnerable sector, 322–24, 327
  executions, 32, 38–39, 40, 71, 95, 97, 263, 276
  failure and surrender, 34, 155, 158–59, 254, 257–58, 261, 296
  hospitals, 36, 315–16
  post-revolution analysis and lessons, 267–68
  preparations, 26–31, 155–56, 198
  prisons/prisoners, 110, 162, 185, 276–77, 318
  social/economic organization, 35–36, 161
  social/political background, 90, 123, 226–29, 259
  support for, 148, 153, 155, 264, 272
  time factor, 273–74
  see also government forces; repression; Revolutionary Committee; revolutionary forces
Octubre magazine, 65, 66–67
Octubre rojo: ocho dias que conmovieron a España (Reporteros Reunidos), 121
Octubre rojo en Asturias (Díaz Fernández), 240, 255, 303–21
Oliveros, Antonio, 80, 81–83, 90, 91, 92, 96, 98, 99–100, 128
Olmo, Rosario del, 69
Ortega y Gasset, Eduardo, 60, 108
Ortega y Gasset, José, 46, 48–50, 56, 60, 84
Oviedo, 31–33, 34, 35, 95, 163, 176, 247, 328
  actions/fighting, 156–57, 260–61
  bombing, 142, 163, 277
  Cárcel Modelo, 110, 165, 276
  destruction, 36, 100, 142, 188
  executions, 39
  and miners/working class, 226–27, 314–15
  university destruction, 165–66, 312
  writers' accounts: Camín, 216–18
  writers' accounts: Díaz Fernández, 311–12
  writers' accounts: Grossi, 157–58
  writers' accounts: Llano Roza, 134–44

Palencia, 103
Partido Radical, 21, 59
La Pasionaria *see* Ibárruri, Dolores
Passionists (Pasionistas), 144–45, 151–52
Peinado, Antonio, 268–69
Pérez de Ayala, Ramón, 60
Pestaño, Angel, 69, 105, 106
Pla y Beltrán, Pascual, 73
La Pluma magazine, 54
Plural magazine, 46
Pola de Gordón, 216
Pola de Lena, 216
Pola de Siero, 219
Popular Front (Frente Popular), 40, 79, 91, 103
¿Por qué fui lanzado del Ministerio de la Guerra? (Hidalgo), 80
¿Por qué Oviedo se convirtió en ciudad mártir: película? (Nuño del Robledal), 240
Posada de Llanes, 219
Post-Guerra magazine, 52, 53, 54, 56
post-Revolution narratives: analysis
  atrocities and brutality, 108–10

autobiographical/biographical accounts, 94–95, 120, 135–36
and causes of Revolution, 94
descriptive/discursive styles, 98–100
exaggerated claims, 96
factual, 79–80, 87–88, 90, 94–95, 96, 101, 112
fictionalized/novelistic, 94
ideological bias and arguments, 85–86, 102
judgement on Republic, 90–91
official reports, 102–13
readership, 98, 101, 102, 108
and socio-economic problems, 96
strategies and techniques, 86–90, 101–02
use of witness reports, 87–88
verifiability of texts, 89–90, 104
post-Revolution narratives: confessions
Documentos Socialistas (compilation), 80, 85, 94, 96
Mi rebelión en Barcelona (Azaña), 80, 86, 87, 88, 94, 96, 100, 101
¿Por qué fui lanzado del Ministerio de la Guerra? (Hidalgo), 80, 81, 86, 92–93, 94, 96, 100, 101
post-Revolution narratives: journalistic responses
Hacia una nueva España (Cossío), 80, 81, 83, 85, 86, 91, 96, 100, 101
Hacia una nueva España en el 1934 (Valdivielso), 80, 83, 91, 92, 94
post-Revolution narratives: political discourses
Asesinos de España (Karl), 80, 84–85, 87, 88–89, 91, 92, 95, 96, 97, 98, 101
Asturias en el resurgimiento español (Oliveros), 80, 81–83, 90, 91, 92, 96, 99–100, 101
Explicación de octubre (Bergés), 80, 84, 93, 96, 101
Hacia la segunda revolución (Maurín), 79–80, 85, 90, 93, 96, 98, 99, 101
Traidores a la Patria (El Caballero Audaz), 80, 85, 88, 89, 91, 92, 95, 96, 97, 98, 101
post-Revolution narratives: repression texts
¡Acusamos! El asesinato de Luis de Sival (compilation), 105–07, 112
'A la opinión pública' reports (Ordás), 103–05, 112
La cárcel por dentro (Quintanilla), 111–12
Los crímenes de la reacción española (S.R.I.), 107–11, 112–13
Prada, Francisco, 175, 176–90, 193, 217, 236, 318
Prados, Emilio, 66, 69, 73
Los presos del "Manuel Arnús": novela (Verdal), 240
press
censorship, 38–39
influence on Revolution, 122, 132
political bias, 72, 128, 224, 253–54
and spread of propaganda, 224
Prieto, Indalecio, 22, 24–25, 97, 105, 106, 126, 140, 214
Primo de Rivera, Miguel
censorship, 52
coup d'état, 17
defeat, 53, 59, 60, 309
economic policy, 18
proletariat, 313–14
literature, 290
see also workers/working class
propaganda
definition, 12
in investigative journalism, 88–89
pre-Revolution, 123–24
revolutionary, 129, 182
S.R.I., 107–08
use by intellectuals, 122, 203
prose literature, 44, 45–46, 64–65, 67
PSOE (Partido Socialista Obrero Español), 19, 21, 22, 23, 25, 35
Federación Catalana, 27
radicalization campaign, 65–66
splits and divisions, 93
publishing houses, 46, 53
Pueblo magazine, 65
Pumariño, Alas, 185, 268, 276

Quintanilla, Luis, 111–12

Radical Party, 81
realism
'new realism', 58
socialist, 68
the Reconquest, 25, 82–83, 150, 218
Las Regueras, 219
Remarque, Erich, 53–54
Repression, 37–40, 71, 72, 261, 314, 328
atrocities and brutality, 37–38, 108–10
investigations and reports, 39, 103–04, 247
political consequences, 79
S.R.I. pamphlets, 107–11
Republic (la República), 79, 80, 85
authors' judgements on, 90–91
cabinet members, 246
evaluation of, 90–91, 130
shortcomings, 94, 279–80
and socio-political problems, 90–91, 93–94
Revista Blanca magazine, 65
Revista de Occidente, 54
La revolución de octubre de 1934 (Núñez), 121, 123, 124–33, 169
La revolución de octubre en España (government report), 120, 121, 122–23, 224–25

La Revolución en Asturias. Octubre 1934 (Llano Roza), 133–44
La revolución fue así: octubre rojo y negro (Benavides), 240, 245–58
Revolutionary Committee, 34–36, 133, 153, 158–59, 270, 278, 282
flight after defeat, 158, 261, 298
local groups, 27, 35–36, 165, 311, 314
revolutionary forces, 225
altruism and bravery, 262–64
arms and weapons, 95–96, 122, 135, 136–37, 140, 159–61, 261, 312–13
critical/negative depictions of, 139–41, 149–50, 313
defeat and flight, 261–62
financial backing from miners' union, 131
food supplies, 36, 311
'Guardia roja', 36
leaders/intellectuals, 131, 132, 149
motives and objectives, 131–32, 182
thieving and pillaging, 186
treatment of prisoners, 162, 185
violence and brutality, 139–41, 146, 161–62, 185, 186–87
women's roles, 263–64
Riego, Rafael del, 37, 229
right-wing politics, 80
1933 election victory, 121, 125, 131, 138, 214
anti-revolutionary campaign, 95, 110–11, 121, 128, 161–62
and Catholic Church, 126
demonstrations (September 1934), 259
and government, 63–64, 79, 80, 131
and patriotism/*Patria*, 91–92, 133, 193
post-Revolution commentaries, 80, 91–92
splits and divisions, 80, 92
and working class, 110–11, 259
see also fascism/fascists; Radical Party
Ríos, Fernando de los, 39, 68, 103
Rodríguez Villamil, José María, 145, 147, 150
Romero Cuesta, José, 120–33, 146, 151
Rosal, Amaro del, 111
Rubinat, José, 133
Rucabado, R., 144, 145
Ruiz Albéniz, Víctor, 54
Russia 66, 68–69
Revolution, 54, 61, 66, 98

Saborit, Andrés, 23, 66
Salazar Alonso, Rafael, 275
Salazar y Chapela, Esteban, 57
Salinas, Pedro, 46, 55
Sama, 32, 34, 35, 36, 266, 272–73
attack on Civil Guards' barracks, 126, 163, 164
destruction of library, 166
killing of priest, 37, 146, 224
Samblancat, Angel, 68, 105, 106
Samper, Ricardo, 23, 25, 92, 131, 168, 214
San Esteban de las Cruces, 163–64, 260
San Lázaro massacre, 265
San Pedro de los Arcos, 38
Sangre de octubre: U.H.P. (Álvarez Suárez), 240
Sangre jesuita. Asturias 1934: Padre Emilio Martínez y H. Juan B. Arconada (Adro Xavier), 175, 202–12
Sanjurjo, General, 24
Santa Cristina de Lena destruction, 128
Santullano, 206–07
El sargento Vázquez (Romero Cuesta), 121, 123–24, 135
Scholes, Robert, 6, 7
Second Republic ('República de los Intelectuales'), 59–62, 79, 80, 85
declaration, 60
and October Revolution, 120
Sender, Ramón J., 54, 55, 57, 58, 64, 68–69, 70, 240, 321–32
Sirval's assassination, 105, 106
Serrano Plaja, Arturo, 70, 73
short stories: analysis, 45, 240, 241, 321–32
characterization and plots, 328, 329
dialogue, 329
differences and similarities, 326–27
documentary aspects, 323
fictional narratives, 323
ideological/political biases/issues, 322, 325, 326, 331–32
literary/techniques quality, 328, 329–30
patriotism and tradition, 322, 331
religious issues, 322, 325, 326, 327, 331
socio-economic issues, 322, 324, 331–32
structure, 328–29
themes, 322, 324
use of symbolism, 330–31
short stories
'El Dios de los niños' (Espina), 322, 325–32
'El guaje' (Sender), 321, 322, 323
'Intelectual' (León), 321, 323–24, 327–32
'Liberación de octubre' (León), 321, 322–23, 325–32
'Xuan, el músico' (Arconada), 321, 327–32
El sindicato católico de Moreda y la revolución de octubre (Madera), 175, 190–99, 337
Sindicato Minero de Asturias, 191, 254
Sirval, Eduardo de, 106
Sirval, Luis de, 38, 70–71, 105–07, 218, 223
SMA (Sindicato Minero de Asturias), 18–19
socialism/socialists, 29, 34, 190
electoral defeat (1933), 138
and left-wing divisions, 93
post-Revolution documents, 80–81
revolutionary preparations/propagada, 132, 138–39, 155–56

Socialist Party, 19, 68, 80, 96, 280, 281
and Alianza Obrera, 155, 156, 157
author criticism of, 300
documents, 80–81
splits and divisions, 255
use of propaganda, 91
see also PSOE (Partido Socialista Obrero Español)
El Socialista magazine, 26, 65, 72
Socorro Rojo Internacional (S.R.I.), 107–11, 112, 113
El Sol newspaper, 48, 60
Solano Palacio, Fernando, 192
Solano, Wildebaldo, 152
Solchaga, General, 34
Soler, Aznar, 69–70
Solidaridad Obrera magazine, 65
Somoza, Eraclio Iglesias, 276–77
Soviet Union *see* Russia
Spanish Civil War (1936–39), 61, 70, 227, 322, 323
and evolution of literature, 44
Spanish government
Cabinet, 94, 288
and the Church, 62
coalitions, 59, 62, 63–64, 79
Cortes, 60, 71
elections, 79, 121, 125, 131, 138, 214
reforms, 62–63, 130–31
see also Spanish politics
Spanish literature
categorization and definitions, 10–14, 337, 338
and history, 4–10
and polarization of society, 326–27
see also novel genre; short stories
Spanish literature development, 52, 336
avant garde, 13, 44, 45–51, 336–37
European political influences, 52–54, 61–62
impact of Asturian Revolution, 70–74
'Literatura de Avanzada', 13, 44, 51–59
new realism, 58–59
poetry, 45, 72–73
'La República de los Intelectuales', 59–62
Russian/communist influences, 54, 326
socially/politically committed literature, 13, 44, 51, 58–59, 61, 62–70
Spanish politics
extreme/moderate divisions, 92, 93
and patriotism/*Patria*, 91–92, 133, 193
polarization, 90, 302
and writers, 84
see also left-wing politics; right-wing politics
SU (Sindicato Unico [Minero]), 19
Sur magazine, 65

Taibo, Paco Ignacio, 2, 12
on the CEDA, 21–22
on food supplies, 36
on Lafuente's execution, 95
on religious killings, 37
on reported rapes, 128
and revolutionary leadership, 35
Vega del Rey fighting, 126
on weaponry, 29–30
Tensor magazine, 65
El Tiempo Presente magazine, 65
Tiempos Nuevos magazine, 65
Tierra y Libertad magazine, 65
Todorov, Tzvetan, 10
Tomás, Belarmino, 33, 34, 38, 141, 217, 224, 232, 269, 275, 308
Torre, Guillermo de, 57
Torrens, Teniente, 230
Traidores a la Patria (El Caballero Audaz), 80, 88
Trubia, 32, 37, 159, 160, 271
truth ('la Verdad'), 86
Turón, 35, 37, 219
attacks/fighting, 136, 229–30
Lasallian brothers (Hermanos de la Salle), 144, 146, 147
religious killings, 37, 120, 122, 164–65, 225–26, 256
Turquesa incident, 30–31, 95, 159, 213–14

UGT (Unión General de Trabajadores), 19–20, 23, 27, 65–66
U.H.P.: la insurrección proletaria de Asturias (Molins), 152–70, 256
Ultra magazine, 45–46
'ultraísmo' movement, 45–46
Unamuno, Miguel de, 60, 71
Unión de Escritores Soviéticos, 68, 69
Unión Republicana, 25
Urrutia, Federico, 127

Valdés, Alejandro, 240, 241, 258–82, 288, 301
Valdivielso, José Simeón, 80, 81, 83–84, 86, 91–92, 94
Valencia, 69, 70, 106, 254
Valladolid, 204
Valle de Aller, 219
Valle del Nalón, 219
El valle negro: Asturias 1934 (Camín Meana), 175–76, 213–36, 247, 255
Valle-Inclán, Ramón María del, 70, 71
Vallejo, César, 69
Vázquez Corbacho, Sargento Diego, 97, 120, 123–24, 128–30, 132, 133, 230, 268
Vega, Carlos, 269
La Vega del Rey
arms factory incident, 30, 94, 159, 269, 313
death of revolutionaries, 33, 126

Verdal, Tomás, 240, 241
vignettes *see* dramatized vignettes; fiction/non-fiction dramatized vignettes
Villafría massacre, 38, 164, 218, 232, 250

White, Hayden, 5, 9
Wolfe, Thomas, 6
women
  viewpoint of Revolution, 298–99, 302
  liberation of, 322, 323
  revolutionary roles, 263–64, 322
  as victims of Revolution 322, 324
workers/working class
  movements 154, 196, 246, 259, 323
  and Oviedo 226–27, 314–15
  peasant disinterest/suppression, 62, 264
  political lessons of Revolution, 196–97
  poverty and discontent, 139, 310, 314–15, 323
  and right-wing government, 110–11, 112
  social/political pressures, 325–26
  and S.R.I. propaganda, 107–08

'Xuan, el músico' (Arconada), 321, 327–32

Yagüe, General (Foreign Legion) 33, 34, 38, 93, 189

zapadores, 133
Zapata, José, 326
Zugazagoitia, J., 52, 69, 71, 111–12